A History of
Eastern Civilizations
Volume I

Lloyd Hoshaw
Rock Valley College

McGraw-Hill, Inc.
College Custom Series

New York St. Louis San Francisco Auckland Bogota
Caracas Lisbon London Madrid Mexico Milan Montreal
New Delhi Paris San Juan Singapore Sydney Tokyo Toronto

A HISTORY OF EASTERN CIVILIZATIONS
Volume 1

1 2 3 4 5 6 7 8 9 0 HAM HAM 9 0 9 8 7 6 5 4

ISBN 0-07-030519-6

Editor: Reaney Dorsey

Cover Design: Jenny L. Friedman

Cover Photo: Lloyd Hoshaw

Printer/Binder: HAMCO Corporation

CONTENTS

EASTERN CIVILIZATIONS TO c.1600

Introducing the World of Asia

The Emergence of Civilization on the Indian Subcontinent

Chinese History and Culture

The Early History of Korea to c.1600

Contents

Early Japan to c.1600

Southeast Asia to 1600

LIST OF ILLUSTRATIONS

Note: *All pen and ink drawings made by Linda Hoshaw-Voss from the author's slide collection.*

LIST OF MAPS

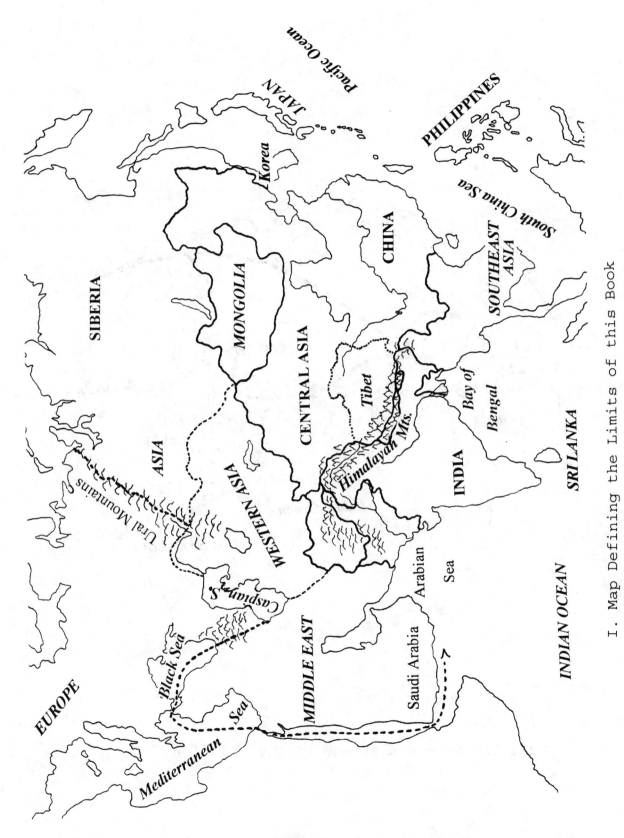

I. Map Defining the Limits of this Book

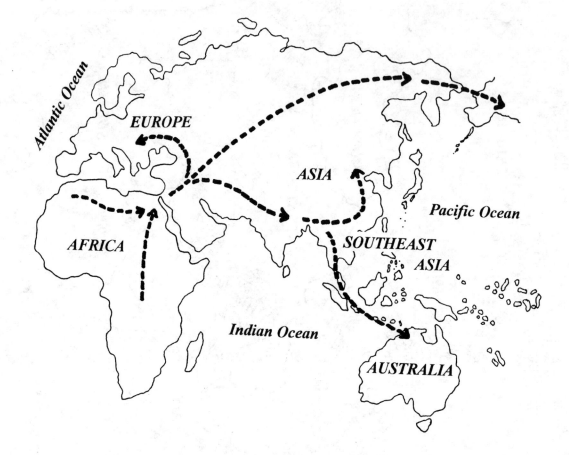

II. The Origin & Spread of Civilization

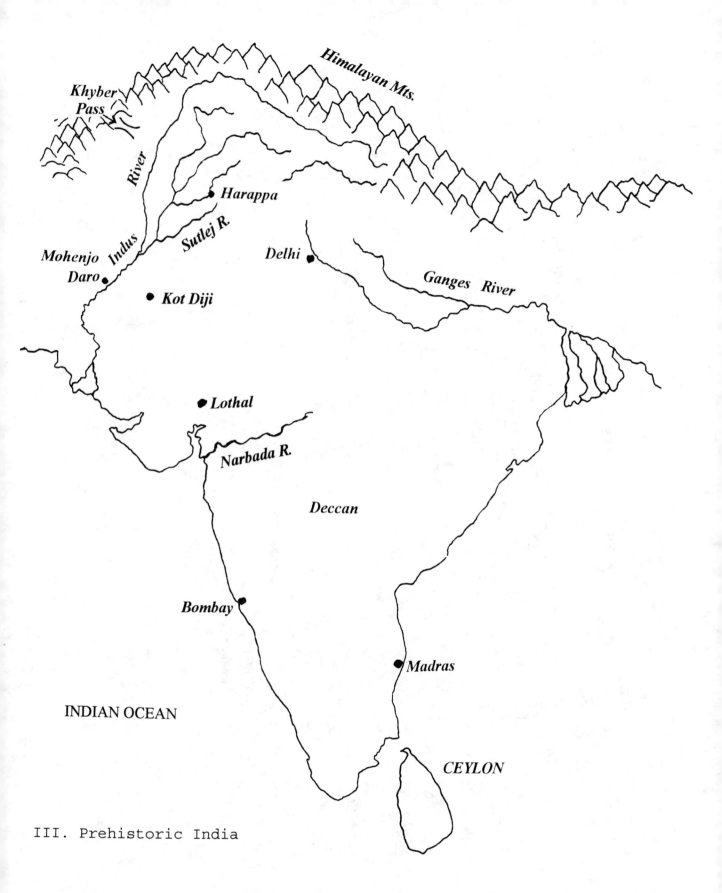

III. Prehistoric India

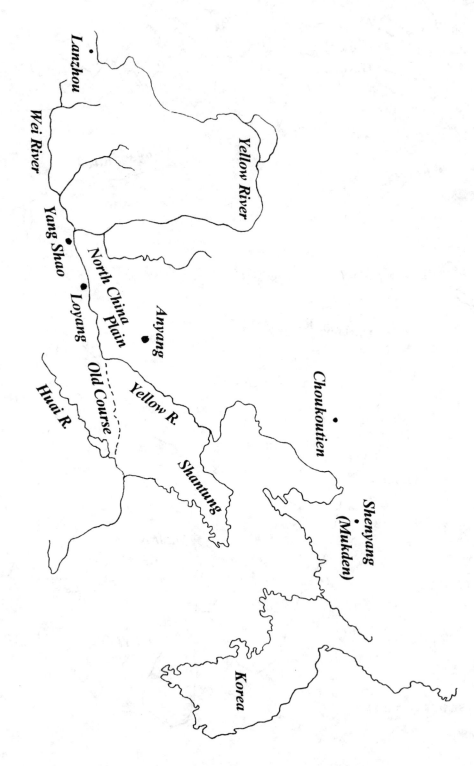

IV. Prehistoric China

x

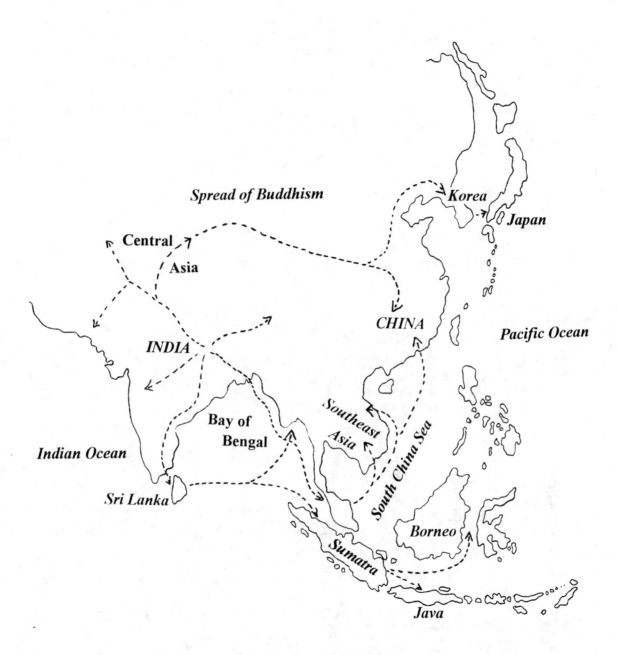

Spread of Buddhism

Central
Asia

INDIA

CHINA

Korea

Japan

Pacific Ocean

Bay of
Bengal

Indian Ocean

Sri Lanka

Southeast
Asia

South China Sea

Borneo

Sumatra

Java

V. Spread of Buddhism

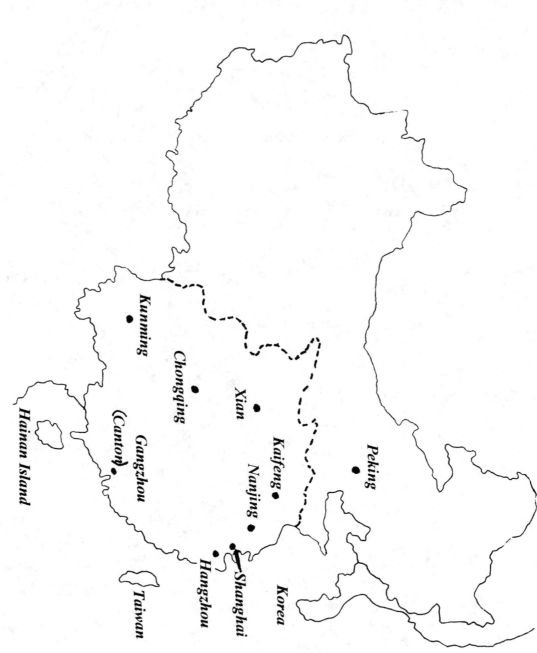

VI. Ming China

Kunming

Chongqing

Xian

Kaifeng

Nanjing

Peking

Gangzhou (Canton)

Hainan Island

Shanghai

Hangzhou

Taiwan

Korea

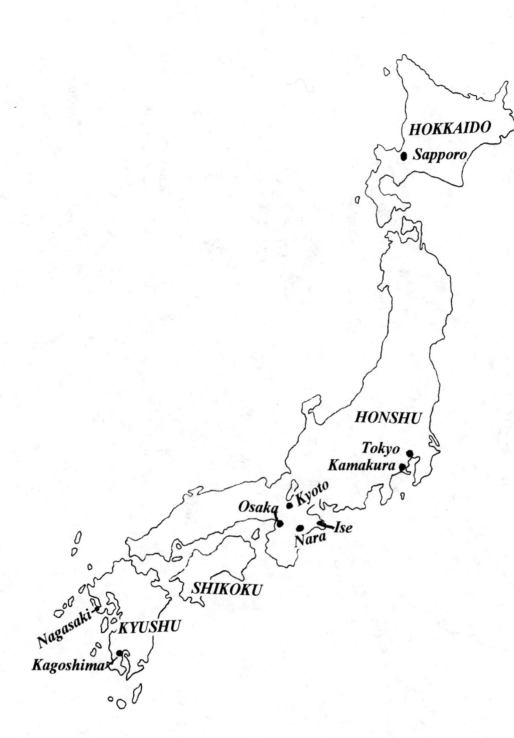

VII. Japan to 1600

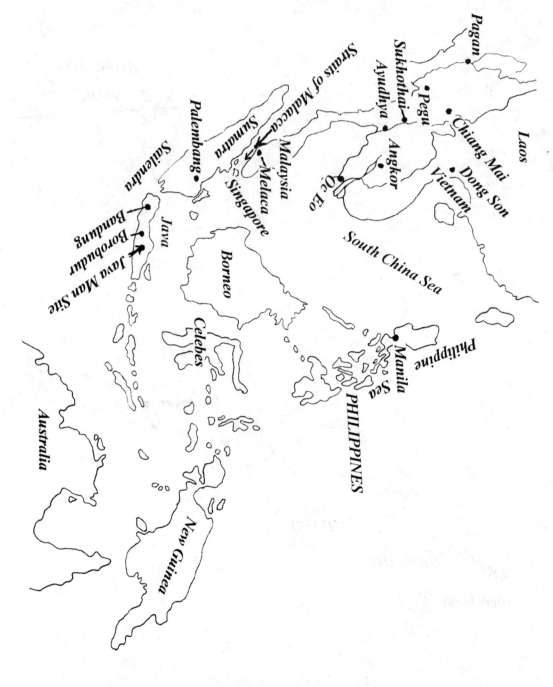

VIII. Southeast Asia to 1600

PREFACE
to
A HISTORY OF EASTERN CIVILIZATIONS

How much should be included in a history of Eastern Civilizations? This is a question which would probably be answered differently by every scholar in the field.

What is the geographic area encompassed within Asia? It is first necessary to divide the great Eurasian land mass into two parts--Asia and Europe. The line is usually drawn along the Ural Mountains in Russia. Beginning on the north, the line follows the mountains south to the Ural River and the Caspian Sea. At the south end of the Caspian Sea, the line turns west through the Caucasus Mountains to the Black Sea. Follow the Black Sea to the Bosphorus including all of Asia Minor (modern Turkey), then south along the eastern Mediterranean Sea to the Suez. The Red Sea separates Asia from Africa.

Within this vast area of Asia live approximately half the people on earth. This same area has spawned three of the world's great civilizations--Mesopotamia (modern Iraq), India, and China. The two eastern civilizations in turn spread to neighboring areas such as Southeast Asia, Korea, and Japan. It is a lengthy history of dynasties which have come and gone along with a sophisticated cultural evolution in the areas of art, architecture, music, drama and religion. All of these areas are both beautiful and interesting for their depth of human knowledge and a better understanding of the cultures of the world today. All of the major religious faiths of the world originated in Asia and spread throughout the world.

The major focus of the first part of the book will be to understand **where** and **how** the people lived in the eastern world. This will include their system of food and agriculture, some aspects of housing, and some of their general religious understanding. Despite the fact that Asia is large, the people are numerous, and their history has been long, most people in the western world know little about Asia. Many still regard it as remote and strange. The very general introductory section will include several comparisons to the western world because our primarily western heritage has centered upon Europe and the spread of that civilization to the Americas.

Even though there are several limitations, the importance of Asia to contemporary America and western Europe cannot be exaggerated. Science and technology of the modern era have made it virtually impossible for any large nation to isolate itself from the world community. The requirements of industrialization, marketing, national security, and competition, have made normal relations between all countries a necessity.

As one begins to study the Asian civilizations in greater depth it becomes apparent that a deeper understanding of each of their cultures alongside our own western tradition brings a much richer understanding of the total world civilization. This is needed in the new world which is taking shape at the close of the 20th century and the beginning of the 21st century. It is then, a matter of necessity in the realm of world peace and world-wide commercial competition on the one hand, and the sheer fascination of exploring old civilizations which have long since passed from the scene (but not until they had made a permanent imprint upon the Asian people), that this study is undertaken.

Such a wide scope cannot possibly do justice to all of the areas of Asia. For that reason there are some major areas which are omitted entirely. None of the area which is known properly

Preface

as the Near East, more popularly referred to as the Middle East, will be included. The vast areas of Australia, New Zealand, and the thousands of islands which dot the Pacific are given very little space. The area formerly known as the Soviet Union, prior to December 1991, has also been omitted. This is not to say that these areas are unimportant. There are very few books in English written on the Asian part of the former Soviet Union. Australia and New Zealand are primarily western cultures which happen to be situated in the Pacific area. Because the Middle East is so complex in historical background and in recent diplomatic history, it deserves a study all its own. Places such as Iran (formerly Persia), and Afghanistan will be brought into the general stream of eastern civilizations wherever appropriate to their association with the East. The main focus of this book will pertain to South Asia, East Asia, and Southeast Asia. Due attention will be given to comparisons and contrasts to the western civilization at appropriate times.

The South Asian area of India, Pakistan, and Bangladesh, often referred to simply as the *subcontinent*, will be the first area to be studied. Even though the Chinese have kept better historical records, the Indus River Civilization seems to be the oldest evidence we have of an organized urban society in South or East Asia. Furthermore, Hinduism is the oldest religion in the South Asian and East Asian areas. Since Buddhism broke away from the Hindu faith, it is important to understand Hinduism as a background to understanding the Buddhist faith, which became so popular in China, Korea, Japan, and Southeast Asia. The earliest written materials in the Indian subcontinent were composed in Sanskrit, a language very similar to the Indo-European languages. Sanskrit and Hinduism were also important in shaping the philosophy and culture of the people of Southeast Asia.

China occupies such a prominent place in world history that it is necessary to investigate its history next. Writing, inventions, the philosophy of Confucius and Lao Tzu, the ability of the people to organize a government, and to defend themselves at their borders, are all important themes in Chinese history. Buddhism was adopted from its place of origin in India, but it was reshaped and developed into a major world religion in China at the same time that it was being phased out in India. Chinese Buddhism, writing, and other major cultural contributions, were all passed on to Korea and Japan and to a lesser extent to Southeast Asia.

Korea, Japan, and Southeast Asia, all have rich historical backgrounds of their own. However, all three of those areas borrowed heavily from either China or India, especially by the 5th or 6th centuries A.D. There is no way to measure which part of the culture came from China or India, or in what quantity. These three major areas of Asia have successfully accomplished somewhat the same approach as the United States, a country which has borrowed heavily from western Europe, but has been selective in what is retained and what is rejected. The end result is an all new culture.

Volume I rather obviously stresses the philosophic and religious backgrounds of South and East Asia. Geographic considerations weigh more heavily in Asia than in the western world, because of the heavy emphasis on labor intensive agriculture to support the high density of population. Village life is much more a part of everyday living than in the United States. The people live close to the soil and to one another. Birth, old age, and death in rural Asia are all much closer to village life than in the western world. The role of women, the basics of government, the survival from one season to another, all occur at the village level. A large amount of the philosophy of the village has been adapted to urban life in Asia.

Preface

For all the joys of becoming acquainted with Asian history and culture, there are also problems. Many of the areas discovered writing rather late in their history. Archaeology is the sole answer prior to written records. This also becomes difficult because many of the buildings were made of sun-dried bricks, bamboo, or other very perishable materials. Cremation, where it was practiced, does not leave bones or grave goods. The wind borne loess soil can often be several feet deep. Floods, accompanied by the shifting course of major rivers such as the Huang Ho in China, have washed away entire villages, or buried them under deep layers of silt. The alkaline soils do not preserve the few remaining pieces of evidence in good condition. When written records do appear they are often little more than the religious and mythological stories of the past. Neither do the written records before the 17th century reveal much about the life of the average individual. It is therefore necessary to offer many general statements.

Volume I is the foundation for understanding Asia from 1500 to the present. The records are still sketchy as late as the 17th century, but by the First World War in 1914, Asian history becomes much more precise. The total story of Asia will require a study of both Volume I and Volume II. The author hopes this will be a pleasant journey.

Finally, it is important to remember that this is a survey course. The text covers a very broad area in a relatively few pages. There are going to be large gaps which are unexplored. Those are areas in which you, the reader, must seek books and read journal articles in the library. There will probably never be a survey textbook of Asia which will include every area and give a complete coverage to every period. This is an important area to **begin** your acquaintance with the world of eastern civilizations.

It should also be pointed out that a study of Asia is not easy. Many of the names of people, places, and events will be very different from those experienced in western history. Even the spelling and pronunciation will vary from one source to another. There had been relatively little interest in Asia beyond commercial traders and missionaries until the beginning of the Second World War. Even now, there are far fewer books and journals available for study in most libraries on eastern subjects as opposed to western history subjects. Still, the challenge will prove interesting, thought-provoking, and very worthwhile as we come to understand a very important part of the world today.

Supplementing the historical narrative account are maps, illustrations, and a list of ***Books for Further Reading***, all of which serve as an integral portion of the historical account. Every effort has been made to include the most recent, and the most authoritative books available that you may enjoy the subject in greater depth and detail.

Professor Lloyd Hoshaw
Rockford, Illinois, 1994

DEDICATION

To my wife Evelyn for hours of proofreading

To my daughter Linda Hoshaw-Voss for all her pen and ink drawings

ACKNOWLEDGMENTS

I wondered as I began to develop this book whether all authors go through as much pain to "get it right" as I have. But every hour of it was a tremendous feeling of satisfaction with the finished product. I cannot help but think of all the things I wanted to include that are not included, especially on the maps. The book has been in my mind for over thirty-six years, but it was not until eight years ago that I began using it as a handout text in my classes. Many students have read it and made both favorable and unfavorable comments. I have tried to change the book to make it a useful tool for acquiring background about the Asian area of the world.

No one ever truly does a project so large without some help and encouragement. I want to thank my secretary, Marge Johnson, who typed on the manuscript for hours before I owned my own computer. I also owe many words of thanks to Dr. George Spencer at Northern Illinois University, and really special thanks to Dr. Leonard H. D. Gordon, and his wife Marge, at Purdue University, for their very helpful assistance. Mr. Kanwal Prashar has read all of the manuscript through the end of India to 1600. His comments and suggestions through the years have been priceless. I would be remiss if I did not mention my several professors who have instilled in me a love of history, especially Dr. Willard Smith at Goshen College, and Dr. Maurice Baxter at Indiana Univeristy, Bloomington.

Several travel agents have given me advice about travel in these areas and helped with the arrangements. Mr. Wilbur Johnson and Mr. Om Kapur deserve special mention. Both family and friends have put up with my long devotion to the keyboard. Some of them have also read at least some of the earlier manuscripts and offered suggestions. Finally, Janet Giles prepared the final Index and made a thousand little changes in grammar and punctuation for which I shall be forever grateful.

At the end of the road, the final product is all mine. The good points, the errors, the little things which were included but should have been left out, and the things which were left out but should have been included. I welcome the comments of every reader of this book, keeping in mind that it is a general survey of a vast area--not an encyclopedia.

Professor Lloyd Hoshaw
Rock Valley College
Rockford, Illinois

INTRODUCING THE WORLD OF ASIA
Chapter 1
THE NATURE OF ASIA'S LANDS AND PEOPLES

There are three outstanding things which are noted by all who visit Asia. The first is the huge distances from one place to another. The second feature would be the enormous numbers of people. The third consideration centers on the great age of everything. Literally dozens of cultures and civilizations have come and gone in Asia over thousands of years.

Our first study will consider the great **Land Mass** of Asia. It is always difficult to make a precise division of the great Eurasian land mass into two parts--Asia and Europe. The line which separates the two is most often drawn from the Arctic Sea in the north in a southerly direction following the Ural Mountains in Russia. At the southern edge of the Urals is the source of the Ural River, which flows south to the Caspian Sea. At the south end of the Caspian Sea the line of separation turns west through the Caucasus Mountains to the Black Sea. At the west end of the Black Sea the line passes through the center of the Bosphorus, the Sea of Marmora, and the Dardanells. The line follows around the curve of Asia Minor (now known as Turkey) and turns south along the eastern coast of the Mediterranean Sea to the Suez Canal. Finally, the Red Sea separates Asia from Africa.

This book will be concerned with the area of Pakistan and the vast area of Asia which lies north and east of that part of Asia. The countries of the Near East--often commonly referred to today as the Middle East will not be a part of this book. This area deserves its own study. Afghanistan will be brought into our consideration as it pertains to the British-Russian contest for power in that area. Neither Australia nor New Zealand, two vast areas within Asia, will be considered. Both of these huge areas have a primarily European-based culture.

Nearly 60 percent of the people on the entire earth live between the line described above and the Pacific Ocean. This same area has witnessed the birth of two of the world's oldest civilizations--India and China. These two great civilizations have in turn spread their learning and culture to neighboring areas such as Southeast Asia, Korea, and Japan.

A **civilization** is often defined as a society wherein there are three major components: the presence of cities and urban life; the development of a system of writing; and a government which makes and enforces laws, collects taxes, and is able to provide for its own defense. Such a civilization at least implies a well-organized agricultural system which is capable of transporting its surplus products to the city for support. Most civilizations also kept records of several kinds-- business records, tax records, written laws, and a history of their achievements, especially their most notable rulers. A society which was not sufficiently developed to maintain most of these characteristics is more properly referred to as a **cultlure**.

It is also interesting that **all** the major religious faiths of the world developed in the broad definition of Asia. All except Judaism, Christianity, and Islam have developed within the area of our study. Hinduism, Buddhism, Confucianism, Taoism (Dowism), and Shintoism are all eastern faiths which will be studied in some detail. The other three great faiths will be studied as they have pertained to Asia. All of these eastern faiths have caught on to one extent or another in the western world.

Introducing Asia

Asia has a rich cultural heritage in art, architecture, music, and drama. Often the arts, the religion, the philosophy, the history, and the laws are all so intricately interwoven that it is practically impossible to separate one area of culture from another. In most cases it is not even desirable to separate them because each area does not encompass its full meaning and stature without the characteristics of the allied fields. This fact is what makes a study of eastern civilizations both interesting and exciting. It is an entirely new approach to life and all its meaning.

THE IMPORTANCE OF AGRICULTURAL PRODUCTIVITY

Since roughly 75 percent of the people of Asia are either full-time or part-time farmers, the wealth of any country often depends upon the amount of good fertile land and the yield which can be coaxed from that land. In all the ages of history up to the late 20th century, a country which allowed its birth rate to exceed its capacity to produce sufficient food in the poor years would ultimately suffer many deaths from starvation.

The English economist and philosopher, **Thomas R. Malthus**, writing in the late 18th century, said that the growth in population would always tend to exceed the growth in food production. He believed that world population statistics would not increase greatly beyond those of the 1790s because famine would always adjust the numbers of people. Malthus believed that poor health would result as a consequence of a poor diet. This would cause many people to die prematurely. But it is obvious that the world today supports a population many times what it was two hundred years ago. Whereas, as late as the 1920s and 1930s there were still huge shortages accompanied by malnutrition and mass starvation, the traveler in Asia today will be surprised to find large quantities of good food such as fresh fruits and vegetables going to waste. Most Asian countries have an abundance of rice for export. What has changed the Malthusian formula in the last two hundred years?

Since World War II the wealthier nations have freely shared their technology with Asian nations via the more specialized missionaries and organizations such as the Peace Corps. Asian farmers who had always been afraid to experiment with new crops, or new ways of growing old crops, were assured that they would not be allowed to starve if they would only try some of the new hybrid seeds. Movies, followed by television programs, demonstrated that there were new and better ways of growing crops and livestock. Commercial fertilizers, herbicides, and pesticides have slowly replaced the old ways. The Asian farmers are still very conservative concerning change. Many fear that the new chemical products will destroy their soil for future generations. They are much more ecologically minded than most American or European farmers.

Malthus attributed many human diseases to malnutrition. By the mid 19th century tremendous strides were being made in the treatment of disease in the western world. Modern medicine assumed a whole new significance following the introduction of sulfa and the antibiotics after World War II. The concept of the germ theory of disease has begun to catch on in Asia but it still has a long way to go. There are many people in Asia who continue to rely upon the old homemade herbal remedies, some of which do work. Others trust their health to the religious remedies since they continue to believe that something has gone wrong in their spiritual world.

Introducing Asia

With plenty of food and the new medical practices there are more children surviving their early years and many more middle-aged people are now living to an old age. When George B. Cressey wrote about China in the 1930s it was a country which claimed about 400 million people. When his book entitled *Land of the 500 Million: A Geography of China* was published as late as 1955, many people found it difficult to grasp such a large figure. Most books dealing with China discussed how that country had moved from 50 or 60 million people at the beginning of the Christian era to 500 million by the mid-1950s. It seemed an incredible number. Today China has more than twice that number with plenty of food for everyone.

But all nations acknowledge that there IS an upper limit to their population growth. Countries such as India have an abundance of family planning options, all of which are voluntary. China has very strict laws governing large families. Other countries are at least investigating ways to control their growing populations. Religlious principles have often been a handicap wherever birth control is involved. Nearly every Asian country believes it has a program to encourage smaller families. The two most populous countries--China and India--have always practiced female infanticide to some extent. Although this practice apparently does still exist, it is now illlegal. However, some expectant mothers are going to a health center with ultrasound and simply aborting a known female fetus. Most western nations believe there are better ways to control the surplus population.

Each of the major areas of study in Asia--the Indian subcontinent, China, Japan, Korea, and Southeast Asia--will be introduced with a section about the geography and the ethnic groups which pertain to that area of the world.

IN SUMMARY

It is always dangerous to draw generalizations in history, perhaps doubly so in Asia. The safest generalization is that there are NO generalizations! Proceeding to summarize our introduction it is safe to say that all the nations of Asia believe they have a population problem. Countries such as China have very strict birth control laws. Every Asian country has some program to encourage smaller families.

Since the late 18th century people have believed that the land could support no further growth in population. However, the river valleys and the coastal areas have rich agricultural resources. Lands which were once in pasture or forest are cleared and plowed to produce more food. This practice has caused enormous erosion problems in many areas. Land which would be declared a total waste from an agricultural point of view in the western world, such as a steep mountainside, is often covered with terraces. The people have called upon the land to do more and with the assistance of hybrid seeds, commercial fertilizers, herbicides, and pesticides, it has. The major problem is that as productivity has increased, the population has increased accordingly.

Finally, the Asia we see today has its roots much more deeply in its own past than do the countries in the western world. As the story of Asia begins to unfold, you will notice the close affinity of the soil, the people, and their culture. Both Dr. Cressey and Pearl S. Buck wrote extensively about the Asian people's closeness to the earth. A trip through any part of Asia will affirm that the people's roots are still in the earth. Our study of Asia will tie the earth, the culture, and the history into one.

Figure 1

4

Chapter 2
THE PREHISTORIC WORLD OF ASIA

AN INTRODUCTION

The question of where mankind originated on this earth and how we came to be as we is now has troubled thinkers for thousands of years. The historian narrates and interprets only mankind's more recent experiences from the time civilization developed. Among other attributes, civilization implies that a body of people have the art of writing. If they have a written account of their accomplishments and failures the historian has something to work from. Whether the written record is on stone, bamboo, metal, wood, or paper, these earliest writings are the primary tools of the historian's craft.

But many cultures developed **before** the writing systems were invented by man. Historians, archaeologists, and anthropologists simply call this period **Prehistoric**. Evidence in this long time period--perhaps as long as 2 million years--is quite sparse and scholars who work in this field are faced with wide gaps and often have many more questions than answers.

Each of the peoples of the world have felt compelled to tell their children how the whole world began and how the first people arrived. They spoke and wrote of the creation as they conceived it having taken place. As we study the various religious faiths of Asia we will cover several of these beautiful stories. Some of them have provided the basis of major religious faiths while others are considered myths in our world today. There are those who would even question the origins as stated in the major religious faiths.

In the western world practically everyone is familiar with the first book of the *Old Testament--Genesis*. *Genesis* is the first of the five books of the *Bible*. They are known as the Pentateuch, which was written by Moses during the forty years of the wanderings of the Jewish people between their release from Egyptian bondage and their entrance into the Promised Land, present-day Israel. Both Jews and Chrisians accept these books as divinely inspired revelation, not from an accumulation of traditions and legends of the Mesopotamian area. However, if one takes the trouble to count back through all the generations cited in the *Old Testament*, along with the lifespan of each, as did Archbishop James Ussher of Armagh, Ireland in 1650, then the *Book of Genesis* covered a period of 2,315 years. Adding the other generations after Moses, Ussher calculated that the creation took place in the year 4004 B.C. Another contemporary cleric agreed and added that the world began at 9 a.m. on October 23!

Scarcely anyone in our modern age would accept that date and time for the creation of the world. Both Christians and Jews have allowed that we do not know how long a "day" Moses was referring to at the time of creation. On the other hand, very few scientists reject all that is in *Genesis*. Indeed, the Bible would certainly be incomplete without *Genesis*; the very germ of all the truth and wisdom unfolded in the remainder of the scriptures is found in the *Book of Genesis*. The opening lines state simply that: "In the beginning God created the heaven and the earth." It is important to remember as we approach the study of the prehistoric record that up to the mid-19th century the *Bible* was interpreted precisely as it was written in *Genesis* Chapters I and II.

Prehistoric Asia

The man who did more to open the scientific conflict with the Biblical account, and to cause people to have questions about their faith, was **Charles Darwin**, (1809-1882). Darwin was an English naturalist and author and is the one most often associated with the scientific and evolutionary approach to creation. There were many other 19th century men who shared his views.

Darwin received his education at Cambridge University where he enrolled in 1827. He spent three years studying for the ministry and in 1831 he was invited to join a scientific expedition around the world. Darwin was to serve as a naturalist on this expedition, which went across the Atlantic, around South America to Tahiti, New Zealand, Tasmania, and the Keeling Islands. It was this trip which convinced him there was an evolutionary process in the development of living things, both plants and animals. He also came to believe that the fittest survived and the weakest died off and disappeared.

The H.M.S. *Beagle* returned in 1836 and Darwin began writing about what he had seen and what he believed. From 1838 to 1841 he served as the secretary of the London Geological Society. In 1837 he began a notebook in which he entered facts concerning the formation of breeds of animals and plants, and describing their natural selection.

During these same years Darwin also began corresponding with other scientists interested in tracing plant and animal origins. Among these were Charles Lyell, author of *Principles of Geology* (1830); Alfred Russel Wallace; and, the American naturalist, Asa Gray. They were, each one, working independently on a theory of evolution and were surprised to learn how closely their work corresponded. In 1858, Darwin and Wallace presented a joint scientific paper dealing with evolution which caused little comment, but when Darwin's book, **The Origin of Species** appeared a year later in 1859, churchmen almost universally considered it contrary to the Biblical account of creation. Darwin followed his first book with one entitled **The Descent of Man and Selection in Relation to Sex** in 1871. By this time nearly every cleric in the western world took issue with Darwin's thesis.

Whether Darwin was right or wrong--and people do choose sides on this issue--he certainly succeeded in setting the scientists to work to either prove or disprove his thesis. No precise and generally acceptable definition of a species and its origins has yet been achieved. Neither do we have a fossil record of how mammals such as whales took to the sea while in other cases fish came to walk on the land. The evolution, strictly from the standpoint of anatomy, from frogs to monkeys to apes to early man looks so logical, but the precise arrangement still lacks a satisfactory explanation of how it occurred. Perhaps if we knew how long the process had been continuing it would be somewhat easier. For all our scientific knowledge, there are still many unanswered questions and many theories.

Beginning as early as 1739, about a hundred years prior to Darwin, the Swedish naturalist **Crolus Linnaeus** classified mankind as *Homo sapiens* in the overall order known as **primates**. Other primates include the lemurs, monkeys, and apes, all of which are a part of the class of mammals. Linnaeus's primary goal was **classification**, not an explanation of our origin. Diderot, Kant, and Laplace, among others, had already hinted at some evolutionary system nearly a century before Darwin had advanced his theory. These early scientists and philosophers reasoned that by whatever means mankind had arrived on this earth in the beginning, there are certain characteristics which set us apart from the other primates.

Prehistoric Asia

Some of the special characteristics of mankind are:

Bipedal locomotion, with upright posture, frees our hands for work. The human hand is a most wonderful tool. Even the largest apes and gorillas use their hands for walking. Their arms are quite long compared to those of people. Furthermore, their spinal column and pelvis areas are about half designed for walking on all fours.

An enlarged brain, which is more than three times the capacity of a chimpanzee, has given modern man a tremendous advantage over the lower animals. Even *Homo habilis*, the tool maker, has a capacity twice that of a chimpanzee.

A different type of dental structure is evident in the size and length of the canine teeth. The same is true of the molars. The canine teeth are made for heavy tearing while the molars are made for grinding fibrous materials. As the teeth and mouth changed, so also did the shape of the face. Furthermore, the heavier teeth required heavier jaw bones, and these in turn required heavier jaw muscles.

In final analysis, we know that humans have changed over the centuries. The brain and teeth seem to have changed as the body changed. We are thinking, reasoning beings who have the physical gifts of many of the lower animals--as the evolutionists point out--but in addition we have a larger storehouse of mental ability. Most importantly, we have a moral sense of what is right or wrong.

Perhaps it is safe to say that no one knows for certain how old the earth is nor when mankind first appeared upon it. Present conjecture says that the earth is 6 billion years old and that mankind first appeared perhaps 2 billion years ago; however, this is only an educated guess. Even under the best of scientific and archaeological conditions we have little more than a few tools and some bone fragments and teeth from our earliest ancestors. The oldest record currently centers in Africa. The oldest remains yet discovered in Asia are Java Man and Peking Man. In order to better understand how these early people have been discovered and analyzed let us first consider the world of archaeology.

THE ARCHAEOLOGICAL RECORD

The word archaeology comes from the Greek *archaia*, meaning ancient things, and *logos*, referring to theory or science. In recent times archaeology has been accepted as a study of the remains of man's past. It is nearly always associated with digging for these remains. As information is revealed during the "dig" the archaeologist must describe, classify, and analyze the artifacts, and endeavor to determine their significance as a part of the history of mankind. From this in-depth study the archaeologist must know scientific information, historical context, and the sociological-anthropological significance of his find. As scientific analysis has expanded so much in recent times it is often necessary to call in a specialist to identify and define the object under study. Radiocarbon-14 dating, which was discovered in 1949, is just one example of the scientific-technological aspects of the field of archaeology today. Excavation, the aspect which the general public sees, is only one part of the story. The archaeologist has become more like the general practicioner in medicine. He must recognize what has been found and then call upon the specialists for modern analysis.

Prehistoric Asia

Archaeology as a discipline had its earliest origins in 15th and 16th century Europe. The Renaissance Humanists became curious about the ruins they found in Greece and Rome. They found that many artifacts were very well preserved in the dry Egyptian climate. Within a short time there were people who had the interest, the time, and the money to begin digging as collectors of past civilizations. Ancient burial grounds and tombs were favorite sites. Both private and national museums sent out teams of people to dig for "nice things" for the museum collection. In these early centuries the artifact was everything. All too often a sizeable share of the culture surrounding the artifact was destroyed in the intense interest of accumulating the most artifacts in the least time and for the least money. Unfortunately, once a digging site has been excavated it is impossible to restore it as it was before the dig began.

Darwin and other scientists caused archaeologists to become interested in the **whole site** rather than just the artifact itself. If more attention were focused upon the surroundings in which the artifact had been found it would take on more meaning. By applying these principles it would be possible to bring the entire site back to life. The British archaeologist Flinders Petrie, who began work in Egypt in 1880, developed a systematic method of excavation which was passed on to others. When Howard Carter and Lord Carnarvon discovered the tomb of the Pharaoh Tutankhamen in Egypt in 1922, the artifacts were removed with the utmost scientific care. The discovery of the Royal Tombs at Ur by Leonard Woolley in 1926 were also very carefully excavated. Petrie, Carter, and Woolley pointed the way to a new and more scientific style of archaeology.

Up to the 1920s a goodly share of the archaeological focus had been upon Egypt, Mesopotamia and the Holy Land, Europe, and there was a small interest in the American Indians. The first significant archaeological interest in the Asian area came in the 1920s when excavations began at Mohenjo-Daro and at Harappa in what is today Pakistan. A few years later came the An-yang dig in eastern China. These directed archaeological and historical interest to Asia. Even though, as we shall see, Eugene Dubois had discovered Java Man before the Indian and Chinese discoveries, he was really ahead of his time and many refused to believe the important find which he had made. At that time there was much emphasis being placed upon the traditional areas of digging and there were also Neanderthal finds in Europe. Before the digs at Mohenjo-Daro, China, and Java there was even a tendency to think that the history of mankind had originated in Europe. But these finds in Asia now meant that historians would be re-writing their account to accommodate these latest discoveries in Asia.

The latest discoveries of prehistoric people have been made by Louis, Mary, and Richard Leakey in Africa at Olduvai Gorge in Tanzania. Some would even place our origin in Africa but it is more than likely that these finds are just one more piece of a giant jigsaw puzzle of our origins.

Those who favor the origin being in Asia believe that earliest mankind appeared in Southeast Asia. Still others claim that mankind evolved in different places in the world simultaneously. The theory accepted by most people who work in the field is that early mankind originated in Africa, then spread across the Red Sea area into the Near East, on eastward into South Asia and China over a period of thousands of years. Simultaneously, another branch moved north into Europe, then spread north and west from the area of present-day Greece or Italy. None of the remains in Europe seem to be as old as those in Africa and Asia.

Prehistoric Asia

There are many problems encountered by the archaeologist and the anthropologist. The oldest bones are such small fragments that it is difficult to draw very accurate conclusions. The richest finds are those which are located in acid soils. Bodies which are buried in highly alkaline soils decompose rapidly. Another important aspect of grave sites centers on the number and quality of the grave goods--the artifacts which are placed with the body for use in the afterlife. Some of the early cultures probably cremated the bodies or left them exposed on a platform in a tree until the flesh was all gone. The bones were then bundled and saved for a time. There may have been a particular day of the year when the entire village went to bury the bones. Or, they may have kept them around until they were lost. In either event, the bones have become so confused that it is difficult to make sense of them. Cremation, of course, leaves very little to analyze.

Another problem encountered today is that some of what were logically the richest sites were raided two or three centuries ago simply to obtain the valuable grave goods. Once destroyed, it is impossible to recreate the exact surroundings of the original site. A problem encountered in a few places, especially China, is that people dug up old human bones, powdered them, then mixed the powder in with various cures and medications. The Chinese often went to great lengths to obtain more old human bones.

Finally, the silent bones do not speak to us as we work daily in their presence. The rich discovery of the terracotta soldiers and horses at Xian, China was located by accident. With wind borne soil (loess) and water borne silt in the river valleys often exceeding twenty or thirty feet in depth, it is possible that we are near an important archaeologic site every day but we do not know about it.

In summary, it should be clear that there are no absolutely clear answers between those who believe in the **creation** theory and those who believe in the theory of **evolution**. Neither is there an absolute answer concerning the **place** where mankind originated. Future generations may develop a better means of detection of sites and analysis of the remains, but today there are simply many educated guesses applied to archaeology and anthropology. Determining **how** a particular item was used often leads to great controversy among experts. Tests such as carbon-14 and other similar tests have taken much of the guesswork out of the field and made it much more scientific. We have made great progress in the last century and logically will progress further in the future.

BOOKS FOR FURTHER STUDY

Allchin, Bridget & Raymond, *The Rise of Civilization in India and Pakistan* (1982).

Basham, A.L., *The Wonder That Was India* (1984).

Cole, Sonia, *The Neolithic Revolution* (1970).

Constable, George, *The Human Dawn* (1990).

Cotterell, Arthur, *China: A Cultural History* (1988).

Fairbank, John K., Reischauer, Edwin O., & Craig, Albert M., *East Asia: Tradition & Transformation* (1989).

Latourette, Kenneth Scott, *The Chinese: Their History and Culture*, Two Volumes in One (1964).

Oakley, Kenneth P., *Man the Tool-Maker* (1972).

Smith, Vincent A., *The Oxford History of India*, edited by Percival Spear (1958).

Stuart, George E., editor, *Peoples and Places of the Past* (1983).

Tarling, Nicholas, editor, *The Cambridge History of Southeast Asia* (1992).

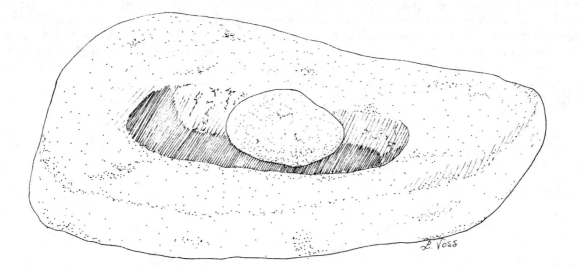

Figure 2

Chapter 3
THE ORIGINS OF AGRICULTURE

The beginning of agriculture has no single, simple origin. At different times and in numerous places, many plants and animals have been domesticated. No one knows how many species have passed into or out of domestication during the prehistoric period. With the number of farms declining in the western world, along with the numbers of people actively engaged in full-time agriculture, it is difficult for us to realize that agriculture continues to draft into its service more of the world's aggregate manpower than all other occupations combined. Nowhere in the world is this more evident than in Asia.

Nineteenth century scholars hypothesized that mankind's development occurred in four stages. In the very earliest stage everyone was a primitive **hunter-gatherer**. Eventually, early people domesticated the dog, sheep, goats and cattle. There were the beginnings of a primitive agriculture in this **pastoral stage**. Eventually, some people began to desire a more settled existence. Rather than going out to gather the wild fruits and berries, and the wild grains, they began to imitate nature by tilling a small plot and growing the crops literally at their doorstep. This changed mankind's lifestyle altogether because it now became necessary to stay in a fixed abode while others took the flocks out to pasture. It was a kind of a mixed way of life.

The greatest change came when mankind moved from this mixed life of partially fixed agriculture and the pastoral stage to totally fixed agriculture. This most often occurred first in the rich river valleys such as the Tigris-Euphrates in Mesopotamia, the Nile Valley in Egypt, the Indus River Valley in Pakistan, and the Hwang Ho (Yellow) River Valley of China. Since this revolution in how the people lived occurred during the Neolithic Age it is often referred to as the **Neolithic Revolution**. Many scholars call this change the **Agricultural Revolution**. During this stage the people improvised many simple tools to assist in the planting and harvesting operations. Simple hoes, rakes, shovels, harvesting sickles, and flails became the universal tools of the farmers regardless of which area of the globe was under consideration. Animals and plants were both bred to accomplish the desired characteristics, generally slanted toward greater yield or productivity.

The final stage of agricultural development is what should properly be called the **second** Agricultural Revolution, which began in Britain during the second half of the 19th century. During this revolution the people invented dozens of machines which would replace the hard physical labor of the farm with mechanical operations, often operated with either steam power or with internal combustion engines. This revolution has continued from the mid-19th century to the present time. It should be pointed out, however, that even though many tilling and harvesting inventions have been pioneered in the western world, there are not many of these tools such as large farm tractors, combines, and other implements employed by the Asian farmer. Farming in many parts of Asia continues to remain in the age of the first agricultural revolution.

In the West, agriculture is carried out on an "extensive" basis. In the East, agriculture is "labor intensive." It is not that power machinery is unknown, it is that the eastern farmer simply does not have the capital to invest in a modern farm tractor or combine. Many could not even afford the fuel for such machines even if they owned one. Since the eastern world is generally overpopulated for their land resources, they tend to employ inexpensive laborers rather than investing in the expensive machinery. In addition large machinery, would not work well on the small fields and rice paddies. One of the reasons that both Stalin in the Soviet Union, and Mao in China opted for large "collective farms."

It seems most likely that mankind developed agriculture as early as 7000 B.C.--roughly 9,000 years ago. The best evidence indicates that settled agriculture began in the ancient Near East, sometimes referred to as Mesopotamia, where mankind first passed from the hunting and gathering stage to the pastoral stage, and finally to a life of settled agriculture. A culture called the Natufians of Palestine had sickles as early as 9000 B.C. We would presume from these archaeological finds that they raised cultivated grains, but there is the possibility that the sickle was used to gather wild grain.

There are good sources which indicate that einkorn, emmer wheat and barley were cultivated in Iran and Iraq as early as 7000 B.C. The Nile Valley, the Indus Valley and the valley of the Yellow River also began to turn to the cultivation of crops at this same time. Domesticated beans, peas, gourds, and water chestnuts were grown at the Spirit Cave in North Thailand by as early as 7000 B.C. The cultivation of pumpkins and gourds in northeast Mexico was also underway by about 7000 B.C. Since each of these areas seem to have discovered some form of agriculture at about the same time, it is believed that each area developed its own system more or less independently. Knowledge of agriculture did not necessarily occur in any one location and then spread to the remainder of the world.

Archaeological evidence concerning the beginning of agriculture in prehistoric Asia is very weak compared to the excellent evidence which we have in Egypt. The Egyptian tombs often had realistic scenes of planting, cultivating, and harvesting. There is no such evidence for any country in Asia. Authorities are divided concerning whether the Mohenjo Daro civilization of the Indus River Valley or the Chinese developed agriculture first. A slight edge is given to China. The final answer is yet to be found.

From early times the preferred crop in northern China was wheat, while rice predominated in southern China. The Chinese also developed the cultivation of the soybean, sorghum, millet, barley, and sweet potatoes. The philosopher Mencius wrote in the 4th century B.C. that there would normally be more grain in the land than could be consumed. That began to gradually change by the first century B.C.. Wastelands in China were being reclaimed for cultivation. By the year A.D. 9 there was an unsuccessful effort to "nationalize" the land and redistribute it to those who had little or no land. By the end of the second century A.D. China was beginning to have shortages which were severe enough to trigger revolts against the government which was believed to be unresponsive to the problems of the people. By about A.D. 1100 China's population had tripled and the situation was desperate. **sericultlure**, the cultivation of silkworms, also began very early in China's history.

Heavy cropping of the land year after year made it ever more difficult to coax enough rice or wheat from the land to feed China's growing population. By the 6th century A.D., a system of "three fields in two years" rotation was established. Night soil, rice cakes, and ashes were used for fertilizer, but it was rice which made China's growing population possible. The same might be said of most of Asia, particularly in the southern climates wherever water was readily available.

Farmers in the western world usually think in terms of innovation and new equipment--along with fertilizer, herbicides, and pesticides--to meet heavier demands for grain. There is evidence of an early Chinese plow with an iron share as early as the 4th century B.C. However, there is no indication that it was pulled by draft animals. It is most likely that people pulled the plow. Cattle-drawn plows did not appear in China until the first century B.C. The harrow and a three-shared plow were both developed by 1279, but Chinese agriculture generally lacked mechanical innovations, and it still does. The same can be said about the remainder of the eastern world. It is not at all uncommon to see people spading a paddy or breaking clods with hand tools.

RICE CULTURE

Rice is an Asiatic tropical grass and is the only semi-aquatic species among the cultivated cereals. Other members of this same general family of plants are wheat, maize (corn), oats, barley, sorghum, and millet. Rice is traditionally thought of as a crop grown under flooded conditions, but certain strains will grow under moist conditions without flooding. Such strains are called upland rices, and they generally yield much less grain than does the flooded variety. There is long-grained rice and short-grained rice. Most of the rice which is grown in Asia is the short-grain variety and is often called "sticky" rice. The crop will grow in most temperate to tropical regions of the world, providing it has water, and it is normally a heavy yielder of grain.

Rice is the favorite crop throughout Southeast Asia and as far north as Korea and the northern islands of Japan. With its heavy yields and the ability to produce up to three crops per year on the same parcel of land in the warmer latitudes, rice is the world's leading grain crop. The recent introduction of the semidwarf strains, with their higher productivity, has greatly increased yields and has made many areas, which were once forced to import grain, now self-sufficient. In an effort to increase production of rice, some countries such as Indonesia even provide the seed for the newer, heavy-yielding varieties.

The origin of rice culture has been traced far back in history, perhaps as early as 5,000 years ago. The first historical record concerning rice is a proclamation by a Chinese emperor in 2800 B.C. whereby he established a ceremonial ordinance dealing with the planting of rice. This would indicate that the crop was already well-established in China by this time. It also indicates the importance of rice in the lives of the Chinese people. Many authorities believe that rice culture spread both east and west from its place of origin. Both China and the Indus River Valley of India claim to have originated rice culture. The Saracens were the first to introduce rice to western Europe during the Middle Ages. Apparently considerable acreage was devoted to rice culture in Europe but rice gradually fell from favor as the grain of choice in the West. In the Far East, most people think of rice first.

It was in Asia where rice became both a staple and **an institution** several thousand years ago. Special offerings, prayers, dances and religious ceremonies accompanied planting and harvesting in many areas. It is rice which makes possible the huge concentrations of populations in the Far East because rice will out yield the other crops even where only two crops per year are possible. The highest yielding crop of all is corn (maize) at about 54 bushels per acre. In almost every instance, corn will only produce one crop per year. Rice yields about 34 bushels per acre and in most of the areas of south and east Asia it is possible to produce two crops per season and in the warmest and wettest latitudes it will produce three crops. Barley only produces about 27 bushels per acre, oats about 25 bushels, and wheat averages about the same as oats. Obviously, the average yields depend a great deal upon the fertility of the soil, the amount of water available, and most important, the length of the growing season. It is said that rice is what makes Asia possible. Without rice there would be mass starvation.

Rice is one of the most labor intensive of all the crops grown in Asia. The crop is started by sowing the seed thickly in a flooded bed. As soon as the seedlings are 25 to 50 days old, these are transplanted to a field or paddy which has been thoroughly prepared. At this stage the seedlings are about six to ten inches tall. During the time the seedlings are growing large enough to "set" in the paddy, the farmer is busy repairing the levees, or **bunds**, so that the paddy can be flooded to a depth of from two to four inches. The soil type should have a solid base of clay or muck which will hold the water during the growing season. The paddy will be stirred several times with a homemade tool which has several large spikes set in it. No weeds should be growing in the paddy at the time the rice is set.

When the seedlings are large enough and the paddy is well stirred, the seed bed is heavily flooded and the plants are carefully removed from the planting bed to be reset in the paddy. Several dozen plants are normally tied together in a clump and are then tossed into the flooded paddy. In many areas of Asia it is considered a woman's job to "set" the rice in the paddy. Each woman takes a clump, then separates off two to five seedlings which are placed in hills three to six inches apart in rows which are eight to twelve inches apart. The women work in long rows across the paddy moving backwards with the newly set rice in front of them. They generally do this backbreaking work wearing broad-brimmed straw hats with their bare feet work through the soft mud. The women often socialize, gossip, tell jokes, and generally seem to have a good time as they work.

Once the rice is set, the paddy is kept flooded during most of the growing season. All of the men and many of the women can be seen going through the rice time after time taking out any weeds or aquatic plants which may compete with the rice for space or nutrients. During this time the crop also requires a great amount of work to maintain the bunds and to keep the irrigation ditches open and the water moving. If the water must be moved uphill, the pumps may be very old styles which have been in use in Asia over a period of thousands of years. A few farmers now employ modern electric or diesel pumps. In the least accessible places the water may have to be carried in buckets.

About 60 days (variable) after setting the rice it begins to flower and then to form grain in a panicle which is somewhat looser than wheat but denser than oats. As the crop ripens the head or panicle begins to bend over, then curls down and eventually it will turn a golden tan which sometimes borders on a rich brown. Once the grain begins to form in the panicle an elaborate system of scarecrows is rigged to scare the birds from the paddy. One of the favorite arrangements involves stringing wires on poles. The wires have ribbons and other items hung upon them so that if a bird approaches the paddy an appointed person can give the wire a sharp jerk. This will make the wire jump all over the paddy and scare the birds away. Most of the rice is harvested just as it passes from green to the tan stage. American farmers would consider this too green to harvest but the Asian farmer wants to harvest the crop before the birds discover the grain. Sometimes storms may also come along which blow the grain down into the water, thus losing a portion of the yield.

As harvest approaches the water is allowed to go down in the paddy so that harvesting is easier. The paddy can still be quite soft to walk upon at harvest time. Almost everyone works barefoot in the fields or else they wear light sandals. Since many of the terraces and paddies are quite small one seldom sees any mechanized equipment used in either the tillage or the harvesting of rice. Even on broad fields rice is virtually all harvested by hand. Garden tractors do exist today but most of them are single cylinder diesels which are rarely seen in the fields; rather, they have a trailer hitched behind them to haul freight. The same is true of large farm tractors.

The Japanese are the most mechanized of all the Oriental farmers. Small motorized combines in Japan work over the paddies moving back and forth like small miniatures of those used in the United States. Some places such as the Philippines do have small portable threshing machines with gasoline engines attached. China has the same type of threshers but they are operated by crank or treadle power. It is not uncommon throughout Asia to see people thresh the rice by beating it across a board or across an old oil drum which has been laid on its side. In this case a large tarp is spread to catch the flying grains of rice.

The most common method of harvesting is to grab a handful of the stalks and cut them off with a small sickle. As soon as a small clump of from three to six inches in diameter is gathered it is taken to the threshing area. There it is either beaten from the straw or the revolving cylinder of the portable thresher does the same task. Where a threshing machine is available they hold the cut end of the small bundle while a rotating drum inside the machine strips away the heads of rice. The rice straw is then laid aside as it will be bundled and stacked later. Every part of the rice plant has some usefulness to the people.

Once the rice grain has been separated from the straw it is gathered in large bags and placed on a trailer to be taken to the village. Sometimes it is placed in baskets and carried by a pole across the shoulder. At this stage the rice berry with which we are all familiar has a coarse husk covering it. In this stage it is called "paddy rice" or "rough rice." In this form it can be used for seed or for cattle feed; however, feeding grain to cattle in Asia is not very common when compared to cattle feeding practices in the United States.

Since the rice crop was harvested before it was totally ripe, it must then be spread out on a pavement to dry. Sometimes it is parboiled and then spread to dry. Some villagers have a cement threshing floor for drying while others spread the rice in a thin layer along the side of a paved highway to dry. The rice is stirred with a rake or a shovel to allow it to dry thoroughly. It is usually sacked up at the end of each day and then spread out the following morning until the drying process is completed.

In order to make the rice usable as human food the next stage is to "mill" it to remove the rough outer husk. This will leave the brown rice berry. At this stage it is perfectly alright to eat because it contains all the natural nutrients of the rice. If it is consumed in this stage it is called "brown rice." Nearly everyone in Asia prefers the white rice. This means that it will be milled further to remove the outer coating of bran. Often they even add talc to the final process to polish the grains to a fine white finish. In this state the valuabe nutrients are gone and all that is left is the starch.

A diet which is heavy in white rice day after day can cause malnutrition diseases such as **beriberi**. It is interesting that if the rice is boiled and dried prior to milling, it retains more thiamin (vitamin B1) and minerals than unboiled rice. It seems that in parboiling, the thiamine, which is largely in the germ and bran layers of the kernel, diffuses into and is fixed in the starchy endosperm. By adding legumes, fish, meat, fruits, and vegetables to the diet the people can also substantially reduce the dangers of beriberi. Unfortunately, there are large areas of the Orient where the diet is very heavy on rice without the other ingredients of a balanced diet.

Beriberi was once quite common throughout the Far East with documentation going back for over 1,000 years. The term is derived from the Sinhalese word meaning "extreme weakness." In what is known as dry beriberi there is a gradual degeneration of the nerves, first in the legs and arms, then of the muscles, and there is a loss of reflexes.

Wet beriberi is more acute. In this form fluid forms in the tissues (edema) and this results in cardiac and kidney failure as circulation slows substantially. In infants breastfed by mothers who are deficient in thiamine, beriberi may lead to rapidly progressing heart failure. This explains in part the high death rate of children in earlier times. Although the wet beriberi is much more serious, it does clear up rapidly once the patient is given thiamine or thiamine rich foods. The nerve deterioration resulting from dry beriberi becomes irreversible if it is allowed to progress too far. It is interesting to note that before 1870, half the Japanese sailors died of beriberi. It was not until the period around 1870 to 1912 that it was both scientifically proven and accepted that beriberi was caused by eating rice without other kinds of foods. Even so, many still died of this malnutrition disease until quite recently. In many countries it is mandatory that the rice be enriched with the proper ingredients before it is sold on the retail market.

Rice is raised primarily as a food product but it does have several other applications and by-products. It is quite common to grind it into flour and use it in many ways similar to wheat flour. The Japanese use rice to make *sake* and in China it is called *wang-tsin*. Both are alcoholic drinks. The hulls, or husks, are used for fuel. The straw is given to the cattle. They nibble at the finer part of the straw while the remainder is used for bedding. Rice straw can be woven into mats or baskets as well as processed into paper. As with all other crops in the Asia, little or nothing is wasted from the rice plant. In the end it is returned to the paddy in one form or another.

It may seem unnecessary to make such a long explanation of rice as an Asian crop, but even a short visit to any Asian country will quickly reveal the extreme importance of this crop in their daily lives. The Asian farmer rises early in the morning to tend his paddy. Many of them then change to a business suit and leave for work in the inner city. Immediately after work he returns home and begins working in the paddy. Men, women, and children all have tasks to perform in preparing the paddy, setting the rice, tending the crop, and harvesting the crop. As soon as one crop is harvested the paddy is immediately prepared for the next crop. The family, the community, and the country are all very much interested in the outcome of the annual rice crop.

SOYBEAN CULTURE

Perhaps the second most important food crop of Asia is the soybean. The origins of the domesticated soybean plant are obscure, but many botanists believe that its cultivation began in central China over 5,000 years ago. The soybean is a legume rather than a member of the grass family as is the case with rice and wheat. Soybeans are treated as a grain crop throughout Asia and these are used as a substitute for other grain crops in the food chain. Unlike rice, soybeans are an excellent source of protein of high biological value. The average soybean seed contains approximately 17% oil or fat, 7% crude fiber, 40% protein, 5% or less sugar, 1.5% potassium, and other smaller amounts of iron, calcium, and vitamins. Since soybeans contain very little to practically no starch, they provide a good source of protein for diabetics, especially in Asia where the people consume such large quantities of rice and cassava.

There are over one hundred different varieties of soybeans known to be cultivated and it is important to remember that some varieties are higher in oils while other varieties are richer in protein. The soybean was first introduced to the United States in 1804, and the U.S. has now become the major world producer. Illinois is the state which grows more tons of soybeans than any other single state. Brazil is the second largest world producer; China is the third largest producer. In the U.S., 98% of the crop ends up as oil or animal feed. The reverse is true in China where about 98% of the crop is consumed by humans and only a few of the by-products are fed to livestock.

Soybeans do well in a warm, moist climate and a fertile soil. They can be grown as far north as Beijing, China and North Korea, and as far south as Southeast Asia. Soybeans are planted directly into the soil as soon as the danger of frost has passed. They are easy to cultivate and are usually harvested in Asia by being pulled up by the roots just before they are fully mature. They are then hung upside down on a fence to dry for awhile. Once the pods are dry they are shelled out and the drying process is completed on a pavement very much like the rice crop. The greatest disadvantage of soybeans is that like wheat, only one crop can be grown in northern latitudes. In warmer climates it is now possible to raise two crops per year due to the development of faster maturing varieties.

Soybeans can easily be milled into flour. The flour can be baked into breads or added to wheat flour recipes for cakes and cookies to give them a firm, less crumbly texture. Soybean flour is often added to ground meat products, ice cream, mayonnaise, and a host of other food products today. Soybeans can be roasted, cooked, and added to many other dishes without substantially altering their flavor. Industrial uses include paint, adhesives, sizing for cloth, linoleum backing, insect sprays, and many are used in the western world for the manufacture of plastics. They are also added to many medications as well as dozens of other applications.

The soybean is used in all of the above ways today throughout Asia. In addition, they process them by taking the dry soybeans and soaking them in water. They are then crushed and boiled. This mixture is then separated into solid pulp called okra, and soya milk. Soya milk is used in its fresh state in China and more often as a condensed milk in Japan. It is very common in Asia to take the fresh milk and add coagulants such as calcium and magnesium chlorides and sulfates, which causes the curds to separate from the whey. The soya milk is poured into molds to allow the carbohydrate-laden whey to drain off. The soft cakes which are left are cut into squares about three inches square by one inch thick and stored under water until used.

In this state the fresh, plain **bean curd** has a texture very much like thick custard and is very bland and tasteless. It is also often called **tofu** in this state. The tofu or bean curd is six to eight percent protein. It is also high in calcium, potassium, and iron. The okra and soy whey are also added to other foods so that nothing is wasted. Even the skin which forms on top of the soy milk as it stands for a while is removed and dried in sheets for use in vegetarian dishes. Dried sheets of bean curd are wiped with a clean, damp cloth when ready for use. This softens them and they are often wrapped around other foods for added protein. The tofu may be grilled, deep-fried, stir-fried, steamed, or eaten fresh. It is more customary to deep-fry the tofu in Southeast **Asia**. It is then threaded onto strings and sold for adding nutrition to soups. These cubes are often rather greasy. Other people use the soybean for bean sprouts but the product is rather coarse compared to the preferred mung bean sprouts.

WHEAT AND OTHER CEREAL GRAINS

Wheat is another favorite food of the Orient. Since rice and soybeans become increasingly difficult to grow north of Beijing, China and in northern Korea, farmers plant more wheat and other grain crops such as oats, barley, millet, and rye. The total acreage of wheat in China is about the same as rice but the total yield is much less, As a consequence, northern China can support far less people per square mile than in the south. In northern China beyond the Great Wall and in most of Manchuria, wheat is planted in the springtime.

White bread is a favorite in these more northern latitudes, especially among the upper classes, in very much the same way as white rice is favored in southern and eastern Asia. But even in these northern Asian areas the people consume far more rice and soybeans per capita than do the people of North America. Poorer soils and/or difficult weather conditions allow rye to be grown where other crops would fail. The rye is ground into flour and baked into very dark breads and pastries. Barley and oats, where they can be grown, are used largely to tide the animals over the long, cold winters.

Beijing, China might be considered the center of the corn (maize) area of China. Farther north in Mongolia and Siberia, the seasons are too short and too cool for corn to thrive. Although corn is grown in southern China where it is possible to raise two crops per year, the people prefer to grow rice wherever sufficient water is available. It should also be pointed out that corn is originally an American crop. It was not grown in Asia to any extent until recent years.

Cornfields in China are of varying size and may also be devoted to grain sorghum, sorghum for syrup, and broom corn. The Chinese raise the corn similar to America except with much more hand labor. The harvest is quite different as they cut the corn and then allow it to cure out while it is flat on the ground rather than husking it from the standing stalk or cutting and shocking it as in America. When the ears are pulled from the stalk they still have the husks on them. They are stored in this way until they are consumed. The stalks and husks become animal feed. It can therefore be said that like other food crops in Asia, nothing is wasted. The idea of boiling corn on the cob is quite recent in the Asian diet. It is also roasted over an open fire.

MILLET

The term millet is applied to a number of small-seeded plants. Millet was originally cultivated by the ancient Egyptians, the Greeks, and the Romans, as well as throughout Asia. It was a popular crop in most of western Europe during the Middle Ages. Records show that it was cultivated in Asia and Africa over 4,000 years ago.

The plants of cultivated millet vary considerably from some which are less than a foot in height to plants which may reach a height of six feet or more. The short millet is often grown in India where it is called *bajra*. The tall broomcorn-type called proso millet is grown in areas where the soil had greater levels of fertility. Since the plant varies so much, it is difficult to describe but on the average it resembles the weed known as "foxtail." As millet matures it forms tiny round seeds in a head at the top of the stalk. The shorter varieties are especially well-suited to the dry, low-fertility areas of India, northern and western China, and southern Siberia. In these poorer areas of Asia, millet is often the primary food grain crop. It can be processed for use very similar to soybeans, or it can be milled to remove the outer hull and cooked like rice. It is often ground into flour for baking. In the West, millet is most often seen as the small yellow seeds which are in bird seed mixtures. Health food stores often stock millet.

CASSAVA CULTURE

Another popular food grown in Asia is a tuber rather than a cereal or a legume. Cassava, or manioc, is a plant which is native to Brazil in South America and was not introduced to the Asian diet until after 1500. It is now widely grown in Indonesia, Malaysia, the Philippines, and Thailand. Cassava contains virtually no protein, fat, or fiber. It is often used to replace rice in the diet but it has even less true food value than white rice. It is practically all starch.

Cassava is easily cultivated, it is immune to most diseases and pests, and produces heavy yields. Some tubers grow as large as 30 pounds each. Since it does fill empty stomachs it is easy to see why this Latin American crop is rapidly catching on in Asia.

Wet-processed cassava involves crushing or rasping the tubers, then allowing the starch to settle. The wet starch is dried in the sun to a point where it can be broken into small pieces. It is then normally tumbled rather than being ground until it turns to flour. In some cases steam is used during the tumbling to form small pellets. In the western world we call these pellets TAPIOCA. Cassava leaves are also edible. They are rich in vitamins, proteins, and calcium but must be boiled to reduce their prussic acid level. The plant also has chemical and industrial applications.

Several kinds of yams and sweet potatoes are grown in Asia. These are also considered very cheap foods and are not consumed frequently by middle and upper class people. It is considered an insult in China to be called "a sweet potato eater."

PEANUTS AS A FOOD CROP

Peanuts are also known as groundnuts, earthnuts, or goobers. Like soybeans, the peanut is a member of the legume family of plants. It is not a true nut. Unlike the soybean which produces pods above ground, the peanut ripens underground. Most of the underground shells, or pods, contain from one to three seeds. Like corn (maize), peanuts are a native plant from the warmer climates of South America. The Spanish and Portuguese were the first to introduce the crop to Asia.

Peanuts need a fertile, well-drained and sandy loam. They produce best in a calcium-rich soil with plenty of water available during the growing season if they are to produce a good crop. A large percentage of the peanuts grown in Asia are irrigated. Furthermore, the crop will not mature north of a line which has less than five months of frost-free weather. If well cultivated the peanut crop produces heavy yields.

19

Pound for pound, peanuts have more protein, minerals, and vitamins than any other crop. They are very rich in fat and high in calories. Peanuts store well over a long period and as a consequence of their many attributes they are popular throughout Asia.

Peanuts in Asia are eaten raw, boiled, roasted, deep fried, and pressed for cooking oil. The tops are used for cattle feed once the peanuts have been removed. Nearly every meal in China either has peanuts or peanut products included. Peanut butter is not commonly consumed in Asia as it is in the western world.

THE MEAT PRODUCTS OF ASIA

Fish is the wonder food of Asia wherever it is available. It is rich in protein, minerals, and the unsaturated fats. The people of Asia seem to have known the value of fish in the diet long before the western scientists figured it out. In countries such as the Philippines and Japan, fish is a heavy part of the diet since the islands are surrounded by the sea. Every morning one can see the fishing boats come in with their catch. The Filipinos set nets for fish along the shore and they are carefully tended. Fish are also important in the diets of coastal China, Indonesia, Hong Kong, Korea, and throughout Southeast Asia. In the Philippines they often catch a minnow-sized fish and dry them on the pavement. These little dried fish are called "dillies," and are stir-fried with a little oil and vegetables.

The fish markets of Japan, China, and Korea are also very important. Fish and rice, along with some fresh green vegetables or an egg makes up a substantial part of the everyday diet of the people from these areas. It is truly an experience for a westerner to visit a fish market in any Asian country. The fish market in Pusan, Korea is one of the largest in Asia. Shop after shop sells fresh fish in the huge market in Seoul, Korea as well. Fish in China is an equally popular food but as one goes into the interior of the country the numbers of salt-water fish diminishes because of transportation and refrigeration problems.

This does not mean that fish are not served. The Chinese have built all kinds of ponds and have separated special areas of their rivers for fish farming. Farm-raised catfish, carp, and other "domesticated" kinds of fish are quite abundant. Seeing a fisherman at work commercially, for family sustenance or for recreation, is a common sight on the many rivers and lakes of the Far East. Fish is a staple of the diet throughout the countries of the eastern world.

There are generally more fish in the markets than are sold each day. The leftover fish are dried and then sold for a much lower price than the fresh catch. Dried fish and several ground fish products can be added to stir-fry dishes to add nutrition. Since the amount of grain and pastureland required to fatten beef cattle is enormous compared to a small rice paddy, it appears likely that most people in Asia will continue to depend upon fish for their meat rather than to seriously consider beef. The land is too precious in most countries to change from grain and vegetables to red meat products. Imported meats are too expensive for the average working class family. Besides, the Hindus have no desire to eat any meat and the Muslims do not eat pork.

Except for the Muslim and Hindu areas of Asia, pork is one of the common meat dishes. Both pigs and chickens are considered scavanger-type animals and are often allowed to roam about scavanging for whatever they can find as well as any leftover table scraps. Pork is especially well prepared in China where the pig has been domesticated for thousands of years.

Asian chickens are a much smaller variety than the ones in America and somewhat skinny as well. All meat products are served quite sparingly, most often as a supplement to soups, stews, stir-fry, etc., not as the main dish such as a large pork roast.

Beef is available but outside of Japan it is generally of poor quality and taste when compared to western standards. The cattle of Asia are more often used as draft animals until they are quite old. Products such as veal and baby beef are almost impossible to obtain in most of Asia. The cow is sacred in India so beef is either very scarce or nonexistant. In many areas it is simply not on the menu. Lamb and goat meat are available in the markets and hotels of Central Asia.

Roast ducks and geese are very popular among those who plan to have a celebration. Peking duck is very popular in China--never mind that the city is now called Beijing. Peking duck is relatively inexpensive for a tourist and it is exceptionally wellprepared. Working class people also indulge on special occasions. The ducks are much more carefully tended than are chickens. Eggs are very popular throughout most of Asia and are fixed in many different ways. Many are mixed into other dishes.

Other meat dishes of Asia which are much less common in the West are octopus, squid, eels, and many other creatures of the sea which are either little known or unheard of in the West. Several Asian cultures also eat dog meat. When these food products are properly prepared, nearly everything in Asia becomes good, tasty food.

FRUITS AND VEGETABLES IN ASIA

In many parts of Asia the vegetables must be thoroughly cooked before they are served because of the bacteria from night soil. This is still true in areas where night soil [*explanation in a later section*] has not been used for up to twenty-five years. Most of their vegetables consist of root crops such as turnips, carrots, rutabagas, and potatoes. Boiled peanuts are a favorite in China. Peanuts are also processed for use as cooking oil. Beans, peas, and lentils of all kinds are very popular. Various kinds of edible seaweed and kelp-type plants are mixed into prepared dishes including soups. The same is true of various kinds of edible lotus, which grows in ponds and along river banks throughout Asia. Vegetables are most often served as a mixture with other foods rather than being served alone.

Fruit is quite abundant in most of Southeast Asia and the Philippines. Pineapple, papaya, mango, various kinds of citrus, kiwi, and many varieties unknown in the West are quite abundant, of excellent quality, and are relatively inexpensive when in season. The Chinese do not grow or serve as many fruits as in Southeast Asia. Even in the southern parts of China, where it seems fruit should be abundant, it is somewhat scarce and often of poor quality. In the northern latitudes an appleshaped pear is quite common but it is generally inferior to either the apple or the pear of the westrn world. Japan grows some fruit and imports large quantities today. Japanese fruit is generally of good quality, but expensive.

FOOD PREPARATION

Food products in Asia are deep-fried, stir-fried, baked, boiled, and steamed. Almost any food can be put through any one of these processes. For instance, a very common food in

Southeast Asia is deep-fried bananas. Almost any food can also be stir-fried with the aid of a little vegetable oil and water. Many products which the western world would bake in an oven are steamed. Noodles are another very common food throughout Asia and are consumed in greater quantities than in the western world.

Properly done under sanitary conditions, any of the foods of Asia are both wholesome and delicious. Water can be a problem in some places, and as a consequence, water should be thoroughly boiled to kill the bacteria. China provides a large thermos of boiled water in each hotel room. It is hot enough to pour out for tea. In India the water is never considered safe for travelers. Everyone should drink bottled mineral water there. Many of the Indian people are also careful. They often carry water purification tablets if they are in doubt. China loves to serve large bowls of thin soup along with plenty of white rice, soft drinks, and beer. Everyone must drink something or risk the dangers of dehydration. Generally speaking, most of Asia is perfectly safe with only a few sensible precautions.

SUGARCANE CULTIVATION

It is believed that sugarcane probably originated in the Southeast Asian island of New Guinea. Its system of cultivation spread along the routes of human migration and trade to Southeast Asia, India, and southern China. The Chinese introduced sugarcane to Java and the Philippines. Long before recorded history, the manner of growing sugarcane had spread to Africa and to some parts of southern Europe.

Throughout these very early years, sugar was a luxury item for the very rich. Some believed it had special healing powers. The age of inexpensive sugar began after Columbus introduced the crop to Santo Domingo, Cuba, and other islands of the Caribbean. By around the year 1600, sugar production had become the largest single industry in the world. With the beginning of the age of inexpensive sugar there were people who consumed huge quantities on a daily basis. The Asians were no exception.

Sugarcane is grown for commercial purposes from "cuttings" which are taken from a section of stalk about twelve inches long with several buds along its length. This section is laid in a shallow trench or furrow, and covered with soil. If the soil is moist the buds will begin to sprout and grow with each one producing a new stalk. Sugarcane can be started from seed but this is not pracatical because the seeds are so small. One grain of wheat would be about the same size as about 100 sugarcane seeds.

A warm, wet, and fertile environment is wellsuited to raising sugar. Water is the most essential since it requires about 100 inches of water per year. If sugarcane is kept well watered it will reach a height of more than 20 feet and become two or more inches in diameter. Some varieties are known to yield more sugar than others. Some are also more subject to disease and insects than others.

In most places of the world, sugarcane is harvested once a year. It is cut close to the ground with a long knife which is usually called a machete. The grassy leaves are stripped off and the stalks are sent to the mill to be crushed between heavy steel rollers. The juice which is squeezed out is strained and cooked down in large vats until it becomes either syrup or solid sugar. The product will not look very attractive since it usually has a pale yellow color. The sugar is ground, then it is spread out to bleach in the sun, or it often will have bleaching agents added to it to produce the white sugar everyone desires.

A new crop will then grow up from the stubble of the old crop. The yield from the second crop will depend largely upon the fertility of the soil. Sometimes several crops can be harvested from a single planting. In other cases, two crops are about all that can be profitably produced until the old roots are ripped out and a new planting is made, usually after the soil has had an opportunity to rest. In fertile soil they harvest a new crop every seven months. Sugarcane in Asia is generally harvested in the fall. Freezing weather will ruin the crop.

Asian farmers usually haul the long stalks to the mill in ox carts, a few in camel carts. A few places have narrow- gauge railways built to transport the stalks to the mill. Farm tractors and trucks are also used in transporting the bulky stalks. In some places sugarcane production is a large plantation project which employs primarily men in the field and women in the mill. In other areas the raising and harvesting of sugarcane is done on small plots with the entire family participating in all the operations. Once the stalks are cut, the small farmer then hauls them to the sugarcane mill in that community.

Sugarcane, like rice, occupies thousands of laborers, often on a whole family basis. Asians consume much more sugar per capita than is customary in the West. Many foods are made unreasonably sweet, especially in the areas where it is grown. The same is true of soft drinks: they are usually very sweet. Beet sugar is not as large a crop in Asia as it is in the United States and western Europe. Beet sugar has only been popular in the western world in the last fifty years.

OTHER AGRICULTURAL PRODUCTS

There are several other agricultural products which deserve mention. **Cooking oils** are made from soybeans, peanuts, cottonseed, and corn--probably in about that order but varying from one part of Asia to another. Some areas use olive oil, but it is not as common as in southern Europe.

Tea is often associated with Asia. Two general kinds are produced--green tea and black tea. Tea is grown in the more southern latitudes and often in the mountainous areas. China, India, Sri Lanka, Java, and several other Pacific islands probably produce the majority of the tea. The Darjeeling area of northeast India, the mountain slopes of Java, and the area around Foochow, China, produce some of the most flavorful teas. The green tea is gathered from the tender leaves at the end of the branches on a large bush. It is carried to the processing center and is simply dried pretty much in its picked state--it still appears green. The black tea is picked in the same manner, crushed and fermented. The fermentation process is very carefully regulated to produce the finest flavors.

Cotton is a big crop throughout the warmer latitudes. It was probably first cultivated in India before the time of the prehistoric cities of Mohenjo Daro and Harappa because cotton cloth has been found at those locations which dates back to at least 3,000 B.C. It is a popular fabric throughout Asia today. The mature cotton is handpicked in Asia, loaded into an ox cart, and hauled to a cotton mill. It is normally harvested in the fall and winter months which is the dry season in much of Asia. It is stacked in great heaps resembling small mountains near the mill.

Both the culture of the plant and the manufacturing process occupies thousands of people. Like all other crops in Asia, no part of the cotton is wasted.

Sericulture, the production of silk from silkworms, is another large agricultural occupation. The origin of making silk is so old that the beginning has been lost in time. Chinese legend claims that the practice was begun when the empress Hsi Ling Shi discovered a silkworm at work just above where she was reclining under a mulberry tree in c.2640 B.C. She noticed that once the silkworm began making the cocoon that it was all a single filament of thread. The empress reasoned that if the silkworm constructed the cocoon in that fashion, then it would be possible to unwind the cocoon.

The empress spent some time figuring out how to dissolve the substance which the silkworm produced to stick it all together. She discovered that they preferred a very clean environment, a diet of a particular kind of mulberry leaf, and the proper temperature and humidity. When the worm is hatched from the egg, it is about one-twelfth of an inch long. They are soon fed a diet of mulberry leaves and the larvae begins to grow. Large larvae grow to a length of three inches.

After feeding heavily on leaves for 42 days, the silkworm begins to raise its head and to shake it from side to side. That motion signifies that it is preparing to form a cocoon. The larvae are then placed in individual compartmennts so that no two worms are able to form a common cocoon. Once their task is finished, they are removed from the tiny compartments and the dormant pupa inside the cocoon is killed. If this is not accomplished, it will later eat through the cocoon and emerge as a moth. The pupa is destroyed by any one of several means. The oldest method is to set the cocoons out in the hot sun which will destroy the life inside. Other means involves suffocation with steam or by passing them through an oven at 210 degrees F. for seven or eight hours.

The process of unwinding the cocoons is referred to as "reeling." The cocoons are first sorted, then they are boiled in water for 10 or 12 minutes. This softens the natural gum with which the larvae constructed the cocoon in the first place. The single filament can then be unwound. These filaments do not need to be spun in the usual sense of working with cotton, wool, or linen. The greater the number of threads per inch the finer the silk product. This can range up to as many as 400 per inch. Silk is sometimes combined with other fibers to produce varying effects. All of the final manufacturing processes of silk have now been mechanized except the care of the worms.

China, Japan, and India are the three largest producers of silk today. The area of central China surrounding the Yangtze River Valley is probably the largest silk producing area in the world. Sericulture continues to require a great amount of hand labor in the initial stages even though the actual manufacturing process has been mechanized. Most silk factories are crowded with fast-moving machinery. A large percentage of the machine operators are women. Silk prints were still being done by hand blocks as late as the 1920s. The cheap labor of China and India are necessary in order to complete the process of silk production from the picking of the mulberry leaves, the caring for the worms, and the manufacturing process. Even though many of the manufacturing processes have been mechanized, women continue to reach into the boiling water to remove the cocoons before reeling.

Asian Food & Agriculture

Tobacco culture is widespread throughout Asia since the crop will grow in many different soils in the temperate zone. Like so many other plants, tobacco was originally cultivated in America. It was first introduced to the Far East by the earliest explorers. The tobacco seedlings are started early in special beds which are covered with glass to protect them from frost. Several thousand plants can be started in a relatively small area. As soon as the seedlings are from four to six inches tall--and providing the weather is mild--the seedlings are removed from the bed and planted in rows in the field. Tobacco prefers a friable, well-drained soil with plenty of nutrients if it is to produce a heavy crop. In modern times the fertility of the soil is carefully measured before planting time and the proper fertilizers are applied. Although much of the planting and cultivating has been mechanized in America, the farmers in Asia plant each seedling by hand and carefully cultivate it until maturity.

Tobacco is a good cash crop wherever the land is not needed for food production. Dozens of different varieties of tobacco have been developed and each one can give the final product a different flavor depending upon the soil type and the manner in which it was culativated during the growing season. Asia does not produce nearly enough tobacco to satisfy its market demands since nearly every man smokes and many women as well. Smoking takes place in all public places such as restaurants and airports. Smoking is allowed on most Asian flights from the time the plane is boarded until it lands. This means that nearly every country imports large quantities of tobacco.

Opium is another cash crop which has occupied many acres over hundreds of years. Even though the international traffic in opium is carefully regulated today, it should be remembered that these laws have usually been passed very recently. There is still a great amount of opium grown illegally. Some of the derivatives from the opium poppy are morphine, paragoric, and codeine, all of which have medical values and are still prescribed today. Unfortunately, many people in Asia have abused the use of opium from the earliest times.

It is even more unfortunate that the British, French, and Dutch trading companies which operated in Asia in the 17th, 18th, and 19th centuries went out of their way to get Asians "hooked" on the opium products. Large amounts were raised in India and then transported to China where they found the most fruitful market. It was very profitable for the trading companies. As more and more Chinese became addicts, their government decided to raise the product locally as a means of eliminating the foreign suppliers. Even though the Chinese government passed very strict laws about opium production, many local officials ignored the enforcement of the laws because the officials could tax opium to obtain revenue for their local government. The elimination of opium from China was never completely accomplished until the period of Chairman Mao. There were millions of addicts as late as the mid-1940s.

Opium culture was a major source of income for Chinese farmers down to the Communist revolution in 1949. It was especially advantageous for those who lived in the isolated mountain valleys where there was no good transportation system out to the large cities. Just as the American frontier farmers who were often far from a good highway could convert their entire corn crop to whiskey and haul it out in a few jugs on horseback, so the Chinese farmer converted his poppy crop to opium and moved it out to market. Although this is strictly illegal in modern China, it still occurs in the area known as the "Golden Triangle" of Laos, the northern regions of Cambodia, Thailand, and Burma.

Asian Food & Agriculture

Rubber is an important agricultural product from Southeast Asia. As a tropical and subtropical tree, rubber grows abundantly throughout Southeast Asia, primarily in Indonesia and Malaysia. Southern India and Sri Lanka also have several large rubber plantations. The rubber tree was growing wild in the forests of South America at the time Columbus discovered America. The Spanish decided to try the trees in their Asian colonies but soon discovered the trees did not grow well in every location. Rubber trees do not thrive above 1,500 foot elevations. Rainfall, humidity, and temperature are also very important. The trees are normally started from large seeds, then transplanated into rows to create plantations. Some trees are grafted with a bud from a high production tree when they are about two years old.

The trees grow quite fast and as soon as they are about six inches in diameter they are "tapped." Some plantation owners use a V-shaped cut but the diagonal cut at about a 30 degree angle is more often used. An initial strip of bark is removed which about one inch wide. The white latex sap runs down the angular cut and is caught in a cup or a small bucket. It has been found that more sap will run in the early morning hours so the trees are tapped at sunrise. The first tap is done about four feet above the ground with succeeding cuts made below that point until the cuts reach near ground level. The older rubber forests are tapped from two to six times per year. Some of the more recent varieties can be tapped as often as every other day. The tree eventually grows new bark over the scarred area and the tapping can go on again. With careful management, a plantation can be kept in production for up to thirty years.

The latex sap is gathered in a tank which resembles the manner in which maple sap is collected in the northern latitudes. The highest prices are paid for clean and uncontaminated latex. From 30 to 40 percent of the milky-white latex is rubber, the balance is water. It must be processed very soon after gathering or the warm climate will cause it to sour. Various chemicals are added to the large tanks which will cause the rubber to form on top as a coagulant. When the rubber has been sufficiently separated from the water, it will be removed and run through rollers to form sheets. These are hung in a smokehouse for about a week. The rubber is then baled into 200 pound blocks for shipment to a vulcanizing center.

The Europeans were interested in this fascinating product from the time they discovered America. They saw the native Americans playing games with a ball made from rubber. Many experiments were carried out for use in waterproofing clothing and similar applications. One of their major problems was that the rubberized cloth became sticky in hot weather and brittle in cold weather. In addition, it had a bad smell. The secret of successfully vulcanizing rubber was finally discovered in 1839 by an American, Charles Goodyear.

Rubber production soared in the 19th and 20th centuries as more applications were discovered for rubber. The advent of bicycles followed by automobiles took rubber out of the laboratories and put the product on the street. There were thousands of acres of rubber plantations operating at full production when World War II began. When the Japanese seized the Southeast Asian area, the rubber supply arriving in the United States and western Europe came to an almost complete standstill.

The tremendous need for rubber products caused the chemists to work overtime to produce a suitable synthetic rubber. Although the early synthetic rubber products were often inferior to natural rubber, further research and development have ultimately produced a product which is now superior to the natural rubber in most applications. There are still many rubber plantations in Southeast Asia. Like so many aspects of Asian agriculture, rubber production is highly labor intensive. A combination of higher labor costs and competition from synthetics has nearly destroyed the rubber business for many farmers.

Palm oil is also a leading agricultural product which is produced primarily in Southeast Asia. The palm oil tree is most often found in Malaysia and Indonesia but it is scattered throughout the Southeast Asian area. There are several different kinds of palms which produce large amounts of oil. The shape of most of these trees resembles a short trunk, seldom over thirty feet, with a lush palm foliage on top. The coconut tree, which most people commonly recognize, is a very tall tree which produces large, hard-shelled coconuts. The palm oil variety is short and the fruits are normally much smaller in diameter. A healthy palm oil tree will produce from two to six bunches of fruit with each one weighing from ten to thirty-five pounds. Each tree may have as many as 1,000 drupes, or fruits, in these bunches or clusters. Each fruit is from one to two inches in length and about one inch in diameter.

The chief reason for cultivating the palm oil tree is obviously the oil. Each of the little fruits has a tough fibrous covering which is removed and pressed separately. The amount of oil produced varies from 30 to 70 percent of its weight. This oil is dark brown and is most often used for soap, candles, and various commercial oils.

The palm kernel oil comes from the inner part of the fruit. Its oil content can run as high as 50 percent by weight. This oil is much lighter and finer and is used primarily in food manufacturing. Several brands of margarine, chocolate candy, and some pharmaceuticals have high concentrations of palm kernel oil. The baking industry used large amounts until very recently. There is now concern that the consumption of palm kernel oil will raise an individual's blood cholesterol levels. As a consequence, the market for palm oil has greatly diminished. Like so many of the other food products, there is practically no waste. The cake which is left over after pressing is fed to cattle. The coarser parts which are unfit for the cattle are added to fertilizers.

SUMMARIZING ASIAN AGRICULTURE

Each of the eastern civilizations faced the same major problems from prehistoric times to the present. Since the majority of people in Asia have no access to shopping centers and supermarkets, each family must raise and gather sufficient food to tide the family over until the next growing season. This is why the monsoon, the rivers, and the lakes are the very lifeblood of survival in Asia. If rain does not fall on a regular basis, then there would be no water for crops and the entire family could conceivably starve. If too much rain fell and caused severe flooding, it could bring death, disease, and wash away terraces and other means of feeding the family. Since the population is at the maximum level which can be supported on the available land, the slightest interruption in the food supply can be disastrous for thousands of people. Transportation facilities in many areas of Asia are also so weak that it is not possible to move food from areas with a surplus to an area which is experiencing a shortage. Life--survival itself--is much more localized than it is in the western world.

It is believed that during the earliest hunter-gatherer stage that people ate a large variety of foods once they knew they were safe to eat. But as rice became more popular, especially in China, people came to be too dependent upon that one crop. This meant that if there were not enough water for the rice and the crop failed there would be mass starvation. Too heavy a dependence upon rice to the exclusion of other food crops could also leave the body weak and malnourished.

Of course it took thousands of years for mankind to progress from the earliest stages of being a hunter-gatherer in the Old Stone Age (Paleolithic) to the New Stone Age (Neolithic) when settled agriculture and irrigation became popular. It is also interesting that settled agriculture seems to have occurred at almost the same time in Mesopotamia, Egypt, India, China, and Southeast Asia. Each area seems to have had its own spontaneous development, although it is just possible that early peoples traveled and communicated over longer distances than we imagine possible today.

Throughout history, planting, cultivating, and bringing a crop to a successful harvest was a major consideration. Crops were subject to insects, diseases, wind storms, and hail in prehistoric and ancient times just as they are today. Harvesting a crop was also a major family operation. Everyone in the extended family who was able to work was assigned some important task to perform. It was always a major consideration to preserve the crop until the next growing season. The great granary at Mohnejo Daro was built with air passages so that the grain would not sour or mold in storage. It was also built like a fortress which would indicate there was a danger of attack by outsiders who might try to steal the crop. The granary was also built above the highest potential flood point of the Indus River. Finally, rats and other rodents were much more numerous in those times than at present. Since rats ruin more grain than they actually eat, it was extremely important to keep the supply protected.

Life was not easy in those early days as mankind learned to plant, cultivate and harvest his food. The domestication of livestock meant that it was no longer necessary to go hunting so often. As wild game became less abundant, hunting became a pastime of the aristocracy more than a necessity of the common people. Over a period of thousands of years, people learned which foods were "safe" and which were not. They learned how to prepare foods so they would be palatable. The control of fire brought an entirely new perspective to food preparation. The secrets of providing the three basics--food, clothing, and shelter--were passed on verbally from generation to generation for thousands of years.

In many rural areas of Asia today it is possible to see agriculture carried out pretty much as it was in prehistoric times. There are more drilled wells today, which have replaced the old open wells. There are more electric and diesel pumps. There are a few farm tractors. But, for the most part rural Asia gets its water from open wells and plows its fields with a team of oxen or a water buffalo. Houses may have electricity, even television, but the construction of the homes in rural Asia has not changed much over the past several thousand years. There are highways, some with hard surface, but automobiles are not plentiful. Visitors to out-of-the-way rural areas are considered somewhere between a nuisance and some kind of curiosity which has just dropped in from outer space.

There is a tendency in the western world to observe this and to want to introduce tractors, electricity, television, new varieties of grains and fruits, new breeds of livestock, commercial fertilizer, herbicides, insecticides, and antibiotics. Such modern measures are often resisted on the one hand because they fear that the crop or the new breed of livestock may not flourish in its new environment. Fertilizers may poison the soil, etc. These communities are extremely conservative. They know what works and they are in no mood to experiment. If it does not work, they are not sure someone will come in to bail them out before they starve. Time passes and agriculture remains pretty much unchanged.

IN CONCLUSION

A study of the role of agriculture in the life of Asia should note that many of the food and agricultural products upon which the people rely for their food supply came from America after 1492. It should also be noted that the people may have a surplus of coconuts. pineapple, sugar, rubber, or palm oil, but many of these have been supplanted by other crops or synthetic substitutes. This often leaves the Asian farmer with a huge surplus of a product which is a glut on the world market. The consequence is a very low price or no market at all.

The western shopper expects to visit a grocery store or a supermarket and find first-class food all wrapped in plastic bubbles, processed and sealed in bottles, or available in the frozen food section. The food is often purchased, prepared, and served without any thought given to how or where that food product was raised. The farmer seems a long distance from the dinner table.

Everyone in the eastern world is quite aware of where the food comes from. They very likely were involved in the planting, cultivation, and harvesting as well as preparing and serving it from its raw state. Those who are inhabitants in the large cities must shop at the bake shop for their baked goods, visit the fish or meat market for their meat, and purchase their fresh fruits and vegetables from the green grocer. Other stores sell spices, dried fruits, and nuts.

Live animals are often slaughtered within sight of the customer. The meat is cut up according to the request of each individual purchaser. Sugar, flour, nuts, dried fruits, spices, etc., are all sold in bulk. Asians often bring their own bags or cartons for shopping. Butchers and other food merchants sometimes wrap the customer's purchase in a piece of old newspaper-- sometimes it is left unwrapped. The only food inspector is the customer. Anyone who wants to thoroughly understand the eastern cultures will do well to remember this close affiliation of the people with the land.

Figure 3

Asian Food & Agriculture

BOOKS FOR FURTHER READING

Beardsley, Richard K.; Hall, John W.; & Ward, Robert E., *Village Japan* (1959).

Blunden, Caroline, & Elvin, Mark, *Cultural Atlas of China* (1983).

Buck, Pearl S., *Dragon Seed* (1942).

Buck, Pearl S., *The Good Earth* (1931).

Collcutt, Martin; Jansen, Marius; & Kumakura, Isao, *Cultural Atlas of Japan* (1991).

Cressey, George B., *Asia's Lands and Peoples* (1963).

Cressey, George B., *China's Geographic Foundations* (1934).

East, W. Gordon; Spate, O.H.K.; & Fisher, Charles A., *The Changing Map of Asia, A Political Geography* (1971).

Ginsburg, Norton, editor, *The Pattern of Asia* (1958).

Miller, Geroge J., editor, *Life in Asia* (1936).

Milner-Gulland, Robin, & Dejevsky, Nikolai, *Cultural Atlas of Russia* (1989).

Myrdal, Jan, *Return to a Chinese Village* (1984).

Rawson, R. R., *The Monsoon Lands of Asia* (1963).

Robinson, Harry, *Monsoon Asia: A Geographical Survey* (1967).

Shue, Vivienne, *Peasant China in Transition* (1980).

Sivin, Nathan, *The Contemporary Atlas of China* (1988).

Stross, Randall E., *The Stubborn Earth* (1986).

Trewartha, Glenn T., *Japan: A Geography* (1965).

Chapter 4
INTRODUCING THE EASTERN RELIGIOUS FAITHS

It has been said that if there were no religions in the world th at we would invent one. Some anthropologists and sociologists rank religion as a basic need of mankind along with food, clothing, and shelter. In a very real sense, everyone worships something. One of the most important aspects of daily life in Asia today is obviously religion. It is not important which country one is visiting, there are Hindu temples, Buddhist temples, Confucian shrines, Muslim mosques, etc. All authorities who have ever studied the excavations at Mohenjo Daro along the Indus River in Pakistan agree that the Great Bath, which was constructed possibly five or six thousand years ago, was not a public pool but a place of ritual purification. The oldest of all the great faiths, Hinduism, has been traced back along the migration route where there have been found the figures of idols and the early Vedic writings. Hinduism, the oldest of all the great religions, probably had its earliest beginnings from six to ten thousand years ago.

Not only are the temples and shrines of the several religions numerous throughout the eastern world, they are used daily by millions of people. The sincerity of the participants cannot be questioned by even a casual observer. There is nothing comparable in the western world. Perhaps the great idol of the western world is materialism and the "joys" of this world. Many people in the western world are looking for immediate rewards and instant gratification. The eastern worshippers in many cases have divorced themselves from the cares and troubles of this world and are in earnest search of the eternal blessings.

The West has not always been as it is today. The people who lived through the Medieval Age were certainly dedicated and devout. Few of the laborers on the great Gothic cathedrals were full-time paid laborers. They were largely ordinary folks who pledged their spare time to build an earthly dream. Perhaps it was Renaissance humanism which changed the West. Some would say that the Protestant emphasis upon capitalism changed our way of life. Others would speculate that it was just plain greed.

It is well to pause and consider that not everyone in the eastern world is totally innocent of materialism and bent on seeking the best route to eternity. There are many in the East who are also greedy and grasping. Some are dishonest. There are others who would steal another's possessions if they thought they could do it and escape. Many crimes are committed in the name of religion. There are likewise those in the western world who are so extremely devout that the things of this world matter little if they can achieve their eternal reward. In other words, generalizations are always dangerous concerning both East and West but in the East one is more likely to see a high level of public religious devotion than in the West.

EXPLAINING THE UNEXPLAINABLE

From the very earliest ages of mankind we have pondered the things which we cannot understand. Often we still have many natural and supernatural phenomena which defy explanation, even with modern science and research. Gravity, for instance, is something we all understand in that when things are dropped they fall to the earth. There are many scientific explanations and laws based upon mass, etc., but the fact remains that we can neither see gravity nor can we cause things to fall up instead of down. In our age of science we simply accept the opinions of our scientists.

Without any knowledge of science our early ancestors were frightened by storms, especially thunder and lightening. To them, the gods were being angry with mankind. Even the analytical Greeks believed that the god Zeus hurled the thunderbolt when he was angry. There are still many in the eastern world who hide when the thunder and lightening begins. They have many ideas on science and the world of nature, including reproduction, which educated people in the West would label very strange. Beyond this, the educated people in the eastern world are every bit as knowledgeable as those who live in the western world. Many of the uneducated are simply repeating the same superstitious ideas which have been handed down through the generations. Beyond studying the movements of the stars and observing the seasons, the people of the East seldom inquired into the basic scientific explanations until in recent times. There was a religious explanation about the **how** and the **why** of things in the natural world which had been passed down from generation to generation for thousands of years.

Although the western world seems far advanced in science and research today, it was not until the 17th century that the western world began to delve deeply into the nature of the universe or how the human body functions. It is well to remember that in some areas of physiology and medicine the Chinese were **far** ahead of the western world until quite recent times. In our western tradition there have been many times since the Renaissance when science and religion have been contradictory to one another. In Asia before the arrival of the Europeans, science and religion were **one**--they were not opposed to one another. Prayers and offerings were made to control nature. Since the arrival of western culture in Asia, there are many people, particularly in the rural areas, who continue to follow the old religious explanations.

EVER PRESENT DEATH

Perhaps people of the eastern world are more religious because death is an ever present visitor to so many households, especially for children under the age of three. In some countries of Asia when an individual dies the body is prepared and cremation occurs the same day. To many people in the West this seems to make life cheap. In still other Asian countries the deceased are "worshipped" as it is said in the West--reverenced or respected might be a better term. In the western world people spend enormous sums on funerals but the deceased are often practically forgotten shortly after the funeral. The western philosophy is a much more "youth oriented" society--it is the "now" generation. Many western families spend large sums of money on toys and nice clothes for their young people, while it is often said that anyone over the age of 40 is already "over the hill." In the East the oldest people are generally the most respected. The entire philosophy of youth, old age, death, and eternity are very different in the East.

Nearly all the people of Asia believe in some kind of reincarnation except for Jews, Christians, and Muslims. This is the concept that upon death the spirit will pass on to another life. Followers of other religions--Jews, Christians, and Muslims--believe in one way or another that we have but one life to live and that this will be followed by eternity in either heaven or hell. For many others in the West, the grave is simply the end. Death becomes a frightening thing for those who believe in **neither** a heavenly reward, nor in reincarnation. For those who do believe in reincarnation, death is only a passage, a transition from one life to another. It is not the end of everything. Since death is always so near to the easterners, they have less to fear than the persons from the West who do not believe they are worthy of heaven.

MAINTAINING THE SOCIAL ORDER

Maintaining the social order in the western world refers primarily to the basic rules of society, such as obeying the principles of the Ten Commandments. Nearly everyone in both the East and the West can agree on such a code of ethics. When such a code is equated to the eternal it assumes a greatly increased significance. At that level it is no langer the law given by Moses, it is a law given by God. **All** the major faiths of the world have some rules similar to the Ten Commandments. However, the eastern faiths do **not** have a concept such as Original Sin as it is stated in the Old Testament. This means that the rules governing eastern society are often made for maintaining a well-ordered society rather than for condemning all mankind from the time of Adam and Eve. This means that personal conduct and sexual matters are viewed in a much different way than they are under Judaism or Christianity.

Along with this social order through a religious approach, every society has many other regulations. These concern the relationship of males and females, parents and children, young and old, buying and selling, working and recreation, which foods are acceptable and which are unclean, and many more day-to-day activities. Such rules might be called the "orders of society." Outside these "orders" or rules are the **taboos**--the actions which no decent person would even dare to consider. Not only would these be considered contrary to the laws of society, they would anger the gods as well. And the eastern gods are very close to the people. Everyone has seen a perfectly healthy person yesterday who is dead today. It is the specter of ever present death. The easterners have lived within these parameters all their lives. It would be risky to violate them.

The western world has millions of people who have defied God and nothing different has happened to them. They feel they are beyond redemption so "live it up." We seldom call upon our neighbor to discuss religion. It is the age of democracy and individuality in the West. If we know someone is doing something very wrong, we either maintain our silence or let the civil authorities take care of the matter. We would find all the rules, restrictions, and taboos of the eastern world very confining. They are much more concerned with being their brother's keeper. The temptations of the free world are so much more interesting to the westerner. For instance, no one in the West can even imagine living within the confines of a caste as it was practiced in India for thousands of years. It was both the religion as well as the social order.

Where is the young person in the West who would want the parents to arrange her/his marriage? This practice has gone on in the eastern world for thousands of years. It has been made unlawful to follow caste rules today, but it did a reasonably good job of maintaining the social order during the several thousand years it was followed in India. Several other eastern areas had similar rules of society.

SACRED AND SECULAR

Everyone has some need of both the sacred and the secular realms of life. If **everyone** devoted one's entire lifetime to sacred pursuits, there would be no one to provide for the essentials of life. For the time spent by each individual in sacred activities, someone must spend some time in such mundane pursuits as raising, harvesting, and preparing food. If everyone became a Buddhist monk and begged for their food, where would the food come from? All individuals and all civilizations must work this balance out for their mutual satisfaction.

The eastern world has a much higher percentage of their people who spend large amounts of time in search of the sacred answers than the western world. That is not to say that the people of the West are necessarily any less concerned with sacred affairs. Earning an income and providing a home and an educational environment for the younger generation contends heavily with spending long hours in meditation and searching for the truth of God's ways. The "job and family" often come first with the people of the western world. In countries such as India, ordinary workmen, houeswives, children, businessmen, and professionals alike, attend the holy services early in the morning, then work for the remainder of the day. A few become full-time mystics. So also in the Buddhist countries such as Japan, where there is a time to work and a time to pray. The same could be said of the followers of Islam, many of whom take time out of their busy schedules to pray five times a day.

Religious retreats and workshops for Buddhists are quite important. People do not join a Buddhist study group solely because such a group might be good for business or politics. Many people in the East are also very involved with business matters. However, within the limited time which they have to devote to their faith, they become totally immersed in the quest for ultimate truth and a realistic relationship with their faith in the eternal. This is certainly true in a country such as Japan today. It was also true in China before the Communist revolution. Religious practices are again returning to China.

Westerners who visit a shrine often see Asian people who clap their hands, toss a coin, say a prayer, and then leave, as somewhat less than sincere. Nevertheless, the worshipper has paid his tribute that day, and that brief moment in the presence of their god was precious to them. They made peace with their god that day regardless of their religious persuasion.

In earlier years the Christian church in the West demanded, and received, a much closer relationship to God via the organized church. Many of the Christian churches today have become more of a social club than a true religious congregation. It should be remembered that Hindus and Buddhists also take up social causes, but they are so earnest in their convictions that they would give their lives for their cause. A good example of this would be those Buddhist monks who burned themselves to death in a supreme sacrifice to end the war in Vietnam. Of course, not all Buddhists in Vietnam became that convinced of their cause. It should also be remembered that not all Christians were burned at the stake or fed to the lions during the early history of the Christian church. Today, very few Christians would volunteer to give their lives for their faith as the early martyrs did. Money, time, and demonstrations are more often the way of the West today.

When we consider religion in the West in our own age, it is customary to measure a country's level of devotion, perhaps improperly, by the numbers who we see actively engaged in church activities whether as clergy or as laity. We tend to think in terms of Christians gathering for worship at the great holidays such as Christmas and Easter. We reflect upon the beautiful organ and choir music of the church. Christians, Jews, and Muslims "gather together" to worship on an appointed day of the week or hour of the day. In the eastern religions we do see large numbers who gather at Mecca to celebrate the Hajj, or those who come down to the Ganges River every morning at sunrise to pray. However, the practioner of his or her faith makes a much more

34

individual choice of when or how that individual worships in the eastern faiths. The service in Hinduism, Buddhism, Shintoism, or Confucianism does not begin at an appointed hour by a great hymn which is collectively sung by the worshippers. Even when the Muslims gather at the mosque at the appointed hours, the primary purpose is prayer--prayer between the worshipper and his or her own God.

Therefore, we can say that religious services are conducted very differently in the East than in the West. This is not to say that either one is more or less significant but they ARE different. Anyone who has attended a worship service in a mosque as the faithful gather for services, or attended services in a Buddhist temple is bound to be impressed. Anyone who attends the early morning services of the Hindus in the open air beside the Ganges River at Benares (Varanasi) is bound to find the service impressive. These are sights which are bound to be forever etched in the memory of a westerner. Perhaps it is safe to say that the evidence of God's presence is just as evident in one of these worship services as it might be in a great cathedral or a synagogue. Certainly no one can deny the deep devotion expressed by all those who have come to worship.

EAST AND WEST
OUR SEARCH FOR FAITH AND UNDERSTANDING

It is always very difficult to explain in clear language the precise variations between the faiths of the East and the West. The explanations of the great faiths are offered in the hopes that the reader will be able to appreciate that there are more similarities between the great faiths than there are differences. Each of the major faiths of the world today have millions of devout followers who are positively convinced that their faith is correct for them and their way of life. Each of the great faiths of the world has been arrived at by thousands of very learned men who have devoted their entire lifetime to study and meditation, sometimes of other faiths as well as their own chosen faith.

In every part of the world there are also those who are the weak ones, the doubters, the agnostics, and the outright atheists. When we say that a country such as India is Hindu, it does not mean that all of the people in that country are practicing members of the faith any more than when we refer to the United States as a Christian nation. However, in India there is probably a lower percentage of actual atheists than in any country of the West. In the same way, many Muslim countries have a higher percentage of the faithful than in the West. But that is a judgmental statement, a very general comment, and to make broad generalizations about the depth of anyone's faith inevitably turns up many exceptions.

MAJOR CONSIDERATIONS CONCERNING RELIGIOUS DISCUSSIONS

One of the major considerations in discussing the great religions must focus upon the basic semantics of each language. Even when two or more people are discussing matters of their own faith in their own native language there are often major differences of opinion. This immediately becomes much more difficult when translation is required from one language to another. For example, the word "god" means something very different from one faith to another, especially when interpreting the variations between a **monotheistic** religion and a **polytheistic** religion. Words like "salvation" become even more difficult to define. For all purposes, each

Introducing Eastern Religions

religion must be studied and understood on the basis of its own definition of terms and concepts. The true scholar of religion will endeavor to understand the language of the faith being discussed as well as the faith itself.

Objectively, religion consists of relationships between basic needs of human beings to be a part of something which is greater than themselves. Each religion endeavors to make the worshipper feel that he or she is an integral part of that basic need. The manner in which we as individuals achieve a feeling of satisfaction as a part of a system of worship is at the very heart of most, if not all, of us and our worship. It is the very foundation upon which our religious faith rests. There is a very close, similar satisfaction between the Christian feeling of being "one with Christ" as there is for the Hindu who has achieved oneness of his individuality with Brahma, even though the two worshippers have arrived at that point through very different means.

Even very devout people have difficulty defining in terms which are understandable to others the very essence of their faith. In the Judeo-Christian world it is difficult to describe God and God's close relationship in concrete terms. There is also so much that the most devout must necessarily accept on faith in any religion. Still, the one who walks close to God soon comes to have a close enough relationship with that faith that those about her or him can clearly sense that he or she is a very devout person. So also is this true of Hindus, Buddhists, Muslims, and the followers of other religions. Considering the complexity of dealing with one god (monotheism) in this close relationship, imagine a person dealing with several gods (polytheism) in such a close personal relationship. This requires a considerable depth of understanding.

To further complicate our understanding of religion, consider that there are many who follow a polytheistic faith but they believe in **animism** as well. Animism attributes a living soul to inanimate objects and natural phenomena. The animist sees spirits and souls not only in the lower animals, but in trees and stones, in the weather, the flowing streams, the lakes and the mountain peaks. Many of the animistic beliefs began many thousands of years ago and have simply been perpetuated to our present time. It should be pointed out that although the animists may be very devout in their belief, they are seldom trying to be close to all of the gods all of the time. The various gods often tend to come and go with the seasons and the needs of the individual. However, respect is paid as they walk past a particular stone or a tree regardless of their immediate need. **totems** are a different variation on this theme.

People in the western world have few totems or animistic thoughts in our modern scientific age. It has only been a few years ago that people were terribly superstitious. In many parts of Asia the scientific explanations are not yet wholly accepted, especially in the rural areas. Often the animistic beliefs have been tied into the major faiths such as Hinduism, Buddhism, Islam, and even Christianity.

It is also difficult for someone who is not from Asia to grasp how a person can profess to be a Christian convert and a Buddhist at the same time. The people who have embraced two or more faiths at the same time have reconciled their interpretation of their faiths with each other in such a way that it is meaningful to them. They do not consider it unusual to be born a Buddhist, to have gone to pray at a Shinto shrine, to be married in a Christian ceremony, and to be buried with a Buddhist funeral service. They have worked this out in such a way that the basic needs of their faith are understandable and satisfying.

Introducing Eastern Religions

Mankind's inability to express sacred reality in concrete or scientific terms is the very mystery which causes the devout to probe more deeply, to meditate more intensely, and to search for the ultimate truth. In early Judaism there was much of this mental probing which took place. As the faith began to take shape and to mature, there was a lessening of the search and a greater emphasis upon mastering what had already been revealed. The early Christian church is a very similar story. The early saints spent thousands of hours thinking, meditating, shaping, then re-thinking every possible facet of the faith. When each of these faiths reached a certain point, the theologians began to accept what had been written as the absolute truth and to refuse to consider any radical new interpretations. Major movements within the church, such as the Reformation, caused both Protestants and Roman Catholics to re-think their faith. Scholars today continue the long search but at a slower pace than in the early years. Religious faiths have come to be more "accepted" in form and theology over the years. This is also true of the Asian religious faiths.

One of the major problems of the "accepted" faith is that it is too often taken for granted. At one time Buddhism was so widely accepted in China that scarcely anyone even questioned the faith. Even the arrival of Christianity had little overall influence. The years following the Communist revolution in 1949 became a severe testing period for Buddhism. Karl Marx had said that religion was a mere opiate of the people. The Chinese Communists decided to stamp out all religions. The temples were closed and the churches were occupied for Party meetings.

After the death of Mao, religion was again tolerated and it was surprising how many parents had taught their children the principles of their faith at a time when it was supposed to be outlawed. Buddhists flocked back to the temples and restored them. Christians gathered again to worship. Although China has many atheists today, there are many families that have survived the time of troubles and consider that their faith is stronger than ever before. Persecution has seldom destroyed any religion. As the early Christian church father, Tertullion, stated, "the blood of the martyrs became the seed of the church."

A crucial aspect of any religion is the interesting mix of sacred mystery, awe, emotion, and fascination. This is well expressed in the Psalms from the Bible as well as the Vedas of the Hindus. "Who is man that God is mindful of him?" We have seen the awesome power of God at an early age through birth, death, storms, etc. Can an humble person really approach God? Would we likely hide our faces if God truly appeared before us? Some are even fearful of praying to God. This "awesomeness of God" is a part of every major faith. To remove all the mystery, the holy of holies, the bar which separates the priest and the laity, between the mystic and the novice, etc., tends to cheapen the faith for many people. Even when God seems to have rewarded us, we still do not fully comprehend **why** we have been blessed.

The matter of prayer--of communicating with God--is the bridge across the gap between the human on the one hand and the sacred and divine on the other. All of the great faiths believe in **some** form of prayer. However, there is a vast difference in the manner in which people of each faith establish this communication. Often Protestant prayers are not terribly well organized but are more of a conversation with God. The Catholic may ask a priest to pray for them or they may seek the assistance of their rosary.

Buddhists also have prayer beads and they employ prayer wheels to assist the faithful in their communication with God. The Buddhist prayer wheels are cylinders which rotate on an axis with a prayer to Buddha contained inside or cast in the metal on the outside of the cylinder. Each turn of the wheel emits a prayer to Buddha. Whether the devout Buddhist is walking around a stupa, turning the prayer wheels as he goes, or spinning a small, hand-held prayer wheel, he is very devout in what he or she is doing. Many Buddhists set up flags with prayers which they believe transmit a prayer to Buddha each time the flag flaps in the wind.

The Hindus who go down to the holy Ganges (Ganga) River every morning to say their prayers, or dash a coconut into a pit to relieve them of their sorrows and problems--all are equally devout. The Japanese tie little prayers to bushes at the temples and shrines, while the Thais tell their problems to a caged bird and then release it so the problem will fly away. Catholics light candles; the Buddhists have a similar ceremony. The Hindu rings a bell after praying, while the Buddhist gains Buddha's attention and favor by burning incense.

Judaism and Christianity, the two leading faiths of the western world, do not have idols. There may be artistic or sculpted images but many churches have banned these as well. The mosques of Islam are allowed only geometric designs. The other eastern faiths are quite heavy on visible images. There are stone Buddhas, wooden Buddhas, terra-cotta Buddhas, jade Buddhas, cast bronze Buddhas, and there is even a life-size statue of Buddha in Bangkok, Thailand which is made of solid gold. The Hindus have dozens of images. There are often frightening warriors as the guardians at the entrance to temples to ward off the unfaithful and the unbelievers. In other words, most eastern religions--except Judaism, Christianity, and Islam--**do** have idols. The three which do not have idols are all philosophical, monotheistic religions. The members of these three faiths must envision in their minds what their God must be like.

IN SUMMARY

All of these are examples of efforts of various people to communicate with the powers which are beyond our earthly comprehension. It is not ours to judge which is the more or less effective--who is the most or the least devout. These numerous religious faiths are practiced today. Most of these religions have been around for two thousand years or more. If we are to understand the peoples of Asia, then we must also understand their basic religious beliefs and their philosophies. The eastern philosophies are all enmeshed in their religious beliefs--philosophy and religion are inseparable. In many cases their ancient history is also incorporated in the same documents.

If our world is to survive in the coming centuries, we must accept that another person's religious faith is sufficient to meet **one's** basic needs even though some of the practices may seem less than acceptable to our own way of thinking. To call some person's faith "pagan" is only going to cause personal anguish to another. In some cases it will invite strife.

Hinduism is the first of the great religious faiths to be studied because it is the oldest of the major organized faiths today and it formed the basis for many of the other faiths of the eastern world.

THE EMERGENCE OF CIVILIZATION ON THE SUBCONTINENT

Chapter 5
THE GEOGRAPHIC CONSIDERATIONS
THE SIGNIFICANCE OF FLUVIAL CIVILIZATIONS

In our study of Eastern civilizations it is important to remember that there were several great civilizations which were developing simultaneously and in different parts of the globe: Ancient Sumer in the Tigris and Euphrates River Valley, ancient Egypt in the Nile River Valley, the Indus river civilization in modern Pakistan, and the early Chinese civilization in the Hwang Ho River Valley in China. Interestingly, each of these civilizations developed in association with a river. Scholars have called such civilizations **fluvial** .

Rivers were important to these early people because they provided transportation. Roads were expensive to build and maintain. Often the roads and bridges on the highways would be washed out by floods. Water transportation was, therefore, their most viable way of moving from one place to another. It is still the least expensive manner of moving heavy freight over long distances. Many of the prehistoric people traveled unbelievable distances on the water. Southeast Asians moved eastward from island to island. Some believe they traveled all the way to the Americas by boats.

Flooding could also be a problem to people who lived in the low-lying areas. Many times their homes were swept away--sometimes even the parcel of land upon which the house stood would be taken as well. But new mud flats formed in another location in the riverbed or the delta region. Those who had been dispossessed by the flood quickly claimed the new island properties and proceeded to build a home on the piece of land which they claimed. All of this required laws and regulations as well as some system of survey to lay out the plots and apportion the land once the flood had subsided.

Rivers also provided a ready supply of water in the dry seasons. It is believed that irrigation began at a very early time. As agriculture began to develop during the late Mesolithic Age and the early Neolithic Age, the settlements began to increase in population. This increase meant that people moved inland from the river itself--too far to carry water. Therefore, a canal would be dug to connect the fields, which were some distance from the river, with the water supply. This required cooperation and probably some kind of rules or laws to tax those who were not able to dig. It would also have been necessary to maintain the canal once it had been created. As the population continued to grow, it was necessary in many areas to build reservoirs to hold the water from the rainy season until it was needed in the dry season. Someone would be required to oversee the apportionment of water so that all the farmers received their fair share from the reservoir. All of this brought on the need for government, laws, and taxes.

Since floods were often a real problem to our early ancestors, they took a keen interest in the seasons and the weather patterns. This led to an early form of calendar long before recorded history. This record would make it possible to anticipate the rising waters and to be prepared to move to higher ground at flood time. A calendar required some system of counting the days, hence a greater interest in mathematics. Early mankind believed that the weather was in some way connected to the sun, the moon, and the stars. Ultimately, some form of zodiac developed. The calendar was also closely tied to religion in each of the fluvial civilizations.

Finally, rivers were an important means of communication. The discoveries and developments which might be made at one location along the river were soon transmitted to everyone who lived in the river valley. In this manner civilization improved generation after generation.

GEOGRAPHIC FEATURES WHICH INFLUENCED INDIA'S HISTORY

The subcontinent of India may be thought of as a giant triangle suspended to the south from the great Eurasian land mass. The subcontinent now contains three important countries-- India, Pakistan and Bangladesh--and several smaller countries and areas such as Nepal, Bhutan and Sikkim. Modern Sri Lanka, formerly Ceylon, is normally included in the study of the subcontinent. The giant Indian subcontinent is properly referred to today as South Asia. From prehistoric times to 1947, the entire subcontinent was treated as a single area, and in those years it was simply referred to as **India**. Altogether it is about one-third the size of the United States. So far as we know it has always had a high density of population.

Modern India is bordered on the east by Myanmar (Burma), Bangladesh and China. India shares a border with Nepal and Bhutan to the north. On the northwest, Pakistan forms the land border and the Arabian Sea forms the remainder of India's western boundary. The Bay of Bengal completes the eastern boundary, while the Indian Ocean is to the south.

The subcontinent has a tremendous natural border to the north--the **Himalayan Mountains**. These mountains, across the north, combined with the seas which surround the other two sides of the huge triangle, have allowed the subcontinent to develop a civilization over thousands of years in reasonable isolation from its neighbors. The influence of China and of other areas in Asia has been very small. During these years of isolation they have developed their own unique civilization in the Himalayan area, along the Indus River and its tributaries, in the valley of the Brahmaputra River, and in the Ganges River Valley. The Deccan to the south also developed a unique civilization separate from the more northern regions. Since the northern part of the subcontinent has been dominated by these three great river systems, it is appropriate to examine each one.

THE INDUS RIVER SYSTEM

Although the majority of the Indus River today flows through Pakistan, it is from the name of the river that we get the term India. The earliest writing about the Indus River Valley is the *Rig Veda*, about 1500 B.C. This is written in the ancient language of **Sanskrit** and refers to the river as the *Sind* or the *Hind*. The Persians referred to the inhabitants as *Sindhus*. The Greeks at the time of Alexander the Great's invasion of the northwestern subcontinent from about 325 to 323 B.C., changed the name of the river formerly known as the *Sindhus* to **Indus** and the people of the area were referred to as *Hindus*. This terminology has been applied to the area since the fourth century B.C.

The earliest settlers in the Indus River Valley did have a pictorial form of writing which was apparently in its infancy. No one has been able to decipher this writing to the present time. For this reason we have no way of knowing what these early people called themselves. Our

40

The Importance of Geography in Indian History

modern terms to denote this early civilization is **Harappan**, because the site is near the city of Harappa, and **Mohenjo Daro**, a term which means "city of the dead." Since there were more than two locations for this civilization it is often referred to as the **Indus River Civilization** since the cities were located in the area of the river and its tributaries.

The Indus River flows through the Himalayan Mountains like a giant serpent, first heading northwest, then plunging south to enter the Arabian Sea, a distance of approximately 1800 miles. Its total drainage area is about 450,000 square miles. This would initially seem to make it a river of immense value as a habitable area for millions of people in India and Pakistan. But unlike many of the other major river systems of eastern Asia, the Indus flows through steep and rugged mountains in the north with little fertile soil on either side. Its source is about 16,000 feet above sea level which makes its current too swift for navigation in the mountain areas. Some of the gorges through which it flows are as deep as 15,000 feet. Small trails cling grimly to precipitous slopes overlooking the river with many gorges from 4,000 to 5,000 feet deep. The annual cubic feet of water which flows through the Indus is about twice that of the Nile and three times that of the Tigris and the Euphrates rivers combined.

Such a quantity of water moving swiftly down the Himalayan slopes would have been terribly dangerous in early times as it made its way across the Sind in modern Pakistan. For thousands of years the river was uncontrolled until the Tarbela Dam was completed in 1975. Below the dam there are four more rivers which flow from the Punjab area of India. The word **Punjab** means "land of five rivers." These tributaries increase the size of the Indus considerably and at floodtime the river may become several miles wide. Fortunately the degree of fall in the river is greatly reduced once it leaves the mountains and enters the plains area.

The Indus carries an enormous amount of silt which can even fill the channel in the plains area and cause the water to seek a new route to the sea. Records indicate it has been changing its course ever since the days of the Mohenjo Daro culture about 4,000 years ago. Generally the shift has been toward the west, a distance of 10 to 20 miles in the last 700 years. The river's channel also changes each year in the delta area as a consequence of flooding.

In the early springtime the Indus River is fed by the melting snow. This is continued throughout the summer with additional water from the melting glaciers, some of which are thousands of years old. When the monsoon rains begin in mid-May to early June, the river receives a second supply of fresh water. The monsoon continues until about mid-August to early September. The river is at its lowest level from mid-December to early March.

The Indus River flows through some of the driest area of the entire subcontinent where they receive only 5 to 20 inches of rainfall per year. This is the semi-desert area which is known as the **Sind**. It is also a very hot area with temperatures ranging up to 120 degrees Fahrenheit in July. This is an area of sand and poor grass. Agriculture has been made possible in several areas with an elaborate system of irrigation canals which date back to the Muslims and the Sikhs. Around 1850 the British built upon these old systems and created the most extensive irrigation system in the world. After the partition of India and Pakistan in 1947, the two countries quarreled over who had the rights to the water of the Indus River system. As the border was set between the two countries, it left most of the sources of water in India and most of the canals and irrigated land in Pakistan. This was finally settled by a treaty arranged by the World Bank in 1960, which split the use of the water between the two countries.

41

The Importance of Geography in Indian History

But even irrigation is not the final answer because salts build up within a few years due to the rapid evaporation of water under the hot sun. Once the soil is full of these salts it becomes worthless for farming for many years, perhaps permanently. Water also seeps from the canals in the sandy soil and raises the water table of the surrounding areas. Sometimes swamps and shallow lakes are formed several miles from the actual area where the irrigation is taking place as the underground water finds an outlet on the surface. These also become salty within a short time.

Erosion is a major problem along the lower course of the Indus. Overgrazing and the exhaustion of the lumber resources many years ago have left the land barren, salty, and subject to both wind and water erosion. Alexander the Great recorded that there were great forests in this same area. As late as the Mughal period in the 16th century, they wrote about going hunting in the forests. Both India and Pakistan now have projects to reforest some of these otherwise worthless pieces of land but it is difficult, expensive, and slow.

Navigation on the Indus was once important but since the end of the 19th century it is limited to smaller craft. Fishing boats do operate on the river and the catch is heavy. Pakistan not only produces its own supply of both fresh water and marine fish, but also exports fish and prawns. Navigation on the river today can be terribly dangerous during some seasons of the year due to timber which is floated down from the foothills of Kashmir.

In conclusion, we have no way of knowing how valuable or how devastating the Indus River was for the early civilization which developed there. Most authorities agree that it was probably very valuable in the early years but of declining value in the later years, perhaps even being the cause for the decline and abandonment of the site known as Mohenjo Daro.

THE GANGES AND THE BRAHMAPUTRA RIVER VALLEYS

These two river systems will be treated together because they both flow into the Bay of Bengal through the same general area. The Ganges River, more properly known as the **Ganga River**, rises in the Himalayan Mountains to the north and west in the subcontinent. From its source the Ganga travels a distance of 1,557 miles to the Bay of Bengal. It drains about one-fourth of the territory of all of India. Its basin supports a concentration of about 300 million people, a population larger than that of any country on earth with the exceptions of China and the remainder of India. The **Gangetic Plain**, across which it flows just south of the foothills of the Himalayan mountains, is the heartland of the region of the subcontinent which is known as **Hindustan**. It has been the cradle of many successive civilizations from the 3rd century B.C. to the 16th century A.D. From time immemorial the Ganga has been **the holy river of the Hindu faith**.

From April to June the Ganga River is fed by the melting Himalayan snows, while in the rainy season from June to September the monsoons cause floods nearly every year. Some years are more disastrous than others. Cities such as **Calcutta** on the Hooghly river, one of the Ganga's tributaries in the delta area, and **Dacca**, the principal city of Bangladesh on the Burhi Ganga, can both have major problems at flood time. The Ganga River and the Brahmaputra join near Goalundo Ghat in the lower river basin to form one stream but with **many** tributary mouths as the combined rivers wander through the wide delta seeking their way to the **Bay of Bengal**. The real estate of this area is in a constant state of change at flood time as old islands and

The Importance of Geography in Indian History

channels are swept away and new ones are formed. The newly formed land is referred to as *khadar* in both Hindi and Urdu. Along the eastern edge of the delta, large islands which are called *chars* are formed. Due to the enormous growth in population in Bangladesh, these areas are quickly inhabited by squatters as soon as they are formed. Areas which are just beneath the water's surface may even be filled in to raise the level above the river. Of course these may very likely be swept away in the next flood.

Major flooding in this region occurs on the average of every eight or ten years today. Every year there are thousands of people washed out of their homes and a few hundred people are killed or die of disease as a consequence of the floods. It has probably always been so. But like the Indus River region, the Ganga and the Brahmaputra have experienced more severe problems in modern times due to logging and cultivation of the land right up to the water's edge. As late as the 16th and 17th centuries the Ganga basin was still heavily forested with large trees and jungles. It was a place where men went to hunt wild elephants, buffalo, rhinoceroses, lions, and tigers.

Virtually all of this natural vegetation has disappeared and the land is now intensely cultivated to meet the needs of an ever growing population. All of the big game has disappeared except for a few Bengal tigers and the crocodiles in the delta region. A few deer, boars, wildcats, and other smaller game survive with difficulty in some of the rural areas. Many tropical birds and fish in the delta area provide an important part of the people's diet. It should be pointed out that India has established a few national parks and managed game preserves to save a few remnants of what was once a beautiful world.

As this intense agriculture and deforestation continues, there is little to hold the waters back as they come rushing downstream to the delta region. Bangladesh is a country approximately the size of the state of Wisconsin. It is said that a severe flood in 1988 placed approximately three-fourths of the country underwater. Even the airport in Dacca closed which meant that relief could come only by boats. The main streams are unrecognizable at this stage--it is all one vast sea or lake! It is not uncommon for as much as 100 inches of rain to fall in the delta region compared to a more normal 30 inches per year in the upper Ganga region.

The Ganga was once navigable as far inland as Agra. Today it is only possible to ascend the river as far as Allahabad. Extensive irrigation canals draw off water which lowers the level of the river during the dry season, while silt from the erosion of the monsoon season tends to fill up the riverbed. There has been very little water power developed to date. The recent construction of the Farakka Barrage at the head of the delta just inside the Indian territorial line has angered Bangladesh. The barrage was built to prevent sea water from backing into the river above the dam. Bangladesh argues that such obstructions of the free flow of the river waters should be operated jointly.

The source of the **Brahmaputra River** is in the high Himalayas of southern Tibet. The river has the name *Tsangpo* (the Purifier) in Tibet and parts of China. It is known as the *Dihang* River as it enters the Assam Valley in northeastern India. After the *Lubit* and the *Dibang* rivers join, the main stream it is then known as the **Brahmaputra** for the next 900 miles as it winds its way to join with the Ganga. The combined waters then continue to the Bay of Bengal. The name "Brahmaputra" means the "Son of Brahma," the Creator in the Hindu religion.

The Importance of Geography in Indian History

The winters are very cold and harsh on the upper tributaries of the Brahmaputra as it works its way out of Tibet, across a corner of China, and into northeastern India in the province of Assam. The Brahmaputra valley throughout most of Assam and into Bangladesh is thought of as a very hot and humid area. Large areas of Assam are still covered with sal forests. The **sal trees** are valuable for their resin production. There are also reed jungles, swamps, waterholes, and floodplains as the river descends southward through Assam. The one-horned rhinoceros, otherwise extinct worldwide, inhabits the swampy area, while tigers and elephants live in the dense jungles just above the water level.

Like the Ganga, the huge river system of the Brahmaputra has yet to be fully utilized and developed by the population. Flood control and the building of embankments did not begin until after the Assam earthquake in 1950. The earthquake loosened huge deposits of soil which came rushing down the river as thick, muddy silt. Even after such a disaster, it was 1954 before work began on the projects to at least modestly control the river. Despite the efforts which have been accomplished so far, the river continues to be a flood problem.

Huge areas of the Brahmaputra Valley are sparsely settled today. A few regions have scarcely been explored! The people who live along the upper reaches of the river have done very little to develop irrigation as compared to most of the other major river systems of Asia. Since there is practically no demand from primitive people of this area for electricity, there have only been two dams built to produce hydroelectric power. The potential of this area is enormous, but India and Bangladesh are both very short on capital for development.

The lower Brahmaputra Valley is used more for navigation than for irrigation. The Brahmaputra is navigable for about 800 miles. It is unnavigable for some distance upstream, then again, it is navigable in Tibet for about 400 miles. The Tibetans move freight and passengers in small boats made of hides stretched over bamboo frames. It also seems interesting that even in our modern age the Brahmaputra River has no bridges throughout its course! Roads and railroads run along it but never cross it. Ferries are used extensively instead of bridges. Truly, this is an area ready for development in the 21st century.

IN CONCLUSION

The study of these three rivers of India--the Ganga, the Brahmaputra, and the Indus--have shown first how important they are in shaping the lives of the people; and secondly, that there remains much work to be done to truly utilize the rivers to their greatest potential. Millions of people live in these river valleys. They depend upon the rivers as a source of water, for fishing, for transportation, for communication, and irrigation. Hydroelectric power has seen all of its development in India since independence in 1947. The people of India are more closely tied to nature--their dependence upon the rivers and the monsoon rains which feed them--than any place else in the world. Wetland rice would be virtually impossible to raise without the abundance of water which is provided almost exclusively by the river systems. Rice culture is an essential crop to support the subcontinent's large and growing population.

The power and force of nature is another factor in understanding the people of Asia. This is a fact which is seldom acknowledged in the western world. Mankind becomes a very insignificant factor when caught in the flood. People in the western world would want to harness these rivers and control them. India is only beginning to give serious consideration to this but they are very short on capital for development. Furthermore, many would probably not want to harness the mighty power of the Ganga, India's most holy river.

BOOKS FOR FURTHER READING

Cressey, George B., *Asia's Lands and Peoples* (1963).

Ginsburg, Norton, editor, *The Pattern of Asia* (1958).

Miller, George J., editor, *Life in Asia* (1936).

Robinson, Harry, *Monsoon Asia: A Geographical Survey* (1967).

Figure 4

Figure 5

Chapter 6
MONSOON ASIA

The introductory remarks have all indicated the heavy reliance of Asia's peoples upon the land. There are many areas of Asia which have fertile land but there is no water for the growing of crops. Rain and snow are absolutely essential in all areas of Asia to provide ample water for the support of the large and growing population in this area. One of the most important factors is the **monsoon**. Those areas which do not benefit from either the monsoons or the rains of the prevailing westerlies are practically uninhabitable.

There is an entirely different weather pattern in southern Asia from any place else around the world. This unusual weather pattern--the monsoon--takes its name from the Arab word for season--*mausim*. There are basically two seasons in monsoon Asia--the **wet season** and the **dry season**. Some would add a third, the cool season, but this occurs during the dry season. There are **two** primary sources for water in Asia--the spring snow melt and the monsoon. In the areas which are not near the mountains, or situated in a northern latitude, there is no spring melt. Even in the mountainous areas they depend upon the rainy season to bring the majority of the water needed for agriculture. The monsoon **is** the primary source of water in southern Asia. Of all the areas which depend upon the monsoon rains, India is probably the most dependent.

Monsoon Asia includes India, Pakistan, Bangladesh, Sri Lanka, Myanmar (Burma), Thailand (Siam), Laos, Kampuchea (Cambodia), Vietnam, Malaysia, Indonesia, the Philippines, East and South China, South Korea, and southern Japan. A corner of Australia is also considered to be a part of monsoon Asia. Southern Malaysia, Indonesia, and most of Australia are in a separate monsoonal system which operates south of the equator where the prevailing winds come from the opposite direction. Most of China and the northern parts of Korea and Japan are more influenced by the prevailing westerly winds which blow across the great land mass of Asia. As this air moves across from the west, starting along the eastern slopes of the Ural Mountains, the air is dry in the summer and quite cold in the winter. Some of Japan and a large portion of China is considered to be in the temperate zone and experiences four seasons very much like the majority of the United States and Europe. The cold winter winds are tempered in southern Korea and Japan because they are surrounded by water.

The monsoons which occur north of the equator are dominated by the prevailing westerly winds and the jet stream. The wind blows from the southwest for approximately six months and from the northeast for the remaining six months. The summer monsoons arrive from a dominant westerly direction and they have a strong tendency to converge and rise. As they do so they normally produce heavy rain--the wet season. The winter monsoons arrive from a predominantly easterly direction with a strong tendency to diverge--they bring the dry season. Each season is the result of differences in annual temperature trends over the land and the sea.

The summer monsoons occur as the sun begins to heat up the land mass of India and Tibet. This warmer air rises and begins to pull in moisture from the cool, temperate sea water. The rising warm air creates a storm center which is strong enough to cause the jet stream to move northward. As this rising air draws the moist air off the Indian Ocean and the Arabian Sea, it creates a low pressure area on the surface which results in precipitation when the moisture-laden air passes over the land. As the great land mass of India and Tibet begins to cool in the late summer, usually late August to mid-September, the cold air diverges, the rains subside, and the farmers go back to working their fields and paddies.

The monsoon rains begin along India's western shores and then they move in a northeasterly direction across the subcontinent until they reach the Himalayan Mountains. There the monsoon tends to follow along the mountains across Bangladesh, Myanmar, and the countries of Southeast Asia. As the monsoon crosses Southeast Asia, it brings rain to Southeast China, Taiwan, southern Japan, and the Philippines. The monsoon rains rise to cross the Himalayas, but the high mountain range acts as a barrier and proportionately little rain ever reaches Tibet, western China, Afghanistan, Tajikistan, Kyrgyzstan, eastern Siberia, or Mongolia. These areas may see gloomy weather and a few sprinkles, but very little appreciable precipitation. The consequence is that these areas have a high percentage of either grassland or desert.

The summer monsoons begin about May 20 in southern Sri Lanka. By the end of May they have progressed north to the southern tip of India. By June 5 they normally reach Bombay. Around June 10 they are as far north as New Delhi. They reach northern India, Kashmir and Ladakh, about July 1 to July 15th. These rains will continue throughout the remainder of the summer months. They tend to come to an end by late August to mid-September.

As the land mass begins to cool in the late autumn there is a secondary monsoon season which affects Sri Lanka, the southeast fringe of India and Southeast Asia. This occurs because the air currents and wind directions reverse as the land cools. This phenomenon brings in the warm, moist air from the Bay of Bengal and it precipitates over the land mass as it begins to cool. This rainy season begins along India's eastern shore about the 15th of October and it slowly moves southward (just the opposite of the summer monsoon). It ends in Sri Lanka around January 1. Although these rains can be especially heavy along the seacoast, they do not normally reach very far inland but they can cause cloudy days and drizzle in the late autumn and early winter.

The monsoon winds blow from the cold toward the warm regions. If the land is warmer, as in the summer monsoon, the wind comes off the cooler sea water toward the warmer land mass as the warmer air rises. In the wintertime, the winds blow from the colder land mass toward the warmer sea water. The best time to be in India to avoid all of the rainy seasons is from about January 1 to March 1.

It should be pointed out that the amount of rain is variable from year to year and from place to place. Topography and other factors combine to make up some complex regional patterns. For instance, it rains little during the summer monsoon season over the water of the Arabian Sea, however, during the winter monsoon it often rains very heavy over the waters of the Indian Ocean and the Bay of Bengal. Heavy rains and local floods are most likely to occur in India during July and August. But, heavy rains often occur in Bangladesh and Myanmar in the late summer and early autumn. There are sections of Indian Rajasthan and southeastern Pakistan which receive very little rain in any season of the year.

Some of the heaviest monsoon rainfall occurs in the Ganga (Ganges) River Valley, which means that this area can support a huge population in porportion to the land. The rich farming area of the Punjab in northwestern India and across into Pakistan is normally driest in November. This area, the Punjab, produces such a large percentage of India's food that it is often dubbed "the breadbasket of India." It is also interesting that the Indian summer monsoon falls on the

Monsoon Asia

peninsular countries of Southeast Asia and later this same area is affected by the Malaysian-Australian monsoon. In other words, Southeast Asia is watered by **both** the summer and the winter monsoonal systems. Western Java has no true dry season because it is also affected by both monsoons but eastern Java is extremely dry during August and September. In conclusion, some of the exact causes of the monsoonal weather patterns are still not thoroughly understood.

IN SUMMARY

The importance of the monsoon rains cannot be overemphasized for India, a country which has been overpopulated for several centuries. Fifty years ago or earlier the failure of the monsoon to provide adequate rainfall left thousands of people facing starvation. More recently there has been much more global cooperation in providing food to starving countries. Since the Second World War, the government of India has taken giant strides to encourage the most modern techniques in agriculture. New varieties of seeds have been introduced, commercial fertilizers are now being used, some herbicides and insecticides are also in use by the more advanced farmers. Electricity and diesel engines have often replaced the team of oxen which used to draw the water from deep open wells to provide irrigation. On the other hand, there are thousands of Indian farmers who refuse to abandon the old ways of farming even though they know there are new and better ways. They prefer to till the soil with their oxen, camels, and horses rather than to use tractors. There are many more who know that they need to change to modern tools and methods but they lack the capital to invest in the latest agricultural techniques. Even with a growing population, India has been able to provide food for their people in recent years.

Indonesia, which has one of the higher densities of population on the island of Java, began shifting to modern varieties of seeds and using fertilizers shortly after World War Two. China began making the shift following the years of Mao Tse-tung when they decided to shift to a form of limited capitalism on the land. Under normal weather conditions, both Java and China have plenty of food for their people. But the one area which is influenced most by the monsoon is the Indian subcontinent. The monsoon makes agriculture possible. The richer the land and the more abundant the rainfall--within limits--determines both where the people live and how they live. This has been true since prehistoric times. It is still true today.

Figure 6

49

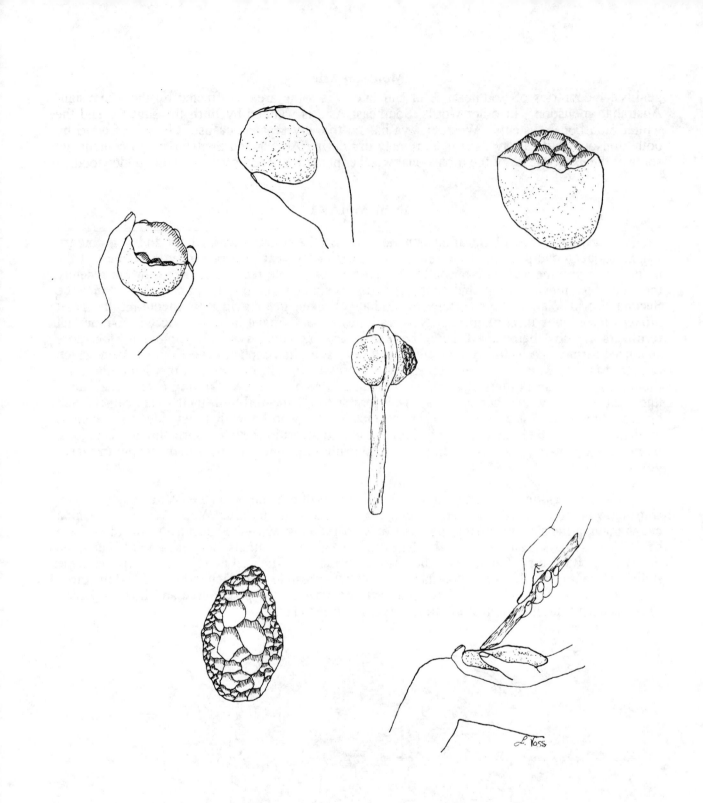

Figure 7

50

Chapter 7
PREHISTORIC INDIA

INTRODUCTION

There are always many problems encountered in doing archaeological work in any given area. India presents several of these which need to be considered in order that you will know that there are handicaps to digging in India. First, all Indians have a sense of the importance of their early history but this must be weighed against taking land out of cultivation in order to do an archaeological excavation in a country which needs the yield from every square foot of tillable land.

Another consideration is that archaeologists often learn a great deal about a culture by examining the grave goods and the method of burial. For hundreds of years the Indian people have cremated their dead, hence there are no grave goods. Many of the sites which have been found there are several feet beneath the present surface of the soil. Not only does this present some difficulties, particularly where the water table has risen, but it also makes one wonder how many **other** sites there are which are buried twenty to fifty feet beneath the surface. This makes the exploration of new sites very expensive.

Countries which are relatively wealthy often subsidize archaeological digs to round out their own national identity. The government of India would be very much interested in such a program but they have struggled since independence to create jobs and to provide new opportunities for their people today. They have not had a large sum of money to devote to archaeology. The monsoons and the extremely hot weather, especially in the summertime, have provided further handicaps to digging. Finally, archaeologists have long been more interested in Egypt, Mesopotamia, and the Holy Land than they have been in prehistoric India.

PALEOLITHIC AND MESOLITHIC INDIA

Many authorities believe that the earliest inhabitants of India lived in the region of the middle Ganges plains in the valley of the Belan river near Allahabad. The neighboring Vindhyan Plateau would have provided the stone for their tools while the fertile flood plain along the Ganges and the Belan rivers would have provided land for crops and fish for their meat. The site known as **Chopani-Mando** on a terrace of the Belan River near Allahabad is the earliest settlement currently known in northern India. The tools found at this site mark it as belonging to the Upper Paleolithic (Old Stone Age) to Lower Mesolithic Age (Middle Stone Age). This settlement has yielded microliths, ringstones, grinders, and querns. These people also produced a fragile, hand-made pottery toward the end of their use of this site.

There is no evidence remaining of the earliest type of housing at the Chopani-Mando site which indicates that it was probably very temporary. Later they began building round or oval huts which ranged from seven to eight feet across to as large as fifteen feet in diameter. There is also evidence that some of the huts were floored with small stones. Flint knapping took place in each of the several huts, since several flakes and cores have been found. The very end of habitation at this site revealed that they ate cattle and sheep or goats along with specimens of wild rice. The conclusion regarding the Chopani-Mando site was that it served a society which was still primarily in the hunting and gathering stage. Although there were bones of cattle and sheep found on the site there is no tangible evidence that these animals had been domesticated at this early date. No one knows when this settlement began, but it appears to have been abandoned in the 9th century B.C.

Two other very early settlements are **Mahadaha** and **Sari Nahar Rai**, both situated at the edge of lakes formed along the Ganga (Ganges) River. Graves were found at both of these sites which indicates that cremation of the dead had not begun at this site by this time. In these two sites, as well as at Chopani-Mando, the huts were clustered quite close together to form a very small village. Both Mahadaha and Sari Nahar Rai appear to have been occupied on an occasional basis rather than around the calendar. Since many animal bones have been found at these sites it is presumed that they were used as seasonal hunting camps rather than as permanent housing. The skeletons were ornamented with pendants made of antler and necklaces and rings were also discovered. These may be the earliest jewelery on the subcontinent. There is obviously much speculation regarding all the Paleolithic and Mesolithic sites of possibly 3,000 years ago.

PREHISTORIC INDIA: THE NEOLITHIC PERIOD

The next link with India's prehistoric past is located only about two miles from the Paleolithic-Mesolithic site of Chopani-Mando on the Belan river. There were two Neolithic (New Stone Age) sites found in this area which are named **Managara** and **Koldihwa**. **Carbon-14** dating has placed these two sites in the 7th century to the 5th century B.C. Both of them have revealed handmade pottery and polished stone tools. Perhaps the most interesting discovery has been the markings of rice on the many potsherds, which have been identified as a variety of **domestic** rice--not wild rice. This would possibly indicate that some cultivation of grain crops was beginning at this location.

Both of these Neolithic settlements were permanent villages with an agriculture-based economy and were occupied continuously over a long period of time. The huts varied from about 9 feet to about 19 feet in diameter. Wooden posts were set in the ground and filled in with bamboo poles and reed mats. The roofs were most likely conical in shape.

Cord-impressed pottery, sling balls, terracotta beads, large storage jars, and vessels for cooking and eating were unearthed at the hut sites. All of these artifacts would indicate an advancement over the Old and the Middle Stone Ages at the Chopani-Mando and Mahadaha sites. It is also interesting that there was a cattlepen at the end of the village which was nearest to the riverbank. Careful digging even revealed hoof impressions of various sizes and ages of their cattle. There can be no doubt that the people of Neolithic India had passed from the "hunter-gatherer" stage to the "pastoral" stage of food supply. The excavation also revealed that some huts had engaged in flint knapping while others did not. From this it can be assumed that some level of specialization and division of labor was developing. But each house had its own cooking, storage jars, querns, etc. About 150 people are believed to have lived at Managara.

Much farther north archaeologists discovered the village of **Burzahom** in the Vale of Kashmir. The climate in Kashmir during the wintertime is very harsh compared to the Chopani-Mando and Managara sites. The housing remains which have been found at the Neolithic Burzahom site were quite different from those to the south. Huge pits were dug into the hard loess-type soil to shelter the people from the winter cold and the summer heat. Although this type of soil does not provide easy digging, the largest of the sixteen houses discovered was 12 feet deep, about 13 feet in diameter, and there was a circular opening at the top about 9 feet in diameter.

It is interesting that some of the pit-style houses were square, but were otherwise of about the same size as the round ones. The people had built a kind of a landing at the top entrance, usually consisting of about three steps. Apparently they used a ladder to descend on down into the living area. Some of the rooms even had plastered walls and evidently provided quite comfortable living quarters compared to living in a small hut. Fires for cooking and for warmth were probably lit inside the pit houses, but there was not any evidence of a heavy use of fuel inside the pit-style house.

Outside the pit houses of Burzahom the digging revealed a series of postholes around the entrance. There was almost certainly some form of structure with a roof, which would have kept out the rain and snow as well as preventing downdrafts of wind into the pit. Such a structure would also have prevented dust and debris from blowing into the living quarters.

There were also shallow storage pits and the excavations indicate that most of the cooking was done at hearths outside the houses. Whereas the Paleolithic and the Mesolithic huts indicated sporadic living, these houses seem to have been year-round habitations over a period of several years. In later years when they no longer lived in these pit houses, they were used to dump the domestic rubbish. Digging through this rubbish has given archaeologists a wealth of information about the people who lived in the area **after** it was abandoned in the Neolithic Age. It might also be noted that there are still some people in rural India who live in varying styles of pit houses.

A second Neolithic phase occurred at Burzahom. In this period the people lived above the ground in houses which were built with posts, mats, and a daub and wattle type of construction. A few of these houses even had plastered floors. No further evidence of these houses has been preserved except for many artifacts such as pottery and many kinds of stone tools and weapons. Among these tools were several rectangular stone "harvester" knives, which were perforated with two holes at one edge. Some knives were shaped the same way, but were made of bone instead of stone. The most interesting thing about the "harvester" knives is that they have also been found in Neolithic digs in China. This obviously leads to more questions than answers concerning any link between Kashmir, Central Asia, and China in Neolithic times.

FROM VILLAGE TO CITY: AN ERA OF TRANSITION

It has been shown that there was a trend evident which indicated that the people were beginning to move very definitely toward village building as early as 5,000 to 6,000 B.C. The period between these early Stone Age people and the great cities along the Indus River is still a great mystery. It is known that sometime between 5,000 and 3,500 B.C. a copper-using, or **Chalcolithic**, culture developed in the northern subcontinent. During this same period of time there is good evidence of an increase in population in the Indus River Valley in the centuries just preceding the Indus River Civilization. The period from 3,000 to 3,500 B.C. is often referred to as the "**Pre-Indus**" or "**Early Indus**" civilization. Several cities which fall within this time frame have already been excavated such as **Rahman Dheri** and **Kot Diji**. So far there has been no direct tie made between these civilizations and either the earlier Kashmir Neolithic settlements or the later Harappan and Mohenjo Daro civilizations. It is logical that there was some tie, but much further archaeology and study are needed to positively fill this gap.

Prehistoric India--The Stone Age Cultures

A SUMMARY OF ARCHAEOLOGY IN NORTHERN INDIA

Our knowledge of Indian prehistory is still extremely sketchy and based largely on surface finds rather than on systematic excavations. From the little we do possess we can say that the people in India passed from a Paleolithic to a Mesolithic to a Neolithic way of life and tool making in very much the same manner as did the other great civilizations such as Sumer in Mesopotamia, the Egyptians, or the Chinese. It is also interesting that many of the Stone Age tools closely resemble tools from other cultures which have been excavated from around the world. Out study of the archaeological sites has so far been primarily in the area from Rajasthan north to Kashmir. There are many prehistoric sites known in southern India, but little has been done there at this time.

ARCHAEOLOGICAL DISCOVERIES IN SOUTHERN INDIA

The outstanding feature of the south Indian development and technology throughout the entire Stone Age period is the development of **megalithic** construction. It has been said that there are about a million of these huge stone monuments remaining in the Deccan alone. Some of them are arranged as huge stone circles which resemble the one in southern England at Stonehenge. There are single upright monoliths called **menhirs**. A third style are the huge **dolmens**, which consist of two or more upright stones which support a horizontal stone slab placed across them. And finally, there are the **rock-cut tombs.**

The rock-cut tombs contain skeletal remains, which is an indication that the practice of cremation had not yet begun in South India during the Stone Ages. The physical type of the skeletons which has been found in these tombs has been identified as the same as many of the present inhabitants of the region. Coarse pottery vessels, apparently for food offerings, were placed with the burials along with a variety of stone ornaments and weapons. The earliest use of metals in this region were of copper, then bronze, and finally the iron and gold objects began to appear. Some believe that the technology for working metal was introduced into South India from some outside area. Nevertheless, these people improved upon it and are believed to be the first people in the world to have discovered how to turn ordinary iron into steel.

CONCLUDING THE ARCHAEOLOGY OF INDIA'S STONE AGE

All archaeological excavations to date indicate a dense population living in South India in these early times. Rice has been identified in the food offerings left in the tombs, thus indicating a well-developed agricultural society by the late Neolithic period. All signs point to a well-organized society, but there is much archaeological work to be done to move beyond these generalizations. The people throughout the subcontinent were slowly evolving a more modern society when they suddenly made a quantum leap to the highly developed Indus River Civilization.

Prehistoric India--The Stone Age Cultures

SUGGESTIONS FOR FURTHER READING

Allchin, Bridget, & Allchin, Raymond, *The Rise of Civilization in India and Pakistan* (1982).

Basham, A. L., *The Wonder That Was India* (1984).

Kulke, H., & Rothermund, D., *A History of India* (1986).

Piggott, Stuart, *Prehistoric India to 1000 B.C.* (1962).

Figure 8

Figure 9

Figure 10

Chapter 8
THE INDUS RIVER CIVILIZATION

INTRODUCTION

Sir William Jones, an Englishman, was the first to take a scholarly interest in the civilization of early India. Jones went to Calcutta as a judge of the British-operated Supreme Court in India in 1783. He was also a linguistic genius who already knew several languages, including Persian, at the time he arrived in India. He soon became convinced that the ancient Indian language known as **Sanskrit** and the languages of Europe, were all derived from a common ancestor. In 1784 he founded the **Asiatic Society of Bengal** and began working with **Charles Wilkins** to translate the *Bhagavad Gita*. It is therefore safe to say that Jones and Wilkins were the fathers of "Indology." Due to the work of these two men, the West began to realize that this distant part of the world also had an interesting history and literature, and, that it was tied to the history of the western world.

As England began to supervise ever-larger areas of the subcontinent, they sent out surveyors under the East India Company. The surveyors began to relate stories of the great Hindu and Buddhist caves, temples, and shrines in the area where the surveying work was being conducted. At the same time they began to discover several very old documents. Two of the men who were working on the translations of these documents, **James Princep** and **Alexander Cunningham**, decided to go and see some of the places from which the documents had come. Even though Cunningham spent thousands of hours both translating and digging, the task was so huge that it was not until the 20th century that archaeological excavation on a large scale really got underway. Nevertheless, Alexander Cunningham is often referred to as the "father of Indian archaeology."

THE EXCAVATIONS AT HARAPPA & MOHENJO DARO

Cunningham's discovery of the ancient cities of the Indus Valley began to excite the curiosity of the British. There were those who believed that it might be as exciting as Egypt or Mesopotamia. In 1901 the British Viceroy, Lord Curzon, appointed a young archaeologist named **John Marshall** as Director General of the Archaeological Survey in India. It was John Marshall who really discovered the Indus civilization in 1922. Between 1924 and 1931, Marshall supervised the systematic excavation of the two most important ancient cities found to date-- **Harappa** and **Mohenjo Daro**.

The second excavation at Harappa and Mohenjo Daro was done immediately after the Second World War by **P. E. Mortimer Wheeler**. There has been little digging of importance done at these sites since the Wheeler excavation due to disputes between India and Pakistan. The ancient civilization is important to both countries and they have not been able to agree on several excavation sites which would require cooperation. India believes the cities are the roots of **their** civilization today, but both sites are located within the borders of Pakistan. The Harappa site is named after the present-day town nearby. Mohenjo Daro means the "city of the dead."

The Indus Civilization

WHAT THE INDUS RIVER EXCAVATIONS HAVE REVEALED

The people of northern India in these early times had already passed through the hunting and gathering and the pastoral stage of development. These had occurred during the Paleolithic (Old Stone Age) and the Mesolithic periods (Middle Stone Age). At the time of the Indus River civilization, they were in a mixed pastoral and agricultural stage of livelihood, most likely in a late Mesolithic to early Neolithic age. The concept of a fixed abode with well-defined field boundaries is very definitely evident at all of the Indus River sites. When this kind of arrangement is evident, the civilization has begun the **Agricultural Revolution**, sometimes also referred to as the **Neolithic Revolution.** Several of the artifacts recovered were made of copper or bronze, which indicates they were in a transitional stage of industrial development as well. When copper and bronze are used by the craftsmen, it is referred to as a **Chalcolithic**, or also an **Aeneolithic** civilization.

This also meant that farmers could now raise more food than they needed to feed their own family, thus the surplus could be marketed in the local town. Soon, the towns increased in size and became cities as the local farmers brought an increasing amount of produce to the city markets. Cities such as Mohenjo Daro with an estimated population of 40,000 people require a great amount of food. Not only was it necessary for the farmers to produce sufficient food to support such an urban area, but transportation vehicles and an adequate highway system was also necessary to move the agricultural produce from the farm to the urban area. Since urban dwellers depended upon the farms to keep them supplied year-round, some system of preserving the food from the months of rich harvests to the dormant months was required.

It is therefore evident that a city such as Harappa or Mohenjo Daro was a very complex society by about 3,300 B.C. This complexity brought a need for laws, a system of survey, the building and maintenence of roads, a calendar, a system of mathematics, and a system of exchange which reached beyond a simple barter economy. It also necessitated a system of government and writing in order to keep simple records. As these ingredients began to appear, the people of the Indus River Valley passed from a simple "culture" to a "civilization."

The earliest remains of settled agricultural communities in India are found in this same area. They date from about the end of the 4th century B.C. Authorities believe that the climate at that time was both wetter and warmer than it is today. The Indus Valley was well-forested in those times and populated with wild elephants, rhinos, and other wild game. The land was well-suited for agriculture and thus provided an excellent environment for the early people who lived in the area. Interestingly, this is the same kind of **fluvial** environment which existed in other early civilizations such as ancient Sumer in the lower Tigris-Euphrates Valley, along the Nile River Valley in Egypt, and the Hwang Ho River in China. Some think that the origins of the Indus civilization may be even older than Sumer and Egypt but scholars have not yet learned to decipher the scanty amount of picture writing which has been discovered so far.

It has now been approximately 5,000 years or more since Mohenjo Daro was a thriving city in the Indus River Valley. Although dates vary somewhat, it seems to have begun sometime between 3,300 B.C. and 2,500 B.C. This same great civilization ended rather abruptly some time between 1,500 B.C. and 1,700 B.C. There are many mysteries remaining about how this area changed from the tiny villages such as Burzahom to become a huge city in a relatively short period of time.

The Indus Civilization

As we endeavor to reconstruct what the Indus River civilization was like, we discover that **both** Mohenjo Daro and Harappa were metropolitan areas where each city was more than three miles in circumference and each supported a population of roughly 40,000 people. Wheeler has found evidence that this civilization stretched for nearly 1,000 miles in length and included both the Indus and its tributaries. The city of Harappa, for instance, was built on the Ravi River, a tributary of the Indus. Recent archaeological evidence indicates that this same type of civilization once thrived far into the Punjab in the east, possibly as far as the tributaries of the Ganga, and as far south as the Narbada River. To be able to organize and to govern so large an area obviously shows that there must have been people in this area who were in the process of developing a civilization for thousands of years before the flowering of Mohenjo Daro and Harappa.

The orderly layout of the streets and the size of the bricks seem to have been regimented by some central authority or planning group because every brick is made to approximately the same dimensions from one end of the valley to the other. They also had a standard system of weights and measures throughout the Indus Valley. Although there is evidence of trade with Mesopotamia and with Africa, there is no indication that they in any way "borrowed" a ready-made civilization from Mesopotamia, rather the cities which they developed were strictly Indian in their characteristics.

When flooding became a problem toward the end of the period of occupation, the people tore down their houses, used them for rubble and fill, and built a new house on top of the remains of the old one. Often they even set the new foundation on top of the old existing foundation and raised the new house to a higher level. At Mohenjo Daro they have unearthed **nine** strata of buildings which were built one on top of the one beneath. In each city they built a **citadel**, but there is no evidence that they either fought one another or that they were challenged by an outside invader who might have come into their area. The only tangible warlike artifacts are several sling balls made of fired clay. With so many similarities between the Indus River cities, it seems obvious that these people lived under some type of government or planning group.

The **citadel** was built on a rectangular earthen platform, which was approximately 600 feet by 1,200 feet in area. They built up a mud brick wall around the outside of this platform area, then filled it with more mud and other debris until it reached a height of 30 to 50 feet. Excavations indicate that there were two phases of construction. In the second phase they raised the platform, then built buildings on top of it. These buildings had thick outer walls and there were no doors or windows on these walls. These buildings were probably public buildings for administration which faced the inside of the citadel, but there are so few remains it is impossible to be certain about this. When the people moved out of their Indus River homes, they left very few articles behind.

Initial speculation was that the platform was raised and the walls were built for defense against the Aryan invaders, but current thinking believes it was more likely it was a measure which they employed against flooding because the entire city was raised at approximately the same time as the raising of the citadel. It is interesting that as they built the entire city higher the brick linings of the wells were also extended upward to the new street level. Now that the ancient cities have been excavated, these brick well-linings appear more like crude chimneys than like wells for drawing water.

The Indus Civilization

Below the citadel was the city itself. The main streets in Mohenjo Daro were about 30 feet wide and quite straight. The side streets then divided the city into large blocks. Buildings covered most of the area, but there were irregular little walkways winding through between the buildings which must have created quite a maze to any stranger. There were **no** stone buildings--only mud brick and fired brick. The fired brick were not fired as hard as most brick today, probably due to a growing shortage of wood, which would have been necessary to increase their hardness. Many were two-story structures. Most buildings had a small, square courtyard with the rooms arranged around it, something like a Roman villa of much later times. The home entrances were usually through the narrow side alleys, and there were no windows or doors that faced onto the wide streets.

Each house had a bathroom and the people bathed by pouring pitchers of water over their heads and shoulders. Each bathroom had a drain which flowed into sewers under the main streets. These sewers ended at open soak-pits outside the city. These must have smelled terribly in hot weather, since they were a kind of open septic field. Inside the town the sewers were covered by large brick slabs, a system still in use in some Asian cities. No such elaborate system of public sewers has ever been found in Mesopotamia or in Egypt from this same time period. It was not until Etruscan and Roman times, about 2,000 years later, that a similar plumbing system came into general use in the western world.

The most striking of all the features unearthed at Mohenjo Daro is the **Great Bath** in the citadel area. It is a rectangular bathing pool about 39 feet x 23 feet in area and about 8 feet deep. The brickwork was beautifully done and it was then sealed watertight with a bitumen substance. The entire bath could be drained by an opening in one corner. There was a cloister surrounding the bath and this gave access to a number of small rooms. Like the "tank" of a later period Hindu temple, the Great Bath most likely had a religious significance. It is speculated that the cloister may have been the homes of priests, but so very little is revealed about their religion that it is necessary to rely upon educated guesses.

Even though most experts believe that the Great Bath has some religious significance there has not been any building discovered to date which clearly served as a temple. Neither have authorities ever clearly identified a palace, although a large rectangular building 230 feet by 78 feet at Mohenjo Daro has sometimes been suggested as a palace. Some believe that the religious leader and the political leader may have been one and the same person--a **theocracy**.

Another interesting discovery is the **Great Granary** at Harappa. This structure, located just north of the citadel, was built up on a platform measuring about 150 feet x 200 feet, and divided into rooms of 50 feet x 20 feet each. The entire granary was obviously designed to be above the possibility of the annual floods. The main crops were wheat, barley, peas, and sesame, which provided edible oil. Many have speculated that the granary was a common storehouse and that the people of the city shared the annual crop, whatever the quantity might have been.

The people of Harappa and Mohenjo Daro also grew cotton, but there is currently no evidence that they raised rice. The products which they did not raise or make were believed to have been imported from Mesopotamia and Africa, especially in the later years. There have been artifacts found in the Indus Valley which have been traced directly to ancient Sumer and they have been dated at 2,300 B.C. to 2,000 B.C. Trade with Africa and Mesopotamia implies that the early Indians were good merchants and that they had a good merchant fleet with sturdy ships to handle such a trade.

The Indus Civilization

So far archaeologists have not found any royal tombs such as those so common in ancient Egypt or the royal burial tomb discovered by Sir Leonard Woolley at Ur in Sumer. A very commonplace cemetery was found at site "R 37" at Harappa. Fifty-seven very ordinary graves were located in this cemetery just south of the Harappa citadel on a slight rise of land. With rare exceptions, the bodies were extended from north to south with the heads to the north. Each grave was large enough to contain an average of fifteen to twenty pots in addition to the body. A few of the graves contained as many as forty pots. This is almost certainly an indication that the people had some concept of an afterlife.

Personal ornaments of one kind or another were often worn by the dead. Among the grave goods were shell bangles, necklaces and anklets of steatite beads, a copper finger ring, and an earring of thin copper wire. Toilet articles such as copper mirrors, mother-of-pearl shells, an antimony stick, and a large shell spoon were also included in the burials. In one grave there was a pottery lamp, and the bones of a fowl were found at the skeleton's feet. Since these grave goods were not elaborate nor were they even of good quality, we assume that the fifty-seven graves were of an average body of citizens and possibly placed there during the last days of the Indus civilization. No cemetery has yet been located at Mohenjo Daro. It is assumed that it is still to be located since so little of the total area surrounding the city has been excavated. The cemetery also indicates that cremation had not yet become a general practice at Harappa.

Nearly everyone who has ever dealt with the Indus civilization has wondered how such a large urban area made a living. How could they have supported such large numbers of people in an urban setting? Some believe the answer lies with the export of cotton, since it is the one crop which was grown at both Mohenjo Daro and Harappa. Fragments of a true cotton textile, which had been dyed red with madder, was found sticking to a silver vase unearthed at Mohenjo Daro. Analysis has shown that it was not wild cotton, but a fiber very similar to that which is grown today. It is speculated that cotton cloth was an important article of commerce which provided that extra capital to support such an extensive population and to pay for the trade items from Mesopotamia. It is interesting that they not only were weaving cotton cloth, but that they understood that the roots of the madder plant would give the cloth a rich red color.

It is almost certain that the dog was the earliest animal to be domesticated and used to assist in hunting. The date which is often cited in Europe is around 8,000 B.C. There is as yet no certainty as to the earliest domestication of the dog in India, but Mohenjo Daro and Harappa both yielded two different types of dog bones. At Harappa a brick was found which had the imprint of both cat and dog tracks before it was fired. Bones of the Indian one-humped camel as well as the domestic ass and elephant bones have been found on these sites. By far the most common animal bones are those of the Indian humped bull, or zebu, and a smaller Indian buffalo. Many of the goat bones indicate that they were similar to the goats of present-day Kashmir. It is possible that goat wool products were also important items of trade.

One inconvenience to unravelling the mysteries of this civilization of thousands of years ago is indicated at the western gateway to the citadel at Harappa. Brick robbers of long ago found the area a fruitful source to quarry free bricks. We do know that there were guard rooms on either side of the gateway, but the details have all been destroyed by those who borrowed the bricks. Some authorities also speculate that these small rooms served a ceremonial purpose but there is so much that is left to speculation.

The Indus Civilization

Archaeologists and historians continue to marvel that such an elaborate system could have survived for over 1,500 years without some overall administrator or central planning office. The search for such a building has long been one of the important goals of those who have worked at the site.

WHEN AND HOW DID THE INDUS CIVILIZATION END?

The Indus River civilization ended some time between 1700 B.C. and 1500 B.C. after thriving for over a thousand years. Scholars are puzzled about the cause of its rapid decline and abandonment in much the same way that everyone is mystified by its rapid flowering around 3300 B.C. The **old** theory was that the **Aryan people** moved into the northwestern portion of the subcontinent by way of the **Khyber Pass** and ended the Indus civilization by military conquest. This theory assumed that the Aryans arrived at the same approximate date as the end of the Indus civilization. It is now known that by the time the Aryans arrived the cities on the Indus were already ghost towns. Furthermore, there is at this time no evidence of a great battle. Since most of the dwellings which have been excavated reveal little or nothing left behind, it seems the people packed their belongings and moved elsewhere. In the event of defeat in a great battle there would be many possessions which would have been left behind.

The **new** theory is that the weather-climatic situation changed abruptly and the Indus civilization was driven out by floods. There is good evidence for this since the city raised its level on nine different occasions. The proponents of the flood theory are greater in number today than the Aryan invader theory. Both theories have their own supporters. And, there are other speculations about the end of the Indus civilization.

It is always possible that as the population of the area grew, the farmers overcropped the land without restoring the fertility of the soil. Eventually it wore out and the people moved elsewhere. Some think that as they cut down the trees for lumber and firewood the forests disappeared. This drove the wildlife away. Furthermore, over-cutting the timber increased erosion and caused the floods to become much worse. This made the site not only dangerous but the farmers were unable to provide an adequate supply of food. Still others speculate that since the inhabitants did use irrigation they may have caused salts to build up in the soil due to the rapid evaporation of the irrigation water upon the soil. It is possible that some future archaeological dig will answer some of these questions.

It is difficult for us today to believe that such an arid area once supported such a large population. The water table of the Indus Valley seems to be slowly rising each year in recent times. As the water rises during the monsoon season the moisture percolates into the sandy soil, the surrounding land, and the ancient ruins. One need not be an archaeologist to determine that this wetting and drying action causes the bricks to deteriorate. The mineral deposits on the surface of many bricks is an indication that the entire brick is also under stress from these extreme seasonal changes in conditions.

Furthermore, the salty soil from the surrounding valley is frequently blown into the ruins, where it sometimes remains a long time before it is removed. This wind-blown soil has a very high concentration of the salt caused by the rapid drying of the moisture under the hot sun following the monsoons. Unless this salty soil is removed from the archaeological site, the arrival of the monsoon rains the following season simply soaks the salts into the porous bricks and sand. Since the site is almost totally exposed, the monsoon rains also wash away some of the remains of the old cities. The local people walk around in the site and on the walls, which are obviously in the process of disintegration.

SUMMARIZING THE INDUS CIVILIZATION

There are still many things to learn about the Indus civilization before the groundwater, the salt, and people walking upon the ruins have destroyed it all. With well over three-fourths of the site still unexcavated, it is altogether possible that many more significant clues will be discovered which will give us a better insight into this civilization of so long ago. All of the writing which has been found so far consists of a large number of seals which have a short inscription written on each one. It is quite likely that there was much more writing than the small amount which appears on these seals. Further excavations may reveal a repository of writing such as a library. Worst of all, it is possible that the writing was all done on perishable materials which no longer exist.

In other civilizations it has been found that writing and religion often go hand in hand. We have little more to work with regarding the religion of these people than we have on their writing. What everyone assumes to be the "ritual bath" at Mohenjo Daro has already been mentioned. However, we have little more than imagination as to how it might have been used or how it fitted into one of their religious services. Several terracotta female figures were found in the excavation which could mean that the worship of a fertility goddess was a high priority. Most of the prehistoric cultures from other parts of the world also have their small clay figures which are obviously female and obviously pregnant. In addition, several stone representations of phalluses, called lingams in modern India, were also found. This could indicate some kind of overall fertility cult, but that is only speculation at this point.

The excavations do not reveal any sudden epidemic of major proportions which swept the people away. Flooding seems to have become increasingly worse. The Aryan invasions began shortly **after** the Indus civilization and for years it was assumed that they were the ones who had driven the inhabitants out of their cities. That theory is no longer considered valid. Neither do we have any tangible evidence that they went to a particular site less prone to flooding. It was not just one city which faded into memory in the Indus Valley, it was all of them. If a central administrative building, a palace, a temple, or a library could be positively identified, it would probably tell us a great deal more about the Indus River cities. Perhaps future archaeological digs will give us additional clues.

AFTER THE INDUS CIVILIZATION

Several very learned scholars have endeavored to trace the evolution of the decline and fall of the great Indus civilization and to show that the people moved into villages in northern India. This theory is based on excavations in the Punjab [northwest India] such as the site at **Bhagwanpura**. The link between the ancient cities and the villages of northern Pakistan and India has been done in part by noting a kind of grey pottery made at Mohenjo Daro during the last years. This very same type has turned up in digs dating just **after** the fall of the great city civilization. After a period of time the people of Bhagwanpura seem to have improved upon this grey pottery by making a finer grade called **Painted Grey Ware**.

The Indus Civilization

Another connection between the Indus civilization and the Punjab villages is that several of the villages were built on a platform near the Saraswati River. The construction principles of the platforms upon which the villages were located is almost identical to the platform construction at Mohenjo Daro except on a smaller scale. The early habitation of Bhagwanpura was quite primitive since the village was composed of mostly rough circular huts of daub and wattle construction and the huts were covered with thatched roofs. The next later stage, now found just above this primitive stage, shows a thirteen-roomed house with walls of solid mud.

Could it be possible that some of the people from Mohenjo Daro or Harappa came here and contributed their construction style to the small village? There seems to have been no in-between evolution at all. Both the simple grey pottery and the much more advanced Painted Grey Ware have been found with this newer building style. In addition, the Painted Grey Ware is also made in the very same shape as the simple grey pottery found at Harappa just before its collapse. For this reason there are many who speculate that the large populations of the cities simply dispersed into several smaller villages.

The houses built in the later stage at the Bhagwanpura site were made of compacted mud, rather than baked bricks as was customary during the later years of the Indus civilization. One of the Bhagwanpura buildings with thirteen rooms was evidently a one-story structure which was similar to many dwellings in an Indian village today. Even the building materials have changed very little over the thousands of years. Other village excavations from the Kashmir area all the way south to the Deccan plateau show many similar characteristics except for local variations in housing style. Tools were changing much more rapidly during this period than housing. Tools which had formerly been made of polished chert and copper soon shifted to all metal tools of copper, bronze, and small items of iron.

THE IRON AGE AND THE RETURN OF CITIES

The second great flowering of cities in India seems to be tied to the **Iron Age**. The antecedents of the simple villages of the Gangetic Iron Age can be traced back to the Indus civilization and forward to the present-day villages and cities. The Painted Grey Ware pottery was continued while a pre-urban period saw the introduction of a new black and red ware pottery.

Small villages of agricultural people have been found at the lowest levels of the archaeological digs in nearly every major city today. The major difference between these villages and those of earlier times is the large number of iron tools which began to totally replace the old stone blades and hoes. One of the city excavations on the Ganga River uncovered an embankment surrounding the ancient city which was very similar to the city walls which were discovered at the Indus River cities. These types of city walls became very common at other cities a little later. Copper, glass, and objects of terracotta, along with bone and ivory arrow points, have been found in these excavations. Marked differences from one archaeological site to another during this period makes generalizations very difficult. Nevertheless, it is proper to think of this as a transitional stage wherein the people were using some of the old ideas from the Indus civilization and at the same time adopting new ideas.

By about 600 B.C. a change took place from a purely village culture to the beginning of a second urban civilization in North India. A novel form of deluxe ceramic ware was introduced at about this time. It has been called **Northern Black Polished Ware**. As this new age of urbanization began to develop, the simple villages of the Iron Age did not disappear, but continued on for a long period. But some villages, especially those situated on strategic highway intersections or near river crossings, began to grow from village status into cities.

One of the major considerations for every Indian family for thousands of years has been how to raise sufficient food to feed itself. As urbanization increased, the farmer had to raise enough for himself and some to sell in the city markets so the urban areas would also have a sufficient supply. At the very beginning of this urbanization movement, there were many of the farmers who lived in the cities in order to have the advantage of the protection of the city walls. They then went outside the walls each day to till their fields. The evidence indicates that in many of the urban areas the houses were spaced far enough apart to raise at least some food right inside the city. The transition from rural to urban was fairly gradual but nevertheless significant.

Rural housing styles have changed very little since the beginning of the Iron Age. Many are still made with formed earthen walls, some with sun-dried bricks, and in recent years more houses are built with fired brick or with a type of concrete blocks. Many of the old style houses are still in use in the countryside. There are even some of the pit houses still in use in the south, a style which even preceded the Indus civilization. The Indian ox or bullock cart still looks very much as it did when the first cameras photographed one of them in the 19th century. There are terracotta toy ox carts which have been taken from the Mohenjo Daro excavation which look just like the ones which the farmers still use today. Some Indian farmers have appropriated old truck axles and wheels for a more modern approach. The same can be said of many of the tools used by farmers--they are almost unchanged from the beginning of the Iron Age. There is, therefore, no recognizable break from the Iron Age tools to the present except for minor modifications.

The Iron Age also saw the introduction of coinage from cast copper and punch-marked silver. A form of writing was begun at this early time but was not well developed until the time of the emperor Ashoka about 200 years later. This early style of writing is known as **Brahmi** and is the direct ancestor of the modern Indian scripts. Life was obviously becoming more complex as religion, politics, law, the arts, trade, communications, warfare and many other aspects of ordinary life were changing.

There is no question that a great increase in population was occurring all across northern India. Outsiders moved in bringing with them the basic principles of their Vedic civilization. It was within this same time period that the caste system began to develop. This increase in population required that much more land be placed under cultivation. Wheat, barley, millet and rice were grown extensively to provide flour for the food on the Indian tables. As more land was cleared of forests and the aged sods were broken, it invited more erosion of the land.

Craft specialization grew in complexity in copper, bronze, and iron. In this stage the people were more fearful of outside invaders than in previous ages. They built massive walls of burnt brick with well-defended gates and a moat surrounding the city walls. Walls such as these served not only defensive purposes but protected the cities from floods as well. In some cases the invaders drove the people of the many scattered tiny villages surrounding the city to seek shelter within the city walls. It is believed that many of the less significant villages disappeared altogether at this time. Although this concept is logical, there is little archaeological proof of this theory.

The Indus Civilization

By the middle of the first millennium B.C., the foundations of the great independent republics and kingdoms of North India had been laid. These kingdoms became the basis of the political structure of ancient India. Although each of these cities varied in power and influence the state of **Magadha** with its capital first in the fortress valley at Rajgir, and later at **Pataliputra** on the Ganga River, became the center of the greatest political unity in early India. From the 4th century B.C. to the death of the emperor Ashoka in 232 B.C., the **Mauryan Empire** was centered in Magadha and controlled the territory from Kandahar to Orissa and deep into South India.

BOOKS FOR FURTHER READING

Allchin, Bridget, & Allchin, Raymond, *The Rise of Civilization in India and Pakistan* (1982).

Basham A.L., *The Wonder That Was India* (1984).

Embree, Ainslie T., editor, *The Encyclopedia of Asian History* (1988).

Kulke, Hermann, & Rothermund, Dietmar, *A History of India* (1986).

Mehta, Dilip, "Mystery on the Indus," *GEO*, August, 1984, page 72f.

Piggott, Stuart, *Prehistoric India to 1000 B.C.* (1962).

Piggott, Stuart, *The Dawn of Civilization*.

Possehl, Gregory, editor, *Ancient Cities of the Indus* (1979).

Wheeler, Sir Mortimer, *The Indus Civilization* (1968).

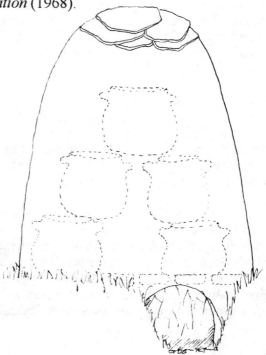

Figure 11

Chapter 9
A BRIEF INTRODUCTION TO HINDUISM
THE EARLY ARYAN PERIOD

The decline and collapse of the Indus River civilization and the subsequent invasions and conquest of the subcontinent by the Indo-Aryan peoples probably occupied more years than we can imagine. Beyond the tiny bits and pieces of history which have been found by archaeologists, along with the linguistic record, there is very little to work with in reconstructing India's early history. There is little concrete evidence before the 6th or 7th centuries B.C.

The best evidence indicates that the inhabitants of the old cities such as Harappa and Mohenjo Daro moved out and formed villages and lived a life based upon subsistence agriculture. Many villages and towns were probably formed, some of which later became large cities while others disappeared from the map. Important families undoubtedly arose, dominated a local area, then they disappeared without leaving a record. Political power and territorial domination were probably an important part of everyday life. Unfortunately, these people, often referred to by the outside invaders as the **Dravidians**--a less than complimentary term--left us no written historical record.

THE DRAVIDIANS

The native Dravidians were a dark-skinned people who were short in stature and had most likely formed a quiet, peaceful society which had already entered the age of fixed agriculture but continued to rely heavily upon their flocks and herds. Except for some of their architectural styles and their pottery, they seem to have carried little with them from the Indus River cities. If they had a system of writing, it has not yet been discovered. Their religion was most likely based primarily upon animism. No Great Bath or religious temple has been discovered which can be traced directly to the post-Indus River civilization. But archaeology in India is still in its initial stages.

THE INVADING ARYANS

Sometime about 1500 B.C. a new element entered the Indus River area. These invaders are known as the Aryans or the **Indo-Aryans**. Like the native Dravidians of the northwestern subcontinent, the invading Aryans kept no accurate written records of this important period of Indian history. These people were primarily in the pastoral stage of development as they traveled from their place of origin through the northwest passes into the subcontinent. It is known that they did have some element of fixed agriculture, but they were primarily a people on the move.

No one knows the details of the origin of the Indo-Aryan invaders, but the linguistic record indicates that they were one branch of people who left east central Europe--possibly the area from the Ukraine to southern Poland--and migrated eastward. Other branches of this same group migrated south into present-day Greece, while a third branch moved westward into Europe going as far as Ireland. The eastward migrating group, the Indo-Aryans later split into two groups. One of these moved southeast into the area of Persia--modern Iran--while the remainder pushed on to the east, crossed the Hindu Kush mountains by way of Khyber Pass, and entered the

Indus River Valley. Best estimates today indicate that the Indus River civilization had just broken up at this time. Since the Aryan invaders had horses and chariots, they proved to be the superior warriors. The local Dravidian population was pushed ahead of the triumphant conquerors.

No one knows why the Aryan people began to move. Since they were in the early stages of settled agriculture it is possible that they were looking for fertile land. Some speculate that the weather had been unfavorable in eastern Europe. There is the possibility that they were looking for more grazing for their flocks and herds. Some believe the population of east central Europe had outrun their ability at that time to produce sufficient food. Perhaps they were short on wood since wood was the major source of fuel as well as building materials. Others believe the various clans had a dispute and scattered rather than face continued warfare in that area. Best estimates date the period of break-up and outward migration around 2,000 B.C. Those who moved west into Europe are known as the **Indo-Europeans**--those who moved east are the **Indo-Aryans**.

If the Aryans were not yet skilled agriculturalists they did settle down in the fertile Indus River valley and established themselves there with fixed abodes and extensive farmland. As their numbers multiplied, and as other Indo-Aryan migrants continued to pour into the subcontinent via the passes through the Hindu Kush mountains, they pushed further east into the Ganges River valley, then they turned south and proceeded as far as the Deccan plateau. This was a slow but steady migration which probably lasted several hundred years. Their migration was probably comparable in some respects to the nature of the Hebrew patriarch Abraham as he wandered with his family and flocks for forty years in search of the Promised Land.

As the Hebrews often had to fight to protect their course of migration in the Fertile Crescent, so also the Indo-Aryans encountered a great amount of fighting along their route to India, and they had to fight the less well-equipped Dravidians for their real estate. Since warfare seems to have occupied a prominent place in their early literature, their warriors, often called the **Kshatriyas**, were very important to both their advancement and their very survival. The Kshatriyas were the number one members of an entire society on the move. The Indo-Aryans looked upon the Dravidian villagers and farmers as inferior people. The Indo-Aryan Kshatriyas were the triumphant victors.

THE IMPORTANCE OF SANSKRIT IN HISTORY

No one knows all the details of the origin of Sanskrit but those who are authorities in linguistics believe that the language developed originally in east central Europe, possibly as many as five to seven thousand years ago. At that early time it was a spoken language. Each of the groups which migrated out developed a written language at a different time, usually to express their religious principles.

Among the first linguists to study these early languages was an Englishman, **Sir William Jones**, 1746-1794. At the same time, a German, **Jacob Grimm** of fairytale fame, began to study the relationship of words in the various languages. Both men concluded that there was a close relationship between the Greek language in the western world and the old languages of Persia and India in the eastern world. Linguistic research since the 18th century has proven that this is true.

The earliest Indo-Aryan written document known at this time is the ***Rig Veda***. The term "Veda" is derived from a Sanskrit term which means "to know." In this case the ***Rig Veda*** refers to a knowledge of sacred information. It is a collection of hymns to the gods when a sacrifice was offered. These hymns were composed and transmitted orally generation after generation for hundreds of years, probably as early as 1800 B.C. By that time it is reasonably certain the Aryans had occupied the lands on both sides of the Indus River.

The **_Rig Veda_** is not only the oldest example of Indo-Aryan writing, it is the oldest religious book in the world. It contains 1,028 hymns which authorities believe were composed between 1500 and 900 B.C., the very time the Aryans were invading northwest India.

The _Vedas_ are the basic scripture of the Hindus and their highest authority in all matters pertaining to religion and philosophy. According to the **_Puranas_**, another Hindu source which was composed between the 4th century B.C. and the 14th century A.D., **Vyasa**, one of the very early wise men of Hinduism, was commanded by Brahma to make a compilation of the Vedas.

Vyasa is reputed to also be the author of the **_Mahabharata_**, another early source of Hindu scripture. One of the very early parts of the **_Mahabharata_** is the **_Bhagavad Gita_**. Since the **_Puranas_** are much more recent writings, they are probably easier to comprehend. They are concerned primarily with five religious topics: the creation of the world; its dissolution and recreation; the lineages of the gods, sages, and kings; the deeds of the royal dynasties; and, the cosmic ages of the world. Hinduism is based upon all of these sacred writings and more. It is a **polytheistic** religion about which it is difficult for anyone not born a Hindu to achieve a very in-depth understanding. It is a lifelong quest for understanding for the Hindus as well.

When the words used in these sacred texts were compared with words in the western world, Sir William Jones and Jacob Grimm noticed many amazing parallels. Although some have tried to define the Aryans as a race, it would be more proper to refer to all Aryans as members of one **language group**. There has been so much intermarriage over thousands of years that it would be impossible for anyone to claim to be of a pure race. By the time the linguists had completed their work on the Aryan language group, they discovered that a total of ten languages all belonged to the same "language tree."

The term "Sanskrit" means perfected or polished which indicates that there were earlier efforts at writing by the Indo-Aryans which pre-date the **_Rig Veda_**. Sanskrit reached its golden age from about A.D. 300 to 900. It was the language of learned scholars throughout the subcontinent. It was applied to religious rituals, philosophy, logic, grammar, medicine, architecture, mathematics, and astronomy for about 3,500 years. Although Sanskrit is one of the official languages recognized in India's constitution today, it has become to modern languages somewhat like Latin has become to western Europe since the Roman era. Like Latin in the history of the Christian church in the West, Sanskrit is the language of the Hindu religion.

THE VEDIC AGE, 1500-500 B.C.
THE EARLY BEGINNINGS OF HINDUISM

Many of the heroic gods of Hinduism were undoubtedly imported by the invading Aryans. Since they considered the native Dravidians inferior people, there are few, if any, ties which can be made between Hinduism and the Dravidian faith except for the point on ritual cleansing. As the migrating Aryans paused for their religious ceremonies, it is possible that a part of their religious service also involved the rites of purification at the flowing streams along the way. Some authorities would like to tie the use of the "tank" in Hindu services to the Great Bath located in Mohenjo Daro. No one knows for sure whether this is true or not, but Hinduism is based primarily upon the customs which the invading Aryans imported into the subcontinent and shaped to form the faith as they understood it at that time. Hinduism is therefore the **oldest** major faith in the world. It was formed at least a thousand years before the birth of Abraham, the patriarch of the Hebrew faith.

Indra was the greatest god of the Hindus in those early times. He was a warlike god and at the same time a god of the weather. He conquered innumerable human and demon enemies, vanquished the sun, and killed the dragon Vrtra, who had prevented the monsoon from breaking. Indra's weapons were lightening and the thunderbolt, very similar to the Greek god Zeus. Indra gained strength for his formidable tasks by drinking **soma**.

No one today knows which plant was used to make soma. The ceremony of gathering and making soma was described in some detail. The stalks of the plant were pressed between stones, the juice was then filtered through sheep's wool. It was then mixed with water and milk. During the sacrifice services, soma was offered first as a libation to the gods, then the remainder was consumed by the priests and the person who was offering the sacrifice. The soma drink was highly valued for its exhilarating effect. Since the entire process of making soma was completed in a single day it is unlikely that it contained alcohol. More than likely it was some unknown member of the hemp family of plants which gave those who drank it a hallucinogenic effect. It was considered such an important part of the early Aryan worship that they created a god called **Soma**. The god Soma was the "master of plants," the healer of disease, and the bestower of riches.

The early gods of the Aryans were chiefly connected with the sky and they were predominantly male. Several of them are associated with the sun--surya. They also created a god named **Surya** who drove across the sky in a flaming chariot similar to the Greek god Helios. There were five other gods connected with the sun: Savitr, Pusan, Soma, Asvins (or Nasatyas), and Visnu. Varuna was supposed to be the highest of all the gods.

Varuna was aware of the deeds of men and he was omnipresent. No matter where one might go, Varuna was always present. He was so pure and holy that simply performing a sacrifice to him would not ensure his favor. Varuna abhorred sin, which covered many things such as lying, evil deeds, anger, gambling, excessive drinking, the influence of wicked men, and any breach of a ritual act. When one prayed to Varuna, it was common to put on sackcloth and ashes and to pray with fear and trembling. Unless one lived a very proper life, Varuna would punish you for your sins. Furthermore, like Yahweh of the *Old Testament*, he visited the sins of the evil person upon his ancestors for generations. Those who crossed Varuna would be caught in his snares and visited with terrible diseases--his favorite was dropsy. One always approached Varuna with total fear and respect. The hymns which were composed to please Varuna sound very similar to the Hebrew Psalms--"who is man that god is mindful of him"? Many prayed to Varuna to be kind and to forgive them for their transgressions. Others wrote poems of praise, again like the Psalms, in hopes of pleasing him.

The Indo-Aryan god, **Yama**, was the lord of the dead. Yama had many characteristics similar to the Hebrew Adam. He was the first man to die. When he traveled to the afterlife, he became the guardian of the "World of the Fathers," a blissful world where the blessed ones who had faithfully performed the rites of the Aryans would live happily forever.

An Introduction to Hinduism

Rudra was a god who was so immoral he could be dangerous. Like the Greek god Apollo, he was an archer-god whose arrows brought diseases to mankind. He was a remote god who lived in the mountains like a hermit. It was Rudra who brought on the storms. Many prayed to Rudra and left offerings to ward off illness and storms. They believed that Rudra knew the healing herbs necessary to cure a sickness.

Of course there were dozens of other gods in the total Aryan pantheon of those early times--a god for virtually every need or purpose. Some of these gods increased in stature over time. Vishnu, for instance, began as one of the rather minor gods who was an attendant to Indra. Later, Vishnu rose to be one the the three chief gods of Hinduism. Indra, on the other hand, tended to diminish in power over the centuries. Indra ultimately became god of the rain, regent of the heavens, and the guardian of the East.

There were hundreds of other deities to whom the Hindu people offered sacrifices, usually animal sacrifices. Each sacrifice was attended by very complex rites. According to the *Rig Veda* these animal sacrifices were paid for by the wealthier chiefs and tribesmen, but even the poor man made his small sacrifice as best he could afford. In the most elaborate ceremonies there were several animals slaughtered on a single occasion. Such large numbers pleased the gods, who then descended to the sacred straw on the sacrificial field to eat and drink with the worshippers. All who attended were then duly rewarded according to the quantity and the quality of their sacrifices.

Such complex and expensive religious ceremonies must have been awe-inspiring to the participants. Some believe that the worshippers were inebriated with the soma drink during their religious ceremonies. In such a state they were able to see wondrous visions of the gods and experience strange sensations of power. They could almost reach up and touch the heavens--they could almost become gods themselves! Only the priests knew the rituals and the formulas whereby the gods could be brought down to the sacrificial area. The priests, therefore, became the masters of a great mystery. Without writing in those early years, the priests memorized the procedures and passed them on from father to son. The priests became the sole intermediaries between the gods and the people.

Once the system of writing was developed, these religious ceremonies and the mysteries of the faith were written down. The priestly class were the only ones who knew the secrets of the faith and they were the ones who developed writing. They were the ones who were in charge of who had access to language and learning. In its widest application, these early writings concerning the faith of the Hindu people and all its mysteries are known as the *Vedas*. These writings incorporated the sacred knowledge of the priests at that time. And, at the same time, the *Vedas* are the literature of the early Hindus. They are very different from the writings of the Chinese, who were much more interested in the use of writing to record their national history. It seemed that the Hindus did not attach any great importance to their history. Religion was the all important consideration.

There are other important Hindu writings besides the Vedas. The *Brahmanas* are explanations of the rituals which accompanied the hymns, chants, and sacrificial procedures. The *Brahamanas* depict the priests as men who could compel the gods rather than imploring them.

An Introduction to Hinduism

The *Aranyakas* are also known as the "forest books" because they were meant to be studied in the privacy of a forest. They also emphasize the mystical aspects of the sacrifice. Books such as the *Upanishads* and the *Puranas* were developed to explain some of the writings of the *Vedas*.

The *Upanishads* were composed between the years c.800 B.C. and A.D. c.300 and are the last major writings considered a part of the revelation of the Hindu faith. There are thirteen *Upanishad* writings which are considered the core of the faith. All Hindu meditation and yoga are from the *Upanishads*. It is the *Upanishad* writings which define Brahman as the eternal, conscious, irreducible, infinite, omnipresent, and the one spiritual source of the universe. Over time the emphasis on the sacrifice began to yield to the ultimate identity of the individual soul known as the **Atman**. The concept of the world soul, **Brahman**, then began to predominate. All of the later Hindu writings began to emphasize the concept of the **Transmigration** of the soul. Brahman, Atman, and transmigration are very important aspects of Hinduism.

The sacred writings of the Hindus were designed to be a total encyclopedia of the faith as well as a guide for theology and worship. All of the secrets were memorized by the priests long before they were written. After writing became common, there were still many of the priests who were known to memorize as many as 100,000 verses. They in turn encouraged their sons to memorize an equal number. Since books were difficult to make at that time, and it was not considered proper to allow the lowest classes to see the sacred writing, the number of copies of the Vedas was never very great. Memorization was still very important.

THE BASICS OF THE HINDU FAITH

It is important to understand the basics of the Hindu faith as it has been practiced in the last one thousand years or more. Hinduism is also the basis of Buddhism and Jainism. Sikhism has also borrowed from this ancient religion. There are three primary gods in Hinduism as currently practiced--**Brahma, Vishnu,** and **Shiva**. Until 1947, the element of **caste** was an important feature of Hinduism. Hindu society was divided into four castes: the **Brahmins,** the **Kshatriyas**, the **Vaisyas**, and the **Sudras.** The people who were not born into one of these four castes were referred to as either **Panchamas** or **Chandalas**. Since all things have a beginning it is appropriate to begin with some of the Hindu beliefs concerning creation.

The creation process began when the self-existent Lord, the first great creator, came out of the darkness as a shining light and began creating. He first created the waters. He deposited in the waters a seed. The seed became a golden egg. The golden egg became as bright as the sun. It was from this egg that **Brahma,** the creator, sprung. Brahma continued in the egg for an entire year. Then he began creation by dividing the shell into two parts by his mere thought. One part of the shell formed the heavens while the other half formed the earth.

It is also interesting that the mythical sage **Manu** claims in his code that he created mankind but not the universe. Manu claims that Brahma is his father. And there are other theories of the creation which are stated in the sacred books of the Hindus. No two of them are alike. Each one of the versions is held to be equally sacred and authentic.

Hindus believe that since the world once had a beginning, so also will it have an ending. We are simply living in one of the four great ages which when taken together span millions of years. The first of these ages--the Golden Age--was the one in which all mankind was equal and happy. In the second age, evil appeared for the first time. By the third age, the numbers of good men and evil men will be equal--they will each struggle for supremacy during this age. In the fourth of the great ages, evil will overcome good and ultimately everything will be destroyed. Mankind will not be given a choice in this final age. At this time, **Vishnu**, the second of the three Hindu gods, will incarnate himself as **Kalki**, the destroyer. The entire world will perish by fire. Most Hindus believe that we are now living in this final age. There is no precise date set but there will be about 425,000 years more of suffering in this final age.

All Hindus believe that they are of divine origin. They believe that before recorded time the gods divided them into four groups which are generally referred to as castes. They claim descent from the person of **Brahma**, the creator. They believe the Brahmins, the priestly caste, originated from Brahma's head. The Kshatriyas, the warrior caste, came from his arms. The Vaisyas, the traders and the agricultural people, came from his thighs. And, the Sudras, who perform the menial tasks, have come from his feet. The people who used to be referred to as Chandalas or Untouchables, are not people in the strict sense of the definition. The other races of men are believed to have sprung out of the darkness which Brahma cast away during the process of creation.

Another very important concept of Hinduism is the soul of man referred to as the **Atman**. The Hindu concept is more of a world view of our individual soul than in the case of Judaism or Christianity. Hindus believe that the one essence which permeates every aspect of the universe is an impersonal, immaterial, unborn and undying spirit or force called **Brahman**. It is the essence of all things, the "Real of the Real," the "world-stuff." There is a universal soul of which all individual souls are an unbreakable and eternal part. This individual soul is referred to as the **Atman**. **Brahman** and **Atman** are one and indivisible. Therefore, we as individual souls, and God as the essence of all things, are **one**. The unity of all life is the only reality. The *Upanishads* repeat over and over this fundamental fact that no matter what we see about us, "That art thou." Western theologians refer to this concept as **pantheism**.

As individual souls living in a world of the senses, we think that each of us and the world itself must exist apart from the one all-pervading soul or essence, but such a belief of separateness is referred to as **Maya**, or illusion. The world of the senses is transitory and exists only as part of the one unchanging Brahman. The illusion of separateness must be completely abandoned before we perceive the truth. While we are living in a state of illusion, we place our faith solely in those things which are transitory and unsatisfying. Hence we are afflicted with sorrow and pain.

We, as individuals, shall never be free from the world's sorrow until we achieve **Moksha--deliverance**. Moksha comes to us through our awareness of the reality of the **one**, the only true eternal life. It is that eternal life which reabsorbs us into the Brahman. This is accomplished only through long experience in meditation, which allows us to completely separate ourselves from this world of illusion. It is impossible to accomplish this in the world of the senses. Therefore, it is necessary for each soul to receive many experiences. Experiences are received only by the incarnation of the soul into many physical bodies. This is the doctrine of **transmigration,** also known as **reincarnation**. This is an essential feature of the *Upanishad* philosophy.

This theory of transmigration began in the early formative periods of Hinduism, possibly three or four thousand years ago. In those early times they talked about the long voyage of rebirth. They said the soul must wander through several worlds in space for a time, then it passes to the world of the Fathers, then to the paradise of Yama. After a time of bliss, the soul travels on to the moon. From the moon the soul goes to empty space until finally it descends to the earth in the rain. The soul then enters plants and becomes food which is finally born again in the fire of a woman. This ancient doctrine seems to rest on another primitive belief that conception occurred through one of the parents eating a fruit or a vegetable containing a latent soul awaiting to be born. The souls which made this long voyage were the fortunate ones, the ones who had prepared themselves through a life of sacrifice, charity, and austerity. The unrighteous were to be reincarnated as worms, birds, or insects.

Not everyone seems to have accepted the transmigration theory right away. However, after time it did work its way into the faith. It would be difficult to say how many Hindus today believe in such a long journey for the soul before it is reborn. But in one way or another, the idea of transmigration from one form of life to another became an important part of Hinduism. There were some sects of Hinduism which taught that all forms of life contained a soul, both plants and animals. It is important to remember that beyond the *Vedas*, the *Upanishads*, and the other sacred writings, there is no church "discipline" in Hinduism, no catechism of what all members must believe. Each Hindu is left to read the holy books, to be taught first by their parents, then by the great gurus (teachers), and they are free to practice their beliefs pretty much on an individual basis. For many who are illiterate, there is only one source, their teachers. In the early years it was very difficult to obtain copies of the holy books. Literacy was reserved for the upper classes.

While we are yet in this world of illusion, all our actions in every aspect of life are governed by an immutable, eternal moral law called **Karma**. Karma can be roughly summed up as the law of action and reaction. Or, as it is stated in the western world, "whatever a man sows, that is what he shall also reap." It is possible to do many good works and to build up a store of merit--that is good Karma. If one is guilty of evil actions, that will build up a store of bad Karma. The very environment into which a person is born, together with one's attending fortune and misfortune, is not due to the whimsy of a capricious God, but to the acts of the individual himself, possibly even in past lives. The Hindu says there is no favoritism in the universe, only immutable law and justice.

When this system of religious philosophy became linked to the idea of caste, the theory of reincarnation fit conveniently--we are born into a particular caste not because of who our parents might be but because the gods directed our soul to the parents whose spiritual level matched our soul's level of achievement at that time. It was possible for a soul to advance from caste to caste, but not during any one lifetime. The caste level to which our soul is reincarnated will depend upon our Karma in this lifetime. This carries another basic concept of the *Upanishads*, that each caste is for learning unique experiences on this earth. The Brahmin who is approaching oneness with the eternal is approaching **moksha**, and will therefore not have to be reincarnated in the world of the senses again unless he commits some terrible error of faith.

THE CASTE SYSTEM

Caste began on the subcontinent thousands of years ago. It has been traced back to the time of the Indo-Aryan invasions. The invaders believed the native inhabitants, the short, dark-skinned people who could never seem to fight an effective battle, were definitely inferior. The term Dravidian means "inferior people." They also called them **Sudras**, a word which labelled them as devils. It is also speculated that the Indo-Aryans were beginning to intermarry with the

74

Dravidians and the upper class feared that this would very likely end their racial superiority. The institution of caste is therefore believed to have begun as a matter of racial discrimination. The Hindu word for caste is **Varna**, which means color. Color and caste became one.

Within a relatively short period of time after caste became accepted by the conquering Indo-Aryans, there were four fixed levels. The **Brahmins** were the priestly caste, sometimes referred to as the "god compellers." The **Kshatriyas** were the warrior caste, the protectors and enforcers of society. The **Vaisyas** were the agriculturalists and the merchant caste. The lowest of the castes were the **Sudras**. They were the serfs and the servants, the lowest members of society. There was yet another group who never deserved to be considered caste. They were called the **Panchamas**, those who had fallen to the lowest status possible. Many in the upper castes considered their livestock to be higher than the Panchamas. The western world has referred to this lowest group as the **untouchables**. There were even those who were considered the **unapproachables** and the **unlookables**. Each of these will now be considered individually.

THE BRAHMIN CASTE

During the period the Hindus call their **Epic Age**, the age of the Aryan conquest of the subcontinent, the warrior caste, the Kshatriyas, held the highest social rank. As the Indo-Aryans moved slowly but deliberately across the northern two-thirds of the subcontinent, the warriors were the number one caste. The great epic accounts of conquest in this period are included in their early literature such as the *Mahabharata*. The conquest is portrayed as the great hero-conquerors--the Aryan master race--overcoming the locals who are always considered inferior. But once the subcontinent was overrun and conquered, the Kshatriyas had little to do. Religion began to assume an ever greater role in the lives of the people.

The Brahmin priests began to add new conditions to the religious faith such as caste. The parameters of the system needed to be carefully defined for each of the four castes. New rites of purification needed to be prescribed for each person within the new caste system. The holy rivers were prescribed and the tank for purification was described in detail. Many of the sacrificial ceremonies were more carefully described. The gods and goddesses were identified pretty much as they are accepted today. Writing was beginning to be more common and they needed men to be the scribes while others would teach the novices. Religion began to assume a much greater importance than protection and conquest. The Brahmin priests moved from the number two position to number one. The Kshatriyas now became the number two caste.

As Hinduism became more complex, the Brahmins began to create a whole body of special attributes which they claimed no one else possessed. One of their most powerful claims was that they were the sole **intermediaries** between the gods and mankind. It was at this time that they developed the concept that they were created from the head of Brahma, therefore they were the highest caste. Since they compelled the gods and controlled the learning, it was only logical that they would become the highest of the castes.

The temple duties, and the wealth they accumulated as priests, allowed them to control more property than the rest of society. They proclaimed that when a Brahmin was born, he was born above the world. A Brahmin was the chief of all creatures in the world. They were divinely assigned to guard the values of society in both the religious and the civil realm. Young Brahmins were taught to believe that whatever existed in the universe was all their wealth. They were entitled to it all by the eminence of their birth. They ate their own food, wore their own type of apparel, and they controlled the alms for those who were in need. Some were so arrogant as to believe that all other people enjoyed life because the Brahmin had willed that it should be so. A few even believed that they were above the gods.

As Brahmins assumed more of these important attributes, the lower castes seemed to approve. After all, they were the god compellors, they behaved like gods here on earth. Their conceit seemed to be unbounded. They taught that every member of a Brahmin's body was a center of pilgrimage. The holy Ganges River was in the Brahmin's right ear. The sacred fire was in his right hand. All the holy places of the world resided in his right foot. The Brahmin's mouth was the mouth of the most exalted of all the gods. This meant that other Hindus had an obligation to feed the Brahmin priests. All of these attributes and powers of a Brahmin were then written in a holy book called the *Code of Manu*. They were treated like gods here on earth.

The Brahmin priests taught that if a man should sell his cow, he would go to hell, but if he gave the cow to a Brahmin as a donation, he would go to heaven. If an entire village should be presented to a Brahmin, then the person who made the presentation would acquire all the merit which it was possible to obtain in this life. Such a gift would bring untold rewards to the giver, including many jewels, a million virgins, and his destiny would certainly be a blissful eternity. A parcel of land given to a Brahmin would guarantee heaven, a house would secure a heavenly palace, and many other rewards were all spelled out in the *Code of Manu*. It was little wonder that the Brahmins became the number one caste--that they exercised control over great amounts of property and wealth.

Since the body of the Brahmin was considered sacred, it was the worst of all possible crimes to injure one of them in any way. Even the king had no right to inflict corporal punishment on a Brahmin. If a Sudra assaulted a Brahmin, the culprit was to be put to death. If he slandered a Brahmin, the penalty was to have his tongue cut off. About the worst thing a Brahmin could do was to pollute himself by touching a person of a lower caste.

There were other "fringe benefits" to being a Brahmin. For instance, his property was too sacred to be taxed by the king. If a Brahmin died without heirs, his property was to be divided among the other Brahmins. A Brahmin could bring a deadly curse upon anyone who offended him. This was so powerful that even the gods were known to have withered under such a curse. Orthodox Hindus were therefore very careful that they should not offend a Brahmin in any way. They were even more respected than the rulers or the gods. As a consequence of such a powerful status in society, there were Brahmins who made unreasonable demands. The people did everything possible to please them.

A Brahmin's life was divided into four periods called **Ashramas**. The first period was known as the student or learning period. As a child he would be raised at home for the early years. By the time he was seven to ten years of age he would be initiated into Brahminhood by a process called the *munja*, otherwise referred to as the investiture of the **Sacred Thread**. He would then be sent to live in the house of his teacher. There he would learn to study the *Vedas* and the sacred law. This period lasted until he had completed his studies, sometimes up to the age of thirty.

Throughout this training period he must obey his master precisely. There were many menial chores such as gathering wood for the holy fire, to learn how to beg for food, to sleep on a low bed, or whatever his teacher demanded. He must treat his master's family with all due respect. The student dared not eat honey, any kind of flesh, or use perfumes or garlands. Women, all sensual desires, singing, dancing, and gambling were all off the limits. He was never to engage in disputes and never to be guilty of a falsehood. There were many other rules which he should learn such as the fact that it was very inappropriate to read the *Vedas* during a natural disturbance such as a thunderstorm.

During the second stage of a Brahmin's life he was expected to return to his father's house and marry a virgin of noble birth. The marriage had most likely been arranged by his parents well ahead of the completion of his learning period. A young Brahmin was not expected to talk to his wife unless it was necessary. Conjugal relations were to be only for progeny and never for pleasure. He was expected to perform all his religious duties, including ceremonies for departed ancestors, and to be a model citizen in the community.

It was also considered appropriate that the young Brahmin should hold a feast and invite his friends to celebrate the end of his student years and the beginning of his married life. The only friends he could invite would be those with a similar caste status to his own. There would be a long list of people in the area who were considered not worthy to have as associates. It was even inappropriate at such a feast to accept gifts from an unworthy person. The young Brahmin should always maintain absolute composure, be benevolent, free from arrogance, greed, and pride. It was during this period that the Brahmin would attend to his priestly duties, succeed his father as head of the family, manage the family property, and raise his own family.

The third stage of a Brahmin's life began when his sons had been raised to manhood in the same manner as he had been raised. It was now permissable, in some areas desirable, to leave his porperty to his sons while he went into the forest to live a life of meditation and asceticism. During this stage he was under very strict self-discipline. This was a period of extreme self-denial. A loin cloth of antelope hide, or even the bark of a tree, was considered sufficient protection. Although most Brahmins were careful about their health and personal appearance through the first two stages of life, it was now considered alright to neglect these because they may be a matter of vanity. He should allow his hair, nails, and beard to grow without trimming. Personal cleanliness was considered akin to holiness in the first two stages of life, but this could also be allowed to lapse. The only possession he was allowed was a begging bowl and possibly one of the sacred books. Self-torture was recommended if it would help him to better understand the absolute. It was a period when many hours would be spent in deep meditation.

The fourth and final stage was when the mature Brahmin was called a **Sanyasa**. By this time he should have achieved complete indifference to the things of the world. He should express no emotions either for favors granted or for any spiteful action against him. He was expected to eat no more than one meal a day. He should have no fixed place to live but must wander from place to place. By this time the old Brahmin was indifferent to his end. He would be looking forward to being absorbed into the Absolute and to escape from the burdens of this world.

There is no way of knowing how many of the Brahmins followed through all four stages of development. Most of them likely finished the first two stages without any great variation. Most of them did turn their affairs over to their sons in the third stage while they spent many hours in meditation. The question which no one could answer today would be how many went into the forest to meditate while neglecting their personal appearance and cleanliness. There are still large numbers of wandering mendicants and Sanyasis in India who have forsaken the pleasures of this world for the sake of identifying themselves with the Absolute. Statistics in India have never been very reliable, so it is difficult to know how many of them are Brahmins and how many are from another caste.

The Brahmins, like the other three castes, had many subdivisions. One of these which should be mentioned were the **Kulin Brahmins** of Bengal province. They claim that they are the purest of all Brahmins. Beginning with only five families who went to Bengal in the ninth century A.D., they have perpetuated their concept of ultrapurity. A Kulin woman never is allowed to marry beneath her subcaste. It is permissible for women from lower subcastes of Brahmins to marry a Kulin man, providing she presents an adequate dowry. This has led to many abuses, since some Kulin men will marry a woman, collect the dowry, then repeat the process several more times. They do not necessarily live with all of their wives, but they do continue to claim them. They usually return to see a particular wife when they are out of money. The father-in-law is expected to contribute even more money.

The abuse of women by the Kulin men has continued for centuries. It is tolerated because each father-in-law hopes that **his** daughter will become the favorite wife and that his **grandson** will become a Kulin. Some Kulin men thoroughly abused their so-called purity status to simply collect a great amount of money from the dowry of each wife. This practice is now illegal.

Another Brahmin subcaste is known as the **Nambudiris** of **Malabar**. According to legend, they were from a group of "pure" Indo-Aryans who conquered the Malabar coast. Whatever their origin, they became the wealthiest of landlords. For many years they enjoyed the privilege of instructing the Rajahs of that area. The coronation of a Rajah was not considered valid unless it was performed by a Nambudiri Brahmin.

The Nambudiris were strict vegetarians. They were very kind to animals, birds, and insects, even though they practiced many cruel measures toward the lower castes. They were polygynists who commonly had more than one wife, a practice which is forbidden today. Only the oldest son of a Nambudiri was allowed to marry and to bring his wives into the family house. His younger brothers lived with him in the same house, but they did not have the right to marry. A younger brother could make an arrangement with a woman of suitable caste, but he must visit her in **her** house only. If there were children from such an arrangement, they belonged to **her** caste. The Nambudiris considered such children to be Sudra, or servant children.

Every Nambudiri demanded exorbitant sums from his father-in-law for the trouble of marrying his Nambudiri daughter. Fathers willingly paid whatever sum was required to have their daughter married off right. The Nambudiri men were known to jealously guard their wife. She was not allowed to go out alone or to talk to any man except her husband. Once a Nambudiri girl had attained puberty, she was not allowed to speak to her own father or to her brothers.

Both Nambudiri men and women were so holy that if they happened to approach certain lower castes within sixty paces, they had to cleanse themselves. They had a servant called a Nayar to walk ahead of them to shout that a Nambudiri was approaching so that the lower castes would get out of the way. A Nambudiri woman used a lady servant to go ahead of her in the same manner. Although the Nayar servants who worked for the Nambudiri were often from the Kshatriya caste, they were treated like Sudras by their employers.

An Introduction to Hinduism

The position of Brahmins in India today is quite different from the traditional ways described above. When the Muslims invaded India they tried to alter some of the Hindu practices, but without success. When the English arrived, it became customary to look the other way. Most English professed to be most interested in the trade and not in the local religion or customs. When India began preparing for independence at the end of World War II, they decided to become a democratic republic. The undemocratic practices of caste did not fit the image of a new India as envisioned by Gandhi and other leaders. **Caste** has been **illegal** since January 26, 1950.

But Brahmin families have carried considerable power and prestige within their community for thousands of years. Many held government positions. Others were lawyers, teachers, and shop owners. Brahmins controlled the majority of the land and wealth in India. It would have been undemocratic to have taken it away from them. As a consequence, many still hold positions of leadership or authority. Since 1947 the Brahmins think of themselves more like John Calvin's concept of the spiritually "elect" within society. They hold a status which might be described as "first among equals." Progress is being made, but since caste was an accepted institution for so many years, change is coming slowly.

THE KSHATRIYAS CASTE

According to Vedic legend, the Hindus believe that a Kshatriya has sprung from Brahma's arms. It was his duty to protect the community from external aggression and internal conflict. They were destined by right of birth to be the soldiers and the kings. The law books make a point that no one but a Kshatriya had the right to rule. He was to be obeyed without question, in all things.

It was also a solemn obligation of the Kshatriya king to treat his subjects as his children. Their prosperity should be his all absorbing care. He should not levy oppressive taxes, and above all else he should see that the Brahmins were well cared for and protected. He should use Brahmins as his closest counselors and always rule wisely.

Courage and fearlessness were essential qualities for all Kshatriyas. If he should die on the battlefield it was believed that he went straight to a heaven maintained for Kshatriyas by Indra, a place filled with celestial dancing girls. For all the other privileges enjoyed by the Brahmins, they were forbidden to go hunting. The Kshatriya was encouraged to hunt because it was considered good training and preparation for war. Since they were allowed to kill for either pleasure or for food, there were many Kshatriyas who were allowed to eat meat.

According to Hindu legend the Kshatriyas became so powerful and arrogant that they began to persecute the Brahmins who they were supposed to protect. One of the legends related how one of the important warriors stole a Brahmin's cow. This led to a war which raged throughout India in twenty-one campaigns until the Brahmins had won the number one position in society. Whether the legend is based on fact seems less important than the fact that the Kshatriyas, who began as the first caste, were demoted to the number two position.

Many of the political leaders in India continue to think of themselves as blue-blooded Kshatriyas. They are able to produce an elaborate lunar and solar genealogy which proves their proper position in the caste system. The Rajputs claim that they are members of one of the present thirty-six "fire-born" clans who are descended from the four clans selected by the gods following the great battle with the Brahmins. Modern research indicates that such political leaders, particularly the Rajputs, were invaders from Central Asia who carved out an area, settled down, took Hindu wives, and built their theory of conquest into the Hindu faith. Genealogy continues to be very important to all members of the former castes in India. This is one reason why caste will not quickly disappear from everyday life.

THE VAISYA CASTE

The Hindu holy books say that the Vaisyas came from Brahma's thighs. This makes them inferior to the Brahmins and the Kshatriyas. It is the duty of the Vaisyas to increase the prosperity of the country. They are considered the lowest of the "twice-born" castes who are entitled to be known as Indo-Aryans. The term "twice-born" means they have gone through the ceremony of the sacred thread. No person in a lower caste is privileged to wear the sacred thread.

In the early years nearly all Vaisyas were agriculturalists. As the needs of society increased, many began to engage in trade and commerce. They were expected to know everything about their particular field of expertise and to be successful in it. There are many of the Vaisyas who are wealthy farmers and businessmen at the present time. Many of those who are engaged in trade and commerce favor gems, jewelry, perfumes, etc., more than other trade items. The acquisition of wealth by this caste was always considered very commendable. Sizeable numbers of the Vaisyas have migrated to other countries such as Burma, Malaysia, and other Southeast Asian countries. The local merchants in these areas are never happy to compete with the Indian merchants. The Vaisya merchants are fiercely competitive wherever they are located. As a group, they are thought of as generous contributors to Hindu temples.

THE SUDRA CASTE

It is estimated that there were more Hindu Sudras than all of the Brahmins, Kshatriyas, and Vaisyas combined. Many believe that the Sudras came from the local Dravidians who became the servants of the Indo-Aryan conquerors. Although they were granted caste status, they were the lowest of all the castes. They were usually considered the servants of the three top castes. The Sudras were the low-paid agricultural and shop workers for thousands of years. They were not only deprived of wearing the sacred thread but they were not even supposed to read the *Vedas* because they would not benefit by doing so. They were not allowed to own land or property until recently. Still, they were expected to abide by all the stringent regulations the same as members of the other castes. One example of this was the regulation concerning the length of the stick which the Indians use to brush their teeth. It was to be twelve inches long for a Brahmin, eleven inches long for a Kshatriya, ten inches for a Vaisya, and only nine inches for a Sudra. It seemed that the Sudra literally came out on the short end of the stick!

In areas where the power of the Kshatriyas and Vaisyas seemed to be in decline, a Sudra leader would sometimes try to muscle in. A few of them even gained top positions. The Maurya dynasty, founded by the great Chandragupta is a classic example. Sudras who were as ambitious as Chandragupta were willing to risk everything they had to gain control. In such cases the Brahmins simply allowed it to happen. When a Sudra official gained a high office, the Brahmins simply failed to enforce the rules which applied. When the ruler was a Sudra, the others in his caste enjoyed many of the same privileges as the upper castes. Often they were allowed to read the holy scriptures, engage in trade, serve in the military, and many of them became artisans and craftsmen. But they were always considered deficient because they did not wear the sacred thread.

THE PANCHAMAS

Technically, the Panchamas were the "outcastes" of India who were not considered good enough to even be servants. Many of the aborigines of India were relegated to this terribly low status. They were probably people who in the early years had no abilities whatsoever. More than likely they were beggars at the time the caste system began.

A Panchama was not allowed to enter a village or town except to do scavenging work. Sudras considered that it was defiling to be touched by a Panchama. But even the Panchamas had their subcastes. The lowest of the Panchamas were called the **Ulladahs**. These people were forced to live totally outside the urban areas. They grubbed their living by hunting lizards and digging edible roots. And, even the Ulladahs had sub-castes.

Another group of the people without caste were the **Chandalas**. These were the children of mixed caste marriages and the children who were born out of wedlock. Even though these children were born to a Brahmin woman from a Sudra father, they were to be considered without caste. They would be Chandalas forever. Many of them even found difficulty being accepted by the other Panchamas. A high percentage of these unfortunates were destined to be beggars for life. The western world referred to these people collectively as the "Untouchables," but the distinctions which they received by others of higher caste designated the lower ones as "Unapproachables" or "Unlookables."

Most Panchamas were considered suitable to enter a village early in the morning or late in the evening--when most people were off the street--to pick up the dead animals or to remove garbage. The Panchamas skinned the dead animals and tanned the hides for leather. It was considered a very "unclean" thing to work with leather. Some Hindus were so pious they refused to even touch leather objects.

At a later time there were some Panchamas who came into the city to dig sewers or to repair streets. Since these people would be working during the daylight hours, it was not uncommon to lay a branch across the street several feet on either side of the work crew--sixty paces was considered a safe distance. In that way the upper caste people had a signal that a Panchama was working ahead and that they should take appropriate measures. If a Brahmin could not avoid using a street where work was going on during the day, he would send a servant ahead to stop work and to move the Panchamas to a safe distance until the Brahmin passed by.

Many other precautions were taken to keep the Panchamas from defiling anyone in the upper castes. Panchamas could not use the village wells, they could not use the temples, nor could they use any of the main streets which led to the section of town where most of the Brahmins lived. Panchamas were not allowed to build houses of wood or stone--only houses of reed or straw mats, or mud bricks. They could never own land. If they became sick they could not find any doctor who would treat them. Many areas even had doctors and hospitals for sick animals but there were none for the Panchamas. They were beneath the animals!

Everyone who lived in the area knew who these people were, except in the largest cities, so it was not very difficult to avoid them. Most Panchamas were so shabbily dressed that they could be recognized from a distance. One advantage the Panchama did have was that they could eat any kind of food because they were outside the Vedic laws! Unfortunately they could not afford anything very good. They usually obtained their food by scavenging the market place after everyone had gone home at the end of the day.

An upper class Hindu who must make a journey through the city on a busy market day would hire a lower caste person to precede him on the street beating a gong and shouting "Ha!, Ha!" at the top of his voice. Those who were defiled by an "Untouchable" should immediately proceed to cleanse themselves by bathing. Both the upper and the lower caste people observed these rules for thousands of years. In actual practice they seldom came in contact with one another.

OTHER ASPECTS OF CASTE

It is obvious that caste and subcaste came to permeate every level or stratum of society on the subcontinent. It seems utterly riduculous to us today that so many of these rules were so well accepted by Hindu society for thousands of years. The principles by which each caste and subcaste lived were instilled in children from birth. Those who violated these rules, at any age, were severely criticized. One could risk losing all one's beneficial Karma by violating any of the rules. Society became very fixed, very static. There was no evident change from one generation to another. The social order **was** maintained! No one dared to even consider changing one small part of this intricate structure. Social pressures toward conformity were enormous. The Brahmins were the primary watchdogs to see that everything remained the same from generation to generation but everyone else was watching, too.

SUMMARIZING CASTE

It is interesting that such a closed system was accepted by people at all levels for thousands of years. The Dravidians apparently had no choice in the early years. Those who remained among the conquering Indo-Aryans were evidently only too pleased to have been accorded the fourth caste status, the Sudras. Those who were the "untouchables" were probably regarded as the outcastes of the Dravidian society as well. Those Dravidians who refused to become the lower rung of the conquering society apparently moved south into the Deccan area. It seems that each caste accepted its fate because that was as high a level as the Karma of a preceding soul had warranted. The greatest revolt against the caste system was led by a young Kshatriya prince named Gautama, better known as Buddha. Buddhism succeeded for a brief period in India, after which the caste system returned.

Your caste was determined by your birth. There was no amount of merit which would gain you a higher caste in one lifetime. If you behaved terribly, it was possible to become an outcaste, but even then you were still considered a part of the caste into which you had been born. Everyone must marry within one's caste and also within the subcaste. Your lifetime of work would be of a nature suitable for your caste. It was totally unacceptable to socialize or to even take food with a person of another caste. Men and women each had their own roles to play within their caste. Everyone was taught to never question the system. Children were taught that "caste was in place long before you were born and it will be in place a thousand years after your death. Just accept it as everyone else does." It maintained the social order in India for thousands of years.

You have noticed how caste became entwined within Hinduism, but caste is only one part of Hinduism, the part which guaranteed security to those within a caste, but stifled any kind of social progress. There are many other aspects of Hinduism which have endured since caste has been legally abolished. Unfortunately, caste outlived its usefulness long before it was abolished. The fact that it was legally abolished following independence does not mean that everyone forgot his or her old caste status.

There are thousands who continue to accept the station in life to which they were born. Many of them seem to have given up hope for a bright future. There are also those from the lowest levels who have gained an education and hold positions of importance today. Many people from the upper levels of society do not object to the system because the lower classes provide inexpensive laborers for them. This situation is compounded by the high birth rate and the overpopulation of the subcontinent. Urban areas are seeing a greater leveling of society than the rural areas. It will take several more generations to work it all out. At least India did set the right course in 1950.

OTHER ASPECTS OF HINDUISM

Members of other religious backgrounds often have difficulty understanding Hinduism because of the vast pantheon of gods which are involved. The three other major faiths--Judaism, Christianity, and Islam--each have only **one** god--monotheism. Hinduism has **many** gods--polytheism--and each has many associates. For the individual with a monotheistic background to try to suddenly grasp the meaning and understanding of Hinduism is probably impossible. Hinduism is a lifetime journey which even Hindus often experience difficulty in fully comprehending.

An endeavor to simplify Hinduism begins with accepting the idea that there are three major gods: **Brahma**, the creator; **Vishnu**, the preserver; and **Shiva**, the destroyer. Each of these three may very likely be represented as having more than two arms, particularly Shiva. This is done to indicate to the believers that the god is capable of much greater assistance than if they were only thought of as having two arms. Further, each arm represents a different facet of the powers of that particular god. Brahma is often represented as having four heads to portray his all-seeing presence. The four Vedas supposedly came from Brahma's four mouths.

In addition to the three gods, each with its several generally accepted images, there is the animal or vehicle on which he rides. Furthermore, each god also has one or more wives or consorts, and each of the consorts has an animal or a vehicle. All of these are thought of as facilitators for the gods in carrying out their powers and duties. It will also be noticed that each god usually holds a symbol in his or her hands. For instance, Brahma's consort is Sarasvati, the goddess of learning. She rides upon a white swan and holds a stringed musical instrument known as a veena.

An Introduction to Hinduism

Vishnu is generally portrayed sitting on a couch made in the shape of the coils of a serpent. He holds two symbols, the conch shell and the discus. His vehicle looks partly like a man and partly like an eagle. It is called the **Garuda**. The Garuda hates snakes and always does good for people. Garuda swoops down to the rescue when we need help the most. Vishnu's consort is the beautiful Lakshmi, goddess of wealth and prosperity. Up to the present time Vishnu has been incarnated here on earth nine times. A few examples are his form as a boar, a man-lion called Narsingha, and as Rama.

The **Rama** visit was intended to portray an ideal man. Rama is the hero of the story called the *Ramayana*. Even Rama needed helpers so the Hindus gave him **Hanuman**, the monkey god. One will often find stone images of Hanuman throughout India. They are frequently found guarding a palace or a fort. Many times there are real, live monkeys inhabiting the place as well. Rama's consort was Sita.

Vishnu's eighth visit was as **Krishna**, the common shepherd boy who became a warrior and a ruler. Krishna is still thought of very affectionately by the working class, especially farm workers, because he is thought of as one of them. The basic sources of Krishna's mythology have come from the epic stories of the *Mahabharata* and other ancient Hindu sources.

The stories tell how Krishna, "dark as a cloud," was born the son of Vasudeva and Devaki. Devaki was the sister of the wicked king of Mathura, in present-day Uttar Pradesh. When the rumor circulated that the wicked king, who was Krishna's uncle, planned to kill the young lad, he was smuggled out of the area and raised by a cowherd named Nanda and his wife Yasoda. Krishna's early life was spent in the simple environment of an Indian cowherd. He is remembered for his mischievous pranks when he was growing up. Krishna was also thought of as a great lover. When he played his flute, the wives and daughters of the cowherds would leave their homes to dance with him and to follow him wherever he went.

Krishna became a hero among the cowherds by killing demons and performing miracles. On one occasion, according to Hindu mythology, Krishna angered the god Indra who thought Krishna was taking attention away from him. In his rage, Indra sent torrents of rain upon the area of Uttar Pradesh as a punishment. Krishna could not bear to see his people suffer so he lifted Mt. Govardhana on his fingertip and held it over the area of Uttar Pradesh for a week. At that point Indra relented and paid homage to Krishna.

When Krishna grew up, he joined with his brother to return to Mathura to slay the wicked king, Kamsa. He then established a kingdom of his own, married the princess Rukmini, and was known as a great charioteer and warrior. Krishna is also identified with two consorts, Radha, the head of the **gopis**, or shepherds, and Satyabhama. At the end of the story, Krishna's brother and son were both killed in a brawl. He retired to the forest to lament his great loss. Shortly after, a huntsman mistakenly thought he was a deer and shot him in his one vulnerable spot, the heel, killing him. Krishna became the god of the pastoral people of India. They turned away from worshipping the severe Indra-dominated Vedic religion to follow a god who was more symbolic of their agricultural environment. Krishna is often portrayed in art with blue-black skin, wearing a yellow *dhoti* (loincloth), and wearing a crown of peacock feathers.

An Introduction to Hinduism

Many Buddhists believe that Vishnu's most recent incarnation was the Buddha. Vishnu's tenth, and final incarnation, will be as **Kalki**. He will appear riding on a horse. This will be a signal that the end of the world is at hand.

Shiva is probably the most popular of the three gods of Hinduism. His vehicle is the bull named **Nandi**, and his symbol is the trident. His consort is **Parvati**. To further complicate Hinduism, Parvati is a good example of one who has more than one facet. The evil side of Parvati is known as **Durga**, the terrible. In this role she rides a tiger and holds weapons in her ten hands. Or, she can become **Kali**, the fiercest of gods or goddesses. In the Kali role she is most often depicted with a string of skulls around her neck. Everyone must sacrifice to Kali to appease her anger. Of course, she is really carrying out the destructive aspect of the god Shiva.

Lest we dismiss Shiva as totally destructive we should remember that he has a creative role as well. Many worship his phallic symbol normally called the **lingam** (lingum). At least one of these lingams will be in every temple dedicated to Shiva. Both men and women leave offerings or flowers to bring them better luck in reproduction.

Like Greek gods and goddesses, the Hindu gods also have children. Of the two children of Shiva and Parvati, the most interesting is **Ganesh**, the one who appears as a human with an elephant's head. Ganesh represents prosperity and wisdom. The legend about how he received the head of an elephant is very interesting. His father, the god Shiva, had just returned from a long journey to find his wife Parvati enjoying a nice conversation with a young man in her room. Without asking questions, Shiva sliced off his head. Then he discovered that he had mistakenly beheaded his own son who had grown up in the god's absence. Parvati was desperate! In order to please his wife, Shiva cut off the head of the first living thing he saw. Since that was an elephant, Ganesh has ever since had the head of an elephant. Then too, Ganesh is often portrayed as having more than two arms to cover his many duties. His vehicle is the rat.

An almost equal number of stories can be told about every god, his consort, the children, and the vehicle. Most Hindu temples are dedicated to either Vishnu or Shiva. There are only two or three temples dedicated to Brahma in all of India. With so many gods, goddesses, and vehicles it is a lifetime of learning experiences to comprehend the faith.

Many Hindus who have been busily occupied in their earning years decide to set out in their later years to learn the mysteries of their faith. These people, who may be from any one of the castes, are called *sadhus*. Some carry a symbol of their search. For instance, if they are searching for Shiva they will carry a trident. Sometimes these *sadhus* gather together, at a place of Hindu pilgrimage. Since many of them are unkempt, they appear to be "Hippies" in the western sense. Every one of these men is in dead earnest. They are often in the last half of their life. The family has been raised and the business or farm has been turned over to a son. Some of them are simply looking for liberation from this world. Some serve as spiritual guides to others. These men are called **Gurus**. Many of them will continue their search until the day of their death. Others pursue the search for a short time after which they return to their family.

The ultimate goal of an individual Hindu is to bring together a complete intertwining and understanding of the three gods until they are able to mentally transport themselves from this world in a religious experience called **moksha** (mukti), achieving "oneness" with the eternal. Moksha, along with the unchangeable laws of *Varnasrama Dharma* all make up the highest achievement of Hinduism. It is like discovering the fundamental law governing the universe. It is a release from all the cares and concerns of this present world. The individual is even released from one's own Karma, one's own individuality, to find peace and oneness with the eternal. It is thought of as a reunion with Brahma. When Buddhists have a similar experience it is called Nirvana.

THE CHAKRAVARTINS

Another aspect of traditional India concerns the rulers-kings-emperors who were called **Chakravartins**. A Chakravartin might be defined as the ideal sovereign or ruler who had passed through all the sacred rites of Hinduism. It was his duty to maintain **varna** (caste), to intercede with the gods, to see that the temples were maintained, to provide rest homes for the holy men, to pray for the prosperity of his people, to protect and defend his people, and to supervise the country's irrigation system.

It should be noted that most of the Chakravartin's duties were religious. At this point, the religion and the state actually became one. Just as the Brahmin priests were "god compellors," so the Chakravartin had the assigned duty to compel his subjects to follow the rules of Hinduism. Each Chakravartin had a vast bureaucracy to fulfill these several obligations. As a reward, the Chakravartin was allowed to live in a luxurious palace and to be surrounded by many beautiful people. The cost for such a system was borne by the agriculturalists and other laborers who lived in the villages. There is no evidence that there were any major complaints. All children were taught that this was the system and they were not to challenge it.

THE RELATIONSHIP OF MEN AND WOMEN

Likewise, the women all held an inferior place in Hindu society, regardless of caste. It has probably been noted that it is a male-oriented faith. Every woman had her duties the same as every man. The men were expected to do the field work and tend to the religious duties. The men would work to build a new home or to repair the old one if necessary. Most men washed their own clothes. They were the head of the household and the chief disciplinarian, sometimes bossing their wife. The men carried the chief responsibility for the religious life of the family. Many of them went to prayers every morning. That was also a good opportunity to participate in politics if they enjoyed doing so.

Women were expected to keep the house, bear the children, prepare and cook the meals, make the clothes and mend them, wash their own clothes and those of the children, and help their husbands in the field whenever possible. Keeping a good house meant, among other things, rationing the grain so there would be enough until the next harvest. They were also expected to make a slip of part clay and part cow dung and coat the floors. This would serve to keep the dust down, since nearly all homes had dirt floors. Women were given the primary responsibility for raising the children and teaching them in the basics of the faith, including proper behavior. The women fed the men first. If there were any food left, the women and girls would eat separately and later. When a man and a woman went to town together, the wife was expected to walk a few paces behind the man--never side by side. They never embraced, kissed, or even held hands in public.

An Introduction to Hinduism

The farm girls went out each morning with a large basket, often twenty inches in diameter or larger, with sides about four inches tall. This was used to gather the dung from the night before. The animal dung was brought home by nine or ten in the morning at which time the mothers and daughters worked together to mix the dung and straw together. The "dung cakes" were usually made from six to nine inches in diameter and from three-quarters to an inch thick. They would be laid up in layers with air spaces between them like a pyramidal stack of dominoes. The cakes were allowed to dry after which they would be used for fuel because even twigs of wood were very scarce in many areas. An alternate method was to stick the dung cake to a south-facing mud brick wall. When the cake fell off it was considered dry enough to burn.

There were a few of the upper class women who learned to read, but literacy for women and girls was considered totally unnecessary. Most wives joined with their husbands in selecting their son's future bride. There is no record of a major women's movement. Like everyone else, the maintenance of the social order was the all important thing. It would be interesting to visit an Indian village to see how this social system functioned.

SUMMARIZING HINDUISM

Hinduism is a very old and a very complex religious faith with thousands of devout adherents today. It is a very polytheistic faith compared to the majority of the faiths in the western world. Caste (*varna*) and religion are intricately intertwined. Village life in early times was based totally upon caste. Caste is a set principle according to the family into which you were born. For millions of people there was no way to escape their caste nor to alter it in any way. The Hindu faith is based upon ancient Sanskrit writings which are among the oldest written material in the world, and those writings are based upon oral traditions which are even older.

The basics of Hinduism were imported into India by the Indo-Aryan invaders nearly 2,000 years before Christ. Although it was almost surely modified to meet the situations which they faced in the early years, once the system was established it became a fixed faith combined with a fixed social system which continued for hundreds of years afterward. Neither the Muslims nor the Europeans were able to alter Hinduism in any major proportions. It was not until the Indians decided to change the caste system themselves following independence in 1947 that it was basically altered. The basic Hindu faith survives today without caste. Except for a few modern mechanical innovations, the village life in most parts of rural India has also changed very little from their early history. Most of the people of India throughout their history have lived either in the village, or closely tied to life in the village. Even the cities are really clusters of villages.

Figure 12

Chapter 10
VILLAGE LIFE IN INDIA

THE STURCTURE OF SOCIETY IN AN INDIAN VILLAGE

A great amount of research has been done in recent years regarding village life in Asia before the arrival of the Europeans. It has been found that only a few things actually changed **after** the Europeans arrived. Even today the fields are still most likely plowed by oxen, seeds scattered by hand, the crop is cultivated by hand, harvested by hand, threshed on a pavement, and dried along the edges of the highways. Perhaps the pavement is concrete and the highway is asphalt instead of a brick pavement, otherwise the process remains the same. Modern trucks pass through from one major city to the next, but in other ways life has changed little for thousands of years. Many rural roads are still dirt, some little more than paths. The single exception to this kind of agriculture and way of life would be found today in the states of Punjab and Haryana.

It has already been noticed that areas such as government, social life, and religion cannot be completely separated in India. One way of looking at Indian society would be to view it as a giant pyramid. The Brahmins and the bureaucrats formed the upper class, while the producers-- mostly farmers, small shopkeepers, and artisans--formed the base of the pyramid. There was **no solid middle class**! This system may seem unfair but that was life--everyone accepted it. Conditions in western Europe were little different until the age of industrialization around 1740.

THE VILLAGE TAXING SYSTEM

In order to support such a hierarchial society, it was necessary to have some system of taxation at the producing level which would support those who were at the top of the pyramid. Since the subcontinent was under so many administrative areas and districts, it is impossible to give one answer which would cover the entire land. It can be said that there was a general understanding that the ruler should not extract exorbitant taxes.

A ruler who demanded too much could bring about a serious revolt throughout his kingdom. It was generally accepted that the taxes should not leave the subjects in poverty nor should the tax policy seriously obstruct trade. The various items of trade which were made by craftsmen and artisans did carry a tax on their value, but the rule was that they should only be taxed once. These taxes were sometimes as low as one-twentieth of their value, while other items may carry a tax of as much as twenty percent. The craftsmen in some cities were also required to contribute one or two days of their production per month to the ruler. Since he could not use such a huge quanatity of items in his household, they were exported to other areas of India or to other countries.

Some of the major roads required that travelers pay a toll to cover the cost of maintenance. The small country roads were maintained by requiring a certain number of days of road work for the monarch each year. The small country roads were maintained by required work days which were levied upon the men who lived in the immediate vicinity and were the most likely to use the road. Some of the larger cities which had heavy walls around them charged a toll to enter the city. Like the roads, this money was used to maintain the city walls, the city streets, and to pay the city administrators.

Village India

The majority of the income for all rulers came from the land tax which was levied on the produce of the farmers. Again, this varied considerably from one part of the subcontinent to another. The most common fraction was one-fourth of the yield from the land--some rulers demanded more and some required less. It also depended upon the needs and the desires of the ruler. A new palace or a new fortress always brought additional taxes, as did a ruler who always had a military campaign underway. Some taxing districts based their taxes upon the estimated yield of the land, then they asked for a fraction of the anticipated yield every year. This was often as low as one-sixteenth of the yield, but that would still be too much in case of severely abnormal weather.

Gold and silver were not unknown in the villages but nearly all the farmers paid their taxes "in kind," that is, they paid their fraction of the tax in the produce from their land. The tax collector came around the very day the farmer began harvesting a field in order to be sure he was receiving his share of the taxes. There were some occasions when farmers were exempted from paying a full share when the harvest was poor. The tax collector wanted to be sure the farmer had sufficient seed to put in the next crop. Another exemption was based upon new land which had never before been under cultivation. That land was exempt from taxes for five years. Any land or produce which was given to a temple was exempt in most cases.

Everyone complained that the taxes were too high, but the rulers justified the taxes on the basis that they granted the people protection. Many taxpayers interpreted this to mean that in times of peace they should not pay any taxes at all. For those who refused to pay their taxes the penalty was the loss of their land. The government had little sympathy with them. On the other hand, if a farmer could show good reason why he happened to be in arrears on his taxes, they were usually granted a year or two to make up the deficit. The tax law also provided that those who did not make good use of their land could be evicted without further cause. All the rulers needed income from some source just to survive. Although the land was owned in small parcels by individuals, the ruler claimed overall ownership of all the land and water resources within his realm of administration. There were those from the lower castes who owned no land at all. They usually worked on the farms of others for a very low wage, or they were peasant farmers who worked on the ruler's private estates.

Most rulers did very well for themselves and many began planning their next palace or fortress well before the one under current construction was completed. It was also considered a very holy thing for a ruler to either build a temple or to maintain one. Sometimes he contributed his entire income from one village within his realm to a temple. This was called a "temple grant" and was considered a very holy thing to do. There were always other rulers who lived at a lower level and maintained lower taxes. In times of famine the rulers often opened their granary storehouse and shared the available grain with their subjects. There are no statistics on the number of people who died of starvation in the period preceding the 17th century. On the basis of the figures from the 19th and early 20th century, the figure was undoubtedly high. A lack of good communication and transportation facilities contributed to this problem. In both good times and bad, the Sudras and the Vaiysas carried the majority of the tax burden.

The taxing system in common usage in the subcontinent was very similar to the manner of raising money in Europe during the Middle Ages. As in Europe, there were many of the tax collectors who cheated the peasants on collection day. One of the favorite tricks was to bring a slightly oversized measure for levying the tax collector's share. It added up over an entire year.

Bribery and corruption of all kinds were common even though it would build up an individual's bad Karma. The money which the monarch received did flow back down through the pyramid as he purchased goods, supplies, and services. Most of the income had originated from the bottom of the pyramid and flowed to the top of the pyramid. When the people at the top spent their wealth, it flowed back down, but it never seemed to reach the lower levels again. Most of the agricultural workers never received anything.

If the tax burden seemed to be excessive in order for the monarch to maintain his court at the level which he desired, he would then try to conquer some neighboring province. In this way there would be more people to support the burden of taxation which he desired. This resulted in much fighting and bickering as every prince saw himself as a rising star on the horizon. It would seem that the lower classes would welcome conquest in order to share the burden, but in actual practice they lost more than they gained. Too often their fields became battlegrounds and their crops were destroyed. Again, this system reminds one of Medieval Europe.

THE VILLAGE LEGAL SYSTEM

The legal system was based upon a multitude of varying levels in each administrative district. There was no common agreement throughout the subcontinent. Most village disputes were settled within the village and within each caste. Various craftsmen in the larger villages and in the cities worked together within their craft area something like the medieval guild system in Europe. They settled most affairs among themselves. The closest evidence available which would correspond to a legal code for everyone came from their religious beliefs in what was proper treatment towards their fellow men. It was somewhat like the English system of common law, but much less formal.

The earliest *dharma*, meaning law or teaching, which was written down seems to have been no earlier than 500 to 400 B.C. Legal codes similar to the western world did not become common until the first and second centuries of the Christian era. Before that time if the parties to the dispute could not resolve it among themselves, the Brahmins stepped in to interpret the law as they understood right and wrong according to Hindu theology. In any event, law was very loosely interpreted and based primarily upon local custom.

Theoretically all the local decisions could be appealed to the ruler, but that depended upon the ruler. Many rulers were not interested in hearing legal cases. Some were constantly off on a military campaign to some far frontier of their realm, since many of the younger rulers saw themselves controlling some vast domain. If the ruler refused to hear a plaintiff's appeal, there was no other legal system of appeal.

Rulers did not normally issue edicts of law on a unilateral basis until after the reign of Ashoka. Even as late as the British period, village law was left almost entirely to the village. This resulted in a reasonably democratic system but it could also prove to be terribly disorganized and uncoordinated. A system of written laws, as that concept is currently understood, depends upon a high percentage of the people being literate. That was not the case in India prior to the 20th century. Many people in the villages today are either illiterate or barely literate.

Each village was governed by a **Council** of about five members. Each council had a **Head Man** who had almost universally received his position by virtue of his caste and by his seniority within his own caste. Beyond this, all the **Elder** men of the village from the higher castes were consulted if important decisions were to be made. These men were naturally conservative and were often reluctant to make any radical changes. Indeed, they considered it their duty to maintain the traditions of the past as nearly as possible from generation to generation. Although the rural villages of India have changed very little from thousands of years ago, the average Indian today believes his country has made great progress in the field of law and taxes. Neither the Muslim invaders nor the British were able to erase much of India's rural conservatism.

EVERYDAY VILLAGE LIFE

Life in the entire subcontinent was based upon the village. Everyone lived in the village and went out each day to work the surrounding fields. The entire social and economic pyramid resided in the village. There probably were no truly typical villages, but each one would have at least one Brahmin family who would be charged with the temple duties. There was usually one Kshatriya family who was the village supervisor, often also the Head Man of the village. He would be assisted by one Kayasth family. These were the clerks, writers, and recorders. Almost every village had one family which took care of the carpentry work. If they did not build a house personally, they would at least supervise the construction. The carpenter family also built the furniture and most of the agricultural tools.

Even though some housewives did their own spinning and weaving, most villages had one clothmaking family which provided sufficient cloth for an entire village. It was also important that each village have one astrologer family. They kept the village birth records which were always necessary to consult before two people could be married.

Beyond these more specialized families, each village would have about fifteen cultivating families--the farmers--who produced ninety percent of the food which the village consumed. The remaining percentage came from the gardens which nearly all villagers maintained, often within or at the edge of the village. Each village also normally had fifteen Sudras families who were the equivalent of the hired hands and day laborers. The village number was completed by three unclean families who served as village scavangers. They disposed of the dead livestock, tanned the leather, made sandals, etc. They were often required to live at the edge of the village and to be careful not to contaminate those within the village who had caste status.

There were always villages which had some special characteristics. For instance, in an area where there were precious stones, there would be more than one jeweler family. Those villages situated along a river, lake, or the ocean had their fisher families. In an area where cotton was the predominant crop, there would be several clothmaking families. Some of them would be involved in spinning, some in dyeing, others in weaving. The surplus jewelry and cloth was marketed in the city in exchange for goods unavailable in the village or for gold or silver. It was this kind of surplus which the European traders wanted to purchase at the beginning of the 16th century.

The villages were almost totally self-sufficient. The items which they did not raise or make were obtained from the closest town or city. The towns and cities were structured on a very similar arrangement to the villages except they were larger and they usually had more crafts people. Most cities were actually clusters of villages or simply overgrown villages which had become larger because they were strategically located at important crossroads, a good harbor, or they were the center of a large administrative district. Many villagers only traveled to the city a few times a year. It was usually the man who made the trip unless his wife also wanted some item which could not be made in the village.

Most village inhabitants were not very well traveled. The country people usually did not feel comfortable in the city. Many people never went more than ten or fifteen miles away from their home in an entire lifetime. There were always a few who traveled for business, for the government, or to peddle goods. The same was true in Europe during the same period. Once or twice a year the tax collector came around. He was most villagers' idea of a real outsider. If a village were located near a large town, then more people went to the once-a-week market, often taking produce or goods to sell.

The towns not only served a market function, but they also provided the administrative organization for the surrounding villages, something like county seat towns in rural America. Towns which were on a major trade route prospered and grew more than those which served only as a marketing and administrative center. Some of the towns became quite large. At the time of the battle of Plassey in 1757, English observers described Murshidabad as being a larger and wealthier city than London. Cities such as that depended for their food and fiber upon the village surplus from the surrounding area. No one ever delineated how large a village needed to be to be declared a town, or how large a town should be to be classified as a city.

THE AGRICULTURAL SIDE OF THE VILLAGE

The largest single number of village residents were tied either directly or indirectly to the land. Although some farmers worked individually in their fields, the most common practice was to work together. Each farmer either owned his own land or paid a rent to work the land of another. Those who were the common day laborers were very poorly paid. Most of the land in the subcontinent would produce two crops per year--one following the monsoon and another as soon as the first crop was harvested. The entire subcontinent was affected by the monsoon. If the monsoon failed, everyone from the individual farmer to the people in the large cities, suffered. Insects and storms could also be devastating. Some farmers over-cropped their land and simply wore it out. However, the Indian farmers discovered the value of barnyard manure centuries before western Europe. It was the productivity of the land which made the subcontinent's huge population possible.

Wheat, barley, and millet were grown throughout most of the subcontinent. Rice was grown where sufficient water was available. Many areas found cotton growing profitable. Sugar cane was a good cash crop. Most of the plowing for each of the crops was done with a simple wooden point which broke up the soil into large clods rather than turning it over as is done with a moldboard plow. The plows did not commonly have iron points until about 600 B.C. The other tillage tools were usually made totally from wood, some of them were very simple. Once a field was plowed it would be largely clods from four to twelve inches in dimension. Many farmers simply dragged a log across the plowed field until the clods were broken up and the field was level. Most seed was sown broadcast, then a log or a clump of brush was dragged across it to mix the seed into the soil. Harvesting took place with a simple sickle with a blade about eight inches long. The grain was threshed by beating it with a flail on a threshing floor, or having muzzled oxen walk over it until the grain shattered from the stalks.

Village India

THE IMPORTANCE OF THE COW IN INDIA

One of the interesting aspects of farm life was the livestock. The most important animal of all was the cow. Cows pulled the plow, they lifted the irrigation water, often they were used to thresh the grain, and they pulled the carts. When a farmer wanted to go to town he took the ox and a cart. Cows provided a considerable amount of milk, the basis for cheese and butter. Butter would soon have become rancid in the intense heat of the subcontinent but they discovered that if it were boiled and the impurities skimmed off it became *ghi* (ghee). In this form it became liquid and it was possible to keep it for a long time. About 25 percent of all the energy consumed in India today comes from burning the cow dung cakes. When the cow died, the hide was tanned and used for leather. Several of the pieces of bone were used for making tools.

On some farms the water buffalo served the same purposes as the cow. The buffalo was more expensive, it required more pampering since it must soak in water for awhile every day, and it did not have the same "holy" aspect among the people as the cow. It is interesting that the buffalo is considered an unclean animal. It is primarily utilized for pulling farm tools, especially for plowing the rice paddies. About sixty percent of all of India's milk comes from the water buffalo.

It is little wonder that the cow became the most respected of all the farm animals, a respect and reverence normally reserved for the senior members of the family. A likeness of the humpbacked cow was found on many of the seals unearthed at the Indus River sites. There were also many bull figurines found, too many to dismiss them as simply children's toys. **Nandi**, the bull, is the sacred vehicle of the god Shiva. A Nandi statue is placed at the entrance of Shiva temples. Krishna is thought of as the "cowherd" god. The cow is the symbol of fertility here on earth. Hindus believe there is a place called *go-loka*, a kind of cow heaven, which is above the heavens of the gods and of mortal men.

Hindu tradition has a story about a primeval ocean of milk which is stirred by the gods. The cow is worshipped at many of India's festivals. Shiva's bulls are allowed to roam the streets unmolested. Both Hinduism and Buddhism use cow's milk in some temple rituals. Many attributed magical and medicinal properties to the "five products of the cow." These are: milk, curds, ghee, urine, and dung. Cow dung is used in the ritual purification of the hearth. Very few people in India will either eat meat or consume any product made from the cow. There are cooks who refuse to even prepare a dish made from the flesh of the cow. Millions in India follow the principle of *ahimsa*--the non-injury of any living creature. This is especially significant because of the Hindu belief in reincarnation.

It is a well-known fact that cows today are allowed to roam freely throughout the countryside and on the busiest city streets. Nearly every community in India today has made some provision for the cows which grow old and are sick. The animal hospitals, which are called *pinjrapoles*, usually have more cows than all the other animals in their shelters combined. The homes for unclaimed cows are called *goshalas*, although they may sometimes be caring for sick and dying animals as well. The *goshalas* accept only cows and are often maintained in connection with a temple. There are *goshalas* with as many as one thousand cows, most of them no longer of any economic utility. The *pinjrapoles* and the *goshalas* are all funded by temples, by contributions, or by private individuals. Since independence, the Indian government has felt obligated by a provision in its constitution, to establish state run shelters called *gosadans*. The cows which arrive at these are kept within an enclosure, sterilized, and generally made comfortable until they die. If they are sick, they are treated for their diseases. The general treatment for cows exceeds that for economically distressed people.

Even though the cattle seem to wander around unclaimed, the majority of the cows are claimed by someone. Often they are simply fed and milked on the street, then they continue to wander the streets until the next milking time. Some Hindus are so dedicated to the holy aspects of the cow that they will not even consume its milk. This is not true of the water buffalo. Nearly everyone consumes the milk from the buffalo. Altogether, India, with three percent of the world's land area, is the second largest dairy producer in the world. Only the United States has a greater capacity.

OTHER FARM ANIMALS

Horses have always been much less common in India than cows and water buffalo. Most of the horses in India are much smaller in size than those in the western world. They are suitable for pulling carts and light wagons, but not for heavy agricultural work. The area of the Sind raises more horses than most of the other areas. Some horses are imported from Persia. The elephant had become a popular animal for heavy work by around 500 B.C. Many of them were captured in the wild and trained by special trainers. They were too expensive for the average villager. The royalty of India thought of elephants as a status symbol. Camels have been used for field work in the drier areas of the subcontinent for many years.

Goats have been raised throughout the subcontinent since the first animals were domesticated. They are useful for both milk and wool, especially in Kashmir. Sheep are also raised for their wool, again in the northern areas of the subcontinent. The yak is useful for both milk and wool in the Himalayan areas of the far north.

Chickens and ducks seem like natural animals for producing eggs. But eggs are not as popular in India as might be supposed. This is probably because the Hindus would not want to knowingly eat a fertile egg. Raising pigs was not unknown in India, but they were never a popular animal because most Hindus considered them unclean. Furthermore, most Indians would not eat meat. Pigs are raised in a few areas today where the inhabitants are Christians. Interestingly, some also believe that fish are unclean. The majority of the Hindus have been vegetarians for centuries. It should be noted that most of the livestock have been kept for milk, wool, or for farm work.

Sericulture, the growing of silk worms, began in India sometime around 400 to 600 B.C. Most authorities believe that the secret of silk came to India from China. Thousands of people are involved in this aspect of agriculture, tending the worms, picking the leaves, cultivating the mulberry trees, and weaving the high-quality silk.

Village India

A VILLAGE SUMMARY

Nearly everyone lived in a village similar to the one which has been described. This was partially for protection from the armies of raiding princes, partly for the sociability which the village afforded, and partly because the people in these early times supported one another much more than in America where each farmer prefers to be independent.

Most of the everyday life in the village revolved around the seasons of the year--the wet season and the dry season. Raising crops was the most important single industry. Everyone lived close to the land. The caste system was carried out even in the smallest villages. The Hindu temple, however small, was an important place for every inhabitant of the village. Each village was almost totally self-sufficient. For most Indians, the village was their life. They often knew very little beyond their own immediate environment.

It was not necessary to journey to the city for medical assistance or to purchase parts for worn or broken machinery as people do today. There were no doctors and there was no machinery. It was basically a very simple life. Since life was a period of hard work for everyone, it was accepted as the norm. People did not complain because hard work was expected of everyone for survival.

Much more could be written about everyday life in traditional India. Although each village had some admittedly unique eastern-style features of its own, it is possible to see an amazing parallel to life in Medieval Europe. Perhaps the major differences center around the caste system, which was so closely related to Hinduism and village life that it is impossible to separate them. There was nothing quite as structured as the caste system in western Europe, even though they too had different social strata with the kings and nobility on the top of the pyramid and the common peasants at the bottom. Another great difference by 1500 was that Europeans were often looking for better ways to grind grain, better recipes to vary the diet, better vehicles for transport, etc. In rural India today, they still use the same style of ox cart which was in use over 2,000 years ago. There are signs of change such as the automobile and the airplane, but for the average rural family, the changes have come very slowly.

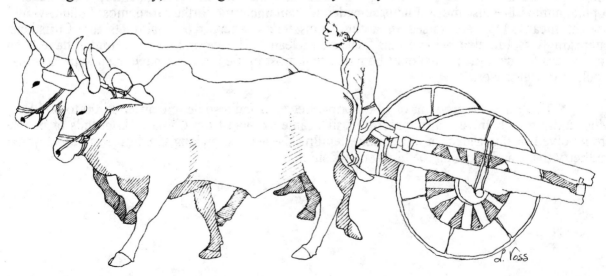

Figure 13

Village India

BOOKS FOR FURTHER READING

Basham, A. L., *The Wonder That Was India* (1984).

Bhardwaj, Surinder Mohan, *Hindu Places of Pilgrimage in India: A Study in Cultural Geography* (1973).

Buck, William, translator, *Mahabharata* (1973).

Campbell, Joseph, *The Masks of God: Oriental Mythology* (1962).

Carmody, Denise L., & Carmody, John T., *Ways to the Center* (1993).

Fenton, Hein, Reynolds, Miller, and Nielsen, *Religions of Asia* (1988).

Hopkins, Thomas J., *The Hindu Religious Tradition* (1971).

Koller, John M., *Oriental Philosophies* (1985).

Kitagawa, Joseph M., editor, *The Religious Traditions of Asia* (1989).

Nikhilanada, S., editor & translator, *The Upanishads*.

O'Flaherty, Wendy D., translator, *The Rig Veda: An Anthology* (1981).

Radhakrishnan, *Indian Philosophy* (1966).

Radhakrishnan S., and Moore, C. A., editors, *A Source Book in Indian Philosophy* (1957).

Smith, Huston, *The Religions of Man* (1986).

Thomas, P., *Hindu Religion, Customs and Manners* (1975).

Welty, T., *The Asians, Their Heritage and Their Destiny* (1963).

Figure 14

98

Chapter 11
IMPORTANT CHALLENGES TO HINDUISM

The Vedic Period from c.1500 B.C. to c.500 B.C. was one in which Hindu culture became fully established in the subcontinent. During this period the Indo-Aryans were migrating into the area and completely overwhelming the local Dravidians. The Vedas were being composed in the Sanskrit. The Kshatriya warrior caste seems to have been thoroughly in control of government, and the Brahmin caste was in control of religion. The Indian subcontinent was divided into several small kingdoms during this approximately 1,000-year period. Although there are only little fragments of information available about this period from a political or historical basis, it seems to have been an era of conquest followed by stability. Even though the subcontinent has had a history of continuous civilization for over 5,000 years, they were not interested enough to make a conscious historical record of it until the time of the Muslim invasions in the 11th and 12th centuries A.D. Most people lived in the villages and concentrated on survival from year to year. It was such a tight system that it was inevitable that someone would challenge it.

MAHAVIRA AND BUDDHA COMPARED

There were two men who challenged the commonly accepted religious solution which was known as Hinduism. These men were **Vardhamana Mahavira**, the founder of the Jain faith, and **Siddhartha Gautama**, the founder of the Buddhist faith. Both of these religious movements are interesting because they both broke away from Hinduism at about the same time, and each one retained several aspects of Hinduism within its beliefs. According to most sources, Vardhamana Mahavira was born in 599 B.C., while Buddha's birth is estimated at about 563 B.C. If these dates are valid it means that Mahavira is about 36 years older than Buddha, a very short time in the total history of India.

Not only did the two men begin their religions at about the same time but there are several other similarities. In both cases they were the sons of wealthy men. Vardhamana's father was a rajah who was wealthy enough that his son neither had to work nor go hungry. His parents were members of a small religious sect which followed Parshava, the twenty-third Jina. Buddha's father was a prince so wealthy that he could afford to shelter his son from the outside world for many years. Vardhamana was born near Vaishali in the present-day state of Bihar in northeast India. Buddha was also born in northeastern India, and both men began their preaching in northern India. Both men were raised in the Kshatriya caste. Both men married and began a regular family life in an aristocratic environment. The records say that Vardhamana abandoned his aristocratic surroundings for an ascetic life when he was thirty. Buddha was almost exactly the same age when he preached his first sermon. Beyond these parallels there are many differences in the mission of each man, even though both men have the same general outlook and approach to life.

THE ORIGIN OF JAINISM

The followers of Jainism believe that the original founder of their faith was a holy man named **Rishabha** who lived millions of years ago. He was the first king on the entire earth and it was Rishabha who created the order of human society. They believe that there was a succession

Challenges to Hinduism--Jainism

of twenty-four **Jinas**, which means a "Conqueror," a "Victor," or an "Enlightened One," who lived down through the ages. A Jina may be thought of as one who has conquered. The very name of their faith, a **Jain**, means one who has conquered the worldliness which is all about us. A devout Jain is the victor over desire and temptation. He is enlightened enough to achieve moksha.

One of these, number twenty-one, was a man named Neminatha, a cousin of Krishna, a very important figure in the Hindu faith who is accepted by Hindus as the eighth incarnation of of the god Vishnu. Therefore, Jainism, through Neminatha, is very closely linked to Hinduism. Vardhamana is the twenty-fourth, and therefore the last, of the Jinas. These Jinas are commonly referred to as **Tirthankaras**, a term which means "ford-markers." They are the ones who mark the safe places to cross to another way of life. Jain temples have statues of the twenty-four Tirthankaras to remind members of the faith that these twenty-four leaders underwent considerable self-denial and sacrifice on the road to Moksha and spiritual enlightnment. Prayers and offerings are made by Jain followers at the twenty-four statues.

During the first twelve years on his search for truth, Vardhamana underwent all kinds of personal self-denial, enduring both bodily and spiritual injury in his search for ultimate answers. In the end he emerged as a renowned preacher and a teacher of many monks. Just as Siddhartha Gautama is commonly called the Buddha, the "Enlightened One," so also Vardhamana is best remembered as **Mahavira**, "the great hero." Mahavira then began a ministry which lasted for another 30 years before his death and final liberation, or moksha. The date most often given for Mahavira's death is 527 B.C. His self-denial was so great that when he died at the age of 72 it is said that it was because of starvation following two days of constant meditation!

Following the death of Mahavira, his followers, who were estimated at more than half a million in 527 B.C., seem to have received some official support from the Maurya emperors of the 4th and the 3rd century B.C. Chandragupta Maurya, c.321-c.297 B.C., the creator of India's first great empire, was believed to be a Jain follower. King Kharavela of Kalinga also gave his endorsement during the 2nd century B.C. From the death of Mahavira to the beginning of the Christian era, the faith spread down the east coast of India as far as Tamil Nadu, possibly as far as Sri Lanka. There are Jains today in every province of India. They are quite strong in the Calcutta and Bombay areas.

The Jains have played an important role in the development of the Tamil culture in the south. One story tells of a Jain leader named Bhadrabahu who led a large group, including Chandragupta Maurya, to Sravana Belgola near Mysore to escape a famine in the North. It is also said that Jain monks preceded Brahmins as bearers of the Indo-Aryan culture in the far south of India.

Another strengthening factor of the Jains in the southern subcontinent occurred about A.D. 79. A major split occurred in Jainism following another great famine in northern India. Food was extremely scarce and several Jains moved from the plain of the Ganges River to southern India. One of these groups, known as the **Digambara,** which means "sky-clad," stayed in the north. They claim to be the true followers of Mahavira and that he wore no clothes at all. The Digambara monks only wear a loincloth when in public--it's the law. They deny the possiblity of women ever attaining moksha, they insist that a truly enlightened Jina requires no bodily sustenance, and they dispute some of the biograpies of the Jinas. They pass their tradition down orally from one member to another.

Challenges to Hinduism--Jainism

The term **Shvetambara** means the "white-clad." These are the Jains who moved to southern India. They wear clothes and are a part of the mainstream of Indian society. The Shvetambaras believe that women can achieve moksha, and women play an important role in this branch of the faith. The Shvetambaras have written their faith down in eleven texts called **Angams**, which means "Limbs." The Shvetambaras have also split into two groups since the 15th century. One of them continues to have images--many of which include Hindu likenesses-- while the other group does **not** believe in images.

Both the Shvetambaras and the Digambaras claim they are the true followers of Mahavira. Although they are only a small fraction of the population, they are represented in every major urban area of India. Jain merchants, professionals, and civil servants hold many very important positions in India.

WHAT THE JAINS BELIEVE

Like Buddha, Mahavira thought of himself as a teacher, a leader, and a guide. He did not ask for deification, although this was established soon after his death. All Jains revere Mahavira. All Jains believe that we **can** know our **Karma**, or destiny through a combination of introspection and behavior. In Hinduism our karma tends to accumulate in other lives as well, but the Jains stress our own karma in our own lifetime. If we live a totally pure life, our karma will also become pure and this will remove any past demerits with which it might be burdened. The Jains believe we can direct this by pure and impure actions. Hindus believe that our karma can be burdened with past experiences in another life. In Hinduism, only the purest Brahmins can hope to achieve moksha. The Jains believe that people from any caste can achieve moksha if they follow the rules of the faith. It should be pointed out that Jains **do** believe in reincarnation.

The Jains say that time endlessly repeats itself like some cosmic wheel. In this wheel there are six ascending spokes followed by six descending spokes. There are regular places on this cosmic wheel for the birth of a **Tirthankara** to occur. A Tirthankara is also referred to as a Jina, "a crosser of the stream of sorry life," or a "conqueror." These Tirthankaras have come to preach the Jain teachings. It is this symbol of a spoked wheel, representing the cycle of life, which has become the national symbol of the modern state of India, even though the majority of the people of India are Hindus. Hindus and Buddhists also have believe in the cycle of lives, although each of the three religions interpret the cycle differently.

Jains believe that there are six **universals**. These are Life, Physical Matter, Space, Time, Motion, and Rest (or non-motion). The first one, Life or **Jiva**, is defined as consciousness. In its unbound state Jiva has four **infinitudes**, which are Perception, Knowledge, Bliss, and Ability. The individual Jiva is bound by **karma**, which for the Jains is an invisible material substance rather than a process of good or evil as it is for Hindus and Buddhists. The intangible force-- **karma**--must always be correct. Any wrong **karma** might multiply and make it more difficult to cause a soul's release. Karma adheres to the **jiva** and prevents the exercise of the four infinitudes.

A very important religious practice of the Jain renunciant consists of stopping the influx of new karma, which they consider basically an evil, or at best a weakness. The greatest challenge is eliminating previously acquired karma from a preceding life. At the very core of Jain renunciant practice are the "three jewels": (1) Right faith, (2) Right knowledge, and (3) Right conduct. Right conduct is then encapsulated in the "**five great vows**" that the renunciant takes upon initiation. **Ahimsa** means the non-injury of all living things. **Satya** means to always tell the truth. **Asteya** is a vow to never steal. **Brahmacarya** refers to complete celibacy for those who plan to become monks. **Aparigraha** refers to the renunciation of all possessions.

It is the first of these five vows--**ahimsa**--which tends to be the most noticeable to non-Jains. This means the strict and absolute practice of not injuring any living thing. This results in total vegetarianism. Since agriculture and many other occupations would likely tend toward the injury of living things, including the insect world, most Jains lean toward the professions, civil servant positions, commerce, and banking. In these occupations the Jain follower is least likely to encounter any form of violence or injury. This matter of Ahimsa is carried to the extent of being careful where one walks to avoid the insects. Many Jains believe that even plants have souls, therefore, they eat only enough to survive. The rules on approved foods is interpreted very narrowly as well.

When carried to its greatest extent, **ahimsa** means that every object of nature has a soul. This includes fire, rain, and even stones. No piece of matter is without it. For the living being, his primary goal in life is to attain salvation. This can best be accomplished by releasing the soul from the matter that comprises the body, whatever that body may be, to a state of eternal bliss at the pinnacle of the universe. Penance and fasting are common practices, employed to bring about the release of the soul. As a consequence of these beliefs, Jains are highly conscious of protecting all souls from injury. This includes the building of asylums and rest houses for sick and diseased animals where they are kept and fed until they die a natural death--the **pinjrapoles** and the **goshalas**.

This belief in ahimsa also results in straining their drinking water in order to avoid drinking any living organisms, the wearing of facial masks to avoid breathing in any kind of life, and many sweep the ground in front of them as well as walking very carefully in order to prevent injury to any small bugs or unnecessary disturbances to souls in the earth and the stones.

IN SUMMARY

Jainism is a very complex philosophy of religion which has only been very briefly described. The Jains can be credited with having made some very basic contributions to Indian belief and practice. The belief in **ahimsa**, or nonviolence, originated with them and has had a lasting effect throughout India. While there is a gap between theory and practice, as evidenced by the continued warfare in India's history, combat was usually guided by humane rules between enemies as well as the regard shown for prisoners. Most Jains are normally very kind and charitable people. They try to avoid violence and would much rather try to assist their fellow humans. This spirit of altruism is stimulated by a desire to be a perfect being.

One of the major Jain changes from Hinduism was the end of the animal sacrifices so prevalent in the Vedic texts. The Jains said that the only significant sacrifice was the one which conquered self, the mastery of one's jiva or karma.

Tolerance is yet another characteristic of Jain thought. The "doctrine of manysidedness" suggests that there are always more than two possibilities to any proposition. In fact, Jains are taught to look for **seven**. To the Jain, it is impossible to view every aspect of a given situation at one time. As a result, other points of view and other religious sects possess a legitimacy that should rightfully be tolerated. Since they avoid agriculture and lean toward professions such as teaching and the civil service, they have had an influence upon Indian thinking and politics beyond their actual numbers. Mahatma Gandhi, a late 19th and 20th century philosopher who was instrumental in winning India's independence peacefully in 1947, was influenced by Jain thinking.

A further contribution was in the field of early literature. Stories with a moral purpose, for example, were composed in abundance in both Sanskrit and in several vernacular languages by Jain monks whose versatility found them writing about scientific subjects as well. Of primary importance also is the Jain contribution to the spread of Indian culture from the northern plains of the subcontinent, where it originated, into the Deccan and ultimately to Tamil country. The kings in the South took Jainism seriously, and it was an influential body of thought among them until new practices challenged its preeminence.

BOOKS FOR FURTHER READING ON JAINISM

Basham, A. L., *The Wonder That Was India* (1984).

de Bary, Wm. Theodore, editor, *Sources of Indian Tradition,*Vol. I (1958).

Campbell, Joseph, *The Masks of God: Oriental Mythology* (1962).

Carmody, Denise L, & Carmody, John T., *Ways to the Center: An Introduction to World Religions* (1993).

Fenton, John Y., **et. al.**, *Religions of Asia* (1988).

Kitagawa, Joseph M., editor, *The Religious Traditions of Asia* (1989).

Kulke, Hermann, & Rothermund, Dietmar, *A History of India* (1986).

Parrinder, Geoffrey, editor, *World Religions from Ancient History to the Present* (1983).

Rapson, Edward J., editor, *Ancient India*, Vol. I of the
  Cambridge History of India, 5 vols. (1922-37).

Rawlinson, H. G., *India: A Short Cultural History* (1952).

Smith, Vincent A., *The Oxford History of India*, edited by Percival Spear (1958).

Figure 15

Chapter 12
IMPORTANT CHALLLENGES TO HINDUISM--BUDDHISM

Only a few years after Mahavira's challenge to Hinduism, another man, **Siddhartha Gautama**, better known as the **Buddha**, challenged the Brahaminism and caste system which were so much a part of Hinduism. Apparently there were other holy men, gurus, and ascetics, who were seeking a better approach to the eternal, but Jainism and Buddhism were the only two whose followers grew in numbers until they became major religious faiths.

THE EARLY YEARS

The founder of Buddhism, **Siddhartha Gautama**, was born the son of the King of Kapilavastu in what is present-day Nepal. His family were members of the **Kshatriya** caste and the **Sakya** clan. He is therefore sometimes called **Sakyamuni**, which means "sage of the Sakya clan." His family name was Gautama. His given name, Siddhartha, means "all my earthly desires are fulfilled." The kingdom of Kapilavstu, where Buddha was born and raised, was just south of the Himalaya Mountains and part of its jurisdiction included what is now northeast India. It is believed Buddha was born about the year 563 B.C., possibly as late as 566 B.C., and that he died about 483 B.C. Everyone agrees that he was eighty years old at the time he died.

There have been many legends which have surrounded the birth of Siddhartha. His mother, Queen Maya, reportedly saw a white elephant the night she conceived. According to the legends of northwest India, the birth of Buddha was irregular because he was born from his mother's side. She died soon afterward and he was raised by his aunt, Prajapati. His father, Suddhodana, was told by astrologers that the young man would become a great ruler if he never had to suffer. If he did suffer, he would become a great religious leader. Since his father wanted him to succeed to the throne, he always kept the young man as sheltered as possible. No real biography of Buddha was written until 236 years after his death, so there are many unanswered questions regarding the details of his life. Many legends about the Buddha grew up during his lifetime and were often embellished over the years which followed.

Since the father loved his son very much, he built three beautiful palaces because he wanted him to be sheltered from the outside world--he would never suffer or want for anything and hence would not be tempted to wander off as an ascetic. Even the servants were selected with the utmost care. He married his beautiful cousin, a princess named **Yasodhara** from another province while he was still a very young man. Several sources say he was sixteen years of age when he married. A son named **Rahula** was born to this marriage when Buddha was twenty-five to twenty-nine years of age.

The family customarily moved from one palace to another with the changing weather seasons. Even today it is not uncommon for a wealthy Hindu to have two or more homes. In traveling from one palace to another he witnessed three things which he had never seen before. The first was an **old** man. The second was a **sick** man. The third was a **dead** man. All accounts relate how Buddha had always been a thoughtful young man, always happy and content. He was surrounded with oriental splendor and luxury, happily married, and he had a harem of beautiful women. But the experience of seeing old age, sickness, and death moved him to a state of anxious and puzzled reflection.

The Basics of Buddhism

On his next trip outside the palace, he saw a monk sitting by the road. The monk seemed quite happy, yet he possessed nothing. This experience prompted him to think more deeply into the true meaning of life in this world. It was not long after this that he seemed to lose all of the joy in living.

THE GREAT RENUNCIATION

In 537 B.C., at the age of twenty-nine, he awoke during the night, looked over his harem and saw the women all sound asleep with their mouths open. Several sources mention that he had as many as 40,000 dancing girls at his disposal! Suddenly he imagined that they were all dead. At this moment he was struck by the concept that all the women, that he--Siddhartha--everyone in the world--we are all mortal flesh and bones as we pass through this world from birth to death. He got up, took a simple yellow robe from his closet, left all his wealth behind, left his family sleeping, and set out to learn the true meaning of life, death, sorrow, and happiness. This action by Buddha was called **the Great Renunciation**.

THE SEARCH FOR TRUTH

Buddha was not the first upper class Hindu to wander away from great wealth and family to seek truth and meaning in life. Many other Indians had followed the same path before him and many continue to pursue the same quest. He quickly left Kapilavastu and wandered south until he reached the kingdom of Magadha, now southern Bihar. In that area he studied under two yoga masters, constantly meditating and trying to get into various positions where he could achieve a state of **moksha**, deliverance from the suffering of this world. All he felt from these awkward positions was discomfort! He decided to give up the yoga approach and to seek deliverance as a simple ascetic.

For the next six years--537-532 B.C.--Buddha devoted himself to the strictest asceticism. He fasted and held his breath until he fainted. When he regained consciousness, he repeated the practice. During this period he was joined by five other mendicants who were also trying to achieve a state of moksha. Buddha came so near to death that the other mendicants feared he would not be able to withstand another fast. At this time Buddha came to the conclusion that he was no nearer to enlightenment than when his quest began nearly seven years before. In fact, as hunger gripped him further, and he saw his body wasting away before him, he came to the conclusion that there **must** be a better way. He ate a substantial meal and took a bath in the river. His five friends continued their fast. They did not follow Buddha.

Buddha again felt totally alone. He also felt guilty for leaving the long course which he had been pursuing. Thinking that he would never achieve moksha, he sat down under a fig tree, more commonly known to Buddhists as a Bo or Bodhi tree. He allowed his mind to range over his experiences of the past seven years. He remembered how his yoga masters wanted him to mentally focus on the celestial spheres outside this world. That had not succeeded. He remembered his fasting for days on end. That had only made him weaker!

The Basics of Buddhism

THE ENLIGHTENMENT--531 B.C.

During that night in May, 531 B.C., as he sat under the Bodhi tree at a place in northern India called Bodh Gaya, Buddha won three knowledges. **First**, the remembrance of his former lives. **Secondly**, Buddha learned of the birth and death of all beings. **Third**, he was aware of the certainty of having finally cast off ignorance and passion, which up to that moment had bound him to the "world of becoming," and had led to successive rebirths. He realized that this was the greatest experience which he had ever undergone. It was **Enlightenment!** It was the kind of experience which brought complete peace and understanding. From this moment on he was referred to as the **Buddha**, the "Enlightened One." Buddha preferred the term **Tathgata** which he interpreted to mean "one who has sought the Truth." The term **Sakyamuni** was often used because it meant he was "the sage of the Sakya tribe." Some of his closest friends called him **Bhagawat**, which means "Lord" or "Blessed One."

As Buddha continued his meditation under the Bodhi tree, he arrived at the **Four Noble Truths**: **First,** human life is an existence of suffering--the human body is very impermanent. **Second**, human suffering is a consequence of our **desire** for things which cannot satisfy the inner spirit. The origin of all suffering is therefore **desire** or **craving**. Buddha believed that the simple attachment to **anything** of an earthly nature would cause suffering. It should be noted that at this point he was following very close to the Hindu philosophy, which taught that what mankind really wants in this world does not really satisfy. The Jain religion followed the same thought.

At this point Buddha began to examine what it is that mankind really desires. He concluded that we want **"being."** Everyone wants "to be" rather than not to be. Normally, nobody wants to die. He also concluded that everyone wants to **know**, to be **aware**. People are normally endlessly curious. The third thing people seek is **joy**. This is the opposite of frustration, futility, and boredom. He further reasoned that of all of these "desires," or "cravings," we want all of them in an infinite degree. That is, without end. We would all prefer **"a reservoir of being that never dies, is never exhausted, and is without limit in awareness and bliss."**

The **Third** of the Four Noble Truths is that suffering can be ended and mankind can be set free by renouncing these worldly desires which are rooted in ignorance. The **Fourth** Noble Truth is that we **can** free ourselves of desire by following the **Noble Eightfold Path**. Buddha referred to this new way of achieving enlightenment as the **"middle way."** That is, it is not total asceticism and self-torture on the one hand, nor is it following the ways of the world on the other. All Buddhist converts are expected to follow the "**Noble   Eightfold Path**."

Since Buddha spent the remainder of his life teaching about the eightfold path the following points are obviously greatly abbreviated. (1) **Right views** or understanding. To see the world as it really exists. To understand our relationship within the world. To have a knowledge of the Four Noble Truths. (2) **Right aspirations** or intentions. Be dispassionate. Seek enlightenment. (3) **Right speech** means to always be truthful. It also means to never say things which would encourage malice or hatred. Everyone should abstain from idle talk. (4) **Right behavior** or action. This point refers to what Buddha called the **five precepts**. One should not take any kind of life, never tell a lie, never steal, take no intoxicants or drugs, do not engage in abnormal sex. (5) **Right mode of livelihood**. A Buddhist follower should earn a living in such a way that it does not harm others. This eliminates hunting, butchering, selling weapons, or doing anything which would injure another. (6) **Right efforts**. Be sincere. Do not have evil thoughts.

The Basics of Buddhism

Nirvana will not occur automatically. (7) **Right thoughts** or right mindedness. Discipline our minds to focus upon worthy ideals or goals. (8) Right contemplation or concentration. Actively work to purify the mind and heart toward unselfishness and compassion.

It should be recognized that Buddhist Nirvana and Hindu moksha are not one and the same. Buddha had been trying to achieve a state of Hindu moksha, which refers to a oneness of an individual's mind with the great brahman spirit of soul--to detach our spiritual core from our bodies to enable it to join with the greater **atman**. Nirvana refers to seeing the world as it really exists--a new kind of ultimate reality, a new awareness. At that moment we see ourselves as very deficient in that reality. The reasoning necessary to adjust the thinking of the individual to the ultimate reality is embodied in the Four Noble Truths. It is necessary under Buddhism to leave this world of birth, misery, and death to achieve complete peace, a state of **nirvana**. The path is open to anyone who can achieve it.

Many recognized immediately that Buddha had outlined a new faith for mankind. His friends commented that he literally glowed with enthusiasm once he had discovered enlightenment. The encumberances and superstitions which had engulfed the people of India for centuries were all stripped away by this new faith. This was especially true of the caste system. Even though Buddha had been born a Kashatriya, he could see **no** place for the caste system in his understanding of enlightenment. He believed that anyone who followed his teachings could achieve the same peace of soul which stripped away desire and prepared one for **nirvana** that he had discovered. This also meant that rituals, ceremonies, or priestly mediators were totally unnecessary.

Buddha **did** believe that every person had a soul, which was somewhat like the Hindu belief in the atman. To state this in western terminology, a concept which would most likely be rejected by both Hindus and Buddhists, there is a mass of "soul" within the universe which Buddha called **Nibbana**, more often referred to by Buddhists as **Nirvana**. Once you have achieved Enlightenment, and can follow it (or retain it), then your mind and soul are in tune with the ultimate for the remainder of your life and for eternity. You have achieved **nirvana!**

If you cannot achieve **nirvana**, then Buddha believed that when you die your soul will return to the greater atman or Brahman and be reborn on earth to try again. Therefore, Buddhism **does** believe in **reincarnation**. If you don't even try to achieve **nirvana**, your soul will have to be born again and again, perhaps in some lower form of animal life. For this reason there are many Buddhists who will kill no animals. Furthermore, a Buddhist should not bring harm to any other living being, the Jainist concept of **ahimsa**.

Buddha did **not** believe in the western concept of a heaven, where each individual soul is rewarded with either eternal bliss or eternal torment. Rather, his philosophy was designed to help mankind adjust to everyday living on this earth. The two most important things in Buddhism concern, mankind's relationship to other people, and mankind's relationship to the universe. The Buddhist believes that those who have not achieved **nirvana** will simply have to be reincarnated until they do achieve that blessed state of adjustment and contentment. The Noble Eightfold Path is designed toward that end.

Finally, Buddha did **not** plan to form a new religion which was centered around himself. He thought of himself simply as a teacher and a monk who was primarily interested in showing others how to achieve the same peace of mind and soul which he had found.

The Basics of Buddhism

BUDDHA'S PREACHING

Shortly after Enlightenment, Buddha proceeded to northeast India to a town, about three miles north of Benares (Varanasi), called **Sarnath**. Nearby was a Deer Park where he taught his first lesson to his followers. Like Jesus of Nazareth at a later date, Buddha surrounded himself with a circle of close friends or disciples. The most beloved of all his followers was **Ananda**. A large monastery grew up at Sarnath, but only a few remains and footings are visible today. The largest single remain at Sarnath is the great **stupa**, which was built by the ruler Ashoka. It is 130 feet high. Near the stupa is the base of Ashoka's memorial pillar. There is a small museum nearby which contains the head of the pillar. This head of the pillar has become India's national symbol. On it is the wheel of birth and rebirth--the symbol of the cycle of life--accepted by Hindus, Jains, and Buddhists.

There were many at that time who thought of Buddha as simply a rebel within Hinduism, a kind of Martin Luther within their faith. They failed to understand that Buddha had done more than re-work Hinduism--he had founded an entirely **new** religion. Also, unlike Hinduism which had **evolved** over thousands of years, Buddhism sprang forth fully grown as a new faith. As this new faith grew in numbers, there were many among the Brahmins who thought of it more as a threat and a challenge rather than just the temporary passing faith of a rebel ascetic. Many Hindus were extremely critical. Rather than striking back, Buddha's message was very calming. His entire attitude was, "why get excited when you are certain that you are right?"

The monastery at Sarnath was the only visible, physical thing Buddha left behind. Like so many great religious leaders, he was not a writer. His only lasting contribution was the **Dharma**, the Doctrine, and his extensive teachings to his followers--all of them oral instructions. Buddha taught the Four Noble Truths and the Eightfold Path to all who would listen. He believed that this was all one needed to achieve **nirvana**.

From the night of his Enlightenment until the day of his death, everything which was taught by the Buddha has been accepted as perfect, homogeneous, complete, and pure. The Good Word of the Buddha is distinguished by four characteristics: first, it is well spoken. Second, it is agreeable and pleasant. Third, it is in conformity with welfare. And, fourth, it is truthful.

During Buddha's lifetime the principles of the faith were taught to anyone who was interested, regardless of caste or sex. It is said by Buddhists that he "set turning the wheel of the Doctrine." The wheel represents the complete circle of life--birth, maturity, and death. This is followed by rebirth through reincarnation and the circle goes on. There were **sixty-one** close disciples who were referred to as the **Sangha**. They were made up of four assemblies: monks, nuns, laymen, and laywomen. Buddha steered clear of discussing subjects such as natural phenomena, whether animals have souls, where God resides, etc. He did not criticize either Hindus or any caste. His faith and the Doctrine were open to those who were willing to work out their lives according to the plan which he taught.

One may well think of Buddha's plan as a blueprint for living. It was not so severe as to bring about starvation nor so easy that one could ignore it in one's daily life. It was the "Middle Way." Those who were the monks and the nuns were distinguished from the laity by their dress, their way of life, and by their understanding of the Dharma (teaching). The clergy were expected to own nothing, but rather to beg for their needs. The laity were simply "on their way" without a fulltime commitment. One of the layperson's duties was to provide food, clothing, or shelter for monks who were in need.

THE LAST YEARS OF BUDDHA

As Buddha grew older, his closest followers became concerned as to the future of their faith. Buddha never mentioned who was to come after him or how the faith was to be practiced by his followers. Apparently he believed that everyone would follow his "Truths" and the "Path" and thereby the faith would be a simple one without any leader or bureaucracy. On one occasion his cousin, Devadatta, offered to replace him as head of the Sangha. Buddha replied that he would entrust the congregation to no one, not even the gods.

At the very end, his most loved disciple, Ananda, expressed a similar hope that the Blessed One would not leave this world before having given his instructions to the community and having designated a successor. The Buddha answered him: "What does the community expect of me, O Ananda? Never having wished to direct it or subject it to my teachings, I have no such instructions for the Sangha. I am reaching my end. After I am gone, may each of you be your own island, your own refuge. Acting in this way you will set yourselves on the summit of the immortal."

When Buddha was eighty years of age, he and his disciples were still on the move. The old Sakyamuni was obviously worn and nearing his end. They stopped for a meal at a peasant's cottage. Everyone, including Buddha, knew the food was tainted. He sent his disciples out, but he ate the food because he feared his host would be offended. An attack of dysentery followed which compelled him to stop just outside the town of Kusinagari in the Malla country. There, lying between two trees in the Upavarta Grove, he went through a long series of meditative states. He expired while he was meditating in the same way as a flame flickers out when it has run out of fuel. Everyone there agreed he had achieved perfect peace through **nirvana**. His last words were, "Decay is inherent in all component things! Work out your salvation with diligence."

Just before he died, Ananda asked him what to do with the body of the Perfect One. Buddha replied: "Do not waste your time, O Ananda, in paying homage to my body. Concern yourself with all diligence and application with your own spiritual welfare." Buddha had never held his body to be worth anything, it was only a body of matter which sustained him in life. It was therefore worth nothing in death.

The Mallas, a local tribe or confederation in the province of Kusinagari, took the Buddha's body and cremated it. The remaining relics were shared among his faithful followers. Within the next few years after his death, these relics were placed in commemorative monuments which came to be known as **Stupas**. The stupa is normally a massive circular structure which is constructed of stone, brick, and/or earth. It is smaller at the top and round like a dome. It is usually surmounted by an umbrella at the very peak. Worshippers can make offerings at a stupa and then circumambulate around the structure. Although stupas vary in size from the very large Svayambhunath Stupa in the Kathmandu Valley of Nepal to small portable ones, they normally are all shaped pretty much the same in India and Nepal. The ones associated with Tibetan Buddhism are more bell-shaped, especially at the top, while those in China take the form of a pagoda.

The Basics of Buddhism

The oldest surviving stupas are the ones in Bharut and Sanchi in north central India. They date from about the second century B.C. Several of the older stupas have been rebuilt to preserve them in a presentable condition. Once all of Buddha's earthly remains had been enshrined in stupas, the Buddhists then decided to place famous texts, or **Sutras**, in these. Some have had spells enclosed, also known as **mantras**. Many of the stupas in northern India, Tibet, and Nepal have large brass cylinders known as prayer wheels all around the perimeter. Faithful Buddhists walk around the stupa and spin the prayer wheels because each one has a **sutra** or a **mantra** cast on its surface. Often there are prayer wheels of over six feet in height which have a wind mill to turn them constantly. Each time the wheel turns it says a prayer to Buddha. It is also quite common to see many flags and pennants near or attached to stupas. These also have prayers which go to Buddha whenever the wind blows the flag.

PRESERVING THE DHARMA

Following the death of the Buddha it became necessary for his closest disciples to consider how they would preserve the **dharma**, or teachings, of their spiritual leader. It was determined to write down some of his most common and frequent teachings. Monasteries were also built to serve both as a place of prayer and study as well as a place to serve the local community, the **sangha**. A body of teaching and practice were adopted with many rules and regulations concerning what a follower of Buddha could or could not do, how one should live, and what to believe.

Those who join the Buddhist faith are expected to be sincere individuals. Everyone who wants to become a Buddhist is expected to take a pledge expressing the **Three Jewels**. The novice promises to take "refuge" from the suffering inherent in this life. They repeat the following three times: "**I go to the Buddha for refuge, I go to the dharma for refuge, I go to the sangha for refuge**." Such is the sincerity of Tibetan Buddhists that many of them completely prostrate themselves before a Buddhist temple or shrine. Unlike some religious faiths where taking the vows to become a monk means that you have pledged yourself for life, the Buddhist monk may agree to serve as a monk for a stated period of time. It is like making a contract for the stated period. All monks are expected to spend some time in a monastery--at least a month. Some do pledge their entire lifetime. Upon acceptance the monk is tonsured, that is, he has his head shaven since that was one of the first things Buddha did when he left the security of the palace as a young prince.

There are **Ten Precepts** which **every** Buddhist is expected to follow. They should: promise never to harm any living thing; never to steal; never abuse their chastity through wrongful acts of sex; not engage in useless or critical speech; abstain from intoxicating drugs or drink; not eat after the midday meal; avoid dancing and rowdy merrymaking; not use perfumes or other personal adornments; not sit on luxurious chairs or sleep in fancy beds; and never accept gold or silver. Those who take the vows to become monks must follow all of the Ten Precepts. The lay people only need to follow the first five precepts.

In addition, there are many other rules which monasteries require of those who are monks. Normally the monks must beg for their food each morning. A monk is only allowed to eat food up to high noon. Both men and women must remain a celibate (unmarried) throughout their tenure as a monk. A monk may possess only what are known as the **Eight Requisites**. These requisites are: one robe with a belt for nuns, a begging bowl for their food, a razor for men to shave both the beard and the head, a needle to mend their clothes, a strainer so they do not drink any living thing, a walking staff, and a toothpick.

There are exceptions allowed under certain circumstances. For instance, in colder climates the monk may own an under garment, an outer garment, and a cloak. In those areas the three pieces count as only one garment. Men in colder climates may also wear a belt, and sandals are allowed. Shoes are allowed as a luxury in the very coldest areas such as the Himalayas. The clothes are most often yellow to orange, or a dull red. A few wear black. The clothes should always be gifts of the lay people to the monk. In poor areas the older monks are often seen wearing well-worn garments. The young novices always have newer robes, which are kept very clean. In hot climates it is permissible to possess a fan.

Each morning the monk sets out to beg his daily food. In silence and with lowered eyes, the monk goes from house to house. When a monk is offered food it should be accepted quietly and be placed in the bowl. As noontime approaches the monk will withdraw to a quiet place to eat his food. People generally will offer the monks rice, bread, and strained water to drink. The use of any intoxicating drinks is strictly forbidden. Fish is permitted only if it was a part of the diet of the lay person who made the offer. Fish should not be specially prepared for monks. Foods such as ghee (clarified butter), butter, oil, honey, and sugar are reserved for the sick, and can be taken "as medicine." Monks may accept an invitation to eat in the homes of the laity. Under no circumstances is a monk to accept gold or silver as a personal gift. Any money given to the temple is used for charity. In a Buddhist country the people expect the monks to come around each morning, so they try to have the food prepared ahead of time. Too many monks in one area could be a burden to the lay people, but they rarely complain because many of the monks do a great amount of charity work.

In the early years the Buddhist monks had no permanent place of residence. Each monk was expected to travel about the country teaching and meditating and spreading the faith. Many lived in the mountains and the forest, in crude shelters which they constructed from readily available materials. In the colder regions they needed more protection. There they lived in caves or in a small hut which they built of local stone. In time, the monks in a given area began to gather together and to form monasteries. There were many who had suffered and died alone in the early years. The monastery provided an opportunity for them to help one another. Even today, many still live alone.

It was pretty well established from the earliest times what a monk should believe in and how he should behave. Intense meditation has always been strongly emphasized. The repetition of prayers and the study of the holy texts has also been emphasized. Even though Buddha wrote nothing, there were ultimately 22,000 volumes collected of his teachings. These are called the **Commentaries.** These provide a lifetime of study for faithful Buddhists. Since monks were never to be involved in political issues, everyone accepted them as the local social workers of the area. Even the monks who lived in a monastery lived a very solitary life. They were expected to meditate and to work out their own personal salvation. When they were in meditation, they were expected to totally disregard society around them, their family, even a spouse or a child. The Hindu practice of yoga is also employed by Buddhists as a detachment from the world about them. Each individual monk was to be able to achieve **nirvana** without either assistance or distractions. In some Buddhist sects there were **gurus** (teachers) who assisted those who were having difficulty.

The Basics of Buddhism

BUDDHISM AND THE WESTERN WORLD

The teachings of the Buddha have been a subject of interpretation in every country of the world. The spread of the faith generally followed along the trade routes. Buddhism was most often introduced through traders who were Buddhists rather than by missionaries. The teachings of Buddha reached as far west as Greece. The Greeks were fascinated by the teachings of Buddha, but very few were converted. The Greeks and other peoples in the western world were evidently content with the polytheistic solutions offered by their gods and goddesses in the early years of Buddhism. The Buddhist missionaries seem to have made no effort to win converts in the West. Buddhism was to be an eastern faith for over a thousand years before it would attract followers in the western world.

BUDDHISM IN INDIA

The **sangha** (community) which Buddha established in northeast India was well in place by the time of his death. Shortly thereafter, five-hundred senior monks met to codify his teachings. Most of them settled in and around the modern Indian state of **Bihar**, which loosely interpreted means "Buddhist monastery." Once they had made a reasonable interpretation which could be agreed upon, they spread out to carry their message to others.

Buddha's religious solution did not attract immediate popularity following his death. It was not a rapidly growing faith in the early years. Upper class Hindus often thought of Buddhism as a challenge to their faith while lower class Hindus lacked the intellectual background to enter into the meditation prescribed by Buddha. Furthermore, most of the lower classes had to struggle to survive--there was no time to meditate.

In 274 B.C., **Ashoka** became the emperor of nearly all of present-day India, Nepal, Kashmir, and part of Pakistan. There is still much to be learned about Ashoka, but from the few inscriptions which we have, originally translated by James Prinsep in 1837, it appears that Ashoka took this vast area partly by inheritance and partly by conquest. Sometime near the end of the conquest, he became a Buddhist. The great leader was apparently appalled by the amount of bloodshed and suffering which occurred in his wars and decided to cease conquest and to divert his life to more peaceful pursuits. Some sources go so far as to say he became a monk, but this seems to be based on inadequate sources. It is clear that he allowed freedom of religion for both Hindus and Buddhists.

With the encouragement of the ruler as an example, the faith began to spread throughout India during Ashoka's reign, 274 to 232 B.C.. His son, **Mahendra**, headed the mission that officially introduced Buddhism into Sri Lanka. It is believed that Mahendra's sister, Sanghamitta, a nun, accompanied him to Sri Lanka about 250 B.C. About this same time period an important monk named Tissa Moggaliputta, organized nine different mission fields of Buddhism.

As Buddhism spread out further from its place of origin, problems began to arise as each monk began interpreting Buddha's teachings differently. Buddha had died in 483 B.C. and by the death of Ashoka, roughly 250 years had elapsed. Time and distance, along with adaptations to local customs and languages, changed what the original sangha had agreed upon. By the time of Ashoka's death, Buddhists operated largely within monastic divisions. Each one thought they had captured the real essence of Buddha and his teachings. By the early Christian era in the West, some of the Buddhist teachings had diverged so far that it is doubtful whether they embodied very much of what the Buddha really taught.

The results were very similar to the splintering of Protestant groups in the western world from 1517 to 1777. It became obvious that Buddhism needed to find some agreement and a common language to express his teachings. They settled upon **Sanskrit** as the official language within India. These teachings were preserved in bits and pieces and were not published in one complete document in Sanskrit until after Indian independence from Britain in 1947. Generally speaking, the **Pali** texts were the basis of Buddhism in Sri Lanka and in the Southeast Asian countries. **Pali** is an early form of the Middle Indo-Aryan language. The manuscripts in **Pali** and in **Sanskrit** became to Buddhism what Hebrew, Greek, and Latin have been to Christianity. Although Buddhism had been popular in India during Ashoka's reign, it began to weaken after his death.

THE SPREAD OF BUDDHISM TO CHINA

The next need for translations of Buddhist texts came from **China**. It is reasonably certain that Buddhism first entered China by way of the **Old Silk Road** and the other trade routes. There were few missionary contacts with China during the early years of Buddhism. Most of the Chinese converts were won by laymen who traveled the trade routes and introduced the faith to other traders and commercial people. The first translations of Buddhist scriptures into Chinese were done by two Indian monks who traveled to China in A.D. 68. The Buddhist scriptures were soon translated from the Indian Sanskrit into Chinese, then printed into books. The Chinese liked the Buddhist philosophy because their government seemed so helpless in assisting the Chinese people in times of natural disasters and famine. The old animistic solutions all seemed to have failed. Buddhism was an opportunity for each individual to work out one's own salvation according to the principles laid down by Buddha. By the 7th or 8th century, Buddhist scriptures were also translated into Tibetan and from the area of western China and Afghanistan it spread north into Central Asia. But it was only a few years later that Central Asia changed to another new faith--**Islam**.

One of the interesting sidelights on the spread of Buddhism into China is that a succession of Chinese Buddhist monks who wanted to learn more about the faith journeyed to India in search of Buddhist manuscripts. Among the most famous of these Chinese scholars were the following: **Fa-hsien, 399-413; Hsuan-Tsang, 630-644;** and **I-tsing, 671-695**. Since Buddhism had practically died out in India by the time the Chinese Buddhists arrived, the account which the Chinese monks in search of manuscripts have given us of India between the 5th and the 7th centuries, is the best insight available today. Furthermore, these Chinese scholars copied and preserved the content of those early **Sanskrit** texts which would otherwise have been lost. Almost as important as the conversion of the Chinese is that the faith spread from China to Korea, and from Korea to Japan. But Buddhism in India, the country where it had originated, was slowly re-absorbed into Hinduism in the centuries following Ashoka.

The Basics of Buddhism

THE CONSOLIDATION AND THE TRANSMISSION OF THE FAITH

One of the very important aspects of early Buddhism was the meeting of **Councils**. Learned monks assembled at these Councils to rehearse and recite the Canon and its commentaries. The **First** Buddhist Council was held at **Rajagrha** (Rajgir, Bihar, India) within a few months of Buddha's final Nirvana. **Maha Kasyapa**, the senior monk, created the first **canon** by questioning the other monks about how they understood the Buddha's teachings and sayings. This was further expounded upon by a monk named **Upali** in his *Vinaya Pitaka*--the Discipline. Still another monk, Buddha's personal attendant, **Ananda**, wrote the *Sutra Pitaka*, a term which means roughly a "Basket of Religious Discourses." There have only been **six** Buddhist Councils held in the 2500 years since Buddha's death. The last one was held in Rangoon, Burma (Myanmar) between 1954 and 1956. Each Council has reviewed the **Pali** manuscripts and has tried to interpret them in as accurate a manner as possible.

Another important aspect of Buddhism has been the monastic tradition. Although one need not join a monastery, and many did not, the monastic way provided an association of individuals who were seeking their own salvation and that of others. Since Buddha had always been very compassionate and democratic, never scolding or dogmatic, the monastery was created along the same principles. **First,** matters of monastic discipline were decided unanimously. **Secondly,** monks owed no obedience. Right from the beginning, each monastery had an abbot at the head. This was based partly upon the need for leadership, and partly upon practicality. They needed someone to examine the incoming novices, and to see that someone who was in need of help would receive it. This was quite a different arrangement from Christian monasticism in the western world where each entering novice promised **Poverty, Chastity,** and **Obedience** for the remainder of one's life.

Beyond simply knowing the rules and practicing them daily, they realized very early that everyone needed help. Therefore, every two weeks the monastery went through a communal **Pratimoksa**. When this practice first began, the monks would meet together to discuss their faults and weaknesses in the faith. Each one was expected to publicly confess his shortcomings to the assembled monks. The monks agreed that to just confess was sufficient and that a promise to correct the fault would be considered satisfactory. Very serious faults could bring penalties, usually a denial of some kind. Later, all faults were confessed privately by one monk to another before the ceremony began. A listing of the faults of the group was then discussed, generally by the senior monk. The **pratimoksa** is one of the most important innovations in the monastic life since the death of Buddha.

THE DIVISION OF BUDDHISM BETWEEN HINAYANA AND MAHAYANA

Sometime about four or five hundred years after the death of Buddha, the early Christian era, the faith began to divide into two major sects--the **Hinayana** and the **Mahayana**. The split seems to have occurred following the third council of Buddhists which was called at Pataliputra by the emperor, Ashoka. Some Buddhists apparently did not think that this council was quite authentic. Although there were some disagreements following the council concerning what the Buddha really taught, there was no sudden breach or major point of disagreement. Eventually there were two factions which developed: the **Mahayana**, which was more liberal with many different paths to salvation, while the **Hinayana** sect became much more of a fundamentalist group, which was convinced they were following the teachings of Buddha. The two sects apparently coexisted in the same monasteries for many years. Ultimately they broke apart.

MAHAYANA BUDDHISM

The **Mahayana** approach to Buddhism is sometimes referred to as the "Greater Vehicle." The followers of Mahayana Buddhism believe that the faith is broad enough to encompass everyone. Mahayana stresses the compassionate concern of the Buddha for humanity, more broadly for all of life. Most Mahayana followers understand Buddha as a religious **savior**. They pray personally to Buddha to assist them in this world. They look upon Buddha as a compassionate prince who became aware of the sufferings and sorrows of mankind. He left his palace and discovered the way to release from the sufferings of this world and can teach us all the way to break the circle of birth, suffering, and death through meditation which leads to **nirvana**. Now that Buddha has shown us the way, it is no longer necessary for each of us to go through yoga, starvation, and a lifetime in meditation. We only need to follow his guide and pray to him to deliver us from evil. This school of thought is the predominant one in China, Tibet, Korea, and Japan.

There are those who may see the evolution of Mahayana Buddhism at about the beginning of the Christian era as making Buddha a Far Eastern Christ. There are, however, major differences to keep in mind. Buddha did not employ miracles in his teaching. He did not claim any aspect of resurrection either for himself or for his followers. Buddha did not claim that he could intercede for his followers in this world or the next. Buddha never claimed to be the incarnation of any God. Finally, he died a very natural death; he was not tortured or crucified. From the beginning of his teaching career to his final hour, he claimed to be only a teacher who wanted to assist everyone to work out their own salvation by achieving **nirvana**.

One of the interesting aspects of Mahayana Buddhism is their concept of the **Bodhisattva**. A bodhisattva is a person who has finally achieved the point at which he could step into **nirvana** but rather than do so he stays on earth to help others achieve what he has achieved. Many people accept a bodhisattva as a reincarnated Buddha. Others believe that a bodhisattva is capable of acting as an intermediary between the individual and the Buddha. A true bodhisattva is incapable of thoughts of hatred or selfishness. There were many people who believed that their ruler was a bodhisattva. Such a claim or title for anyone, from a ruler to a guru working with others, gave them a great amount of power and authority. There were many who worshipped the bodhisattva as a saint.

The highest Mahayana ideal is the bodhisattva who sacrifices himself for others. Many would say that it is a sacrifice for a ruler to forego **nirvana** in order to stay and rule on this earth. And, there are cases of bodhisattvas who have truly given their life as a physical sacrifice. For instance, there was the one who gave his body to a famished tigress to prevent her from eating her cubs. During the 6th century there were some Buddhist monks who decided to burn themselves for a holy cause. In preparation, they would first eat fatty foods for a long time so they would burn better. In a like manner, there were some monks who burned their bodies as a protest to the war in Vietnam. Since total liberation of the mind from the body is a great accomplishment, there have been Buddhist monks who would wrap a string soaked in oil or fat around the finger several times at a joint. They would then light the string and watch it burn. When the fire went out, they would pull the finger off.

116

The Basics of Buddhism

It will be recalled that Buddha also pushed his life to the very brink through starvation and other acts of self-enforced misery before he received enlightenment. But after enlightenment, he taught that there was a "Middle Way" which did not require such tactics. The Buddhists who continue to take such actions which could lead to death are very careful to characterize them as acts of "sacrifice" rather than suicide. All Buddhist sects proclaim that they are opposed to suicide.

One of the sacred texts which was written well after Buddha's death is called the *Lotus Sutra*. This work calls upon all Buddhists to sacrifice themselves if their religion is in grave danger. On one occasion there was a Buddhist martyr who truly believed that the faith was endangered. He first punched his body full of holes, poured oil in them, sealed the holes with wax so the oil would not run out, then set fire to himself. This was an action of a bodhisattva who believed that his body was dust compared to the principle for which he died. Such acts are rare in the Buddhist community at any time in their long history.

A true bodhisattva should possess the thirty-two physical characteristics which were special to the Buddha. Every parent examined their newly born son to see whether he possessed those special characteristics. These marks were the following: (1) well-set feet, (2) wheels with a thousand spokes on the soles of his feet, (3) large projecting heels, (4) long, thin fingers, (5) soft hands and feet, (6) netted hands and feet, (7) prominent ankles, (8) limbs like an antelope, (9) his hands should reach his knees when he is standing, (10) his private member is in a sheath, (11) his color is a golden glow, (12) he has one hair in each skin pore, (13) the skin is soft, (14) he has black hairs which curl to the right, (15) he stands very straight, (16) there are seven prominences on his body, (17) his chest is like that of a lion, (18) the space between his shoulders is filled out, (19) his height is equal to his outstretched arms, (20) his shoulders are both even, (21) he has a keen sense of taste, (22) he has a lion-jaw, (23) there are forty teeth, (24) his teeth are shiny white, (25) his teeth are all even, (26) there are no gaps between his teeth, (27) he has a large tongue, (28) his voice can vary from as soft as a cuckoo to that of Brahma, (29) very black eyes, (30) long eyelashes like an ox, (31) there is white hair between the eyebrows, and (32) his head is well shaped.

In addition to the thirty-two characteristics there were eighty other "minor marks" such as having copper-colored nails, having well-hidden sinews, and he should have extra long earlobes. Sculptors often tried to incorporate as many of these body marks on the Buddha's statues as they knew. According to legend, the Buddha had all these special marks on his body. These same signs are searched for in Tibet when it is time to name another Dali Lama.

HINAYANA BUDDHISM

The Hinayana school of Buddhism is the predominant one in Southeast Asia. The term Hinayana means the "Lesser Vehicle," or sometimes the "Lesser Raft." They think of themselves as the more conservative and the more personal approach to finding **nirvana**. They believe that is how Buddha went out as an individual to seek enlightenment. In this approach there are many more individuals who seek enlightenment alone than in the Mahayana, where they are more inclined toward a monastic community. The followers of the Hinayana sect believe that **only** monks and nuns have any hope of achieving Nirvana. They spend a large percentage of their time in concentration and meditation. They regard Buddha as both a teacher and a saint. They

The Basics of Buddhism

are the "fundamentalists" of the faith. Often the followers of Hinayana are referred to as the **Theravada** school, the "Doctrine of the Elders," the way of the **theras**.

The Theravada followers do not have the concept of the bodhisattva, but they have a similar arrangement called the **Arhat**. Someone who has achieved this state of enlightenment has gone as far as is possible in this world. The term **Arhat** means "one who is worthy." Today they are often referred to as "saints." The Theravada branch of Hinayana Buddhism does not consider the image of Buddha to be as important as do the Mahayana followers. In Sri Lanka it is commonly accepted that anyone who pledges to become a monk should consider it a lifetime commitment. In the Southeast Asian countries such a long commitment is not required. In Thailand and Cambodia **all** young men are urged to spend at least one rainy season as a monk in order to receive moral instructions from the elders.

Church and state are closely allied throughout Southeast Asia. In Burma there is a council made up of leading Buddhist monks and laymen. They operate as a guiding advisory group for Buddhism throughout the country. They are closely supervised by the state. Burma discourages all other religious faiths.

In Thailand the head of the **sangha** (community) is chosen by the heads of all the major monastic groups. He is then approved by the ministry of education and finally appointed by the king. As **sangharaja** (Sanga ruler) he makes appointments to other important positions in Thailand with the approval of the government. Lay people commonly look to the monks for the basic precepts of correct living. Devout followers of Buddhism also maintain a small shrine in their homes, go to lectures on doctrine, and go on pilgrimages to sacred Buddhist sites. They hope to gain extra merit by refraining from sex, not eating after noon, using no perfume, they do not enjoy music, or do anything which seems luxurious during the special holy days.

Many devout Buddhists use small hand-held **prayer wheels**. These are cylinders of varying sizes. The prayer wheel always has an axle which will allow the wheel to turn freely. Prayers to Buddha are carved or molded on the outside and prayers or mantras may be written on parchment and placed inside the wheel. The theory is that every time the wheel turns it says a prayer to Buddha. These are most common in Southeast Asia, Nepal, Tibet and Ladakh in northern India. The hand-held models have a small weight attached to one side of the cylinder which will allow the prayer wheel to spin with a slight wrist motion.

Prayer beads are also common in Buddhist countries. The purpose of the beads is to help the individual to focus upon his faith, to concentrate more completely, and to meditate. Many worshippers prefer the repetition of mythical sounds and word combinations such as "**om**" or phrases such as "**Om mani padme hum**," which means roughly, "Oh jewel in the heart of the lotus." **Sutras** are sacred scripture, sayings attributed to Buddha. A **mantra** is a tool for spiritual meditation. The Buddhist term **mandala** refers to a diagram, literally a circle, which is projected into the mind of a worshipper. It is a spiritual map for meditation. The object of the meditation is to reach the center of the circle. A **tanka** is very similar to a **mandala** except that it is printed on rectangular piece of cloth. It generally has a "doorway" painted in each corner. The worshipper enters through one of the doorways and seeks to find the center of the **tanka** through meditation. The center of the diagram is often a figure of Buddha. **Prayer beads, sutras, mantras, mandalas, and tankas** are all tools of meditation for the Buddhist. Although they can be employed by those of the Mahayana following, they are central to worship for the individual who follows the Theravada school of Hinayana Buddhism.

The Basics of Buddhism

Statues devoted to Buddha did not become common until the second or third century before the Christian era. Authors have attributed the likenesses of Buddha to the Hellenistic influence of Alexander the Great. It is now known that there were likenesses of Buddha before the invasion of Alexander the Great. It is difficult to tell today how much the Ghandara school of northwest India was influenced by the Greek sculptors and how much they were influenced by the Roman traders who arrived at a much later time. Modern research indicates that Alexander probably had less influence than was originally believed. In any event, Buddha is most often portrayed in a "lotus meditative position." That is, he is sitting with his legs crossed, his back is upright, he is looking straight forward or slightly down, and he has a contented smile. He is obviously in deep thought. And, there are other statues of average-size Buddhas, very skinny Buddhas, enormous Buddhas several feet in height, reclining Buddhas, jade Buddhas, and solid gold Buddhas.

One type of statue was modeled on that of the Greek statues of Apollo. In this version, Buddha has a bump on top of his head. The Greeks always added this to the top of Apollo's head because he was the wisest, the most intelligent, of all their gods. Since Buddha was a very wise man, the Hellenistic sculptors gave Buddha a similar addition to the top of his head. In other versions there are dozens of little curls on top of Buddha's head. All of these turn to the right in keeping with the thirty-two marks of the great man. One legend states that these are not really curls of hair but small snails which took pity on Buddha who was seen sitting in the hot sun while he was meditating. The snails crawled on top of his head to cool it from the rays of the sun. Many Buddhists do worship at the great Buddha statues throughout the world. Many have small versions on their family altar. The Tibetan monk would prostrate himself before the statue, while other Buddhists would only venerate the memory of Buddha. Like all other religions, there are varying degrees of devotion depending upon both local customs and the individual.

Throughout Southeast Asia the monks are close to the lay family. When the child reaches puberty, the monks conduct what is called a **tonsure** ceremony. This is repeated when a young man enters the order. Weddings and funerals are also Buddhist affairs. This may seem to be a very close tie between the family and the religion. It is. Both the people and the religion want it to be that way. The rules of the faith are adhered to closely by most of the inhabitants in a Buddhist country.

There are many joyful times in countries where Therevada Buddhism is the leading religion. A holiday called **Wesak**, usually celebrated in May, is a triple commemoration of the Buddha's birth, enlightenment, and death. Another celebration is the feast of the offering of robes and alms to the monks. This occurs at the end of the rainy season. The New Year festival is yet another period of celebration, which is filled with special dances, games, and contests. Of course, Buddha is celebrated and the equivalent of our New Year's resolutions are made. And there are many local festivals which bring additional happiness to the people where either the Theravada or the Mahayana sects of Buddhism predominate.

TANTRIC BUDDHISM

During the last years Buddhism was a viable religion in India, it became much more involved with **Tantrism**. Tantrism grew out of Hinduism. It is the belief that a collection of certain mystical teachings, regarding creation and destruction, should be worshipped as divine spirit emanating from a Vedic god, who attains his highest power in union with his wife. This

The Basics of Buddhism

included magical incantations, gestures, and diagrams. Such a union would heal illness, avert evil, and impart mystical powers to the believer. Tantrism became especially popular in northeast India, especially in the Bengal area. Kali, one of the consorts of the Hindu god Shiva, was to be worshipped for her female reproductive powers.

Tantric Buddhism is an outgrowth of the Mahayana branch of Buddhist interpretation. Buddhism first entered Tibet from Kashmir sometime about A.D. 630, but it was not widely accepted until the end of the 8th century. It is named the "thunderbolt vehicle" by the Tibetans. It gained its most notable success in Tibet where the concept of compelling a god or goddess to do or not to do a particular thing merged in with the ancient pagan rites in Tibet which were known as **bon**.

The **bon** religion, which was being practiced in the 6th and 7th centuries in Tibet, employed the expertise of a **shaman** to invoke spells, to dance wildly, to see visions of the gods, and all the while he beat loudly on a drum. Such a practice is referred to as **theurgic**--it is an art or science of compelling a god to do or not to do something. It was most often invoked at the birth of a child, the purification process of driving evil spirits from a home, the attempt to cure illness, or as a part of the rites for the dead. Since the common people were all **bon** followers, they saw the Buddhist ceremonies of invoking spells and casting out evil as very similar to their own religion. Many of them worshipped the goddess **Tara** at public festivals. Tara was a kind of mother goddess to whom common people could appeal for help. Tibet's music and dance developed largely out of the Tara festivals.

A typical Tantric Buddhist meditation combined many of the **bon** and Hindu practices. The monk began by bathing for purification. He then took refuge in the three jewels, a common practice for any Buddhist meditation. The next step was to try to take on the identity of a deity. They meditated upon this until they had achieved that identity. Hand gestures and mental exercises were numerous in the process of achieving the level of the selected deity. At the moment they had identified with the deity, they became an enlightened Buddha. Such a process would employ the use of all kinds of Buddhist scriptures, **mantras**, **mandalas**, and **tankas**. Most often these were conjured up in the mind of the meditator. Such a meditation could require many hours, perhaps many days, to reach the state of enlightenment.

In Hinduism and Buddhism the meditator was often assisted by a **guru** or teacher. In Tantric Buddhism the **guru** was called a **LAMA**. The **lama** was a teacher who had achieved Buddhahood, but was there to assist the monk who might be having difficulty finding his way. It was not uncommon for a monk who was meditating to experience total blank areas in his view of the cosmos while meditating. There also were vast numbers of "divine beings" to cope with in meditation, some of them peaceful while others could be positively terrifying. Each of the demons also has consorts and children, each with a different character. In a sense, the lama assisted the monk in compelling the gods to help him in achieving enlightenment--to awaken the Buddha-nature within. Tantric Buddhism, therefore, became a merger of regular Mahayana Buddhism with the god-compelling nature of bon, and with the assistance of a lama. A lama came to be viewed as the fourth "jewel" of Buddhism. Many young men joined the monastery as young as nine and spent their entire lifetime in study, prayer and meditation. Many of them became experts at manipulating the gods and goddesses. Approximately one-fourth of the Tibetan population was engaged in religion before the communist takeover.

The Basics of Buddhism

Tantric Buddhism became popular in Tibet not only because it seemed to easily adapt to the bon worship, but also because it was supported by the kings. The kings had pretended to be the tie between heaven and the people, and when the kings adopted the new faith it was readily accepted. Interestingly, when the power of the kings declined, the head of the leading monastery--the Drepung monastery--came to be known as the **Dalai Lama**. The kings always seemed too busy with a military campaign, or with other pleasures, to be troubled with ruling Tibet. The Dalai Lama simply assumed those responsibilities.

As the abbot of the Drepung monastery assumed more political power, it came to be commonly accepted that he was a reincarnation of the previous abbot. The followers of this concept believe that when a ruling abbot died his soul went to the great **atman**, or supreme soul, and from that **atman** would be born the next leader of the faith--the next Dalai Lama. By the 15th or 16th century the Dalai Lama had become both the political and spiritual leader. Tibet became a **theocracy**.

Tantrism spread from Tibet to western China, some areas of northern India, Mongolia, and Afghanistan. The term "Dalai" is a Mongolian term which means "ocean." It suggests that the Dalai Lama has the breadth and depth of wisdom of the entire ocean. This is especially interesting since Tibet is a landlocked country located far from any sea. The tillable land averages around 14,000 feet in elevation. The terms Dalai Lama, Royal-ba Rinpo-che, mean the "Great Precious Conqueror." Close ties were maintained with Mongolia in the early years. This brought one political control to a vast area of Inner Asia at a time when the Chinese government was weak. So great was the power of the Tibetan Dalai Lama that the "Great Fifth" Dalai Lama built the majestic winter palace known as the **Potala Palace** in **Lhasa**.

In 1705, the Mongols overreached their friendly relationship, ousted the Dalai Lama and ruled Tibet on their own. China considered this a military threat, which led the Qing Emperor Kangxi to send an expedition to expel the Mongols. China claimed they were only helping the Tibetans, but in the end they left representatives who simply dominated the political sphere of Tibet for the next 200 years.

When the Qing (Manchu) Dynasty fell in the revolution of 1911, the thirteenth Dalai Lama led his people to expel the remaining Chinese. This restored the independent state of Tibet in 1912. When the thirteenth Dalai Lama died in 1933, there was a great search for a new one. A young boy, born in 1935 of Tibetan parents who were living in China, seemed to measure up to the qualifications for a Dalai Lama-Bodhisattva-god-king. He was enthroned in 1940, but Tibet soon encountered political problems.

The Communist forces took over China in 1949, and in the following year they began moving into Tibet, which they claimed was a part of China. There was no way the Dalai Lama--the spiritual head--or the Panchan Lama--the political head, could fight back the thousands of Chinese, who were well-trained, well-equipped, and seasoned soldiers, who began occupying Tibet. The Dalai Lama reached an agreement with the Chinese which allowed their army to occupy Tibet, but left the political-religious organization intact.

The true story of this occupation varies greatly depending upon whether you follow the Tibetan account or the one given by the Chinese. Apparently, the Tibetans would not cooperate with China on plans such as the collectivization of agriculture. This led the Chinese government to assume control of the political sphere. The Dalai Lama's situation was complicated by several factors. First, Tibet had no real army. Secondly, there had been many Communists who had already infiltrated his country.

The third problem was that the other leading nations of the world were deeply involved in the war in Vietnam and the struggle to keep communism out of Southeast Asia. Everyone felt sorry for Tibet, but the Dalai Lama received no support to expel the Chinese. At that point the Dalai Lama and at least 80,000 of his followers fled to India and Nepal. The Dalai Lama considers himself the leader of a government in exile with headquarters in Dharamsala in northern India. He thoroughly expects to return some day to rule Tibet. Although China is firmly entrenched and has no intention of leaving. Tibetan monks continue to agitate against the Chinese but their struggle has little chance of success at this time.

OTHER RELIGIOUS FAITHS IN TIBET

THE MANICHAEANS

During the years that Tibet was on good terms with Mongolia, the area of their control reached across the Old Silk Road. This brought the Tibetans into contact with several other religious ideas. Among these were the religious teachings of the **Manichaeans**. This religion originated in Persia (Iran) as one of the odd combinations of Christianity and the old Persian religions. The Manichaeans said that Jesus and Mani were both prophets who preached that the world is filled with cosmic conflict between the good--the realm of light, and the evil--the realm of darkness. The lusts of the flesh come from the realm of darkness. Therefore, everyone should become an ascetic. They also believed that all matter was inherently evil. This religion was popular during the last years of the Roman Empire. It arrived in Tibet from the western traders who operated on the Old Silk Road.

NESTORIAN CHRISTIANITY

The **Nestorian** religious faith also came into Tibet via the traders on the Old Silk Road. Nestorius was a patriarch in Constantinople during the 5th century. He taught that a divine and a human personality were joined in Jesus Christ in a perfect harmony of action. The Nestorians claimed that Mary, the mother of Jesus, was a very human person and should not be called the Mother of God. This doctrine was totally unacceptable to the Roman Catholic Church. The teachings of Nestorius were condemned, but the faith had many followers in Central Asia.

THE INFLUENCE OF HINDU SCIENCE ON RELIGION

The Hindus believed that "if a thing is worth doing, it is worth doing well." They probed the very depths of everything, even to the point of actually splitting a hair. Hindu science was superior to most aspects of western science prior to the 17th century. Hindu scientists and religious leaders alike probed the mind and the relationship of mind and body. Some aspects of Yoga delved deeply into the control of bodily functions by the mind. They trained themselves to stop breathing, to stop the heart, and to reverse the flow of digestion. They also studied the weather and the movement of the planets.

The Basics of Buddhism

The inquiring minds of the Hindus probed into the secrets of sex with the same frank, open-minded thoroughness which characterized their conduct when dealing with astronomy, physics, medicine, architecture, or mind-body control. They imposed no crippling taboos on their research nor did they feel in any way inhibited when talking of sex or matters allied to the sexual processes. To them, sex was a normal function of nature, and, like all other functions of nature, there was a great deal about it which was hidden and mysterious. Like all their other scientific inquiries, they were curious about sex.

The frankness of the Hindu findings are outlined in the popular Indian book, **The Kamasutra of Vatsyayana**. The Hindu interest in sexual matters is also vividly and realistically displayed through the stone carvings on the temples at **Khajuraho**. Several of these portray amorous couples engaged in sexual acts in a variety of poses. It is said that the ectasy on the faces of the couples symbolizes the supreme bliss resulting from the union of the male and the female principles of the universe. But matters of sexual inquiry and the power of sexual union goes back to scenes uncovered at Mohenjo Daro and the Copper Age in India. And, it is not only in India that such scenes have been found. These are found all over Asia and in many parts of Europe. It was the Medieval church which imposed the Christian taboo on open sexual discussion.

It is important to note that the Khajuraho temples are located only eighty miles from the very center of Tantric Buddhism in India, the same variety which next went to Tibet. The Khajuraho temples were built by both Hindu and Jain sponsorship during the 11th and 12th centuries, a time when Tantrism was quite popular in Tibet. It is little wonder that the mysticism of sexual union should become a part of the Tibetan plan of meditation.

A SUMMARY OF TANTRISM IN TIBET

Tantrism in Tibet is a very complex religion. Its earliest foundations reach back to the animistic Bon religion of the Tibetan people. This was combined with the regular Mahayana Buddhism with a strong emphasis upon the monastic ideal. It incorporated the Tantrism drawn partly from some branches of Hinduism and from the later years of Buddhism in India. Tibetan Tantrism was also influenced by the Manichaeans and the Nestorians who traveled on the Old Silk Road. The concept of the guru as a lama was borrowed from the Hindus and the Buddhists of India, but the idea of the lamas as reincarnated former lamas is a Tibetan one. The use of mantras and mandalas were not entirely new, since they were used by both the Indian Hindus and Buddhists. The employment of a tanka to unravel the mysteries of the faith seems to have originated in Tibet. Tibetan Tantrism is probably one of the more difficult religions for the westerner to understand, largely because it is made up of so many complex beliefs which were borrowed from various sources.

THE ROLE OF WOMEN IN BUDDHISM

The role of women in the Buddhist faith is very different from either Hinduism or Christianity. Buddha taught that all human beings are equal, men and women, rich and poor alike, and that racial differences do not matter. There were evidently several women who followed his teachings during his lifetime. He said that women were capable of enlightenment the same as men. This was very different from the Hindu belief that women could **not** achieve moksha, rather they must be reborn as men if they ever hoped to attain this high goal.

The equality of women was a major stumbling block for the Hindu men. But for Buddhist women, it opened a whole new horizon. Women now had several options other than marriage. Women could join a monastery, they could teach, or they could preach. They could do all kinds of social work. None of this was open to a single woman within Hinduism. Hindu women were expected to marry and to have children, and to care for their husbands and their family.

Buddhists viewed spouses as "near equals." Buddhists thought that the man was still the head of the household simply because someone must head it. All responsibility within the household should be equally shared. Decisions on almost every topic could and should be shared. Married women were allowed to inherit property and widows could remarry. The Hindu practice of suttee was totally out of the question.

REASONS FOR THE DECLINE OF BUDDHISM IN INDIA

Hinduism was the universal faith in India when Buddhism came upon the scene. Upper class Hindus viewed Buddha as a Kshatriya prince from northern India who could not wait to be reborn as a Brahman. He therefore left his home and family to seek enlightenment on his own. The Hindus would agree that Buddha was a very wise man, but he should have remained a Hindu, and should have worked within that faith. Since his doctrine was so very different, he was guilty of leading many good people astray. Buddha's greatest error, the Hindus said, was that he opposed caste and that he believed that women could become equal members of the faith. This, was pure heresy to an orthodox Hindu. They believed that such ideas would lead to class revolution and the destruction of the social order. Be patient, the Hindu would counsel, and your opportunity will come through reincarnation. Rather than begin a militant campaign against the Buddhists, the Hindus elected to simply wait until such heretical ideas would fade away. As people became disenchanted they would return to the Hindu majority.

Although the Buddhists had no other ruler who was as active in their support as Ashoka, they were still doing well at the opening of the 7th century. Most of them were wealthy and the religious institutions owned a great amount of property. At the same time that their religious fervor waned--since they felt very secure--their support by kings and princes disappeared. The Mauryan Empire, 321-185 B.C. was generally a good time. The Gupta Age, 320-499, saw a great revival of Hinduism. The Buddhists were too slow to revive their movement and to confront the obstacles which began to appear. By the 11th or 12th century the Hindu pressures upon the Buddhists in India became quite strong. By the 16th century there were very few Buddhists remaining in the subcontinent.

Beyond the revival of Hinduism as the true faith in India, a second threat came with the invasion of the Huns, who showed no respect for either Hinduism or Buddhism. Since Buddhism was not as firmly entrenched in India, they suffered the greater loss. The third challenge came from the invasions by the Muslims in the 11th and the 12th centuries. They destroyed both Hindu and Buddhist religious sites, often replacing them with a Muslim building on the same location. Islam dealt the final blow to Buddhism in India.

The Basics of Buddhism

SUMMARIZING BUDDHISM

Buddhism began when a young Hindu prince named Siddhartha Gautama left his worldly life behind in the "Great Renunciation" to seek truth and enlightenment. None of the routes which he tried gave him enlightenment until one night it all became very clear--Siddhartha Gautama became the Enlightened One, the Buddha. There were Four Noble Truths. Mankind is doomed to be born, to suffer, and to die in an endless cycle. This can be broken and Nirvana can be achieved if the individual will give up desire and follow the Eightfold Path. He taught this "Middle Path" to his disciples who he instructed to pass the plan of salvation on to others.

The faith grew slowly in the first 250 years after the death of Buddha. The simple plan became much more complex as the years passed. The Hinayana, or Theravada, approach was conservative and puritanical. It tried to follow the teachings of Buddha as the monks understood them. The Mahayana approach was much broader and less demanding of the lay followers. Those who became monks were, of course, held to higher standards. Mahayana Buddhists stressed the value of belonging to a monastery, at least for some time, and doing many good works. The most complex of all the approaches came to be known as Tantrism, sometimes referred to as Lamaism in Tibet.

Buddhism originated in northeast India on the border with Nepal. It spread to the northwest into Kashmir, followed the Old Silk Road into Tibet, China, Korea, and Japan. The faith enjoyed its finest hour in India under the emperor Ashoka of India. In the later years of his reign he sent his son as a missionary to Sri Lanka. Buddhism moved into the entire Southeast Asian area from Sri Lanka. Even though it gathered millions of followers in eastern and southeastern Asia, it had no attraction for the peoples of Europe or Africa until recent times. It is also interesting that there are very few Buddhists today in the country where it all began, India.

BOOKS FOR FURTHER READING ABOUT BUDDHISM

Bechert, Heinz, & Gombrich, Richard, editors, *The World of Buddhism* (1984).

Burtt, E.A., editor, *The Teachings of the Compassionate Buddha* (1955).

Campbell, Joseph, *The Masks of God: Oriental Mythology* (1962).

Carmody, D.L., & Carmody, J.T., *Ways to the Center* (1993).

Ch'en, Kenneth K.S., *Buddhism, the Light of Asia* (1968).

Drege, Jean-Pierre, & Buhrer, E.M., *The Silk Road Saga* (1986).

Fenton, John Y., *et. al.*, *Religions of Asia* (1988).

Gettelman, Nancy Moore, *The Himalayan Journey of Buddhism* (1989).

Guenther, Herbert, *Buddhist Philosophy in Theory & Practice.*

The Basics of Buddhism

Guenther, H., & Trungpa, Chogyam, Edited by Michael Kohn, *The Dawn of Tantra* (1988).

Hume, Robert, *The World's Living Religions*.

Kalupahana, David, *Buddhist Philosophy, A Historical Analysis*.

Kitagawa, Joseph M., editor, *The Religious Traditions of Asia* (1989).

Mascaro, Juan, translator, *The Dhamapada: The Path of Perfection*.

Parrinder, Geoffrey, *World Religions from Ancient History to the Present* (1985).

Rao, Nina, Photos by Storm, K.R., & Van Gruisen, J., *Ladakh* (1989).

Rajavaramuni, Phra, *Thai Buddhism in the Buddhist World* (1984).

Ross, F.H., & Hills, T., *The Great Religions by Which Men Live* (1956).

Smith, Huston, *The Religions of Man* (1986).

Thondup, Tulku, Translator, *Enlightened Living: Teachings of Tibetan Buddhist Masters* (1990).

Walpola Sri Rahula, *What the Buddha Taught* (1967).

Watson, Francis, *A Concise History of India* (1979).

Zwalf, W., *Buddhism, Art and Faith* (1985).

Figure 16

Chapter 13
ZOROASTRIANISM

This religion is different from the other religions of India because it began outside India and came into the country, not by conquerors as did Islam, but by **refugees** who were fleeing persecution in their native Persia--modern Iran. The Indians garbled the word applied to these people which should have been "Persian," and called them **Parsis**, also known as **Parsees**.

While most religious faiths have been based on either one god--**monotheism**--or many gods--**polytheism**--this religion stresses the importance of **two** great forces in the world. One of these is the God of **Good** who they call **Ahura Mazda** or ORMUZD, and the other is the God of **Evil** who they call **Angra Mainyu** or AHRIMAN. Such a concept of world forces is called "**Dualism**."

The environment of ancient Persia was a harsh place to make a living in agricultural pursuits. Many people prayed and made offerings to a multitude of gods in order that their crops would grow, their animals would stay healthy, and the people might prosper. It was a kind of demanding nature worship they had created. But most people were required to spend long hours tending their crops and animals; they could not afford to spend very much time praying and making offerings. Therefore, a priestly class, developed composed of men who were supposed to know the correct prayers to be made for everyone in the tribe, thus freeing the majority for manual labor. Since the priests often performed **magic** to accomplish all the good things the people wanted, these men were referred to as the **Magi**.

According to the Zoroastrian legends, in the year 660 B.C., the chief magician in Persia, a man named **Durasan** had a dream that a child had been born who would grow up to destroy idol worship, banish sorcery, and end magic. Durasan soon discovered that the child had already been born to parents of the Spitama clan in the city of Azarbijan, and that he had been named **Zarathustra**. It was the Greeks who much later changed Zarathustra to Zoroaster. The word Zarathustra means "one who possesses golden camels."

As far as the chief magician Durasan was concerned, this young man was a threat to his own position as a Magi as well as to all of those who made their living making idols. The magicians and idol makers immediately set out to find the young man. When Durasan and his followers found Zarathustra, they took him to the temple and placed him on the blazing fire of the altar. To their surprise, the child played happily in the flames as though he were sitting in lukewarm water. Not content, they next placed him in the path of a large herd of cattle. The first cow that came near Zarathustra stood over him while the entire herd passed around on every side and he emerged uninjured. Still one more effort was made to eliminate the child--they abandoned him in a den of wolves. Miraculously, none of the hungry wolves even came near him. Durasan and his followers were truly amazed, but they continued to put him to the test for some time.

By the time Zarathustra was old enough for school, his parents sent him to learn the art of healing. He then went out to minister to the poor and the sick among his people. While he made his daily rounds, he began to reflect upon the health and disease dilemma. He considered joy and sorrow, life and death, light and darkness, and good and evil.

Zoroastrianism

During the years Zarathustra practiced healing, he had married and had children. But as more time passed, these eternal questions begged for an answer. Finally he told his wife, **Havovee**, that he wanted to go to the top of Mount Sabalan to live as a hermit and to seek answers to these nagging questions. No one knows for sure how long he was living in a state of solitude. Some say that he left his family at age 20 and spent the next 10 years in his search. Still, he found little in concrete answers. Then it suddenly came to him that "From good must come good, and from evil must come evil." The good cannot create evil nor can evil create good even though they try magic and prayer. These two forces created a state of **dualism**.

Zarathustra, however, did not believe in eternal dualism. He believed that the God of Good, **Ahura Mazda**, who had created the world with purifying fire, cleansing water, fruitful earth and sweet smelling air, was at war with the God of Evil, creator of sickness and pestilence, pain and death. If people would do good and ally themselves with Ahura Mazda, they would be able to triumph over **Angra Mainyu**, the God of Evil, and then only the God of Good will rule the world. But it is important to remember that the God of Good needs mankind to help him conquer evil.

Even though Zarathustra was beginning to sort out his beliefs, he stayed in his mountain retreat for some time. The revelations he received during the ten-year search were later to be called the **Gathas**. And, many other revelations came to Zarathustra, the most notable one included a face-to-face meeting with Ahura Mazda. In this meeting he was told that there would be **a Day of Judgment** and Good would triumph over Evil. As soon as he had all these things organized in his own thinking, he decided to return to the people to preach **the faith of Mazda**, a religion which would lead the world from darkness to light, from suffering to joy, and from evil to good.

Although the entire religion was abundantly clear to Zarathustra, the people preferred to continue to pay the Magi rather than to believe in his new religion. Not even his own family would follow him in renouncing the old polytheistic gods. After trying unsuccessfully to gain a following over a ten-year period he decided to move on to Balkh, a city in Bactria, where he asked for an audience with the king.

"And who are you?" asked the guards at the Royal Palace of King Vishtaspa.
"Go, and tell King Vishtaspa that I, Spitama Zarathustra, have come to preach the True Religion, the religion of the Holy One, Ahura Mazda, and to turn him and his court away from the worship of idols to the worship of the Beneficient One."
And as a sign that he was the True Phophet of Ahura Mazda, Zarathustra stretched out his right hand. In his palm a ball of fire burned brightly, yet the hand was not burned.
The guard went at once to inform King Vishtaspa. And the King said, "Go, bring him in!"

The king called a meeting which included the High Priest, the other Magi, and all the learned men of the kingdom. They asked Zarathustra the most difficult questions imaginable, such as "when would all the world become good?" Zarathustra answered that men must first ally themselves with Ahura Mazda. As the king's best magicians began an even deeper cross-examination, Zarathustra began relating his personal revelation with Ahura Mazda and quoted the conversations verbatim and in the third person.

When King Vishtaspa had heard all of Zarathustra's revelations, he called in the Royal Scribes and ordered them to write down on parchment all that Zarathustra had related. The

Zoroastrianism

resulting writings became the book called the *Zend-Avesta*, which means the Law and Commentaries. This has been the holy book of the Zoroastrians ever since this time.

By the end of the 7th century B.C., the Zoroastrian faith was quite well established in Persia--by the 7th century A.D. it had almost disappeared. Zoroastrianism therefore had its peak during the middle of this 1400-year period. Their greatest enemies were first the Greeks and then the Muslims.

The greatest period of Greek interest in this religion came during the time of the Greek historian Herodotus and the philosophers Plato and Aristotle. Although the faith was a matter of great curiosity for a time in the western world, it never really caught on. Renewed interest by the West did not revive until early in the 18th century, when some of the English, who were stationed in India, obtained a copy of the *Zend-Avesta*. It was largely a matter of curiosity at that time, and they failed to take the time to translate it. Ultimately it ended up in a collection of "books of a strange nature" at the Bodleian Library at Oxford University. A French language scholar who was visiting the library happened to notice the book and decided to learn how to read it. This man was Anquetil Duperon. Duperon traveled to India, lived among the Parsis for ten years and translated a copy for the French Royal Library. It was soon translated from the French into several of the modern languages.

The best we can tell from the sources now available, Zarathustra was about 42 at the time he converted King Vishtaspa. Once the religion was established, it soon spread south into Persia and as far west as Greece. It is said that the Greek philosopher Aristotle was very much interested in the faith. Ironically, it was Aristotle's student, Alexander the Great, who was the first to persecute the sect by ordering all the copies of the *Zend-Avesta* burned so he could replace the Zoroastrian faith with that of the Greek gods and goddesses.

After the death of Alexander, the Greek influence in Persia soon waned and the *Zend-Avesta* was reconstructed from a few remaining fragments and from memory. For the next several years the religion again flourished until another adversary arrived on the scene--Islam. It had been Muhammed's goal to establish the Muslim faith in the Arabian peninsula, but his successors set out to conquer the whole world in the name of Allah. By the middle of the 7th century A.D. the Muslims had conquered Persia and they immediately began persecuting the followers of Zarathustra. Again, the *Zend-Avesta* was destroyed and many people were killed for their faith. Several Persians decided to escape to India and they took their religious faith with them. This is the origin of the **Parsis** in India today. There are only about 140,000 in the world and about 115,000 of these live in Bombay and the surrounding area.

WHAT THE ZOROASTRIANS BELIEVE

The first principle of the Zoroastrian religion is that the world was created with both good and evil. All good things have come from **Ahura Mazda** and all bad or evil things are from **Angra Mainyu**. All of mankind was created by Ahura Mazda. Each person is given **the power of free will** to choose between good and evil. If all of mankind would only ally themselves with Ahura Mazda, than Angra Mainyu would be conquered.

Zoroastrianism

If any person wishes to become an ally of Ahura Mazda, it is required that they must first cleanse their heart and mind of all evil. It is quite proper to pray to Ahura Mazda to make us better or happier, but one should never pray for evil against someone else.

All Zoroastrians believe in the "Day of Judgment." That is when all the followers of the faith will share a happy, joyous life here on earth. It will really be a kind of heaven here on earth. When we die, both the good people and the evil ones will have to cross a bridge. The good people will all go on to heaven and those who do evil will fall off the bridge into the dark pit of hell. It is therefore very important for each of us to discipline ourselves to have only good thoughts, good words, and good deeds.

The Zoroastrians believe that the man who has a wife is far above the ones who do not. Those who have children are far above those who do not. Zarathustra said that at the end of time there would be a savior, a *Sayhoshant* who would revive all the dead. At this time those who did good would be rewarded but those who did evil would be punished. And, once the savior, Ahura Mazda, has arrived, he will reign forever more.

One of the important Zoroastrian ideals was to achieve ahimsa. This is virtually unattainable in this world where there is such an abundance of evil. Nevertheless, we can continue to cherish the thoughts well thought, the word well spoken, and the deed well done.

Zarathustra strongly condemned two of the three forms of sacrifice most prevalent in his age. He detested all sacrifices involving blood. He was completely opposed to the drinking of Soma during sacrifices, a practice which evidently was common throughout the Middle East at this time.

The third sacrifice, which **was** retained, was the fire sacrifice. Zoroaster said that fire was the only true path to immortality because it was the symbol of Justice. Because Ahura Mazda created fire, water, and earth, none of these should be polluted by man. Therefore, it is improper to either burn or bury the dead. This is why the Parsis utilize giant silo-like structures known as **"Towers of Silence"** or **"Towers of Peace."**

According to the religious practice of the Parsis, once a death has occurred, a dog is brought before the corpse. It should be a "four-eyed" dog, that is, it should have a spot above each eye because the Zoroastrians believe that this increases the efficacy of its look. The rite should be repeated five times a day. After the first time, fire is brought into the room, where it is kept burning until three days after the removal of the corpse to the Tower of Silence. The removal of the body to the Tower must be done only during the daylight hours.

The interior of the Tower of Silence is composed of platforms built in three concentric circles--one each for men, women, and children. The corpses are exposed naked on these platforms within the silo. The birds then enter the open-topped towers and pick the flesh from the bones, usually within an hour or two. The bones are allowed to dry in the sun within the tower. They are then swept from the platforms into the central well. In earlier years, the bones were kept in an ossuary known as the **astodian** to preserve them from rain and the animals. The use of the ossuary is no longer practiced today. The Parsis consider this manner of disposing of the dead as non-polluting.

Zoroastrianism

The morning of the fourth day is marked by the most solemn observance of the entire death ritual. On this day the Parsis believe that the departed soul reaches the next world and appears before the deities who will then pass judgment over it.

LATER INTERPRETATIONS

Like all the other great religions, Zoroastrianism has changed a great deal over the years. Since the time of Zarathustra, they have become experts in dream interpretations, astrology, and magic. The religion stirred considerable discussion and conflict right from its inception. The old priests of the Magi constantly worked to make the new faith look ridiculous. It is said that Zarathustra was murdered by a priest of the old religion when he was 77 years of age. Even though Zarathustra was very strict in interpreting the faith to his followers, he always claimed to be a prophet. He never assumed any god-like stance. Almost immediately after Zarathustra's death, his followers believed they would have to make compromises with the old religions in order to salvage a part of their new one. Many changes and interpretations have followed.

Zarathustra taught in a form of Middle Persian called **Pahlavi**. As was mentioned earlier, when he converted King Vishtaspa, the court scribes wrote down the first form of the *Zend-Avesta*. But with the death of Zarathustra, the destruction of the *Zend-Avesta* and other early writings by both the Greeks and later the Muslims meant that what remains to us today is very likely **not** what the faith was about over 2600 years ago.

The last great pre-Islamic empire which ruled over Persia from A.D. 224 to 651 was known as the **Sasanid Emprie**. During this period, Zoroastrianism was the official state religion and many more changes came about. This period saw the first major editing of the *Zend-Avesta*, and at the same time the holy book was also provided with a commentary in Pahlavi, the vernacular of Persia in those years. There were many men who had revelations and wrote about their beliefs during the Sasanid period.

One of the interpretations since Zarathustra is the belief that the history of the world has been divided into four periods of 3,000 years each. In the first period the world was not yet created. At this stage everything was embryonic and perfect. During the second stage the sky, sun, moon, and stars were created. It was following this time that primeval man appeared and was called "Mortal Life." During this second stage, the ox also appeared, and the ox was able to create other things. Interestingly, evil first appeared with the arrival of mankind during this second stage.

The third period saw evil rise up in triumph and kill both man and ox. The fourth period saw the beginning of religion and the birth of Zarathustra. After these four periods, the Zoroastrians predicted there would be a new savior who would appear as a descendant of Zarathustra. Zoroastrians also believe there will be successive saviors every millenia until the last savior will bring about the Last Judgment and the advent of a new world.

At the time of Zarathustra, young people were initiated into the faith at about the age of fifteen. That has now dropped to seven in an effort to save more of the young people for the faith before they go astray. The ceremony of binding the sacred girdle is called *kusti*, which means the newborn, and from this time forward the young person is expected to be responsible for his or her actions. A strong emphasis is placed on maintaining all the laws of purity as set forth by the faith so the individual does not fall under the spell of Angra Mainyu, the Evil One.

Many of the Parsi concepts of heaven, hell, salvation, the Good Shepherd, resurrection, and the last judgment were developed many years before very similar ideas were incorporated into Judaism, Christianity, and Islam. Their idea of a bridge to heaven as in Islam, was hundreds of years before Muhammed. From the beginning of the faith, prayer was recommended five times daily. The Zoroastrians began the religious concept that each person will be judged after death according to the Book of Life, which is a record of all the good things and all the bad things which have occurred during one's lifetime. It is this record which determines the eternal destiny of each individual. Judaism, Christianity, and Islam all have adopted some variation of this concept. Zoroastrians celebrate several holidays throughout the year, some of which are remarkably like the Jewish, Christian, and Muslim holidays.

IN SUMMARY

Most of the Parsis in India today are businessmen and professionals. They hold responsible positions, but they do not represent a growing religious group, since most Parsis have small families, they do not accept converts, and many of their young people are marrying out of the faith. There are more Parsis in India--about 115,000--than in any other country. Although there are several in Iran, they have been persecuted there ever since the Muslims took over what was then known as Persia in A.D. 651. Other than their religious beliefs, they have been quite thoroughly Indianized, just as most other immigrants to India.

BOOKS FOR FURTHER READING

Campbell, Joseph, *The Masks of God: Oriental Mythology* (1962).

Basham, A. L., *The Wonder That Was India* (1984).

de Bary, Wm. Theodore, editor, *Sources of Indian Tradition* (1958).

Carmody, D. L. & Carmody, J. T., *Ways to the Center* (1993).

Parrinder, Geoffrey, editor, *World Religions* (1983).

Rawlinson, H. G., *India: A Short Cultural History* (1952).

Thapar, Romila, *A History of India* (1966).

Tinker, Hugh, *South Asia, A Short History* (1966).

Chapter 14
THE HISTORY OF INDIA FROM THE IRON AGE THROUGH ASHOKA

INTRODUCTION

It continues to be difficult to untangle the political and economic history of India just before the time of Buddha, during his lifetime, and immediately thereafter. It should be clear with the discussions on Hinduism, Jainism, Buddhism, and Zoroastrianism that the people of the subcontinent considered religion the most important single factor in their lives. The period preceding the time of Ashoka in 273 B.C. is always difficult to portray in a very accurate manner. The names of the political rulers, geographic boundaries of the various states, and the economic conditions of the subcontinent always took second place to religion.

In general, northern and eastern India had four great kingdoms in those years. They were **Kosala, Vatsa, Avanti,** and **Magadha**. There is more information about Maghada than any of the others. Southern India seems to have been organized into an even larger number of small kingdoms. A reasonably safe generalization is that all of these kingdoms were ruled by strong-men who seized power by violent means, then used their power for their own purposes.

It is also known that these militarily inclined rulers had little or no administrative ability. There is good evidence that their kingdoms were poorly organized with many of the taxes being raised by force. Each one concentrated largely on expansion of his own kingdom. None of them could afford to administer a peaceful reign, since he would soon have been overrun by his neighbors. Several of them supported one or more of the holy men who roamed the Indian countryside in those years, hoping that the gods would be on their side. Some authors refer to this era as India's medieval period, since it has many of the same characteristics as the Medieval Age in the West. Among the differences between these two historic eras would be that the Indian Medieval Age occurred nearly 2,000 years before the western Medieval Age.

THE CULTURAL INTERACTION OF THE EAST

As Buddhism began to spread to Tibet, China, and Southeast Asia, the scholars of the faith in those areas wanted to return to the original sources. They believed those sources would be found in northern India and Sri Lanka. Interestingly, culture moved in both directions as this research was carried out. The Indian subcontinent had been quite isolated up to this point with oceans on two sides and the Himalayan Mountains separating them from the rest of Eurasia on the north. India began to learn the culture of the outside world and the outside world learned from India.

Among the things India began to learn from the world beyond their borders was a sense of political history outside and beyond the strictly religious approach given in the Vedas, the Upanishads, the Ramayana, etc. The Age of the Vedas drew to a close and a new era began to emerge with these outside contacts.

INDIA AT THE TIME OF ALEXANDER THE GREAT

The kingdom of **Maghada** was one of sixteen ancient North Indian states traditionally mentioned in Buddhist sources. Its center was located in what is now Bihar state. Strategically situated along the middle Ganges, Magadha dominated North India from the 6th century B.C. to the 8th century A.D.

According to the best available sources, the first famous king of Magadha was **Bimbisara**, who ruled from about 546 to 494 B.C. He built his capital at modern-day Rajgir, and consolidated his power through matrimonial alliances. By all accounts, he was a good administrator. His encouragement of trade on the Ganges led to general prosperity throughout northern India. Bimbisara's reign was terminated by his assassination by his son, who took over the area of Magadha sometime between 494 and 498 B.C.

A long succession of Magadhan rulers is given in various religious documents and it is interesting how many of their rulers were assassinated by their sons, who then succeeded them on the throne, a practice called **parricide**. It was the ruler Kaloshoka, who reigned from about 396 to 368 B.C., who moved the Magadhan capital to **Pataliputra**, modern-day Patna, on the Ganges River. A dynasty called the **Nandas** were ruling Magadha from 346 to about 324 B.C., and it was the Nanda forces which met the Greek and Macedonian forces who were invading the subcontinent under the leadership of Alexander the Great.

EAST MEETS WEST
THE BACKGROUND OF ALEXANDER THE GREAT

The dates of **Alexander of Macedon** are 356 to 323 B.C. He was the son of King Philip II and Olympias of Macedonia. Alexander also claimed that he was descended from the gods Herakles and Achilles. As a young man Alexander became infatuated with Greek mythology and the writings of Homer. He received the best education possible at the time, studying under several Greek scholars, and for a period of three years, he studied under the notable Aristotle.

Early in the reign of his father, Philip II, the process began of unifying the disjointed Greek city-states and joining them with Macedonia for the purpose of presenting a united front against the Achaemenid Dynasty, better known in western history as the **Persian Empire**. Even though the Greeks had defeated the Persians in 479 B.C., peace was not formally made until 449 B.C. There were many times when the two forces clashed during this thirty-year interval. The Greek city-states lived in constant fear the Persians would return and conquer them. This was especially true when the Greek city-states fell into a civil war known as the Peloponnesian War, 431 to 404 B.C. Philip II of Macedonia moved into the power vacuum following this war and began pulling the city-states into one confederation for the purpose of defeating the Persians. Philip's plans were almost ready for action when he was assassinated during his daughter's wedding party. The task of defeating the Persians then fell to his twenty-year-old son, Alexander.

Alexander spent the next couple of years establishing a power base in Macedonia and Greece, then he began his wars of conquest. He left Macedonia in 334 B.C. and for the next eleven years, he conquered the greatest empire which had been known up to that time. The war between Alexander and the Persians quickly became a battle between two great armies--the Greeks and Macedonians versus the Persians.

The Persian king, **Darius III**, fought hard and well, but Alexander continued to win victories and to expand his holdings within the Persian realm. It almost seemed that Alexander was either some kind of a god or under the supervision of a god as he won victory after victory, often against outstanding odds. And Alexander cultivated the image that he was a god as he swept through the remainder of Asia Minor, Syria, Phoenicia, the Holy Land, Egypt, on west as far as Lybia, then he resumed his march to the East. The fall of the Persian capital at Nineveh in 331 B.C. marked the end of the Persian Empire as an organized government. At this point he had accomplished what he had set out to do.

Had Alexander stopped at this point and consolidated his gains, he would be remembered as a great conqueror and a great ruler. However, he had a burning desire to push northeast from Persia, across Parthia and into Bactria in South-Central Asia. It is believed that he was driven by some, perhaps all of the following motives. Alexander wanted to be sure his empire encompassed **all** of what had ever been claimed by the Persians. Since they had claimed a portion of the Indus River valley, it meant that he would have to conquer that area before he could turn back.

Some have said that Alexander wanted to push beyond the Indus because he had heard that it was not very far to another sea, which he believed would make it possible to sail on around the world and return to Greece from the West. It should be mentioned that there were other Greeks at this time who believed the world was round. Others said that Alexander had been told that the Indus River crossed a vast desert and provided the source of the Nile River in Egypt. One of their reasons for believing this was that the Indus had crocodiles and so also did the Nile. In any event, there can be no denying Alexander's great interest (and ignorance) in geography.

One of the most important reasons Alexander wanted to conquer the eastern world was to spread the Greek culture throughout that area. Alexander had always been totally captivated by Greek culture, and he had inaugurated his plan by building a model city at one of the mouths of the Nile River. That city--Alexandria, Egypt--became an example of the greatest city of learning in the world for the next several centuries. It is known that he then founded at least **fourteen** more cities, all of which he named "Alexandria," scattered throughout his vast realm. The one which was the farthest to the northeast was in Bactria, several miles beyond the ancient city of Samarkand. The easternmost Alexandria in the subcontinent was founded in the area presently known as Kashmir. Through these several cities there developed a new **Hellenistic** style of art and literature. The one which was established in northern Pakistan and India was known as the **Gandharan School** of art.

ALEXANDER'S CONQUEST OF INDIA, 326 B.C.

Alexander the Great arrived in India by pretty much the same route as the other invaders--by way of the Hindu Kush mountains and the **Khyber Pass**. In order to prepare for the invasion of India in **326 B.C.**, Alexander sent the bulk of the Macedonian army under his close friend and companion, Hepaestion, over the Khyber Pass and on down the Indus River. Alexander took the remaining units on another route north of the Khyber Pass in order to secure the flank of his main army. The Macedonian forces encountered stiff opposition from the Indian hill peoples, but he successfully swept around, then rejoined Hephaestion, who had arrived ahead of him and had already succeeded in building a bridge across the Indus River.

By the time his army was consolidated in northern India, the men began saying that India extended on eastward to the end of the earth and was inhabited by giants and elephants. Perhaps this belief came as a consequence of their Indian adversary, King **Porus** of the Punjab. By all accounts Porus was a giant of a man who stood almost seven feet tall. The Punjabi army also used elephants, more elephants than the Macedonian forces had ever seen on any previous occasion. Of course Alexander loved the challenge of finding out whether India was really inhabited by giants and elephants.

The foot soldiers probably thought they had marched to the end of the earth by the time they had arrived in India. It is estimated that his army had marched 17,000 miles since they had left Macedonia. Still, the system of supply which had originated with his father, Philip II, was so efficient that they even received a fresh shipment of equipment which had been sent all the way from Macedonia. For day to day living, the Indus Valley and its tributaries were lush farmland at that time, and Alexander had no problem in obtaining food supplies at the local level.

His first target city was **Taxila**. The king of this area, who the Greeks called Taxiles, had already consented to join Alexander, so this was a logical place to locate a hub on the Indian side of the Khyber Pass. The Kashmir kings had also thrown in their lot with Alexander, which left only King Porus of the Indians as his first really great opponent.

Spring rains had caused flooding of the **Hyphasis** River, now known as the Beas, and King Porus, whose domains stretched eastward from the Hyphasis, took up a strong position across the river from Alexander's advancing army. His army numbered approximately 35,000 infantry, 4,000 cavalry, 300 war chariots, and 200 elephants. This seemed quite a formidable force to challenge in a frontal attack. Some of Alexander's officers had suggested crossing on rafts and defeating the enemy in a head-on battle. Instead, Alexander planned to take a portion of his army upstream under the cover of darkness with the intention of falling quickly upon Porus's flank.

In order to disguise this operation, Alexander had his men create a huge stockpile of material on his own side of the river. He assigned many of his men to building large rafts, presumably for the frontal attack on the Indian forces. Every night he launched some rafts while he moved his cavalry right to the shore. Porus responded by shifting his forces up and down his side of the river night after night in anticipation of an attack. Finally, Porus's men became weary of all of Alexander's deceptive moves and they just sat and waited for Alexander to attack.

This reaction was exactly what Alexander had hoped they would do. He had already selected a place where there was an island in midstream large enough to conceal his entire force if he should be surprised by Porus. Alexander then left the majority of his army in place facing Porus under a trusted officer named Craterus. Alexander then took a selected force of about 5,000 cavalry and 10,000 infantry, including many of his best skirmishers, and made the planned sweep around Porus's flank at night. This **Battle at the Hyphasis** has often been considered one of Alexander's best planned campaigns.

As Alexander left the main forces behind, he moved some distance back from the river bank in order that his men would not be detected by the Indian scouts. A heavy rainfall during the night further helped to muffle the noise of marching men. Alexander had already arranged to have boats and rafts moved to the crossing point. Everything was assembled to move across the river at dawn. The ability of Alexander's engineers to construct, in sections, a fleet large enough to transport a force of about 15,000 men and 5,000 horses continues to amaze modern military historians.

Alexander personally led the flotilla in a thirty-oared boat, which towed a raft bearing the royal foot soldiers. When they passed the end of the island, they were spotted by the Indian scouts, who rushed back to inform Porus. The Macedonians made a mistake that night which could have proven fatal. Instead of disembarking on the eastern shore of the Hyphasis River, they found themselves on yet another island. Rather than re-assemble and float across the remaining channel, they decided to ford the remainder of the river, a very difficult task for armed men. There were some deep places where the water was up to the horses' necks.

Porus now knew that he had two Macedonian armies to fight, but he did not know which one was the larger. He first spent too much time deciding how many men he would send against Alexander's force on the east side of the river and how many he would keep for a frontal attack. In his final decision, Porus sent too few men under his son. The force sent to meet Alexander advancing along the riverbank was only 2,000 cavalry and 120 chariots. Evidently Porus believed this was only a feint to distract his attention. His son's forces ran into trouble right away. The heavy rain during the night caused the chariots considerable trouble as they were often stuck in the mud. When the two forces clashed, the Indians lost 400 cavalry and all the chariots they had sent in this contingent. Even more importantly, Porus's son was killed in the engagement. It had been a case of too little, too late, and with the wrong kind of equipment for the situation.

At the same time as Alexander closed in on Porus's main force, the Macedonian troops began crossing all along the river front. The next mistake Porus made was to ignore the Macedonians who were crossing the river, evidently believing that Alexander had the bulk of his army on the eastern shore already. He turned his army to engage Alexander's small but victorious army and allowed the main Macedonian center to cross and to engage his forces from their rear.

The Indian army quickly re-deployed to meet this new situation. Porus placed his infantry in the center and his cavalry on the wings--about 30,000 infantry and about 2,000 cavalry on each wing. The elephants were positioned about 50 feet apart in front of his infantry in a line stretching for almost two miles. He placed 150 chariots on each wing and ahead of the infantry. The really frightening thing for both the Macedonian men and their horses were the huge elephants with armed men on their backs.

This was a crucial moment in the battle! Had Alexander made even a small error he could easily have been destroyed. He decided to push the Macedonian infantry forward towards Porus's center and then to hold at that point. His plan was to fight the main battle with cavalry tactics by moving sizeable numbers of his own cavalry right along the Hyphasis River. They were now facing the left flank of the Indian army which was under the command of King Porus.

As Porus saw this action taking place, he shifted his right cavalry section around behind his infantry to counter the Macedonian cavalry so they could not slip between the Indian forces and the river. This action left very few Indian cavalry on the Indian right. As the Indians saw their cavalry ride around behind them, it is believed the infantry took this as a sign to retreat, and they began to do so. This major shift in defense by the Indians allowed their lines to break just enough for Alexander's forces to get behind the rear of Porus's army, and all the way across to the Indians' right flank. At this same moment, Alexander's cavalry launched a frontal attack upon the Indians' right flank.

Porus's army was then caught between two of Alexander's best cavalry units. Alexander's cavalry drove hard against the Indian lines and they began to fall back in confusion. By this time Alexander's infantry closed in around the elephants so they were caught in the center of the battle and unable to maneuver. At this point the elephants began to panic and in their fright they trampled more Indian infantrymen than even the Macedonians were able to put out of the battle. Many of the elephants lost their riders as the huge beasts stood up on their hind legs. Now, without riders or direction, the elephants began moving towards the rear as the Macedonians poured a heavy fire into the still tightly massed Indian infantry. Alexander ordered his infantry to lock shields and to attack.

There were still several Macedonian troops on the west side of the river as a reserve. These men crossed the river and began pursuing the fleeing Indians. Twenty thousand Indian infantry and three thousand cavalry fell in the Battle of the Hyphasis. Porus lost two more of his sons in this battle against the Macedonian forces. Alexander calculated his losses at about 300 men. The brave Indian leader continued to fight to the very end. He was ultimately wounded, but did not flee the battle site. Alexander later had him brought to his camp. He asked Porus how he would like to be treated. Porus replied, "as a king." Alexander was so impressed by his bravery that he allowed him to rule northern India jointly with Taxiles.

The Battle of the Hyphasis was Alexander's last great pitched battle. The word of this battle spread among the Indians and there was no major prince or king who was willing to challenge him. Shortly after the men had rested from this hard battle, Alexander announced that he wanted to push on east until he found the end of the earth. By this time the men thought they were already far enough from Macedonia and Greece. A three-day standoff ensued as Alexander tried to convince his men how important it was to push on. Ultimately, the mortified Alexander gave in and turned his army back west. There were still many confrontations along the way from small local Indian armies, but no more major battles. His army suffered terribly as they crossed the Gedrosian Desert of southern Persia, now Pakistan and Iran. It is probably a miracle that anyone survived all of the travels and the many battles.

There can be little doubt that Alexander the Great wanted to Hellenize India and to rule over it. Had he stayed there and become an Indian ruler, he would probably have wanted to push on eastward as soon as he could gather an army which would be willing to follow him. Before he left the Punjab he founded two cities. **Nicea**, which means "Victory," was established on the battlefield where he had defeated Porus. The second city he named **Bucephla** at the point where he had begun to cross the Hyphasis River. Bucephla was so named because the horse which he had ridden throughout all his campaigns, "Buccephalus," had died of exhaustion and old age along the riverbank. He also created three new provinces, which he called *satrapies*, to link his Indian conquests to the remainder of his empire. Taxila was given control of the area near the strategic Khyber Pass. Porus was given control of the Upper Indus in the area of the Hyphasis River, a tributary of the Indus River. The third area included the territory around the mouth of the Indus, which Alexander named the Sind.

India From the Iron Age Through Ashoka

The cities in these three areas were garissoned with Macedonian and Greek veterans of the 120,000-man army of Alexander. Once Alexander had departed from the Indus areas, the generals he had left behind became nervous and restless about what they considered an untenable position so far from relief and in a hostile country. Some of these generals considered their positions so dangerous that they packed up and moved back to Asia Minor even before Alexander's death in 323 B.C. Within a decade after Alexander's famous victory, there were only a few Macedonian and Greek troops left in India.

THE LEGACY OF ALEXANDER THE GREAT IN INDIA

Alexander's conquests changed the course of world cultural history by producing a fusion of Greek and Eastern civilizations. We call this new era the **Hellenistic Age** in western history. It was no longer strictly Hellenic (Greek), it was a **new** Hellenistic (Greek-like) civilization. In the long run, his venture into India was of less importance than was the Greek influence in other parts of Asia, such as the Near East. There was at first a real interchange of cultures between the cities he founded as new Alexandrias, but even this grew dim with time. Within a hundred years of Alexander's conquest, the impact was pretty well diminished in the East. Perhaps his campaigns had a greater impact upon the West, particularly in mathematics and in medicine.

Alexander had provided more stable settlements in Bactria--present-day Afghanistan--and in South-Central Asia, than he had in India. He had originally left this area under the control of Euthydemus, a Greek, and it was Euthydemus's son, Demetrius, who began a re-conquest of India in 180 B.C. Demetrius established a Greek-Indian dominion within his conquered area in cooperation with the descendants of Ashoka. Alexander's city of Nicea had already disappeared by this time. Bucephala thrived as a trading center for some time, then it too vanished so completely that neither city has ever been positively located.

Demetrius encouraged many of the Bactrian Greeks to settle as far east in India as the Ganges River area. Most of these Bactrian Greeks lived between the Kabul Valley in modern Afghanistan and the Hyphasis River in the Gandhara area. They brought their Greek gods and culture into India, but were eventually cut off from the West by Chinese nomadic invaders known as the Kushans in the first century A.D. Most of these Greeks, now surrounded by Indian influences, were absorbed by the Indian culture. Still, it is significant that Greek-thinking people stayed in this area for about three hundred years. There is no way to measure the cultural impact which transpired during these centuries.

THE GANDHARAN PERIOD AND THE KUSHANS

One of the most important developments which occurred as an outgrowth of Alexander's Indian campaign was the Indo-Hellenistic school of art known as the **Gandharan School**, which was referred to earlier. This style of Indo-Hellenistic art flourished in northwestern India, Pakistan, and Afghanistan from the 1st to the 5th century A.D. Much of the Gandharan art was directed toward visualizing Buddhism. Prior to Alexander's invasion, Buddhism had few images of the great relilgious teacher. Most Buddhists did not think images were in keeping with the great philosopher's teaching. The Greeks could not conceive of any religion without some visual representation. There were also many raised-relief carvings of the life of Buddha from his birth until his death.

India From the Iron Age Through Ashoka

Around the first century A.D., Gandharan art was given an additional push by the Kushan rulers. The Kushans had originated around **Gansu, China**, then spread to the south. One of their rulers, Kujula, united several of the Kushan chieftains, then pushed south of the Hindu Kush Mountains where he ruled for many years. The Kushans borrowed many ideas from the Macedonian soldiers in the area of **Bactria**--present-day Afghanistan and Tajikistan--regarding religion and culture. Since the Kushans maintained trade ties with China, the Gandharan style of art spread along the entire course of the Silk Route in Central Asia.

The so-called "Golden Age" of the Kushans reached its peak under the ruler **Kanishka**, often regarded as one of the four great powers of the world during his age. Unfortunately, we do not have precise dates of Kanishka's reign, probably sometime between A.D. 78 and 225. During his reign of about twenty-five years, he changed the legends on his coins from Greek to Bactrian, an Iranian language written in modified Greek characters. The fact that Greek disappeared from the coins at this time indicates that any lingering influence of the Greeks in the northwestern subcontinent had pretty well disappeared. The coins did continue to include the deities of the Greeks, the Iranians, and the Indians. Best estimates place the period of the last petty Greek ruler at around 50 B.C., well before Kanishka. He is known to have been a Buddhist, and he convened the **Fourth Buddhist Council**, probably in Kashmir, and is thought of as second only in importance to Ashoka in the spread and popularizing of Buddhism.

Since the kingdom of the Kushans was situated astride the **Old Silk Road**, these pro-Greek, pro-Buddhist people had a tremendous impact on history. Not only were they in a favorable position to control the thinking of whoever lived within their domain, but they also profited economically. This, is evidenced by their vast hoards of gold coins found in India. These included coins from almost every country from China to Rome. The Kushans also controlled the fertile valleys of the Oxus, the Indus, and the Ganges-Yamuna river systems. Such a profitable situation made it possible for the Kushans to subsidize the Gandharan and the Mathura schools of art. Poets and philosophers also received royal patronage as did the crafts people. Truly, Alexander's conquests in the East had far-reaching effects for over three hundred years following his death.

Many trade goods in northern India have been traced to western origins. Many eastern ideas of government and military tactics were shared with the West. The Greek influence was seen not only in sculpture, but also in architecture. Elephants and camels were introduced for a time in the Greek military line-up. Even though governance of the eastern areas became rather shaky by the end of the first century following the death of Alexander, trade continued down to about the time of Christ. By this time, the Romans picked up the trade where the Greeks had left off. However, the Roman merchants relied upon the caravan routes to obtain the lovely trade items from India and China. Few, if any of the western merchants ever ventured into India or China to obtain these trade goods themselves. Damascus in Syria became a hub of the trade routes. Tyre and Sidon on the coast of the eastern Mediterranean became important trading centers, which were frequented by the Romans in search of the eastern trade goods. Byantium, present-day Istanbul, also served this trade until it was finally closed off by the Seljuk Turks in 1453. The demand for eastern goods, especially the spice trade, became so great and the prices were so high that Columbus was encouraged to set sail in search of the goods of the East in 1492.

India From the Iron Age Through Ashoka

THE MAURYAN EMPIRE

Just before the time of Alexander's invasion of India, the leading power in northeastern India was one of those short-lived kingdoms named **Nanda**, about 346 to 324 B.C. Nanda and his family seem to have been thoroughly disliked throughout the Ganges River valley--the area of the old Magadha Empire. At this time a strong young Indian leader, named **Chandragupta Maurya**, appeared on the scene. Little real factual information is available about his early life. One account suggests that he was the son of the last Nanda king by a woman of low caste. With the assistance of a minister named Chanakya and the Brahmins, Chandragupta overthrew the other contestants for the throne and took control of northeast India. Several other Indian states then cast their lot with Chandragupta Maurya. Within a relatively short period of time Chandragupta and his followers were in control of approximately the northern half of the subcontinent. The part they lacked was the northwest corner, which included the land along the Indus river valley. Chandragupta established his new capital in the same city as the old Nanda capital of Pataliputra about 321 B.C., just after the death of Alexander the Great.

One interesting legend says that Chandragupta actually met with Alexander the Great while he was in India, but this is totally unconfirmed. In any event, Chandragupta did not challenge the Macedonians during Alexander's lifetime. However as soon as it was known that Alexander the Great had died in 323 B.C., Chandragupta planned to seize the northwest area and to add it to his realm. He first consolidated his position in South India, then, when he believed the time was right, he began his campaign in the northwest.

By 305 B.C., most of the area Alexander and his Macedonian army had conquered had reverted to the control of local Indian chieftains. Since the Macedonian Satrap, **Seleucus Nicator**, was threatening to invade India again to re-establish western control, Chandragupta moved a huge army into place, which not only stopped the advance of Seleucus, but pushed him back towards the passes in the northwest.

At this point Seleucus reached what seems to have been a friendly settlement. The terms were: first, Seleucus was to receive a gift of 500 elephants, which he planned to use in the Macedonian-Greek army; second, Seleucus was to receive the hand of Chandragupta's daughter in exchange for leaving the area of northwest India to the Indians. This point was significant in the Hellenistic exchange of cultures. To marry an Indian princess was entirely in line with Alexander's frequent encouragement to have his men intermarry with Asian women of high rank. Finally, Chandragupta agreed to allow Seleucus to send an ambassador to his court at Pataliputra. The man selected for that post was **Megasthenes**, c.350-290 B.C..

Chandragupta Maurya died c.300 B.C., after turning his throne over to his son, **Bhadrabahu**, better known in western history as **Bindusara** (not to be confused with **Bimbisara**). Like Chandragupta's youth, the demise of the old ruler is also believed by many to be a legend. The Jains have told how the great ruler decided to abdicate in favor of Bindusara. It is said that Chandragupta converted to Jainism, traveled to southern India, and there he died of a self-imposed starvation. Although this was one of the Jain practices, there is no proof that Chandragupta even became a convert to the Jain faith.

Bindusara developed a great interest in the products of the western world. Only a few fragments of history remain regarding his reign from about 300 B.C. to about 272 B.C. The

India From the Iron Age Through Ashoka

Greeks of his time referred to him often as **Amitraghata**, which means "killer of enemies." Doubtless there were many people who wished to test Bindusara to see whether he was as strong a ruler as his father Chandragupta Maurya. He is credited with putting down a number of internal uprisings and expanding the Mauryan Empire to the south through several campaigns in the Deccan. Bindusara pushed his line of conquest through the Deccan and as far south as Mysore. He is generally considered a good ruler and a powerful unifier of the subcontinent. Only the east coast province of Kalinga, and a few other isolated areas, were not under his control. This task was left for his son, Ashoka.

Apparently Bindusara remained on good terms with the western Seleucids throughout his reign. One anecdote says that he wrote to the successor of Seleucus, **Antiochus I**, asking to buy some figs, some Greek wine, and a sophist. Antiochus replied that he was sending the figs and the wine, but that the Greeks were not in the habit of selling sophists.

Our best insight into the Mauryan dynasty has been provided by the Ionian Greek, **Megasthenes**, who served as an ambassador to the Mauryans under both Seleucus Nicator and Antiochus I. While at the Indian embassy he wrote a famous book entitled *Indika*, an account of the geography, government, customs, social structure, superstitions, and history of North India during his tenure there. His office at Patalaputra became a listening post from which Megasthenes traveled throughout the area observing the Indian people and their ways. It is the only first-hand account by an outsider of what India was like under the Mauryans. Today it is considered an opinionated account, but it was used by Strabo, a Roman historian who wrote *Annals*, an important source in the first century B.C., and by the Greek historian Arrian as late as the second century A.D. Arrian's works included *A Life of Alexander the Great* and *Indica*, a description of India. Very few of the men from the western world who did make the long journey to India ever bothered to write about it so far as we know.

THE REIGN OF ASHOKA

Sometime about 272 B.C., Bindusara was succeeded by his famous son **Ashoka (Asoka)**. Ashoka ruled from about 272 to 232 B.C., and is probably the most famous of all the Indian rulers before or since. Before the close of his reign Ashoka controlled all of India except the far southern tip which remained under **Tamil** control. There is one thing in particular which sets Ashoka apart from the other rulers of his time--he loved to post his edicts on stone pillars for everyone to see. Several huge rocks and pillars have been discovered from one end of his realm to another with various messages carved upon them. When taken together, they present a remarkable picture of a ruler of this time in India.

These stone edicts show a man who was very much involved with virtually every aspect of the well-being of his subjects. Several of the stones were placed alongside the roads where they crossed the border frontiers coming into his realm, evidently with the intention of informing all who crossed the borders what he expected of subjects and visitors alike. The national symbol of India today is taken from one of the capitals of one of these stone pillars, which is located at Sarnath in northern India. Not only do the boundary stones describe his empire, but his reign is also recorded in Sanskrit and other contemporary writings, and in the Pali chronicles of Sri Lanka (Ceylon).

Turning to the Buddhist sources, they tell how Ashoka usurped the throne, killed all possible rivals--which seems to have included several brothers--and began his rule as a tyrannical

142

despot. None of Ashoka's stone writings have even a hint of such behavior. According to Ashoka's own accounts of his reign, he greatly expanded his empire after he came to power. There were a great number of lives lost in these wars of conquest. Ashoka has gone down as a firm ruler, especially in his earlier years. It is logical to assume that there were many who had to learn the hard way what it was he expected of his people.

However terrible those first years may have been, after reigning for eight years the great ruler seems to have undergone a great conversion experience. At this juncture he embarked on a totally new policy. One of his own decrees told of his change of heart following the conquest of Kalinga. He claimed that his armies had taken 150,000 prisoners and had killed 100,000 others as well. Apparently this appalling number bothered his conscience. From all accounts he made an abrupt change of course in his reign and began to follow a more "righteous" policy. He announced that he would forgive anyone whenever possible. Ashoka claimed to have even reasoned with the "forest tribes," not an easy group to deal with in our own age. Such a forgiving policy was to be in effect from Ceylon to the south to Greece and Egypt to the west.

According to all the histories which deal with Ashoka's reign he became a **Buddhist** at about this time. Although some think he became a monk, there is no evidence that this was true. He not only gave up war at this point, but also posted edicts suppressing the royal hunt, and stressed the sanctity of animal life. He strongly supported the doctrine of **ahimsa**, the non-injury of both men and animals.

Some have claimed that the sacred feeling toward the cow began with Ashoka. However there is very good evidence that cows were held in high regard long before the time of Ashoka. At the same time he also banned the use of animals in ritual sacrifices. The Buddhists had **never** practiced animal sacrifices, but it was used in some Hindu rituals. He even regulated the slaughter of animals for food. He named some species which could not be killed under any circumstances. He suggested that everyone should substitute pilgrimages to holy places in place of the royal hunting parties. There are those who claim that his decrees were the beginning of vegetarianism in India. Again, this was a practice long before Ashoka. In conclusion, Ashoka was evidently one of the most popular rulers up to that time and many who wrote about him in later years credited him with much more than he deserved.

During this period, Ashoka's edicts express an active social concern, a religious tolerance, an observance of common ethical precepts, and the renunciation of war. In the name of **dharma** he lamented that he had caused so much suffering as a consequence of his conquests. It is also interesting that he made no effort to compensate those who had been the victims of war. Neither did he volunteer to free Kalinga or to grant them their independence.

So far as we know there were few who questioned the sincerity of the king on religious matters. In one of his famous pillar edicts he advocated that everyone should follow the Buddhist **dharma** (teaching) for the greatest welfare and happiness of the people of the realm. The king promised that he would follow it as well. Since Buddhism had been only a tiny minority of the Indian population up to that time, Ashoka gave the faith a tremendous boost.

It seems that everyone praised him for his toleration of other faiths, particularly the Hindus. He even had temples built to an unpopular sect composed of a group of ascetics who roamed around India wearing no clothing whatsoever. He was deeply concerned by the raids conducted by the wild, uncivilized tribesmen, but rather than killing them off as previous kings had done, he made a serious effort to convert them to Buddhism. But for all his regrets about killing and warfare, he never mentioned any effort toward a reduction in the size of his army.

Ashoka revealed his practical side on many occasions and by many actions other than just locating edict stones and pillars of his laws throughout his realm. For instance, one of his edicts mentioned that he had fruit trees planted along the roads so they would provide both shade and fruit to the weary traveler. He also had wells dug along these same roads for those who might be thirsty in India's hot, dry weather. Furthermore, he had rest houses located at the wells so that people could stop and rest before traveling on. He believed that it was important to maintain some semblance of law and order along these roads. He therefore created several new administrators called "Officers of Righteousness," who were ordered to travel throughout the provinces and see that good, orderly relations were maintained throughout the realm.

In the 13th year after his coronation he instituted regular circuits of his officials to proclaim the moral law. The following year he appointed *dharma-mahamatras*, or censors of religion and morals. It was the duty of these Officers of Righteousness to check on what was going on within India's borders. What this amounted to in the end was a good, logical system of morals designed for the peace, fellowship, and well-being of the subjects not only of India, but of any realm.

The sensible rules his subjects followed during Ashoka's reign, were primarily the teachings of Buddha. As mentioned earlier, it is very difficult to tell just how much he might have been involved in this religious faith. It has been said that he sponsored a Great Council of the Buddhist clergy at the capital in Pataliputra where they codified the *Pali Canon*. As soon as this was accomplished there were missions sent throughout the length and breadth of India, and beyond, to proclaim the *Pali Canon* of Buddhism. Most authorities agree that he sent his son, and possibly his daughter, to Sri Lanka (Ceylon) to convert them to Buddhism. In any event, Ceylon became Buddhist at this time, and it is also considered the beginning of civilization in that country. It was during Ashoka's reign that Buddhism became a strong religion in Kashmir, Nepal and in Southeast Asia. Ashoka even sent missions throughout the Hellenistic world, but these missions were not successful in converting any number of people in the western world.

Perhaps Ashoka's most important religious act was the final division and redistribution of the bodily relics of the Buddha. His own record says that he had eighty-four thousand **Stupas** built during his reign. This does seem to be quite a sizeable number, but the relics of the Buddha were broken down to little more than a single hair or a thread from Buddha's garment. When they lacked any more authentic relics of the Buddha, the stupas had a famous scripture or a sacred mantra enclosed within it. Since it had been over 200 years since the death of Buddha, several of the earliest stupas were in need of repair. Ashoka had some of these completely rebuilt. Most of these became important Buddhist pilgrimage sites in India and Nepal.

The *Pali Canon* which went to Ceylon became known as a basic source on Buddhism, even to the present time. Ashoka personally toured his realm and offered moral advice to his subjects as he traveled. Most of his edicts and teachings were composed in a derivative of Sanskrit called *Prakit*. This language was first deciphered by **James Princep** in 1837. One of the edicts from the Kabul River area was in Aramaic, the language of Syria and Palestine. Another one was discovered in 1958 near Kandahar, Afghanistan's second largest city. The interesting thing about the Kandahar edict is that it is in both Greek and Aramaic. As Alexander the Great had wanted to spread Greek culture throughout Asia, so also Ashoka wanted to spread

Buddhism throughout both Asia and as far away as Greece. Each man was about equally successful beyond his own realm. Ashoka **was** responsible for fastening Buddhism upon India and its neighbors for the next several years.

A SUMMARY OF ASHOKA

It is difficult to write a fair and accurate summary of the reign of Ashoka. His thirty-seven year reign from 269 to 232 B.C. was unquestionably the most important and the most dramatic of the Mauryan dynasty. In his own lifetime he seems to have been considered a great man, but he was so very different from those who had preceded him and those who followed, that we must allow that not everyone fell into step behind the great ruler. He sent ambassadors to Antiochus II of Syria, Ptolemy Philadelphos of Egypt, and to the Greeks. Some credit his son, Mahendra, with the world-wide mission of spreading Buddhism not only to Ceylon but also into Southeast Asia. Other missionaries carried the faith both north and east from India. All of this seems to have had the blessings and encouragement of Ashoka. It is therefore safe to say that his primary contribution was the stimulus he gave to the moral and ethical principles of Buddhism.

Other rulers who followed Ashoka did not seem to either understand or to be able to implement the fine art of being kind and gracious along with being the absolute ruler who could get others to do their bidding, even when they followed Ashoka's well-established pattern. Some favorable Buddhist accounts say that the king lost his grip on affairs in his old age. Perhaps this was simply a part of the aging process. It is fairly well accepted that he ended his years in a Buddhist monastery. Some say that his peaceful policy was far too advanced for the age in which he lived. In any event, the Mauryan dynasty only lasted about fifty years after the old king's death. Had he dug the grave for his own dynasty by his policy of peace and fairness in an age of force and violence?

Ashoka's most important contribution to India today would be the edict stones which tie the 3rd century B.C. to India's present. And, the most important one of these is the Sarnath Pillar with its four lions turned back-to-back and the endless wheel, which was selected by the Indian Republic as its national emblem.

LIFE IN MAURYAN TIMES
THE POLITICAL AND LEGAL SYSTEMS

The political system that governed Mauryan life is described in considerable detail in an account of the period known as the *Arthasastra* which has been attributed to **Kautilya**, a contemporary of Chandragupta. It may have been written, or perhaps revised, under a later emperor but it does provide us with a rare source for that time period.

The center of Mauryan power was vested in the monarch, who was an absolutist ruler although he was assisted by a group of advisers. His security included numerous bodyguards and secret passages and hidden staircases in the royal palace. Dress and processions were elaborate and often with great pomp such as the perfuming of traveled roads with incense. The primary ministers in the central administration at Patilaputra were the treasurer and the chief collector.

145

India From the Iron Age Through Ashoka

The empire was divided into four provinces, each governed by a member of the royal family. For smaller units, such as the districts, groups of villages, and the village--the smallest political unit--local people were selected to govern. The importance of revenue collection was important at every level, including the village. The village accountant was responsible for land and boundary registration and taking the census of people and livestock, while the village tax collector saw that the proper taxes were paid. Even the village headmen were responsible to these two officials. In the cities the administration was similar to the village except on a larger scale. This arrangement clearly emphasized the importance of collecting sufficient money to maintain the state.

The Mauryan legal system was severe as measured by contemporary western standards. The courts usually had a group of magistrates whose jurisdiction was divided between civil and criminal cases. The civil magistrates administered the contracts, marriages, inheritances, and boundary disputes. The criminal jurisdiction utilized witnesses to determine a person's guilt or innocence. It should be remembered that torture was also used frequently by the Mauryan dynasty in criminal cases.

Punishments included fines or imprisonment and were based upon one's level within the caste system. For example, the murder of a Kshatriya usually cost the guilty party a fine of 1,000 cows, a Vaishya would cost 100 cows, and a Shudra would only cost 10 cows. The cattle would be given to the monarch, who would distribute them to the relatives of the slain. For those who were too poor to pay the fine, the penalty was to labor for the state. The death penalty was also employed, especially in serious crimes such as plotting against the king or being so bold as to enter his harem! There was also a Chief Justice, but in the final analysis, the emperor had the last say, particularly if the case involved him in any way.

Although the doctrine of nonviolence had its roots in ancient India, it did not assure the elimination of war or capital punishment. Conflict among the independent states of India was commonplace, especially in the years following Ashoka. Often military combat had a sport-like quality to it. Victory only required reverence and tribute from the vanquished kingdom.

The mainline of a state's military force was a group of hereditary troops who were often supplemented by mercenaries, allied troops, enemy deserters, merchant soldiers organized to protect caravans and trading posts, and tribesmen for jungle warfare. While all classes participated in military activities, most of the hereditary troops came from the Kshatriya caste.

The armies were mobile, but slow. In addition to the infantry, chariots and cavalry were both used in combat, but the most important feature of the ancient Indian military establishment was the elephant "cavalry." The elephants could be used for protection in defensive maneuvers and would add great force in an aggressive attack. However, if the enemy held firm and poured a heavy fire into the elephants, they could be routed at that point. Alexander the Great's forces used this tactic against King Porus's elephant forces.

Weaponry in the early Indian arsenal included the bow and arrow, swords, lances, iron maces, and battle axes. Many cities built sophisticated fortifications with a wall encircling the entire city and square towers with roofed balconies. Up to three wide moats surrounding the walls was not uncommon. These heavily fortified cities were so secure that storming the defenses was not a common practice. Most often the attacking forces surrounded the fortress and attempted to starve the defenders into submission. The appropriate time for a battle or a seige was normally determined by a religious rite in consultation with the astrologers.

THE MAURYAN ECONOMY

The economy of the Mauryan dynasty developed a bustling craft manufacturing industry which was supported by a guild system. Many merchants actively engaged in extensive trade. The centralization of the Mauryan government, accompanied by a good road system, contributed to the development of the economy. The base of the entire system rested upon the members of the guild system. Not all workers were in the guild, since some of the artisans were employed by the state in such vital industries as weapons-making and ship-building. A few artisans operated independently of the guild. For the majority who did belong to the guild, there were many financial benefits. In time, membership in the guilds became hereditary.

The guilds were organized along craft lines on a very similar basis to the guild system which developed in western Europe in the late Medieval and Renaissance periods. The primary skills around which the guilds were formed included pottery-making, metal-work and carpentry. The power of these organizations pervaded every aspect of craft production. They set their own quality standards, work rules, and selling prices. In due course, when a money economy developed, the guilds engaged in banking. Coins were minted and circulated along with foreign currencies, but not on a large scale until after the Mauryan years. The merchant class expanded considerably during the Mauryan dynasty. This expansion added a considerable amount to the state's revenue through both direct taxes and the payment of tolls for moving goods over the public roads.

THE TAXING SYSTEM

The largest amount of government revenue, however, came from the **land tax**, which had already been developed before the Mauryan period. At least one-sixth of the crop produced in a given year--some sources suggest one-fourth--for fertile lands, was owed to the government. Whatever the tax, it was not as heavy as the percentage figures might imply. Exemptions and remissions were frequent. Newly tilled land, for example, was not taxed during the first five years. Tax remissions were granted for bad harvests as well as to villages which worked cooperatively on a public project. Moreover, not everyone was taxed. Learned Brahmans and ascetics were among that privileged group. In addition, lower rates were applied to religious organizations, and to some extent the difference was made up by the extra taxes required of the untouchables. Taxes other than those placed on land were fixed on water, which was obtained from the state for irrigation. Livestock, dairy produce, and agricultural crops rarely escaped taxes. Homes, shops, and certain industrial equipment were also the object of taxation.

LIFE AFTER TAXES

The family's relation to the state was close in that the state took care of the poor, the elderly, and the families of soldiers and workmen who died in service. The "welfare state" practices of the Mauryan dynasty are evident in the government regulation of waste disposal and medicines. State assistance was also given in times of famine through the distribution of grain and seeds. The people were also protected against the sale of imperfect goods by unscrupulous merchants. A worker who lost his job through no fault of his own was entitled to receive compensation. In general, the administration of the Mauryan Empire was thorough and sophisticated.

The life of the average Indian in Mauryan times was apparently a good one. Most of the people were well-dressed. There was time for the men to engage in sports. Everyone participated in the festivals where they would be entertained by dancers, singers, and actors. Many men had an opportunity to travel, but always for business purposes.

The "extended family" saw more than one generation living within one home. This allowed the young people to gain advice from the older generation until the older generation was no longer able to care for themselves. At that time, the elderly were cared for by the younger generation until they died.

A marriage could be dissolved either by mutual consent or by a lengthy absence of one spouse. The status of an unmarried woman, or a widow, continued to be very bad. In the case of a widow, her former husband's family would not want to care for her, nor would her own parents want her to return home. In the case of wealthy men, it was possible to take an additional wife. If both parents died and there were no male heirs, adoption could be legitimized by the king. Everyone had grown up within this framework and everyone accepted it without question.

Figure 17

India From the Iron Age Through Ashoka

BOOKS FOR FURTHER READING

Basham, A. L., *The Wonder That Was India* (1984).

The Cambridge History of India, 5 Volumes (1922-1937).

de Bary, William T., Editor, *Sources of Indian Tradition*, Vol.I (1958).

Ferril, Arthur, "Alexander in India: The Battle at the Edge of the Earth," *The Quarterly Journal of Military History*, Autumn, 1988, page 77ff.

Marshall, Sir John, *A Guide to Taxila* (1960).

Nehru, Jawaharlal, *The Discovery of India.*

Rapson, Edward J., editor, *Ancient India*, Vol. I, *Cambridge History of India.*

Rawlinson, H.G., *India, A Short Cultural History* (1952).

Smith, Vincent A., *The Oxford History of India* (1967).

Thapar, Romila, *A History of India*, (1983).

Figure 18

Chapter 15
INDIA FROM ASHOKA TO THE END OF THE MEDIEVAL PERIOD

It was unfortunate for India that the Mauryan Empire did not last very long after Ashoka's death in 237 B.C. For several years the records are foggy, but about 185 B.C. Pushyamitra, commander-in-chief of the last Mauryan, assassinated his master and founded the **Sunga Dynasty**. Pushyamitra ruled India from 185 to 172 B.C.

The most important change under Pushyamitra came in the area of religion. The Mauryan rulers had been strong sponsors of Buddhism throughout most of India. The new ruler opposed the Buddhists and endeavored to restore Hinduism. A growing anti-Buddhist reaction began with the Sungas in 185 B.C. One might have hoped that the Sunga dynasty would have restored order to India, but after the firm rule of Pushyamitra the same fate fell to the Sungas as to so many other Asian dynasties--there was much quarreling and a short-lived **Kauna Dynasty** came to power. Within forty-four years (28 B.C.), they too had failed. Furthermore, each succeeding dynasty after the Mauryans had ruled over a smaller and smaller area.

Throughout this period of weak and quarreling rulers, India was plagued by many invaders. The most powerful of all these invaders came from the northwest and were known in India as the **Kushans**. These same people were known as the **Yueh-chi** in China. Around A.D. 40 the Kushans crossed the Hindu Kush range of mountains and conquered the entire Punjab area as far east as Benares (Varanasi) and as far south as the Deccan. The greatest of all the Kushan rulers was **Kanishka**.

Kanishka (Kaniska) is known as the founder of the second Kushan dynasty. The area of their control included not only approximately two-thirds of India, but Afghanistan, part of Kashmir, and on into Central Asia as well. Although he was referred to as one of the four greatest rulers of his period, it is interesting that little is positively known about him. He reigned for either 23 or 25 years, beginning probably in A.D. 78. Even his capital is uncertain, but most likely it was at Peshawar in present-day Pakistan.

As **a Buddhist**, Kanishka is remembered as the one who spent vast sums in the construction of several Buddhist monuments and convened the Fourth Buddhist Council in present-day Pakistan. The result of this conference was that many of the most important authorized commentaries on the Buddhist canon were prepared and were then engraved on **copper plates**. Theoretically, these should have lasted to the present time. Unfortunately, they have been totally lost. But the Chinese had made copies of the plates, then translated these into Chinese characters. Most authorities agree that it was Kanishka who first introduced Buddhism into Central Asia, and that the Chinese picked up the faith from that area. The first evidence of Buddhism in China dates to this time. Furthermore, the beginnings of Mahayana Buddhism have been associated with the fourth Buddhist council.

Since the Silk Road ran through the center of Kanishka's empire there was a considerable amount of trade between the Kushans and the Romans in the West as well as with China. Kanishka was also a heavy sponsor of the Gandharan school of art which was centered in northern Pakistan, especially around Peshawar and Lahore.

From Ashoka to the End of the Medieval Period

The Mauryan Empire had been a highly centralized form of government, but the Kushans were much more federal. Kanishka and his descendants were more like the kings of Medieval Europe, since they had many lords and vassals serving under them. Sometime around the year A.D. 200, the entire Kushan system collapsed, most likely from a combination of factors such as incompetence, an internal challenge from more powerful barons, an over-extension of territory in an age of poor communications, and possibly no small amount of local nationalism. The Kushans had taken in so many diverse groups that some were certain to want their independence.

The third century A.D. is often considered the beginning of the classical age of Indian civilization. By this time, the language, literature, science, philosophy, etc., were all well in place in India. The caste system was also well established.

THE GUPTA AGE--320 to 510

The founder of this dynasty was **Sri Gupta**, who began assembling a small state in northern India in the third century. About the year 320, **Chandragupta I** (320-335) appeared on the scene as a great ruler over this area. When Chandragupta married a Licchavi princess from the area around Benares in the north, the dynasty assumed considerable prestige.

Chandragupa's son, **Samudragupta** (335-375), succeeded to the throne and began a struggle of conquest which, according to his pillar at Allahabad, caused him to exterminate nine kings and five monarchial states. What he endeavored to do was to create a circle of tributary states as a buffer zone to protect his own capital at Pataliputra, present-day Patna. Those kings who would join with him were allowed to rule their own little kingdoms in peaceful subservience so long as they paid their annual financial tribute. The others were apparently crushed.

Samudragupta's son, **Chandragupta II**, ruled India from about 375 to 415. He took over large portions of western India and formed a marriage alliance with a ruler from as far south as the Deccan. He is generally remembered as the ruler who consolidated the empire, which by this time included all of the subcontinent except for a small area in the far southwest. Chandragupta II was a great patron of the arts and letters. Scholars such as **Faxian**, a Chinese Buddhist monk who visited India in search of Buddhist documents and relics, reported that India was a secure and prosperous empire.

The Gupta empire reached its zenith in the period of **Kumaragupta I**, 415 to 455. Considering the expansionist tendencies of all the preceding Guptas, it is remarkable that there were **no** military campaigns during the reign of Kumaragupta! It was an era of peace with splendor for almost four decades. By the end of his reign, there were numerous groups who constantly tested the frontiers of India, probing for a weak spot. The Pushyamitras put pressure on the southwest while the **Hunas**, better known as the **Huns** in our western history, began to threaten the northwest.

Kumaragpta's successor, **Skandagupta**, spent a large portion of his reign, from about 455 to 467, along the frontiers trying to save the empire. He succeeded in holding it together, but several internal power struggles began following Skandagupta's death in 467. The ten year civil war (467-477) prevented the various factions from uniting against their common enemies, the foreign invaders. In 477, **Budagupta** pulled the pieces of the empire back together until his death in 495. Then, following Budhagupta, a combination of weak rulers, internal quarrels, and

Huna pressure, all joined to take its toll. Sometime between 510 and 530 the entire subcontinent reverted to dozens of little principalities with little or no cooperation.

EVALUATING THE GUPTAS

Compared to the severe brutality of many Asian rulers, the Gupta Age was remarkably mild. Although the Guptas were the unquestioned rulers during most of the period from 320 to 510, the system was quite decentralized. Local social and religious groups, trade guilds, etc., appear to have enjoyed a great amount of autonomy. The legal system was liberal and the death penalty was not imposed. The Chinese monk, Faxian, indicated that there was freedom of movement and the trade routes were generally safe. The economy was excellent during most of the Gupta years. Their coinage, called **dinars**, was based on the Roman standards of coinage of those times. Many of the gold coins are still considered works of art on their own merit.

Literature, science, technology, and the arts were all encouraged. Classical Sanskrit was at its height. Two national epics of India, the *Ramayana* and the *Mahabharata*, along with the major *Puranas*, all assumed their final form. Other works on religion, philosophy, dance, drama, mathematics, and astronomy were produced by the Guptas.

Many Indian scholars in modern times refer to the period of the Gupta empire as the "golden" or "classical" age of Indian history. The long period of nearly 200 years was one of almost total peace and security accompanied by religious freedom and toleration. Since the Guptas maintained a favorable trade balance, there was economic prosperity throughout the period. The decentralized nature of the Gupta Empire allowed each provincial area to freely develop its own cultural characteristics. It was truly one of India's greatest ages.

INDIA AFTER THE GUPTAS

There was a scattering of famous rulers through Indian history following the Gupta era. One of the most famous was **Harsha**, 606-647. He created a more consolidated rule in northern India than anyone had been able to provide for many years, but he could not control the area south of the Deccan line. He was a great patron of literature and personally wrote Sanskrit dramas. Harsha favored Buddhism as a religion, and it was during his reign that a Chinese pilgrim visited India and wrote a biography of the great ruler. His court poet, a man named Bana, also wrote a biography of Harsha.

Harsha has been remembered as a just ruler and one of the last great patrons of Buddhism in India. Among his many contributions was the founding of Nalanda university. As one of the most liberal of all rulers, Harsha went to the confluence of the Ganges and the Yamuna rivers once every five years to distribute his entire treasury.

From Ashoka to the End of the Medieval Period

INDIA'S MEDIEVAL PERIOD

The term *Medieval* **period** in the history of India has the same meaning as in western history. It is a "**middle**" period of history between two more important periods. In the case of India, it refers to the period between the Mauryan and Gupta period and the beginning of the Muslim period.

From about 650 to 1300 India saw a period of great dynastic rivalries. After the death of Harsha in 647, the country divided itself into a large number of separate states. Ultimately, the **Pala Dynasty** established itself in Bengal, in northeast India. This dynasty was also known as one of the last to support Buddhism in India. Most of the remainder of India was moving toward the restoration of Hinduism. The Pala Dynasty rose to power around 750 and ruled over the northeast until the middle of the 12th century. To further complicate the history of the subcontinent, the first wave of **Muslim** Arabs moved into the area of the Sind--present-day Pakistan on the lower Indus River--in 711.

The concept of an independent kingship began to develop in India during the Gupta and post-Gupta period. Even though the Hindus and the Buddhists worshiped many kinds of gods and goddesses, the kings of India were **never** regarded as gods. King and emperor worship had long been customary in the area of Mesopotamia and modern-day Iran and Iraq up to the time of the Muslims.

During the post-Gupta years there were many rulers who were men of low caste--and foreigners--who had won their thrones by usurpation, assassination, or military conquest. This would normally have been too much for devout Hindus to have accepted, since these men did not have the proper caste for the job. It was not uncommon for the Brahmins to provide the new ruler with an acceptable genealogy to make him look legitimate. This was one avenue for the Hindu community to bow to the inevitable and still preserve their own social norms and values. At the same time, this practice contributed to the stability and order of the political environment. None of the rulers of this age were great lawgivers. Rather, it was the king's duty to maintain the ideal fabric of society as described in the great legal and religious texts. This meant that while the king's powers were being defined by the Brahmins, caste fastened itself more firmly upon India. The kings needed the Brahmins to give them religious support--they in turn supported the caste system.

THE DEVELOPMENT OF SOUTHERN INDIA

The kingdoms of southern India were even less centralized than in the north. One good example of this was the **Chola Dynasty**, which was based in the Kaveri River valley and its delta. The Chola rulers were divided into two groups: the earlier Cholas ruled South India in the first few centuries A.D., while the later Cholas reappeared as minor chieftains in the 7th century. By the 9th century A.D., the Cholas had again become the greatest power in southern India, and by the 10th and 11th centuries they moved into Sri Lanka. By 1025, they raided the maritime ports of Malaysia, Thailand, and as far away as Sumatra. They also pushed northward in the subcontinent. Rajendra I, who ruled from 1012 to 1044, claimed that in one of his northern expeditions, his armies reached the Ganges River. Perhaps with their weak system of decentralized nationalism they had tried to do too much. The Chola defeat by the Pandyans in 1279 marked the end of Chola rule.

The **Pandya Dynasty** ruled over the far southern "tip" of the subcontinent. This area was inhabited largely by people who spoke **Tamil**, the oldest of the Dravidian languages. With so many wars occurring during this unsettled age, the Pandyas had to fight to survive. At one time they were taken over by the Cholas, but as the Chola power declined, the Pandyas again became important. Their overseas trade was quite profitable, especially their trade with Southeast Asia. Like so many of the other small states, their independence was later lost to a Muslim sultan named **Malik Kafur** in 1329. Their city of Madurai, near modern Madras, was already South India's oldest urban area.

Other great Indian rulers in South India during this medieval period were those of the **Pallava Dynasty**. It is believed that they were Brahmins who came from North India as early as the 2nd century. By the late 3rd or early 4th century they ruled a sizeable amount of land in the south, but were almost constantly at war with the Cholas and the Pandyas. They built several beautiful temples and produced beautiful Sanskrit literature. The last effective Pallava ruler was Nripatunga, who reigned from 869 to 900.

When the Muslims took over Madurai in 1329, they secured much more than just another city. The Hindus had come to Madurai for centuries to worship at the 14-acre Pandya temple of the goddess Minakshi. Many of the Tamils were so unhappy with the Muslims that they decided to leave southern India entirely and to migrate to northeastern Sri Lanka. From there they spread Tamil influence throughout Southeast Asia. Although many of the Muslim rulers were quite generous in their treatment of the Hindus and Tamils when they first took over, they began to increase restrictions as they became more established. South India would never be quite the same again.

During this same time period, approximately 650 to 1300, the **Rajputs** came into prominence in the western portion of northern India. The word Rajput is derived from the Sanskrit term **rajaputra** which means "son of a king," and refers to the male members of a caste of northern and west-central India. In modern India the Rajputs have many occupations and professions, but the traditional occupation of the Rajput caste in those years was **warfare**.

According to the Kashmiri chronicle entitled ***Rajatarangini***, compiled about 1150, the Rajputs were divided into thirty-six great families. Later sources indicate that these families belonged to three great clans: The Suryavansa, or Solar Clan; the Somavansa, or Lunar Clan; and the Agnivansa, or Fire Clan. All three clans continue to claim they have maintained their genealogies very carefully, but they do in fact vary substantially. By the late medieval period, 1300 to 1700, the most famous of the Rajputs came from Rajasthan. Many of these Rajputs allied themselves with the Mughals and provided the emperors with wives and a steady stream of loyal soldiers throughout much of the 16th and 17th centuries. There were others who fought fiercely against the Muslim invaders. Little by little the Muslims began to gain both power and credibility among many of the Indians.

Besides sharing myths of descent, the Rajput warriors adhered to a common code of conduct called **Kshatriya-dharma**, roughly translated as "the way of the warrior." This code required the Rajput man to die the "good death," which meant on the field of battle, and to maintain his personal honor and masculine integrity in all situations. Likewise, the Rajput women had their own code, the most exacting demand of which was for the woman to join her dead husband on the funeral pyre and become a **sati**, or **suttee**, which means a "virtuous woman," by perishing in the flames.

During a long and losing military siege the Rajput women were even known to commit their bodies to fire **before** their husbands rushed out for a final, fatal onslaught against the foe. Such ritual mass suicides were called a **jauhar**. It was not a rarity, but was quite commonplace as the Muslim sultanates closed in upon the Rajput kingdoms. Some of the most famous **jauhars** occurred in 1303, 1535, and 1568. The English viewed this as both primitive and disgusting. Although they outlawed both **sati** and **jauhar**, the practice continued down to Indian independence. Even though India's constitution outlaws **sati**, it is still performed occasionally.

A SUMMARY OF THE PERIOD OF MEDIEVAL INDIA

We have now surveyed a few of the many, many kings and small states of India which existed between the end of the Guptas and the coming of the Muslims. Many of the modern historians have referred to this jumbled age of history as India's MEDIEVAL PERIOD. The reader should be cautioned that even though there were many principalities and rulers, it is very different from the period of Europe's medieval history, which was transpiring concurrently. The major difference between European medieval history and Indian medieval history is that Europe merged into an era of modern nation states, whereas, India was conquered by the Muslims. That could have united the entire subcontinent under one great power, but like the Christian nations of Europe, the Muslims could never agree among themselves. The South most often went its own way and developed a culture quite different from that in the North. Most historical accounts tend to focus more on northern India.

BOOKS FOR FURTHER READING

Basham, A.L., *The Wonder That Was India* (1984).

de Bary, Wm. Theodore, editor, *Sources of Indian Tradition* (1958).

Kulke, Hermann, & Rothermund, Dietmar, *A History of India* (1986).

Rawlinson, H.G., *India: A Short Cultural History* (1952).

Smith, Vincent, *The Oxford History of India* (1967).

Thapar, Romila, *A History of India*, Volume I, (1966).

Tinker, Hugh, *South Asia, A Short History*, (1966).

Chapter 16
THE BASICS OF THE ISLAMIC FAITH

INTRODUCING ISLAM

Understanding the Islamic faith is important to comprehending the events which occurred in the next period of Indian history and then throughout the eastern world. Islam is the second largest religious faith in the world today. It originated in present-day Saudi Arabia, but it has adherants in virtually every country of the world. Its impact at the close of the medieval period in Indian history is beyond measure. It would be impossible to follow India's history during the Delhi Sultanate, the Mughal period, or the present history of India, Pakistan, and Bangladesh, without a complete understanding of this faith.

ORIGIN and SPREAD

Islam originated in the area known variously as Arabia, the Middle East, or the Near East. Archaeology indicates that from the very earliest time the deities of that area were most likely images which represented the power of the sun, the stars, and the moon. Other special deities which have been discovered represented fertility, a good harvest, a good hunt, etc. Much of this is based on meagre information which dates back several thousand years and cannot give us many positive facts.

Among all the polytheistic peoples of those times there was one man who was singled out in both the Hebrew *Old Testament* and in the Islamic *Koran* as a **monotheist**--the patriarch **Abraham**. Apparently Abraham was a wealthy desert chieftain who lived in the vicinity of Kadesh with two wives, one named Sarah, and another named Hagar.

Abraham's first wife, Sarah, was childless. She knew that Abraham wanted a son to succeed him very much to succeed him, so she encouraged her husband to take one of their maidservants named Hagar as a wife. Abraham then took Hagar as his concubine and she had a son who was named **Ishmael**. [Genesis Ch.16] Ten years later, when Sarah was quite old, she also gave birth to a son who was named **Isaac**. Sarah feared that Ishmael would claim to be the heir to Abraham's estate so she did what any number of women would do, she pleaded with Abraham to have the concubine wife, Hagar, and her son Ishmael banished. [Genesis, Ch. 21]

After much nagging by Sarah, Abraham agreed to banish Hagar and Ishmael from his house. They wandered about in the hot sun for a long time. Hagar was utterly depressed. She sat down on a rock and began to weep because she feared they both would die from heat and thirst. Ishmael stood beside his mother, kicked the hot sand, and at once the fresh waters of a spring began to gush forth. It is said that this very spring still flows today. "And God was with the lad; and he grew, and dwelt in the wilderness, and became an archer. And he dwelt in the wilderness of Paran: and his mother, Hagar the Egyptian, found him a wife from the land of Egypt." [Genesis, Ch. 21:20-21]

The Hebrew Bible tends to leave the story of Hagar and Ishmael at this point, but the Islamic tradition continues the story by telling how Abraham heard of the miracle of the spring of water in the desert. He went to Hagar and Ishmael to see for himself and Abraham was greatly impressed. He built a cubic temple called the *Kaaba*, which means a cube, near the spring. Then

The Islamic Faith

Abraham placed the **Black Stone** in the eastern corner of this temple. The Black Stone was said to have been handed down to him as an inheritance from Adam--the one thing which had been carried by Adam and Eve when they were banished from the Garden of Eden. Every **"True Believer"** of Islam faces this stone, regardless of where they are located throughout the world, when they pray.

Hagar and Ishmael stayed near the Kaaba and prayed daily while facing the Black Stone. As Ishmael's family grew, they became a great nation. According to Islamic beliefs these are the non-Hebrew people of the Middle East today. The city which grew up around the Kaaba was called **Mecca**. For centuries, people came to Mecca to kiss the Black Stone and to drink the sacred and healing waters of the Spring of Ishmael.

The Hebrew people settled in the area of present-day Israel. They also trace their lineage back to Abraham through Isaac. The Hebrews believe they are God's chosen people and through both good times and adversity they have remained monotheistic. The children and descendents of Ishmael not only worshipped the Black Stone but also the sun, the moon, and the stars. They were very much involved with astrology. They also filled their temples with idols--360 idols--so they would have one for each day of the year. There were many other "sacred stones," "sacred palms," "sacred hills," etc. Each tribe had its own religious idols in addition to those of all of the others.

Even though each tribe became quite different from the others, there were several points they all shared in common: first, the Kaaba, the small building which Abraham originally constructed; second, the Black Stone; third, the Spring of Ishmael. A fourth point they all agreed upon was that they were the descendents of Abraham and Ishmael. Finally, the city of Mecca became the sacred city for all believers.

The Arabic peoples came to have many divisions in spite of the things which they shared in common. Corruption also crept in as merchants became rich selling the spring water. All kinds of sorcerers appeared as did soothsayers, stargazers, and swindlers. Each competed with the other to get the business of the pilgrims who came to see the Kaaba and the Black Stone. Mecca was also known as a city of heavy drinking and general degradation. It was into this environment that **Muhammed** was born about **A.D. 570**.

Before proceeding further, we should clarify the several terms which have been applied to this faith. The name of Mohammed has been accepted throughout the western world for centuries, but it should more correctly be **Muhammed**. He was born into the Koerish tribe, which was one of the leading tribes in Mecca in either 570 or 571. Many people in the non-Islamic world call this faith Mohammedanism. Nothing could be further from the truth! Such a term implies a worship of Muhammed. The followers of Muhammed worship the one all-knowing, omnipotent god, **Allah**. In the West we use the term God, Yahweh, or Jehovah as the **same monotheistic** concept. According to Islam, Muhammed did not even shape this religion--God did. Muhammed was simply his servant or prophet here on earth.

The term **Islam** is derived from the Semitic word *salam*, which means primarily "peace," but in the secondary sense, to "surrender." In its full connotation, Islam means "the perfect peace that comes when one's life is surrendered to God (Allah). The corresponding adjective is **Muslim**. It is therefore proper to refer to this faith as either Islam or Muslim but **never** as Mohammedanism.

The Islamic Faith

By the time Muhammed was born about 570, the Arabs were living a primarily tribal life. It was a fierce struggle to gain possession of a little wealth in this barren area. No one felt any real obligation outside his own tribe. Muhammed's father died a few days before he was born. His mother followed when he was six. He was cared for by his grandfather, but he also died when Muhammed was nine. After that he was raised in the house of an uncle, who forced the young Muhammed to work hard tending the flocks.

The biographical materials on Muhammed were collected **after** he died. It is therefore not clear how historically valid these may be. It is said that he was of a sweet and gentle disposition, inclined to be sensitive to human suffering, always ready to help others, particularly the weak and the poor. His sense of honor, duty, and fidelity won him titles such as "The True," "The Upright," and "The Trustworthy One." The word Muhammed alone means "highly praised."

As the young man grew up, he became very concerned with all the pointless quarrels, the fighting and death, the immorality of drunkenness, gambling, and prostitution. Silently, broodingly, his thoughts turned inward. When he reached maturity at age 20, he changed from tending flocks for his uncle to working for a caravan operator. At age 25 he changed jobs to work for a wealthy widow named **Khadija**. Muhammed was so sincere, dependable, and honest that Khadija came to trust him with the most sensitive missions. Even though she was fifteen years older than Muhammed, Khadija came to love him and later they were married.

Fifteen years of happily married life transpired before Muhammed began his years of ministry. Since they ran an honest business, they became moderately affluent. Muhammed then had time to leave the city of Mecca to go to a huge, barren rocky mount on the outskirts of the city known as Mount Hira. There was a cave in this huge rock where Muhammed went to escape from the din of the city. He thought deeply about the mysteries of good and evil, love and hate, and many other thoughts. He decided within his own mind that he would reject anything which seemed evil. As his thoughts turned to Allah, who he considered **the God**, and with vigils of concentration often lasting all night, especially in the hot month of **Ramadan**, he came to the realization that there is no other God but Allah. [*al* means "the" and when joined with **Illah** "God" it means **The God**.]

Muhammed seemed to find peace and strength in that cave. Sometimes his wife or family members accompanied him. Then, one night when he was at the cave alone--the Muslims call it the "Night of Power and Excellence"--a strange peace came across him as he slept. Then a voice commanded him to "Cry!" [Some translate "Cry!" as "Read!" or "Write!"] Three times the voice called out. On the third time Muhammed answered in terror, "What shall I cry?" The answer came back:
"Cry--in the name of thy Lord!
Who created man from blood coagulated.
Cry! Thy Lord is wondrous kind
Who by the pen has taught mankind
Things they knew not because they were blind."

When Muhammed awoke from his trance, he felt as though the words he had just heard had been branded on his very soul. He was terrified and rushed home to tell Khadija. He even considered that perhaps he had gone mad. Khadija tried to calm him down and shortly afterward she became his first convert. They both wondered whether the voice would return again, and it did--many times. Muhammed's life was no more his own from this point forward.

Khadija sent for a scribe with an excellent reputation to record these voices from the angel who identified himself as **Gabriel**. The scribe's name was **Abu Bekr**, and he became a convert as well. Gabriel told Muhammed to go out and preach. In his preaching he proclaimed the beauty and the wonders of God's world. Muhammed criticized the people's wayward lives. He preached about the sins of drunkenness, gambling, and prostitution. He told the story many times how he was just an ordinary man who Gabriel, as God's agent, had sent to proclaim a message. The people wanted a miracle, some proof that he was truly receiving messages as Allah's agent here on earth. Muhammed told his listeners that his faith was not a faith of miracles, but a new way of life. The only miracle was the *Koran*, a book dictated by the angel and recorded by Abu Bekr.

Muhammed's early converts were his wife and family, some household servants, Abu Bekr, and a few others. Nearly everyone in Mecca opposed Muhammed's teachings for several reasons. Perhaps the most important reason was that Bedouin pilgrims came for miles to worship at the Kaaba and the 360 other religious shrines in and around Mecca. Since Muhammed demanded that his followers should have **positively no idols**, it was too great a sacrifice to the Meccan citizens to give up the lucrative business of selling idols.

Another great sacrifice he asked of his converts was an end to the gross licentiousness of his day and to live a pure and holy life. It seemed they were all enjoying their wayward lives too much to give it all up for an ordinary camel driver who thought he had seen a vision. Furthermore, true followers of the faith could not use alcoholic beverages in any form. All of these reasons for opposition to Muhammed and his message of purity touched the local businessmen in Mecca and their pocketbooks. That was what Mecca was all about at Muhammed's time--making money from the pilgrims and the caravan drivers. Besides, his insistence that all men were equal in the sight of Allah did not appeal to a society which had a certain level of caste even though it was not as structured as that in the Indian subcontinent.

The people of Mecca were certain that Muhammed was out of touch with reality. Perhaps more importantly, he was definitely dangerous to their economic well being. Laughter, ridicule, and derision became more severe. Actual abuse and threats then became more common. When the followers of Muhammed's faith prayed, they believed that everyone should wash one's hands, feet, and mouth. Their critics would throw dirt on them as well as all kinds of filth when they were preparing for prayer. When Muhammed and his converts remained undaunted by all of this ill treatment, the critics threw stones and beat them with sticks. Sometimes they would be tied out in the hot sun with no water. Then their critics offered them water if they would curse Allah and give up their silly religion.

The story of the suffering of Muhammed and his early followers reminds one of the early years of Christianity. Muhammed himself never flinched or wavered. On the contrary, the more he was persecuted, the more devout he became. At the end of three years of preaching and persecution, he only had forty converts; after ten years he had several hundred families--hardly what we would call a mass exodus from the old faiths to the new one.

One of the major blows in Muhammed's life came when his wife, Khadija, died after twenty-six years of marriage. Nevertheless, Muhammed believed he had a mission to fulfill, so he continued to preach. He had more visions, which Abu Bekr recorded, and Muhammed continued to preach. The number of his listeners slowly increased. More and more his sermons changed from general criticism of greed and sinfulness toward singling out a particular group. He became quite critical of the merchants and political leaders of Mecca. Ultimately, they plotted to kill Muhammed.

THE HEGIRA

Muhammed learned of the plot and fled from Mecca the night of **June 20, 622**. This date is still called the **Night of the Flight** and it is known as the *Anno Hegira*. Many Muslims still date their calendar from this time, writing it A.H. and the current year since 622.

The city to which Muhammed and his followers fled was about two hundred miles from Mecca and known at that time as Yathrib. It was later changed to Medina al Nabu, which means "the kingdom of the Prophet," now shortened simply to **Medina**. In this smaller, more rural town he won many converts. The religious faith we know as Islam was organized while they were in Medina. They also created an army to not only protect his followers, but to go out and conquer new areas for the faith of Allah.

Within eight years after his flight from Mecca, Muhammed decided he was strong enough to return. Although he had fled under cover of darkness, he now returned in broad daylight at the head of an army of thousands of followers. Many Meccans fled the city even before he arrived because they feared his revenge.

His followers smashed the chapels which housed the three hundred and sixty idols, but the Kaaba and the Black Stone remained untouched. There were many shopkeepers who had fled Mecca in such great haste that their wares were left exposed. Muhammed instructed his followers to molest nothing. A few days later some of the people crept back into the city to see what was going on. They were not harmed. He preached every day and the remainder returned when they saw he was not taking revenge, only destroying the idols. His army of True Believers grew at an alarming rate. Within two years he controlled all of Arabia. Muhammed died in A.D. 632 just ten years after he had been forced to flee for his life.

WHAT THE PROPHET MUHAMMED TAUGHT

Muslim theology is embodied in their holy book, which is known in the western world as the *Koran*, more properly spelled *Qur'an*. It was revealed to Muhammed by an angel of the Lord, generally referred to as Gabriel. It was copied down by a faithful scribe and convert named Abu Bekr. It is composed of 114 *suras*, or chapters which are of varying size. Each **sura** has a name such as "The Opening," which is the title of the first chapter.

This short *sura* is referred to as "the Lord's prayer of the Muslims:"

In the Name of God, the Merciful, the Compassionate
Praise belongs to God, the Lord of all Being,
the All-merciful, the All-compassionate,
the Master of the Day of Doom.

The Islamic Faith

We only worship You and to You we appeal for help.
Guide us in the straight path, the right way,
the path of those who You have blessed,
not of those against whom You are wrathful,
nor of those who are astray.

This theme is repeated many times throughout the Koran. In fact, to most westerners the book appears to be a kind of a re-write of a lot of the Old Testament stories dealing with Abraham, Noah, Moses, and Jesus as well as the story of Adam and Eve. The creation story is especially interesting as it is told in the Koran. Like the Old Testament, Muslims believe that man was created by God from clay. After that Allah created the other creatures of the world. Just as God has created each of us and given us life, so also will each of us surely die. Muslims do believe in a day of Resurrection, when the faithful will be raised up from the dead and judged in a final Judgment.

Non-Muslims often find that reading the Koran seems terribly repetitious, since many phrases are repeated over and over. It is said that many Muslims have committed the entire 114 chapters to memory, and the devout quote from the Koran many times. In the Christian world we generally believe that if we read the *Bible*, we will believe. The Muslim first believes and then he reads the *Koran*.

Westerners have taken the Koran apart for years in an endeavor to understand Muhammed and his place in Arab history. Much has been said about the Muslim's acceptance of Jesus as a prophet, but they cannot accept Jesus as the Son of God. Neither does a Muslim accept the Holy Spirit as a part of the faith. To accept God, Jesus, and the Holy Spirit would, in the mind of the Muslim, be worshipping three gods. One of the most fundamental of all Muslim beliefs is that there is but **one** God, Allah, and Muhammed is his prophet. Furthermore, all Muslims believe that Muhammed is the *last* prophet God will send to mankind. Similarly, the Muslim believes in the Virgin Birth, but that Mary was a human being and nothing more. God simply chose her to deliver the baby Jesus, who became a great prophet.

There are several verses in the Koran which will be interesting to both Christians and Jews, particularly in the light of modern events. Some of the verses warn Muslims to not enter into too close a relationship with Jews and Christians because they are only friends of each other. Muslims should never fear to fight for their faith. "If there should be a hundred patient men among you they will be able to overcome two hundred of the enemy." But they should be patient because God will be with those who are patient. God is all-knowing and wise and He cannot be tricked. Believers must continue to fight the unbelievers totally, because God is with the godfearing.

Like so many other great religions, there are many sects, but they all go back to the Koran and the teachings of Muhammed for their ultimate sources. From that point on, each sect interprets the Koran according to its own conscience and revelation. Some of the variations within the faith began very early because the Koran had only been written in manuscript form during the life of Muhammed. The first authoritative version was organized by the Caliph Othman about 20 years after Muhammed's death, sometime in the early 650's. It was several centuries later before the version in Arabic script was gradually written and interpreted as it is today.

The Islamic Faith

The Koran was the first book ever really printed in Arabic. Several translations were made in the West, the first one in Latin in the 12th century, but this particular version was not printed until 1543. The first one to be translated into Italian appeared in 1547. The Italian version was translated to German in 1623, then from German to Dutch in 1641. A French version which appeared in 1647 was translated into English in 1649. There have been several other efforts at translation since 1649. The Egyptian translation, made in 1919, is generally regarded as the most authentic one by many Muslims. Devout Muslims claim that there is only one authentic version, the one which was given to Muhammed at the beginning of the faith. They also believe that the Koran must be read in Arabic because all others are false translations.

The western world has only recently begun to do in-depth, serious study of the Islamic faith, a faith which is followed by nearly one billion people in the world today. Islam is also one of the fastest growing faiths throughout the world today.

WHAT THE MUSLIM BELIEVES

The Muslim Creed consists of **Five Articles of Faith**:
1. Belief in one God.
2. Belief in the angels.
3. Belief in the revealed books
4. Belief in the prophets
5. Belief in the Day of Judgment.

There are **Five Pillars** which are the obligations of every good Muslim. The most important is to profess one's faith by saying the *Shahada*: "There is no God but God and Muhammed is his Prophet." Other cardinal points are based upon the **Five Pillars**, which are required of every true believer. Among the other requirements are the following: to pray **five** times each day; to pay a tax for the poor; to fast, particularly during the month of Ramadan; and to make a pilgrimage to the holy city of Mecca at least once during one's lifetime.

An individual may make private prayers at any time, but there are five public times when collective prayers are led by an **Immam.** The first prayers are just before sunrise. The second prayer time is just after noontime. A third session is held in the late afternoon. The fourth prayer period is immediately after sunset. The final public prayers are held two hours after sunset. Many Muslims follow all five times very faithfully. All participants remove their shoes when they enter the **Mosque.** They wash their hands, their feet, and their mouth just outside before entering the building. They then kneel facing Mecca regardless of where they may be in any part of the world. Everyone recites the first *sura* (chapter) of the Koran, then there are other prayers and readings from the Koran. If a Muslim is at home, he or she will have a small altar. If they are traveling, they carry a small prayer rug, which is rolled out at the appropriate prayer time wherever they happen to be.

Fridays in a Muslim country are special days. Both men and women "dress up," and the men wear black hats. It is the equivalent to Saturday for a Hebrew or Sunday for a Christian. Stores and factories normally close, especially where Islam is the predominant faith. The prayer given just after noon will include a sermon, called a *khutba*. It will be given from the pulpit which is called the *minbar*. Special occasions, such as the **Month of Ramadan**, bring special

163

services and special prayers. Everything associated with the Islamic religious service, including the Koran, should properly be done in Arabic. In this way the devout can depend upon knowing what is going on in the service regardless of where they may be in the world at that hour.

All Muslims must also pay a tax called the *zukat*, or "purification" tax. This tax is payable on food grains and money income each year. The money raised by this tax is spent primarily on the poor and the needy. During the first two or three hundred years of Islam, church and state were one. Since this is no longer universally true, it has been left to the individual conscience to pay the correct sum rather than the state coming around to collect it as a tax. Giving gifts to charities are encouraged in many passages of the Koran.

The fifth month of the Muslim calendar is called **Ramadan**, which means "Scorcher." It was already a holy month among the Arabic people before Muhammed, but since the Koran it has become a very special time. According to the Islamic faith, the "Night of Power" or of the "Decree," occurred on the 27th of Ramadan. This was the first time the angel Gabriel appeared to Muhammed. It is said that although Muhammed had prayed for guidance in his troubled world, he thought of running when Gabriel appeared. However, every place Muhammed looked he saw the angel in front of him.

During the month of Ramadan every Muslim is expected to abstain from drink, sexual activity, any alteration in the body, or anything which might be contrary to the Koran or the teachings of Muhammed. For the 29 days of the month of Ramadan the Muslim may not eat in the morning once a white thread can be distinguished from a black one. In the evening, one must wait until the same rule applies--no food throughout the day. Those exempt are the very young, the very old, the sick, and the pregnant or nursing women. Persons on an extended journey may also be excused. The sign for ending Ramadan is the first sighting of the new moon. If the sky remains clouded at this time, the fasting is prolonged until the new moon appears. The Muslims use a lunar calendar, which means that the beginning of the month of Ramadan will vary a little bit from one year to the next.

Many people say additional prayers at night during this month. Fasting is generally considered a good penance at any time of the year. The feeding of one poor man during the month of Ramadan, "for those who can afford it," is also considered a very pious act. It is customary for a rich man to throw a huge feast at the end of Ramadan. The tables are heaped with food and everyone, rich and poor alike, are invited to attend.

A pilgrimage to Mecca during one's lifetime began many years before Muhammed. In those times there were many caravan routes which passed through Mecca to the nearby seaport of **Jidda** on the Red Sea. There are somewhere around 200,000 people who live in Mecca today, but the pilgrims often add another 200,000 or more. Only one occupation is allowed in Mecca today and that is the tourist business with its attendant manufacture of religious articles. Since Mecca and Medina are now located in Saudi Arabia, their government believes they have a solemn responsibility to maintain law and order and to police the area, especially during the official *Hajj*, or pilgrimage, which is made every year from the 7th to the 10th of their **month of Zu'i-hijah**. Every Muslim is expected to make this pilgrimage at least once in his lifetime. If he is unable to make the journey, he may substitute a relative or close friend. However, there is really no substitute for making the pilgrimage in person.

The Islamic Faith

The limits of the city of Mecca are set by pillars along every road coming into Mecca. **No non-Muslim may enter the city beyond the pillars located about six miles outside the city on every entrance**. There are five elements of a proper pilgrimage which are the *sine qua non*. Without these, it is cheating and not a true pilgrimage.

First, every pilgrim must stop at the limits of the holy city and put on two seamless garments like large towels or sheets called the *Ihram*. One is worn around the loins and the second covers the upper torso.

The second requirement for pilgrims is the *waqfa*. This involves "standing before God" in the hot sun on the **Plain of Arafat** on the afternoon of the 9th day of Zu'i-hija. The "standing" lasts from 2:00 p.m. to sunset. Many have fainted during this act of reverence. Others have "cheated" by being driven out for only the closing ceremony at sunset. In any event, the ceremony **must** be done bareheaded. In modern times they have allowed umbrellas. Once the sun has set, everyone rushes to Muzalifa, where the pilgrim performs the sunset prayer and the evening prayer. He will spend the night there. An evening meal is served after which each pilgrim gathers 49 stones from the riverbed of Wadi Muhassab.

The third element of a proper pilgrimage takes place early the following morning. It is called the *rami* or "stoning" of the *Aqabat al Kabir*--the "Great Devil."

The next stage of the *Hajj* following the "stoning" is to go to Mecca to perform the *Tawaf*. This is a ceremony whereby the pilgrim runs around the Kaaba three times. Then he goes around the Kaaba slowly four times--a total of seven times. The Kaaba is a very old building which is built of solid granite. It is forty feet by forty feet by forty feet high. Muslims believe that Abraham and Ishmael built the original Kaaba of stone. After this Ishmael was taken to nearby Mina, where Abraham planned to offer him as a sacrifice to the Lord, but was prevented by an angel who showed Abraham a ram caught in a thicket. The ram was then offered as a substitute. [*See Genesis Chapters 12-25 for the story of Abraham. The story of the sacrifice is in Genesis 22: 9-13*. In the Old Testament it was Isaac who was nearly sacrificed.]

Following the completion of the *Tawaf* the pilgrim should perform the *Sa'i*, also called the *sa'y*. This involves running between Safa and Marwah seven times, beginning at Safa and ending at Marwah.

One of the rules upon entering Mecca for the *Hajj* is that the pilgrim may not cut his hair, trim his fingernails, have any sexual relations, wear any cosmetics, perfume, or lotion, or do anything which might change the state of his body. At the completion of the ceremony he may shave his head if he so desires. In actuality, he will most likely snip off a wisp of hair. The pilgrim may now remove the *Ihram* and dress in ordinary clothes. The pilgrimage has been completed.

Once the pilgrimage has been fulfilled, there will be many feasts to attend in Mecca. Most pilgrims buy souvenirs of the trip to show off to their friends. Each man who has completed the pilgrimage can now add the word *Hajji* to his name. In many Muslim countries it is customary for the pilgrim to even paint one outside wall of his house white, then in colored paints he will create a mural depicting all of the events in which he participated from the time he left home to go to the airport until his return. The mural will obviously include the Kaaba and all the other holy places. It is a matter of the greatest pride not only for himself, but for his family and friends alike. Every man in a Muslim country hopes that some day he can do the same kind of pilgrimage.

It should also be mentioned that the stream called the Wadi Muhassab which runs near the Kaaba is not a huge river by any measure. However, when heavy rains fall, there is a tremendous runoff. This has destroyed the Kaaba on several occasions. It is always rebuilt to the precise size as the original, as nearly as possible, and with the same stones, which are gathered up just downstream after the flood. In 1950, the courtyard of the great mosque near the Kaaba was also flooded to a depth of seven feet! At times like these the freshwater and sewage systems often mix, which forces everyone to boil the water for the next several weeks.

An adequate freshwater supply is a huge problem during the month of the pilgrimage. Many pilgrims like to bathe in the reservoirs serving the city. A small snail in these waters causes a parasitic disease called *bilharziasis*. Measures are being taken to alleviate the water problems to make the pilgrimage as safe for everyone as possible. As the number of pilgrims has grown steadily through the years, there are such large numbers arriving in Mecca for these few days that many are crushed or suffocated by the dense crowds.

THE ISLAMIC SHARI'A

The *Shari'a* is the most important and fundamental religious concept of Islam. The term means "a path to the watering place," or in our terms, the application of all of the above points to one's daily life. It includes both the doctrine of belief and the practice of law. And, it is well to remember that during the first two or three hundred years of the Islamic faith, the belief and the law--the church and the state--were really one and the same.

There are four bases of the *Shari'a.* The most important is the Koran, the sacred book as revealed to the Prophet Muhammed by the angel Gabriel and recorded by the scribe Abu Bekr.

The second of the four bases is the **Suma**. This term means "the Way." It encompasses the total teachings of the Prophet Muhammed. It is grouped into six collections of what Muslims call "the Tradition." There were many people associated with Muhammed during his lifetime who wrote accounts of his teachings. Only six of these have been considered authentic enough to be preserved. They are sometimes referred to as "the six genuine ones."

The third base of the *Shari'a* is the universal agreement called the *Ijma*'. This refers back to the history of Islam--that is, how things were actually done at the very beginning of the faith. Since the majority of the Prophet's friends came from Medina, they were the ones who claimed they knew best what Muhammed had in mind. This has been complicated by the fact that in the lifetime of Muhammed, there were certain things allowed into the practice of the faith which were just plain animism. But, to get the faith going, Muhammed was forced to make some compromises. The early Christian church had done the same. Some Muslims considered those early compromises to be valid, even though they were contrary to the Koran--after all, the Prophet had allowed it.

Finally, the *Shari'a* involves thinking through any changes in Islam's historic traditions by analytical reason. The learned Muslim doctors often debate a fine point of theology for many years before deciding to either accept it or reject it. Sometimes these changes involve modern

166

matters in society, such as whether a good Muslim can ride in an airplane, or, is he bound to a camel. Is it permissible to watch television, and to use many other modern innovations? Often the learned doctors debate so long that some Imam rides in a plane and this either speeds up the decision or the man is declared a heretic. The penalty is often execution. Many Muslims from both high and low stations in life often get in serious trouble in a very innocent way.

Many of the Muslims who choose to bolt the *Shari'a* have been known to group together to form a new sect--there is protection in numbers. But the word "sect" is a term abhorred by all Muslims. They prefer the word "school." One of the first to form their own school were the **Sunnis**. They like to think of themselves as the true followers of the Prophet's way. Generally speaking, they are an ultra conservative, puritanical group who try to follow the precise teachings of Muhammed the Prophet so far as it has been interpreted by the learned doctors of Islam. They will go to great lengths to preserve the faith and to maintain its purity.

A second major split is the school commonly called the **Shi'ites**. This group is smaller in numbers than the very "orthodox" Sunnis, but they are very active and vocal. They originated as followers of the **Caliph Ali** around 657. They believe that the Caliph Ali was the infallible **Imam** in whom there resided a divine charisma restricted to the house of Ali. They are the Persian reaction to the Omayyads in the West. It is a little like the split between Roman Catholicism and the Eastern Orthodox faiths. The Shiites also believe that the 12th Imam, Muhammed al-Muntazar--who disappeared in 878--is still living and will reappear just before the last day to save the world.

Followers of "The Twelve Shia" are located chiefly in Iran, Iraq, Pakistan, and Lebanon, with some scattered throughout the Middle East, including Syria. The Shiites claim their own version of "The Tradition" and they have evolved their own system of law. Some have even gone so far as to say that they have had a new revelation and re-written portions of the *Koran*. They further believe that one need not go to Mecca. It is possible instead to visit the tomb of a Shiite saint such as Ali at Najaf in Iraq, or of Fatima, sister of Imam Riza at Qom, Iran. And, there are other smaller schools of thought on Islam.

SUFISM

Sufism is a form of Muslim mysticism which began in Iraq and Egypt in the 8th or 9th century. The word **Sufi** seems to have come from the Arabic word for wool--*suf*. Since many of the early Muslim ascetics wore coarse wool garments, they were referred to as "Sufis." The Sufis were also known as the "poor in spirit," or *fuqara*, which is the plural of *faqir*, and in the Persian language, *darwish*. The English did not understand nor did they respect this religion in their early contacts with the Sufis in India. The English garbled these terms and called the followers "fakirs" and the "Dervish." The Sufis are important to understanding Asia because when the Muslims began entering the subcontinent they brought many Sufi beliefs with them.

Every Muslim must believe that there is only one absolute reality--Allah. The Sufi believer carries this one level beyond to believe that there is a "oneness of being," or what westerners call **monism**. The *Koran* includes phrases such as "wherever you turn, there is the face of God." It also refers to the God-spirit in each of us and in everything about us. This is not **pantheism** as that term is used in the western world, but rather the essential aspect of God's oneness and that he has no parts. The Koran also says that all things in creation will suffer extinction and yet there remains the face of the Lord in all its majesty and beauty. Every Sufi therefore believes in the ultimate extinction of all things in the world other than God.

When every Muslim prays, he bows down and prostrates himself before God in ritual prayer--it demonstrates an undefined humility of the individual before God. But for the Sufi, prostration is the absolute extinction of the ego so that God can see only the true self remaining. When the Sufi purifies himself before prayers, it is intended to be an **absolute** purification. Everything is washed away except the purity of God within. In this sense, the Sufi is a Muslim puritan.

Beyond these philosophical differences, the Sufi follows all the same practices of Islam that every other Muslim follows. He prays five times a day, he pays alms, fasts during the month of Ramadan, and he hopes to make the pilgrimage to Mecca sometime during his lifetime. The Sufi abstains from alcohol, lives a wholesome sex life, avoids wild parties, and tries to be a religious model within the community.

The roots of Sufism began at the time of the very founding of the Islamic faith by Muhammed. Every Muslim had to live a model life in those early years because every non-Muslim was watching this new religion to see what faults would occur. But by the third century after Muhammed, many were becoming much more liberal while they continued to claim to be Muslims. Sufism was founded at that time as an effort to combat worldliness and to restore the faith to the time of Muhammed. It was a kind of "evangelical" movement, an effort to purify the faith.

Muhammed had recommended the recitation of several litanies a specified number of times each day. In order to make certain that each litany was recited the correct number of times, the Sufi first used knotted cords, then they turned to prayer beads. The repetition of these litanies by following the rosary-like beads often caused the Sufi to get into a rhythmic movement of the body as he recited. This practice was carried to the Indian subcontinent by a Sufi mystic named Muinuddin Christi, who died in 1236. A few years later another mystic named Jal-ud-din Rumi began using various dance movements to recite the litanies. This practice was called the *dhikr* or "remembrance" exercise. It can be performed alone or with a group, silently or aloud. The *dhikr* consists of reciting one or more of the ninety-nine names of God as understood by the Muslims and the Sufis. Altogether, the religious practices of the Sufis have been designed to bring them into an intimacy with God which cannot be experienced in any other way.

Another devotional exercise similar to the *dhikr* is the one called the *sama*. This involves the musical recital of religious poetry and is often accompanied by the chanting of verses from the Koran. It was only a matter of time until the Sufis combined the *dhikr* and the musical *sama* with the rhythmic, chant-like music, then they added a dance. This fast-moving religious exercise was called "**whirling**." Their religious dances caused them to be called the "**whirling dervishes**." They believed that adding the fast dance to this form of worship aided their ability to concentrate on the litany in very much the same manner as the Sufi who was following his prayer beads. The difference between the two services is that the tempo is much faster in the dance. As the religious fervor builds up, the whirling dervishes dance faster and faster.

There are many Sufis who believe that mankind was created by God because of God's need to be known and loved. They believe that God continues to create and to destroy every day but God has never changed. As they search to know this great God through the prayers, litanies, and dances, the believer receives a divine blessing from God, which is an experience similar to achieving moksha or nirvana. They call this the **baraka** or "blessing." If one has experienced the *baraka* it will survive forever, even after the death of the holy person. It is therefore a wonderful thing to visit the tombs and shrines of great Sufis who are known to have experienced *baraka*.

By the eighth century the Sufis were a well-established branch of Islam. A leading Sufi holy man would often attract a huge following. These religious groups are referred to as "fraternities." When their leader dies, the fraternity will elect another holy man. Such leaders were often referred to as a **shaik**. Although some shaiks followed their predecessor's teachings, there were others who were known to change many of his philosophical concepts. This has led to many different Muslim beliefs throughout the world. Best estimates place the number of Sufi branches alone at about seventy.

Sufism continues today as one of the extremely influential religious movements in the Islamic world. Sufism has tried to stay somewhere within the mainstream of the Islamic movement. Many of them attend regular prayer services and in large cities they are often known only to other Sufis. There are some Sufis in every country which has a Muslim population. They are strongest in Afghanistan, Central Asia, Bangladesh, India, and Southeast Asia.

MUHAMMED'S SUCCESSORS

Muhammed died at Medina on June 8, 632, without leaving any instructions for the future government of the Muslim community. Naturally, there was a power struggle. After lengthy argument, it was agreed to recognize **Abu Bekr** as the leader of the community. This was ratified on the following day by most of the Prophet's followers, but not all. Muhammed's son-in-law, **Ali**, husband of Muhammed's only child, a daughter named **Fatima**, held out for several months but ultimately, he gave in to Abu Bekr.

Abu Bekr took the title *Khalifat Rosul-Allah*, which means "successor of the Messenger of God." This term has been shortened to simply *Caliph*. It took him a while to stabilize internal revolts, then he launched out on a campaign of conquest of additional territory. The Muslims had come to control virtually the entire Arabian peninsula during the lifetime of Muhammed. By the time of the death of Abu Bekr in 634, the Muslims controlled land in what is today Israel, Jordan, and Iraq.

The second caliph was **Omar**, 634-644. He finished the campaign in Syria, then added Egypt. The Islamic armies of these Arabs were composed entirely of tribesmen mounted on camels and horses. Their traditional tactic was to form a long line, rush the enemy as they showered them with javelins, then wheel back to a prearranged base line from which they would repeat the operation time after time until the enemy lines began to crumble. On a given signal they would switch from javelins to a short sword and close in for hand-to-hand combat.

The forces led by Omar never carried siege equipment for cities or forts--it would only have been a burden considering their style of attack. They planned to capture the cities by storm, treachery, or blockade. They preferred to fight on the edge of the desert rather than to break down the walls of a fortified city. Since they were out in the open, they could always break and leave if the enemy were too formidable. Often their enemies used the same tactics but seemed to be less effective. The forces of Allah had spirit! Muhammed and the early caliphs, such as Bekr and Omar, often led their troops into battle in person.

When Omar was stabbed by a Kufan workman in the mosque at Medina in 644, he was succeeded by **Othman**, 644-656. He used the Syrian and Egyptian fleets on the Mediterranean to launch his attack upon Turkey. It was Othman who was caliph when the first official copy of the Koran was ready. He ordered all other versions destroyed, a move which caused a revolution. He was killed when his house in Medina came under seige.

Ali, Muhammed's son-in-law became caliph in 656 and continued to guide the faith until 661. His entire tenure was one constant power struggle, and he was killed in 661. He had hoped to pass his powerful office on to one of his sons--Hasan, also known as Husain--but his son failed to gain control. Hasan retired to Medina and died there in 669. His descendants busied themselves with the supervision of the holy places at Mecca and Medina. They are called *Sharifs*.

Following the death of Ali, the son-in-law of Muhammed, the Muslims were led and governed by **three** major groups who ruled in a style similar to the great dynasties in western history except that they exercised almost complete control over the religious affairs of the people within their jurisdiction. These were: (1) The Omayyad Caliphs, (2) The Abbasid Caliphs, and (3) The Ottoman Caliphs. The term "caliph" simply means the civil and spiritual head of a Muslim state who is a successor of Muhammed. The Caliph System was abolished in 1924.

There continued to be much in-fighting for the control of both the faith and the real estate, but after the first 200 or 300 years, real estate and political matters seemed more important than religious matters. The leaders of the Arab states became political-military leaders much more like the kings in western Europe. However, they continued to **use** religion as a power over the people, to direct "holy" wars, and to acquire even more real estate because "it was the will of Allah."

By 732, Islam had pushed across North Africa, crossed over to Europe at Gibraltar, crossed the Pyrennes Mountains and proceeded northward toward Paris. They were met by the Frankish leader, **Charles Martel** at what is known as the **Battle of Tours** (actually closer to Poitiers) in **732**. There they were finally defeated and eventually pushed south of the Pyrenees. They occupied central and southern Spain and Portugal for the next 760 years. During this period they were known as the *Moors* in Spanish history. Ferdinand and Isabella finally drove them across to Morocco in 1492.

By 1500, Islam still reached from Morocco and Portugal on the Atlantic to Southeast Asia, China, and the Philippines in the Pacific area. Their last significant threat to western Europe came when they were encouraged, without a tremendous amount of persuasion, to attack **Vienna**, the stronghold of the Holy Roman Emperor Leopold I. From July 17 to September 12, **1683**, in what is known as the **Siege of Vienna**, western Christendom struggled for its very life. The Christians in western Europe were understandably frightened, particularly the Catholic world.

The Turkish grand vizier, **Kara Mustapha**, led some 300,000 Turks in the siege of Vienna. Pope Innocent XI tried unsuccessfully to induce Louis XIV of France to aid Leopold against the Turks, but Louis XIV was more interested in weakening the power of the Holy Roman

The Islamic Faith

Emperor and enhancing the position of France in western Europe. The pope then appealed to **John Sobieski** of Poland to come to Emperor Leopold's defense. Sobieski finally consented, provided Charles of Lorraine joined a combined army which would include the electors of Saxony and Bavaria, along with thirty other German princes.

By the time the combined European forces reached Vienna, the Muslim Turks were already beginning to tunnel under the walls of the city. Sobieski's 80,000-man army formed along the top of the Vienna hills and drew off some of the Turks from the beleaguered city. On the morning of September 12 the Turks attacked Lorraine's forces and the battle raged for fifteen hours before the Turkish battery on the Isle of the Danube was silenced. Without artillery support and badly battered, the Turks began to withdraw from their line of trenches. About the same time, an artillery shot hit the red tent of the Grand Vizier and it was blown up. He managed to escape while thousands of the members of his routed army were slaughtered or taken prisoner. Reports stated that it took the armies defending Vienna a week to collect the booty left behind in the Turkish camp.

The Muslim Turks backed away from Vienna toward the southeast, but continued to occupy a sizeable amount of the Balkan Peninsula until 1821. By this time the **Ottoman Turks** were in control in Turkey. When they proved to be both weak and corrupt rulers, the **Greeks** were the first to decide to declare their independence in 1821. This resulted in a long and bloody war but in **1830** the Turks recognized Greek independence and the modern boundaries were established for the country of Greece. The Islamic Turks have continued to hold a small portion of what was once a sizeable area in the Balkans. Their principal city on the European side of the Straits is modern Istanbul, formerly known as Byzantium and Constantinople.

THE ROLE OF WOMEN IN ISLAM

Like Hinduism, this is primarily a faith for men. The women's role should be confined to maintaining a good home, raising children, and providing a mother's nurturing care. Women do **not** need to be highly educated, just enough to cope in the marketplace and to care for the children. Even in our present age there are Islamic countries where women are still forbidden to drive an automobile. In the conservative Islamic countries the women literally should not be seen. They are asked to wear long black dresses which nearly reach the ground. They should wear a covering over the head, also black, and a veil across the face with only the eyes showing. This has been common practice for many years. Women are allowed in the mosques providing they are not having a monthly period. That would be considered a very polluting circumstance. Once inside the mosque they may join in prayers, but not mixed among the men on the main floor of the mosque.

These rules do vary from one country to another and from one family to another. In some Islamic countries the rules have become much more liberal in recent years. Even under the best of circumstances, an Islamic woman who wears shorts, uses makeup, or goes out in public with her head uncovered would be considered of very low social status by not only the men, but by most of the women as well. Peer pressures toward conformity are very strong. Many Islamic countries now encourage women to achieve the equivalent of a high school education in the western world. More Islamic women have been earning college degrees than ever before. Rural areas are generally much more conservative than the urban areas. The trend toward the educated woman has only begun in the last half of the 20th century.

The Islamic Faith

Some women are beginning to join the professions, especially teaching, and some are becoming involved in medicine, architecture, business, and other similar areas. Where women work in gainful employment, they are rarely paid the same amount of money for the same job as the men. It is not an uncommon experience for women who do begin to make progress toward equality in a country to see the trend reversed when the government experiences a fundamentalist reaction. Governments continue to be very much male oriented. When such a reaction occurs, there are some men who even bar their wives from going shopping or being seen in public. Pakistan has elected a woman as the head of state. This has been a notable exception in the 1990s. The military there is still the seat of power.

Many of the marriages are still arranged in the conservative Islamic countries. The women have little to say about the man who has been arranged for them. Divorce is very easy for a man. A simple note left on the table--or he may pack a suitcase with some things for his former wife and leave it at the front door. This is a signal that she is "finished." He often keeps the sons while his wife will get a daughter. Alimony and child support are virtually unheard of. Unless the woman has an education, she will be left in dire straits. Even then, her lower pay scale will cause her to have many financial problems.

It is alright for a man to take a second wife, if he can afford it. His first wife will simply learn to get along. Some men have affairs on the side, but if a woman is caught in adultery the law in most Islamic countries requires that she be stoned to death. Total equality for women in Islamic countries is still a long way from realization. The role of women is rather interesting because Khadija, Muhammed's wife, played a leading role in founding the Islamic faith.

A SUMMARY OF THE ISLAMIC FAITH

The Islamic faith was founded by Muhammed, a simple caravan worker who was faced one night by the angel Gabriel, who commanded him to write down the message he would bring. Muhammed could not write, but he employed Abu Bekr, a scribe, to accompany him and to write down the message. This became the holy book of all Muslims--the Koran.

The faith grew slowly in the early years. In 622 Muhammed and his converts were driven from Mecca to Medina. A few years later they returned with an army and secured Mecca for their followers. They have never lost the city to any foreign foe since that time. The faith which was always on the defensive in the early years soon took the offensive. They spread their religion across North Africa and twice threatened Europe. At the same time, they spread across South Asia. By the 10th and 11th centuries they were already heavily involved in the Indian subcontinent. From there they spread to Central Asia, China, and through Southeast Asia as far as the southern islands of the Philippines. The faith generally followed the trading routes. Islam is one of the fastest growing religious faiths in the world today.

Members of the Islamic faith believe in **one** god, **Allah**. They believe that Muhammed was only his prophet--his messenger here on earth. Good Muslims pray to Allah five times each day. They believe that all the earth belongs to Allah. The place where one stops to pray is considered holy ground. The Muslim only needs to face Mecca from any point around the world. A mosque is convenient but not necessary. Every mosque is marked inside which way faces Mecca.

The Islamic Faith

Muslims believe that all men are equal in the sight of Allah. Wealth, position, color, or education mean nothing. At the same time, women are relegated to a low position in Islam. They do believe in a life after death in much the same way as Jews and Christians. There will be a Judgment Day followed by a heaven or a hell. Our individual behavior will determine our eternal fate.

Good Muslims will abstain from corrupting influences such as intoxicating drinks. They will be truthful in all instances. They do believe in charity for the less fortunate, yet few Islamic countries have the equivalent of a government welfare system, social security, or a health care system. That is an individual responsibility. Kindness should be extended to all other people and to animals as well. The sixth *sura* of the *Koran* does include an Islamic version of the Ten Commandments.

At the present time, Islam is the overwhelming choice of faith across North Africa. There are heavy concentrations of Muslims scattered throughout the continent of Africa. It is the faith of choice throughout the Near East/Middle East area, except for Israel. Pakistan has the highest percentage of Muslims at 97 percent. Close behind is Indonesia with 89, and Bangladesh with 87 percent. Even though the subcontinent was divided three ways in 1947--India, Pakistan, and Bangladesh--to accommodate the religious preferences, India still has 11 percent of its population as Muslims. The islands of Fiji are 8 percent Muslim, and Islam is the official state religion in both Malaysia and the Maldives.

In addition to the above countries, there are Muslims in rather sizeable numbers in the former Soviet Union, Outer Mongolia, and China. Current and reliable statistics on these countries are not available. Many of the African countries are Muslim. Rather sizeable numbers have migrated in recent years to the various West European nations, Canada, and the United States. Several violent political incidents have occurred in India's history from the tenth century to the present which makes some understanding of Islam necessary.

BOOKS FOR FURTHER READING

Armstrong, Karen, *Muhammad, A Biography of the Prophet* (1992).

Campbell, Joseph, *The Masks of God: Oriental Mythology* (1962).

Hitti, Philip, *The Arabs: A Short History*.

Hitti, Philip, *Islam and the West*.

Hodgson, Marshall, *The Venture of Islam*.

Irving, Washington, *Mahomet and His Successors*.

Kitagawa, Joseph M., *The Religious Traditions of Asia* (1989).

Lewis, Bernard, *Islam and the Arab World*.

The Islamic Faith

Lewis Bernard, *The Arabs in History*.

Parrinder, Geoffrey, Editor, *World Religions from Ancient History to the Present* (1983).

Schacht, Joseph, *An Introduction to Islamic Law*.

Smith, Huston, *The Religions of Man* (1986).

Stewart, Desmond, *Early Islam*.

Von Grunebaum, Gustave, *Classical Islam, 600-1258*.

Von Grunebaum, Gustave, *Medieval Islam*.

Watt, W. Montgomery, *Muhammad at Medina*.

Williams, John, Editor, *Islam*.

The Koran.

The Bible, especially the Book of Genesis.

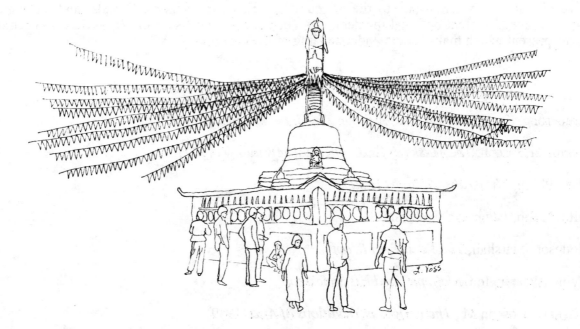

Figure 19

Chapter 17
FROM THE EARLY MUSLIMS THROUGH THE TIME OF AKBAR

THE EARLIEST MUSLIMS IN INDIA

The first Muslims to arrive in India were trading men and commercial operators. No exact date is known of the very first convert in the subcontinent, but it is assumed that it was quite soon after Muhammed founded the faith, almost certainly by the time of the Prophet's death in 632. Muslims began appearing at Bombay and several of the coastal ports on the western coast of the subcontinent south of Bombay.

The first wave of Muslim Arabs who came to set up a new colony moved into the **Sind** area, just west of the Indus River, in **711.** Their leader was **Muhammed bin Qasim**, a fantastic young man who completed the conquest of the lower Sind at the age of seventeen. Within a short time he had moved north to the Kashmir area. At this time he was recalled and executed. The rumor at the time was that he had molested some of the slave girls who were meant for the caliph. Today it is believed that he was executed because his father-in-law had lost out in a political struggle. Even though Muhammed had come as a conqueror, he was very popular with the Hindus since his Brahmanabad Declaration granted both religious and economic freedom to the Indian people.

The invasion by Muhammed bin Qasim is important to the western world because the Muslim scholars were quite impressed by the level of learning they found in the Sind and in India generally. The Hindus were far ahead of the rest of the world at that time in their knowledge of astronomy, medicine, and math. The game of chess came from India as well. This Indian culture was transported back to Mecca, Damascus, and other important cities in the Middle East. Within a short time the Arab traders had moved this new knowledge on into the western world. East met West through this important connection. Very shortly the Indian manner of counting and numbers was adopted in the western world where the numbers were referred to as "**Arabic numerals**." Everyone agreed that this was a far superior system of mathematics compared to the old Roman numerals or any one of a number of other mathematical systems in current useage. The people of India have never received proper credit for this simple but extremely easy system of numbering. The same is true in other fields such as medicine, astronomy, and even chess.

INDIA AT THE TIME OF MAHMUD OF GHAZNA

It will be recalled that the Indian subcontinent was very weak and power was divided among several Rajput kings at the close of India's medieval period. These kings could never seem to coordinate their defenses when it was necessary; however, they had managed to hold the Muslim advance at the Indus River until the 11th century. At that time they were faced with a new foe, **Mahmud of Ghazna**, who began an invasion from the northwest with his Afghan and Central Asian forces.

Mahmud of Ghazna, 971 to 1030, became the head of the **Ghazhavid Dynasty** which had its capital city at **Ghazna**, a city located just south of Kabul in present-day Afghanistan. Mahmud and his Muslim followers controlled an empire which stretched across Asia from the Tigris River on the west to the Indus River on the east. It did not include the southern portions of modern Iran and Iraq. It seemed to the inhabitants of the subcontinent that he continually campaigned into the Punjab and Sind areas of what is today Pakistan with his troops, sometimes reaching far to the east into modern India. Their chief motive was looting the area rather than permanent occupation and control. The Ghazhavids did not actually control the area beyond the Punjab, but they continued to haul the booty back to Ghazna.

The Ghazhavid dynasty had risen in the Middle East under circumstances very similar to those which have been a continuing theme throughout that area. It was an unsettled period and many independent dynasties sprang to life to fill the void in leadership. The people of the Punjab and the upper Ganges River valley considered him a Muslim fanatic. He reduced northern India to such a devastating state that the entire northwest was open to other Muslim invaders.

One memorable occasion seemed to the Hindus to be totally beyond all the other horrors he had brought upon them. Mahmud and his forces crossed the desert from Multan to the temple of Somnath. The Shiva temple there was known to house a huge Hindu idol in the form of a **lingam**, or phallus, that was washed daily by water brought by faithful runners from the Ganges river which was several miles away. The temple was served by 1,000 Brahmin priests and 600 musicians, dancers, and attendants. These were in turn supported by the offerings of innumerable pilgrims and by the revenues of 10,000 villages owned by the temple. The Muslims, of course, detest any kind of idols, especially one which they considered utterly disgusting.

Mahmud ordered that the entire temple complex be razed. At least 50,000 Hindu worshippers are said to have laid down their lives in defense of their deity. He followed the demolition of the temple by looting all the nearby villages. Mahmud's cruel and inhuman behavior has often been cited as one basis for the Sikh religion, a new religion which was formed in northwest India to counter all invaders.

To many Indians, Mahmud was simply a raider and a bandit--or worse. In his own mind, he was a zealous upholder of Islam who conducted holy raids against idolaters and heretics, especially those who he considered politically or theologically dangerous. What he accomplished by his numerous raids was the final destruction of the remainder of several governments in northern India. It is generally accepted that these campaigns of Mahmud were the opening wedge for Muslim expansion into the Indian subcontinent. Beyond his wars of conquest, Mahmud was a Sunni Muslim who patronized poetry and learning and built magnificent palaces.

THE SULTANATE OF DELHI

Mahmud's descendants were driven from Ghazni by a rival Muslim power known as the **Shansabanis of Ghor**, also sometimes referred to as the **Ghurids**. They forced the Ghaznavids to abandon Afghanistan and to take refuge far to the south in the Punjab area. Even there they were not safe for very long. A new leader named **Mohammed of Ghor** invaded northern India and conquered as he went. By 1192 he controlled all of northern India as far to the east as Delhi. After a brief time his army moved east again through the Ganges River valley into the Bengal area. About this time, 1206, Mohammed of Ghor was assassinated by Muslim heretics. His general, **Qutbud-Din Aibak**, (also known as Qutubbin Aibak) founded the dynasty known in India as the "**Slave Kings**" of Delhi. It is probably better known as the **Sultanate of Delhi** by the Muslims. This Sultanate lasted until Babur laid the foundations of the **Mughal Empire** in 1526, an empire sometimes referred to as the **Moguls**.

The Muslim Period in India

The term "Slave Kings" is a reference to the fact that Qutbud-din Aibak was a trained slave military officer owned by Mohammed of Ghor. It was a common practice for this group of Muslim leaders to buy slaves--mostly Turks--and train them for specific military assignments. Slavery came to be totally accepted among the Muslims in Central Asia, Afghanistan, and the Punjab area. Many of the slaves were very efficient and ultimately rose to positions of great importance in the Sultan's army. The military officers often said they would rather invest in a good slave than to have a son because the first loyalty of the slave was to his master. On more than one occasion during the period of the Delhi Sultanate, when a Sultan died the strongest military man was a slave who took over the control of the government. Such strong-minded men as the slaves did rebel on occasion.

Throughout the 13th century, the Muslim control of northern India was extremely precarious. In many cases it was a military occupation, which was effective only in the neighborhood of a Muslim garrison or a military force. Because of the numerical inferiority of the invaders and the vastness of the subcontinent, there were large areas that necessarily were left in the hands of the Hindu chiefs. Furthermore, there were both good and bad sultans in Delhi. Since the Hindu leaders were badly divided at this time, they were unable to throw the hated Muslim invaders out. Instead, each aspiring Hindu or Rajput leader tried to unseat the Delhi Sultanate alone. Each time they lost. Perhaps an even greater problem for the Delhi Sultanate than the Rajput leaders was that there was an abundance of Muslim leaders who hoped to carve out a piece of northern India for their own empire. As a consequence, the Sultans of Delhi were almost constantly at war fighting either Rajput leaders or other Muslim leaders who wanted their empire.

During the period of the Khaljis dynasty, one of the Sultans, **Ala ud-Din**, pushed into the Deccan area carrying the Muslim faith and urging everyone to accept the Koran. No united opposition faced him as he literally forced conversion upon thousands of people. Ala ud-Din's general, the eunuch **Malik Kafur**, easily penetrated far to the south in the subcontinent, always carrying the Muslim faith with him.

The period of the Delhi Sultanate attained its greatest extent in the year 1330 under **Muhammed ibn Tughlak**, 1325 to 1351. By 1330 his government and administration stretched from Kashmir in the far northwest to the southern tip of the subcontinent. In 1339, Mohammed decided to move the capital from Delhi to Deogiri, now Daulatabad, in the Deccan area. He hoped to control most of India from this south-central location. Deogiri seemed a logical choice not only because of its central location but there was a remarkable fortress on a rock about 600 feet high. The center of wealth of his sultanate was still in the north which meant that administration from the Deccan proved impossible without modern communication systems such as the ones available in the 20th century.

Muhammed's successor, **Foriz Sjaj**, 1351 to 1388, made little attempt to recoup the provinces which had seceded from the sultanate of Muhammed ibn Tughlak, many of which had departed because of the sultan's extreme cruelty. India became a patchwork area of small principalities ruled by ambitious Muslim military men. But India was not totally Muslim. There were several pockets of native Hindu strong-men who managed to hang onto their small pieces of real estate. This was the general situation when a new strong leader named **Timur**, more correctly "Timur i Leng," which means "Timur the Lame," arrived on the scene. He is better known in the western world as **Tamerlane**.

The Muslim Period in India

TAMERLANE, 1336-1405

Tamerlane was born at Kesh about 50 miles south of Samarkand in Transoxiana, present-day Uzbekistan. The *Memoirs* of Tamerlane are now considered to be a forgery, but there was little else written about him at that time. They portray Tamerlane as a leader of expeditions following Amir Kazgan, the governor of Transoxiana, who died about 1357. Tamerlane was first appointed as a minister to Ilyas Khoja, but this was too boring. He deserted his job and wandered around, building an army of his own and ultimately he conquered Transoxiana. After leading several internal revolts in that area, participating in assassinations, and by other "illegal" means, he proclaimed himself sovereign and the restorer of the Mongol Empire.

For the next several years Tamerlane and his army moved about freely over the Central Asian area, the Middle East, Mesopotamia, and as far west as Turkey. Finally in 1398, he decided to attack northwest India. By this time Tamerlane was over 60 years of age and still going strong. He crossed the Indus River on September 24, 1398, then marched to Delhi leaving a trail of carnage in his wake. The army of Muslims assembled under **Muhammed ibn Tughlak** was destroyed at **Panipat** in the northwest on December 17, 1398. Tamerlane then reduced Delhi to such ruins that it took more than a century to recover. By the following April, 1399, the old leader was back in his own capital beyond the Oxus River. Besides all his destruction, he carried an enormous quantity of spoils out of India.

The Indian people were greatly relieved in early 1400 when Tamerlane decided to head another way, this time to defeat and occupy Damascus. In 1401, Baghdad was taken by storm and 20,000 citizens were massacred and many of the city's old monuments were destroyed. After capturing Turkey from the European Knights of Rhodes, he received offers of submission from both the Sultan of Egypt and from John VII, the co-emperor of the East. He returned to Samarkand in 1404, made preparations to invade and conquer China, but he fell ill on the way. Tamerlane died on January 19, 1405 at Otrar at the age of sixty-nine. He had lived a full and active life which seemed to thrive on conquest and plunder. The subcontinent was greatly relieved by his demise.

Tamerlane's body was embalmed, laid in an ebony coffin, then sent back to Samarkand. There it was buried in a sumptuous tomb called **Gur Amir**. He had already arranged for the division of his empire between his two sons and his grandsons. After years of struggle the youngest son, Shahrukh, reunited the area over which his father had once ruled. It constituted a large portion of northwest Asia, the Middle East, and what he had plundered in northern India.

Tamerlane was, in a very real sense, the beginning of the end of the Delhi Sultanate. As a Mongol, he had caused so much destruction in Delhi that it is difficult to say that the surrounding area was ever able to totally recover. Like his father, Shahrukh was more interested in what he could take out of northern India than in unifying the area and governing it in the manner of the earlier Sultans. The people of India, including many of the Muslims, thought of the Mongols as gross outsiders. Furthermore, the Sultanate was left in such a weakened condition that Hindu military men tried to seize the opportunity to recover their land. And, there were other Muslim military men who wanted to control northern India.

The Muslim Period in India

SUMMARIZING THE EARLY MUSLIM YEARS IN INDIA

The Delhi Sultanate had dozens of very interesting leaders beyond the few who have been mentioned. This relatively brief period in the long history of India is a very important turning point because it introduced an entirely new religion and philosophy into the subcontinent which placed the Hindus on the defensive for the first time in their entire history. Jainism and Buddhism had been peacefully tolerated and then ultimately reabsorbed. That approach did **not** work with the Muslims. They came as conquerors and they forced their faith upon untold thousands of people. They did not fade from the scene even when they were challenged by the next great invasion of the subcontinent, the Europeans.

Like all of the invasions of the subcontinent up to this time, the Muslims arrived overland. Some of the armies came across through Persia (Iran) and many of them penetrated from the north and west with their roots in Afghanistan and Central Asia. The Indian Rajput leaders could have joined together at an early stage of the invasion and expelled the foreigners, but each prince or king wanted all the glory and refused to cooperate with other Indian leaders to provide a united front. This made it easier for the outsiders to gain a foothold.

One of the great contributions of the Muslims was that they often did accomplish the unification of the majority of the subcontinent under one administrative unit, a situation which the Indian people seldom seemed to be able to do themselves. Another contribution of the invaders was that they served for many years as the middlemen between the spices, teas, and silks of the East and the markets of the West. Not only did merchandise travel along the trade routes but also culture, especially the "Arabic" numbering system. Much of this trade and cultural communication was interrupted during the period of the Christian Crusades, which began in 1095.

The Crusades was an effort by the rising western nations to capture the Holy Land from the Muslim Turks. Ultimately the trade between East and West ended and forced the European world to look for another route to the riches of the East. The Muslim situation continued to remain a knotty problem in the subcontinent at the time of Indian independence in 1947. Tempers continue to flare on occasion between the Muslims and the Hindu population of India.

THE EARLY MUGHAL PERIOD

BABUR, 1526-1530

Babur is the first Mughal ruler of India. The word "Mughal," often spelled "Mogul," is a corruption of the word "Mongol." There was a tendency, following the years of Tamerlane, for the Indians to dub all foreign invaders Mongols whether they were from Mongolia or elsewhere. Babur claimed he was a descendant of Tamerlane on his father's side, and of Genghis Khan on his mother's side, another reason why they thought of him as a Mongol.

Babur was born as Zahir ud-Din Mohammed, the son of the ruler of a small principalilty called Ferghana, a portion of Transoxiana. This was a very important area in those years because of the caravan routes which linked China and India in the eastern world, with Damascus, Syria and the western markets. These caravan routes, often referred to as the **Old Silk Road**, carried a great amount of culture as well as merchandise. One of the branches of this commercial highway, often called the **Grand Trunk Highway**, led from the Calcutta area of the subcontinent all the way across northern India and joined the Silk Road at Samarkand. Not only was this an easily accessible highway for goods, but it provided an easy invasion route for armies from Central Asia.

Babur's father died when he was only twelve but he soon learned which side to be on in the many palace revolts which followed--he became a "survivor." By 1504 he had brought the period of unrest at the palace which followed his father's death under his complete control. At that time he decided to move his capital to Samarkand, the same city which had served as the capital of Transoxiana in the days of Tamerlane.

But for all the young man's leadership abilities, he was defeated by another Muslim who seized Samarkand and forced Babur and his army of followers to search for another suitable city. He began to conclude that his future would be only constant warfare if he tried to reconquer Samarkand because it was wedged between the aggressive Usbeks from Central Asia on the north and the equally aggressive Persians to the south. In order to survive at all, he adopted the military tactics of the horsemen of the north and the culture of the Persians. As the Usbeks grew increasingly stronger, he accepted an invitation by the ruler of Lahore to help him fight local Muslim militarists.

India proved to be a much easier area to conquer and hold than the Samarkand area. Babur adopted guns and lightweight mobile field artillery while the Indian forces were still using archers in their field battles. The Indians did have heavy artillery mounted on their forts, but no mobile field pieces at this time. Babur met the Sultan of Delhi in a battle near Panipat in northwest India. The Sultan was certain he could defeat the forces of Babur by simply rushing Babur's line. Babur's forces fired their light artillery into the Sultan's advancing lines while his cavalry swept around both ends of the Sultan's infantry. Suddenly the Sultan was faced with one army in front of him and another behind him. Sultan Ibrahim Lodi and most of his men died on the battlefield.

Using the treasury of Sultan Ibrahim Lodi, Babur bought more guns and light artillery. He also levied taxes upon those who he had just conquered, again using his annual tax money to purchase still more guns. With a confident and winning group of followers who were all equipped with the latest guns and mobile artillery, many Indian armies were ready to surrender before Babur even challenged them to battle. Unlike the Mongol raiders such as Tamerlane, Babur treated the people of his newly conquered area as his subjects rather than an area to simply be raided and looted. Many of his generals wanted him to take the loot and return to the northwest to triumphantly reconquer Samarkand. A few did leave but most of the highest officers stayed with Babur in India. They were carving out a new empire.

HUMAYUN, 1508-1556

When Babur's son was old enough to command an army, he was given control of the Afghanistan area to guard the northwest passes against any surprise attack from the several strongmen from Central Asia. Once Babur was in full control in Delhi, Humayun joined him there. When Babur died, Humayun succeeded him officially in 1531. Other military men saw that there was a lot of wealth in northern India and they decided to challenge Humayun's control of the Delhi area. On one occasion Humayun lost his empire to the Afghans for a fifteen-year period between 1540 and 1555. Some have said that he was a weak ruler because he was an opium addict who spent too much of his time and energy on his habit.

A son, Akbar, was born during the years Humayun was in exile in Persia. In the face of many handicaps, Humayun was able to hold his army together and when the Afghan ruler, Sher Shah, died, he returned to claim his throne in the Delhi-Agra area. He again ruled over that area of northern India from 1555 to 1556. It is interesting that the warrior who had fought so many battles died at a relatively young age when he fell down the stairs of his library in Delhi.

AKBAR, 1556-1605

Akbar was only 13 when his father died. Since his father was on the move with his army a great deal, there was no time for Akbar to be educated. When he took over the throne he was illiterate. Since he could not read, he was forced to sharpen his memory to compensate for his lack of formal schooling. Akbar was a man who loved to discuss any and all topics with all of those who came to see him. He managed to merge the book learning of others with the practicality of ruling and ultimately earned for himself the title of **Akbar the Great**.

One of Akbar's first acts had to be to quiet all of the palace revolts and intrigues which were initiated because of his young age. As soon as he had stabilized the palace he decided to marry the daughter of the Rajput maharaja of Jaipur. This pacified a considerable number of his Hindu opponents, who hoped that the Hindu wife would win him over to her faith. Those who continued to oppose him, he eliminated without mercy. Those who agreed to submit to his authority received very generous treatment. He was known to play the Muslim leaders, the Afghan leaders, the Persian leaders, and the Hindu leaders off against each other to his own advantage. It soon became obvious that it was more profitable to be on Akbar's side than against him.

Akbar knew that there would be many Hindus who would oppose him because of his Muslim faith. He surprised many of them when he abolished a hated poll tax which had been levied against all non-Muslims. He also abolished a tax which the other Muslim conquerors had levied upon those who were Hindu pilgrims to their holy shrines. One of his favorite topics for discussion was religion--any religion. The Hindu scholars were granted equal time with all others to present their beliefs. They were somewhat amazed that he did not try to force Islam upon them but could defend his own faith along with all the others. The first Jesuit missionaries had arrived in Delhi by this time. They also met with Akbar to try to win him to the Christian faith. He told everyone that he preferred the "religion of God."

Since one of the major problems of the Muslims in India from the beginning had been the challenge of other Muslim leaders who hoped to seize control, Akbar enlisted the assistance of many of the Rajput chiefs to serve with his army. He wanted to recapture the area of Samarkand and Central Asia, but decided he would rather not risk the loss of northern India in what he knew would be a long and difficult campaign. Such a campaign would also require very heavy taxes and Akbar believed he could build a more powerful state for himself by holding taxes low and building up a strong peasant class. During the years of his reign the population of India has been estimated at 140 million people, most of them agricultural peasants. There was also a large urban craft sector.

The Muslim Period in India

Akbar never demanded more than a one-third share from a peasant's land. This was determined by an accurate measurement and survey of the fields. He also saw that the taxes were properly levied and fairly collected. Not only had the other Muslim rulers extracted all they could get from the peasants but so had the Hindu leaders. To be sure that his governors and other officials were administering their areas properly he had people who regularly visited the outlying areas to bring him reports. A new currency based on silver was introduced. With the peasants happy and prosperous, with the Rajputs pacified, and with only a few foreign conflicts, Akbar's Mughal empire was the envy of many of his neighbors who seemed to be constantly at war.

By the time Akbar was 34 years of age he had expanded his empire to again include a large portion of the Sind on the west side of the Indus River. His empire also stretched from the Himalayan Mountains on the north to the Deccan in the south. Much of this was taken with little or no warfare. At the time of his death, Akbar controlled 15 provinces, which were ruled in a peaceful and orderly manner without exercising the extreme acts of cruelty and seizure of property from those who were weaker, as had so many rulers who had preceded him. Although he said he wanted to be a "just ruler," he would still have been considered an absolute monarch by western standards. He was the supreme umpire on all questions. His forty-nine year reign is one of the longest in all of India's history. India had been so badly ruled for so many years they needed someone like Akbar. Unfortunately, his son Jahangir rebelled against him in his later years.

It was Akbar who was ruling in northern India when the first European traders arrived. None of them went inland to trade in those early years, but depended rather on the Indian merchants bringing the goods out to the ports where they could pick them up. Even though Akbar's long reign was one of the best in India's history, the Europeans commented about the over-population, the dirt, and the disease. They obviously compared a very idealistic view of Europe against what they found in India. Not every city of Europe was a beauty-spot in the 16th and early 17th centuries. India would be changed by these western contacts and trade with the West in the years following Akbar.

THE ACHIEVEMENTS OF AKBAR

Even though Akbar was illiterate, he did many things to add to the culture of India. His generous policy regarding religion not only ended most of his conflicts with the Hindu leaders, it also caused many of them to examine the new faith within their midst in a more objective manner. He ordered many of the Hindu scriptures translated into Persian, a policy which formed the beginning of the language known as **Urdu**. He established new schools designed to blend the Indian and the Persian cultures. Akbar expressed a great interest in history. Much more was accomplished in the way of historical records, than had been the case of others, who had been given a better education. He was fascinated by the study of astronomy and supported further research in that field. All kinds of art were appreciated. It was Akbar who began the policy of architectual building on a massive scale, a policy which almost bankrupted the empire under Shah Jahan.

One of Akbar's largest architectual monuments was the construction of an entire city at **Fatehpur Sikri**. Although Akbar had wonderful intentions when he commissioned the building of an all new capital about thirty miles west of Agra, it turned out to be all wrong. The red sandstone buildings were designed to be a blend of the native Indian style rather than to be the typical Muslim type of architecture. This was evidently done with the thought that it would appeal more to the local populace. The problem which developed in this beautiful all new capital city was that there was not enough water available at the site to maintain its viability. The local people knew that water was not plentiful in the area, but Akbar wanted the capital built at the place which was inhabited by a Muslim holy man who had correctly predicted the birth of his son and future heir. The buildings were scarcely finished when the site had to be abandoned in 1586! Fatehpur Sikri today is a ghost town inhabited only by tourists.

There were several other interesting and very beautiful buildings built during the reign of Akbar. One of the first was the tomb of his father, Humayun, at Delhi. A fort and a palace in Agra completed the major building plans of Akbar. The importance of this passion for building is that it started the Mughal leaders who followed Akbar on the road to an ambitious building program which was well beyond the people's ability to support at that time. The epitome of all the Mughal buildings is the Taj Mahal, which was constructed after Akbar.

THE ARRIVAL OF THE EUROPEANS

By the time of Akbar's death in 1605, the Europeans were arriving in ever increasing numbers. The Portuguese came first, then the Dutch, the French, and the English. Although the earliest of the European traders worked out of the seaport towns along the coast, by the time of Akbar they were beginning to penetrate farther into the interior. The Europeans were the first invaders to the subcontinent who had arrived by sea. All the others had come by land via the passes in the Hindu Kush mountains. The Europeans also brought a new religion--Christianity-- which they often presented more forcefully than would be considered reasonable today. India would be forever changed.

THE EARLY YEARS OF THE SIKH RELIGION

The story of India before 1600 would not be complete without at least a brief mention of the **Sikh** religion. The founder of Sikhism was a man named **Nanak**, 1469-1539. There is very little actual source material about the life of Nanak. The first accounts were written in the period of fifty to eighty years after his death. These accounts are more in the form of heroic ballads than the life and sayings of the founder. The two most accepted works are the *Adi Granth* and the *Vars*. The *Adi Granth* contains nearly 6,000 hymns which were composed during the years of the first five gurus.

Like so many of the religious leaders of India, Nanak grew up a very ordinary individual with an unusual interest in religious matters. He married, raised a family, then at about thirty years of age he had his first vision of God. He proclaimed that there should be neither Muslim nor Hindu but an entirely new faith which would merge the best characteristics of the two major faiths. He traveled more widely than most of the other religious founders, always preaching religious reconciliation.

There have been a total of **ten gurus** altogether since Nanak. The last one was a religious leader named Gobind Rai, Guru from 1675 to 1708. None of them were very popular with the leaders of either Hinduism or Islam. The general Hindu attitude was that the Sikhs would ultimately see their errors of belief and return to the Hindu fold in much the same manner as the Buddhists. The Muslims took the opposite view of stamping out the heresy by persecution and by executing the leaders, a practice which produced many martyrs of the Sikh faith.

The first Guru to become a martyr to the Sikh faith was **Arjun Mal**, the fifth guru from 1581 to 1606. Arjun Mal is also very famous among the Sikhs because he completed the compilation of the *Adi Granth*, their holy book, and he had a temple built in the middle of a huge tank at **Amritsar** as a repository for the *Adi Granth*. That temple is formally called the Hari Mandir, but it is better known as the **Golden Temple**.

Following the death of Arjun Mal, the sixth Guru, Hargobind, 1606-1644, decided to arm the Sikhs. Since they were unable to convert very few Muslims to their faith, along with a considerable amount of persecution at the hands of the Muslim leaders, they came to view the Muslims as one more of the dozens of invaders who had entered the subcontinent by the northwest passes. Most of the Sikhs lived in that northwest area of the Punjab. Their religion of reconciliation of the faiths changed in the early 17th century to an active opposition to **all** foreigners. The story of the Sikh struggle will be continued in the period following 1600.

BOOKS FOR FURTHER READING

Basham, A.L., *The Wonder That Was India* (1984).

Camerapix, Editors, *Spectrum Guide to Pakistan* (1989).

Craven, Roy C., *Indian Art: A Concise History* (1976).

de Bary, Wm. Theodore, *Sources of Indian Tradition* (1958).

Guru Gobind Singh Marg, *The Great Pilgrimage*.

Ikram, S.M., *History of Muslim Civilization in India and Pakistan* (1989).

Kitagawa, Joseph M., *The Religious Traditions of Asia* (1989).

Lattimore, Owen & Eleanor, editors, *Silks, Spices and Empire* (1968).

Myers, Bernard & Copplestone, Trewin, editors, *The History of Asian Art* (1987).

Parrinder, Geoffrey, editor, *World Religions from Ancient History to the Present* (1983).

Rawlinson, H.G., *India: A Short Cultural History* (1952).

Chapter 18
A SUMMARY OF INDIAN HISTORY TO 1600

The journey through India is always a long one. There are two major river valleys to consider--the Indus and the Ganges. The Indus is very important because of the ancient civilization which developed in that area. The Ganges River valley has been important throughout Indian history because of its religious significance. No other river in the world is imbued with such a powerful religious impact. In addition, its large drainage basin provides food for millions of people. The area south of the Deccan, is also important but most of the great historical movements have transpired in the northern half of the subcontinent.

The journey through Indian history to 1600 has introduced seven religions--Animism, Hinduism, Jainism, Buddhism, Zoroastrianism, Islam, and Sikhism. Four of the seven have originated in the subcontinent. Two of the four--Hinduism and Buddhism--are major religious faiths today. Although the Zoroastrians and the Muslims came from outside the subcontinent, they are important religions in India. The Greek historian Herodotus once said he thought the Egyptians were the most religious of all peoples. Herodotus had never visited India.

Egypt left us a better record of their civilization than has prehistoric and ancient India. The dry climate, the mummification of the bodies, and the records carved on stone have endured throughout the ages. In India the archaeological record is more difficult. Many of the bodies have been cremated. When an archaeological dig is exposed, such as the one at Mohenjo Daro, the heavy monsoons begin to destroy it before the task is even completed. Although the ancient peoples of India used some stone, the primary building material has been brick throughout the centuries. Brick does not withstand the test of time and weather. Finally, the Egyptians **did** have writing. There was writing at Mohenjo Daro but there is so little of it, and it has not been deciphered at this time.

If some of the lists of rulers, and the details about them seem sketchy, it is because the leaders were preoccupied with religious considerations more than they were with maintaining an accurate historical record of their own age. As a consequence, there have been many political leaders who have come and gone about whom we know little more than a name today. In some cases even the name is missing. There was no importance attached to history except as it pertained to religion.

India is still a nation of farmers. Yes, the cities are large and overflowing with people, but the basis of the economy depends upon the hard-working peasants to feed an over-populated land. It seems that the subcontinent has always been over-populated. With no solid manufacturing base during any of India's historic periods, they are unable to earn cash to purchase food from abroad. It must either be produced within the subcontinent or the people will go hungry. A good monsoon is essential to maintain life in India. The stress on village life and agriculture may seem exceptional to outsiders but a few months in India makes the relationship of the people to the land abundantly clear. In fact, India may be thought of as a nation of villages. Even the large cities are actually clusters of villages.

Everything in India appears to be very old. Even the new buildings soon acquire an antique patina and blend in with their surroundings. A building in America which is one hundred years old is considered an antique. In Europe, a cathedral or other structure which is one

A Summary of India to 1600

thousand years old is considered a national treasure. In India there are so many things which are thousands of years old, especially in the religious realm. Time is simply measured in different proportions than in the West.

India was isolated from the remainder of Eurasia for centuries because it is surrounded by water on two sides and the high Himalayan mountains arch across the northern areas. Even though the passes have been high and difficult, invaders have been filtering into the subcontinent by way of the northwest passes for over 3,000 years. The consequence has been a mix of nationality groups and many local languages and dialects. Those who invaded were almost always "Indianized" within a short time. The one great exception has been the Muslim invaders.

The Muslim invasions have always been considered a foreign intrusion by the Hindus. The early Muslims were interested in India primarily for the wealth and material resources it offered. When the Mughal rulers arrived on the scene, they introduced a strictly monotheistic religious faith which was just the opposite of the very polytheistic Hindu religion. Many conversions of the Hindus to Islam were effected by force. Tempers still flare between the two religious groups.

But the Muslims probably did more to tie India to the outside world than any other group of invaders up to the 12th century. The other invaders had moved into India, took roots and stayed. The Muslims established trade routes with the West via the Grand Trunk Road going northwest into Central Asia where it connected with the Old Silk Road. This route was so effective that Europe came to depend upon the silk from China and the tea and spices which arrived from India. India profited not only from the goods which they produced and sold, but also by acting as middlemen shipping spices from the area of Southeast Asia. When this trade was finally cut off following the capture of Constantinople--now Istanbul--in 1453, the Europeans had already become so dependent upon those goods that Columbus and others launched out to find new routes to the riches of the East.

Even though the journey through India's history, religion, and culture has been a long one, many of the basic principles will apply to the study of China, Southeast Asia, Korea, and Japan. In fact, many of the religious and commercial contacts of Southeast Asia were almost exclusively with India in the early years. Hinduism still flourishes in Bali, Indonesia. The great temple at Borobudur in east-central Java is Buddhist. Buddhism also followed the Silk Road into Central Asia and on to the east through China. From China it traveled to Korea, and from Korea to Japan. Islam followed some of the same routes via India to Southeast Asia and as far east as the southern islands of the Philippines. The arrival of Europeans is the next major chapter in the history of India.

CHINESE HISTORY and CULTURE to c.1600

Chapter 19
THE INFLUENCE OF GEOGRAPHY UPON CHINESE HISTORY

Early mankind in China developed a civilization which was very much like the settlements in other areas of the world. Sumer, Egypt, and the Indus River civilization were all classified as **fluvial**--they were all founded along rivers. China's earliest known civilization was no exception. It also developed along the **Huang Ho** River in northern China. Slightly later in time a second area of development in China occurred along the **Yangtze** River in Central China.

THE HUANG HO RIVER

The Huang Ho is known as the Huang He in Pinyin Chinese. It is better known in the western world as the **Yellow River**. This river is the most northerly of China's important rivers. The Yellow River begins in the eastern highlands of Tibet, it passes just south of the Gobi Desert crossing both Tsinghai and Kansu provinces. It then passes through Ningsia Hui and Inner Mongolia, Shensi, Honan, and Shantung provinces before emptying into the Gulf of Chihli, a part of the Yellow Sea. Its total length is 3011 miles.

For the most part, the Huang Ho is unnavigable except to small boats. In a few areas the river plunges through cascading and narrow gorges, but for most of its length it becomes a flat, shifting, turbulent, and muddy stream. The term "Yellow" comes from the fine, **loess** soil that it carries with it to the delta. It often overflows its banks and sends floodwaters rushing across the North China Plain. It has caused so much destruction that it has been called **"China's Sorrow"** and **"The Ungovernable."** The Yellow River drains a total of 288,000 square miles of northern China's territory.

The upper reaches of the river consist of a rocky area which has already been badly eroded of its topsoil by both wind and water. As the little streams and gullies feed in more than their share of topsoil, the river begins to wind its way across the northern plains of China. The rich loess soil is yellowish to brown and has been largely wind borne from the deserts and plains of Mongolia over thousands of years. The strata of this soil varys from 160 up to as much as 500 feet deep. The river has cut deep valleys through this loose soil while at the same time it carries huge quantities of the easily eroded soil in the form of silt. Some of the silt is deposited in one place and some in another while the river at the same time often creates an entirely new channel. Ultimately, large amounts of the fine yellow soil are washed out to sea.

There are approximately 110,000,000 people who live in this unfriendly environment and depend upon the rich soil and the water, whenever it can be utilized, for their survival. Eight large cities line its banks. This is why floods in the Yellow River valley are so devastating. Efforts through the years to build dikes along the banks to control the flooding have been only partially successful. Once dikes are constructed, the silt soon fills the bottom of the channel so that the river will carry less cubic feet of water. This necessitates building still higher dikes. As the dikes are continually built higher it means that the river is crossing the land as much as 33 feet above the surrounding fields and villages!

The Geography of China

Even a small break in the dikes allows millions of gallons of water to pour out across the land. Some people have even built their homes on top of the dikes. In other places, such as a bend in the river, it is virtually impossible to control the water at flood time. The river's swift current chews away at the soft loess soil on the bend and in some cases it goes through to form an entirely new channel. Some of these have been truly dramatic shifts, such as one which occurred in 1852, and in another incident in 1947. As a consequence of these major shifts and the floods, the people live in fear each time there is a dramatic rise in the river's level. Since 1949, a combination of flood control, coupled with reforestation and grassing in the gulley areas, has helped to control some of the flooding. Nevertheless, the river is practically uncontrollable when the waters reach flood stage.

The delta of the Huang Ho begins approximately 160 miles from its mouth. It spreads out over an area of about 950 square miles. The delta is swampy and much of it is covered with reeds and is not useful for agriculture as are most of the other river deltas in Asia. A sand bar at the mouth of the river impedes navigation by boats, since there is only about four feet of water over the sand bar at low tide. In the century from 1870 to 1970 the delta has pushed into the sea an additional average of 12 miles each year. One portion of the delta pushed 51 miles between 1938 and 1949. The Yellow River carries one of the heaviest silt contents of any river in the world, about 57 pounds of silt per cubic yard of water compared to 2 pounds for the Nile River. The Yellow River is the world's muddiest river. A flood in 1887 covered 30,000 square miles, a severe tragedy in itself, but entire villages were completely buried under the heavy silt.

The irrigation system of the Yellow River is one of the earliest formal irrigation systems in the world. There are over 4,000 miles of waterways which can bring water to about 10,000 square miles of land--some of them are large enough to be navigable. The **Grand Canal**, which cuts across the lower Yellow River, runs for more than 1,100 miles from Peking (Beijing) in the north to Hangchow in the South. The **People's Victory Canal**, completed in 1953, runs for 30 miles parallel to the Beijing to Hankow railroad, and links the Huang Ho River just north of Cheng-chou with the Wei Ho River. This substantially improves navigation between Hsin-Hsiang and Tientsin and provides a network of irrigation channels in those same areas.

A one million kilowatt power station and dam is located at Sanmen-hsia (Three Gate Gorge) about 130 miles west of Chengchou. The reservoir behind the dam is 120 miles long and this makes it possible to greatly extend the length of navigation on the lower river. There are currently plans to construct more dams and reservoirs along the river to serve a dual purpose--flood control and the extension of navigation.

Regular records of the floods, etc., in the Yellow River valley have been kept since the 6th century B.C., but there are some ancient Chinese writings regarding the river which extend back to the 3rd millenium B.C. The archaeological record indicates that the Yellow River valley is the site of the oldest Asian civilization.

THE YANGTZE RIVER

The Yangtze River is the longest of all the rivers of Asia, and it is the fourth (some sources say the third) longest river in the world. There is a sizeable difference in the figures quoted on its entire length. They range from 3,434 miles to 3,900 miles. From its source in western China to its mouth, the Yangtze crosses twelve provinces or regions, including Tibet.

The Geography of China

Five large cities have developed along its banks, each of them with a million or more people. Roughly 300 million people live in this river basin and its tributaries.

The Yangtze River has many names to the Chinese people. The Ch'ang Chiang (long river), and the Da Kiang, which means Great River, are both popular in China. The English tried to have it named the Blue River (except that it is more brown than it is blue); but the name which seems to be the most acceptable to everyone is the Yangtze, so named by the Europeans because it flows through what was once the ancient fiefdom of Yang.

The river basin of the Yangtze is generally divided into three parts: the upper courses, the middle courses, and the lower courses which also includes the delta. Some authors prefer to treat the delta of the Yangtze as a separate entity.

The upper courses of the Yangtze have a high degree of fall throughout most of the river's origin. Winter snows, rain, and melting glaciers make this water reasonably clean and clear. Huge, steep gorges are often too narrow for even a footpath along the side of the river. There are several self-sufficient, isolated villages scattered along this portion of the river. Some of them are almost totally isolated from the remainder of China. Within these valleys the people conduct their daily lives far from the remainder of China or the world. They have their own language and culture and are known to ignore some of the laws passed in Beijing. They have been like this for centuries.

The middle course of the river has so many variations in channel and topography that it is difficult to describe in simple terms. The tributaries begin to add volume to the main channel. This means that the Yangtze becomes wider, sometimes from 1,000 feet to 2,000 feet, except where it passes through the gorges. There it increases in both depth and speed. The area of the gorges between I-pin and Wu-han is both picturesque and navigable. Most of the "tourist" boats use this area but there is a heavy local freight and passenger traffic as well. The Shangsia Gorges, sometimes referred to as the "Three Gorge Area," is in this central course of the river. There are limestone cliffs which force the river into a channel about half as wide as above the gorges and up to 600 feet deep. The Yangtze is very deep throughout its course compared to the silt-laden Yellow River. The Yangtze runs from 100 to 300 feet deep for most of the distance from the area of the gorges to the sea. It is said to be the deepest river in the world. The river is fast moving throughout its course with treacherous currents and eddys requiring skillful pilots to navigate its entire length.

The soil is fertile in the middle course of the Yangtze, the summers are hot and the winters are mild. There is an annual rainfall of from 40 to 60 inches. Many Chinese call the Yangtze Valley the "Land of Plenty." Szechwan Province is in the very center of this region. In addition to crops such as cotton, maize, rice, etc., **sericulture**--the raising of silkworms--is a major sideline which employs several thousand people. Generally speaking, this is a wealthy area of China.

The lower course of the Yangtze--from Wu-han to the sea--is generally a slower, wider river with vast plains on either side. This region is known for its highly developed agriculture and industry. The weather is very favorable for farming, since there is an abundance of water and the soil is rich. If flooding does not interfere excessively, it is possible to obtain three crops per year from a single plot of land. Almost half the crops grown in China are grown in the Yangtze basin. Seventy percent of the total gross volume of Chinese rice comes from the Yangtze Valley as well as much of their cotton. Many people refer to the lower Yangtze Valley as the **"Rice Bowl of China."**

Another feature of the Yangtze River in its lower course is that it is connected with several large lakes. These lakes tend to slow the swift current, provide tons of freshwater fish, and serve as recreational areas as well. In several places along the river's lower course there are huge dikes constructed to control flooding. Some of these began before recorded history and stand as an example of mankind's constant struggle with nature, a theme often expressed in Chinese art. Altogether there are about 1,700 miles of dikes along the lower Yangtze River.

The Yangtze's volume of flow in cubic feet per second is nearly twice that of the Hwang Ho (Yellow) River. Fortunately its flow is moderated by the reservoir effects of the lakes in its lower course as well as some reservoirs which have been built for irrigation. It is much less muddy than the Hwang Ho (Yellow) River because the soil structure is different, plus the fact that the vegetation is much more firmly secured throughout its course. Still, it carries up to 300 million tons of alluvium to its mouth annually. This causes the delta to extend itself into the East China Sea by as much as an entire mile in some years. If the delta deposits create a blockage of the river's mouth during the monsoon season, a huge build-up of water occurs in what is referred to as a "flood wave." Severe flooding then occurs on a sudden basis and without warning.

At flood time the delta region is often completely submerged. These floods correspond with the South China monsoons, which begin in March or April and sometimes last for 8 months. Rainfall during this period averages 43 inches. The river reaches its highest level in August and its lowest level in February. There can often be six- to eight-week intervals without rain during the dry season. For this reason it is necessary to build reservoirs to catch the surplus during the rainy season. An elaborate system of canals and smaller channels feed the water to the fields and paddies. In spite of the uncertainty of life in these circumstances, people continue to return to the lower Yangtze and the delta regions as soon as there is tillable land visible following a flood period.

Tides from the East China Sea influence the Yangtze River for 250 miles upstream. Since these tides can vary from six to as much as twenty feet it becomes a factor in both daily living and navigation. Dock facilities, for instance, must be able to adjust to the sharp variations in tides as well as the flood levels. At flood time these variations can be as much as 65 feet between high tide and low tide.

Repeated flooding along the Yangtze River has been disastrous on several occasions. According to ancient records the worst flood occurred in 2297 B.C. The records say that on that occasion it rained hard for many days until the Yangtze, the Huang Ho, and the Wei all overflowed and submerged almost the entire North China Plain, turning the area into a huge sea. Reasonably accurate records from the period beginning in 206 B.C. until A.D. 1960 show a total of 1,030 floods. In these years flood waves caused by silt blockage at the mouth of the Yangtze, plus heavy rains, caused the river to rise above the dikes.

Under such severe flood conditions the dams are destroyed and reservoirs are rendered useless. In 1931, and again in 1954, cities as far upstream as Wu-han, 700 miles from the coast, have gone under water to depths of six feet to as much as twenty feet and remained at this level for over four months. Under such circumstances the diseases connected with water pollution lead to a great amount of sickness and death as well as the water damage to buildings, factories, food storage, and farmlands.

In terms of the river's importance for transport, there are millions of tons of freight and millions of passengers who use the river annually. All kinds of vessels from 10,000 ton displacement ocean going ships to Chinese junks and sampans ply the river over some 35,000 miles of waterways including the many tributaries and canals. The river is navigable as far as I-ch'ang for ships of 2,000 tons. Even Chungking, which is far inland on the river, is considered a major port city.

The untapped resources of the river center around utilizing its enormous volume of water per day for hydroelectric power. Damming the river could provide even better irrigation possibilities as well as regulating flooding. Navigation on or across the river with its swift current is tricky at normal water levels, nearly impossible when the river is running at full flood capacity. Serious thought has been given to the possibility of further developing the river, but the capital necessary for such a massive project is low at this time. The dams would have to be built on the upper and the middle courses of the river because the lower course and the delta are too flat to dam. If these areas were dammed it would cause a great amount of the tillable land to be taken out of cultivation. The deep gorges and the upper course of the river and some of the upper tributaries would be a logical place to begin. Plans have been drafted to dam the area of the Three Gorges, but there is much opposition to this.

BOOKS FOR FURTHER READING

Cressey, George B., *Asia's Lands and Peoples* (1963).

Blunden, Caroline, & Elvin, Mark, *Cultural Atlas of China* (1983).

Danforth, Kenneth C., *Journey into China* (1982).

Ginsburg, Norton, *The Pattern of Asia* (1958).

Sivin, Nathan, *The Contemporary Atlas of China* (1988).

Figure 20   192

Chapter 20
PREHISTORIC CHINA
THE DISCOVERY OF PEKING MAN

When Asia began opening up to the western world following the early contacts with Europe and America, everyone was fascinated by how very **old** everything seemed to be in China. It was only logical, therefore, that the oldest of men might also be found in China. When Eugene Dubois discovered Java Man in 1891, the search proceded in earnest all over Asia, especially in China.

The story of the discovery of early mankind in China began with a German naturalist, **K. A. Haberer**, who went to China to study Chinese history and culture. It was not very long until he learned about their so-called "**dragon bones**," which were ground to a powder and mixed into various medications. Haberer began collecting these bones and within a relatively short time he had collected over a hundred different kinds. These included hyenas, wild boars, tigers, etc. One tooth seemed remarkably human and in 1903 he took his collection to Max Schlosser at the University of Munich. Schlosser confirmed Haberer's hunch that it was a tooth of either a man or of an unknown ape.

Nearly twenty years passed before the pursuit of early man was again taken up in China. A Swede, **Gunnar Andersson**, followed up on Haberer's discovery, which was located 25 to 30 miles southwest of Peking. Digging began in **1921** at a place called "**Chicken Bone Hill**," one source for the old bones which were being used for medicinal purposes. Once the workers understood more fully the purpose of Andersson's dig they informed him that there was a more plentiful source of human bones at a place called "**Dragon Bone Hill**" on the other side of the village. They changed digging sites and the workers began turning up bits of broken quartz among the limestone deposits almost immediately. This was a strong clue that early man had carried the quartz there for toolmaking purposes.

Dragon Bone Hill was one of two limestone hills which overlook a river just outside the town of **Choukoutian**. Today one can see that the hill is deeply scarred. This is a consequence of two factors: first, the town had quarried the hill for many years for its limestone; and, secondly, archaeologists have removed about a half million tons of limestone and earth to obtain better access to the prehistoric bones of Peking Man.

Among the early finds at the upper levels of the dig they came across many bones of wild animals. The weather of this area had fluctuated over the ages between being warmer than today to being pretty much as the present weather patterns--very hot in the summer and very cold in the winter. The area was well forested **500,000 years ago** when Peking Man first began using this cave. The surrounding forests were inhabited by bison, sabre-tooth tigers, leopards, brown bears, black bears, red dogs, and wolves. On the plains to the southeast there were wild horses, deer, elephant, woolly rhinoceros, striped hyena and cheetah. Bones from all of these were found as they began to open the site.

Digging soon concentrated inside an enormous cave in the side of the limestone mountain. It measured 460 feet from east to west, 130 feet from north to south, and it was 130 feet from the floor to the ceiling. The upper layers of the cave where the dig began were found to contain bones and artifacts about 200,000 years old, a marvelous discovery had there been little more.

As the archaeologists dug deeper, the age of the bones increased until they were bringing out items which dated to about 500,000 years ago. The remains of Peking Man were found in many of these lower strata. In one corner at the very top were some skeletons of only 15,000 years ago. It should be pointed out that Andersson believed this cave held the secrets that he was looking for, bones even older than Java Man. They continued to dig for four years before they found much more than simply "evidence" of early human habitation. Up to that point the dig had revealed largely animal remains and encouraging indications--little more.

The first break came in 1926 when two teeth were found which Andersson believed to be human teeth. He turned them over to **Dr. Davidson Black**, head of the Anatomy Department at the **Peking Union Medical College**, a school founded with Rockefeller Foundation funds. Dr. Black was one who had believed for many years that modern man's ancestor originated in China. With no more than the two teeth to back his claim, Black announced to the world the following year, 1927, that a new species of primitive man had been discovered. He named the new find *Sianthropus Pekinensis*, the Chinese man of Peking. It was fortunate that more fossils were found, and on December 2, 1929, **Pei Wen-Chung**, head of the Institute of Vertebrate Palaeontology and Palaeoanthropology in Peking, discovered the first skullcap.

The skullcap was found at the bottom of a hole about 100 foot deep. The men were so excited when it was found that even though it was a little after 4 P.M. they decided to remove it rather than to wait until the following morning. Part of the bone cracked while it was being removed, an indication that it was very old and fragile. It was also an indication how excited everyone was to make a very important find. The piece had to be thoroughly dried to make it firm enough for the move from the dig to the research unit in Peking. They chose to dry and harden the fragment over a charcoal fire, a process which required a full day and two whole nights. Such an important find excited the scientific world as well. Within a very short time there was money coming from the Rockefeller fund and from other sources interested in archaeology.

The entire hillside at Choukoutien's Dragon Bone Hill was eventually sliced off. Some 20,000 cubic meters of earth were removed by 1937. Parts of more than 40 men, women, and children were found. These included 5 skulls, 9 skull fragments, 6 facial fragments, 14 lower jaws, and 152 teeth. All of the skulls found shared one interesting characteristic--they were missing the underneath surface of the brain case through which the spinal cord passes.

This has obviously led to many questions by anthropologists and archaeologists. Was Peking Man a cannibal who ate the brains of those he killed? If this might be true, why were the tops of the crania not bashed in? Others believe they carefully removed the head upon the death of a relative, opened the fragile bottom section and ate the brains to insure that this knowledge and spirit would continue on in the family. Some think they had some form of a religious ritual. Still others point out that this area is thinner and it simply decomposed with time or was damaged or crushed from the pressures of the earth above over thousands of years of time. Since the bones are so old, it has been impossible to make a definite announcement about this feature.

All scholars do agree that the skulls found at Choukoutien's lower levels date to about 400,000 to 500,000 years ago. They are considered slightly younger than *Pithecanthropus*

Prehistoric China--Peking Man

erectus, which was discovered in Java, but before the people known as the *Neanderthals* from western Europe. Many archaeologists continue to believe that there will be discoveries in China in the future which will be even older than the Java Man remains.

Another fascinating discovery at Choukoutien was that Peking Man was using fire! This includes even the earliest ages of occupation. There were thick layers of ash, burned and charred bones, and hearths in several parts of the large cave. These fires helped to not only provide some heat in the cave in wintertime but they kept the wild animals out as well. It is speculated that a band of twenty or more individuals returned to this cave year after year. One of the ash layers measured 22 feet deep. Considering that there have been 10 hearths identified it must have been a smoky environment. It is not possible to tell definitively whether they cooked their meat or not.

There was no evidence of the control of fire in the case of the Java Men who lived from 100,000 to 200,000 years before the Peking Men. Approximately 100,000 stone tools and fragments were also found in the large cave area alone. Most of these were worked from quartz. These consisted of the same basic Paleolithic "tool kit," which most people of these early times used--axes, scrapers, awls, crude knives, and hammerstones. All the tools have been worked by chipping, or percussion, in the usual Paleolithic style.

Dr. Davidson Black died in 1933 at the very height of these discoveries. Dr. **Franz Weidenreich**, a German anatomist, was asked to replace Dr. Black in 1935. Two more years of digging followed, then in 1937 the war came to Choukoutien. Fortunately, Dr. Weidenreich had the foresight to make plaster casts of many of the most important bones. When the war broke around him, Weidenreich prepared to leave China and come to America with his drawings and the plaster casts. Things happened more quickly than anyone could have anticipated and it was 1941 before he could get away.

The Chinese scientists who remained did not know what to do with the real human bones. Both they and the western scientists believed the bones should stay in China--they actually belonged to the Geological Survey of China. At the last minute it was decided to ship them to the United States until after the war. They selected 175 of the most significant ones and carefully packed them into boxes after Weidenreich's departure in 1941. This work of packing the bones was done by **Claire Taschdjian**, a young German lady who had come to China in 1934 to work under Weidenreich.

Ms. Taschdjian also made both solid and hollow casts of the several pieces before they were packed. She realized how important these materials were to everyone in the world of scholarship. Box "A" contained the *Sianthropus* remains while Box "B" contained the remains from a more recent discovery called the "Upper Cave." The latter discovery were estimated at 10,000 to 20,000 years old. Both boxes were marked "Property of Peking Medical College," padlocked and left in the college storeroom. Claire Taschdjian never saw these boxes again.

Just before the Japanese arrived in Peking the U.S. Marines came and removed Box "A" and Box "B" and gave the keys to Claire Taschdjian. Within a week of when she had packed the boxes, the Japanese came to the Medical College and began to go through everything. They began cleaning out and throwing away anything which they did not value. This included the stacks of bones and bone fragments which were not packed into the two boxes. It was told later how the Japanese simply threw these bones and other artifacts on a heap and the local Chinese peasants gathered them up. The bones were probably sold for medicinal purposes among the Chinese during the war years which followed.

Claire had packed each bone very carefully into a cardboard box, then into the two redwood chests. The Marine commander, Col. William Ashurst, evidently thought they looked too Chinese in the redwood chests to pass for American baggage so he ordered them repacked into regulation Marine footlockers in November 1941. The footlockers were then sent out in the baggage of William Foley. The lockers were scheduled to go to the port city of Chinwangtao where they would wait at the Marine base, Camp Holcomb, until a troop ship arrived to remove all Americans and their property from China.

The Marine footlockers were next loaded on a train which required three days to cover the 140 miles from Peking to the port. At the same time the *U.S.S. President Harrison* crossed the Yellow Sea to pick up the remains of the American presence in Peking. The ship was scheduled to reach the port of Chinwangtao on December 11, 1941. The footlockers were removed from the boxcars when they reached Chinwangtao, along with the other Marine baggage, and were placed in the infirmary and laboratory at Camp Holcomb.

But Sunday, December 7, 1941 arrived before the *President Harrison*. The day the Japanese attacked Pearl Harbor was actually Monday, December 8th in China. Camp Holcomb awoke to a Japanese takeover--the Marines had waited too long to escape! There were only 18 Marines at the base, but they got out the guns, piled the footlockers up to make a defensive position and waited. At 10:40 a.m. Col. Ashurst in Peking gave the defenders orders to surrender to the Japanese. No shots were actually fired. The fate of those footlockers after December 8, 1941, is one of the world's greatest mysteries.

There was a lighter, a large flat-bottomed boat, which capsized in the harbor at Chinwangtao. A few people believe that perhaps the bones of Peking Man was a part of the lighter's cargo. The *U.S.S. President Harrison* was run aground shortly after the captain learned of the Japanese attack on Pearl Harbor. There is no record that the footlockers with the bones were ever placed on the ship.

The most likely fate of the bones of Peking Man is what happened to the other old bones at the Medical College--the Japanese probably wanted the footlockers for their own use, they simply dumped all of them they found, took what they wanted, and placed the remains in a heap for the local Chinese to scavange. The bones of Peking Man probably ended up on such a heap. Such acts often happen in wartime.

Near the end of World War II American planes bombed Chinwangtao and several warehouses along the waterfront were burned. It is remotely possible that the footlockers with the bones of Peking Man were still in those warehouses at that time. Since the *President Harrison* never arrived, it is impossible that the bones were ever placed on that ship as many would like to believe. At the time the Americans surrendered at Camp Holcomb they were promptly marched off to prison camp. They were allowed to carry only a few personal effects. No prisoner of war carried a footlocker! Some remembered the Japanese loading things from the camp onto freight cars as they were leaving. It is also possible that these cars with their cargoes were shipped to any number of places in China and then simply lost in the fury of wartime conditions.

Prehistoric China--Peking Man

FOLLOWING THE RUMORS

Since World War II there have been dozens of rumors about the fate of Peking Man's bones. Christopher G. Janus from the United States was one of the first tourists to visit China following the Nixon visit. Janus has spent much time and money researching the final known hours of the bones. Others, too, including the U.S. State Department and the F.B.I. have looked into the matter. So far all research has proven fruitless.

There are those who believe that the bones **did** somehow come to the United States and that the person who has them is holding them for ransom. Some of those who have contacted Janus in response to his ads have said that they know exactly where the bones are and they want a very large sum of money to reveal the location of the Peking Man bones.

All of these leads which have been followed are of a very suspicious character. One of the rumors explains how the Chinese refugees brought the bones with them to Manila, a very unlikely place to go in wartime. If the refugees were still in China through the war, it still does not explain where they were kept during those years. Another story says that Chiang Kai-shek obtained the bones and had them moved to Taiwan when he left Mainland China. If Chiang knew of the whereabouts of the bones, it seems reasonable to assume that he would have wanted them on display before he died in 1975.

There are others who say that the bones are in Hong Kong. However, **all** rumors have so far proven false. Of course Christopher Janus believes the bones are still in the hands of some as yet unknown person. Each country which was in any way involved with the bones has accused the others of knowing where they are but witholding the information. As the years pass it is increasingly likely that no one knows where those original bones are located.

BOOKS FOR FURTHER READING

Chang, Kwang-chih, *The Archaeology of Ancient China* (1986).

Creel, Herrlee G., *The Birth of China (1937)*.

Janus, C.G., & Brashler, W., *The Search for Peking Man* (1975).

Kwang-cheh Chang, *The Archaeology of Ancient China* (1986).

Lanpo, Jia, & Weiwen, Huang, *The Story of Peking Man from Archaeology to Mystery* (1990). [This is probably the most complete account of the digging at the Peking Man sites.]

Treistman, Judith M., *The Prehistory of China* (1972) .

Watson, William, *Early Civilization in China* (1966).

LEGENDARY ORIGINS OF THE CHINESE

No one knows how the people of the Peking Man era explained their origins. When the Chinese began to think in historical terms, they said that their origin began with ten legendary figures during the most ancient times dating back to the first millennium. The most important of these are the three who were both sages and rulers. One of these three was **Fu Hsi** who taught the people how to hunt. A second important sage was **Shen Nung**. He taught the Chinese how to cultivate the five grains, invented the plow, and established the markets. The third sage was **Huang Ti**. His inventions included boats and oars. He also told the Chinese how to clear the hills and plains of trees and brush.   He cleared the country of wild and dangerous beasts, and he is credited with originating music. Many of the royalty claimed they could trace their ancestors back to the time of Huang Ti.

The Chinese claim their first two dynasties were the **Yu** and the **Hsia**, but no one has yet been able to positively identify any one person as a ruler from this very early period. The **Shang** dynasty, sometimes also known as the **Yin**, which began about 1766 to 1123 B.C.. is currently the first dynasty of record. But even these dates are only approximations and nearly all our information comes from archaeology for these early times.

THE EARLY CULTURES OF CHINA

The evidence of archaeology in northern Asia indicates that early mankind in that area began on the North China Plain along the course of the **Huang Ho** (Yellow) River as a typical **fluvial** civilization. Archaeology came late to China, and it was not until the twentieth century that archaeologists began to unearth a variety of sites. Three distinct cultures have currently been identified as the foundation of a continuous development that culminated in the Chinese civilization familiar to us in the earliest written records.

THE YANG-SHAO CULTURE

Paleolithic origins began to be well established with the discovery of **Peking Man** and the tools of his age. Consequently, we know that an early form of man was able to sustain himself in northern China some half a million years ago. What is of greatest interest, however, are the sophisticated tools and household items of the **Neolithic period**. In northwestern Honan province, in the village of **Yang-shao**, not very far from the center of China's earliest dynasties of the Shang and Chou, some beautifully decorated pottery was found. It was painted with black, red, and white decorative patterns in a spiral. The skillful designs and the balanced form of the pottery suggest the use of a potter's wheel. This illustrates the advanced development in the Chinese culture which had taken place sometime before 2000 B.C.

Eventually, examples of the **"Painted Pottery"** or **"Yang-shao"** culture, as it is known, were discovered elsewhere in China. Besides the pottery, other remains of Neolithic mankind in China were found that reveal their practice of domesticating dogs and pigs, weaving cloth, and their ability to make implements for war or the hunt. Of particular interest, are the skeletal remains, which differ very little from the modern northern Chinese people. The **Li** style pot was a hollow, three-legged cooking utensil which suggests continuity between this early culture and the much later Chinese civilization.

Also in the Honan province area is the site known as **Chengchow**. Chengchow was a walled town of about one-quarter mile by one mile in size. The huge walls varied from 19 to 55 feet thick at the base. Archaeologists have found several tombs, workshops, kilns, shops for casting bronze, several kinds of weapons, personal items such as hairpins, objects of bone and ivory, and of course there were thousands of pottery shards. Some of the interesting finds were several baked clay stamps made in a design which became quite popular for the next several years.

THE LUNG-SHAN CULTURE

What appears to be a second late Neolithic culture sprang up along the China coast in Shantung Province near **Lung-shan** and spread southward to the city of Hangchow. There, another form of pottery was discovered. It was largely finished in shiny black, and the site also contained evidence of domesticated animals and other implements common to Neolithic man. This second development is now identified as early China's **"Black Pottery"** or **"Lung-shan"** culture. In other words, there have been two basic cultural forms in northern China: the **Yang-shao** to the west and the **Lung-shan** in the east.

THE SHANG PERIOD CULTURE
1766-1123 B.C.

A third early cultural form was discovered near **An-Yang** in Honan province. The An-Yang site is located along the Huan River. It is here that the Shang leadership of China's first verified dynasty had apparently maintained the archives of its department of divination. Numerous fragments of jade and inscribed oracle bones and tortoise shells, along with exquisite bronze vessels and stone implements have been discovered at An-Yang. Objects made of glazed pottery and bronze seemed to be abundant even at this early age, about 1397 B.C. There were houses which had huge timbers, palaces, governmental offices, and ancestral shrines unearthed at the An-Yang site. The tombs were large and their contents contained those everyday things one would likely need in the next world. There have also been some chariot burials unearthed at this site.

The archaeology thus far indicates that the sites at Chengchow and at An-Yang were well organized, hierarchial states with a king at the top of the hierarchy. He was followed by many important nobles, all of whom lived in elaborate palaces. It also appears that the kings were important religious as well as political leaders. They looked for assistance and information on how to govern from divinations, which were directed to their departed ancestors. The supreme god was **Ti** and there were several lesser divinities. No one knows how universal the worship of ancestors might have been at this early date, but it appears to have been used constantly by the royal family.

Archaeologists have regarded these three distinctive cultural forms as quite separate entities. It was contended that the Yang-shao culture developed first, followed by the Lung-shan culture of the East, and that still later the Shang dyansty culture began independently of the

Prehistoric China

former two. More recently, however, an archaeologist at Yale, Chang Kwang-chih, has given strength to the belief that there may be a greater linkage between the Yellow River farmers of Neolithic times and the earliest form of Chinese civilization in the classical age. The Lung-shan culture, he believes, may have been the forerunner of Shang society. The exact region where, and the process by which this transition took place, is as yet uncertain.

While northern China experienced the early stages of man's development, southern China was not devoid of human activity. Civilization in southern China has a different origin and it did not become part of the later mainstream Chinese civilization. Chipped stone implements have been found in China's extreme southern provinces. These Upper Paleolithic implements, and the recently discovered evidence of man in southern China, were an extension of developments which took place in Southeast Asia. The Mesolithic Age sites located in southwestern China also reveal a Negroid type population similar to an earlier one in Southeast Asia, as contrasted to the Mongoloid group in the North. The development of metallic tools and weapons at a very early time have also been discovered in South China.

It is known that the Chinese developed a calendar earlier than most other civilizations. This early calendar was based upon the lunar system of a 30-day month and 360 days in a year. There was an additional month added to the year whenever the calendar became seasonally dislocated. This was called the 13th month and could be added at any time within the regular twelve month calendar. Although it appears awkward by our modern standards, they were able to maintain a calendar which fit the seasons. Keeping the calendar correct, recording sunrises and sunsets, eclipses, etc., was the duty of a team of royal astronomers, who were maintained by the king. One Chinese scientist claimed that he had records spanning a period of 152 years from 1313 to 1161 B.C. Interestingly, his records showed the solar year to be 365 and one-fourth days!

Chinese historical tradition claims that during the reign of the ruler Wu-ting the days were divided into seven parts, but in Tsu-chia's time they were divided into 10 parts, an indication that the Chinese were already favoring a decimal system. The decimal system was soon transferred to all units of measurement as well as to time. The Chinese standard unit of measurement in this early time was equal to 1.7 centimeters today.

The king, with the advice of his astronomers, told the official superintendents when the various tasks were to be performed--plowing, sowing, harvesting, road work, etc. Even the tools for work and agriculture were stored by the authorities, and were issued to those doing work each day. Like many other primitive societies, the harvests were kept in the royal granaries and grain was drawn out for each family according to their needs. Such close administration was maintained by a whole hierarchy of administrators who were responsible to the king. The outlying territories were given out as fiefs, largely within the royal family or to deserving generals and the king's office-holders. These "vassals" owed the king military assistance in exchange for their grant of land. They were also required to pay tribute, and supply manpower for public works.

The peasants in those early times used hoes and mattocks, which were made primarily of wood but given a point of stone or shell. Spades and a foot plow were also in use. The water buffalo, whereof there seem to have been many wild ones at this time, were beginning to be domesticated, but there is no concrete evidence that they were used to pull a plow or that the simple pull-type plow had yet been invented.

Prehistoric China

The one crop common throughout China in the Shang dynasty was **millet**. **Rice** was cultivated in China perhaps 5,000 years ago, but it is generally believed to have been secondary to millet in these early times. The rice crop required 180 days from seedtime to harvest during the Shang dynasty. It was not until the 11th century A.D. that **Champa rice** was introduced with its much shorter maturity time. It was the Champa rice that made two crops per year were possible, depending upon the latitude. As the maturity time shortened it was therefore possible to double the annual yield of rice from the same acreage. Interestingly, China's population has always risen to fill, or often over-fill, the grain supply. From earliest times until quite recently, China suffered from starvation unless nature was most cooperative. Like India, southeast China is heavily dependent upon a good summer monsoon. In the past few years there have been varieties of rice developed which will yield three crops per year in the southern parts of China. This, along with stringent birth control, has actually given China some rice for export.

It was during the Shang dynasty that goats and fowl were domesticated and trained elephants were used for heavy building projects. The water buffalo became a common sight working in the rice paddies. Some irrigation was practiced in these early times, especially in the Huang Ho River valley, but nothing compared to the amount of land under irrigation in modern times.

THE BRONZE AGE IN CHINA

There is evidence that bronze-making began in China as early as the Xia dynasty, the 21st to the 16th centuries B.C., since primitive knives and drills have been found from excavations of those early times. By the early Shang period there is good evidence that the technique of casting small bronze objects had been accomplished. Later they moved into spear points, arrowheads, hardware for chariots, and hardware for harness. It should be noted that bronze objects during the Shang era were largely for military purposes, not for domestic use or for agricultural purposes. These tools of the household and of agriculture continued to be primarily Neolithic stone, bone, shell, wood, etc.

Most bronze domestic pieces were extremely heavy, most likely very expensive, and found only at royal sites. Many of the bronze finds of the Shang era, 1766 to 1123 B.C., have been of such quality that some authorities believe the technique must have been imported from someplace in the West, where bronze work had already developed around 2500 B.C. Lately, however, a few primitive bronze pieces have been found, which establishes an evolution of the working of bronze in China. All styles to date are strictly Chinese in style, which causes other authorities to believe that the Chinese discovered the technique totally on their own. One added point favoring Chinese origins would be that virtually all bronze work in the western world leaned heavily toward the "lost wax" method, whereas, nearly all Chinese work of this early time was poured into molds of at least two parts and cast in the mold. The "lost wax" technique of bronze casting seems to have first arrived in China rather late--about the 5th century B.C.

Prehistoric China

SERICULTURE

Another aspect of early Chinese civilization concerns the process of the manufacturing and trade in **silk**. There seems little question that **sericulture** is one of China's distinct contributions to the world. There is a Chinese legend that over 4,000 years ago, **Lei Zu**, wife of the Yellow Emperor, Huang Di, was resting under the mulberry trees in the garden of her palace when she heard a rustling in the leaves. Looking up, she saw silkworms spinning their cocoons. She took one in her hand and found how fine and shining the silken thread appeared. It was so soft and flexible that she wondered whether it would be possible to wind it off the cocoon and weave it into cloth. "How wonderful such a cloth would be!" At least some variation of this story has been told in China for thousands of years. Not only was China the first to weave silk cloth, but for hundreds of years other countries could not overcome the obstacles of tending to the worms and keeping them healthy.

Whether this legend is true or not, there is evidence that the Chinese had begun to weave cloth from hemp fibers as much as 2,000 years before they began to work with silk. Evidence of this is found in a basket of woven hemp excavated at a Neolithic site in Zhejiang province in 1958. Also, jade carvings in the shape of silkworms were often placed on funerary objects which were later discovered in the tombs of the Shang aristocrats. Finally, the written characters for "silk" and "silkworm" have been found scratched on oracle bones from that same early time. In the centuries following, sericulture flourished under government sponsorship. At one point in Chinese history the people were even allowed to pay their taxes in silk. Much of this silk was exported to provide capital for the expensive tastes of the various kings and emperors. It is also significant that the capital of the first Chinese emperor was at **Xian**, the city which was also the eastern terminus of the **Old Silk Road**.

AN INTRODUCTION TO WRITING AND LANGUAGE IN EAST ASIA

No one knows who invented writing. Neither do we know when or where it began. Most authorities who study the origin of writing would say that it very likely was started by drawing pictures to represent objects, animals, or people. Chinese pictographic writing is believed to have begun during the Shang period, possibly around 1400 B.C. Writing in Mesopotamia and Egypt had begun nearly 2,000 years before this time, but there is no real evidence that China borrowed from those areas because the Chinese characters are so different from either Mesopotamia or Egypt that it must have been developed independently. A system of phonetic writing, which was developed by the Phoenicians and is still in use in the western world, does not seem to have had any influence upon China at all. The Chinese system originated primarily as a pictographic or ideogramatic system and it has remained that way to the present time.

Most of our current knowledge of Shang dynasty writing comes from inscriptions on bones and the upper shell of the tortoise. Both bones and shell were employed for sacred and profane use. Over 162,000 of these are scattered around the world in public and private collections. One of the largest discoveries of these "oracle bones" came in 1936 when 17,096 were located in a single pit. A few bones were among the great mass of tortoise shells. Three hundred of the the shells and bones were very complete. The inscriptions on a large percentage were incised against a scorched area, but some were written with a brush, using cinnabar, a reddish pigment derived from mercuric sulfide crystals, which occur as a natural ore of mercury

Prehistoric China

in some parts of China. Generally, there is both a question and a response written on these oracle bones. For instance, "What about this year's rice crop?" The answer might be, "Greatly favorable." Questions were also asked about health, success in war, whether the ruler would have a son or a daughter, etc. It should be mentioned that the Greeks and other early civilizations used a similar system of divining the future.

The mechanics of the oracle bone system meant that the question would be posed, then the tortoise shell or the shoulder blade of an animal was heated, sometimes totally but often with the hot end of a stick. As the cracks formed, a shaman or priest would interpret the meaning of the cracks. Obviously, the accuracy of such a test depended upon the skill and knowledge of the person who made the interpretation. The system very likely was as accurate as some of our long-range forecasts today, otherwise, it would never have continued for over a thousand years in almost every one of the early civilizations. Once the interpretation had been made, it was written on the bone, or tortise shell, possibly for future reference.

Other evidences of Shang writing indicates that many things were written down such as receipts, contracts, tax records, etc. They were written on flat strips of bamboo because paper was not invented until a later date. Although none of these have survived to the present time, we know that they used the bamboo strips because they have been graphically illustrated on the sides of beakers which **have** survived. It is probably safe to say that the early pictogram writing had its antecedents which reach back much farther than the Shang period.

Like all other languages, including modern English, French, or German, the Chinese writing has made some changes since the earliest times. On the other hand, it has probably changed less throughout the ages than most other languages. Chinese writing is also interesting in that there are between 3,500 and 4,000 characters which were developed to represent individual words rather than sounds. Basically, they break down into three types: (1) pictographs, which can be recognized for what they are supposed to represent, (2) ideographs, which represent ideas, and (3) compound characters, one part of which indicates how the word is to be pronounced.

Chinese writing has had a profound influence upon nearly all the languages of East Asia today. Even though the people of China may speak several different languages, they have all adapted their **written** language from the same basic characters. The **Sinitic** languages include Chinese, Vietnamese, Thai, Burmese, and Tibetan. Not only are each of these different from the other, but even in Chinese there are several different dialects, especially as one travels from North China to South China. The Communist dictator, Mao, tried to force everyone in China to learn **Mandarin Chinese**, but even with all the power of the state behind the effort it was not succeeded.

The **Ural-Altaic** languages of Asia include Japanese, Korean, Manchurian, Mongolian, the Turkic languages, and, in Europe--Finnish and Hungarian. Although Japanese, Manchurian, and Mongolian may have some similarities in writing, Korea developed its own system, and of course the Finnish and Hungarian are written with an entirely different alphabet.

Prehistoric China

THE WARS OF THE SHANG DYNASTY

Organized warfare can first be noted in the Shang period, although it undoubtedly existed much earlier. Standing armies of 3,000 to 4,000 men seems to have been common during this period. On some occasions these armies grew to as many as 20,000 to 30,000 men who were conscripted for service. Some battles involved as many as 13,000 soldiers. There are no records yet discovered which show how the Shang were able to bring so many together for war and to support them over a sustained period of time. Nevertheless, their military power evidently gave them a very decided advantage over the less advanced tribes who lived around and among them. It is believed that many of the Shang kings engaged in almost continual military expeditions. Plunder and tribute became one way of financing the royal economy. Slavery was also very common under the Shang rulers.

Some of the Shang rulers kept large, well-stocked hunting preserves which included many wild animals. Since these animals were not all native to China, they must have been imported. It is presumed that the nobility believed that hunting was a good practice for war. Two-wheeled chariots drawn by two horses as well as four-horse chariots have been found. These indicate that mechanical ability was quite advanced by this time. The nobility either rode in these chariots or on horseback for both hunting and for war. They carried bronze spears and halberds, and in warfare they were protected by shields and helmets. Other troops and conscripts were supplied chiefly with composite bows that shot arrows tipped with points of bronze, bone, or stone. One inscription on a bone dated in the 12th century B.C. tells of a successful military campaign against a state on the western marches in which the booty included 1,570 prisoners, 2 chariots, 180 shields, 15 pieces of armor and a few arrows.

LIFE AND SOCIETY IN SHANG TIMES

The successful wars of the Shang period created a class hierarchy. The king and the officials of his court lived in spacious houses within the city wall. Rows of wooden pillars were set upon foundation stones which supported the roof. Homes of the upper class were built above the ground while the peasants lived in hovels which were dug partially or totally into the earth. The fortunate ones dug their homes into the side of a hill. Most Shang cities were built upon hills. From 90 to 95 percent of the population belonged to the lower class or were slaves. There is little evidence of a middle class. Nearly everyone worked on the land. The only exceptions were the soldiers when they were engaged in warfare and far from their land. With few exceptions, the claim to land was based upon military service.

Life was cheap in Shang times as far as children were concerned. Many children never saw their first birthday. **Infanticide** was practiced by both upper and lower class families with baby girls being the most likely victims. The upper classes wanted boys to succeed them in the power structure, and the lower classes also wanted boys to work since they would earn much more for the family. Infanticide was most common during times of famine when food was scarce. Upper class girls nearly always had their feet bound so they would always have tiny feet, a practice which continued into the 20th century.

The Shang also practiced human sacrifice. In one large Shang tomb archaeologists found the decapitated bodies of humans, horses, and dogs, as well as ornaments of bone, stone, and jade.

Prehistoric China

One could speculate that such a mass grave was a consequence of either war or criminal activity, such as plotting the overthrow of the government. However, this does not explain why they would have included the ornaments of bone, stone, and jade in their graves since jade was both expensive and considered a sacred rock. Could such a grave site have been some kind of human sacrifice for religious purposes? No one knows the answer to this ancient puzzle.

It is known that when a king died, hundreds of the lower classes were slaughtered and buried with him, along with those who were his faithful servants. Although he probably wanted many servants in his household in the after-life, it is altogether possible that some of his close friends considered it an honor to go into the next world with their king. Since writing during the Shang period is still largely confined to oracle bones, it is impossible to understand their religion and the social pressures present much beyond these inscriptions. Archaeologists and anthropologists continue to work toward answers as to **why** so many people joined the king in death. Almost certainly those of the working class were **not** volunteers. At least we can be quite certain that the Shang **did** believe in a life after death. It is also known that humans were sacrificed when a new palace was finished or an altar was built. There may well have been other human sacrifices such as important religious festivals.

Industry and commerce centered around silk, agriculture, and handicrafts. There is good evidence at archaeological sites such as Changchow, An-yang, Xian, and other sites, that trade goods often moved long distances. There is a small amount of evidence that they traded as far away as India, Mesopotamia, and possibly as far as present-day Lebanon. Cinnabar, a red sulfide of mercury which was used as a dye, was traded throughout China.

Other remarkable signs of progress place the Chinese as pioneers in building roads, and the **Grand Canal**, which was begun as early as the Shang dynasty. The Grand Canal is a masterpiece of engineering nearly as great as the Great Wall. Both achievements were not completed until later, but it is believed that their antecedents dated back to Shang times. There is no evidence at this time which would show that food was moved through their transportation system in times of famine. Rivers were used extensively for moving freight as far back as prehistoric times. When the Yellow River flooded each summer, it disrupted both transportation and communication as well as washing away entire villages. Life was hard in Shang times and most of the people lived close to the land and had little contact with the outside world.

There is a tradition that in the reign of Ti-hsin, the last ruler of the Shang, there was a period of extreme drought. Many dragon dances were conducted by the priests, but it seemed to do no good. According to the Chinese historians, this was interpreted as a portent indicating failure on the part of the king and he was overthrown. It is more likely that after a few hundred years of the same family, they became soft, inefficient, and corrupt.

A SUMMARY OF PREHISTORIC CHINA

Prehistoric China's earliest people were hunter-gatherers who lived in caves such as the one at Choukoutian south and west of Beijing (Peking). Today there is very little of the Paleolithic or the Mesolithic Ages--some 400,000 to 500,000 years ago--to focus upon. Beginning in the Neolithic Age there are many more archaeological finds which help to begin the story of early mankind in China. Recording the past--history--has always been very important in

Prehistoric China

China. Religion played an integral part in everyone's lives. Religion in these early times was primarily an **animistic** faith.

The Shang dynasty lived on the edge of recorded history, but much of that period is still largely mythological. Perhaps future archaeological digs will begin to close the vast gaps we do not understand concerning the long period between China's earliest ages and the finds of the Neolithic Age. The deep loess soil and the frequent floods accompanied by the changing course of the Huang Ho River have made archaeology very difficult. An unstable government in China from 1912 to 1949 also slowed the process of discovery.

Writing as a means of recording the divination of the oracle bones for future reference began during the Shang period, 1766 to 1123 B.C. The Chinese knowledge of writing then spread to most of East Asia. Trade and commerce have always been an important factor in Chinese society. The Yangtze River reaches far into the interior as a navigable river. The Huang Ho (Yellow) River is less valuable for navigation, but its water is necessary to support life in the rich loess soil of northern China.

The Chinese, therefore, developed a civilization which was closely tied to the land and water resources. At some very early time they began using their tin and copper resources in the manufacture of bronze. Unfortunately, much of their metal production in these early years was utilized for warfare rather than improving the lot of their citizens.

Figure 21

Prehistoric China

BOOKS FOR FURTHER READING

Blunden, Caroline, & Elvin, Mark, *Cultural Atlas of China* (1983).

Chang, K. C., *Early Chinese Civilization: Anthropological Perspectives* (1976).

Chi Li, *The Beginnings of Chinese Civilization* (1968).

Cotterell, Arthur, *China: A Cultural History* (1988).

Cotterell, Arthur, & Morgan, David, *China's Civilization* (1975).

Creel, Herrlee, *The Birth of China* (1937).

Eichorn, Werner, *Chinese Civilization* (1969).

Fairbank, John K., *China, A New History* (1992).

Fairbank, John K., Reischauer, Edwin O., & Craig, Albert M., *East Asia, Tradition & Transformation* (1989).

Fitzgerald, Charles P., *The Horizon History of China* (1982).

Gernet, Jacques, *A History of Chinese Civilization* (1987).

Gernet, Jacques, *Ancient China from the Beginnings to the Empire* (1968).

Keightley, David N. editor, *The Origins of Chinese Civilization* (1983).

Kolb, Albert, *East Asia* (1971).

Kwang-chih Chang, *The Archaeology of Ancient China* (1986).

Loewe, Michael, *The Pride that was China* (1990).

Schirokauer, Conrad, *A Brief History of Chinese and Japanese Civilizations* (1989).

Treistman, Judith, *The Prehistory of China* (1972).

Watson, William, *Early Civilization in China* (1966).

Figure 22 208

Chapter 21
THE CHOU DYNASTY
c.1122-256 B. C.

INTRODUCTION

The **Chou Dynasty** also known as the **Zhou**, ruled from about 1122 to 256 B.C. They were a tribe on the western frontier, an area which had long been a battleground between the civilized Shang and the more primitive nomads. Led by a **King Wu**, the Chou tribe took this opportunity to strike the famine-weakened Shang. They formed a coalition with eight other states, and it required twenty years of hard fighting, along with much suffering, but the Chou prevailed. In the final battle for the Shang capital, it is said that blood flowed like a river through the streets while thousands of survivors fled in every direction. Some believe it was these refugees who may have introduced the Shang culture to **Hunan province** in the south and **Manchuria** and **Korea** to the north and northeast. King Wu allowed the last of the Shang family to retain a small parcel of land near modern Kuei-teh in Honan to continue the ancestral rites while the Chou occupied the remainder of China.

The Chou established their capital at **Hao** near **Xian**. They then parcelled out the territory to the near family and to favored generals. Each member of the family and the military held their land as a kind of fief. Altogether there were about 1,773 such fiefs at the beginning of the Chou dynasty, and of course each one owed dues to King Wu. By dividing the land into such small tracts, it guaranteed that no one of the "barons" would have enough resources to launch an attack against the monarchy.

For the next two and one-half to three centuries, 1122 to 771 B.C.--the dating is uncertain--there were thirteen Chou kings. And, just like the Shang, at the end they were overthrown by enemies from the outside who discovered they had grown rich and soft. The ruling king was slain, but like the Shang, the family established a new capital, this time on the Lo River. The Chou family never recovered from this disaster of 771 B.C., and although they continued to rule over a fair amount of real estate, the final blow did not fall until 256 B.C. But in the interval the Chou continued to lose both land and the respect of the people. The feudal powers around them ignored their capital at Lo-yang. By 403 B.C., there were only seven states of what had once been a mighty kingdom. In 221 B.C., **Shih Huang Ti** pronounced himself the first emperor of the family of **Ch'in** and the Chou came to a close. The circle of history had been repeated. After ruling a goodly share of China for over eight and one-half centuries, this somewhat barbaric tribe, which took over China in 1123 B.C., considered themselves very civilized by 256 B.C.

LIFE AND CULTURE DURING THE CHOU DYNASTY

The face of China changed a great deal during the Chou years. Early in their reign it was reported that the king had killed 420 stags of different kinds and wild boar, as well as two tigers and nine wolves, and all of that in a single month! The Chou monarchs traveled widely, living off their vassals, and checking on their administrators. Each successive king only lived in his predecessor's palace until he could build a new one. Such an expensive court caused more and more land to be cleared and heavily cultivated in an effort to meet the royal demand for taxes.

The Chou Dynasty

Furthermore, each vassal thought of himself as a mini-king, and tried to construct palaces and cities to rival those of the king. Tax burdens were excessively heavy as a consequence.

In the later Chou period, 771 to 222 B.C., also referred to as the **Eastern Chou** because of the location of their capital, many of the vassals blamed the king for their weakness. Noblemen struggled with one another hoping in each case that they would come out the top man and turn the tide around. It did not work and the fighting and disruption only weakened the Chou further.

Even with such heavy taxes, many nobles taxed their subjects even more to build defensive walls against their neighbors and against nomadic tribes who raided into their realm because they heard the Chou were weak. Some states created state monopolies in universally needed staples such as salt, iron, and liquor. Even the weather changed toward a cooler, drier climate in the north. The first recorded reservoir to store water in China was built around 600 B.C. near Shou-hsien in Anhwei. This reservoir was about 40 miles in circumference and provided irrigation for approximately 1,000 square miles of land.

As the Chinese irrigated the land it would soak up less water in the event of a heavy rainfall. Furthermore, more trees were cut and grassy areas were placed in cultivation. The consequence of such a policy led to severe flooding by the 4th century B.C. Everyone agreed they must build dikes. In 487 B.C. the state of Wu, centered near Soochow, dug the earliest canal to connect the Huai with the Yangtze River. Ultimately there were 288 miles of feeder canals, which provided both transportation and communication as well as irrigation. Even though the tax burden was terribly heavy to finance all of these internal improvements, it was this area of northeast China which became the grain center of China and the greatest area of growth.

Commerce and industry increased considerably under the Chou. In theory, the nobility were supposed to be above engaging in trade, but in actual practice they became excellent businessmen. The first noble to receive a fief in the Shantung area promoted its silk textile industry and encouraged handicrafts. China's silk industry was soon centered in the Yangtze Valley. Embroidery was already beginning as a people's art and very shortly the Chinese merchants developed a sizeable market in this offshoot of their textile industry.

A fifth of the world's bamboo grows in China--some 300 different varieties. The Chinese have probably used bamboo for the last 6,000 years or more. In southern China, almost every house had bamboo items such as furniture of all kinds, cases, baskets, brooms, chopsticks, and boats. Sometimes even their houses were made of bamboo. The people in southern China spent long hours weaving palm fiber, cattail stems, rice straw, wheat straw, and rattan as well as bamboo. A large market developed during the early Chou era for all kinds of items made of bamboo and woven straw products. The merchant entrepreneurs capitalized upon this demand and the market area soon expanded throughout China.

Commercial and industrial centers developed in the north where certain areas became known for their copper, textiles, salt, fish, and after 500 B.C., iron. By as early as 550 B.C. the rich merchants of Chiang, the capital, could decorate their carriages with gold and jade. One scholar has estimated that by the year 300 B.C. the city of Lin-tzu had a population of at least 370,000. Some of the merchants became as rich as the noblemen. But the nobles had other desires. They built beautiful palaces and pleasure houses as well as providing elaborate tombs and maintaining a lavish court. At least they employed many of China's growing population.

The Chou Dynasty

Up to this time most of the trade had been handled by local barter arrangements. The great increase in the need for money for all the palaces and tombs led China into a money economy. Cowrie shells, both real and imitation, were China's first medium of exchange. Copper and gold coins replaced the former barter system in trade outside one's local area. Some of the earliest coins were shaped like knives and other everyday items, but in time the round coin, frequently with a square hole in the center, replaced the earliest coins. The scope of this Eastern Chou trade is shown by the fact that the knife coins have been dug up as far away as Korea. The acceptance of coinage was not immediate and barter continued to be relied upon in the local markets for several centuries.

The era of the Eastern Chou, 771 to 222 B.C., was a busy and a growing time in spite of warring nobles, pressures from without, and seeming weaknesses of the government. We have seen the tremendous increase in trade and commercial pursuits, so also was there a tremendous increase in the intellectual life. The need for literate people to serve as scribes, archivists, judges, diplomats, temple priests, etc., exceeded the supply available. Education was admired by everyone. The teachers were at the pinnacle of prestige at this time. All kinds of writing--poetry, political theory, law, music, mathematics, medicine, agriculture, and the list could continue--all were held in high esteem.

AN AGE OF PHILOSOPHERS

Some of the greatest minds China has ever produced appeared in this period. Many of China's political philosophers were associated with the government and most seemed to recognize that there were some grave problems. Unfortunately, there were few viable solutions.

So far our study of the religions and philosophies of Asia has dealt primarily with the religious environment in India--Hinduism, Jainism, and Buddhism, as well as some of the minor religious groups. Islam and its sects such as Sufism became a major consideration once the Muslims began to invade the subcontinent by the 10th century. China also witnessed the development of some major religious philosophies which were unlike the other religious persuasions.

There are three major faiths which are of Chinese origin. The oldest of the three is **Taoism**, sometimes spelled **Dowism**. This religion was founded by **Lao Tzu** who lived during the period of about 600 to 500 B.C. The second great faith which originated in China is **Confucianism**. This was founded by **Kong Qui,** better known in the western world as **Confucius**. His dates have been reasonably well established as 551 to 479 B.C. The third purely Chinese faith is known as **Meng-Tzu**, founded by a scholar known as **Mencius** who lived about 371-289 B.C.

A fourth great religion in China is **Buddhism.** This faith originated in India under the leadership of a young prince named Siddhartha Gautama, who lived in the same general time period as the great Chinese philosophers. Buddha's dates are most often given as 560 to 483 B.C. Buddhism arrived in China at a much later date.

There is the story, although not positively confirmed, that Confucius went to see the archivist, **Lao Tzu**, at the Imperial Library. Confucius, still a young man, put on his most elaborate gown to meet the old scholar. The story goes on to say that for all the questions which the young Confucius asked, Lao Tzu turned them around to ask Confucius, or he gave the question the total brush-off. There are some scholars who believe that this story may be true.

TAOISM

Of the four major religions of China listed above, **Taoism** is considered the oldest. The founder of this faith was **Lao Tzu**, also spelled Lao-tze and sometimes Lao-tse. The name is translated to mean "Master Lao" or sometimes "the Old Master." Lao-tzu is not only the oldest but probably the second most significant of the Chinese philosophers, Confucius ranking number one. At the present time scholars have still not been able to establish precisely where or when Lao Tzu was born, or where or when he died. There are a few who doubt there ever was a Lao-Tzu. Some of the stories about him will help explain the lack of confidence in the legends about Lao-Tzu.

It seems Lao-Tzu was born about 604 B.C. in China. Legend says he was conceived by a shooting star, carried in his mother's womb for 82 years (which would make it the longest pregnancy on record), and he was born a wrinkled old man with white hair. It is said that he was never a youth, he was always very old.

Lao-Tzu was immediately recognized as a very intelligent and insightful person. He was appointed the keeper of the official government archives where he already knew virtually everything in the records. After several years on this job, where he supposedly discussed philosophy with the younger Confucius, he climbed on his water buffalo and rode off to the West in search of solitude in his remaining years. When he arrived at the border to his province, he was recognized by the guard who pleaded with the Old Master that he had failed to leave any written records of his teachings and beliefs.

Realizing this was the case, it is said that Lao-Tzu then took the time to write a small book of only 5,000 characters which is called the *Tao Te Ching*, which means **The Way and Its Power**. The guard then pleaded that he wished to accompany Lao-Tzu and to be his servant. Lao-Tzu consented and they both rode off through the now unguarded border post, and neither was ever heard of again. Rumor says they were headed toward Tibet.

This small book, ordinarily referred to simply as the *Tao*, is the heart of the belief in Taoism, which is pronounced "**Dowism**." Actually, Taoism consists of two distinct movements, one **a philosophy** called *Tao-chia*, or the Taoist school, and the other **a religion** called *Tao-chiao*. There is a tendency in the western world to melt the two together. The basic idea embodied in the *Tao Te Ching* is **naturalism** in the sense of *wu-wei*, which literally means "inaction." As interpreted by a Taoist we should take no "**unnatural**" action. The best thing to do is to follow the "path" or "way," and that is precisely what the "Tao" means--the way.

If one asks, "What is the way?" then Lao-Tzu would say that it cannot be perceived because it exceeds the senses. It can be known only through mystical insight which cannot be expressed in words. "The way" not only pertains to the individual and the ordering of their own life, but to the universe itself. It is the driving power in nature, the order behind all life, the spirit which cannot be exhausted. Tao is behind all and beneath all, the womb from which all life springs and to which it again returns. Since Tao is a spirit rather than matter, it cannot be exhausted. The more we draw upon it, the more it will produce.

The Chou Dynasty

The *Te* in the title of Lao-Tzu's little book refers to the way of **power**. Power can be used in more ways than one. Some Taoists believe that the "power" should be used to order the gods, to accomplish our desires, but this is not a common interpretation today.

Another approach of Taoism believes that the power of the universe is basically psychic in nature. If an individual is willing to practice yoga very stringently, it is possible to become receptacles of the Tao. This would give the recipient a certain calm within the world which would radiate out to others and thus show them the way. Those who followed this philosophy did have many devotees in the five centuries before the birth of Christ, but this approach has now died out.

The most popular of the three "power" approaches and the one subscribed to by most Taoists today is the approach whereby the individual tries to bring their life into tune with nature and the universe. Self-assertiveness, competition, and ambition must all be given up as well as material goods or goals. **Selflessness** is an honored condition. Material nature is all bad. The follower of this philosophy should not work to acquire material things because they only tend to corrupt. They should try to make friends with nature rather than trying to control it. In following this approach to the *Te*, one must use the resources of the subliminal mind to release one's self. One should sense the ebb and flow of life and nature, then adjust to it rather than trying to direct it.

In other words, make friends with nature rather than trying to conquer it, dominate it, or control it. Civilization for the sake of civilization is condemned. Travel beyond the necessities of food is discouraged. Stark simplicity is encouraged. All of this thinking had a profound impression upon the Chinese. It shows not only in their philosophy of life, but in their art and architecture.

It is no accident that the 17th century "Great Period" of Chinese art coincided with an effort to portray philosophical Taoism in art. Painters took nature as their subject, and before assuming brush and silk they would go out and live in the forest with nature, lose themselves in it, and become one with it. Many times we see mankind depicted by the artist as being very small, floating down a rapid stream between towering mountains. Man is so helpless against nature and yet the artist shows him calmly riding his raft as though he too were a part of the natural setting. Other scenes show the breadth and depth of a scene or a beautiful flower or tree, sometimes with a small solitary figure observing it all passing before them. Even in our own time, it is said that one of the inspirations of Frank Lloyd Wright was the fact that Taoist temples never stand out from the landscape but rather are nestled against the hills, tucked back under the trees, and blend in with the environment. So also should mankind blend in with nature, identify themselves with it and allow the *Tao* to work through their lives.

The Chinese symbol which portrays **Yin and Yang** is a symbolic representation of this feeling--man and nature in harmony--man and the eternal in harmony. It may also be thought of as a polarity in the world between good and evil, active and the passive, light and dark, warm and cold, summer and winter, positive and negative, male and female, etc. Even though life is full of these polarities, the individual can learn to complement and counterbalance these forces. In the western world the concept of Puritanism has tended to paint things black and white, whereas the Taoist sees harmony in nature and much more gray area as one of the polarized areas tends to blend in with the other. In the end, life and death are seen as relative phases of the Tao's embracing continuum. The natural world does provide for us in both life and in death.

213

The Chou Dynasty

CONFUCIANISM

Lao-Tzu may be the slightly older Chinese philosopher, but **Confucius**, 551 to 479 B.C., is certainly the most **famous**. **As a teacher, philosopher, and political theorist**, his ideas have deeply influenced the civilization of all of Eastern Asia. It is sometimes difficult to assess the true Confucius since so many fanciful legends and sayings have been attributed to him. Nearly everyone knows a few "Confucius say...." lines, whether the philosopher ever actually said the statement or not.

As best we can tell, Confucius descended from a long line of minor nobility who became impoverished long before his birth. His family name was Kong Qui. The Confucius we know in the West was Latinized by Jesuit fathers in the 16th century. They took the Chinese title of **Kong Fuzi**, which meant Master Kong, and came up with the word Confucius.

Confucius was born in the state of Lu on the Shandong Peninsula. He was orphaned at an early age and grew up with little or no formal education because of a lack of money. He seems to have been diligent and probing and to have educated himself. He then served in a minor civil service position, some say as a local minister of crime, others say he was an accountant, but in any event he became famous and respected by teaching the sons of middle and upper class men to prepare them for civil service positions. It is said that he tutored as many as 3,000 disciples.

It was his teaching for which he is remembered rather than for his outstanding leadership in the civil service. Apparently, he was much too idealistic for the men who were his superiors. In his later years he is credited with editing the classical books of history now known as the *Wu Jing*, or the Five Classics. Confucius had a great desire to preserve the history and style of governance of the former kings, especially of those from China's Golden Age, in order that his followers would understand the true basis and philosophy of government and power.

Like Buddha, Confucius was troubled by all the misery and suffering he found in the world. Much of this centered around the feudal style of warfare among the principalities, which was prevalent throughout China. China was nominally a united country under one king, but anyone could see that the king was only a figurehead or a puppet. The real power was held by the feudal princes. The feudal nobility constantly warred and jockeyed for position, hoping they would ultimately become the number one prince in China. Taxes were very heavy in order to support all the military campaigns. Armies marched to and fro, destroying crops as well as lives. Starvation was very common.

After observing all this suffering, Confucius dedicated his life to changing the system. He concluded that government, which heretofore had been managed for the pleasures of the rulers, should be managed for the happiness of their subjects. More concretely, he advocated the reduction of taxes, making punishments for criminals less severe, an end to needless wars, and a streamlined and dedicated civil service. His lifelong objective was to occupy an important administrative post in which he could put his theories into practice. Since so many of the Confucian theories ran counter to the policies of the local princes, he was never given a top policy-making post and remained the scholar-teacher. Many of the rulers considered Confucius "odd," while others considered him positively dangerous. Even the rulers in his native state of Lu paid little attention to his admonitions.

The Chou Dynasty

Apparently he had only a few students when he began teaching some of the basics he believed should be the foundation stones of any government. He does seem to have understood the basic qualifications rulers would look for in their new civil servants. The records indicate that he had above-average success in placing his students, even though it was said he could not get a civil service position for himself until he was fifty years of age.

Confucius taught his students the essentials of the position they wished to fulfill, and beyond this they were taught to think and to maintain high moral and ethical standards. Added together, it is fair to say that the students of Confucius were trained in **wisdom** rather than pure facts.

By the time that Confucius was in his fifties, it seemed that he had trained and placed so many well-qualified students that his own fame merited an administrative post. Unfortunately, he was given a position with a great title but no real authority to make changes. As soon as he recognized that his job was more of an honorarium than a real job, he resigned in disgust. Armed with his knowledge of administration, he traveled throughout China looking for a ruler who would more or less turn over his state for management according to Confucian principles. Needless to say, he found none. Some of his disciples implored him to return to his native state of Lu. Finally at age 67, he did return to Lu where he continued teaching until his death at the age of 72.

The Confucian method was apparently similar to that of the Greek philosopher, Socrates. He conversed with his students in both small groups and individually. He studied the character of each disciple and sought to develop the total man. Sincerity and high ethical standards were transmitted to all his students. In addition to statecraft and administration, he asked each student to study history, poetry, and music. He set up human relations type conflicts and had his students develop solutions, while he acted as a coach. He was neither dogmatic nor authoritarian. He strongly emphasized that every educated person had both the right and the duty to think and to make decisions for themselves. The real importance of Confucius is this awakening of education and its application to real situations. This system undermined the very basis of authoritarianism. It was really the world turned upside down for the princes, nobles, and the upper aristocracy.

Everyone can agree that Confucius was a highly principled man. He felt that somewhere in the universe there was an element or a force on the side of what was right and ethical. He was a religious man by all accounts, but like most Chinese he gave little attention to metaphysics, epistemology, or logic. He gave no credence to superstition. He was very systematic. He always liked to hear all sides of an issue, to think it through, discuss it thoroughly, then come to a conclusion. Humanity was also central to the Confucian philosophy. He said that: "Virtue is to love men and wisdom is to understand men." Whatever else we may say of Confucius, he had no design to start a new religion centered upon himself.

Confucius regarded mankind as one large family. Therefore, sincerity and reciprocity should be one's guiding principles. To help another person to succeed or to become established was to be considered a mark of success for one's self. In accord with these ideas, he believed that the state should be a wholly cooperative enterprise with everyone from the ruler to the lowliest peasant working as a team for the good of all. In his own age the aristocrats often believed that they were descended from the gods--that they were divine--an idea running through many Far Eastern philosophies and religions.

215

The Chou Dynasty

Everyone varies in their talents, but Confucius believed that anyone was capable of becoming educated. Therefore, he laid very great stress on education designed to develop abilities and to strengthen character. He believed that at least the basics of education must be given to even the humblest of citizens. In this way society could select from all the students those individuals who were best qualified to fulfill the Confucian plan to improve society. Furthermore, since the state was a cooperative enterprise, an enlightened citizenry was necessary to permit it to operate effectively. Finally, Confucius believed that war was evil because of all the suffering it entailed. Occasionally a nation would have to go to war for self defense. In such cases, he believed that when war must be prosecuted, it should be done vigorously. The army should be well educated and be entirely clear as to **why** it was fighting and thoroughly convinced of the justice of its cause.

It seems to be the common fate of great men to have their ideas distorted by posterity. So it was with the great philosopher of Lu. It was not until the **Han Dynasty** came to power, 202 B.C. to A.D. 221, that the Confucian principles were truly applied. By this time Confucius had been dead for nearly two centuries. People selected from his teachings those things with which they agreed and discarded the remainder. One of the most lasting contributions of Confucius also came long after his death in 479 B.C. It is a collection known as the "Four Books," consisting of four ancient Confucian texts that were used as official subject matter for civil service examinations in China from 1313 until 1905. These "Four Books" also served to introduce Chinese students to the more complex Confucian literature, the *Wu Ching*, otherwise known as the "**Five Classics**."

Many people worshipped Confucius as a wise sage, another Moses, or Jesus, or a Buddha. He was so all-knowing he must have been a gift of heaven. Stories even circulated about experiences his mother had before the Great Sage was ever born. Works which were purportedly written by Confucius were, in our words, canonized. Confucius supposedly had a saying for everything. All of life could be managed successfully simply by following the sayings and teachings of Confucius. [Note: There is little positive evidence that Confucius personally wrote anything original.]

Filial piety, or respect for one's parents, became a major Confucian contribution. The story was told that although his father died while he was quite young, his mother gave him every educational opportunity. Parents, especially aged parents, should therefore be respected. Respect for the older parents led to respect for **all** of one's ancestors dating back many years before. In other words, **ancestor veneration**. We have seen that cremation was a common method of disposing of the dead in India, but in China the dead were **buried**. Since everyone does return to the soil from which we came, Confucius reasoned that everyone was entitled to a burial plot when they died. Even though it may be small, it should not be disturbed.

The matter of cemeteries has been a problem the various communist leaders of China have really had to wrestle with because in some areas of China up to 10 percent or more of the land was devoted to cemeteries. At least Confucius **did** make the Chinese reflect upon whether they were doing a good job or a bad job as a parent, civil servant, or community leader. The feeling in China continues to be that your children and grandchildren will never respect you if you either did evil things or were a failure in life.

Education should become a primary goal of the state according to Confucius. By the 20th century the enormous increase in population made total education impractical--really impossible--but the desire was still there. Many families made tremendous sacrifices collectively to send just **one** of their promising sons to school, hopefully as far as it was possible for him to profit educationally. Later, many came to America in the early 20th century hoping for a good education for their children. Education for everyone is still a goal of the present Chinese government.

The Chinese Civil Service grew out of the Confucian system of education. The Confucian book called ***The Analects*** became **the** book, the basis of **all** education. The goal for the past several centuries has been to create the dream of Confucius of hundreds of years before. That is, that the very best of China's youth should serve the government. The democracy envisioned by Dr. Sun Yat Sen used much of this philosophy, but it was never implemented for several reasons. When Mao arrived on the scene following World War II, he replaced the Confucian philosophy by saying that hard physical labor was the answer. The major form of education during the Mao years consisted of indoctrination sessions based upon ***The Sayings of Chairman Mao***. Students from the schools and colleges were put to work in the fields or on public projects. Today, Mao's little book is hard to locate in China. The Confucian principles of a strong educational program have now returned, but Confucius is no longer as popular with the masses as he was before 1949.

For centuries **the close tie between the Chinese and the earth** meant that many should have the opportunity to own land. Consequently, when a man died his land was split among perhaps two or more sons. When one of these sons died the land was again split among his sons, etc. China became a patchwork of "garden plots" because of this intense desire for land. Soon, no one had enough land to make a living. Many barely survived even in good times. This problem came upon China **indirectly** as a logical consequence of the Confucian ideal for the ownership of land. The Communists tried to remedy this through collectivization, but this never provided sufficient food for the growing population. Today, China is again moving in the direction of private ownership (more often private management of public property), but with strict government regulations.

Confucianism stressed **other educational attributes** beyond being the good prince, the good administrator, or the good civil servant. They taught peace, music, painting, poetry, and of course, history. Self-contemplation and self-improvement were strongly stressed. They wished to portray to the world the greatest civilization ever. They valued the respect which was granted to them by the rest of the world. Unfortunately, these fine attributes of the liberal arts and an honest civil service were practically cast away as China entered the mechanical age of industrialization and materialism. A large part of their mechanistic view of life came from western businessmen and politicians, not from Confucianism. China today is looking toward a middle road between Confucianism and crass materialism.

It can be seen, then, that China's religion is an intellectual path as taught by Confucius, the Middle Way as taught by Buddha, and the non-materialistic path of adjustment to nature as taught by Lao Tzu. Mencius also made his contribution, similar to the others, but Confucianism, Buddhism, and Taoism became the big three in China.

The Chou Dynasty

MENCIUS

Mencius, 372 to 289 B.C., was given the name **Meng Tzu** at his birth. Mencius was a Confucian, and is sometimes referred to as the second major figure in classical Confucianism. He devoted his entire life to the study of Confucius. Then he went **beyond** Confucius in advocating many **democratic reforms**. Mencius lived toward the close of the Chou period, when the ruler and the government in general experienced an era of weakness and corruption. He was especially troubled by the lack of a real central authority and the disregard of the rulers for the welfare of their subjects. He laid out a program which is more or less a Chinese version of Plato, plus Thomas Jefferson.

Mencius advocated that all states should be ruled by philosophers. He said that all the people were entitled to good government. If the ruler did **not** give the people a good government then they would have every right to replace that ruler with another who would. Thomas Jefferson referred to this as "the right of revolution." Mencius never moved beyond the philosophical stage. The Chou rulers obviously did not like what he said and paid no attention to him. Consequently, their corruption and inefficiency caught up with them and they were thrown out in 256 B.C.

OTHER FAITHS IN CHINA

Religion often follows the trade routes, and that certainly was the case in China. Confucianism, Taoism, and the teachings of Mencius were the native Chinese religions. Then, Buddhism, Islam, Christianity, and Judaism came into China via the trade routes. There were two major routes--by land and by sea. Traders moving along the Old Silk Road brought religion as well as trade. So also did those who visited the port cities.

Islam never overwhelmed China as it once engulfed India. It did gain a firm foothold in nearby Southeast Asia. Mosques were built in the large maritime cities such as Canton and Quanzhou. Several mosques were also built in northern China, including Xian, but Islam never gained a large following at any time. The Muslim population of nearby Mongolia is about 4 percent today but was once higher. It was on the western fringes of China that Islam experienced its greatest expansion, probably related to the strong following in many of the Central Asian nations.

Christianity in China dates back to the **Nestorians**, a Syrian Christian sect. They first appeared in China in the 7th century when a Syrian named **Raban** introduced the faith at the imperial court in Xian. According to a stele found at Xian, there was a Nestorian monastery built there in 781.

Roman Catholic missionaries arrived in China from Rome in the 16th century. Among the first Christian missionaries to leave a lasting impact were **Matteo Ricci** and **Michael Ruggieri**, two Jesuit priests in the 1580s They established a mission at Zhaoqing in the Guangdong Province of China. Later, they were invited to the imperial court in Beijing. Roman Catholicism has been strong in Beijing from the end of the 16th century.

The Chou Dynasty

Protestant churches in China today have about the same relationship to the general populace as the Catholic Church. The first really large number of Protestant missionaries went to China in the late 19th and the 20th centuries. By the turn of the 20th century, there were several thousand Protestants and Catholics doing mission work in China. So great was their influence that the imperial government came to view them as an invading army, even though these early missionaries did much good and had little or no political aspirations. Western governments often asked China for increasing trade concessions and along with these, the right to protect the missions in the country. China saw such a request, along with Christianity, as an effort to introduce an entirely new lifestyle into their "superior" society. The government feared that western science, the new mechanical and industrial innovations, along with western approaches to education, different morals, and a new religion would totally change China within one generation. In the end they were right!

Protests against Christianity were about all the old imperial government of China could manage. The Revolution of Sun Yat Sen was little better. When the Communists took over in the late 1940s and early 1950s, the new government was very atheistic. According to the founder of Communism, Karl Marx, all religions were little more than an "opiate of the people." The Communists said that since the Christian church had been used as a tool of the ruling class to perpetuate oppression, they were opposed to **all** faiths. During the Cultural Revolution of the 1960s, the Communists closed all religious establishments, forced the monks, missionaries and priests to work at hard physical labor, and they used many of the churches for schools, libraries, offices, museums, restaurants, and warehouses. A few were just allowed to crumble in ruins without further use. Christian churches are again allowed in China, but within state regulations and restrictions.

Another small religious minority in China were the **Jews**. Historians today are uncertain about the date of arrival of the first Jews in China, but most likely as early as the Han dynasty, possibly around 206 to 220 B.C. They probably came from Persia or Palestine working as merchants selling cloth from the western markets. Their most permanent settlement was at **Kaifeng**, probably before 1127. They spoke Persian and built their first synagogue in Kaifeng in 1163. They seem to have been at their peak during the 16th and 17th centuries. The Chinese records show that many of the Kaifeng Jews rose to become military commanders and scholar-officials, but most of them were involved in merchant and commercial pursuits. They placed a high value upon education and were sometimes referred to by the Chinese as "people of the book." It is believed that they never numbered more than about fifteen hundred, and although they tried to maintain their separate identity, they did intermarry and some took Chinese surnames.

The Chinese regarded the Jews as a Muslim sect. After the 16th century their isolation from the main body of Jews in Palestine and in Europe caused them to become lost in the ways of the Chinese people. By the end of the Second World War the racial assimilation of the Chinese Jews was almost complete. A couple of hundred in Kaifeng still claim Jewish descent. There were a few other Jews who came to China from Russia, or from other western nations, largely as merchants. Most of those outside the Kaifeng area settled in the large port cities, such as Shanghai. Altogether there were probably never more than about 25,000 Jews in China at any one time. Those who continued to follow the faith generally migrated to the new state of Israel following World War II. Many probably died for their faith in the early years of Mao's communist regime. There are only a few dozen Jews remaining in China today.

A SUMMARY OF RELIGION IN CHINA

The Chinese were generally thought of as a religious people in the centuries preceding the Communist revolution in 1949. There were many followers of Confucius who believed that the only hope for mankind was a civilization based upon the ways of the ancients, especially their ethical standards and the wisdom of the classics. Lao-Tzu's Taoism was also very popular. He said that mankind should learn to conform to the ways of nature and the universe. Mencius stressed the essential goodness of man, but reserved the right of revolution against a persistently unjust ruler.

Other Chinese philosophers of the same general period, such as Chuang-Tzu, who died about 300 B.C., said that the best way to govern was through non-government. Mo Ti, a philosopher between Confucius and Mencius, believed that institutions should be submitted to the pragmatic test--were they of any benefit to society? He also believed that T'ien, or Heaven, loved men and that all men should therefore love one another. Yang Chu, a contemporary of Mencius, believed that men should no longer trouble themselves with either society or the hereafter, just live for their own pleasures because the grave would be the end. And there were others. Never again was Chinese philosophy so creative. Although Communism destroyed an entire generation of philosophically minded individuals, many of these religious and philosophic concepts are returning as China seeks to rediscover its past. The Chinese philosophers accomplished for the eastern world what men like Socrates, Plato, and Aristotle did for the western world.

Membership in a religion is viewed differently in Asia than in the western world. The term "religious affiliation" would be more appropriate than "membership," which implies that the member's name is listed. Many Chinese find good points in several different religious faiths. Taoism, Buddhism, and Christianity, along with a respect for elders, which is adopted from Confucianism, all seem to mingle together in the faith of a single individual. Even though the Communists were convinced that religious beliefs were totally dead by the close of the Mao era, there was a remarkable revival of all religions in China by the 1980s. Chinese women are widely accepted in the ministry of all religions in China. Whereas religion was once the very heart and core of Chinese life in earlier times, China is still officially an atheist state--religions are simply tolerated within limits.

LIFE IN A CHINESE VILLAGE

There are many different Chinese villages to be considered. There are those situated along the rivers, those in the delta regions, those on the wide plains of China, and those which cling to the side of a mountain. There have also been villages which have been predominantly involved in textiles, or tea processing, or ceramics. Although everyone in China is tied very closely to the soil--everyone has a garden if there are a few square feet of free soil--China has been somewhat more occupationally specialized than has India for several centuries. China also has a long history of commerce, both overland and maritime. It is therefore difficult to characterize a "typical" village.

Rural villages in China south of the Yangtze River all grow rice if the land can be irrigated and the soil will support the crop. Since rice produces more grain per acre, per year, it is the food crop which has become totally institutionalized in China. Rice and food are essentially one and the same. Any crop which will produce so heavily also removes many nutrients from the soil each year. As China's population began to grow, it became obvious that they could not allow the soil to lie fallow for a season to recuperate as was customary in western Europe.

Faced with this knotty problem the Chinese reasoned that the soil nutrients do not simply vanish once a crop is removed from the land, they simply are not returned to the soil to feed the next crop. Since the rice crop, and other food crops, are consumed primarily by people and animals it made sense to return both animal and human waste to the land. Barnyard manures from the livestock, the waste from vegetable and fruit crops, human waste, and everything which came from the land should be returned to the land. Therefore, the Chinese were among the first in the world to discover the need to recycle any and all waste products to the soil from which it had come. The year this system began has been lost to history. It was several centuries before western Europe began to understand the need to rebuild the soil.

All of the waste products were traditionally placed outside the door on a neat pile. When the pile reached a height of from four to eight feet, it would be sealed over with clay. This caused the pile to heat within a sealed area and all the waste products broke down to a rich, dark compost. As the fields, garden plots, and paddies were prepared for the next crop, the pile was crumbled and distributed as evenly as possible over the growing area. This could be repeated time after time over thousands of years because the nutrients were never lost.

The wastes were also collected from the cities. People placed their waste at the doorstep in a "honey pot" where it would be picked up each morning for recycling. This system was often called **night soil**. Its chief disadvantages were that it did create an unpleasant odor--but one which was accepted as normal--and some of the more dangerous bacteria did not perish in the composting process. This did transmit diseases in China but children usually built up an immunity to the germs within a few years. Those who did not simply perished. It should be pointed out that China has replaced this arrangement today with commercial fertilizers in most areas.

Since the soil has always been such a precious commodity to the Chinese, they are much more ecologically conscious of damaging it than are western farmers. Many Chinese farmers are still reluctant to experiment with new fertilizers, herbicides, or insecticides. Farmers in the American Midwest often feel that a good corn or bean crop is impossible without a heavy application of liquid nitrogen. This type of farming is still resisted by many farmers in China. They would likely ask how to remove the product from the soil if they decide they do not want it there.

China's agricultural production south and east of the Yangtze River depends heavily upon the monsoon. Rainfall in China varies from as much as one hundred inches to less than four inches per year. The kind of crops grown depends directly upon the rainfall. Wherever possible, the favored crop is **always rice**. Chinese farmers go to great lengths to store water during the wet season for the rice crop during the dry season. Reservoirs and irrigation canals to make rice cultivation possible date back to at least the Chou dynasty, possibly even earlier. The land along the rivers and streams has always been the most highly valued throughout Chinese history. Population density maps tend to parallel the supply of water. This is true even on the windward and the leeward mountain slopes.

The Chou Dynasty

Both temperature and rainfall patterns in China show tremendous variations. India's weather pattern is relatively simple with ocean on two sides and the mountains arching across the top. Virtually all of India is governed by the monsoon. Since China is much larger than India there is more room for variations. China's western areas are very continental and very barren. This results in very cold, dry winters and very hot summers. If an area of northern China is in a location where the summer wind currents blow off of a sizeable body of water, there will be ample rainfall for agriculture. If this is not the case, then the crops will be confined to wheat, rye, or millet. Beyond these crops the land is barren and grazing is the only occupation possible. Although a few areas of China receives heavy snows in the winter, the prevailing westerlies blow across a huge land mass without an ocean and the air is frigid and dry. Winter dust storms are much more likely than snowstorms. This does leave a rich deposit of loess soil, but unless there is water, crops are still impossible.

The final factor which governs China's agricultural pattern is the temperature. Rice can be grown north of Beijing, but it is not profitable. The weather is too cool and the season is too short, especially in the inland areas. South of Beijing the rice crop is much more prolific. Most of China's rice comes from the area south of the Yangtze River. The far northern areas of Mongolia have too short a growing season for most crops, regardless of how short their growing season. These areas are confined largely to grazing, forests, or mining. Many areas of the far north have very sparse populations.

On the opposite corner of China is Tibet. In the Tibetan area the latitude should provide a year around growing season, but this is altered by its high elevation, which causes cool summers and very cold winters. Tibet is also out of the main patterns of summer rainfall. There are valley regions in Tibet which can produce a crop from the spring and summer snow melt. Western China is very cold in the winter, very hot in the summer, and very little rain or snow at any season.

The seasons in China are also varied. Southeast China is in a monsoon pattern of wet and dry seasons, whereas northern China is an area of four well delineated seasons. Central China sometimes is caught between the two. Winter wheat is the number two crop in China. It is raised from the Yangtze River valley north to Beijing. Spring wheat is raised in the area from Beijing north.

A much larger amount of beef, pork, chicken, and mutton is consumed in China than in India. Most regions of China either get their fish from the sea, the rivers, or they have fish farms. Fish and pork are the leading foods in China and have been for centuries. Even though tractors are becoming more common in China, the buffalo or the ox as a beast of burden is still quite common. Most of the tillage of fields and paddies has changed to either animal or tractor power. There are less people doing hard physical labor in the fields than was true in the older ages. Before 1600 a high percentage of the labor was done by people. China has always been more labor intensive than the western world.

Chinese social life changed very little for thousands of years. The two major events which changed China were the coming of the Europeans and the Communist revolution in 1949. In all the centuries of Chinese history, the father was unquestionably the head of the house. Like all other Asian cultures, Chinese women were expected to look dignified and to manage the household affairs. Many young girls had their feet bound tightly at an early age so they would have delicate little feet. Neither men nor women cut their hair in the early days, and the older men rarely shaved. A long white beard was a mark of envy and respect by the younger generation. Everyone was expected to listen to the dictates of the older men and women. They always knew best. All marriages were arranged by the parents. Birth control was seldom practiced by any of the married couples because children were considered an asset, especially boys. Too many girls in one family often led to female infanticide. There were some areas where infanticide was a common practice, while in other areas it was practically unknown. Since the Chinese buried their dead, and because of the Confucian respect for ancestors, the cemeteries were highly revered and protected. The cycle of birth to death was followed in an extended family setting for thousands of years.

Figure 23

The Chou Dynasty

BOOKS FOR FURTHER READING

Creel, Herrlee G., *Confucius and the Chinese Way* (1949).

Creel, Herrlee G., *The Birth of China* (1937).

Fenton, John Y., *et. al., Religions of Asia* (1988).

Fairbank, John K., editor, *Chinese Thought and Institutions.*

Kitagawa, Joseph M., editor, *The Religious Traditions of Asia* (1989).

Koller, John M., *Oriental Philosophies* (1985).

Lau, D. C., *Lao Tzu: Tao Te Ching* (1963).

Lin Yutang, *The Wisdom of Confucius* (1938).

MacHovec, Frank J, translator, *The Book of Tao* (1962).

Merton, Thomas, *The Way Chuang Tzu* (1965).

Mote, Frederick, *Intellectual Foundations of China* (1989).

Schwartz, Benjamin, *The World of Thought in Ancient China* (1985).

Waley, Arthur, *The Analects of Confucius* (1989).

Waley, Arthur, *Three Ways of Thought in Ancient China* (1969).

Welch, Holmes, *Taoism: The Parting of the Way* (1957).

Wing-Tsit Chan, *A Source Book in Chinese Philosophy* (1963).

Chapter 22
THE PERIOD OF THE WARRING STATES
450-221 B.C.

The last centuries of the Eastern Chou were so troublesome, with so much conflict, that it has gone down in history as the period of the **Warring States**. One is often forced to wonder whether such times of troubles, a period of over two centuries, caused people to think more deeply about society, and whether the same leaders might have been as productive in an era of peace and stability. Or, was it the introduction of **iron** in this same period--a much less expensive weapon system than bronze--which caused all the warring? Since bronze had been reserved primarily for weapons and religious purposes in the Shang and earlier Chou periods, did the application of iron cause men to form larger armies with more weapons and to act more recklessly? Perhaps it was the invention of the crossbow during this period which added to their warlike nature. We do know from archaeological evidence that the Chinese suddenly moved far ahead of the rest of the world in their iron making technology during this time period.

These questions have troubled Chinese historians for centuries. Precise answers continue to elude the researcher. It is known that iron tools did appear for agricultural purposes during this period. Throughout the Shang and the earlier Chou periods, even grain was still harvested with stone sickles. The application of iron to farm chores such as cultivating and harvesting must have brought enormous changes in the way people lived. The farm tools were undoubtedly more expensive, but they were so much better that it almost surely increased agricultural production and accelerated up harvesting, a crucial point in case of bad weather.

Craftsmen suddenly had available tools such as the spoked wheel, the wire saw, and the diamond drill for working everything from wood to jade and marble. Chopsticks replaced the fingers in polite society. Both ink and brush were improved for the scholar and the painter. The use of lacquer was perfected, and many objects, such as swords, bowls, musical instruments, and wooden figures, were all beautifully decorated. Objects of glass came into use, mostly as works of art. It was during the last two centuries of the Chou dynasty that the two-humped camel was brought into China from central Asia, along with donkeys and mules, to work the route which came to be called the **Old Silk Road**.

The trade routes also introduced new ideas from the West and from India. A new knowledge of geography began to be evident, since even Japan was mentioned along with the countries on the caravan routes. They still clung to the idea that **China was the center of the universe** and everything else was just outlying territories. By the 4th century, their astronomers had mapped 1,464 individual stars. This was 200 years before the Hellenistic astronomer Hipparchus (146-127 B.C.) who only found 850 stars. Solar eclipses, comets, meteors, and shooting stars were also recorded because they were believed to be signs and portents. The Chinese stated the **Pythagorean geometrical theorem** in what is believed to be the oldest book ever written on mathematics. The Greek philosopher and mathematician Pythagoras was active around 530 B.C., slightly ahead of the Chinese. We have no way of knowing whether the Chinese borrowed their ideas from the Greek world or whether they developed the theorem independently. They did develop their own system of figuring fractions and how to multiply and divide fractions. Geometry became one of several areas of study in the school of **Mo Ti** at about the same time Euclid was working in mathematics in Greece.

Figure 24

226

Chapter 23
THE MIDDLE PERIOD OF CHINESE HISTORY
THE CH'IN, 221-207 B.C.

One after another the Eastern Chou states fell to the warring leaders. By 316 B.C., the **Ch'u** and the **Ch'in** were the only two remaining powers. Fighting from chariots was abandoned in favor of fast mounted cavalrymen who fired crossbows. The **Ch'in** group of warriors won the struggle to control China about 223 B.C.

The **Ch'in**, also known as the **Qin**, ruled over a large portion of present-day China under the leadership of a powerful young man known in Chinese history as **Prince Cheng of Ch'in.** Once he had conquered most of China in 221 B.C., he took the title of *huang-ti*, "august sovereign." He is better known as **Shih Huang Ti**, c.259 B.C. to 209 or 210 B.C., the **First Emperor**. He is also known as **Qin Shihuangdi**. Shih Huang Ti rose to power at a relatively young age in much the same manner as other young rulers of the Warring States period, it was just that he played the game better and won the largest realm. He declared himself emperor in 221 B.C. and held that position until his death in 209/210 B.C. His domain stretched from the great bend of the Yellow River to areas south of the Yangtze.

One of his first actions was to divide the area of his control into 36 military districts, sometimes called "commanderies," with five or six more added as his control broadened. Each commandery had officials who were subject only to the emperor, a major difference over all previous systems. The old systems had allowed friends, relatives, and military men to control various areas as vassals who owed allegiance and paid taxes. The problem with the old system was that even trusted family members often tried to secure permanent control for themselves, and many succeeded. Under **Shih Huang Ti** all power was with the emperor and no power was shared. He was truly the **the first emperor of China**.

Shih Huang Ti shifted officials from one commandery to another and requested the most powerful families to live in the capital city where he could watch them more closely. Those who caused him trouble, including robbers, etc., were assigned to the borders to hold the nomads back. It was a little bit like being sent to Siberia during the early years of the Soviet Union. Watchtowers, complete with a signal system for both day and night operation, were built into a defensive system across the north. Sections of the Great Wall were united and fortresses were built at strategic locations to keep out the nomads from the north. It should be made clear that Shih Huang Ti was not the originator of the Great Wall, as some books imply, nor was he the one who finished the wall. The Great Wall which remains today is largely the work of the Ming dynasty many years later.

The emperor was very much interested in consolidating his empire and getting everyone to agree with him on a common Chinese culture. He was interested in a prosperous empire as well as a strong one. The roads and canals he had built not only speeded the movement of his military, but they also stimulated trade throughout his empire. Many of these major projects were suggested by his most competent advisor, **Li Ssu**, who was later declared grand counselor.

Other measures which Shih Huang Ti enacted to stimulate business and trade included the adoption of a uniform system of weights and measures. This even included a standard length for all chariot and cart axles. He ordered the first standardization of the Chinese writing script, and all laws were made uniform throughout China. This was the first time there had been so much uniformity throughout such a large area of China. To be sure that his orders were being carried out he conducted a series of Imperial Inspection Tours.

As the tours progressed he would offer sacrifices to the gods to assure peace and safety for his empire. He was a very religious (and superstitious) man who believed he was divinely appointed to rule the first united China. He constantly searched for men who were known as magicians or alchemists who could do mysterious things in their laboratories. One of his greatest interests was in finding the elixir of immortality. Some believe he traveled as far as Japan in search of such a magic elixir. Stone tablets with ritual inscriptions were ordered erected as he passed through the country.

All of the above points should be applauded since very few countries were so progressive. But there was another side to the First Emperor. He positively could not stand criticism. When several of the Confucian scholars were critical of his search for the elixir and his interest in magic, he decided, with the suggestion of his grand counselor, Li Ssu, to destroy all of their books except books on agriculture, medicine, and history. In 213 B.C. he held a special ceremony which is usually referred to as the "**burning of the books**." All books which **he** thought were unsuitable, for whatever cause, were collected by the emperor's men and burned. Learned men, teachers, monks, etc., who refused to be subservient were assessed very heavy penalties. There were still a large number of non-conformists so the emperor sentenced 460 of them to be buried alive! Emperor Shih Huang Ti died just a few years later. Since he had not made adequate safeguards for the succession, the empire faltered as two strong men wrestled for control. Within three years, the Ch'in era was over.

Although Shih Huang Ti had maintained some historical records, it was the historians of the Han period who wrote most of what we know about the First Emperor. Since it was in their interest to make the former dynasty look bad, it is difficult today to know how accurate some of their stories may be. No one can question that he was a strict and forceful ruler whose sense of punishment would be totally unacceptable today. Everyone gives Shih Huang Ti credit for unifying China for the first time and his dedication to uniformity throughout the state.

THE CEMETERY AT XIAN

The emperor Shih Huang Ti had arranged for an elaborate funeral for himself. There is good evidence, but not totally conclusive, that he had his ministers, family members, slaves, and horses buried with him as some rulers had done centuries before. It is not yet clear whether **all** were killed on the day of the funeral or whether some were added to the burial area as they died from natural causes at later dates. The site is still under excavation and evaluation.

We do know that the First Emperor had no intention of entering the next world alone. It was his plan to be accompanied by at least 8,000 clay warriors who were buried nearby. The terracotta soldiers were not discovered until some peasants who were digging a well began to unearth them in 1974. Each human figure in this large cemetery is approximately life size. They wear a variety of uniforms and body-armor, but all have knee-length robes, turned up lapels and breeches. Their hair is done up on top of their heads and all have some form of a moustache. Virtually all carried weapons but these have since decayed.

The Ch'in Dynasty

The clay figures were found 16 feet below the surface in a vault made of pounded earth walls and a wooden roof. It appears that General Xiang Yu, who plundered **Xian** in 206 B.C. opened the vault and burned the roof. This is why some of the figures have toppled over. Most of the men stand 5 feet 11 inches tall. This was probably slightly larger than real life at that time. The lower part of their bodies is solid clay, but the upper part is hollow. They were originally painted, but this has now almost totally disappeared. Three beautiful chariots, each drawn by four clay horses, have been found so far. The harness ornaments for the horses were made of pure silver and gold. In summary, this discovery is considered the equivalent to the earlier discovery of King Tut's tomb in Egypt.

Figure 25

Figure 26

Chapter 24
THE HAN DYNASTY, 209 B.C.-A.D. 220
ESTABLISHING THE DYNASTY

In 209 B.C., only a year after the death of the First Emperor, a revolt broke out in the old Ch'u area. Several other rebellions followed in quick succession throughout the empire. Most of the rebel bands were led by men who claimed they were defending the cause of the royal line or else one of the older Chinese states which the Ch'in had destroyed at an earlier time. Finally, the rebel general, **Hsiang Yu** wiped out the last of the Ch'in armies in 206 and enthroned a Ch'u prince as emperor. He tried to revive the old Chou system of governing China, but this did not work out, and Hsiang Yu was soon challenged by another rebel general named **Liu Pang**.

It was **Liu Pang**, 256-195 B.C., who succeeded in creating a lasting dynasty where the First Emperor had failed. His descendants reigned until A.D. 8, a time span of over two hundred years. After a brief usurpation the dynasty was again resurrected as the **Later Han**, which continued from A.D. 25 until 220. The two Han empires approximately parallel the period of Rome's prestige in the West. They ruled China longer than any other single dynasty.

Liu Pang took the name **Han** as the dynastic name of his new dynasty from one of the major tributaries of the Yangtze River. His throne name, Han Kao Tsu, means "High Progenitor," a title which plainly indicates his intention of having the people see him as a powerful unifier of China, similar to the role which Shih Huang Ti had played. Kao Tsu wanted to create a Chinese empire for which all Chinese could be proud to call themselves "Han". In this he succeeded because even today the Chinese refer to themselves as "**men of Han**," and the Japanese and Koreans refer to the Chinese writing system as "the Han characters."

Kao Tsu was a rough commoner who had no aristocratic ties. He knew how he had come to power--by military might--and he knew he must constantly remind the people that he would allow no one to challenge his authority. On the other hand, he reduced the severity of punishments and lessened the tax burden. It had now been several years from the Chou period and he saw that those who wanted to return China to the earlier Chou times had not fared very well. He therefore chose to build upon the work of the Ch'in instead. The Confucian scholars were returned to their jobs as teachers and scholars but not to government service. Taoism was the favored philosophy of the emperor at this time. Nevertheless, the Confucians were so grateful for their treatment that they became chroniclers of every important event which transpired. Music, art, and dance were heavily subsidized. As a consequence of these changes, the people were much more willing to give their allegiance to the Han dynasty than they ever had to the Ch'in.

Kao Tsu still had many small kings and barons controlling Chinese lands. Unless these men could be brought into his system of governance they would likely cause him the same kinds of rebellious problems which previous dynasties had experienced. Kao Tsu's goal was to make these men his vassals or to defeat them. By the time of his death in 195 B.C. he had pretty well established the fact that henceforth only members of the imperial clan--his own close family members--could be vassals of the emperor. He also set about reducing the powers of the kings of the outlying territories by placing restrictions upon their powers and reducing their territories. Without as much territory they also found that they had smaller revenues. From the time of Kao Tsu, the Han imperial power was centered in the imperial city at **Lo-yang**.

The Han Dynasty

There were problems of governance which arose during the Han years in addition to the consolidation of power within the imperial family. The succession to the throne had long been a problem for Chinese rulers. This became a complicated situation on several occasions because the Han emperors often had many consorts. The emperor traditionally recognized one of his consorts as the **future Empress Dowager** as soon as he had selected one of her sons as his successor. He would make her a dominant figure at the court and upon the accession of her son, she could claim the full "Empress Dowager" title. This arrangement became a problem from the very beginning. When Kao Tsu died, his empress became the real ruler of China and came close to usurping the throne. She, and members of her family, dominated the court until her death.

Another major problem for the Han came from the pastoral peoples of the North. The Chinese called these warlike peoples the **Hsiung-Nu**. They were most likely a Turkish-speaking group of people who came to dominate the area from western Manchuria through Mongolia and southern Siberia and southwest into Chinese Turkestan. Later they moved westward placing pressure against the later Roman Empire. The Romans referred to these people officially as the **Hunni**; we know them better as the **Huns**.

They were powerful enough that on one occasion in 201 B.C., they entrapped Liu Pang and forced him to pay heavy subsidies in silk, wine, grain, and food in order that he might be set free. A Han palace maiden was given to them in marriage on a later occasion. These people from Central Asia rode fast horses and were capable of out-flanking the Chinese army, which was primarily infantry.

Tired of being harassed by these nomadic raiders the emperor **Hsiao Wu-ti**, often referred to as Emperor **Wu**, 141-187 B.C., arranged a combination of tribes to fight the most powerful segment of the Hsiung-Nu. By conducting raids deep into their territory he managed to bring them in check. The Chinese historians claimed that in 121 B.C., Emperor Wu's forces killed or defeated 19,000 of them. On still another raid he seized 80 chiefs, and in 115 B.C. he captured another 300 of their men. These same nomadic raiders often caused trouble in northern Korea. It was at this time that China began taking a position on protecting Korea as a safeguard along their own northeastern border. This showed that the Han Chinese meant business against the Hsiung-Nu nomads. At this time, several other nomadic tribes joined the Han, probably for protection. The Han gained the respect of the people who lived around their borders. The size of their area of administration was about the same as that of Rome at its peak, and the Han Chinese were enjoying about the same level of wealth.

Hsiao Wu-ti, the "Great Martial Emperor," extended the **Great Wall** far to the west and all the way to the Yellow Sea on the east, hoping to prevent "end runs" by the fierce nomadic raiders to the north and west. By this time the Great Wall reached almost to Bactria. Emperor Wu tried to make an alliance with the Scythians to the west to control the Hsiung-Nu but they were not receptive. Later, the Sythians were defeated by these same people, the Huns. Had the Sythians been receptive, and had they then teamed up with Rome, the history of the world could have been very different.

Trade flourished in Han China. Silk and other Chinese products moved west, where they were traded for several of the western products such as grapes and alfalfa. The Old Silk Road was made safe for merchants, and when the Romans conquered Syria in 64 B.C., they discovered

Chinese silk. Soon there was a market for this beautiful product as far west as Portugal and Britain.

Emperor Wu also wearied of the pressures from aristocrats to place their sons in government positions. He turned to the Confucians to occupy some of the positions. They were found to be capable administrators and the number of Confucians increased, virtually all of them obtaining their positions by civil service examinations based upon the classics. The Confucian principles were finally accepted.

Other intellectual contributions of the Wu reign saw an expansion of educational opportunities for ordinary young men to obtain an education. Those who showed talent were given scholarships, if necessary, to attend the Imperial Academy. The best and the brightest were selected from the Academy for the civil service openings. At this stage the educational process seems to have been reasonably democratic. Later, the families who were already in the government service manipulated things to see that their sons received the highest levels of education so the jobs could be passed on within the family.

THE HAN INTERIM PERIOD

During the Han Interim Period following the death of Hsiao Wu-ti, the power of the military seemed to decline and corruption was an everyday affair. A coup resulted and one of the leaders named **Wang Mang** became emperor from A.D. 9 to 23. He made many reforms, but the bureaucracy seemed to be stronger than the emperor, a situation already forseen by Emperor Wu. The nobility had paid no taxes under the Han. All of the building and the military had been supported by the peasants or by taxes on merchants. Merchants were not allowed in the bureaucracy, and by this time the peasant children were unable to afford the basic education necessary to pass the civil service exams. As a consequence, the children of the nobility formed the majority of the civil service. When the bed of the Yellow River made major shifts due to flooding, and heavy taxes resulted in general impoverishment, everyone except a few large landholders became very angry. Naturally, they blamed the government for their problems. The merchants encouraged the military to attack the capital and the emperor was killed.

For the next two years there was anarchy. It took several years to restore peace and to pull the empire back together again. It was not until A.D. 36 that peace was restored and it was not until 73 that China was again the thriving country it had been under the former Han. By 221, many of the same internal problems which had brought the earlier Chinese rulers and dynasties to a close also brought the Han dynasty to a close.

AN ASSESSMENT OF THE HAN DYNASTY

It has been said that during the Han dynasty from 202 B.C. to A.D. 221, China came of age. Even during many of the troublesome times, it seemed that China was learning and growing. Education became so commonplace that by the middle of the 2nd century A.D. there were 30,000 students who were studying in the capital at **Lo-yang** alone. Beyond the oracle bones, stone carvings and bronze inscriptions, the Chinese were writing on thin, flattened strips of bamboo. The earliest books were called *jian ce*, or bundles of bamboo slips. A single volume was made up of many of these strips fastened together with silk threads or thin strips of leather. During the

The Han Dynasty

Warring States Period, 475-221 B.C., the silk book or scroll came into use. Its major problem was the high cost of silk.

During the Han dynasty, the **first paper**, pretty much as we know it today, appeared. This early paper was made from hemp rather than cotton or wood. An excavation in Shanxi province in 1978 turned up the earliest hemp paper book to date. It was mellow, but not brittle, and in quite good condition. It is hard to assess the intellectual impact of this new writing product--paper. Block printing did not arrive in China until the Sung (Song) dynasty, 960-1279, therefore, the writing of the Han period was all done with a brush on paper. This was another quantum leap in the conservation and the spread of knowledge.

Along with the invention of paper came China's first dictionary, the **Shou wen**, which explained about 10,000 characters. Alchemists began to make discoveries which were found to be useful in both medicine and industry. The pseudoscience of alchemy was now moving toward modern chemistry. Most importantly, all of the new experiments and findings could be written down on inexpensive paper and then passed on to future students. Emperor Wu established the first imperial university in 124 B.C. A century later it had 3,000 students.

Confucius, 551 to 479 B.C., was venerated by the Han scholars as the wisest man in history. Since Confucius considered the Chinese classics and philosophers the most important single branch of knowledge, and since the civil service exams were based upon this same theme, the students spent an inordinate amount of time studying the things of the past. This educational program was extremely short on subjects such as higher math, engineering, chemistry, etc. In a sense, Confucianism became the philosophy of the state.

As outlined by Confucius, the civil service examination should be based on the **Five Confucian Classics**. History was extremely important and each dynasty set the scholars to writing a chronicle of its predecessor. University scholars began the **Historical Records**, also known as the **Shih chi**, a voluminous work of 130 chapters. Even though the educational system was somewhat unbalanced when compared to a broad, liberal arts background there was a great stress on education. Teachers were just one level below the gods in Han China. It was unfortunate that the middle and lower classes seldom had the opportunity to rise to the top.

Even though the heaviest stress in the educational world centered around passing the civil service exam, there was a great number of creative discoveries such as paper, a primitive seismograph capable of detecting earthquakes, the adaptation of water power to grind grain, the discovery of the process for making porcelain, and the horse collar, an invention which was not discovered in Europe for another 1,500 years. Han art was very creative and realistic. It was much more realistic in that it portrayed ordinary life whereas the older art had been primarily religious and decorative. Their astrologers were becoming astronomers--they even discovered sunspots. At the close of the Han period, China surpassed the level of technological development anyplace else in the world.

EAST-WEST TRADE

It was during the age of the Ch'in, 221-207 B.C., and the Han, 202 B.C.-A.D. 221, that the East and the West began to discover one another. By the time of Christ and the Roman emperor Augustus, trade was established between Rome and India for luxury goods such as ivory, pearls,

The Han Dynasty

spices, dyes, and cotton. The Indian traders established commercial ties with China. This trade was then interrupted by the Parthians, whose kingdom extended from the Euphrates River to the borders of Bactria. When the Parthians cut the trade routes, the Romans valued the goods of the East so highly that they traded by sea.

The trade between Rome and the East at that time followed a land route via the Sinai and down the Red sea to the Gulf of Aden. It then went by sailing vessels from Aden, across the Arabian Sea to India. A Greek mariner named Hippalus, who was engaged in this trade, discovered that the monsoon blows from the southwest from May to October, and from the northeast between November and March. The bad weather of the monsoons interrupted the regular trade schedules, so the Romans decided to eliminate the troublesome Parthians who had been blocking the land routes. This was only partially successful since the tough fighters of northern Persia, modern Iran, did set the eastern limits of Roman territorial expansion. Part of the trade did resume on an overland basis, but the Parthians demanded a price to allow the goods to pass. The land route allowed one round trip every eight months.

Due to the many difficulties of the land route, the trade by sea continued. As early as the emperor Augustus, 27 B.C. to A.D. 14, the Romans were sending a ship at least as far as Aden every year. Shortly after 100 B.C., the Chinese set up the **southern** Silk Road whereby they could deal with the more peaceful Kushans in the area of Gandhara, India, and Afghanistan rather than the difficult Parthians. Silk flowed along this route from China to the Indian Kushans, then on to the Roman sailors, across the Arabian Sea to Egypt, and across the Mediterranean Sea to Rome. From Rome, their merchants and peddlars sold the goods throughout the Roman Empire for over a hundred years

Beginning in the 3rd century A.D., contact between the East and the West began to decline until it literally came to a standstill. It was not revived again until the 15th century. Among the several reasons for this decline is the overthrow of the Han dynasty in A. D. 220. The Han had always been such a great power that the smaller nationality groups which lived around their western border had regarded them with awe and fear. Once the dynasty was destroyed, the various Central Asian powers began to assert themselves. They no longer feared mighty China. The Kushan Empire, which had dominated the area of northwestern India, Afghanistan, and the southern areas of Central Asia, weakened and fell at the same time. There was no longer any state powerful enough to guarantee the safety of the caravan routes.

Finally, the Roman Empire began its decline and ultimate fall at this same time. The Roman economy had been draining gold out of the country for several years in order to purchase the luxury goods from the eastern world. There was an internal weakness in the fabric of Rome's social culture. This was followed by the invasions by the "barbarians," who were pushing west and pushing south due partially to pressures upon their eastern borders by the Huns and the Mongols. Thousands of these barbarians had already infiltrated Rome's borders over the years until one of them finally took over in 476. This was more than an already weakened Rome could endure. There were no great leaders to emerge to save the day. Rome fell to the barbarians. The trade with the East virtually ended until it was revived following the Christian crusades, which began in A.D. 1095.

Figure 27

236

Chapter 25
THE PERIOD OF DISUNITY FOLLOWING THE HAN

THE SIX DYNASTIES
221-589

For the next 368 years there were troubled times in China. The old empire first split into three parts. There was the **Wei** in the north, the **Wu** in the central part, and the **Shu** in the southern Szechwan area. The three-part division lasted from 221 until 265. In 265, China was temporarily pulled back together by the **Tsin**, 265 to 317. During the 52-year period of the Tsin, the Mongolians and other ethnic peoples began to penetrate the poorly defended passes in the Great Wall. The northern Wei was the first to be toppled. Many Chinese moved south ahead of the invaders. As the Mongolians came deeper into China, there were many who tried to move ahead of them until the Han Chinese became more and more impacted in the south.. It was under these circumstances that the "**Six Dynasties**" ruled China from 347 to 589 from their southern capital of **Nanking**. Many northern dynasties came and went, but the southern Chinese came to think of themselves as the remains of the one true Chinese race.

The period of the Six Dynasties was nothing like the so-called Dark Ages of western Europe. Many of the Mongolians liked the Han civilization and wanted to adapt to it and live under its benefits rather than to loot it and destroy it, as was the case of the barbarians in the West at this same time. The problem in the north generally was that the invaders were good soldiers but poor administrators. They did not want to trust the Han Confucian bureaucrats. The Mongol system simply failed to function properly without bureaucrats. If they wished to enjoy the benefits of the old Han culture, it was necessary to adopt many of the Confucian principles.

In such a troubled time there were many who sought refuge in religion, more specifically, **Buddhism**. The faith had been in China for some time, but the number of converts grew rapidly during this period. Many of the northern monarchs espoused the foreign faith as well. It was at this time that the Chinese missionary monk, **Fa-hsien** (Faxian), went on a pilgrimage which required nearly fifteen years and took him through nearly thirty countries. He, and four other Buddhist monks, traveled to the sacred Buddhist sites in Gupta India and Sri Lanka and returned with new Buddhist scriptures.

Travel at that time was slower but the monks took their time because they wanted to learn the Sanskrit so they could understand and interpret the scriptures they had discovered. Furthermore, there were no copy machines--all the work of copying had to be done by hand. By the time the Sui had reunited China in 589, Buddhism had become an integral part of China's life. It altered other faiths such as Confucianism and Taoism, and Buddhism began to express itself in Chinese literature and art. By 589, Buddhism was more powerful and more prosperous than it would ever be again in China. It was an important unifying force in China very much as Christianity was in western Europe during the Middle Ages.

New discoveries in medicine, mathematics, astronomy, botany and chemistry occurred during this period of disunion and turmoil from the 3rd to the 6th century. Trade with India revived and the Chinese knowledge of the outside world increased. Cartography was developed by **P'ei Hsiu**, 224 to 271. These new fields of study were stressed by the Buddhists much more than under the Confucian system of stressing the classics as a means to an end--a bureaucratic position.   Local histories were written and the Chinese did not forget that they were once **one** people.

THE SUI
589-618

Three hundred and sixty-eight years is a long time to dream of a reunited empire. The Sui rulers were active Buddhists who embarked upon extravagant plans to rebuild the country and to recover the territory which had been lost at the end of the Han period. The **Grand Canal** was extended from Tientsin in the north to Hangchow in the south. They rebuilt the Great Wall to protect the north. They even moved China into a new area of conquest--Southeast Asia. There they forced two different kingdoms to pay them tribute. The Sui conducted a raid against Formosa (Taiwan) and conducted **unsuccessful** raids against Korea and the Eastern Turks in Mongolia.

Rebellions within led to five years of fighting which in the end cost the emperor his life. At least their short period of rule covering 29 years, 589 to 618, taught the Chinese that they **could** be unified again.

Figure 28

Chapter 26
THE TANG DYNASTY
618-907

The first task of the Tang dynasty was to consolidate their hold at home. Having accomplished that, they decided to reopen the war with Korea. That war continued into the 660s, but ultimately they annexed a large percentage of the peninsula and held it for a time. Even though Korea did not belong to China continuously from this time, China continued to think of themselves as a kind of guardian over that country, since they did not want Korea to be occupied by either the Mongols or the Japanese.

The Sui had begun contacts with Japan and these were continued under the Tang. Culturally, the Japanese felt quite inferior to the Chinese during these years and wanted to upgrade. Both students and merchants from Japan went to China, especially Buddhist monks. Buddhism had arrived in both Korea and Japan by way of Chinese missionary monks who followed the trade routes. Since Confucianism and Taoism had mingled with Buddhism in China, the monks introduced all three ways of thinking into Japan. It was the Buddhist tradition which took the deepest roots in both Korea and Japan.

The second Tang emperor also carried Chinese expansion into Central Asia. He defeated both the Eastern and the Western Turks in **Mongolia** and secured that huge piece of real estate for China. He then turned south and the ruling princes of both **Bokhara** and **Samarkand** recognized Chinese suzerainty. The Chinese power was experienced either directly or indirectly from the Caspian Sea on the west to the Pacific in the east.

The next move by the Tang was against **Tibet**. In this case, Tibet allied with the Mongolians and before it was over, China was faced with the possibility of an invasion themselves. Ultimately, a truce was arranged whereby the Chinese sent a royal princess for marriage in Tibet.

Quite obviously, the Tang were heavy on territorial expansion. By the time of China's second Tang emperor, their borders were larger than they had ever been before. Much of the newly added territory was not very useful for agriculture, but the Tang emperors believed it still had to be conquered and governed in order to make Tang China safe from invaders.

Confucian bureaucracy returned at this time along with its heavy emphasis upon a classical education and the civil service examinations. The system of bureaucracy became so entrenched at this time that it remained with only a few minor changes until the Revolution of 1912. With control over areas stretching farther to the west than ever before, Chinese merchants followed their armies to the farthest borders of the empire. Trade flourished throughout China under the Tang.

New religions followed the trade routes into China. **Mazdaism, Nestorian Christianity**, and **Manichaeism** all established places of worship in China and began translating their sacred works into Chinese. Not to be outdone, Chinese Buddhists continued to travel to India and Ceylon (Sri Lanka) in search of documents and to visit holy stupas and temples. Once conquest ceased, there followed a wonderful period of peace throughout China. Peace and leisure saw a resurgence of **all** the arts. So many wanted copies of formerly hand-printed books that the block printing of books and prints became popular at this time in order to meet the great demand.

The economy was quite good in the early Tang years. The Tang emperors established rules for regulating markets, licenses were issued for business, and more roads and canals were constructed. Tea culture and new varieties of "wet rice" came into cultivation. With the heavy yield and short maturity time, rice became virtually an **"institution"** in China from this time forward. The area from the Yangtze River valley to the south became a huge "rice bowl" and the population of the area increased accordingly. The government had granaries built to store grain for future periods of famine. Even though food was more abundant, the Chinese peasant worked hard, lived in very poor housing, and saw little future in life except for more hard work.

By this time there were many merchants who were able to send their sons to school, help them get good civil service jobs, and move up the ladder of success. Trade attracted many foreigners--more than 100,000 in Canton alone. Most of them were Hindus, Persians, Arabs, and Malays. Many foreign merchants also operated at the capital of China, now **Chang'an** (present-day Xian), the city of "Everlasting Peace." The capital grew to over a million people under the Tang Dynasty. Some have referred to this period as "**The Golden Age of China**."

It seemed that prosperity and education tended to call for ever more prosperity and more education. China's society became layered with the emperor and his family equal to the royalty of the western world. The bureaucracy filled an area of what might be called the upper middle class, and then there were all the peasants, who worked the small plots of ground, some of which were individually owned and some were not. Like the society in India, it was a giant pyramid with the peasant, artisan, craftsman class supporting the heavy bureaucracy and royalty at the top.

At this same moment in history, 618 to 907, Europe was still struggling through the Middle Ages. Europe had its layered society, but they did not have the huge number of very well educated bureaucrats to assist in running the state. Indeed, many of the European kings could not even read or write during this period; therefore, the affairs of state in the West were handled by court favorites supplemented by a few people who had received a small amount of education in the cathedral schools, which were designed primarily for training people for clerical jobs or the priesthood within the church.

Educationally China was miles ahead of the West. Literature, poetry, music, art, and architecture--all flourished in China. The Chinese of this period firmly believed that the lessons learned from the past would serve as a guide for the future. History was preserved with that view in mind as well as the nationalistic aspects, which were popular in both China and the West. *The Understanding of History* was published in the 8th century in China, and the *Study of Institutions* appeared in the 9th century. Many local histories were written as well. The only comparable offering in the West was the English history known as the *Anglo Saxon Chronicle*, which began during the reign of Alfred the Great, 849-899.

Tang sculpture and painting also reflected this age of national smugness and prosperity. The religious work was largely done by, or commissioned for, Buddhists. There was a tremendous demand for Buddha statues--large ones for temples and small terracotta ones for the home altars. The Chinese Buddhist statues clearly show the influence of the Greek-Gandharan style of Bactria, one of the areas on China's new western frontier. The Chinese gave Buddha a more Chinese look in his face, but the remainder of the statue was quite close to the Gandharan style. The Confucian scholars condemned Buddhism as a "barbaric" faith with idols, and tried to persuade others accordingly, but it was the age of Buddhism.

Most of the secular art focused on realism. There were those artists who painted and sculpted very realistic people, horses, and other animals. Some of this realistic art was used in the tombs of the wealthy. They especially enjoyed scenes of servants and dancing girls who would make life pleasant for them in the unknown world. They also memorialized their younger years when they enjoyed going hunting. Art, both sacred and secular, tended to show compassion for human concerns. The Chinese have always placed a high value on humility, a pity for human suffering, a love of natural beauty, and the inevitability of old age and death. Rather than the wheel of life, so popular in India, the Chinese have often characterized the perfect gentleman as like a willow tree--the older they become, the lower they bend.

Many have said that the Han Empire was the age of prose; the Sung empire was the age of painting; but the Tang empire had the greatest **poets**. **Li Po** and Tu Fu, both seventh and eighth century poets, are classified as a part of China's classical period. Li Po, a Taoist, wrote of beautiful mist-filled valleys, high and rugged mountains, rushing streams, and waterfalls. It was the Chinese Taoist close connection with nature brought a little closer by poetic images. Li Po was known to sometimes take more wine than he should in order to open his mind to new images. It was said that the great poet drowned in the Yangtze River in 762 while trying to embrace the image of the moon.

Tu Fu was more of a realist. A Confucian, Tu Fu held several minor government posts and traveled throughout China on his own, whereas Li Po had often been ordered to leave a province or be killed. Although assigned to various geographic areas, Tu Fu loved the capital city of Chang'an. His poem "**Autumn Meditation**" reflects on the beautiful new capital city. Many consider Tu Fu the greatest of all Chinese poets. And, there were many others. All the poets reflect the freedom and happiness of people in the Tang years. But, like all great epochs in history, the Tang seemed to outlive its usefulness to the people and it passed from history.

THE SLOW DECLINE OF THE TANG DYNASTY

There is more information on the decline and fall of the Tang dynasty than any other in Chinese history. Waste and corruption in office led to rising taxes which hit the peasant class the hardest. Many peasants left the land to work in the cities where they could earn more money and pay less taxes. Those who simply abandoned their land saw it revert to the landlords, but with no one to work the land, there was less income and less food for the growing urban populations. Food prices climbed higher. With less tax money from the land--and **land** was the chief source of government income--government services declined and morale was poor among both the civil servants and a poorly equipped army. The working classes who were called upon to support the state were very disappointed in their government. Everybody seemed to be unhappy. Many wondered whether the emperor had lost his "**mandate from heaven**."

In 751 the Muslims took Turkestan. Shortly after this the Tibetans raided and sacked the capital city of Chang'an. When the country appeared weak, even though there was still much strength remaining, other hawks descended for the kill. The Mongolians had anxiously awaited this hour. They now moved south across the Great Wall into China.

The Tang Dynasty

The monarchy was in desperate need of both money and soldiers. A decree issued in 845 attacked the wealthy Buddhist monasteries. Instead of providing relief to the poor or other charitable activities, several monasteries had gone into money-lending at high rates of interest, a practice which made them very unpopular with many of the people. Therefore, when the government decided to dissolve about 4,600 monasteries and 40,000 shrines, it hoped it could divert this revenue to the state coffers. It did not work out as they had projected. There were roughly 260,500 monks and nuns who had to shift almost overnight from sacred to secular employment. The job market could not possibly absorb so many within a short period of time. The economy had already been weak and this action obviously weakened it further.

Many citizens also decided to take desperate measures. A frustrated intellectual led a revolt which lasted from 875 to 884. This group blamed the merchants for their woes, especially foreign merchants. They marched south and murdered several thousand foreign merchants in Canton, then marched north and captured the capital city of Chang'an. It took the government nearly nine years to suppress this uprising. When many prominent citizens and military commanders realized how weak the government actually had become, they formed their own little armies and became, in effect, kings within the Tang empire. Several of the peripheral areas split off or else made deals with their neighbors outside China in order to gain some measure of protection. Some of the lists of Chinese rulers separate each of these areas of the Late Tang period into several separate groups.

In 907, one of the military commanders who was fed up with the system killed all of the court eunuchs, deposed the ruling emperor, and took over the throne. Originally the eunuchs were only court attendants, but in the Late Tang years they seemed to dictate to the emperor how he should run the empire. Although some eunuchs were educated, most were illiterate and self-seeking men who gave the emperor bad advice. The eunuchs paid dearly for their exercise of power--the same price the emperor paid for failing to exercise his power.

If we survey the Tang period, we see that the first 50 to 100 years were periods of tremendous territorial expansion, intellectual achievement, and generally good government. Art and culture flourished as did religion. The Tang seemed to have plateaued after about a century, maintained a high level for another century, then literally skidded out during their third century.

One of the most interesting "characters" in all of Chinese history was a woman, **Wu Zhao, 627? to 705**. Ms. Wu came from a locally prominent clan in modern Shanxi Province. She first entered the palace around 640 to serve as a low-ranking concubine to the second Tang emperor, **Taizong**, who reigned from 627 to 650. It is believed that the third Tang emperor, **Gaozong**, who ruled from 650 to 683, fell in love with Ms. Wu while the second emperor was still living. According to tradition, all the concubines were to have their heads shaved upon the emperor's death and then enter a Buddhist convent, but not Ms. **Wu**. According to one account the new emperor was paying a visit to the Buddhist convent when he needed to go to the lavatory. It was sheer coincidence that the beautiful, talented, and scheming Ms. Wu was in the right place at the right time. Within a year she had won the new emperor's heart and was serving as his concubine.

Ms. **Wu** rose in favor with the new emperor by always seeming to be in the right places in the palace. By 652 she had borne at least one son to Gaozong and began scheming to displace the emperor's legitimate but childless wife, the empress Wang. One day she told the emperor that his empress was guilty of sorcery, murdering her baby daughter, and plotting to poison the emperor.

The Tang Dynasty

The emperor showed his appreciation for Ms. Wu's excellent detective work by demoting the empress Wang and marrying Ms. Wu. Since the emperor was incapable of making the decisions which Ms. Wu believed were in the best interest of the emperor and of China, she dominated the court by sitting behind a silken screen and telling him what to do.

The emperor "ruled" in this fashion for the next twenty years. When he died, Ms. Wu installed two of her sons as successive puppet emperors, but then deposed them both, an unprecedented action for anyone in China up to this time. There were many conspiracies and these were ruthlessly suppressed. She seemed to have spies everyplace. Her real dates of power are given as about 660 to 705. In 690, at the age of 62, she declared **herself** emperor, the only woman ever to rule China in name as well as in fact. She referred to her rule as the "**Zhou dynasty**" and assumed all aspects of the title of an emperor. She even moved the capital from Chang'an to Luoyang. For the next fifteen years she systematically liquidated most members of the Tang dynastic house in a cruel reign of terror.

The Confucian historians disliked her because she did not follow the old aristocratic system with which they had become so dependent and comfortable. Instead, she relied far more upon the examination system than her predecessors. This brought in a larger number of officials from the great and lesser clans of the eastern plain and the South, none of whom had been involved in the government before this time. Since she selected only a very few from the northwestern clans, as had been the practice for several years, the Confucians distrusted her motives. Apparently, she was most interested in anyone who could do the job and would be amenable to her will. This seems to have resulted in a great amount of competition among the old civil servants at the court and the new appointees. Many chose sides in a kind of the "ins" and the "outs" of the court. Overall she seemed to be a remarkably able monarch who managed to gain at least the tacit support of the Chinese people. It was during Ms. Wu's reign that virtually all of Korea came under China's control. Border uprisings were put down without mercy.

But Ms. Wu did have some weaknesses, one of which has already become evident. It was said that she kept a cosmetics salesman around the court, ultimately elevating him to the position of commander-in-chief of the armies on the northern frontier. Another pair who were close to the old empress at the court were two young brothers who wore thick white powder on their faces. She liked the boys so much she appointed their younger brother a governor. This was too much for the military, who rose up and decapitated the two "white faces."

Wu did win over the Buddhists. At least one Buddhist monk was reputed to be her lover. A Buddhist prophecy said a woman would be born who would rule over a great empire. They were convinced that Ms. Wu was fulfilling that prophecy. In fact, they declared her to be a divine incarnation of the Buddha. The Tang capital was renamed the Divine Capital, and Ms. Wu assumed the special title of "Holy Mother, Divine Imperial One." Finally, in 705, the old empress, now 78 years of age, was too feeble to have any more affairs and was unable to govern. She was replaced at that time by a restored Tang dynasty.

Ms. Wu was succeeded by her son, **Zhongzong**, but the government never seemed to work out as successfully for her son. He was first dominated, then poisoned, by his own Empress Wei. Empress Wei and her allies sold bureaucratic offices, greatly swelling the central government bureaucracy and ushering in an unprecedented era of corruption. In 710 a young military leader named **Xuanzong** moved against the Empress Wei and replaced her with his own

The Tang Dynasty

father, **Ruizong**, who he claimed was the rightful heir to the throne. In 713, **Xuanzong** led another coup and established himself as the Tang monarch.

Xuanzong ruled China from 712 to 756, the longest and the most glorious epoch in all Chinese history. He was commonly known by the name of Minghuang, "the Brilliant Emperor." Even so, by the end of his reign it became obvious that the Tang dynasty was suffering from a lack of strong leadership.

Xuanzong's reign began with a series of reforms designed to strengthen the regime and to restore a healthier balance of power between the throne and the court. The massive corruption of the preceding decade was ended, political decision making became more open to official scrutiny, and the efficiency of local government was improved. The administration of the provinces was improved and the perennial problem of famine was addressed by reviving a coordinated system of granaries to provide food in time of emergency. Military power was strengthened, especially along the frontiers, and the Tibetans were defeated.

Xuanzong's court reflected a new elegance and pageantry in keeping with its new prosperity. The emperor was a lively patron of poetry, music, dance, and the arts. A new kind of court music incorporated a combination of the old Chinese ritual and popular music with foreign tunes from India, Iran, and Central Asia. The new music was so popular that by the mid-ninth century the old Chinese music had entirely disappeared. The new musical style was in turn exported to Korea and Japan. Work in bronze and jade reached a high point. This new level of culture also penetrated the areas of Chinese occupation in the Korean peninsula. Again, the Koreans passed this on through their contacts with Japan. Truly this was a high point in Chinese history.

This was followed by Xuanzong's pursuit of mystical Taoism and Tantric Buddhism. He began to pay less attention to matters of state and turned the governance of China over to his chief minister, **Li Linfu**. Li became a virtual dictator, who delegated a great amount of military power along the northern and northeastern frontiers to **An Lushan**. A grant of so much military power to one man caused jealousy among the other military commanders, who decided to reduce the power of An Lushan following the death of Li Linfu. An Lushan decided to strike a quick military blow which would establish his position as the head of China.

The conflict with the other generals--especially Yang Guozhong--soon turned into an open civil war. In 755 An Lushan captured one capital, Luoyang, and early the next year he captured the other capital, Chang'an. This forced the emperor, Xuanzong, to flee from his own capital to southern China. En route, the military escorts mutinied, killed several who were close to the emperor, and ordered him to also kill his favorite concubine, the beautiful and talented Yang Guifei. Seeing no choice in the matter, Xuanzong ordered his beloved strangled, a tragic end to a sequence of events which got totally out of control. This event led to generations of Chinese poets, painters, and dramatists who retold the tragic story of Xuanzong and Yang Guifei in countless versions. Late in 756 Xuanzong was deposed by his son. He died a few years later, a totally broken man. The Tang dynasty would never be the same again.

An Lushan was, for a brief time, the man behind the throne who controlled the military organization. In 757, he was killed by one of his own sons, who then had to fight numerous contestants for the control of the military. The civil war was ended in 763, but it had done irreparable damage to the Tang dynasty. The result was that the central government had lost direct control over a large part of the country. In order to survive, the government had to surrender much of its power to the military governors in the provinces. These men tended to go their own autonomous ways. The central government headed China in a symbolic way but the real power was with the military governors.

The finances of the central government now depended largely upon what the governors wanted to send to the emperor. Most of them kept the bulk of the local revenue for themselves. Although the southern provinces were more faithful, it was not enough. The government declared a monopoly on salt production and distribution in an effort to add to their revenue. Since this brought in a sizeable amount of money, the government then extended monopolies to wine, tea, and lacquer. These various monopolies provided an important segment of revenue.

Land tenure changed in the later Tang dynasty from the emperor owning all the land and then apportioning it out to trustworthy individuals, to the local governors now handling land distribution to their own advantage. In the late 8th and 9th centuries a free market system of land ownership began. This made it possible for the rich and the powerful to control large amounts of rural lands. They in turn had their lands worked by poor peasants who lived in villages and farmed the land like serfs for the great landowners.

THE LAST YEARS OF THE TANG

During its final eighty years the Tang was only a shadow of its former self. Flooding disasters in the Yangtze Valley added greatly to the misery of the already downtrodden peasants. Banditry and rebellion engulfed much of southern and central China. A salt smuggler named **Huang Chao** accumulated enough capital to equip an army and lead a rebellion from 875 to 884. His forces first swept south to Canton (Guangzhou), then north to the capital at Chang'an. This rebellion caused a terrible loss of life and an economic disruption from which southern China did not easily recover. From the fall of Huang Chao in 884, the central government ruled in name only. The real power drifted even more to the regional regimes, most of which were for all purposes independent.

In times such as the Later Tang, there are always plenty of people at all levels who wish to place the blame on someone else. There was a tendency to again blame the concubines and the eunuchs for all that was wrong in China. Hundreds of these people were slaughtered for solely political purposes. The **Khitan**, a tribe of people from the north who spoke a Mongol tongue, swept into the northern part of China and established themselves in **Peking** (Beijing) in 938. They ruled the northern one-third of China under the name **Liao** for nearly 200 years.

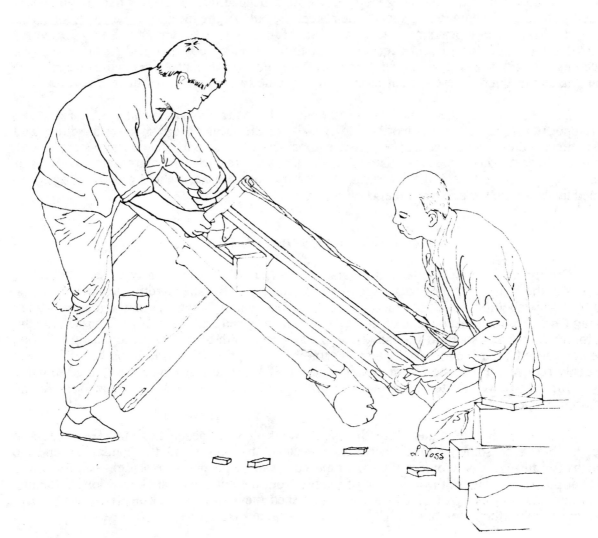

Figure 29

Chapter 27
THE SUNG DYNASTY, 960-1279

The **Sung** dynasty, also known as the **Song**, was founded by **Zhao Kuangyin**. who ruled from 960 to 976. Zhao was a great military leader who was proclaimed emperor by his troops with the title of **Taizu**. China had suffered nearly a century of strife and disorganization following the declining years and the final break-up of the Tang Dynasty. The Six Dynasties period and the early Tang were in many ways the last phase of **ancient** Chinese history. The late Tang and the early Sung which followed it in 960 formed the first phase of later Chinese history. It was during this transitional period that a culture developed which remained characteristic of China until the opening decades of the 20th century. From that perspective, the Sung dynasty could very well be labeled **Early Modern China**.

The early part of the Sung dynasty, 960 to 1126, saw the capital city located in the central Yellow River valley at **Kaifeng**, a northern city. Consequently, it is often referred to as the period of the "Northern Sung." The later part of the Sung dynasty, 1127 to 1279, saw the capital moved to **Hangzhou** (Hangchou), about 110 miles south of Shanghai and the Yangtze River. The city was founded in A.D. 606 and it soon became the center of China's rice and silk culture. Trade abounded from the beautiful harbor city of Hangzhou, since it was located on the East China Sea and later became the southern terminus of the Grand Canal. The reason for the move to the relatively new city was the conquest of the North by a new group called the **Jin dynasty**. The period from 1127 to 1279 is therefore known as the "Southern Sung."

The first leader of the Sung, **Taizu**, proved to be not only a skilled militarist but a talented administrator who set China on a new course. He created a professional army of career soldiers whose officers were rotated on a regular basis and were under **civilian** control. This brought to a close the "strong man," or "warlord" era, which had been so damaging to the Later Tang. The conquest of the southern provinces was relatively easier than in the North. Two powerful provinces in the north--the Khitan state of Liao, and the Xixia state around Gansu--caused considerable problems for the Sung conquerors. Ultimately, the Sung had to make substantial tribute payments in silver and silk each year to maintain a hold in that part of China.

The Sung emperors wanted a strong, centralized state from the emperor at the top all the way down to the most local level of administration. At the top level of central administration there were three branches: (1) Finance, (2) Army, and (3) Secretariat. There were many overlapping responsibilities, checks and balances, and there were administrators who checked to be sure the administration was conducted fairly and honestly. At both the central level and the local level there were officials who were judicial intendants, fiscal intendants, military intendants, and those who were intendants of transportation and monopolies. All of these were very closely organized and supervised from top to bottom. As clumsy as this may sound, it all seemed to work for the Chinese. Furthermore, it provided a model of government which other dynasties tried to follow most of the time until western influences and greater democratic needs and demands reshaped it.

There are several reasons why the Sung dynasty is referred to as the Early Modern period of China. It was an age when political parties which operated similar to those in the western world were beginning to form. There was more argumentation among the governing officials, concerning future policy, instead of court officials aligning themselves with some powerful eunuch or court concubine who controlled a faction close to the emperor. There were many of the eunuchs who were powerful enough to make or break the emperor's own policy announcements. By bringing political issues out into the open for debate it also took the power away from the local military warlords who had been able to dictate their own policies within their areas of control.

Under the more open political environment the status of the commoners began to rise at the court, which witnessed a corresponding decrease in the power of the aristocracy. During the early Sung period, they decided to re-write the civil service examinations in an effort to discover new talent to run the government, a policy which ended some--but not all--of the bureaucrats arranging to pass their jobs along to their sons. The civil service under the Tang had become an aristocracy of its own which worked in conjunction with the eunuchs and concubines.

Trade began to increase under the more stable government of the Sung dynasty. Hard money was scarce and in 1024, the Sung introduced paper currency. It was a great boon to trade, and much safer than trying to move a quantity of gold. There were those, especially peasants and shopkeepers, who did not want to accept the paper currency for several years. Eventually, everyone was pleased to accept it on a par with hard currency. China was one of the first of the major nations to introduce paper currency on a wide basis. However, there was a problem with counterfeiters right from the beginning.

A new era in literature and philosophy began with fiction and drama in addition to theological tracts and history. Artistic drawings often accompanied the literary works. Another area of literature opened up which covered various educational opportunities for study beyond the ancient classics. One of these areas was a new interest in scientific topics. The Confucian scholars now admitted that there could be other fields of study as well as more than one interpretation of the Confucian canon. The world of scholarship became more broad minded and much less provincial than in the Tang and earlier periods. All of the new and more practical approachs to the world of learning gave greater rise to a general literacy than ever before. All of the new learning and open politics would appear to make the Sung period a delightful time to be living in China. There were problems!

The fact that the Sung could not totally control the northern area but were required to pay tribute was not because they had not tried. The size of the army more than tripled until in 1041 there were about one and a quarter million men in uniform. This absorbed three-fourths of the government's revenue as well as leading to several disputes among the militarists and the generals. Support for such a huge army was borne primarily by the peasant and worker class, and it appeared they might revolt.

The first reformer to appear was **Fan Zhongyan** who attempted to institute several reforms in 1043-44. Fan was an honest and sincere man who was opposed by the conservatives, who were vehemently against **any** changes. As a consequence this first reform movement died. The government tried to make government finances balance by drastically reducing government activities, but this proved an inadequate answer. The huge army simply consumed the national budget. Deficit financing was unknown.

The next reformer was **Wang Anshi** who was able to effect major changes in China between 1069 and 1085. The secret of his success was the support of the Emperor **Shenzong** who reigned from 1067 to 1085. Wang's reforms began with major changes in the land

The Sung Dynasty

assessments. An age old problem in China was that huge amounts of money was traditionally skimmed off by bureaucrats between the point where the peasant paid his just taxes and the money arrived in the capital. Wang Anshi introduced new schemes for assuring that the money due the central government arrived at the royal treasury.

One of these schemes included a new system of bookkeeping at all levels of government. By placing new priorities on budgetary items, he was able to more nearly balance the budget. It was a case like all governments--as the bureaucracy grew and inflation slowly increased, the cost of government went up. There were new weapons to purchase and as better equipment became available it cost enormous sums to re-equip China's large army. This was partially offset by creating local militia units so there would be a military available in time of need without maintaining such a large standing army.

Since the mass of the peasants had been terribly unhappy, the new tax assessment policy made the levies seem more fair, even when the emperor asked for more money. The government began to provide low interest-bearing loans to the peasants so that many of them could acquire the land they had worked for generations rather than become simply serfs who were controlled by the rich landlords. The government established pawnshops to replace the several private ones which were known to charge exorbitant rates of interest. The government also eased the burden of the peasant class, who had been asked to do road and bridge work for several days each year. Taxes were now levied to pay a regular crew of men to maintain the highways and bridges. As an increasing number of civil service jobs were opened at the local level, there were more of the sons of the peasant class who could qualify for these entry-level positions. The number of government schools in the villages and towns were increased to make education available to a wider range of people than ever before.

These "Wang reforms" were the most sweeping reforms China had witnessed in a thousand years. Although no one today could argue against most of these changes, nearly everyone was unhappy, especially the military and the civil servants. To change the civil service exams was tantamount to attacking religion itself, but with the emperor's support, Wang ousted those civil officials who opposed him. The same was true in the military establishment. But ultimately the arch conservatives like Ouyang Xiu, and later, Sima Guang, gained power. There was much factionalism and Wang's men were ousted.

The emperor **Huizong**, who reigned from 1100 to 1125, was one of China's most cultivated men. A great painter and calligrapher, Huizong left much of the governance of the realm to his chief counselor, **Cai Jing**. Towards the end of Huizong's reign, there arose two major problems. The first was a revolt in 1120 throughout the northern provinces which was led by **Fang La**.

It is not certain whether Fang La was a **Manichean**, but he has often been identified as one, and he certainly had the support of this strange religious group. The founder of **Manichaeism** was a man named **Mani** who was born in A.D. 216 in northern Mesopotamia. The sect was not popular with the rulers of any of the countries, but has generally had an appeal to the people of the lower economic classes. Manichaeism combines Gnostic spiritualism, Zoroastrianism, and some elements of Buddhism. It spread to the West, including North Africa, where the young St. Augustine practiced it before his conversion to Christianity. In the eastern world it was a favorite in some areas of Turkestan and China. It has been condemned by Christians, Muslims, Zoroastrians, and Buddhists, but it still survives in isolated areas to the

249

present time. On the positive side, the Manichaeans have composed many beautiful pieces of literature and poetry.

Fang La dubbed himself the "Sage Duke." He conquered a piece of northern China and proclaimed himself the ruler over it. He referred to his reign as the **Yongle**, or "Everlasting Happiness." He said he was protesting exorbitant taxes and rapacious officials. The Chinese Manichaeans saw him as a mystic leader and many began to support Fang La's new government. Although his revolt lasted less than a year he became a folk hero and a martyr. Worst of all, he weakened the Sung defenses along the northern frontier.

Another more serious threat occurred in a Jurchen state to the north of Liao in 1115. There a warlike group called the **Jin** arose and began to attack the Liao in 1115 from their northern border. The Chinese, who had always wanted Liao for themselves, attacked the Liao from the south. In 1122 the Chinese and the Jin agreed to divide the Liao territory between them. Scarcely had the ink dried until the Jin moved to take all of Liao, then the Jin moved against the Chinese capital at Kaifeng. It was such a surprise that the emperor Huizong and his heir were both made prisoners by the Jin before they could escape.

Sung Chinese loyalists regrouped in the South and proclaimed a younger son of Huizong as emperor. At that moment this was thought of as a temporary measure until Huizong could be released. In the end, Huizong was **not** released and the younger son, **Gaozong**, reigned from 1127 to 1162. Gaozong was the emperor who decided to move the capital far to the south at the port city of **Hangzhou** while at the same time the Jin established their capital at **Peking** (Beijing). From this time period, A.D. 1234 onward, China would remain divided into two parts for the next several years. The term "Northern Sung" refers to the period **before** the move to Hangzou, and the "Southern Sung" refers to the period **after** the move to Hangzhou.

Although the Sung officials talked a lot about regaining the north, there was only one general who really made any effort to accomplish that mission. When general **Yue Fei** reached the Luoyang area, a good start toward recapturing the north, he was recalled to Hangzhou and executed. A treaty was made with the Jin in 1142 after which the Sung government made annual payments of tribute to the Jin as they had previously done to the Liao. It is hard to say how long such a static situation might have endured except that a new ingredient in the military-political world entered the scene--the **Mongols**.

In 1215, the same year King John of England signed the Magna Carta, the **Mongols** captured **Peking** from the Jin. The Mongols continued their conquest until they had the state of Xixia and began attacking the Sung along their northern border. Although the Mongols had already captured much of Asia, the Sung fought them for 40 years before they, too, eventually lost. Sung resistance finally collapsed between 1273 and 1279, and **Kublai Khan** became the emperor of China.

LIFE IN THE SUNG PERIOD

By the year 1100, China's population had already reached 100 million people! Modern analysts have wondered how the country could possibly support so many when western Europe had only a fraction of this number. The answer centers around two factors-- first wetland rice cultivation, and secondly, improved methods of pumping water. As wetland rice was proven to

The Sung Dynasty

outproduce either dry land rice or wheat, the farmers began selecting and breeding new strains of rice as well as introducing a drout-resistant rice from Southeast Asia, which also matured much earlier. China quickly went from a one crop per year type of rice culture to two, and in a few cases, they could harvest three crops per year in the southeast. In order that the land would not wear out from such heavy cropping they began returning everything to the paddy which could possibly enhance its fertility, including "night soil."

Most of the rice at this time was grown in the southern half of the country and that was also the area of the greatest population growth. Not only did a wealthy peasant or land owner believe that he could support one more child, he thought he needed another one to help care for the rice paddies because rice is a very labor-intensive crop. Whereas the Yangtze Valley and the southeast coast had supported one-fourth the total population in the Tang and early Sung period, by 1080 they had **half** the total population of the entire country. Nearly all of this increase was engaged in agriculture. Some people owned their own land, but most of the people were either tenants who paid the landlord a rent, or they were peasants attached to the land of wealthy landlords. Apparently the ownership of the land varied throughout time as well as from one area of China to another.

There was also a great growth in commerce under the Sung dynasty. Port cities, whether on the coast or along rivers such as the Yangtze, had the most rapid rate of growth. All kinds of boats were improved and the production of iron and textiles made remarkable advances. From a material point of view, the people in Sung China were better off than anywhere else in the world.

It was an era of great inventions, great craftsmen, and entrepreneurs. Silk, lacquer, and porcelain reached their highest levels of technical perfection. Cotton for clothing was used widely while in other parts of the world cotton was a luxury cloth which sold for about the same price as silk did in China. Ceramicware entered the overseas trade. By around the year 800, the Chinese had discovered how to coke bituminoius coal, something which did not happen in western Europe for over 500 more years. The Chinese even developed explosives to mine the coal! All of these advances brought a huge demand for consumer goods, both from within China and from the outside world.

With so much going in the business world the Chinese were the first to develop credit on a widespread basis. Bankers and brokers first appeared in the Sung period. The minted copper coins which had been used in China for centuries proved totally inadequate. Unminted silver was used sometimes, but it was paper currency in both large and small denominations which made such a large scope of business possible. Paper currency had first come into use in China during the late 9th century, long before it was used in western Europe. The paper bills were at first redeemable certificates of deposit so that merchants would not have to carry large amounts of cash when traveling. In 1024 the Chinese government issued its own notes and they were accepted very much as our present day currency.

Various areas of China were known for their own type of production in both manufacturing and in agriculture. Tea, sugar cane, and other "luxury" foods became quite commonplace. Chinese trade routes went to most parts of Asia in the Sung years. Overseas trade was facilitated by huge ships which were propelled by both oars and sails. The **compass** was first reported in China in 1119. Taxes were revised to shift the burden away from the peasants toward the newly rising areas of commerce and business by around 1200. By 1300 the government received less than half its taxes from the land.

The Sung Dynasty

As people experienced such an increase in living standards, the entertainment places in the large cities began to stay open from dusk to dawn. Jugglers, acrobats, storytellers, musicians, fortunetellers, and the beginning of theater, all thrived under the Sung. Wine shops and restaurants were found in the larger cities as well as commercial hotels for the traveling merchant.

But along with the fun there were problems. For instance, sanitation and safety problems arose. Fire was a constant problem. Communicable diseases spread very quickly in the densely populated areas. Crime began to rise. But Europe was still asleep in the medieval period at this time. The age of the Crusades was just beginning to open the eyes of the crusaders that there was a world beyond their little villages and towns.

Education came to have a much greater importance during the Southern Sung period. Throughout the Tang and Northern Sung period the government had been controlled by a few aristocratic families. By the Southern Sung period these old and fixed lines began to break up. By about 1200 many government officials came from the local provincial gentry. Education was the key to these changes.

The Southern Sung began to use the Confucian style examination, especially the *jinshi*, with its continued heavy emphasis on the classics, history, and literary skills, as a method of selecting officeholders. Nepotism and other inside connections now were less important than knowledge. The landowning-merchant class could now send their children to school and expect that if they could pass the examinations, they would end up with lucrative jobs. Furthermore, they could now marry above their social status, buy more of the recently available consumer goods, and then send their children to school for even better public or private jobs.

Printing from large wooden blocks had begun at the end of the Tang period but reached its full proportions during the Southern Sung. This meant that books were now less expensive than hand-printed ones. The gentry could now afford them, and their children began school with a decided advantage over those families without books or education. Both Chinese classics and the Buddhist canon were published in their entirety. Entire encyclopedias, and even ghost stories, were now set on permanent wood blocks. During the late Sung period, **moveable type** appeared with ceramic letters rather than metal type as was used in the West at a much later date. In fact, it was 1455 when Gutenberg began printing in the western world. But for the Chinese, the woodblock print was considered **art**, whereas the moveable type was used for more utilitarian type of printing.

The new emphasis on education during the Sung period not only made knowledge more widespread, but the shift from an aristocratic to a middle class civil service caused a shift toward civilian interests over the military interests, urban interests over rural, and native Chinese culture came to be thought of as much higher than any non-Chinese culture. This movement has sometimes been referred to as "**Neo-Confucianism**," a kind of ethnocentrism which permeated the entire Chinese society for the next several centuries.

Neo-Confucianism was an important route to success in government or private employment but it should not be thought of as a new religion. Buddhism became the acceptable faith of nearly all the Chinese during this time. However, the Neo-Confucian principle of perfecting oneself before trying to reform the world had many adherants in China. A great

The Sung Dynasty

emphasis was therefore placed on seriousness and reverance, and the study of history and the classics indirectly reinterpreted the Confucian teachings until the quest for knowledge and personal perfection became a kind of a new religion in and of itself. During this time much emphasis was placed upon the proper study of **history**. A Chinese historian named **Sima Guang** wrote a history of China from ancient times through the Tang. This was not the first comprehensive history of China, but it was exceptionally well done. Sima Guang checked all the sources and explained why one was more reliable than another.

The new interest in history and the classics served as a stepping stone to an important position and created a further interest in China's antiquities. It seemed that everything from the past was brought out and studied. This included bronze vessels, mirrors, inscribed stones, etc. The Sung wanted to know how old they were and their relationship to their own time.

Overall, the Sung dynasty was an age of great growth in population, culture, and inventions. The result was that China under the Sung was probably the most intellectual nation in the world during the period from the 10th to the 13th centuries. They certainly did have a high standard of living and they were conceited and proud of it. When the first Europeans arrived during the 16th and 17th centuries, they were quickly reminded by the Chinese people and government that the Chinese were the most intelligent people in the world. They firmly believed that the emperor's palace was the actual center of the world and that all other rulers owed **them** the highest respect. But the Mongols to the north and west never accepted the idea that the Chinese were any better than any other people.

Figure 30

254

Chapter 28
THE MONGOL DYNASTY, 1279-1368

The Mongols were a people of the Altaic language group who inhabited the steppe region north of China and from the western tributaries of the Yellow River to Lake Baikal for centuries. Originally the term "Mongol" referred to only one of a small group of eastern Mongolian tribes, but it was one of their leaders, born into one of these eastern tribes, who united these many peoples to the north and west of China into one powerful group. Although they often disagreed among themselves, they appeared to the Chinese and to Europe as one powerful and united people. The Mongolian leader who first pulled all of the tribal factions together was **Genghis Khan**. From Genghis Khan on, people in both Asia and Europe thought of **all** the people from this area as Mongols.

The Mongols had never kept a history up to the time of Ghengis Khan, so we know very little about their background except that they were a nomadic people who depended for their livelihood on flocks of sheep, goats, horses, and sometimes camels. They followed regular routes each year as they migrated from one good pasture area to another with the changing seasons. The basic governmental organization was tribal with a leader who was responsible for assigning pasture areas. This same leader organized groups of mounted men to attack settled regions from time to time. Often they controlled large areas north of China by very militaristic and dictatorial methods. The Mongols depended upon the income from these raids upon settled communities for a portion of their livelihood, as well as tribute or protection money, which the communities of northern China paid them.

The Chinese generally considered the Mongols simply as a nuisance people who lived along their northern frontiers. They were first mentioned in the Tang period, 618-907, but it was the 12th century when they began to worry the Jin dynasty just north of China, probably because their numbers were growing substantially at this time. What the Mongols needed was a good leader with organizational ability. That leader was Genghis Khan.

GENGHIS KHAN

Genghis Khan was born about 1162 into a family under the leadership of Yesugei, a chieftain of a minor Mongol clan. Genghis Khan's father was murdered by a rival tribe when Genghis was only eight years old. His mother taught the young man the essentials of becoming a chief to follow in his father's footsteps. Beyond the principles of hunting and warfare, she taught him the importance of creating a network of loyal friends and allies before he went to war. Genghis became quite adept at winning friends, using them, then turning against them when they were no longer needed. Very early in his life it became plain that **he**--Genghis Khan--wanted to be the **one** ruler of **all** the Mongols. In these early years of campaigning he assembled a trustworthy army known as the *nokod*, which he rewarded with the spoils of war.

Genghis Khan's first act was to crush the **Tatars** who had murdered his father. Having accomplished that mission he defeated several other Mongol tribes in rapid succession. By 1206, the other chieftains endorsed Genghis Khan as the ruler of **all** the Mongols. One of them later decided to rise up against Genghis after 1206 and he was promptly defeated. Genghis ordered his loyal men to execute the leader by breaking his back.

The Mongol-Yuan Dynasty

Much of Genghis Khan's success was in his well-organized military. His army was divided into groups of one thousand, each group headed by a nobleman. By placing the military under his hand-picked nobility, he broke up the old petty factionalism of clan and tribal leaders. Other noblemen were appointed to raise the large sums of money needed for his army. It was the first time, so far as we know, that the Mongols had ever really paid taxes--and they were collected in full. This was an entirely new military compared to the old Mongol system in which each man had provided his own weapons and fought pretty much at his own pleasure with his own set of rules.

Genghis Khan also had an effective **spy network** which infiltrated areas he planned to conquer well ahead of his army. When he was ready to make a move, his men were trained to engage almost totally in offensive action. Most of his army consisted of mounted cavalry. They were extremely well-trained and mobile. Beyond striking by surprise he employed psychological terror extensively. It was not unknown for him to kill everyone in a town which had resisted his conquest. As a consequence, many of his opponents surrendered without resistance in the expectation of a better bargain. Some historians believe Genghis planned to conquer the entire world, but it is more likely that one successful campaign simply led to the next. Genghis Khan and his army seemed to thoroughly enjoy warfare, especially since they always won.

Once all the Mongols were under his control, he attacked the areas of northern and western China along the edge of the Mongolian territorial claims. He used the excuse that the **Xixia** people, also known as the **Tanguts** and the **Da Xia**, had been discriminating against the Mongols in their trading practices. This Buddhist group of people also controlled the eastern terminus of some of the important trade routes. By 1209 the Xixia people could no longer resist the Mongol advance. They gave up the fight on a promise that they would pay an annual tribute and become a vassal state to the Mongols. This was important to Genghis Khan's empire-building plans because the Xixia were situated across many of China's trade routes to the western world. It was a good source of income.

The Xixia were geographically close to the Jin who were just to the north of the Xixia territory and situated along China's northern boundary. Unfortunately for both the Xixia and the Jin, they had never cooperated. Had they allied together when the Mongol threat had originated, Genghis Khan would have had a difficult battle. Having finished the Xixia off, Genghis Khan turned against the Jin, and by 1215, Genghis Khan captured their capital at Yanjing, also known as Peking or Beijing.

The following year, 1216, Genghis Khan sent an embassy and a trading caravan to one of the rulers in Central Asia with the anticipation that he could establish trading ties in that area. Instead of being received in a kindly manner, the Central Asian ruler ordered the Mongols murdered. He then sent a second group of envoys asking that the shah who ruled over that area hand over the guilty murderers. These envoys, too, were murdered. That provoked a declaration of war. It was 1219 before Genghis thought his army of 200,000 was ready to move against the shah **Ala al-Din Muhammad**.

As the Mongol army moved west, they took along huge catapults capable of hurling stones large enough to crush most city walls. City after city fell to Genghis Khan, and by 1220 he had caught up with Shah Muhammad. The shah was forced to pay a stiff penalty for the murder of the Mongol envoys. The old shah died the following year, 1221, and was succeeded by his son **Jalal al-Din**, who took a small detachment and fled to North India. This opened all of Central

The Mongol-Yuan Dynasty

Asia to Genghis Khan. He stayed in that area from 1222 until 1225, stabilizing his conquests and sending out smaller armies into the surrounding areas to receive their subservience as well. Two of his generals went west into the state of Georgia while conquering most of the area of the Crimea. Far away on the eastern end of Genghis Khan's empire, another general conquered Korea and forced them to pay him tribute. Still another of his generals attacked the Jin, who had risen up again thinking that all the Mongol armies were in Central Asia.

Although the Jin uprising was put down, the Xixia also decided to revolt. Genghis Khan had depended upon troops from the conquered armies to supplement his Mongolian forces. When the Xixian ruler refused to send troops, Genghis asked that he send his son as a hostage to the Mongols. This too was refused. Genghis headed for Xixia in 1226 to put them in their place but he died on the way east in August, 1227 without accomplishing his mission.

The body of Genghis Khan was transported to Burkhan Khaldurs, "Buddha Cliff," a mountain range in northeast Mongolia. In 1229 the great leader was appropriately laid to rest along with forty young women and forty horses, that were sacrificed at the tomb. We would certainly wonder about such a cruel conqueror today. Did he have any religious scruples at all?

It is interesting that one of his first considerations when he began his conquests was religious toleration. With so many diverse religions within his empire, he recognized that good relations with the religious leaders would facilitate his control over the local people of each area. He was also known to have eagerly met with religious men to discuss their beliefs. He was generous to Taoists, Muslims, Nestorian Christians, Buddhists, and others within his realm.

Since Mongols often lacked administrative skills, he often used foreigners in his government. Since the Mongols had no written language, he employed a Turk to create a written language based on the **Uighur Turkic** script. He also employed Uighur tutors for his sons, advisers, secretaries, and interpreters. Rather than make all the diverse cultures into the Mongol style, he either allowed them their own system or actually adopted it as his own.

The Mongols had never had a law code before Genghis Khan. His *Jasagh*, which was really more of a set of rules than a true law code, reflects the nomadic characteristic of the Mongol people. Since Genghis was such an absolute ruler, we must assume that the *Jasagh* was a reflection of his own views. It prohibited religious discrimination as well as favoritism toward any one religion. He carefully outlined how a centralized military organization should function. The base of his centralized military was built upon the metric system, that is, a base of ten. For instance, Mongol troops were to be divided into units of tens, thousands, and ten thousands, each with its own military commander. The commanders were obliged to carry out the orders of the Khan without question. All of these rules were based upon what Genghis Khan thought of as practical considerations.

Less practical or totally absent were some of his rules about taxes, land ownership and land inheritance, the duties and rights of tenants, and the word **commerce** was never mentioned. He provided **capital punishment** for civilians who might injure his soldiers; soldiers who failed to follow orders; and his rules prohibited the washing of clothes. Truly, it was more of a nomadic code than one for an emerging nation.

Perhaps the most serious omission in the *Jasagh* was the lack of a precise and orderly means of succession. In the years preceeding Genghis Khan, the Mongol leaders simply met, raised some names, and then decided on their new khan a couple of years later. He must have thought that his newly installed nobility would accomplish the task of filling a vacancy in the top office in the same manner as the old tribal chiefs.

Genghis had three sons and one whom he had adopted. Each one had his strengths and his weaknesses. Apparently Genghis favored his third son, **Ogedei**, a man who was fairly flexible and recognized that a good system of administration was needed to govern a country which stretched from Georgia in the Black Sea area to China. Ultimately, Ogedei was the choice of the nobles, but it took them two years to come to that conclusion. By that time the country was in a mess. People were no longer paying their taxes, revolts were cropping up all over, and Genghis's youngest son, **Tolui**, challenged Ogedei for the throne.

Ogedei (1186-1241) was finally able to assume the full leadership role in 1229. He was the first Mongol ruler to adopt the title of *khaghan*, which means "khan of khans." His reign continued to expand into China's territory. He crushed the rebellious Jin dynasty forever, and followed that by seizing all of North China in 1234. He then returned to pacify Korea in 1235. During these early years of his reign, he also mounted campaigns on the western end of his empire. There he conquered a large share of Russia and Armenia, which was added to the Mongol holdings in Georgia. His troops ranged as far as Hungary and Poland, but he did not effectively control these latter areas.

As a ruler, Ogedei established a reasonably efficient civil administration to govern his vast domain. Confucian scholars were recruited to serve as bureaucrats. North China was given an equitable tax system. Finally, Ogedei built a new capital fit for a ruler over the largest realm in the world at that time.

The new capital was built at **Karakorum** along the banks of the Orkhon River in what is today the Mongolian People's Republic. It had been only a tent city at the time of Genghis Khan, but Ogedei ordered that city walls and a palace should be built in 1235. It was a beautiful city by the standards of that time. Later it was completely destroyed, some say by the Ming Chinese in 1388. There was also an effort by another Mongol named Khalkha, to rebuild Karakorum in 1585, but this seems to have failed. Karakorum became an almost unidentifiable place until it was rediscovered by archaeologists in 1948.

In the last years of Ogedei's reign he became a heavy drinker, lost interest in the business of running his government, and in 1239 he turned over the financial administration of North China to Central Asian merchants who overtaxed the Chinese people. The peasants had to go to the merchants, many from Central Asia, for loans at such usurious rates that they became slaves of the merchants.

When Ogedei died in 1241, there was another long break before his young son succeeded him in 1246. Since the prince was still young, his mother, Ogedei's widow, **Toregene**, served as the regent. Young Guyug only served two years, a brief and ineffectual reign from 1246 to 1248. During this troubled time, the sons and grandsons of Genghis Khan spent most of their time quarreling about who would succeed to the throne. The ultimate winner was Mongke, the oldest son of Tolui, who was the oldest grandson of Genghis Khan.

Mongke installed a new government at Karakorum and reasserted the authority of the office of *khaghan*. After several years of family feuding, the empire's internal affairs were again in a total mess. Mongke began his reign by ordering a new census of the entire realm. He re-introduced a regular system of tax collection, and mobilized huge armies. By 1252, he sent his brother **Hulegu** to complete the conquest of western Asia. Four years later, 1256, Hulegu destroyed a group known as the **Ismalis**, better known as the "Order of the Assassins," and destroyed their strongholds in northwestern Persia, present-day Iran. Baghdad fell to Hulegu in 1258, and the inhabitants were put to the sword. Enamored with his successes in Persia, Hulegu moved on westward until he was stopped by the Egyptian Mamluks at the **Battle of Ain Galut** in Syria in 1260.

While brother Hulegu was so successful in the West, Khan Mongke reopened hostilities with Korea. The Koreans despised the Mongols and would revolt at any opportunity. The long quarrel over the succession gave them another opportunity. The Koreans tenaciously resisted-- Khan Mongke even had to commit his reserves--but in the end the Korean king was forced to acknowledge the Mongols as overlords.

Beginning in 1252, Mongke sent another brother, **Kublai**, to fight the Sung Chinese. Kublai and his able military commander, **Uriyangkadai**, were meeting with great success along the western and northwestern Sung frontiers at which time Mongke entered China with a second Mongol army. Fortunately for the Chinese, Mongke died in August of 1259.

The Mongols still had been unable to agree upon an orderly method of succession, and when Mongke died they quarrelled among themselves for twenty years! Mongke's brother, **Kublai**, believed the throne was his, while **Arigh Boke**, his youngest brother, had the advantage of being the commander Mongke had left in control of the capital city at Karakorum. The civil war which resulted found most of Genghis Khan's grandsons and their friends, relatives, military commanders, etc., all choosing which of several armies they would join in this fight amongst themselves for the ultimate control.

The final decision was finally made among the two commanders in the east--**Arigh Boke** and **Kublai**. It was **Kublai** who had won enough support from the wealthy Chinese to wear down his youngest brother, whose followers consisted largely of the much poorer and less numerous Mongolian tribesmen. In 1264, the final decision gave the rule to Kublai. He first pardoned his brother Arigh Boke, then executed him for "rebellion."

THE GOLDEN HORDE

The **Golden Horde** refers to the extension of the Mongol Empire into western Russia and Poland. When Genghis Khan died in 1227, he gave the westernmost portion of his empire to his oldest son, Juchi. But Juchi died before his father, so it was Juchi's son **Batu** who took over in the west and proceeded to expand his territory through a series of brilliant campaigns against the Slavs. It is therefore **Batu** who the Russians think of as the **founder of the Golden Horde**. These Mongol conquerors who controlled vast areas of Central Asia as far west as Russia from the 13th to the 15th centuries are also known in Russian history as the **Tatars**.

The Mongol-Yuan Dynasty

TATAR RUSSIA

In 1240, Batu sacked and burned the Russian capital at Kiev, and by the end of that year he controlled most of European Russia. In the campaign in central Europe, one Mongol army defeated King Henry II of Silesia at Liegnitz on April 9, 1241, while another Mongol army led personally by Batu defeated the Hungarians at Mohi two days later, April 11. It was at this time that the Mongols plunged into another dynastic squabble over the succession, so Batu moved back east where he established the **State of the Golden Horde on the lower Volga River at Sarai Batu**. Later, the capital was moved upstream to **Sari Berke**, a city of 600,000.

There is often a tendency to think of the Mongols and the Golden Horde as primitive warriors. **Sari Berke**, now known as Saray, a city about 30 miles east of Volgograd, was a city of beautiful mosques, water mains, centrally heated houses, and public baths. There were **no** other cities like this in the western world in the 13th century. At its peak the Golden Horde's territory included most of European Russia from the Urals to the Carpathian Mountains, and, to the east and north it extended far into Siberia. On the south the Golden Horde's lands bordered on the Black Sea, the Caucasus Mountains, and the Persian territories of another Mongol dynasty known as the **Il-Khans**.

This was a tremendous amount of real estate and one may well ask why they continually kept conquering more. The answer probably rests within two words--**plunder** and **power**. It was certainly not agricultural land because they already had more than enough of that in China. Furthermore, as a nomadic people they had always concentrated on animal husbandry in the steppes, primarily horses, and they had never been known as tillers of the soil.

The Mongols/Tatars customarily raided and looted the more developed civilizations of the West. They carried off what they could, then sometimes they left the region for several years before they would return. In other areas, they settled down among the Turks, the Persians, and the Slavs and adopted their culture. Their subjects in Russia, Moldavia, Greece, Georgia, and Armenia were forced to pay taxes. Since the Tatars knew so little about government they often employed the people they had overwhelmed to collect the taxes for them.

Those Russian princes who were anxious to learn to live with the Tatars often obtained permission to collect taxes for the Golden Horde because this not only gave the Russians some experience in government but they were allowed to retain a portion for their services. The Golden Horde did engage in trade with the East, as well as a north-south trade which extended from southern Russia to Mamluk Egypt, and as far west as the Italian city-state of Genoa.

The Black Death of 1346-1348, along with the murder of the man who was to have been the succeeding khan, greatly weakened the Mongols in their western areas. The Russian princes who had been collecting the taxes and consolidating power with their own people saw this as an opportune time to strike out for freedom. They defeated the Tatar general Mamay at the Battle of Kulikovo Pole in 1380. In the end, Mamay was replaced not by a Russian, but by his own ally, **Timur** in 1395. Timur then destroyed Sari Berke and deported most of the region's skilled craftsmen to Central Asia. This destroyed the lucrative trade the Horde had established with Europe and Africa. It also gave the Russian princes in the north an opportunity to take over some of that former trade and to build their own state of **Muscovy**. Within a surprisingly short period of time, Muscovy was powerful enough to resist the power of the Golden Horde.

The Mongol-Yuan Dynasty

In the 15th century the Golden Horde disintegrated into several smaller khanates--the Astra, Kazan, and Crimea khanates. The last of these, the Crimean Khan, was destroyed in 1502. But the nationalistic feelings of these areas has continued to the present time as exemplified by several of them who are seeking their independence from currently established countries. The Mongols continued on in the eastern world. Their areas of Inner and Outer Mongolia are dominated today by people who are descendants of the earlier Mongol peoples.

The Mongols failed to retain their control in the West largely because of their inability to agree upon the succession to the throne. The death of a ruler always led to internecine struggles which left the throne vacant from two to ten years each time there was a vacancy, a luxury which no state could afford even in those times. Government by assassination was often the accepted rule. The area of Central Asia over which they established their rule was too vast with too sparse a population and too weak of a transportation and communication system to be governed effectively. Basically, it broke down into the following areas: China, Mongolia and Central Asia, southern Russia, and Baghdad and the Middle East. Any one of these was a huge area. Perhaps it is amazing that they accomplished this as successfully as they did.

KUBLAI KHAN

Kublai Khan was born on September 23, 1215, the son of **Tolui**. Tolui was one of the sons of Genghis Khan and his mother was **Sorghaghtani Beki**, a **Nestorian Christian** noblewoman of the Kereit tribe. The western world considered the **Nestorians** to be a heresy beginning in the 5th century. This religious interpretation of Christianity began as a result of the teachings of an eastern patriarch of Constantinople named **Nestorius**. Nestorius was probably a good, original thinker, but he had often been at odds with the established church. Born in Germanica, Syria he entered a monastery near Antioch at a young age and became a very zealous Christian.

Nestorius first quarreled with the church fathers over the title *Theotokos*, "Mother of God," when referring to the Virgin Mary. He said that Mary could rightly be called the "Mother of Christ," but not the "Mother of God." St. Cyril, bishop of Alexandria, saw this as a denial of the oneness of Christ and God, therefore the bishop said this was a dangerous heresy. Nestorius proceeded next to say that there were two distinct persons in the Incarnate Christ--one human and the other divine. Nestorius was so convinced that he was right that he asked the Emperor Theodosius to call an ecumenical council to debate the issue. Such a council was held at Ephesus in 431, and Nestorius was condemned before he even arrived at the council. He refused to retract his beliefs and was deposed. Nestorius was ultimately exiled to the Great Oasis in the Libyan Desert where it is believed he died in 451. He had only been a patriarch for about three years, 428 to 431, but his teaching had widespread effects.

The Nestorian heresy survived long after the death of Nestorius. Kublai Khan's mother was but one example of a Nestorian Christian. Most Nestorians were strong-minded individuals who set their life on a certain course, were convinced they were right, and never wavered. Such was Sorghaghtani Beki's positive approach toward raising her husband Tolui's four sons. Both parents believed that the Mongol leaders had done them a great injustice in naming Ogedei rather than Tolui as the successor of Genghis Khan because Tolui had spent virtually his entire life helping his father win the military victories which had made him so great. While the father had been in the field fighting, the mother prepared her sons for power.

Sorghaghtani's success was not only in grooming each one of her sons for an important place in the Mongol empire, but she was recognized by her contemporaries as the greatest woman of her age. The Persian historian Rashid al-Din wrote that she was "extremely intelligent and able and towered above all the women in the world." A Hebrew physician named Bar Hebraeus said, "If I were to see among the race of women another woman like this, I should say that the race of women was far superior to that of men." Sorghaghtani Beki certainly did raise some strong-willed Mongol men.

The oldest son of Tolui and Sorghaghtani, **Mongke**, ruled as the Great Khan from 1251 until his death in 1269. Mongke was the last to base his capital at Karakorum in central Mongolia. It was under his rule that the city achieved an unprecedented splendor, and his empire expanded at a rapid rate. The Mongol Empire under Mongke became so large and so diverse that he was the last great Khan capable of exerting real authority over **all** the Mongol conquests.

Kublai succeeded his older brother and ruled China from 1260 until 1294. The next brother, **Hulegu**, destroyed the Abbasid dynasty which had governed much of the Middle East since 749. Hulegu then established his own dynasty in Persia. **Arigh Boke**, the youngest son, ruled the Mongol homeland until the death of Mongke.

Not only did Sorghaghtani prepare her sons intellectually, she acted wisely in forging alliances with several of the Mongol nobles who could assist her sons to power. Although she was a fervent Nestorian Christian, she assisted and supported Muslims, Taoists, and Buddhists providing they would advance the family cause. She won over the Chinese people who feared that the Monguls would take their rich farmland and convert it to pasture for their horses. She not only allowed the Chinese to continue farming the land but she actually promoted agriculture in China. She also allied with Batu, the ruler of the Golden Horde in Russia, to assist her son Mongke to be enthroned as the Great Khan in 1251.

Apparently, **Kublai** was greatly affected by his mother's attitudes and policies. He did not pillage his conquered territories, but rather granted them a considerable amount of local autonomy. The men of his Mongol court did not always possess the necessary administrative skills, so he recruited a corps of Chinese advisers to establish an orderly and equitable system of taxation which would improve their agrarian economy. He even managed to persuade many who had fled North China when the Mongols invaded that it was now safe to return. He was so tolerant of various religions that he used Confucians, Buddhists, Muslims, and Nestorian Christians as advisors and executors of his policies. When he decided to build a summer residence in Kaiping, 36 miles west of the modern town of Dolon Nor in Inner Mongolia, he built it in the Chinese style. He renamed it **Shangdu**, which means "upper capital" in Chinese. This city is presentday Kaiping.

MARCO POLO

It was this fabulous capital at Shangdu which **Marco Polo** visited in 1275. Marco Polo was born in 1254, possibly in Venice or nearby, and became, so far as we know, the West's first traveler to visit China and then to write a book about his visit. When Marco was still a child, his

The Mongol-Yuan Dynasty

father and his uncle set out for the East. Both men were merchants with business ties in Constantinople. In 1261, the two men wanted to move on east from Constantine's city to visit Sudak, a Venetian colony in the Crimea where they seem to have had a branch of their business. Once they had settled their business in Sudak, they decided to journey on east to Sari Berke, the city which was the capital of the Golden Horde along the Volga River. They were welcome at Sari Berke and stayed there for about a year.

About the time the Polos arrived in Sari Berke, the Mongols began another of those dynastic struggles which made it seem unsafe to return to Europe the same way they had come. The two men chose rather to circle around the Caspian Sea to the east and found themselves next in Bukhara in Central Asia. This time they stayed three years. While they were at Bukhara, some agents of Kublai, the Great Khan of China, persuaded the Venetian merchants to accompany them as they returned to what was then called Khanbaliq, the modern Beijing. They questioned the Chinese envoys about the safety of such a long journey, but they were assured that the Mongols controlled all the land from the Crimea to the Pacific Ocean and that the Great Khan would be pleased to see them. The Chinese agents explained that the Muslims had built a barrier between Europe and the Far East, but the Mongols had now opened that barrier because they controlled it all.

The Polo brothers decided the men were telling the truth so they joined the caravan and headed east, thereby becoming the first Europeans in medieval times to enter China. Kublai welcomed them and asked them many questions about the western world. They were so impressed that they stayed for several years at the court of the Great Khan, but unfortunately they left no record of their experiences there. Kublai Khan allowed them to leave and asked them to take letters to the pope asking him to send learned missionaries to instruct his subjects concerning their Christian faith.

Their journey back to Venice followed the caravan routes westward across Asia. Pope Clement IV had died in 1268 and no new pope had yet been appointed, so there was no real need to deliver the Khan's letters in Rome. But Venice must have seemed a very mundane city following their years in China and two years later the two men decided to return. This time they took Niccoli's son **Marco**, then 17 years of age. By the time they arrived in Syria, they heard that Gregory X had been elected pope, so they returned to Rome to deliver the letters from the Great Khan.

The Polos delivered the letters as they had promised, but the pope said that he could only spare two Dominican missionaries, who only accompanied the three men a short distance until they said they found the journey too arduous and turned back. The western world obviously missed an opportunity to reestablish communication with the Far East at this time.

Their second journey to the East began in Syria in 1271, and again they followed the trade and caravan routes. They arrived in China at Kublai Khan's palace at Shangdu in **1275**. Marco Polo and Kublai Khan seemed to get along quite well from the start. He studied Chinese and was even entrusted by the emperor to various diplomatic missions in different parts of the khan's realm. Marco made careful notes of where he had traveled, what the cities were like, the customs of the people, and what kinds of crops they grew.

Most of the places Marco Polo mentioned later in his book have been located. He also claimed he had been the governor of Yangchow province for three years, but this cannot be verified. It does seem certain that he was some kind of agent, deputy, or administrator for the khan. He also seems to have exaggerated a story about his father and his uncle advising Kublai Khan about the conquest of a city in South China. Marco also said he visited Cochin China, present-day Vietnam, as well as Burma and India. The three men served Kublai Khan for 17 years and were beginning to want to return by that time. The khan was growing old and they knew of the bitter contests for power which ensued when a ruler died. But Kublai Khan had found the Europeans useful to him and he did not want them to leave.

The opportunity for the Polos to leave China came in 1286, when the Persian Mongol ruler lost his favorite wife. He sent agents to Kublai to send another wife from his Mongol tribe in the Far East. The problem was that this was a long and arduous journey and apparently more dangerous for a young princess than for merchants. The decision was, therefore, to send her by sea. The Polos begged to accompany this mission and Kublai Khan consented. He gave the Polos friendly messages to the pope and the kings as far away as England and France. The naval expedition left port, probably Fukien, in early 1292. They moved down the coast of China, around Malaysia and past Sumatra to the Nicobar Islands, Ceylon, and western India and arrived at Hormuz in 1294. The three Venetians and the bride all seem to have survived the dangers and the diseases of a sea voyage in the 13th century. Interestingly, the old khan of Persia who had ordered the bride died in 1291, so she married his son, Ghazan Khan.

The Polos finally arrived back in Venice after an absence of 25 years. Even their relatives failed to recognize them. Supposedly, they brought back much wealth. Very shortly after their return, a trade war broke out between Genoa and Venice. Marco joined the war to defend his city but was held captive by the Genoese for a little less than a year. While he was waiting release, he met an able writer who recorded Marco's dictated story of his travels. Marco seems to have had access to his abundant notes which he had kept from the very beginning of his eastern journey. *The Book of Marco Polo* was regarded as partly the marvels of another world and partly a result of a man with a strong imagination. He was not taken very seriously in his own age except as a terrific storyteller.

Marco Polo died on January 8, 1324, leaving behind a book, a wife named Donata, and three daughters. The detailed information concerning distances, topography, customs, etc., did not appear outside his book until the printing of the *Catalan Atlas* in about 1375, about 50 years after the death of the great explorer. It is said that Christopher Columbus had a heavily annotated copy of the Latin version of the atlas in his possession. Most other navigators had simply heard about Marco Polo, but were not greatly interested. Had Europe followed up on the trips of the Polos and have established ties with the Far East, it would have been more difficult, perhaps impossible, for the Muslims to have closed off trade with China. Most historians believe that the closing of this trade after the Turks captured Constantinople in 1453 was a major factor in the desire to find another route to the riches of the East. The voyages of Diaz, Vasco da Gama, and Columbus were all efforts to find a water route to China and the spices and other riches of the East by circumventing the land-based caravan routes.

CHINA AND THE MONGOLS UNDER KUBLAI KHAN

We have seen how Kublai and his youngest brother Arigh Boke struggled for the throne between 1260 and 1262. The real basis of this dispute was between those Mongols who believed that conquest and pillage was the proper way of life as Genghis Khan had shown while he was the

The Mongol-Yuan Dynasty

ruler. They believed they could have control of the entire Eurasian land mass if they only continued conquering and pillaging as they forged ahead. Kublai and his faction of Mongols were more inclined to consolidate the winnings of the past, properly administer the area and reap the benefits. Kublai Khan won this struggle.

It probably seems easy for us to follow Kublai Khan's rise to power, but he had plenty of fighting during his regime, first to get the throne, and then to retain it. In 1268 his cousin Khaidu took over much of Central Asia. Another challenger was a Nestorian Christian named **Nayan**, who rebelled in Manchuria in 1287. Leading a force of approximately 200,000 men, Nayan was too powerful to be ignored. Kublai personally crushed the Manchurian rebellion and executed Nayan. It was about this same time that Kublai concluded that he must be more belligerent, more like his grandfather. The Mongols loved every one of Kublai's military expeditions. This led Kublai to conclude that a very long period of peace would probably cost him his throne.

Both his uncle Ogedei and his brother Mongke had tried to pacify the Southern Sung but they had met with little success. Kublai employed two Muslim engineers who brought his army a knowledge of artillery. They then laid seige to the Sung stronghold of **Xiangyang** in 1273. They were soon successful, so they moved on to the Sung capital of Lin'an in 1276. In 1279 the last Sung emperor drowned in a naval engagement off the southeastern coast of China. All of China was now added to the vast area under Kublai Khan's control. As early as 1272 he had named his Chinese dynasty the **Yuan**, but he did not achieve final and total control of the Southern Sung until 1279.

Kublai was more interested in moving his frontiers to the south than to the west at this time. It is difficult to find the real reason for their Southeast Asian campaign, possibly just the expansionist mood of the Mongols. There was a flurry of peoples who lived in southern China to flee ahead of the advancing Mongols. These refugee people followed the valleys from China into the Southeast Asian peninsula rather than live under the Mongols.

The Thai people were among the first to push south into what is now northern Thailand. The Burmese people from southwestern China, the Lao people, and those who now live in northern Vietnam were all originally peoples from the southern fringe of China who arrived in the rugged terrain of the Southeast Asian peninsula seeking refuge from the advancing Mongols in their march south across China. After several campaigns from 1277 to 1287, Kublai Khan compelled **Burma** and **Champa**, present-day Vietnam, to accept the sovereignty of the Mongols. Thailand was not invaded, but they and the Laotians both paid the Mongols tribute to keep them out of their areas. Even today, Southeast Asian countries fear and dread the Chinese.

Having placed enough fear in the people of Southeast Asia that they would pay him tribute, Kublai Khan's next campaigns were against **Japan in 1274** and **1281**, both of which ended disastrously. In both cases the Japanese met the Mongol invaders at the shoreline to put up a stiff resistance, but a typhoon, which the Japanese called a "divine wind," or *kamikaze*, destroyed much of the Mongol fleet, especially on the second expedition. In 1292 Kublai Khan tried to capture **Java**, but without success. He was growing older and there were problems of administration in China which seemed more important than launching another military campaign.

During these years a rebellion by a Chinese official named **Li Tan** in 1262, caused Kublai to distrust many of the Chinese administrators. He then turned to non-Chinese foreigners to try to better control China. But too much paper money had already been issued. Inflation and taxes were high and many Chinese were unhappy. Conflicts between the Buddhists and the Taoists re-emerged. Kublai also had a brief anti-Muslim campaign. His Japanese and Java ventures had cost a lot of money and showed no returns. The Mongol people were the type who thought conquest of foreign territory should be made daily. Without new territory added to the realm, the people thought the Great Khan was losing control.

After Kublai's favorite wife, Chabui, died in 1281, and his son Zhejin, who had been groomed to succeed him, died in 1286, he seemed unable to face the problems as he had in his younger years. He began to both eat and drink in enormous quantities. In his last years he was fat and often drunk. Kublai Khan died in 1294, a sad and disillusioned old man.

THE LEGACY OF KUBLAI KHAN

Kublai's ambition to create a well-governed and unified empire composed of numerous nationalities, ethnic groups, and religions remained unrealized at the end. This was due in large part to his own Mongol supporters who loved war and plunder more than governance, stability, and peace. Still, Kublai Khan was the first of the Mongol conquerors to truly make the transition from simple conqueror to enlightened ruler.

Kublai Khan's greatest contribution was as a great ruler of China. He reimposed Confucian rituals and provided tax exemptions to Chinese Confucian scholars. However, he did **not** reinstitute the Confucian civil service exams because he wanted to be free to include some non-Chinese administrators. These men would have needed to know the Chinese classics in depth to have passed the exams. Marco Polo, his father, and his uncle would all have been a part of this group of outsiders who held various offices in the Yuan government. In 1267 Kublai Khan shifted the capital city for his entire empire from the Mongol city of **Karakorum** to **Khanbaliq**, present-day **Beijing** in northern China. The Chinese were very much in favor of this move as it seemed to again place them at the center of the universe. They were **not** so pleased when he imposed a four-class system of society upon them which placed the Mongols in the top class while the Chinese were placed at the bottom.

The Great Khan did give special aid to the Chinese peasants to help them produce more food. In the 1280s he extended the Grand Canal to Beijing in order to get sufficient grain from South China to his growing capital in the North. He was very favorable to commerce since he wanted a prosperous country. He encouraged merchant associations and organized a postal system. Since Kublai was a great builder, he often employed foreign architects and craftsmen to work for him.

As a patron of culture, Kublai offered a government position to **Zao Mengfu**, one of China's greatest calligraphers and painters. He ordered a Tibetan Buddhist lama to devise a written script that could be used for all of the languages throughout the Mongol lands. This was a brilliant idea, but one which obviously did not succeed. He revised the law code of China in 1291 so that it would be somewhat more lenient. Chinese drama, medicine, and astronomy gained during his reign. Each was improved by foreigners who came through his realm, and he managed to utilize their talents to enhance his Chinese empire.

The Mongol-Yuan Dynasty

THE LAST YEARS OF THE YUAN DYNASTY IN CHINA

The Mongol conquest of North China had begun during the reign of Genghis Khan, 1167 to 1227. By 1234 the Jin dynasty was conquered and the Mongols appointed military-civilian overseers to rule the North. It was Kublai Khan who completed the conquest of South China, built two capitals in the North, and totally controlled most of what is present-day China by 1279. Although preceding Mongols had often claimed China, Kublai Khan was the first to effectively rule the area.

The term **Yuan Dynasty**, which means "origin," came into use as early as 1272 to ensure the Mongols a legitimate place in the future succession of Chinese dynasties. One important characteristic of Kublai Khan's reign was that there were no civil service exams held in China which used the old classical tests. After the great ruler's death in 1294, the Chinese let it be known that they very much preferred the old system over the Mongol *yin*, or privilege arrangement. The emperor Renzong, 1311 to 1320, allowed the old Confucian examinations to be reinstituted. Mongols were still favored over the Han Chinese for the most important positions. Emperor Renzong was also the first Mongol emperor who was able to read and write Chinese. Still, government business in Yuan times continued to be written in Mongolian.

There were no Yuan rulers who equaled the ability of Kublai Khan in the following years of the Mongol or Yuan dynasty. Court factionalism, succession struggles, and a weakening military began to show that the Yuan dynasty was weakening. There were too many court assassinations and coup d'etat's. The emperor **Yingzong** (Shidebala) was one of several who were assassinated. In 1328 a civil war broke out in China between two rival Mongol claimants. The emperor **Mingzong** (Khoshila) held the throne for six months before he was assassinated. In 1332 there was again fighting for the throne of China. The victor in this struggle was **Shundi** (Toghon Temur) who took the throne after deposing his younger brother, Irinjibal, who had ruled for only fifty-three days.

The Mongols had a practice of military offices being handed down from father to son. Many of these men were not as capable as the military men under Kublai Khan. The old system of military garrisons even ceased to exist in many areas, or, where the garrisons did exist they proved to be weak and ineffective. When the **White Lotus Rebellion** broke out in 1351, the success of this uprising encouraged other Chinese to revolt once they saw how weak the Yuan dynasty really was by that time. A Mongol named Shundi (Shun Ti) thus became the **last** Yuan ruler. In 1368, **Zhu Yuanzang**, a rebel leader of peasant origin, established a new dynasty called the **Ming. The Ming** ruled China from 1368 to 1644.

EVALUATING THE YUAN

The Yuan dynasty in China must be viewed as typical of a government of occupation which ruled over a conquered people. They made just enough concessions to the Chinese to prevent full scale civil war. The four-tiered system of social classes let the Chinese know that they were at the bottom of the scale and the Mongols were on top when every "Man of Han" knew that the Chinese were the greatest of all people. Many of the top government offices were staffed by Mongols only. But in actuality, there were insufficient Mongols with the proper education or administrative ability to fill these top posts. In those cases, the Mongols found

The Mongol-Yuan Dynasty

Chinese who were willing to assume Mongolian names and learn enough of the Mongolian language to "get by." Most of the best educated Chinese boycotted the political jobs because they did not want to be associated with the Mongol Yuan government. These scholars turned to study and writing, a course of action which left non-scholarly Chinese clerks to do some of the most responsible work for the Mongols. The consequence of this was a weak administration at the top.

Literature and the arts did reasonably well in Yuan times. The Yuan period is often known as the **"golden age"** of Chinese drama with 171 plays dating from this period still in existence. Some scholars today believe that the best educated Chinese turned to writing drama or literature because they refused to work for the Yuan rulers. Authors evidently thought it was safe to express their opinions in writing, and there never was any literary inquisition to look for dissidents, since most Mongols could not read Chinese.

Painting also flourished during the Yuan years. The Mongols had many portraits painted. Horses were one of the artists' favorite subjects. Again, as in the case of writers, the best artists refused to serve the Mongol royal court. Some of the painting was actually quite uncomplimentary of the regime, but as in literature and drama, the Yuan did not censor Chinese art.

In the area of religion, the Mongols were at first very neutral, but interested in all the religions. In time they turned against Islam and leaned more toward Buddhism. Kublai Khan was interested in keeping Tibet neutral while he conquered southwest China. In 1253 he invited a leading Tibetan lama named **Phags-Pa** to visit him. Phags-pa stayed for a long period at Kublai's court and in the end converted Kublai and several of the court to Tibetan Buddhism. One of the convincing arguments in the conversion was that the Yuan rulers were Buddhist universal emperors, hence, they were the legitimate rulers for China, a kind of supranational, world-view religion which suited the Mongols, since they ruled over such a large area. After their conversion, the Yuan continued to tolerate the other religious faiths.

In some cases an evaluation of the Mongols is as important for what they did **not** do as what they did do. One case would be the ruler Ogedei after he had conquered an especially prosperous section of North China. He immediately announced that he planned to tear out the dikes, the dams, and the canals which had been so carefully constructed for growing rice. He fully planned to convert North China into a huge pasture area for horse raising. The Chinese scholars all pleaded that such an action would be disastrous for his Chinese subjects. Both his mother and his brother finally convinced him that this would not be a practical course of action.

When Kublai Khan took over in North China, he actually encouraged new agricultural techniques. Kublai established a Bureau of Agriculture in 1270 specifically to promote and improve both agricultural productivity and the quality of life in the rural communities. It was not that the Mongols necessarily appreciated farming so much as it gave them an opportunity to tax the farmers for much more than they could ever have made from horse farming on an open range. With all their military and expansionist tendencies, the Mongols needed an economic base to finance their operations. Even with the Yuan encouragement of agriculture in North China, the population of that area declined from over 100 million to about 60 million during the Yuan years. It would have been a **much** greater decline had Ogedei have carried through on his plan.

Many of the Chinese would have looked upon the Mongols as just another ruling family **except** for taxation. Taxation of the Chinese by the Yuan was heavy by any standard. This was made worse by the Mongol tax administrators who were usually ill-prepared for their job, and secondly, they had no finesse in their collecting tactics. Most often they were frankly brutal. As they saw the situation, they were victorious foreigners collecting tribute from a weak and conquered people. About the middle of the Mongol-Yuan period, they discovered that they could "farm out" the taxes. Central Asian Muslims, many of whom belonged to merchant associations called **ortaq**, were employed as financial advisors at the Mongol court and as collectors as well. They showed no mercy in collecting as much as they could because they were allowed to keep any amount over their assigned quotas. Fortunately for the Mongol rulers, the Chinese directed their criticism of taxes at the Central Asian **ortaqs** rather than toward the rulers. These merchant collectors were therefore a buffer between the Mongols and the people, while at the same time the Mongols received the desired amount of money.

When the Ming dynasty began under Zhu Yuanzhang, they continued the Yuan practice of sons inheriting their father's military rank and command. They continued the census registers not only for tax purposes but also to permanently classify the population into social and occupational categories. All of these practices were hated by the Chinese and could well have been abandoned with the new dynasty.

The positive side of the Mongol carryover into the Ming times was the postal system. Another important contribution of the Mongols was an excellent system of roads as compared to other parts of the world during the 13th and 14th centuries. The Muslims had given the Mongols a great amount of information on astronomy and mapmaking. All of this was also passed on to the Ming.

It is interesting that the Mongols seem to have melted back into their nomadic, pastoral ways with remarkable ease when the Ming dynasty took over in 1368. It is hard to say precisely how much of the more sophisticated Chinese civilization they took back to the steppes with them. Many of their descendants returned to China in 1644 when the Manchus defeated the Ming. There was probably very little, if any, carryover during those years. From 1644 to the present, the Manchus, closely linked to the Mongols, have also been closely linked to China's history.

The Mongol-Yuan Dynasty

BOOKS FOR FURTHER READING

Blunden, Caroline, & Elvin, Mark, *Cultural Atlas of China* (1983).

Cotterell, Arthur, *China, A Cultural History* (1988).

Cotterell, Arthur, *The First Emperor of China*.

Cotterell, Arthur, & Morgan, David, *China's Civilization* (1975).

Creel, H. G., *Confucius and the Chinese Way* (1949).

Fairbank, John K., *China: A New History* (1992).

Fairbank, John K, Reischauer, Edwin O., & Craig, Albert M., *East Asia, Tradition & Transformation* (1989).

Fitzgerald, Charles P., *China: A Short Cultural History*.

Fitzgerald, Charles P., *A Concise History of East Asia*.

Froncek, Thomas, editor, *The Horizon Book of the Arts of China*.

Gernet, Jacques, *A History of Chinese Civilization* (1987).

Hopkirk, Peter, *The Great Game: The Struggle for Empire in Central Asia* (1992).

Komroff, Manuel, editor, *Contemporaries of Marco Polo* (1989).

Legg, Stuart, *The Barbarians of Asia* (1970).

Loewe, Michael, *The Pride That Was China* (1990).

Marshall, Robert, *Storm from the East: From Genghis Khan to Kublai Khan* (1993).

Meyer, Milton W., *A Concise History of China* (1994).

Schirokauer, Conrad, *A Brief History of Chinese and Japanese Civilizations* (1989).

Waldron, Arthur, *The Great Wall of China from History to Myth* (1990).

Chapter 29
THE MING DYNASTY, 1368-1644

The **Ming dynasty** was founded by **Chu Yuan-chang** (Zhu Yuanzhang) in 1368. Chu was not a part of the old Yuan dynasty, but he had risen to power by military conquest rather than by right of birth. He was born in 1328, the son of an itinerant farmer and the daughter of a master sorcerer; he was a very ordinary person for that time.

Floods and famine often swept through the area where he grew up as a consequence of the uncontrolled Yellow River. The dikes seemed to break nearly every year between 1327 and 1344, and as the men gathered together to repair them they had ample opportunity to socialize and to air their complaints about the government. Sometimes they would work for as much as eight months of the year on securing the dikes. It did not seem to the peasants that the **Yuan dynasty** was very interested in the problems of the Chinese farmers, and they often talked of insurrection.

During this same time, a secret society known as the **Red Turbans** began to form under the leadership of a man named Chang Shih-ch'eng. By 1355 another leader named Han Lin-er proclaimed himself the first emperor of what he hoped would become a "new" Sung dynasty. Since **Chu Yuan-chang** became an orphan at the age of sixteen, he decided to take refuge in a small Buddhist monastery near Feng-yang city. Just as he was seriously considering becoming a monk for the remainder of his life, the Yuan military forces destroyed the monastery.

Unemployed and with no place to stay, Chu set out as a wandering beggar for the next three years. Floods in 1352 caused famines and rebellions again, and by this time Chu decided to join the Feng-yang branch of a secret Manichaean-Buddhist society, which had dedicated itself to the overthrow of the ruling Mongol Yuan dynasty. It should be pointed out that there were dozens of these revolutionary groups scattered throughout China, especially in the southern part. Most of them simply adopted a name and were known locally as religious organizations, but they were really a front for opposing the Yuan dynasty. Chu's group was known as the **White Lotus Society**.

The White Lotus Society combined native folk religions, Manichaeaism, Buddhism, and Taoism to form an extremely militant society. They were willing to go to battle with fanatic devotion to their cause--a China freed of Mongol rule. It was a similar type of political-religious militant society which was behind the Boxer Rebellion at the turn of the 20th century. Some parts of China had fallen under the Mongol Yuan rule as early as 1272, but they did not control all of China until the time of Kublai Khan, 1260 to 1294.

These years were the peak of Mongol power and after the time of Kublai Khan a decline set in within the Yuan dynasty. Even the Mongol military was in a state of decline. Customs such as inheriting military offices, accompanied by a succession of rulers due to court assassinations and the misutilization of Chinese intellectuals in the administration of the government, were enough to test any government. On top of these problems the Mongols had always been looked upon as hated foreign invaders, who were more interested in pastoral pursuits and world conquest than in the everyday problems experienced by the Chinese people. Flood control, which would have benefitted the Chinese farmers, was not a high priority with the pastoral-minded Mongols. It was within such an environment that the revolts gained momentum.

The Ming Dynasty

With so many revolutionary groups in the countryside, the Mongol military was soon proven to be weak and on the defensive. They knew they were not loved by the Chinese people, so they resorted to ridiculously harsh punishments for any person or group who opposed them. Evidently they hoped that by fear they could make up for what they lacked in numbers and ability.

Chu initially had no military experience, so he became a guard at the household of the leader of the local White Lotus rebels. He then married the White Lotus leader's daughter, an action which gave him an inside connection with the rebel organization. Chu was given more and more leadership tasks and he performed them all very well. He rose to be a general of their growing forces and by 1356 he had captured the important city of **Nanking** (Nanjing) in the Yangtze River valley. Although he said he favored the newly proclaimed Sung dynasty of Han Lin-er, Chu began building his own power structure, branching out from his center in Nanking, and within a short time he had won control over the central Yangtze River valley.

Since he was such a successful leader, the Han area to the north and west as well as the Wu area to the east, were shortly under Chu's control. As his power and prestige grew, he announced his **new** dynasty would take control of **all** of China beginning in **1368**. By this time he had decided to name his new dynasty the **Ming** because the word meant "brightness," one of the Manichaean principles of faith. He established his capital at Nanking and surrounded the city with some twenty miles of walls which were sixty feet high.

His military forces expelled the Mongol Yuan court from Peking (Beijing) in September 1368, and Chu began trying to establish his legitimacy by rebuilding the badly shattered countryside throughout China. He ruled over China from 1368 to 1398 under his throne name of **Hung-wu**, which means "vast national glory." He was the only peasant to found a major Chinese dynasty. He chose January 1368 to announce that he was taking over control of China because he believed he had a sign from heaven that this was a favorable time.

Hung-wu's first task was to bring about government stability and recovery from Yuan neglect and seventeen years of civil war. He had an army of around 2 million men, a tremendous number to feed and clothe. There was a distinct feeling that any smaller number would tempt the Mongol Yuan dynasty to try to stage a comeback. All of the expenses of the Ming state were therefore kept as low as possible in the early years in order to allow the people to invest more in the rebuilding of China.

Hung-wu recognized from the outset that high taxes would only drain the people of the capital they needed to rebuild their country. Citizens were compelled to do many of the duties of governance which would have been normally associated with paid civil officials. Hung-wu's method of administering his empire was based on a very old system whereby groups of ten families were responsible for collecting the taxes and maintaining public order. It was a local self-management system which the wealthy people unfortunately soon learned to exploit to their own advantage by forming groups of ten rich families.

The rich families simply agreed among themselves that they would turn in a low tax amount. The peasants tried to contribute their fair share with the consequence that they were called upon to pay more and more until many lost their land. Many of the rich were also able to pass the burden on to their workers, but the independent peasant had no way to shift the tax

The Ming Dynasty

burden. This lack of a good civil service system was one of the basic weaknesses throughout the Ming period. Even though there were severe penalties for both civil servants and lay workers who were guilty of either dishonesty or factionalism, both practices were all too common. With a small civil service there were too few officials to catch the ones who cheated. Recognizing this basic weakness, the number of Ming officials assigned to enforce the laws increased throughout the entire Ming period.

The early Ming wanted to expand their boundaries to the north and the west, largely as a protection from the Mongols, who they expected might very well return. They therefore pushed the Mongols back through Shensi, Kansu, and Inner Mongolia. By 1387 they had pushed northeastward well into Manchuria, then they pushed to the west into Central Asia the following year. During the same period, Ming armies moved on into Outer Mongolia beyond Karakorum and almost reached Lake Baikal by 1388. When trouble arose in the southwest, they ventured into that area to pacify the aboriginal tribesmen on the Sino-Burmese border.

During the 276 years of the Ming era, 1368 to 1644, there were a total of seventeen emperors. It was one of the longer reigning and also one of the most successful dynasties in Chinese history. Of the seventeen emperors, the first one, Hung-wu, proved to be one of the strongest and most colorful personalities in all of Chinese history. During his thirty-year reign he established policies which lasted to the end of the dynasty, several carried on to the Revolution of 1912, and a few traces of the Ming continued until the Communists took over in 1949. The Ming gained considerable respect among the other nations by Hung-wu's firm policies. In the early years of his reign there were rulers, or their ambassadors, from Korea, Mongolia, East Turkestan, Burma, Siam (Thailand), and Nam Viet (Vietnam) who regularly acknowledged his overlordship.

Hung-wu even altered the religion of China in order that people would worship and offer sacrifices to the Lord of Heaven and the Empress of Earth, according to his view of the cosmic order. He dreamed of a China made up of quiet villages, obedient officials, and a modest livelihood for everyone. He stressed education for more of the young men than ever before in China's history. Agriculture was revitalized, especially through projects to control flooding and by building irrigation projects and canals. Hung-wu was well enough regarded that his temple name after his death was "great ancestor," a fitting tribute for a peasant boy in the 14th century who had become emperor.

The road to the top is never an easy path, and in 1380 Hung-wu began a trial against his old companion in arms who had helped him seize power. He accused his former friend and partner of treason, of planning a rebellion, and at being in contact with the Mongols and the Japanese. Over 15,000 persons were involved in the trial. At the end, Hu Wei-yung was executed. In 1390 he reopened the trial and yet another 15,000 were involved, and again there were about 15,000 people who were executed.

Hung-wu was succeeded by his grandson, who was much less successful right from the outset. Within a short time he was overthrown by his uncle, the Prince of Yen in 1402. Yen took the throne name of **Yung-lo (Yongle)**, which means "Perpetual Happiness." Yongle ruled China for twenty-two years, 1402 to 1424. This reign was nearly as vigorous as that of Hung-wu. He first subjected Nam Viet, now North Vietnam, then he began an extended campaign against the revival of Mongol power in the north. Yongle sent his eunuch, admiral **Cheng Ho** (Zheng He), to demand tribute from as far away as East Africa.

The Ming Dynasty

He also moved his capital city from the more centrally located Nanking to the northern city which had been taken from the Mongols and named it **Paeking**. This later proved to be a flawed decision because it placed the capital of China too close to his Mongolian enemies in the north. They always thought of Peking as "their" city and looked forward to the day it would again be their own. During these years of expansion, conquest, and rebuilding, the Chinese were blessed with prosperity and stability for nearly a century.

Among the most memorable accomplishments of Yongle's reign were the seven expeditions of the fleet under the command of admiral Cheng Ho between 1405 and 1433. Among the ports of call were: Vietnam, Java, Sumatra, Malacca, Ceylon (Sri Lanka), Calicut, Cochin in southwest India, Siam (Thailand), Ormuz at the entrance of the Persian Gulf, Aden in the Arabian peninsula, Somalia on the east coast of Africa, and other stops along the East African coast. It should be pointed out that they called on some of these ports several times during the years Cheng Ho was admiral of the fleet. Commercial vessels also followed the fleet and China enjoyed a lively trade with all of these areas and cities.

These voyages were possible because Cheng Ho's fleet was composed of several dozen huge **junks**, which carried a total complement of over twenty thousand men on each expedition. The Chinese fleet was highly regarded in those years. Rich and powerful China was the envy of the East Asian world. Japanese pirates scarcely dared to intrude in the coastwise shipping of China.

The maritime expeditions not only stimulated trade and commerce, but also there were several books of geography written during this early Ming period. The title of one of their books at this time says a great deal about the Chinese--*Treatise on the Barbarian Kingdoms of the Western Oceans*. China considered all non-Chinese as "barbarians." The Chinese were convinced that they were the center of the universe and that they were superior to all other peoples. With such a fine fleet and led by a very capable admiral, it is interesting to speculate about the future of western Europe had Cheng Ho decided to travel around South Africa and sail to Europe in 1405. Neither the Portuguese nor the Spanish had any ships capable of such an extended journey at the beginning of the 15th century. The Chinese had been building ships of this type from the 11th century, far ahead of European maritime development.

In the late 15th and early 16th centuries there were several weak emperors who preferred to turn the duties of governing China over to the court eunuchs. These men on some occasions actually exercised more power than the emperor. One example of this is the eunuch, **Wang Chen**, who convinced the emperor **Cheng-t'ung** to start a military campaign against the western Mongols, the **Oyrat**, in 1449. The Oyrat leader, **Esen Taiji**, ambushed the Imperial army, captured the emperor, and laid siege to Peking. The Ming Defense Minister, **Yu Ch'ien**, forced Esen to leave Peking, then **he** ruled China for eight years under emergency powers and set up his own "interim emperor," 1449 to 1457. When the interim emperor fell ill, Cheng-t'ung moved in, resumed his throne, and Yu Ch'ien was executed as a traitor. Although there were other weak rulers, this was the only occasion where there was a total disruption of power during the Ming years.

By the 1540s it was obvious that the Ming empire had passed its zenith. The Oyrat, or western Mongols, had met the Ming army and they had discovered that it was not invincible. Soon thereafter the Mongols began conducting raids along the borders where they thought there might be a weak spot. At the same time, the Japanese, who had paid tribute to China during the

The Ming Dynasty

early Ming period, now began to raid the coastal areas of China, especially in the wealthy Shanghai area. Sometimes these Japanese raiding parties followed the Yangtze River far inland, taking what they wished and demanding tribute from the people in the delta area. Some even predicted that China would fall to the Oyrat as they moved in from the north while the Japanese troubled the eastern coast.

By the 1560s the Chinese realized they must get organized or collapse. They fought both the Oyrat and the Japanese repeatedly until the invasions of their territory eased off. This 16th century Ming revival saved the dynasty for about another century. The **Longqing** (Lung-ch'ing) emperor, who reigned from 1567 to 1572, restored order with the assistance of several outstanding government assistants and capable generals. When Japanese forces under **Toyotomi Hideyoshi** invaded **Korea** in 1592, the Ming came to the defense of their Korean neighbors. This seemed to be an excellent opportunity to weaken the power of Japan before they were at the very borders of northeast China. The Korean conflict dragged on from 1592 to 1598, at which time Hideyoshi died and the Japanese withdrew from Korea. The last half of the 16th century was the final hour of greatness for the Ming.

HOW THE MING WERE GOVERNED

Most historians believe that the collapse of the Ming dynasty was in some way associated with certain basic weaknesses in the very way they were governed from the beginning. The local self-management style of government provided more liberty than the people were able to manage during the early Ming years. Although this style of government was partly due to the fact that the first emperor, Hung-wu, had no money, it was also due to Hung-wu's peasant upbringing, which caused him to be suspicious of the well-educated *literati* in China. Since he had come from simple origins and had risen to the top, he believed that any ordinary person could handle any civil service job which might be vacant. Therefore, there was little need for well-trained civil servants.

As time passed, the bureaucracy in China did grow--even during the thirty years of Hung-wu's reign--largely because the self-management style lent itself to too many opportunities to render less than the government had asked. Furthermore, the government was filled with too many incompetent people. These people tended to form cliques among themselves with the consequence that in some reigns, it seemed that they spent more time fighting among themselves than they did in accomplishing the task for which they had originally been employed.

It is easy to say that China was over-bureaucratized during the later Ming dynasty. However, it should be remembered that it required a huge bureaucracy to operate a country with 13 provinces, each as extensive and populous as many modern European states today. From 1407 to 1428 Nam Viet was a 14th province. Furthermore, each of these provinces was about as different from one another as are the modern European states. The vast expanses north-south and east-west were difficult to govern, since there were no transportation arteries except for the rivers and the Grand Canal. The first capital, which was situated at Nanking from 1368 to 1421, was more heavily populated and more centrally located geographically, than was Peking. Peking was a poor choice because it was too close to the Mongol frontier and the area was much more sparsely settled than was the Nanking area. Peking was so difficult to supply that it was one of the major reasons for rebuilding and extending the Grand Canal.

The Ming Dynasty

In the early years there was a unitary Secretariat who worked directly with the emperor. From 1380 on, the emperor served as the sole coordinator of the various branches of government because he did not think he could trust the Secretariat. Neither did he trust close family members who were sometimes found to be plotting his overthrow. Holding the supreme central power over all aspects of the government gave the emperor total absolutism far beyond anything which was ever exercised by Louis XIV of France or the Divine Right Monarchs of England. The basic problem with absolutism has always been that it works reasonably well with an intelligent, hard-working, well-organized monarch. It was a terrible choice when the monarch was weak or uninterested.

When the Ming dynasty, began there were five chief military commissions under a Chief Military Commission, an arrangement which paralleled the Secretariat. This too came under the emperor's authority in the 1380s. Military men were stationed throughout the empire--especially along the borders, near Peking, or other strategic cities. These were divided into units called guards and battalions. Whenever possible they were assigned state-owned agricultural lands. This provided for their pay and supported their families; it was intended that their sons would follow their fathers and join the military in order to retain their land from generation to generation. If the sons did not volunteer to serve in the military, then the family lost their land. This led to many abuses and many of these farms, which were once good producers, either fell dormant or ended up in the hands of opportunists. This left other family members destitute.

At the lower levels of the military--the farm tenant and soldier level--the military was very loosely structured. It was thought that they would have a minimum period of training and border duty while the remainder of their time would be spent farming. Training under this system became weaker as the years passed, and even though they were at the borders where they were needed, they could be easily overrun by the better-organized and better-trained Mongols.

The military who lived in these frontier areas might have been strengthened had the emperor allowed members of the royal clan to head the units. Fearing palace type revolts, he used coordinators in each province to oversee the organization and training of the farmer-militia groups. They soon became known for the top-heavy bureaucracies they built up and for the small amount of training and coordination they actually provided. As a consequence, the military stagnated from the mid-fifteenth century onward. At first they supplemented the lack of recruits with conscripts, and at the end, they had to rely heavily upon mercenary soldiers. This system proved to be no match to counter the Qing (Manchu) invaders.

THE MING CIVIL SERVICE

Beyond the local self-management arrangement, the Ming used the Sung system of civil servants, who were theoretically selected on the basis of their scores on written examinations. Again, members of the Imperial clan were usually excluded from these offices, a practice which kept many able people from serving in the top administrative posts. Eventually, high-ranking civil officials were able to place one son in the civil service by hereditary right, and beginning in 1450, wealthy civilians were allowed to purchase civil service positions at the lower levels. Most of the men who purchased their offices were never able to climb to true administrative positions.

Every third year the government held week-long exams at the provincial capitals to construct their civil service lists. It was impossible to even take the exam unless you were first certified by your teacher that you were ready. Once appointed to a lower echelon position, the men were evaluated regularly and required to pass more exams in order to move to higher positions.

Civil service examinations were heavily weighted toward a general knowledge of the Chinese classics and history. In the early Ming period, there were many questions designed to test the applicant's ability to apply the knowledge of his classical education toward solving practical problems of governance. Towards the end of the Ming period, the tests became highly stylized and formalized in a pattern called the "eight-legged approach," a style which tended to discourage creative and original thinking.

The government established many schools at the district level and they subsidized students to prepare them for the difficult exams. This system was designed to assist sons from the poorer families to move into government work. After about 1500, there were also many private academies in which scholars prepared students for the exams. Either system of education was quite costly for the parents, especially the private academies, with the consequence that children from poorer families were rarely able to compete equally. It meant that the Ming civil service was composed of a group of elite and very conservative people.

Once a candidate had been appointed to the civil service, position there was a great amount of favoritism and factionalism, a problem which became much worse in the last fifty years of the dynasty. Nevertheless, there was more social mobility in the Ming civil service than in the preceeding Sung or the succeeding Qing periods. Perhaps the greatest abuses were in the system of court eunuchs, who were usually well-educated but selfish men who tried to manipulate the court life to their own best advantage and advancement. Since court eunuchs are no longer used by heads of state, it is well to consider the eunuch's place in Chinese court life.

First of all, the eunuchs were considered to be "safe" men to have around the palace because of the many women, both family and mistresses. Since they were often very close to the monarchy as they maintained the palace and the grounds, they became almost a part of the family. They were men the emperor came to feel that he could trust. It was this close position from which some of the eunuchs learned about plots against the imperial family and alerted the emperor to the problem before it had an opportunity to develop. Since a few of these plots originated within the royal family, it was only natural that the emperor came to rely more on the court eunuchs than he did on members of his own household.

Not only did they win the emperor's confidence, but within fifty years from the beginning of the Ming dynasty, they were heading naval expeditions, leading the army, overseeing provincial governors, administering the appointments and promotion of officials, and heading the emperor's cabinet and secretariat. The most important area which came under the control of the court eunuchs was the secret police. From this powerful position, they were guilty of extortion and blackmail, but clever enough to keep such scandal away from the emperor. Unfortunately, the emperor approved all their acts without bothering to investigate personally, a practice which only corrupted them more as the years went by. It was also unfortunate that most of these powerful men came from the northern areas and in the later Ming period, they were often uneducated. Worst of all, they often gave the emperors bad advice.

The Ming emperors lived a life of luxury with their most difficult tasks often being the decision whether to add another building to the Forbidden City, or how to rebuild one which had already been built. Too much of this system of leaving day-to-day governance to the eunuchs and other court favorites carried on down through the Qing dynasty, through the years of the Republic, and it was finally abolished by Mao. Under this system, the governance of the people drifted farther and farther from both the people and the men who were responsible for China's defense and welfare. It appears that even though these do-nothing people were purged by the Communists in the early years after 1949, they have reappeared in a different form as an "inner circle" of the Communist party favorites with many benefits unknown to the hard-working people of China.

Nearly every Ming emperor used his powers in an abusive way at some time during his reign. Imperial clansmen, provincial warlords, palace women, and palace eunuchs were known to use their greatest ingenuity in order to win personal concessions. These strong men, sometimes including the emperor in one faction, built up groups of supporters who represented their way of thinking. Such factions spread down through the extensive bureaucracy until every reign had two or three such factions operating, each trying to persuade the emperor that their approach was best. It was not unlike the devious planning of some politicians in the western countries in this same time.

The true cause of the people was only a minor consideration as each faction fought to get to the top, and once on top, they had to fight to stay there. If the one side became vocal or open in their opposition to the emperor's favorites, then at that moment he would purge the sulking and unhappy faction because he did not want political enemies, a practice which created many enemies among those who had been banished. It then became necessary for the emperor to execute the ringleaders of the opposition, sometimes a dozen people, or on occasion, several hundred people. The Ming emperors probably exercised more absolute power than any other dynasty in Chinese history. If you wished to survive in the Ming civil service, it was terribly important to belong to the winning faction.

MING FOREIGN POLICY

Both the Ming emperors and their Chinese subjects assumed that the emperor was everyone's overlord. No one in China ever really assumed anything different. This caused a problem of assimilation of non-Chinese people around the land borders. It also caused a problem with foreigners, both those from other Asian countries as well as Europeans, who were there because of their interest in the Chinese trade. Consequently, they usually designated from one to three special ports to deal with foreign trade. Ning-po port was reserved for Japanese traders, Ch'uan-chou was reserved for contacts with Taiwan, and the port at Canton served the area of southeast China. Furthermore, each foreign envoy brought proper gifts on the proper day according to the Chinese calendar. Once all the gifts had been exchanged, the businessman was then allowed to do business in China.

The Chinese sold silks and porcelain while they purchased spices, tea, and horses. The balances were paid in copper and silver. Foreign demand for Chinese goods was strong, since the prices were quite reasonable and the high quality of the goods meant they would sell well in the consumer market. The emperors knew that foreign traders marked their goods up, so they placed limits on the amount of trade goods a foreign merchant could purchase on any one trip as well as the time lapse between trading missions.

The Ming Dynasty

European traders found this arrangement very strange, but in the early contacts they were forced to follow the Ming government's requirements or smuggle. The Chinese trade goods were made by skilled craftsmen who were virtual perfectionists. The men who were most skilled were forced to work in either Peking or in Nanking, a policy which was costly to those who were required to go to the capital at least once a year to work. Some craftsmen were required to live in the capital the year around to supply the emperor's demands for high quality goods.

There were about 27,000 of these master craftsmen in the early Ming period, but it fell by more than a third by the early 17th century. Each of these master craftsmen had from three to five men who worked for him, but it should be noted that the number of master craftsmen decreased at a time when the population had increased and the foreign demand became much greater. By the end of the Ming dynasty, there were even less of these highly skilled persons. The reason for their decline centered almost totally around what they were paid by the state. Like the small peasant farmers, the empire's effort to limit any rise in prices kept their pay ridiculously low. Low wages proved to be a special hardship to both farmers and craftsmen due to inflation in other aspects of the economy.

The Chinese always feared a resurgence of the Mongol power, and rightfully so. The Great Wall, already in place when the Ming came to power in 1368, was reinforced and extended to its greatest length during the early Ming period. Shortly after the Ming drove the Mongols back, the Mongols began a quarrel among themselves concerning who would lead their forces. Three major antagonistic groups emerged during this period. The **Oyrat**, or western Mongols, the **Tatars**, or eastern Mongols, and the **Urianghad tribes**. The Urianghad tribes became reasonably well integrated with the Chinese, which caused a lessening of vigilance along the borders of present-day Manchuria and Inner Mongolia. In the weaker years of the Ming dynasty, these areas served as a base of operation for the Oyrat to infiltrate and dominate. It became a matter of policy for the Mongols to test the Ming defenses on a regular basis. Aside from their usual vigilance regarding the Mongols, once the Ming borders were established, most of the Ming emperors were unaggressive, a policy which the Mongols interpreted as weakness.

Another major foreign problem concerned the Japanese marauders. They worked the coastline of China looking for wealthy cargoes to confiscate and they also raided up the river valleys. This caused the emperors to order more strong fortresses to be constructed along their eastern and southeastern shores. China's foreign policy also worked to maintain the overland trade routes from the West because this brought them needed revenue.

Several areas around China's borders, such as present-day Vietnam and Korea, often had dynastic struggles going on. China tried to stay free of all of these. The most expensive campaign conducted outside China's borders was the assistance they gave to Korea in the later Ming period. The Japanese were very anxious to establish a foothold on the Asian continent and they selected Korea, probably because of its close proximity. Japan's real goal was mainland China, especially the area of Manchuria. China's policy throughout the Korean situation was directed more toward keeping the Japanese away from their frontier at the Yalu River than any real act of friendship. The Ming emperor had every reason to send an army against the Turko-Mongol empire of **Timur** (Tamerlane) at Samarkand, especially after Timur murdered some Chinese envoys and planned to capture a piece of China for his own empire. Generally speaking, Ming foreign policy was **defensive** rather than offensive.

The Ming Dynasty

The major exceptions to the nonaggressive policy of the Ming was the first emperor, Hung-wu, 1368 to 1398, as he established his frontiers, and Yongle, 1403 to 1424, as he sent his admiral Cheng Ho throughout Southeast Asia and as far as the east coast of Africa. Yongle also added Nam Viet to China in 1407, but it reverted back to local rule in 1428. After Yongle, the emperors adopted the philosophy that since everything in China was far superior to foreign things, there was no need to go outside the country for any reason. Ming policy centered more on China for the Chinese and the idea that the Forbidden City-Temple of Heaven area was the center of the universe. Foreign trade decreased considerably in the later Ming years.

In accordance with this policy there were several Ming emperors who feared the Chinese people would be contaminated by the "barbaric" customs of foreigners. It was therefore decreed that private dealings between Chinese traders and foreigners were forbidden. Neither were Chinese traders allowed to make foreign voyages. At one time these rules became so strict that even Chinese coastal fishing and trading was disrupted. The prohibitions became so unrealistic, unpopular, and unenforceable that by the mid-fifteenth century the Chinese businessmen engaged in widespread smuggling. Some of the smuggled "barbaric" goods even reached the royal household. By late Ming times there were thousands of Chinese living in Southeast Asia and Japan who were engaged in this illegal trade on a full-time basis. The Ming court then closed all seaports except Canton, and by the 1540s they built coastal defenses against foreign traders. It should be remembered that the Ming attitude toward foreign people and foreign trade goods up to this time had pertained primarily to **Asian** traders from countries such as Japan, India, and the countries of Southeast Asia.

IMPORTANT CHANGES IN POPULATION

Population statistics from Ming times can only be viewed as "best estimates." The Chinese did maintain official census figures, which would indicate the population remained steady throughout the Ming years at about 60 million people. Modern scholars believe they have evidence which indicates there was a substantial growth to 100 million and perhaps as high as 150 million people in China. Once the frontiers were established, there was both foreign and domestic peace, which remained unbroken for long periods of time. Rice and cotton yields increased during the Ming era due to earlier maturing varieties which had been introduced in Sung and Yuan times. Economic times were generally prosperous during the Ming period, an environment which encouraged larger families. American food crops such as peanuts (groundnuts), corn (maize), and sweet potatoes may have arrived too late in the Ming dynasty to have been significant factors in the population trends, but the addition of these crops certainly did influence the following Manchu or Qing period.

Perhaps the most important shift in population occurred early in the Ming rule. The vast North China Plain was quite underpopulated, while the opposite was true of the southeastern areas. North China was predominantly rural while the area of South China tended to be urban. The rehabilitation of the North China Plain became a high priority of the early Ming emperors. The first two emperors resettled peasants on the northern lands on an extensive scale. Several agrarian development programs were encouraged by the government such as water-control projects along their river basins. The Grand Canal reopened in 1415 following extensive work to connect the capital at Peking with the most populous region in the southeast.

The Ming Dynasty

THE GRAND CANAL

The **Grand Canal** (Da Yunhe in Pinyin, or Ta Yun-Ho in the Wade-Giles) connects the Yangtze River at Chen-Chiang in the Shanghai area in the south, with Tientsin and Peking (Beijing) in the north--a distance of **1050 miles!** This is the world's longest man-made waterway, and since construction was begun as early as the 4th century B.C., it is probably the oldest. The oldest section connected the Yangtze River with the city of Ch'ing-chiang, which at that time was in the Huang Ho Valley when that river followed a far more southerly course than it does today. In those early times the Chinese called it the Shan-yang Canal.

Many additions and improvements have been made to the Grand Canal through the centuries. When the Yuan (Mongol) dynasty ruled over China from 1279 to 1368, they made Peking their capital city. They needed a reliable route to move grain to Peking from the more heavily producing areas of southeast China; therefore, during their reign they extended and greatly improved the waterways which connected Peking with the Huang Ho River.

At the beginning of the Ming dynasty, 1368 to 1644, the location of the capital was changed from Peking to Nanking, the first major Chinese city to come under Ming control. But in 1403 they planned to move the capital back to Peking. At this time the canal was rebuilt and joined with the Wei River. This system was expanded by widening and building lateral canals and this network of canals was used until about 1868 at which time it was abandoned. Again, in 1934, the Nationalist government rebuilt and expanded the size and depth of the canal to accommodate medium-sized steamers. Between 1958 and 1964 the Communists enlarged and straightened the canal once more to accommodate ships up to 600 tons. Another section was also similarly improved south to Hangchou, a distance of over 100 miles south of the Yangtze River-Shanghai area.

The hundreds of tons of freight which move on this canal annually improve the utility of both the Huang Ho and the Yangtze Rivers, the Wei River, and the areas along the coast. It has also provided a waterway for the transport of millions of passengers, and as a source of water for irrigating areas which would otherwise have no source of water in such large quantities. Entire cities have evolved along the course of the Grand Canal and its tributaries. This has attracted millions of people to the north who could not otherwise be supported solely by locally grown crops. Its importance to both transportation and agriculture makes the Grand Canal as important as the major river systems of China.

Another important factor in populating northern China was government policy. Colonists who agreed to move north were provided with seeds, tools, and animals--a kind of Chinese Homestead plan. Furthermore, they were exempted from taxes for three years. Once the capital finally moved to Peking in 1420-21, and the people could see that the heavy investment in developing that area was underway, then others willingly migrated to the north. The large building projects in the Forbidden City adjacent to Peking was a further encouragement. People did not believe that the government would ever pull out and leave them there without protection from the various Mongol groups of invaders. Even though rice cultivation was more difficult in the area around Peking, there were several other crops which did well on the North China Plain, such as wheat, soybeans, sorghum, and later, corn.

281

The Ming Dynasty

Approximately 10 percent of the population lived in the North during the Yuan period, compared to 40 percent in the late Ming period. It has already been mentioned how land was also available for soldiers and their families who wished to settle north of Peking from the earliest Ming times. The government very much wanted to populate this area because it believed that the settlement of both military and civilian families would help to hold China's enemies to the north in check. It should also be noted that when the Ming government withdrew its subsidies for those who moved north in the late 15th century, the population declined as well as the spirit of the inhabitants. Many felt abandoned, especially when the Manchu Ch'ing pressed along the northern front. In spite of the sizeable shift of population into the northern areas, the southeast remained the most populous, the wealthiest, and the most cultured area in Ming times.

MING DYNASTY FINANCES

Since the Ming were short on finances in the early years and wanted to hold down taxes, there were many jobs such as police, tax collection, road work, etc., which were divided up among local citizens rather than maintaining a staff of full-time employees. Besides taxes through work, people could pay their taxes with either grain or money. In the early Ming period, a majority of the people preferred to work out their taxes, but by the later Ming period, this shifted to most people paying their taxes with money. The emperors also preferred money because the in-kind services were often done by people who had no knowledge of what they were doing. Besides, money is much more convertible.

Copper coins were the most prevalent among ordinary folks. In 1375 the government paid some of its bills with paper currency which was nonconvertible into copper, silver, or gold. As a consequence, the paper money soon lost its value. Perhaps the greatest problem with the paper money was that the government issued far too much. Since the government used the paper currency to pay many of their bills, they also began to allow the people to use it to pay their taxes in most years. Precious metals were not used in commercial exchange until after the mid-sixteenth century when silver began to circulate for large business deals, especially bulk silver. The Ming government also levied taxes on trade, craft shops, salt, wine, goods in transit, etc. Private capitalism was **not** encouraged by the Ming since they considered that economic area to be an Imperial prerogative. The Ming government tried to control all areas of business and agriculture.

MING CULTURE

The first observation on Ming culture is that the emperors wanted centralized thinking in **all** areas of their society the same as in their governance. Accordingly, they sponsored artists, craftsmen, philosophers, writers, etc., who would produce their work according to Ming specifications. Much work was produced by people who seldom asked questions, but produced what the state desired. Some of this work was well done within the specified parameters laid down by the state, but often it was not very original. This has led many to characterize the Ming era as an age of bureaucratic monotony and mediocrity. This generalization would be correct for those who followed the guidelines of the state, but not everyone did. Every age has its nonconformists and the Ming years were no exception.

The Ming Dynasty

Perhaps the Ming dynasty's most remembered, and most visible contribution, was in the field of fine arts. **Cloisonne**, the process of filling enamel in the raised relief on metal vases and other objects, then firing it, reached a high level of artistic accomplishment. Ming porcelain ware superceded the Sung dynasty's monochrome work with beautifully decorative polychrome works. The best known style of the Ming period continues to be the blue-on-white decor, plain at first but later becoming floral and abstract. The "willow pattern" porcelain ware created a huge demand on the western market and continues to be popular to the present time. The deep cobalt blue coloration used on genuine Ming porcelain is considered a great collector's item today.

The rulers of the Ming dynasty wanted everyone to follow the Neo-Confucian philosophy of the great Sung thinkers. Taoism and Buddhism during the Ming period declined into ill-organized popular religions which strayed far from the original philosophies. Some tried to merge Confucianism, Taoism, and Buddhism into one faith. Rampant iconoclasm (idol destruction) was another approach, while **Li Chih**, 1527-1602, debunked all aspects of Confucian morality. He was extremely critical of almost everything, and he seldom bothered to be polite in his attacks. Sometimes the government took action against these far-out thinkers, but there were so many religious dissidents with so many different ideas that enforcement according to the government's rules was very near to impossible.

Ming prose and poetry was supposed to follow the style set by the early Chinese masters of previous dynasties, but again there were those who went their own ways. One of the better known scholars was **Kuei Yu-Kuang**, who wrote simple essays and anecdotes about everyday life. Ming novels and fiction were often far departures from the old masters, particularly in the late Ming years. In the field of writing, it should also be noted that there were several efforts to create encyclopedias of herbs, flowers, animals, military science, technology, and medicine. An anthology of all the esteemed writings of the Chinese heritage from the very earliest times was completed in a very scholarly way in 1407. It was known as the *Yung-lo ta tien*, a monumental work which contained over 11,000 volumes. It was too much for even the Imperial government to consider printing! It did, however, preserve many old writings which would otherwise have been lost.

Most of the portrait artists followed traditional Chinese styles except for four painters who were less and less inclined to follow government patterns. As the Ming period progressed, there was more and more self-expression painted into the portraits. Finally, operatic drama emerged as a new art form in Yuan times and developed more fully during the Ming era. Members of the Imperial clan and other highly respected scholars wrote for these plays, a consideration which gave them increased respectability. Another form of Ming opera aria is remembered for the popularity of its "sing-song girls." Most Ming drama can be characterized as having an air of sentimental romanticism.

THE DECLINE OF THE MING DYNASTY

There were several things which began to come together in the 17th century which brought about the final decline and fall of the Ming dynasty. One of the most important of these was the six-year war against the Japanese in Korea, 1592-1598. Even though it did not seem to the Koreans that China was helping enough, China's tax system was not sufficient to arm and equip a modern army to meet the Japanese, who were using the latest weapons at that time. China did succeed in keeping the Japanese from using Korea as a staging area to invade northern

The Ming Dynasty

China, but otherwise the war could not be called a success. Fortunately for both China and Korea the Japanese government decided after the death of Hideyoshi to simply withdraw their troops from Korea.

At the same time that the Chinese were fighting the Japanese in Korea, the people from Manchuria began attacking the Ming outposts. Concurrently the various hill tribes in the far southwest of China, including the Thais and the Burmese, began a war against the Ming. The Ming armies were successful in all of these campaigns, but it was a terrible financial drain on a very disorganized tax system. The Ming were now beginning to realize that the tax privileges and deferrments they had granted through the years to favored gentry deprived them of essential revenue.

The officials who were supposed to be advising the emperor and administering the government could never seem to agree among themselves. There was a great amount of wrangling among the court officials and civil servants. Throughout the emperor Wan-li's long reign from 1573 to 1619, the partisan controversies increased to the point that he began to use eunuchs as advisors rather than the regularly trained court officials. Even they could seldom agree on policy. There was no question that China had problems--the question was how to solve them.

When the old emperor, Wan-li, died, his successor only lasted one month. The next emperor, Tianqi, 1621 to 1627, survived longer, but he was too young and indecisive at the time he inherited the throne to pull the empire back together. He hated the tasks associated with governing and rarely called a meeting of his ministers. In desparation he virtually turned over complete totalitarian powers to his court favorite, **Wei Chung-hsien**, the most notorious eunuch of Chinese history. Wei purged many officials who were calling for reform and replaced them with inexperienced men who earned their positions largely through flattery. The officials who were demoted ended up in terrible prisons where most of them were tortured until they died, still professing their loyalty to the emperor. In the meantime, the emperor enjoyed himself as a master craftsman of elegant furniture which he even lacquered himself.

The Ming government, greatly weakened economically and politically, was suddenly faced with its greatest challenge of all--another barbarian threat from Manchuria. An ambitious young leader named **Nurhachi** launched his first campaign against China in 1583. This was just before China became involved in the Korean campaign to prevent the Japanese from taking Korea.

Nurhachi had only nominal success in the early years, but as the internal strength of the Ming weakened as a consequence of fighting on two fronts--sometimes three fronts--the forces of the Manchurians became stronger. In 1616, Nurhachi proclaimed a new dynasty. He followed this with overwhelming victories over the Ming forces in 1619 and again in 1621. Through these campaigns, he gained control of the entire northeastern part of China which was north of the Great Wall.

The new emperor, **Ch'ung-ch'en** (Sizong) reigned in China from 1627 to 1644. He banished the court favorite of emperor Tianqi, Wei Chung-hsien, but failed to stop the partisan bickering within his bureaucracy. In desperation he changed the head of one bureaucracy 116 times in 13 years. No one was certain of their position. Everyone feared making a wrong decision which meant it was safer to make no decisions at all. The corruption and the infighting had become a way of life at the very pinnacle of the government. China was dying from the inside while the barbarians kept moving south of the Great Wall.

The **Jurchen** tribes under the leadership of **Nurhachi**, 1559 to 1626, eventually came to call themselves the **Manchu**, or the **Ch'ing**. They are also properly known as the **Qing** dynasty. By 1629 this persistent group of warriors were threatening Peking. They returned to the city again in 1638. By this time the Ming government seemed to be prepared to write off Manchuria, at least temporarily if need be, but they were not prepared for any Qing encroachments south of the Great Wall, including Peking. It seemed that the Ming bureaucracy could not be brought back to life in their hour of need. There was no money. There was no strong military leader. Finally, a domestic rebel named **Li Zi-cheng**, 1605? to 1645, captured the capital in April 1644, and the emperor committed suicide. At this time, the Qing seized the throne for themselves. It is considered that the Ming dynasty ended in **1644**.

The remaining Ming forces moved south ahead of the advancing Manchurian Qing army, but they were so badly splintered by this time that they put up little resistance. There were those who held small geographic areas of control in the name of the Ming for another generation, but it was useless. The last resistance on the mainland died out following 1662. Another faction under Cheng Ch'eng-kung, better known as **Koxinga**, held out on the island of Taiwan until 1683.

THE ARRIVAL OF THE EUROPEANS

The first Europeans arrived in Ming China in 1514, 130 years before the collapse of the Ming empire. China was one of the main reasons why Columbus had set out 72 years previously to find a new route by sea to the riches of this vast land. By 1514 the Portuguese were already established in India, but there was a certain magnetic interest about things which were "made in China." The earliest Portuguese outpost in China was at **Macau** in **1557**. This gave them an opportunity to trade with the nearby major city of **Canton** (Gangzhou). Even though the early merchant-traders did not have an official license to trade with the Chinese, the Chinese were just as anxious to trade with the Europeans. The trade was profitable for both parties. Within a few years the Dutch, the English, and the French were also interested in the China trade.

As always, the missionaries followed the trade routes. The newly founded **Jesuit Order**, anxious to establish itself, sent the earliest missionaries. **Francis Xavier**, a Spaniard, was the first to arrive in Canton in **1552**. He was ill when he arrived, having already visited Japan, and he died in China shortly after arriving. Others missionaries followed in the next few years.

SUMMARIZING CHINA

The people of China have always lived where the land is rich and fertile. The southeastern coastal plains and the river valleys have always been preferred with the highlands coming in second. The high plateaus and the mountainous areas are the least desirable since they are not capable of supporting a large population. China has always favored large families, especially of boys, who can work in the rice paddies to provide a better living for the entire family.

The Ming Dynasty

In the archaeological digs to date, the earliest centers of population were in the central and lower Huang Ho (Yellow) River valley. As more land was brought under cultivation and the forests were removed, the loose loess type soil became more likely to erode and the Yellow River became more likely to flood. The challenge of living in the river valleys caused the Chinese to very early try to out-think nature by providing dikes, reservoirs, irrigation and navigation canals, and granaries to store grain in the good years so people would not starve in the lean years. Crop varieties were also developed to gain more food from the same amount of space. They engineered the Great Wall to hold back their less civilized neighbors to the north.

Writing developed in China about 4,000 years ago. Some of the earliest writing was for religious purposes, but the Chinese developed a sense of history and nationalism long before most other civilizations in the entire world. A sense of beautiful and informative writing has long been a tradition in China. This was made even more important by the emphasis which Confucius placed on knowing the ancient classics. Unfortunately, even though the Chinese have discovered many practical inventions, they have lacked in the application and manufacture of these goods because they were more interested in literature than in science, math, and engineering.

The Chinese appreciation of beautiful literature has extended to beautiful works of bronze, porcelain, gold, silver, jade, and even many applications of bamboo and jute. Painting, which has often been influenced by their philosophic beliefs in mankind as a part of nature, certainly ranks exceptionally high by any standards. China has its own great philosophers who rival those of India or of the western world. They were one of the earliest areas to develop a system of writing to express their ideas in literature and art. All of these cultural benefits have influenced East Asia, especially Korea and Japan, and to a lesser extent, Southeast Asia.

The Chinese have stressed conformity of writing, standard weights and measures, high standards for craftsmanship, etc., at least since the time of the First Emperor. Current writing, regardless of the time of composition, has been judged against the great classics which predate Confucius. This has given the Chinese a sense of national unity which is more powerful than any other country of equal size. This is best expressed in their belief that they are all "men of Han."

For all of China's assets, there have been weaknesses and liabilities through the centuries. Democracy has never been a tradition in China. Throughout history they have preferred a strong leader at the helm to guide them through troubled times. Generally speaking, they have lacked this leadership as each of the dynasties eventually faltered and failed. China has also shown a great weakness in never providing an orderly system of selecting a successor to rule over them. Their government advisors have too often been selfish people who have often taken advantage of a weak ruler. The concept of a parliament is foreign to them. There have been occasions when their weakness of government would not have been important except that they have had unfriendly neighbors on their northern borders.

The Ming Dynasty

BOOKS FOR FURTHER READING

Blunden, Caroline, & Elvin, Mark, *Cultural Atlas of China* (1983).

Chan, Albert, *The Glory and Fall of the Ming Dynasaty* (1982).

Chan, Wing-Tsit, *A Source Book in Chinese Philosophy* (1963).

Chang, K. C., *Early Chinese Civilization: Anthropological Perspectives* (1976).

Chang,Kwang-chih, *The Archaeology of Ancient China* (1986).

Cotterell, Arthur, *China, A Cultural History* (1988).

Cotterell, Arthur, *East Asia: From Chinese Predominance to the Rise of the Pacific Rim* (1993).

Cotterell, Arthur, & Morgan, David, *China's Civilization* (1975).

Creel, H. G., *The Birth of China* (1937).

Creel, H. G., *Confucius and the Chinese Way* (1949).

Danforth, Kenneth, *Journey into China* (1982).

Eichorn, Werner, *Chinese Civilization: An Introduction* (1969).

Fenton, John Y., *et. al., Religions of Asia* (1988).

Fairbank, John K., *China: A New History* (1992).

Fairbank, John K., Reischauer, Edwin O., & Craig, Albert M., *East Asia, Tradition & Transformation* (1989).

Fitzgerald, Charles P., *The Horizon History of China* (1982).

Gernet, Jacques, *Ancient China From the Beginnings to the Empire* (1968).

Gernet, Jacques, *A History of Chinese Civilization* (1987).

Hopkirk, Peter, *The Great Game: The Struggle for Empire in Central Asia* (1992).

Huang, Ray, *1597, A Year of No Significance: The Ming Dynasty in Decline* (1981).

Komroff, Manuel, editor, *Contemporaries of Marco Polo* (1989).

Legg, Stuart, *The Barbarians of Asia* (1970).

Loewe, Michael, *The Pride That Was China* (1990).

The Ming Dynasty

Marshall, Robert, *Storm from the East: From Genghis Khan to Kublai Khan* (1993).

Maspero, Henri, Translanted by Kierman, Frank A. Jr., *China in Antiquity*.

Merton, Thomas, *The Way of Chuang Tzu* (1965).

Meyer, Milton W., *A Concise History of China* (1994).

Mote, Frederick, *Intellecltual Foundations of China* (1989).

Schirokauer, Conrad, *A Brief History of Chinese and Japanese Civilizations* (1989).

Schwartz, Benjamin, *The World of Thought in Ancient China* (1985).

Sivin, Nathan, *The Contemporary Atlas of China* (1988).

Spence, Jonathan, & Wills, John E., Jr., editors, *From Ming to Ch'ing: Conquest, Region, and Continuity in 17-Century China* (1979).

Treistman, Judith, *The Prehistory of China* (1972).

Waldron, Arthur, *The Great Wall of China From History to Myth* (1990).

Waley, Arthur, *The Analects of Confucius* (1989.

Waley, Arthur, *Three Ways of Thought in Ancient China* (1989).

Watson, William, *Early Civilization in China* (1966).

Welch, Holmes, *Taoism: The Parting of the Way* (1957).

Yutang, Lin, *The Wisdom of Confucius* (1938).

THE EARLY HISTORY of KOREA to c.1600

Chapter 30
THE GEOGRAPHY OF THE KOREAN PENINSULA

Korea is a large peninsula surrounded on three sides by water. It is separated from Japan by the Sea of Japan on the east, by the Yellow Sea to the west, and by the Korea Strait on the south. Two rivers are generally thought of as its land border on the north--the **Tumen** and the **Yalu**.

Korea is situated approximately between the parallels of 35 degrees south and 42 degrees north; about the same as North Africa and Spain, or in North America, it would correspond to the area between North Carolina and New York City. The size of North Korea is slightly smaller than Pennsylvania, while South Korea is somewhat larger than Indiana.

A spine of mountains known as the **Taebaek-Sanmark** runs along Korea's east coast. Generally speaking, the peninsula faces **west** with the important port city of **Pusan** on the southeast corner. Several other mountains are scattered throughout the peninsula. The peninsula is dotted with peaks throughout so that it is impossible to find a place with a clear view where there is not a mountain, often in all four directions. Modern Korea has no active volcanoes at the present and it seldom suffers earthquakes such as those experienced in nearby Japan.

Mineral resources include coal, iron ore, copper ore, tungsten, graphite, limestone, gold, and silver. Many of the richest mineral resources are in the northern areas while the majority of the agricultural land is in the south. Some gold is found throughout the peninsula.

Due to its mountainous terrain, only one-fifth of the land is suitable for agriculture. Most of the agricultural land is around the coastal area, the river valleys, and the fertile valleys between the mountains. In South Korea the climate will generally allow two rice crops a year. Most of the forests are in the more rugged northern area. The hydroelectric potential is also mostly in the north.

The climate of Korea is both humid and continental. The warm, humid weather in the south compares very closely to the weather in Georgia, while the north is more like Maine in the wintertime. Even though it is not situated that far north, it is the cold winds which blow into North Korea from Siberia which causes the extreme winter cold. Korea also has a definite rainy season in the summer but relatively dry winters. There is generally plenty of rain for raising crops throughout the peninsula, although this varies from about 25 inches in the northern interior to 60 inches along the southern shores. Korean farmers prefer to raise rice whenever possible, and the hot, moist summers are well suited for this crop, especially in the southern latitudes.

Figure 31

Chapter 31
PREHISTORIC KOREA

PALEOLITHIC KOREA

No one today knows the exact year when mankind first arrived in Korea. Modern dates are based totally upon archaeological evidence, which did not really get underway until as recent as 1933. The first significant Paleolithic site was at **Tonggwanjin** in the far northeastern corner of the peninsula. This was followed by excavations in North Hamgyong province in 1962. In 1964 there were new Paleolithic sites discovered in South Ch'ungch'ong province. Since 1964 other widely scattered Paleolithic sites have been discovered. The most recent of the dates on these sites vary from 20,000 to 30,000 years ago, with the oldest sites ranging from an estimated 400,000 to 500,000 years ago.

Some of the recent digs have revealed human bones, but primarily they contain tools of stone and bone. During the Paleolithic Era the stone tools were all chipped by percussion. Although it is sometimes difficult to determine the use of some of the tools, or flakes, others were clearly used for knives, scrapers, awls, and gravers, along with handaxes and choppers. At one site there is good evidence that a kind of Paleolithic tool "factory" existed. All evidence indicates that by sometime about 20,000 years ago the people lived together in communities, probably for protection as well as hunting. Some of their shelters were inside caves, some were placed under an overhanging rock, while others were built on level ground. Apparently they all selected home sites which faced the sun and sheltered them from the wind.

The early Koreans were quite obviously living in a **Hunting and Gathering** age, which means the people subsisted largely on fruit, vegetables, berries, edible roots, and honey. Their meat would necessarily have been mostly small game and fish.

In summary, life in Paleolithic Korea was not that different than in other parts of the world during the same time frame. Since archaeology in Korea has only begun in recent years it is possible that later discoveries will indicate that the people were more advanced during Paleolithic times than we had originally believed.

MESOLITHIC KOREA

There have been no definite Mesolithic remains found in Korea. As the last Ice Age began to recede, sometime about 8,000 B.C., small game and deer began to appear. It is believed that the settlement of early man in Korea during this period followed the small game. Rivers flowed full and the lakes were filled during this period. Various types of bows came into usage to hunt the game. While some hunters used simple bows, others attached sharpened stone points to either wood or bone shafts. Stone tools were in a transition stage between chipping during the Early Mesolithic, but they shifted to flaking during the Late Mesolithic Age.

Prehistoric Korea

NEOLITHIC KOREA

By 5,500 B.C. the majority of the ice had melted and substantial numbers of people moved into Korea, most of them coming from the area of present-day Manchuria. The Neolithic people flaked the flint and chert for most of their tools and weapons. Their pottery was small, simple, and most of it was undecorated. That which did have any decoration was made by placing small strips of clay on the outside of the pots and bowls. This design was evidently added so these vessels would not slip through wet and greasy fingers. Pottery of this type has been found scattered throughout the entire peninsula.

Beginning sometime about 4,000 B.C. the Koreans began making pottery incised with a geometric "comb-like" pattern. Some of these patterns appear as waves of water, probably because they received much of their protein from the rivers and the sea. There are also incised zig-zag patterns believed to represent thunderbolts. They considered lightning to be the heavenly force which started all of creation.

The Korean incised pottery was gray in color with a V-shaped pointed bottom which could be set in the dirt floor. Other pots had rounded bottoms to set on the surface of the floor. This same comb-shaped pattern in pottery has been found in archaeological sites throughout the peninsula. Nearly identical pottery has also been found in Siberia, Inner Mongolia, and Japan. This has led to the theory that culture flowed from northeast Asia through Korea and on to Japan. Painted design pottery which dates to about 2,000 B.C. also seems to have entered the Korean peninsula via China. By this time most of the pottery was made with a flat bottom rather than a pointed or rounded bottom. This early pottery is the only evidence we have of their artwork today.

No one can be certain the Paleolithic people who inhabited the peninsula before the Ice Age were the forefathers of present-day Koreans. Most authorities believe they probably were **not**. But those who entered Korea from about 4,000 B.C. to the present were almost certainly the forerunners of present-day Koreans. Migrants continued to enter the peninsula from China and Manchuria until as late as 400 B.C.

LIFE IN STONE AGE KOREA

Life in early Korea was rather simple as the people settled mostly in the river valleys and along the coastal areas. Marine life and small game such as rabbits as well as deer and wild boar were also hunted. This is often referred to as the Hunting and Gathering stage. Archaeological evidence shows that Neolithic Koreans lived in both caves and in pit dwellings. Pit dwellings have been found which were both round and square, and set about five feet in the ground. Four or more posts were set around to support a thatched roof. The fire pit was in the center of the house with a hole in the thatched roof for the smoke to escape. Their large clay pots with pointed bottoms were generally set in the floor around the fire pit. At some of the sites they were also placed near the door.

Since several of these dwellings have been discovered clustered at a single site, it has been speculated that the early Koreans had some form of communal life. The basic social unit was the family. Beyond this, it was the clan organization. Apparently each clan had a **totem** around which the members could rally. Our earliest records shows they were governed by a **Council of Nobles** with a chieftain who was selected by his clansmen. This position was **not** hereditary but was retained by merit. Most of the hunting, gathering, and their primitive agricultural work was performed in common during the Neolithic Age.

Each clan community was an economically independent and self-sufficient entity. Each clan delineated its own area of hunting and gathering. As separate as each community seems to have been, the evidence is strong that they traded items such as flint or chert for tools and other items. Marriage partners also came from other clans but not as a regular practice. Larger social configurations, or tribes, were composed of several related clans.

THE KOREAN RELIGION

There has always been a close connection between Korean art and religion. The early Koreans believed that the force which began creation was the lightning bolt. There were many other beliefs which were closely associated with things in nature among the early Koreans. The birth of one of their earliest kings, **Pak Hyokkose**, was supposedly from an egg. His very name, "Pak" meant "brightness." They said that as a child of the sun, light radiated from his body.

Animistic beliefs also abounded throughout the peninsula. They believed that every object in the natural world was possessed with a soul. All souls were immortal, including mankind's, so they buried the articles a person would normally use on a day-to-day basis in their graves with them. The animistic belief was carried to the extent that even the mountains, the rivers, and the trees had souls.

Nearly every Korean worshipped the sun's soul because the sun brought good fortune to people. Darkness was another situation--that was where the evil spirits and misfortune dwelled. No matter how careful one might be it was always possible to be infested with an evil spirit. There were many intermediaries, sometimes referred to as **shamans**, who possessed the ability to drive off these evil spirits and invoke the gods to bring about a happy outcome. Both men and women served as shamans.

The ceremonies conducted in early Korea to drive away the evil spirits or illness were referred to as a **kut**. Clanging cymbals and the steady thump of an hour-glass drum would begin to draw the people to the "possessed" house. The shaman would then put on the costume of a particular god. The drummer would play while the shaman would sing an invocation. The shaman would then stretch out his or her arms and begin to dance, gracefully at first, lightly moving to the music. A sudden burst of drumming would set the shaman jumping. The shaman would then pound at the air and kick up her or his curled toes toward the ceiling.

Soon the gods would descend into the possessed shaman and begin to speak through his or her lips. The gods would remind everyone present of their wondrous powers. Then the gods would berate the sponsoring family for skimpy offerings and past neglect. The people in the household would talk back if the criticism seemed to be unjust.

Ceremonies of this type were carried out frequently--with variations appropriate to the situation, and for several reasons. A shaman was often called in because the family wished to communicate with their departed ancestors. Sometimes after a spell of bad luck the family would conclude that the house should be cleansed of evil spirits. In other cases their conscience may have been bothering them for having forgotten to make appropriate offerings to the gods each day. On other occasions the shaman was called to rectify a marital problem or perhaps the parents and children were not getting along.

Shamans were often consulted to be sure that the parents were selecting the proper marriage partner for their son or daughter. This was a very serious matter. In later Korean history a shaman was sometimes called to a house for something as simple as asking whether their son would find suitable employment. This was also a very important question once the son had spent years in school and had applied for a civil service type position. All schooling was private which meant that most families had to make great sacrifices in order to send their sons to get the best possible training. And of course they called upon the shaman for any mystery or problem which the family could not understand.

Many educated Koreans today say that **shamanism** and the **kut** no longer exist. Nevertheless, the kut ceremonies have continued to be held for many years since prehistoric times. Koreans today say that it is a good way to bring people together for a few hours of partying. It is much more prominent in the rural areas than the urban areas today. Undoubtedly, there are those who still feel some power from these ceremonies.

Spirit Posts, also known as "devil posts," were female symbols something like small totem poles. Supposedly they represented the fertile "Great General of the Underground." These spirit posts were placed along pathways, in front of the house, at an intersection of two highways, etc. Most of the spirit posts are found in the museums today, but a few are still seen in the countryside. There are also neo-shaman scarecrows placed in the fields. They are designed to not only scare away birds but evil spirits as well.

In general, all of these shamanistic and animistic ideas are more alive in the countryside than in the cities today. Even in Seoul, however, the shamans celebrate traditional holidays with a day-long kut to the Dragon King of the Han River. Apparently, shamanism is a greater attraction to Korean women than to men. Many women offer rice cakes and a glass of water to the house gods. Or, they may wrap a small bundle of pine needles and wedge it somewhere in the house for the same reason.

Most shamans in Korea today are women, and generally there are more women than men who attend a kut. Often the men give wine, rice, and delicacies to the family's ancestors in filial piety; or, dedicate their offerings to parents and grandparents beyond the grave. Appeasing the household gods is largely the women's responsibility. In olden times there is every evidence that the men were equal participants. Anthropoligists also believe that ceremonies such as the kut were quite frequent from prehistoric times down to the early twentieth century.

Archaeologists have also uncovered small clay figurines in the shape of an animal which is believed had some religious meaning. Another interesting discovery is the sculpted face of a person and a mask made almost entirely of shell. It it quite evident that the various art forms were all closely tied to the religious life of the Korean people. Future archaeological digs will undoubtedly tell us much more about the early peoples of the Korean peninsula.

Prehistoric Korea

BRONZE AGE KOREA
c. 800-400 B.C.

Since so much of our knowledge of early Korea depends upon archaeology, it is necessary to rely upon an interpretation of their artwork and their tools which have survived. There was obviously some cultural continuity between the Neolithic Age and the Bronze Age. Some geometrically decorated pottery from the Neolithic times continued on following the introduction of bronze in the 9th or 8th century B.C. Geometric motifs also appeared in the decoration of bronze daggers and mirrors. This ultimately gave way to the more characteristic pottery which has a brownish-red color and is largely undecorated. Tombs also became much more elaborate in the Bronze Age. Large dolmen structures were combined with numerous large upright stones known as menhirs. Some authors refer to this period as the megalithic age.

The Bronze Age Korean people constructed their homes on the upper slopes of the hills and mountains overlooking the valleys below. The cultivation of rice, especially in southern Korea, began during this period. Both crescent-shaped sickles which were used to cut the rice and stone hoes have been found. The manner of cultivating rice and the tools which have been discovered are the same as those which were used in China. Hunting for small game and fishing continued throughout the Bronze Age.

Both the Bronze Age tools and accessories, as well as the dolmen tombs with their capstones weighing up to 70 tons, were clearly for the rich. No ordinary Korean could have afforded the cost of purchasing the tin and copper tools, or the labor to build tombs incorporating such huge stones. Bronze daggers, tools, mirrors, etc., would also indicate an upper social class with considerable wealth. The graves of commoners continued to contain stone, shell, horn, and bone for tools, weapons, and fishhooks. It is therefore presumed that the Koreans of this period had a stratified society, probably based upon a rich class and a poor class.

KOREA'S EARLIEST HISTORY: FACT AND MYTHOLOGY

According to Korean mythology, a man named **Hwanung**, the Son of the Divine Creator, came to earth in a pine forest. First a bear, then a tiger, came to Hwanung and requested to become human beings. He gave each of them twenty pieces of garlic and a piece of artemisia (probably either wormwood or some strong-smelling herb or foilage) and told them they would become humans if they would eat these two products and remain out of the sun's light for one hundred days. Both animals ate the food and went into their respective caves. The tiger became restless and reappeared in the light and it remained a tiger. The bear remained in its cave the entire one hundred days and when she emerged, she became a woman.

The woman's first wish was to have a son. She prayed under a sandalwood tree where Hwanung breathed on her and shortly she bore a child named **Tan'gun**. Tan'gun's reign as the first human king began in **2333 B.C.** The Republic of Korea officially begins its calendar on that date. They simply add 2,333 years to the western calendar when figuring what year it is in Korean history.

Tan'gun is not only credited with being the first king, he also taught the early people agriculture and how to live with each other. Many think the bear and the forest story probably originated much earlier among the peoples of northern Asia and was carried into the peninsula by the people who migrated into Korea at a very early date.

Still another significant legend relates the story of **Kija**, a Chinese sage who they say emigrated to Korea in **1122 B. C.** This story tells how Kija, a descendant of the Shang dynasty, supposedly brought 5,000 followers and introduced Chinese culture into Korea. Some researchers believe that there may be some validity to the Kija legend because of the tremendous influence of the Chinese civilization upon the Korean people. They say that once Kija was established, Tan'gun resumed his spirit form and disappeared. The problem with this story is that 1122 B.C. seems quite early for the Chinese migration into Korea. Since the Tan'gun story was not written until the 13th century, no one can verify whether it is correct.

THE BEGINNING OF WRITTEN RECORDS IN KOREA

The first historical records of any validity date back to about 108 B.C. when the Chinese established four colonies in northwestern Korea. One of these was **Lolang** (Lelang). The capital of Lolang, which was at P'yongyang, was the most prosperous of the four. Each of the four tribes was composed of a federation of many clans. Even in 108 B.C. there are still more suppositions than there are facts. [*Note: It should be pointed out that there is a Han River in both Korea and in China.*]

When the Later Han dynasty collapsed, one of the Korean tribal states took over the territory governed by Lolang. The leading Korean tribe which eventually overcame the Lolang, as well as some rival Korean chieftains, was the **Koguryo**. By the time the Koguryo had grown into a kingdom with a centralized government and overcame the Lolang in the northwest, it was already the 4th century A.D. Even though the Koguryo were often at war with the Chinese, the Koguryo adopted Chinese weapons and Chinese governmental organization. This group of hill people were very aggressive. Their men were well-drilled and skilled militarists. They not only dominated the northern half of the Korean peninsula, they also controlled all of Manchuria in these early years.

The Chinese influence upon Korea probably began as early as the Bronze Age, but an increasing influence became apparent during the Early Iron Age. Political institutions, writing, burial customs, and technology, all owed a heavy debt to the Chinese Han civilization--202 B.C. to A.D. 221. This civilization first infiltrated from the northwest via the settlements around the Yalu River. Once Chinese culture had moved south of the Han River in Korea it began to change into an all new culture--the Korean culture. The three Han states of the area in southern Korea soon surpassed their tutors to the north. Agriculture, based on rice culture, animal husbandry, fishing, and hunting were all important.

It was during this same timeframe that the clans and tribes turned to kings to head their government. Chinese records indicate that there was an upper aristocracy, a commoner class, the lower class, and the slaves. The elite lived in heavily walled towns which were somewhat like those in medieval Europe except a few hundred years earlier. This princely class dominated their own area of jurisdiction and the subjects who were under them. Although the early kings were elected, this soon gave way to a hereditary monarchy. By the 3rd century A.D. there were **Three Kingdoms--Koguryo** in the north, **Paekche** in central and southwestern Korea, and **Silla** in the southeast.

Chapter 32
KOREA FROM THE END OF THE PREHISTORIC TO c.1392

INTRODUCTION

There is a great amount of Korea's earliest years which will probably remain a mystery forever. Whatever the origins of their people, the Korean peninsula's history was greatly enriched at an early date by an aggressive **Han emperor**, **Wu Ti**, whose army swept through **Choson** (Korea) in **108 B.C.** and implanted many lasting elements of Chinese culture. The chief Han outpost was located at **Lo-lang**, now known as P'yongyang. Many Chinese families were encouraged to move into Korea where they attempted to reproduce the civilization of their native China. As these families grew prosperous through trade with their homeland, they encouraged the arts in which master craftsmen left a fine legacy of exquisite talent from the Han era of China. This became a vigorous colony, carefully organized into districts, and perpetuated under Chinese control for almost four centuries. Despite the fall of the Han dynasty, the Chinese leaders in Korea were able to sustain themselves in power. Eventually, the challenge of the new Korean states slowly brought the demise of the Chinese rule by **A.D. 313**.

THE PERIOD OF THE THREE KINGDOMS

During the period from the first century B.C. to the fourth century A.D., three kingdoms rose to political leadership in the Korean peninsula, thus uniting the various tribes that had migrated into the Korean peninsula from Manchuria. These three kingdoms were **Koguryo** in the North, **Paekche** in the Southwest, and **Silla** in the Southeast. A fourth smaller state named **Kaya** was also formed in the South between Paekche and Silla. The small state of Kaya became closely associated with Japan, and it was known to them as Mimana.

The three Korean states--Koguryo, Paekche, and Silla--were able to establish themselves during the same period as the Chinese colonization in the area of Lo-lang. Many of the Koreans feared that China would overwhelm the entire peninsula, but the Chinese confined their political domination to the Lo-lang area after Wu Ti's conquest. It was this failure on the part of the Chinese to dominate further which allowed the three Korean kingdoms to develop. Evidently, the Chinese were interested primarily in securing a trade outlet at that time rather than adding territory. As trade moved between China and Korea, so also culture flowed into Korea which resulted in a gradual Sinification of the peninsula.

CHINESE CULTURE IN KOGURYO

Seasoned by conflict with both their neighboring tribes and the Chinese, Koguryo developed into the peninsula's largest and most Sinified kingdom. Their state was located in the far North end of the peninsula, close to the Chinese culture. In that location, Koguryo served as a transmitter of Chinese traditions, such as Confucianism, throughout the entire peninsula. The sophistication of China's bureaucracy, law, science, and taxation system appealed to the people of early Koguryo and they adopted and modified Chinese advancements in these areas as they chose. It also became necessary to learn to read and write the Chinese language. This opened the entire area of Chinese literature to the Koreans. Art and music also moved from China into the Korean peninsula.

By A.D. 372, Buddhism began to be advocated in northern Korea. When the capital of Koguryo had moved from the Yalu River region to Lo-lang (P'yongyang) in 427, the process of cultural absorption became even more thorough. Fine artistic remnants of the period, such as wall paintings and stone sculpture, give evidence of a talented and imaginative people who were fascinated by Chinese techniques. From the end of China's Lo-lang outpost in 313 until 668, Koguryo had been politically powerful and militarily expansive toward her smaller, weaker, and less Sinified neighbors.

THE RISE OF PAEKCHE

Korea's most productive agricultural lands to the southwest became the area of the second most important state in early Korean history, Paekche. Frequent warfare with Koguryo, especially in the fourth and fifth centuries, resulted in many defeats that forced Paekche to shrink its ambitious boundaries, move its capital progressively southward to Puyo by 538, and seek allies either with the Silla to the east, Japan across the Korean Straits, or with China. An early tribute relationship with southern China brought Buddhism to Paekche by about 384. This was later followed by more general cultural exchanges and with trade. Although we know relatively little about Paekche's early government and society, this late fourth century contact may have been the source of a Chinese-style bureaucratic kingdom. Since Paekche was buffered from China on the north by Koguryo, the primary flow of Chinese culture to Paekche was via the maritime route to the peninsula's southern area.

THE FOUNDATIONS OF THE STATE OF SILLA

The least Sinified and the least centralized of the three kingdoms was Silla. Held together by a loose confederation of tribal leaders, it was finally unified in the late fourth century by a strong and determined king. In the sixth century, several Chinese institutions and a burst of aggressive energy became characteristic of this small state. Buddhism had been brought to Silla in the late 5th century by two monks traveling from Koguryo. It was made the state religion by a converted monarch in 527. Again, selected elements of China's political system were adopted, but they did not replace traditional practices in Silla.

The bureaucratic ranks of the Chinese hierarchy, for example, were superimposed on Silla's hereditary caste system, which divided society into groups (most would call them castes) identified as **"Bone-Ranks."** The military establishment, however, was not affected by the evolutionary growth of Chinese practices. The warrior class of Silla continued to dominate rather than adopt a Chinese-style peasant army. Artistic evidence of the perioid, especially the pre-Buddhist era, further reveals the comparative slowness of Sinification.

During the sixth century the Kingdom of Silla began to expand. They first moved toward the neighboring small state of Kaya in 532, followed later in 551 by a joint venture with Paekche against Koguryo. After some gains in Koguryo's southern region, Silla broke with Paekche and in gratitude for their assistance against Kaya, they took some of Paekche's territory as well. These latter moves brought Silla into control of all of the Han River valley and gave it access to

Korea's west coast. Within a short time the Kingdom of Silla began a more direct contact with China. When China was united under the Sui dynasty in 589, following centuries of political disintegration, the Chinese armies advanced into the Korean peninsula where they met determined resistance by Koguryo.

It was not until 660 that a stronger T'ang dynasty, at the request of the Silla, decided to strike against Paekche by sea as part of a strategy by the Silla to outflank Koguryo. China's large military commitment to this operation succeeded in defeating Paekche by 663. Growing weakness in Koguryo's leadership also made that kingdom vulnerable. After almost 70 years of sustaining Chinese onslaughts, Koguryo was defeated by the Chinese T'ang armies in 668. With its rivals defeated, T'ang China and Silla then turned on each other. Supported by the conquered Korean groups, Silla was able to force China's withdrawal and consolidated their position in less than ten years throughout the Korean peninsula south of P'yongyang. The increased contacts with China through these several years brought further Sinification to the Silla. The T'ang court dress and governmental structure were adopted in the Kingdom of Silla by the middle of the 7th century. By the century's end, Silla had, in effect, become a tributary state of China, at least from a **cultural** point of view.

KOREA FOLLOWING THE UNIFICATION BY SILLA

The unification of Korea by the Kingdom of Silla brought to a final close the old and fragmented political arrangement of the Three Kingdom Period which had so often been absorbed in warfare. As the Chinese meddled in Korean affairs, and as the Koreans "used" the Chinese to accomplish their own goals, Korea adopted many Chinese cultural characteristics. Some of these became a part of Korea by choice while others were absorbed unconsciously. Many Koreans recognized, reluctantly in many cases, that China under the T'ang had a superior civilization. While Silla searched for ways to perfect its own character, they ultimately adopted many of the Chinese ways as a matter of self-defense against China. The Chinese gifts of culture and civilization were seldom truly appreciated by the Koreans.

GOVERNMENT AND SOCIETY

As the Silla adapted the Chinese governmental model to their own immediate needs, they divided the peninsula into nine provinces. These were further subdivided into a little more than 100 districts, 300 counties, and an indeterminate number of villages. **Kumsong** on the Kyongju plain in the southeast corner of the Korean peninsula continued to serve as the Silla capital. To assure closer regional control, five subsidiary capitals were erected. The bureaucracy required for these governmental units was quite large. Unlike China's civil service system based upon a Confucian model, Silla's government was staffed by the socially elite. Although an examination system was adopted by 788, only aristocrats were eligible to participate. The old "bone-rank" system of the Silla now came to predominate throughout Korea.

The government of Silla also attempted to control land ownership and establish a tax system similar to the Chinese example, but before long these efforts failed. In other words, the growing move toward Sinification was often limited by native traditions that had deeper roots. A similar pattern was also followed in Japan.

Korea from Prehistoric to c.1392

By the middle of the 8th century, the strength of the Silla began to weaken. An erosion in social stability had taken place in which the nobility fragmented into rival groups. At the same time, "bone-rank" distinctions began to fade. The once aristocratic warriors, called *hwarang-do*, deteriorated into nonentities. Quarrels and intrigues frequently plagued Silla's leadership between approximately 750 and 900 when a series of revolts and attempted palace coups took place. Further disruption in Silla power occurred as powerful merchants upset the old social order through their growing influence.

THE LATER YEARS OF THE SILLA KINGDOM

One of the more colorful figures of the later Silla Kingdom (ninth century), whose career illustrates both the social changes which were taking place and the resistance to it by traditionalists, was **Chang Po-Go**. After a trip covering a few years in China, Chang returned to Silla and proposed that he be allowed to set up a naval base at Ch'onghae on Wando Island off Korea's southwestern coast. His purpose was to prevent the seizure and sale of Koreans into slavery in China. His report of such activity, and increasing piracy, sufficiently concerned the leaders of Silla to go ahead with the project. In 828 Chang was made Commissioner at Ch'onghae and commanded a small army which seems to have been his personal mercenaries. From this position--in command of a naval base that happened to have been on the main trade route betweeen China, Korea, and Japan--Chang Po-go created a commercial enterprise that dominated the Yellow Sea traffic.

It was not long before Chang's wealth gave him entree into important government circles. In the course of a royal succession struggle, Chang allied with **Kim Ujing** and committed his troops in battle in exchange for the promise that his daughter was to marry the new king or his son. After a successful military venture, Kim did accede to the throne, but he died three months later. His son, **King Munsong**, planned to fullfil the earlier agreement by marrying Chang's daughter. The Korean court, however, objected very strongly because this would be an infusion of common blood into the royal line. The pressures became so great that the new king was forced to cancel the marriage. The consequences of this episode were grave. Without Chang's expertise, Silla's profitable maritime activity came to a close. This cut off a valuable source of wealth at the very time the Kingdom of Silla was already growing weak.

THE END OF THE SILLA PERIOD OF UNIFICATION

By the latter portion of the 9th century, peasant uprisings, tax collection failure, and civil war characterized the Korean scene. Dissident factions then tried to resurrect the old kingdoms of the period before unification. A state called Later Paekche was formed in the Southwest while the state of **Later Koguryo** (to be known as **Koryo**) formed in the North. These "Later" kingdoms existed for a brief period, thereby recreating a newer version of the old Three Kingdom period.

Wang Kon, the founder of the state of **Koryo**, emerged from this troubled period in Korean history as the most powerful rebel king. In 935 he succeeded in bringing about the downfall of the greatly weakened Silla Kingdom. The next year he eliminated Later Paekche, uniting Korea once again under a dynasty that was to last more than four centuries.

THE KORYO DYNASTY
935-1392

Koryo is really a shortened version of Koguryo. It was from the word "Koryo" that the English later established the name **Korea**. General **Wang Kon** of Koryo established four regional capitals. The central capital was located at Kaesong, the eastern capital at Kyongju, the northern capital at P'yongyang, and the southern capital at Seoul. Of these four, Kaesong (also known as Kaeju, Song'ak, and Songdo), was the most important.

Wang Kon maintained a basically Chinese style of government. The officials were chosen through highly rigorous civil service examinations. There were separate civil and military bureaucracies, and the civilians were more highly regarded than the military because many of the military had come from the commoner class and lacked the scholarly qualifications held to be essential to the Confucian ideal of enlightened rule.

The state continued to own all lands, which they viewed as the historic cornerstone of political and financial stability. Private land ownership was not recognized--it all belonged to the monarchy. Land was assigned under a rather elaborate formula in such a way that control could not fall into the hands of a few aristocratic families. Some lands were held directly by the royal household, some by the temples and monasteries, some by public officials, and the rest was "leased" to individuals.

Despite all the precautions, approximately two centuries of relative calm was disrupted by the gradual ascendancy of aristocrats who, by means of intermarriage with the royal line, had gained an excessive amount of power in the government. These upper class families engaged in many court intrigues which ultimately undermined the authority of the kings. The resulting chaos at the royal court led to a military seizure of the government in 1170.

The military takeover was led by General **Chong Chung-Bu**, who had been awaiting his opportunity after one of the civilian officials had scorched his whiskers. Once he took over power he ordered a wholesale massacre of high ranking civil officials. Many others in the military supported General Chong Chung-Bu, while there were those who saw an opportunity in the break-up of governmental authority to try to seize power for themselves. The result was two decades of rebellions which were joined by the peasants and the slaves. The army officers reduced the powers of the monarch to little more than a puppet. They appointed many commoners who had little education or training for the high positions they held in the government. The period of Confucian civil service exams was temporarily ended.

Such political anarchy also encouraged many of the aristocratic families to transfer public lands to their private estates. Many individuals joined military groups which promised to grant them protection in exchange for goods or money. Many Buddhist monasteries formed their own private armies to protect their holdings, since many people had given grants of land to the various monasteries. State revenues declined to practically nothing at a time when the government needed ever more money to bring order out of the chaos. The Koryo Kingdom was wide open to foreign invaders.

THE MONGOL INVASIONS

The T'ang Dynasty in China had posed as Koryo's protector for many years, but when they suffered weakness, which was followed by collapse at this same time, Korea was forced to contend with the powerful tribes from the north without any Chinese assistance. As a consequence, the last one hundred sixty years of the kingdom were especially turbulent. It was a period when waves of Mongols laid waste to large areas of the country with seemingly little resistance.

Once the armies of the Mongol leader Ogedei had conquered northeastern China, the Mongols decided to gain the submission of the Koreans for all time to come. Although the Mongol armies had forced their way through northern Korea and had extracted promises from the leaders on previous occasions, the Koreans proved to be a stubborn-minded group who seized every opportunity to reassert their independence.

The Mongol campaign to conquer Korea began in earnest in 1231. Their army, bent on revenge for Korean misbehavior, crossed the Yalu River. They were even more cruel this time than in their previous raids. Still, each time the Mongol armies thought they had crushed the Koreans, the Koreans struck back. After ten years of warfare involving outright murder and unimaginable pillage of the countryside, the Koreans were again forced to accept a peace in 1241. It is difficult to say how much longer Ogedei might have continued his killing campaign in Korea, but he decided to draft another peace in order to expand his territorial holdings against the Chinese Sung.

With all the suffering the Koreans had endured, they still refused to keep the peace with the Mongols. One area after another of the little peninsula bravely rose up against the hated Mongols until after nearly thirty years of resistance, Koryo was the last to capitulate to the Mongols in 1259. The Mongols had not only defeated them militarily but they had destroyed and carried off so much of the wealth that there was no longer an economic base. In the single year of 1254, about 206,000 Korean men were said to have been carried into slavery by the Mongols.

In 1259 the northern part of the country was incorporated into the Mongol Empire, soon to be known as the **Yuan Dynasty, 1279-1368**. Following 1259, the royal house of Koryo became a branch of the Mongol ruling family through intermarriage between Mongol kings and Koryo princesses. The crown princes of Koryo were obliged to reside in Peking, the capital of the Yuan. There they were for all purposes hostages to assure the good behavior of the people of Koryo. In addition, Koryo was forced to pay heavy tribute, which included large numbers of virgins for the Yuan monarchy. During this same time period the Yuan under Kublai Khan tried to invade Japan in 1274 and again in 1281; both campaigns were unsuccessful. These ambitious military campaigns of the Yuan were paid for in part by heavy levies upon the Koreans.

THE LAST YEARS OF THE KORYO

The Koryo Kingdom regained their national freedom when the Chinese **Ming Dynasty, 1368-1644**, overthrew the Mongol Yuan dynasty. Once the Yuan had been driven from Peking, the people of Koryo split into two rival factions--those who favored staying with the Mongols, and those who favored joining with the new Ming dynasty. This issue was finally resolved when a **pro-Ming** general named **Yi Song-gye** seized control of the government. General Yi had become Korea's most popular and powerful military leader in the last years of the weak and corrupt Koryo dynasty. He had built his popularity base by fending off a group of Chinese bandits who were known as the Red Turbans. At the same time, the Korean coast was being invaded time after time by Japanese pirates. Yi Song-gye seemed to be the only military leader capable of keeping both groups at bay at the same time.

In 1388 the weak Koryo ruler sent General Yi north to repel a group of Ming military opportunists moving in from China. No one in Yi's army was terribly excited about their prospects for success. Everyone recognized that the real problem in Korea was the internal weakness of the Koryo dynasty, otherwise the Chinese and the Japanese would not have been so eager to snipe at the Korean borders. There were also some who believed the corrupt Koryo had been too friendly with the Mongols, that they should have resisted more intensely. Instead of heading north to repel the Ming, Yi and his army marched upon the Korean capital at Kaesong and began a four-year campaign to take over the government.

The first step was to seize Kaesong and install the king's son on the throne. With the support of his military, the general began a reform program throughout his area of control in Korea. When the Koryo leadership proved reluctant to change their ways, Yi ousted the last Koryo and took the throne for himself in 1392. The Yi dynasty ruled Korea for the next 518 years!

A second major change in Korean life began even before Yi took over total control in 1392. The Buddhists had been such a strong power behind the old Koryo throne that they were eased into the background and replaced by Yi's Neo-Confucian supporters. Buddhism was Yi's own religious persuasion, but he realized that the Buddhists were too closely allied to the old regime, they never paid their share of the tax burden, they practically ran the Koryo regime as the power behind the throne in its later years, and as a consequence, they became very unpopular with the Korean people.

THE ROLE OF BUDDHISM IN KOREA

Buddhism first arrived in the Korean peninsula via the most northern of the three kingdoms, Koguryo, in about A.D. 372. The Koreans had become familiar with the ancestor worship several years before Buddhism, but they saw the two philosophies as compatible. It was Buddhism which became Korea's first sophisticated and truly institutionalized religion. Buddhism gradually moved south through Korea until it permeated the entire peninsula by the 7th century. In the end, it probably had the greatest impact upon the southern part of Korea, where so much time and money was spent on the faith in the form of temples and monasteries that it tended to weaken the central government. Buddhism became the state religion during the Silla period from about 661 to 918. When the Silla dynasty weakened and was overcome by the Koryo, Buddhism continued as the state religion and the Buddhists gained in both political influence and economic power.

Buddhism was the one aspect of Chinese civilization which had the most appeal in Korea by the close of the Koryo dynasty. Nearly everyone claimed they were Buddhists, whether they practiced the faith or not. While Confucianism was also popular, it only seemed to offer guidance for mankind in his immediate environment. Buddhism served as a more satisfying explanation within the spiritual and eternal realm. The popular and optimistic **Mahayana** version of Buddhism was the one which came to prevail in Korea. Large monasteries, stone and brick pagodas, and bronze statuary were all executed by Korean craftsmen with an artistic brilliance as great as any in China. Many wealthy aristocrats had given land to the Buddhist temples and monasteries with the consequence that the Buddhists supported the monarchy in virtually everything, and the monarchy supported Buddhism.

The Buddhism of Korea leaned toward a faith of simplicity and the promise of security and a better life. The **Pure Land** sect was one of the most popular because they made salvation easy to attain. **Son**, also soon to be known as **Zen**, which emphasized meditation was also attractive because it did not require a complex interpretation of the sutras. The Koreans incorporated a certain amount of magic incantations to Buddhism, such as those in the old Korean **Kut** ceremonies. Korean Buddhism, therefore, became a religion tailored to suit the Koreans and their own background. There were thousands of Koreans who treasured Buddhism in their individual lives to such an extent that they contributed enormous amounts of both time and money for the support of the Buddhist religion.

By the close of the Koryo dynasty, most of the land in Korea was owned by either an aristocrat or a Buddhist group. Ordinary Koreans could scarcely afford to own even a small plot because the land taxes were very heavy in order to support the aristocracy and the Buddhists, both of whom were exempt from almost all forms of taxes. Since the upper classes would not pay taxes if they could possibly avoid doing so, the Koryo financial basis weakened and with the undermined economic system, the entire country suffered. It was the fragile economic situation in the Koryo Kingdom, plus a succession of weak and ineffective rulers, which had attracted the outside invaders. The Korean people were looking for a more fair and forceful ruler who would keep the enemies out and allow an opportunity for ordinary Koreans to own land.

CHRISTIANITY IN KOREA

Christianity arrived in Korea by an interesting route. Whereas most aspects of culture arrived in Japan via Korea, Christianity arrived in Korea from Japan. When the Japanese military forces entered Korea under Hideyoshi in 1592, one of the generals named **Konishi**, was a Christian. A small Christian congregation was established in the southern tip of Korea during the late 16th century but it did not last very long. When the Japanese evacuated Korea in 1598, the Christians returned to Japan with the army. Christianity was associated with the detested Japanese and had no recognizable following until it was reintroduced by a Roman Catholic scholar named **Yi Tukso** as late as 1777.

Chapter 33
KOREA UNDER THE YI DYNASTY, 1392 TO c.1600

Yi Song-gye ruled Korea from the time his military coup succeeded in 1392 until his retirement in 1398. He decided to call his country **Choson**, a term which had been used for many years to describe their peninsula as the land of the "morning serenity" or "morning calm." The dynasty which he established ruled Korea, with only a few interruptions, from 1392 until 1910.

One of the first things General Yi did was to order the destruction of all land registers. He then confiscated the private estates of the rich and aristocratic Koryo leaders along with the privileged holdings of the Buddhist monasteries. This action broke up the large landholdings, but it did not endear him with either the old aristocrats or the Buddhists, who had gained a considerable amount of power in Korea by 1392. With no support from either the upper classes or the most popular religion in Korea, General Yi had to build a new power base.. He had little choice but to support those who had supported him in the coup--the **Neo-Confucians**.

THE NEO-CONFUCIANS

This **new** interpretation of Confucius had begun in China during the late Sung period, 960-1279. By about A.D. 1300, the basic concepts of the new interpretation of the old philosopher had been pretty well formulated. It was brought from China to Korea by a Korean scholar named **An Hyang** following his visit to Peking during the time of Kublai Khan. An Hyang acquired many Confucian documents and books which gave the old Confucianism an entirely new interpretation in Korea.

The new interpretation of the teachings of Confucius said that the world was composed of "*li*," which acts like natural law, and "*qi*," which is the material force in nature. These principles are then revealed in the lives of humans in such a manner that everyone tends towards "goodness." Unfortunately, individuals can be disrupted in these feelings by greed, the quest for power, wealth, etc. These characteristics tend to obscure mankind's original nature of goodness. Therefore, everyone should cultivate the qualities of seriousness, reverence, and goodness. The investigation of things in this world was alright, providing it did not distract one from the quest for goodness.

Within a few years after An Hyang introduced these ideas in Korea, they began to be accepted by the civil servants. They believed that the course which the Kyoro dynasty had been following would ultimately lead to the destruction of the Korean society. Neo-Confucianism was not immediately seized upon by the general public, but Yi Song-gye found they would support his coup because he represented that movement toward reform which they had not had from the ruling Koryo aristocrats. Even though Yi Song-gye was a devout Buddhist, it became a political marriage of convenience for both factions.

Within a relatively short time the Neo-Confucian philosophy began to catch on because Yi Song-gye gave the people a strong and stable government. Many of the Neo-Confucians came to believe that **they** were destined to be the interpreters and custodians of this new interpretation of Confucius as the servants of the powerful new government. They believed that the Chinese and the Japanese had both strayed from the basic Confucian concepts. They believed that only they--the Koreans--had the true and orthodox approach to Confucianism. They also came to believe that all western peoples were "barbarians" because they did not practice Neo-Confucianism.

But many of the older civil servants soon indicated that they were quite content with the **old** interpretation, and they made it quite clear that they were quite reluctant to change to the Neo-Confucian concepts of faith. This resulted in a total of four bloody purges of mostly Buddhist civil servants, but there were some nonconformist Neo-Confucians who did not fit the new philosophy of government. The politician who emerged on top during this difficult time of readjustment within the Korean government was **Yi Hwang** (T'oegye), usually regarded as the leading political philosopher of Neo-Confucianism during the Yi dynasty. Even after the purges there were more factions which developed within the Neo-Confucians. Some of the Neo-Confucians became convinced that the chief force in the world was "*li*," while others were just as convinced that it was "*qi*." They were not content with an explanation of a balanced system.

Korean philosophers continually probed the inner depths of this dualism in Neo-Confucianism. These arguments occupied the best of Korea's intellectuals. Nothing else seemed important at that time except which of the two forces in the world was the most powerful. Thousands of hours were consumed on the finest points of interpretation. It was a situation very similar to the scholasticism which flourished within the Christian church in Europe at approximately the same period in history. Perhaps it was well that the Koreans did take the time to think through their faith at this moment in history because in the modern and materialistic world which was just ahead of them, there would be very little time for thinking about metaphysical problems and solutions.

THE YI DYNASTY CONTINUES

It would have been overly simplistic to believe that all was going to be smooth sailing for Yi once he had seized power. The Neo-Confucians and the working classes did favor his rule. On the other hand, he was opposed by the members of the ousted Koryo dynasty. Even though they were weak, they represented some very important people in Korean society.

Yi was opposed by the Buddhists for their loss of offices and prestige as a part of the inner circle in the outgoing dynasty. He was opposed by all those who had lost land in his reapportionment program. And, sometimes Yi could not avoid becoming involved in the arguments among the various Neo-Confucian factions concerning the world force question.

Among Yi's strongest points were that he often asked advice of other government officials and followed their recommendations, something the old regime had never done. He ruled largely as a figurehead leader rather than as a military dictator. The Koreans were not accustomed to this style of government and some interpreted it as a weakness. One of his most important contributions was that he ordered that the many rules and laws for the country should be written down. Every individual from the most powerful officials to the lowest officer at the local level in Korea understood their relationship to the government, their limits of power, and the laws by which they were governed.

In an effort to completely separate his new dynasty from the old one, Yi moved the capital from Kaesong to **Seoul**. A new class of young scholars who shared Yi's ambitions were

Yi Dynasty Korea

appointed to serve in Seoul as well as officials in local government offices. The men who served in the outlying local offices were called *yangban*. Under Yi's new style of governance these officials were granted the power to make many decisions which would formerly have had to be referred back to Seoul for a final answer. The rules under which each of the *yangban* operated were spelled out in the village codes. Those who were successful administrators among the *yangban* were granted land for their services. Since land ownership was a very precious right in Korea, this created a new landholding class which was very loyal to the Yi government. In later years the *yangban* became guilty of the very same abuses as the former Korean officials.

As Yi grew older his sons began a bloody struggle among themselves for the control of their father's kingdom. Most Koreans sided with one of the sons or another, which resulted in a rather restricted, but nevertheless bloody, civil war. Korea was no longer the land of the "morning calm." This was very disheartening to the old ruler and in 1398 he decided to resign altogether. He retired to a Buddhist monastery for his remaining years, where he died in 1408.

KOREA'S RELATIONS WITH CHINA

Once the Ming were firmly established in China, they began working out good relations with their neighboring countries. Gifts and ambassadors were exchanged between the two countries early in the Yi dynasty. Since the Yi dynasty gave Korea a strong and stable government there were no more major invasion threats from China. China began to refer to Korea as their most important *shu-kuo* country. This meant that Korea was a "dependency" of China. Today this would be considered a degrading designation. At that time it was considered an honor to be accepted as a *shu-kuo* of China. China was the greatest power in the world at this moment in history. They also granted *shu-kuo* status to Vietnam, Siam (Thailand), and Burma (Myanmar). All other countries were considered "barbarians."

KOREA'S WAR WITH JAPAN

The *shu-kuo* status of Korea paid off for both China and Korea in the 1590s when Korea refused to allow **Hideyoshi's Japanese army** to cross their territory on his way to invade China. **Toyotomi Hideyoshi,** 1536-1598, was completing the reunification of Japan when he announced his desire to conquer a portion of China by invading via Korea. It had been a long and bitter struggle in Japan, but Hideyoshi evidently believed that he could export a high percentage of his warriors to fight against the Chinese and thus get these men out of Japan where they might otherwise be competition for him in his period of consolidation. He also seemed to believe that Japan was on sufficiently good terms with Korea that they would give their consent to using Korea as a highway in his conquest of a piece of Chinese territory. This assumption was probably based on the fact that Korea had not really been involved in any major military action since the Yi takeover in 1392, a period of two hundred years. Besides, the power behind the throne was the Neo-Confucian civil service, which was basically committed to a peaceful policy.

Hideyoshi miscalculated the Korean intentions. When the first Japanese troops landed at Pusan in April 1592, the Korean opposition began to take shape, but they found themselves inexperienced in the arts of warfare since they had enjoyed two centuries of peaceful existence. Furthermore, the seasoned Japanese soldiers carried muskets they had purchased from the Portuguese. The Koreans began a retreat to the northern part of the peninsula as the Japanese army, now composed of about 158,000 men, were in close pursuit. Most Koreans felt totally helpless and just allowed them to move north. Just twenty days after landing at Pusan, the Japanese army captured Seoul. The Yi ruler and his family fled the capital city amid the jeers and insults of the crowd, escaping just ahead of the Japanese army. When Japan captured P'yongyang in the north in July, it should have been the end of Chosun.

The remarkable thing about this war was that the Korean army had done so poorly and their navy had done so well. **Admiral Yi Sun-sin** achieved several of the greatest triumphs of any military officer in any nation. When the admiral learned of a probable invasion from Japan, he immediately began fitting out his ships for battle. No one had ever designed ships quite like those which he began to build in preparation for a likely battle with the Japanese fleet. The ships were around one hundred feet in length and twenty-five or thirty feet wide. All the Korean ships were propelled by oars and even though they were quite heavy, they were still very maneuverable.

The really outstanding feature of this new style of navy designed by Admiral Yi was that all previous ships had an open deck. Admiral Yi ordered that the open area should be totally covered with heavy iron plates which had sharp spikes protruding from them to discourage anyone from climbing on board--a giant metal umbrella covering the top to protect the men beneath from all projectiles as well as potential boarders. Each ship carried up to twenty-six cannons, each of which could be aimed through gunports. Even the oarsmen were protected from enemy fire by an ingenious design. Each ship also had a heavy iron ram built on both the bow and the stern, and there was the head of a turtle projecting from the front of the iron canopy on each ship. They looked like huge turtles moving through the water. The ships even had a mechanism to generate a heavy screen of sulphur smoke so the the Japanese would not be able to immediately recognize what the Koreans were going to do next.

Within three months time, Yi's navy was able to sink about 200 of the Japanese ships at sea. He then cruised boldly into the port of Pusan, which the Japanese had taken over to supply their army in Korea, and managed to sink or disable over half the 500 ships which were there. With the **"turtle fleet"** on the loose around the perimeter of the peninsula, it was unsafe for the Japanese to consider any other landings or supply ports for fear of attack by this new-style Korean navy. Truly, Yi Sun-sin's ingenuity had saved Korea from a complete Japanese take-over.

The naval operations gave the Koreans time enough to begin organizing **"righteous armies"** led by local members of the gentry and Buddhist monks. The royal family had grown so soft without any major threat in two hundred years that they did not know what to do next. The pacifist Neo-Confucian government officials were almost totally oriented to the internal development of Korea. Since they had not faced a serious outside force in two hundred years, they seemed totally puzzled about what to do next. This was complicated by many factions within the government bureaucracy, each of which believed they had the only correct answer! They finally did agree among themselves to get an appeal off to Ming China for assistance.

In the meantime, China had been watching the Japanese invasion of Korea with some interest and finally figured out that **they** were the real target. They finally sent an army of 40,000 which helped the Koreans to retake P'yongyang in February 1593. Japanese forces were pushed just south of Seoul and at that point the joint Chinese-Korean army could not budge the Japanese any further south. Neither could the Japanese regain the initiative. The war was stalled.

Yi Dynasty Korea

A four-year period of talks then opened between the Chinese and the Japanese in Japan. Hideyoshi demanded that the Chinese acknowledge defeat and that they send a Chinese princess to be the wife of the Japanese emperor. They also demanded trade concessions in China which they hoped to exploit into a permanent foothold as they had done over the years in the Pusan area of southern Korea. Finally, the Japanese demanded that Korea cede their four southern provinces to Japan and offer members of the royal family as hostages. At the same time, China agreed to recognize Hideyoshi as "king" of Japan, providing he agreed to become a vassal of the Ming emperor. Since Hideyoshi could not read the Chinese messages, he had to rely on his interpreters. When he discovered that they were not making the Chinese terms clear to him, and that Japan would become a vassal of the Ming emperor, he had the Japanese negotiators executed and he resumed the war against Korea in August 1597.

It was not quite the same victory march it had been in 1592. Korea's "righteous armies" were now much better organized. The Korean "turtle navy" resumed taking its heavy toll of Japanese troop and supply ships. The Chinese Ming armies had anticipated a renewal of the war and they were there to assist the Koreans. The Japanese advance stalled again, just south of Seoul. A combined Korean-Chinese navy led by Yi Sun-sin managed to defeat a much larger Japanese fleet, a battle in which Yi Sun-sin lost his life. It would be difficult to predict what the next move would have been, but it all took a dramatic turn in September 1598. The Japanese leader, Hideyoshi died very suddenly at age 62, some believed over grief and worry that the Japanese armies were unable to forge ahead victoriously.

After a two-year internal struggle, Hideyoshi was succeeded in Japan by the more peaceful Tokugawa regime in 1600. The Japanese generals in Korea informed their government that they foresaw a long and difficult war. The more peaceful Tokugawa leadership concluded that the war in Korea was not their highest priority and ordered the troops withdrawn. In 1609 they made a treaty with Korea which formally ended the struggle.

TAE KWON DO IN FAR EASTERN DEFENSE

A final interesting note about the struggle with Japan which began in 1592 concerns the so-called "righteous armies." These were an outgrowth of centuries of unarmed self-defense which seems to have had its roots in China. Korean *tae kwon do* is one of several uniquely Far Eastern self-defense tactics. Some of the other similar methods are judo, kung fu, karate, and a style of fencing called *kendo*. The Korean tae kwon do is a highly developed form of kicking, punching, and skilled grappling with an adversary. It does not involve weapons. Many of the other Far Eastern methods of self-defense, especially the Japanese, do use weapons such as swords, *kyudo* (archery), and they adapted firearms when they became available. Still others trained the peasants in self-defense by utilizing everyday agricultural tools and knives. One form of Chinese exercises called *tai chi* does not necessarily involve any physical resistance but rather prepares the individual for a state of utilizing the entire body in a combination self-defense and mental conditioning exercise.

Virtually all the Far Eastern self-defense techniques stress the mental preparation, usually by practicing meditation. The trainee is urged to know and understand their weaknesses, then to concentrate on overcoming them. This mental and spiritual development is every bit as important as the physical development. They often stress the ultimate development of every part of both the mind--through spiritual exercises--and the body-- through physical exercises. The object is to train the body to react completely without even thinking about the action. Even diet may be included in the complete program. Nearly all of the self-defense methods are closely tied to Taoism and Buddhism.

The "righteous armies" of Korea had begun centuries before in the heroic defense of their homeland against the many invasions of the Mongols, especially during the 13th century. Even though the Mongols probably slaughtered as many as twenty million Korean people, the Koreans continued to conceive ways of killing the hated invaders. The Korean court held out on Khanghwa Island for an entire generation without considering surrender. They concluded it was better to resist and die than it was to submit and live the remainder of their lives in a state of dishonor. All of the Far Eastern self-defense systems are strong on maintaining one's personal honor.

This same spirit of self-defense was developed again by the "righteous armies" in their fight against the Japanese. The Neo-Confucians had been opposed to many of the tae kwon do principles during their long years of peace, but enough of the basics had been kept alive by private individuals and by several of the Buddhist monasteries to form a basis of resistance to the Japanese invaders in the 16th century. This spirit of fighting against the most uneven odds was also characteristic of the "turtle navy" when on one occasion twelve Korean ships challenged about three hundred Japanese ships--and won!

THE LONG RANGE OUTCOME OF THE JAPANESE-KOREAN WAR

There were several long range effects of the war between Japan and Korea from 1592 to 1598. One of these was that the Yi dynasty never fully recovered from the event. They seemed unable to check the Japanese advance in any way. Had it not been for the guerrilla tactics of the "righteous armies," which had been organized on a local militia basis, and the "turtle ships" of Admiral Yi Sun-sin, the Koreans would have surely become a reluctant addition to Japanese territory.

The general Korean public had suffered terribly during this war. Their crops and livestock had been devastated either by battles or by the Japanese foraging parties. The Japanese often resorted to a scorched earth policy of burning the countryside as they advanced. This included everything from peasant huts to temples and public buildings. Entire cities were put to the torch, destroying many priceless ancient treasures of art and culture. Many important Buddhist manuscripts were lost as a consequence of the war with Japan from 1592 to 1598.

More importantly, thousands of people had died of either direct military action or of starvation. Tax revenues fell off by two-thirds, a circumstance which placed the Yi dynasty in great economic jeopardy. Many ordinary landowners lost their land due to their inability to pay the rising taxes. This land was purchased inexpensively by the *yangban* officials or by the various members of the Yi family dynasty. This allowed the *yangban* to build a landed aristocracy similar to that which had existed at the beginning of the Yi dynasty except that the land was held by the civil servants rather than by the royal aristocrats and the Buddhists.

This war also had a huge impact on the general course of East Asian history. The Koreans came to realize how weak they really were compared to the Japanese. They also realized that they would almost surely have lost the war had it not been for the sudden death of Hideyoshi and the assistance of the Ming Chinese. But while the Chinese were assisting the Koreans, the **Jurchen Manchu invasions** began to occur on China's northeast borders. Although the Ming had given good military assistance to the Koreans, they seemed unable to stop the flow of Manchurians into their northeast provinces. Ultimately, these people took over all of China as the Manchu or Qing dynasty.

By 1627, the Manchus under General Nurhachi were able to force Korea to give up their alliance with the Ming and to shift sides. The *shu-kuo* arrangement with Ming China was dead. It was a second military-diplomatic defeat coming within a few short years after their defeat by Japan. At the same time, Japan came to assume an overly inflated view of themselves and a generally aggressive attitude toward their neighbors, China and Korea.

SINIFICATION AND BUDDHISM

Throughout the period of Silla unification, only the framework of the Chinese political model was adopted, but interest in other aspects of Chinese civilization had been more pronounced. New ideas in medicine and astronomy fascinated the Koreans, as did the Chinese science of **geomancy**. By this pseudoscience the Chinese tried to explain all aspects of the universe and our daily lives by what they considered a "scientific" approach. This involved the drawing of lines on paper--sometimes connecting dots drawn at random with lines--in order to predict the future. They believed that the proper combinations of dots and lines could determine the best day for a wedding, the best day to plant crops, or the very center of the universe. Chinese and Korean scholars began to exchange information in all of these areas. Culture was definitely migrating from China into Korea.

A brisk trade brought Chinese textiles, weapons, and artistic crafts to Korea. Most significant among the trade items were the Chinese books. It was through the Chinese books, as well as the Korean students who traveled to China, that a further knowledge of Confucianism, Buddhism, and other concepts were transmitted. Because the Koreans did not have their own written language, all Korean scholarship was recorded in Chinese characters. Slowly and in a cumbersome form, the Koreans devised a system by which selected Chinese characters were used to serve as a syllabary to transcribe Korean words.

THE ARTS IN KOREAN

The artistic talent of the early Koreans was established long before the arrival of Buddhism. Subterranean tombs of the pre-Buddhist period, hidden for centuries from pilferage, have revealed numerous gold objects with jade and imported blue glass ornamentation. The golden crowns, bracelets, rings, buckles, and similar items of personal luxury, were apparently common among the upper classes in Korea and suggest a richly talented society led by a wealthy aristocracy.

Once Buddhism was introduced to Korea in the late 4th century, Buddhist art followed and dominated cultural creativity thereafter. We can also see in Korea the persistence of cultural influences as Buddhism and its art spread from India. The Hellenistic forms of Gandhara sculpture, art, and learning--accompanied with the modifications which were made in Inner Asia and China--have all been recognized in Korea.

Since Buddhism was first experienced in the early Koguryo period, it is in that early period that the first examples of Korean Buddhist art have been found. Ceramic figures of the Buddha and various bodhisattvas, show a decided Chinese Han influence. The cultural migration from China also brought colorful wall paintings, especially in the tombs. These tomb paintings illustrate both impressions of the supernatural world and events of their daily life. Musical reed, string, and percussion instruments from Inner and East Asia were brought to Koguryo. All of these seem to have inspired dancers who are depicted on the wall paintings. Architectural strides were also rapid with both pyramid tombs and stone columns, all of which indicates a highly sophisticated engineering ability.

In Paekche, Buddhism was introduced only a dozen years later than in Koguryo, and by the 6th century it had reached even greater heights. Gilt bronze Buddhas and bodhisattvas were made, which were obviously influenced by the styles of southern China and the Northern Wei. But the greatest advance in Buddhist art occurred after the Silla had unified the peninsula. Numerous monasteries, skillfully erected, have paintings and statuary that reflect the creativity of the period. While the perishable wooden structures and paintings have largely succumbed to wars and accidents, stone-carved Buddhas, lanterns, and animals, as well as metal figures and huge monastery bells, all remain. Some of these objects are exceptionally large. The oldest bell from the Silla period dates from 725, and weighs over 3,000 pounds. The various influences from Inner Asia are also numerous during the period of the Silla dynasty.

In addition to the Buddhist art, other skills were developed in the period of the Silla dynasty. Cloisonne was developed in the 6th and 7th century. Woodblock printing is believed to have begun in the mid-eighth century. Numerous examples of pottery, largely unglazed and with simple designs, are also among Silla's artifacts.

THE KOREAN LITERARY DEVELOPMENT

The early system of writing Korean words in Chinese, known as **Hyangch'al**, was in use in the 6th century. It was especially important in the recording of Buddhist chants so that the magical power inherent in the incantations would not be lost. Prose writing in this period was largely narrative, and the powers of Buddhist priests and dragons that were believed to give guidance to men were prominent themes. One of the best examples of the scholarly tradition of the Silla period was the work done by **Ch'oe Ch'iwon** (d.857). As a young man he lived in China and gained entrance to the T'ang bureaucracy for ten years. After his return to Silla, he worked briefly in the government, but resigned and wandered around until he settled in a monastery in the southeast. Many of his writings commemorated Buddhist monks, a fact which brought further recognition to this popular religion. His Chinese-style poetry had a lasting audience.

The absorption of Chinese culture, dominated by Buddhist influences, and the creative art that it stimulated in many areas, established a consistent pattern. While the basic forms were adopted, those that clashed too strongly with the native experience were modified to be more Korean. It was an innovative rather than a wholesale duplication of Chinese culture which became characteristic of the "borrowing" experience. As this Buddhist-dominated culture from

Yi Dynasty Korea

China was transmitted to Japan, often via Korea, the Japanese continued the Korean practice of altering the Korean culture to suit their cultural choices. Curiously, it was from Korea--and by Korea--that a high percentage of Chinese culture made its way across the Korea Strait to Japan.

SUMMARIZING KOREAN HISTORY & CULTURE TO 1600

Since the Korean peninsula stands at a geographic crossroads of East Asia, a point where Chinese, Japanese, Manchurian and later the Russian cultures try to mix with the native cultures of the peninsula, it was inevitable that there would be controversy and conflict. The Chinese and the Japanese each wanted to exercise the dominant control of this geographic area. The Chinese, just across the Yalu River, were unquestionably the dominant influence through the Han period. By the early Ming era, China adopted what they referred to as the *shu-kuo* principle of a dominant China in a protective "big brother" role. During the same period the Japanese sent many merchants and colonists into the southern end of the Korean peninsula to act as an internal force to persuade the Koreans that Japan was their best friend. At the same time, many Japanese pirates continued to raid into Korea's coastal area.

As time passed a high percentage of the Koreans favored the quieter Chinese approach to the bombastic and forceful nature of the Japanese contacts. By the early Yi dynasty, beginning in 1592, it seemed that the Chinese had won their point. Throughout all of Korean history, there have been factions which have supported one foreign group or another.

It is also important to remember that even though northern Korea during the Lo-lang period was dominated by Chinese cultural pressures until as late as 313, and the peninsula was formally invaded by the Japanese in the late 16th century, the Koreans have always thought of themselves as first as **Koreans**. Like the Japanese, the Koreans do import foreign cultural ideas, but they have rather successfully "Koreanized" the imports. That has included both Buddhism and Confucianism.

From the early 4th century until the beginning of the Yi dynasty in 1592, the Buddhists exercised the most control over the people by infiltrating the higher government circles. They were certainly the power behind the throne through the Koryo period while the Confucianists were pushed into the background. With the Yi dynasty the roles were reversed. The Buddhists were in disfavor and the Neo-Confucianists filled the civil service offices and became the intellectual power behind the throne. Offices were given out by civil service exams, and often land was granted along with the office, to create a new *yangban* class. As the Yi dynasty progressed over time, the Neo-Confucianists became just as much a burden to good government as the Buddhists had been in earlier times. Nevertheless, the Neo-Confucians forced the Buddhists to build their temples in rural areas. For many years Buddhist monks were even forbidden to enter Seoul for fear they would stir some subversive activity. The *yangban* virtually closed the civil service to those of lower social estate than themselves.

The Koreans adapted many other aspects of Chinese culture besides Buddhism and Confucianism. The Chinese techniques of casting bronze and working with ceramic products were often improved upon by the Koreans to such an extent that their work was some of the finest in the world in both fields. Many aspects of natural science were also imported into Korea from China. One of their most important imports was the invention of printing with moveable type. This led to a kind of Korean renaissance in learning during the Yi dynasty.

Yi Dynasty Korea

One aspect of the Chinese learning which the Koreans did **not** appreciate was the Chinese system of writing. In 1443 the Koreans invented their own alphabet--called *Onmun* with 28 letters--which was designed to replace the Chinese writing. It was based on a phonetic system taken from the spoken Korean. The Neo-Confucian scholars, often known as the *literati*, who had been schooled in the Chinese classics were extremely critical of the new "common" alphabet, but the writing system has endured to the present. This has led to a dual system whereby the classics are studied in the old system, but all other composition is done in the new alphabet.

The writing system is an excellent example of Korea's dependence upon their Chinese neighbors for so much of their scholarship but adapting it to their own patriotic and nationalistic purposes. The Japanese invasions of 1592 and 1597 nearly wrecked their country but the Japanese were impressed with the workmanship of the Korean master craftsmen and forcibly removed them when they left the peninsula in 1598. These men were taken to Japan to train Japanese craftsmen in bronze casting and especially in the field of ceramics. Many books and manuscripts, along with the process of printing with moveable type, were also taken to Japan where they provided a tremendous enrichment of the Japanese culture during the Tokugawa period.

BOOKS FOR FURTHER READING

Berger, Carl, *The Korean Knot: A Military-Political History* (1964).

Eckert, Carter J., *et. al, Korea Old and New: A History* (1990).

Fairbank, John, Reischauer, Edwin, & Craig, Albert, *East Asia: Tradition and Transformation* (1989).

Ha, Tae-Hung, *Guide to Korean Culture* (1968).

Henthorn, William E., *A History of Korea* (1971).

Henthorn, William E., *Korea: The Mongol Invasions* (1963).

Joe, Wanne J., *Traditional Korea: A Cultural History* (1972).

Ki-baik Lee, *A New History of Korea* (1953).

McCune, Shannon, *Korea's Heritage, A Regional and Social Geography* (1956).

Myers, Bernard S., & Copplestone, Trewin, *The History of Asian Art* (1987).

Palais, James B., *Politics and Policy in Yi Dynasty Korea* (1980).

EARLY JAPAN TO 1600

Chapter 34
THE GEOGRAPHY OF THE ISLAND NATION

INTRODUCTION TO THE JAPANESE ISLANDS

It is virtually impossible to begin a study of Japan in either prehistoric or modern times without a consideration of their geographic separation from the great Eurasian land mass. Japan is a group of nearly four thousand islands which form an arc from northeast to southwest along the coast of Eurasia for a distance of 1,735 miles. Many of the islands are totally uninhabitable. About 95 percent of the people live in the four main islands--**Hokkaido, Honshu, Shikoku,** and **Kyushu.** The settlement of the Japanese islands began before the last Ice Age but the ancestors of the Japanese people who inhabit the islands today arrived in much more recent history than the people who inhabit the Eurasian mainland. Much of Japan's culture flowed from China via Korea to Japan.

GEOGRAPHY AS A FACTOR IN THE HISTORY OF JAPAN

The people who inhabit Japan today originally came from China, Manchuria, and Korea thousands of years ago. The very nature of their isolation across the Sea of Japan from the Eurasian land mass has given them a separate identity from their distant relatives on the mainland. Japan may very well be thought of as a nation with a separate eastern identity from the people of China or Korea in much the same way as England, which is geographically positioned on the far western end of the Eurasian continent. In the case of England, they are located only 21 miles across the Channel from the coast of France. Japan is located approximately 120 miles from the Eurasian continent at the Straits of Tsushima. This has not only given the Japanese a separate cultural identity, but has allowed them to develop a far different and more unique eastern culture than the difference between England's culture and that of western Europe. Whereas England has often **wanted** to be considered a part of Europe, Japan has never aggressively pursued a desire to be like China or Korea even though they have borrowed heavily from those cultures.

All of the islands of Japan have literally risen from the sea by volcanic action. Of Japan's 265 volcanoes 36 are considered possibly active, although only 20 are recorded as having erupted since 1900. The best known of all of Japan's volcanoes is Mount Fujiyama, better known simply as Mt. Fuji, with an elevation of 12,389 feet. It last erupted in 1707 and is now considered dormant. The Showa-Shinzan volcano on Hokkaido just became active in 1944. All of the Japanese islands are simply mountains formed by once active volcanoes which began erupting beneath the sea and continued spewing out lava until they rose above sea level. The islands actually stand in two of the deepest trenches of the sea--the Japan Trench, which is 27,600 feet below sea level, and the Bonin Trench, which is 33,926 feet below sea level.

Tens of thousands of years ago the Japanese islands were joined to the mainland, but over several thousands of years, the Sea of Japan has risen since the last Ice Age, thus separating the island chain from the mainland. The rising of the sea, the volcanic action, and the shifting of the huge plates beneath the earth's surface has made Japan exceptionally prone to earthquakes. The

The Geography of Japan

shaking of the earth topples the fragile, combustible homes onto the hibachi burners used for cooking and heating. Gas lines also rupture from the shocks. A very serious earthquake on September 1, 1923, started a fire which destroyed most of the Tokyo area. The reports said that over 100,000 people lost their lives, but by 1930 the city was largely rebuilt. As a consequence, Japan was one of the first nations in the world to begin dictating building construction codes to make their buildings--particularly the multi-story buildings-- earthquake-proof, so far as possible. As many as 1,500 earthquake shocks per year have been recorded, but many of them are very slight.

The distance from the north edge of Hokkaido Island to the southern end of the Ryuku Islands is roughly the distance from Quebec in Canada to Palm Beach in Florida. This distance gives Japan a great variation in climate. Tokyo, for instance, is in roughly the same latitude as New York and Chicago in the United States, but the climate is much milder. Compared to Europe, Tokyo is about the same latitude as Gibraltar in southern Spain, but the climate is generally cooler. Since the entire nation is surrounded by water, temperature extremes are moderated.

The summer rains and the winter snows develop over the Sea of Japan and the Pacific Ocean. Japan has an interesting combination of monsoon rains in June and July in the southern latitudes and heavy winter snows along the coast of the Sea of Japan in the wintertime. The weather on Hokkaido Island in the north is influenced by the Siberian Highs, which sweep across the Sea of Japan and can dump as much as 24 feet of snow in a single winter. These winds from the northwest can also drop temperatures to as low as minus 30 degrees Fahrenheit. This leads to collapsed roofs and other major problems associated with winter weather. The heaviest snows and the heaviest rains fall on Japan's coastal area facing the Sea of Japan.

Farther to the south, the frost line is in the Tokyo area, depending upon the weather, and wintry storms can sweep into the Tokyo area as late as March or April, sometimes dropping snow on the city. Hard freezes are not normally experienced very far south of Tokyo. Most of the winter months are normally bright and clear with little rain or snow, but strong, cold winds in the winter are a characteristic of the Tokyo area. Southern Japan depends upon the spring and early summer rains, along with the snow melt, to provide water for their rice crop. Since the rivers are short and often go rushing out to sea, it is difficult to build large reservoirs for water storage for the cultivation of rice or other crops.

The southern islands of Japan, Kyushu and the Kuriles, are frost free and farming continues around the calendar. All of Japan is likely to experience **typhoons**, especially during August and September. Kyushu and the Kanto plain are the areas most at risk. Three or four typhoons per year are not unusual.

The weather in Japan is influenced by many factors--the sea, the altitude, the latitude, the air currents, and the water currents. The warm **Japan Current** moves northeast along the coast of Japan and warms the eastern shores of the islands very much as the Atlantic Gulf Stream warms the coast of Florida. At the same time, a second ocean current, which is cold, moves southward from Siberia into the Sea of Japan and around both sides of Hokkaido Island.

The Japanese climate is also influenced by the mountains, which form the central spine of the islands. Although Japan has many of the characteristics of monsoon Asia in the southern islands, the four main islands do experience all four seasons comparable to those in North

The Geography of Japan

America and Europe. Winter descends upon Japan about mid-December, but by early February, there are signs of an early spring. The temperatures never fall to freezing in Okinawa far to the south, but Hokkaido does not experience spring until six to eight weeks after Tokyo.

Japan is about one-twentieth the size of the United States and less than one-fifth of that is tillable. It almost seems that nature added the tillable soil as an afterthought. The majority of the people have always lived on the fertile plains since before recorded history. The **Kanto Plain** of the Tokyo area and south is the most important with one-fourth of the Japanese population living in that area today. The Kanto Plain is far enough south that some farming continues the year around on its roughly 5,000 square miles of area. Large areas are now covered with permanent plastic greenhouses while other farmers use temporary greenhouses which are set up on the rice paddies once the crop is removed at harvest. The greenhouses produce vegetables during the chilly winter months until it is time to begin another season of planting rice.

The **Kansi Plain** of about 500 square miles is much smaller. It is located in the Kyoto-Nara-Osaka area. The Kansi Plain was one of the earliest areas of settlement in Japan and was known in earlier Japanese history as the **Yamato Plain**. There are three or four other smaller plains areas of level soil, every one of which is utilized to its fullest potential. The land surface of Hokkaido is rolling in many places, but most of it is not beyond agriculture. Beyond these areas, some have terraced the mountainside, which was popular in the ages preceding World War II. Since that time there has been an increasing amount of mechanization of agriculture and some terraced areas have even been abandoned as impractical because the farmers cannot use their expensive mechanical implements. Rice is the favorite grain crop, except in the north, where the farmers grow wheat.

Japan's total coastline is longer than that of the United States. It is no surprise, therefore, that the people have engaged in fishing and trade from the earliest times. There are a few plains along the coastal areas which are also suitable for farming. There are not many rivers and those that do exist are generally short--the longest is under 300 miles--and they are not adapted to navigation as are the rivers of mainland Eurasia. However, they do provide considerable hydroelectric power today.

It is quite obvious that such a scarcity of good tillable land restricts the grazing of large numbers of livestock. Fish and other seafood products have become the number one meat choice in Japan for many centuries. Buddhists prefer a non-meat diet, but they do allow fish in Japan. The staple foods of Japan are rice, fish, eggs, and vegetables.

The Japanese also consume many kinds of noodle dishes which are made from both rice and wheat. Soybean curd is most often mixed with many of the dishes to add nutritional value. Green tea (**cha**) is their most popular drink, along with beer (**biru**), and rice wine (**sake**). Soft drinks such as CocoCola have become popular in recent years.

Agricultural pursuits tend to concentrate on producing the staples of the Japanese diet. With about 7 percent of the land totally inaccessible and 68 percent of the surface covered with forested mountains, there is only about 13 percent of the land which can be utilized under any circumstances. Another 8 percent is suitable only for grasslands or orchards, while another 4 percent is covered with housing, factories, or transportation facilities. With so little tillable land in proportion to the population, Japan, like most of Asia, has practiced **intensive** rather than **extensive** agriculture for centuries. Again, like most of the other Asian countries, Japan's chief

The Geography of Japan

crop is the labor intensive cultivation of rice. Even Japanese rice is now harvested with combines, the only Asian country to employ machines in the place of hand labor. For the last 2,000 years the Japanese have tried to harvest two crops per year, not necessarily both rice, on plots so small they would be considered gardens by most American farmers. The government is currently trying to encourage larger plots and more mechanization instead of the intensive hand labor. In earlier times when Japan's population was smaller, the farmers owned larger tracts of land and they depended solely upon that land to produce food for themselves and for their family. Most farmers today hold a second job in the office or the factory.

Throughout most of Japan's history the population was relatively sparse compared to China, and Japan traded relatively little merchandise with China or Korea before the Christian era. Nearly all their trade was coastwise shipping with other Japanese ports until the 19th century. Farming and fishing in those times were more than just Japanese occupations--they were a profession designed for survival. Although Japan was not heavily urbanized in early times, they nevertheless depended upon agricultural surpluses to provide food for the markets of the urban areas.

Although Japan does import large quantities of food today, the Japanese farmers continue their tradition of coaxing every grain of rice from the ground and every pound of fish from their waters so that they only need to import the lowest possible amount each year. The self-sufficiency they nurtured over thousands of years has become something of an institution with their well-organized union farmers. To import food is to have failed their native land. This has also tended to control their family size through the centuries. With over 124,000,000 people, they have an annual population growth rate of only .35 percent, one of the lowest of any country in the entire world.

Figure 32

Chapter 35
PREHISTORIC JAPAN: ARCHAEOLOGY & MYTHOLOGY
INTRODUCTION TO THE EARLIEST PERIOD

The Japanese call their homeland **Nippon** or **Nihon**, which means "**The Land of the Rising Sun.**" It was Marco Polo who approximated the name of the archipelago east of China as **Chipango,** or **Zipango**. When the western cartographers described this Far Eastern land, they eventually Latinized Marco Polo's title to Japan. The Japanese accounts of their own history came much later--about the eighth century A.D. The two earliest accounts are called the *Konjiki*, 712, and the *Nihon Shoki*, 720. Neither one is considered more than pure mythology. The reason they are given serious consideration by anyone is that they contain the mythological story of the creation of Japan, the beginning of the Japanese line of emperors, and the very foundation of their national religious faith known as **Shintoism**.

A detailed account of Japanese history cannot be traced back nearly as far in Japan as it can in China or in India. This certainly does not mean that there were not any peoples in the islands but rather that we know very little about the earliest ages of Japan. Archaeology has revealed a great amount since the Second World War and there are undoubtedly many more revelations to be made in future years.

THE PALEOLITHIC AGE

Since the Japanese began writing their history somewhat late in comparison with many other countries, it is necessary to rely largely upon the archaeological record for their early history. The **Paleolithic Age** (**Paleo**=old--**lithic**=tool age) in Japan extends from about 28,000 to 10,500 B.C. During this stage of the development of mankind, the tools were adapted from natural shapes by striking one stone against another in order to fashion a better tool. Since shell mounds are associated with the Jomon sites, it is presumed they not only consumed a great amount of shellfish but that many of the shells were also fashioned into tools. It was during the Paleolithic age that the Japanese islands separated from the continental shelf about 12,000 years ago, as the ice from the last Ice Age melted and formed the Sea of Japan and the Tsushima Straits separating Japan from Korea.

During the years preceding the separation from Eurasia, the principal land bridges to the continent were at the northern and southern extremities. Temperature considerations made the southern route through Korea an easier one than the northern route. As long as the land bridge existed with Korea, it is well accepted that the earliest settlers in the Japanese archipelago came via the presentday Korean peninsula and crossed to the Japanese islands where the Tsushima Straits are now located.

Authorities believe there were many arrivals moving into the Japanese islands during these early years. Paleolithic artifacts have been unearthed at the **Iwajuku Site** on the Kanto plain. These artifacts indicate that the earliest invaders may have arrived as early as 200,000 B.C., which is well before the melting of the last glaciers. The pottery finds at this site have been dated to about 10,000 B.C., dates which antedate those generally accepted for the earliest Chinese pottery, thus indicating that the Japanese had already developed their own method of firing pottery. Core and chipped flake stone tools have been found in some of the archaeological sites which have been opened since World War II. But, as in many other areas of the world, the Paleolithic Age is still a dim and shadowy past.

We know very little about the religious beliefs of the Paleolithic inhabitants of the Japanese islands. Clay figures representing men and animals have also been found in association with the shell mounds. Since a large number of clay female figures have been found, it is believed that they practiced some early form of fertility goddess worship. All of the clay figures were fired at a comparatively low temperature. Some anthropologists believe that since several of the figures have broken limbs that their religion included some kind of sympathetic magic whereby if a person broke an arm or a leg, then the figurine was similarly broken in the belief that it would help heal the patient. There is also evidence of an increasing use of magic towards the end of the Paleolithic period. Archaeology indicates that they most likely followed an **animistic** worship of large trees, special stones, mountains, and streams. Their dead were buried in the soil in a fetal position.

The Paleolithic Japanese lifestyle was a part of the early "Hunting and Gathering" stage rather than fixed agriculture. They were far enough advanced to build houses with thatched roofs and bark walls which were partially dug into the soil. There was a hearth in the center of the floor plan, and evidently there was a hole in the roof to allow the smoke to escape. As hunters and gatherers, they would have been required to range widely for food. Their houses were, therefore, more than likely their winter place of abode or temporary hunting camps.

THE JOMON CULTURES, c.10,000 B.C.-c.200 B.C.

The **Jomon Cultures** are considered to have originated in the **Mesolithic** (Middle Stone Age), and continued into the **Neolithic Age** (New Stone Age). The **Early Jomon** began about 10,000 B.C. and extended to about 3,500 B.C.. The **Middle Jomon** was from 3,500 B.C. to 2,400 B.C., and the **Late Jomon** period extended from 2,400 B.C. to about 200 B.C.

Any form of settled agriculture is clearly lacking in the two earliest Jomon periods but was probably begun during the late period, sometime between 2,400 and 1,000 B.C. So far, this is speculation and no one can be certain. Most of the Jomon period was given over to hunting, fishing, and gathering rather than by settled agriculture as in China. Since historians and archaeologists have found many similar patterns between Jomon Japan and the early Korean period, it is believed the people passed back and forth and shared a somewhat common culture. By the Middle Jomon period the stone-polished tools were of excellent quality. The "rope pattern" pottery became so characteristic of the Jomon period that the word "**Jomon**" means "rope pattern." Their pottery style was an obvious continuation from the Paleolithic period.

Their bulbous-shaped pottery with the rope pattern was built by hand and shaped to be partially buried. All kinds of jars, both large and small, were used for storage. It also was created with a flat bottom so it would support itself. The pottery was fired at a relatively low temperature. Modern archaeologists and anthropologists believe the twisted cord was impressed on the outside of the soft clay before it was fired in order to improve the grip of the cook who might want to pick it up with greasy hands, since the people in these early times had not yet discovered the process for making soap! The clay figurines of the human form were "soft fired" in the same way as the pottery. Several hundred Jomon archaeological sites have been excavated throughout Japan and the Ryukyu Islands.

Skeletal remains indicate that the Jomon people were tall, averaging five feet six inches. Life expectancy was probably short, perhaps as little as fifteen years on the average. The numbers in the islands began to grow during this period until they were between 125,000, and at their peak, possibly 250,000. After about 5,000 B.C. the numbers began to decline for several years. Several reasons are offered as speculation for the decline.

The standard Jomon house was small with living space for about four to eight persons. There was a fire pit with an oven in the center and a makeshift grass roof. Like the Upper Paleolithic houses, these structures were evidently little more than camps built for protection between hunting expeditions. Houses of this type were most often grouped into small villages of between six and ten dwellings. In the Late Jomon period the houses came to be a little more substantially built. There were no major advancements over the Paleolithic Age.

A great amount of our knowledge of the Jomon period comes from their shell mounds (midden) called *kaizuka*. From the size of these mounds it appears that the entire community placed their shells and bones in huge heaps along with the broken tools, discarded weapons, pottery shards, and discontinued jewelry. So far there have been about 2,000 of these shell mounds located, and all are relatively well preserved in Japan's acidic soils. Over 90 percent of the animal bones which have been found were of deer and wild boar. The seafood diet included tuna, mackerel, oysters, and other mollusks. In eastern Japan they fished for salmon as well. They used hooks, harpoons, gigs, and nets. Rafts and dugout canoes served as fishing vessels. The hunters relied on polished stone and bone spears and clubs. Their technology **had** advanced to the use of the bow and arrow. The dog was the only known domesticated animal, probably trained for hunting.

THE YAYOI CULTURE, c.200 B.C. to A.D. 300

The Yayoi culture has been so named because of the Tokyo street where several examples of their more advanced pottery was first discovered in 1884. Additional finds of this style of pottery were soon discovered in other parts of Japan. Apparently this culture began on Kyushu Island and then spread to the north. As the Yayoi moved in--most likely from China--the Jomon seems to have moved nort until eventually they reached Hokkaido Island, where Jomon culture continued to survive until as late as the Meiji period in the 19th century.

The Yayoi pottery style was beautiful with simple lines. It was much more delicate than the Jomon pottery because it was created on a **potter's wheel** instead of hand-built. Some jars have scenes which were worked into the soft clay before it was fired. The Yayoi pottery was fired at a much higher temperature than the Jomon pottery, a technique which made it much more durable. The Jomon had begun placing their burials in huge jars, a practice which was continued by the Yayoi. This culture seemed to use the huge jars for the storage of all kinds of food items as well as burial jars. It is altogether possible that these jars were needed because of leaky thatched roofs as well as to keep the rats out of the stored grain. Rats were an enormous problem in all of Prehistoric Asia.

Prehistoric Japan

There were several other important changes which occurred during the Yayoi period besides the pottery. Wet-rice agriculture arrived in Japan during this six-hundred-year period, probably introduced from China or Korea. Fixed rice paddies very likely meant the eventual end of the "Hunting and Gathering" age and the beginning of Fixed Agriculture, an event which began a much more settled society. Irrigation required considerable preparation to construct dikes and canals to channel the water where it was needed, when it was needed, and in the quantity that it was needed. The beginning of wet-land rice probably occurred first in the naturally swampy areas which would not immediately have interfered with hunting, but it provided a much greater amount of inexpensive food.

With plenty of rice to eat, and wild game still abundant, the population on the islands began to increase. Within a relatively short period of time the population in Japan had outrun the food supply. This meant that more rice would need to be planted, thus forcing the farmers to level more land so it could be flooded for paddies, build more dikes, and provide for more irrigation to feed the rising population. Raised granaries and thatched-roof houses, which were durably constructed, were now frequent sights in a growing number of peasant villages. By the end of the Yayoi period, the population had risen to ten or fifteen times what it had been during the Jomon period. Wet-land rice, a rapidly increasing population, and a much more settled agriculture, therefore, all occurred within a relatively short period of time in Japan. This short evolutionary era can be compared to the long evolution of agriculture during other times in Japan as well as in other areas in Asia.

Another Yayoi innovation was a great increase in their knowledge of **metallurgy**, so much so that the Yayoi period is often referred to as **Japan's Iron Age**. Bronze had arrived in Japan sometime during the first century B.C. It was used primarily for weapons, mirrors, and ceremonial bells. Iron arrived about A.D. 200 and was quickly made available for weapons, agricultural and woodworking tools, and household uses such as knives, all of which contributed to lifting the level of civilization during this period. The iron technology is thought to have come from Korea, while much of the technology for the bronze bells and other metal items came from China. At the outset, the iron was used almost exclusively for military weapons. Japan has a small amount of iron, which was worked with charcoal in the early times. By the 19th century, the Japanese had exhausted their iron and much of their timber resources at the very moment they were entering the industrial age.

Another improvement in the Japanese lifestyle was the invention of looms used to make rough hemp cloth. As the age moved forward, both the weaving techniques and the materials improved until by the end of the Yayoi Age, the Japanese were making excellent quality textiles.

Finally, social and political organization also began to show remarkable changes during this six-hundred-year period. Social classes began to develop in the southern part of Japan while political groups formed into strong clans. The division of society into a ruling and a peasant class appeared at this time. There is also evidence of the beginning of an early system of tax collection, a sure indication that there was some form of a fixed government.

THE TUMULI CULTURE, c. A.D. 300 to 600

There were several waves of immigrants who moved to Japan from both China and Korea in these early times. The **Tumuli culture** refers to a group of several waves of migrants who arrived in Japan from Korea. They crossed the strait into Kyushu Island, then moved north to the Kansai Plain (**Yamato Plain**) around Kyoto, Nara and Osaka. Whereas the previous invaders had been more or less peaceful tribes who were looking for new opportunities, the Tumuli immigrants came as mounted warriors with helmets, armor, and iron swords. These invaders are called the "Tumuli" because of the large tombs they constructed.

They built stone tombs for their priest-kings, then covered them with large mounds of earth. They are almost identical to the stone tombs of Korea from which the warrior invaders had departed. The stone tomb of **Nintoku**, A.D. 303-399, in the Osaka area, was constructed 1,100 feet in length and over 100 feet in height with the entire area enclosed by moats. The grave goods which were placed with the body were very similar to those found in the Korean tumuli. Clay figures called *haniwa* surrounded the burial. The style of garments worn by the clay figures, as well as their weapons, tell us a great deal about how the people lived.

CHINESE-JAPANESE CONTACTS
THE YAMATAI CULTURE, c.A.D. 300-c.600

Not only were the Koreans interested in migrating to Japan, but so were the Chinese. The Chinese historians recorded their first **diplomatic** contacts with Japan as having transpired in A.D. 57, although there were probably some unrecorded diplomatic contacts before that date. During these early contacts the Chinese referred to Japan as the land of **Wa**, which means a dwarf.

One of the earliest Chinese writings which refers to Japan in any depth is entitled ***The History of the Wei Kingdom***. This portion was written about A.D. 300. It refers to the Japanese people as those who conformed closely to their laws. The record shows that agriculture and fishing predominated at that time. They described the land of **Wa** as a country having an area called **Yamatai**. This area had a warm climate, plenty of fish and grain, but no horses, cattle, or other large animals. No one is even positive where the state of Yamatai was located, but the area around modern Nara, Kyoto, and Osaka seems to have more supporters than any other.

The Chinese said that the first real ruler was a woman who was an old shaman named **Himiko** (Pimihu) who had come to power following nearly a century of warfare. She was apparently assisted by a younger brother. When Queen Himiko died, she was buried in one of the huge Tumuli graves with over one hundred slaves. A man then tried to take over and rule, but he was murdered and there was no peace until the old queen's young sister, Iyo, assumed the throne. The Chinese historians who described these events in the land of Wa also took note of the great interest of the Japanese people in the practice of tatooing the body. They seem to have regarded the Land of Wa as a rather curious place and the stories as a novelty. It is therefore uncertain how accurate their records may be.

After the Himiko period in Japan, the fighting resumed, according to ***The History of the Wei Kingdom***, but one clan, the **Sun**, seems to have been the strongest of that early period of history. Each clan appears to have claimed some divine attribute, but the Sun line claimed descent from the sun goddess **Amaterasu Omikami**. More modern research indicates that the Sun line gained their advantageous position by utilizing the technology of Korea and China in constructing more deadly weapons than their enemies.

Prehistoric Japan

It is well accepted today that most of the Yamatai political institutions centered on a complex of "clans" which were called *uji*, which means lineages. Each clan had probably formed around the various families and tribes which had moved from the mainland to Japan, each one with its own family of leaders and each with its own deity. Titles known as **Kabane** within the clans and the proper genealogical records seem to have been very important. Various occupational groups were attached to each of the powerful clans, and these occupational groups performed services or produced goods or products for the clan to which it was attached. Some of the finest artists and artisans during the Yamatai period rose in status because of their ability to create beautiful mirrors, masterpiece weapons, and other metal objects. This was evidently a well-organized society which became increasingly stratified over time. Titles and rank were extremely important to the Japanese during these years.

The late Yamatai leaders became involved in Korean affairs at the request of the Koreans. In these times the Koreans were divided into three kingdoms--the **Paekche,** the **Koguryo,** and the **Silla**. Since the Koreans often fought one another--or the Chinese--the Japanese were only too eager to assist one group against another in the hopes that they might gain a foothold in Korea. It is believed that it was through this Korean connection that the first **Buddhist** images entered Japan sometime during the 6th century. Late in the 6th century the Yamatai were replaced in Japan by the Soga clan. By this time, Buddhism had been in the process of development in Korea for centuries before its arrival in Japan. The traditional date for the introduction of Buddhism into Japan is 587. The Buddhists in Japan urgently pressed to replace the native Japanese faith--**Shintoism**.

SHINTO--THE WAY OF THE GODS

According to the sacred Shinto scriptures--the **Konjiki** and the **Nihon Shoki**--there were many gods who lived in the heavens. One day two of them decided to descend to earth. These were **Izanagi** and his younger sister **Izanami**. At that time the earth was only a mass of brine-- some accounts say it was formless primeval mud. The gods in heaven commanded Izanagi and Izanami to solidify the earth from the briny deep. As they stood on the bridge which connected heaven and earth, they lowered their jeweled spear into the brine, or mud. As they lifted the spear, the drops which fell from the spear formed the Japanese island of Onogoso. The couple then came on down the bridge from heaven and erected a heavenly pillar. As one went around the pillar one way, the other came around the other. When they met, they began to procreate. The consequence of their procreation was the birth of the other islands of the Japanese archipelago. They then named each island as it was born.

When they had completed this task, there were the heavens above with its many gods and goddesses, the earth below, and the underworld beneath. The gods and goddesses traveled between all three realms until one day a huge earthquake rolled a stone across the entrance to the underworld and the bridge to heaven was shaken and broken.

After forming the islands of Japan, Izanagi and Izanami began to give birth to the **Three Illustrious Children** of Japanese mythology--the **sun goddess**, the **moon goddess**, and the **storm** (wind) **goddess**. Izanami died in the process of giving birth to fire. Izanagi was quite upset about his wife/sister's death. He decided to follow her to the underworld. However, he discovered that this was a very unclean place and he realized that he was terribly contaminated simply by being there. He began washing and cleansing himself in an effort to again become a

Prehistoric Japan

pure god. As he washed his left eye he gave birth to **Amaterasu**, the **sun goddess**. She is the most important of all the Japanese goddesses. As Izanagi washed his right eye he produced the **moon goddess**, Gakko-bosatsu. When he washed his nose he produced the **wind** or storm **goddess** named Susanoo. In addition to these three goddesses, there is a large pantheon of other Shinto gods and goddesses.

The sun goddess--Amaterasu--had many escapades with the moon goddess and the storm goddess. Ultimately, Amaterasu had a family. Her grandson's name was **Jimmu Tenno** who became the first Emperor, or **Mikado**, of Japan. The rulers who had preceded Jimmu Tenno have always been characterized as mighty warriors. Jimmu Tenno was different from the other warriors because his grandmother was Amaterasu, the sun goddess. This made him a divine god, a Shinto belief which was not tarnished since his birth, **February 11, 660 B.C.** (the first day of Spring) at Kashiwara, the first capital of the Yamato state of Japan. Interestingly, the date for Jimmu Tenno's birth was arrived at by using a Chinese calendar for calculation.

The Japanese histories claim that as head of the Yamato state, Jimmu Tenno ruled over 121 political units in Japan. It will be mentioned later that there were periods in Japan's history when the emperors did lose their military might and their political power in the centuries following 660 B.C., but the emperor was **always** considered the divine embodiment of the gods here upon earth until the close of the Second World War, 1945.

Since 1945 there are many Japanese who are very confused about their national religion. The nation continues to be referred to as the **Land of the Rising Sun**, and the symbol of the sun is still on the national flag. The emperor is highly revered, but he has not been considered divine since Hirohito gave up that aspect of his power at the end of the war. Japan was required to disestablish Shintoism as the national faith because it was considered too nationalistic and too militaristic. Shinto shrines are no longer maintained by taxes, but rather by freewill offerings. Some believed the temples would fall into a state of disrepair and vanish with time, but they have been well maintained.

It is interesting that in the very early prehistoric times the Japanese do not seem to have even had a word for religion. When writing appeared in the 8th century, they began assembling the earliest copies of the sacred scriptures. These were completed in A.D. 712, quite late in comparison with the other great religious faiths. Writing was not invented by the Japanese but was borrowed instead from the Chinese. And, along with the Chinese writing came Buddhism, Confucianism, and Taoism. Add these new religions to the Shinto belief with the emperor as the grandson of the sun goddess, combined with the animistic nature worship which the Japanese people had practiced for generations, and it is easy to see the manner in which the complex religious beliefs of the modern Japan began to unfold.

Like Judaism, Shintoism is inextricably bound up with history. Prior to World War II the Japanese child was born into this complex of religious beliefs which have been tied to their national history. It was a kind of Manifest Destiny of the race, the faith, and the nation. All of this was drilled into Japanese children from birth. All else in life must accommodate to this one concept of a national religion. It overpowered both Buddhism and Christianity. It tended to overlay and to undergird all other beliefs. The state religion was always **first**! Since the Second World War the Japanese have reshaped their nationalistic image and have reconsidered their religious beliefs. It is a process which continues to the present time.

Prehistoric Japan

Another facet of Shintoism inculcated a profound love of nature. The very stones and flowers, the trees and streams of Japan, all are associated with rituals and prayers which had special meaning for them. The adoration of the rising sun was followed traditionally since Jimmu Tenno ascended the throne to become the first emperor in 660 B.C. The date 660 B.C. is also the **Year One** of the Japanese era.

Since Amaterasu, the sun goddess, had given birth to the ancestor of the first emperor, sunrise became a favorite time of day for young and old alike in Japan. Many still rise early to greet the morning sun while others go to the Shinto temple to seek a blessing for the coming day. There are many temples, all very beautifully and naturally set upon and within the landscape in order to capture the maximum beauty of the rising sun. Even houses are often arranged to take the greatest advantage of the rising sun. These principles of Shintoism were magnified further by the Taoist philosophy of leaving nature undisturbed whenever possible.

The Shinto temples have no idols and no images. People **do** bring offerings such as mirrors, food, or spears, as well as leaving money. They pray for their immediate needs. They adore **Amaterasu-om Kami** not only for the sunrise, but for all things that grow or flow. Flowers, forests, and streams are considered especially significant. These are also the most preferred subjects for an artist to paint, songwriters to eulogize, photographers to photograph, and many prayers are offered along the same theme. It is therefore fair to say that the beauty of nature has become a part of the Shinto religion. It is more than something to be admired; it must be experienced. Whatever is beautiful in nature **is** the Divine.

The Shintoist's love of nature cannot be overemphasized. There is no better way to learn this faith than to be in intimate contact with nature and to rely upon it as a teaching and a healing power. Since the Japanese have taken far better care of their environment than most areas in the West, one need not seek after the divine because they endeavor to be surrounded by it. Thousands of parks are available throughout the country where people can go to seek solitude and meditation. They believe that there is no evil in nature. That which is evil has been caused by the fact that people have abused the balance of nature. All natural appetites are good. They only become evil when they are indulged in to excess.

There are several other characteristics of Shintoism which tend to set it apart from other religious faiths, not because other faiths do not believe in the same principles, but because Shintoism places a special emphasis upon them. They condemn theft and lying, incest and adultery, bestiality and witchcraft. That is because such practices are **not** the way of nature.

Shintoism has the *Code of the Knight*, also known as the *Code of Bushido*. According to this code the true believers should always have **courage**. They teach courage to the children as early as they can understand the concept. Children who cry when they are injured are reprimanded. They teach their children that "it is true courage to live when it is right to live, and to die when it is right to die." **Cowardice** is condemned as a sin. The Shintoist would say that all sins, great and small, may be forgiven except two: cowardice and theft. And, along with courage is **loyalty**. Until recently, a Shintoist's first loyalty was to the emperor. After this it extended to members of one's immediate family, to the community, and to future generations.

Cleanliness also has a special place in the Shinto ritual. It is very important to be purified at a Shinto temple. Most Shinto temples are near a stream or a lake to make purification a simple matter. To be unclean is considered a sin, it is an offense to the gods. An outgrowth of this approach has made bathing in Japan both a purification and a religious rite. The bathroom in each home is intended to be an inviting place. Many people spend as much as two hours bathing between the hours of five and seven preceding the evening meal. There are fixed ceremonies concerning bathing. There are even holidays which are devoted to bathing.

Other thoughts which predominate Shinto thinking is the concept that life is good. The gods have been good to Japan and to its people. There should be no place for grumbling or complaining. Whatever may seem impossible today will all be less important tomorrow.

In addition to the above concepts of Shintoism there are several other fundamental beliefs. An individual should not transgress the will of the gods. They believe that to honor the goodness of the gods will avert misfortune and heal the sick. Confucianism crept in to remember one's obligations to the ancestors. It is also very important to never transgress the decrees of the State. Even though others become angry, we should learn to control our own anger and never forget that each person has limitations. If one engages in business, it should always be done with energy, never slothful--if it is worth doing at all, it is worth doing right. Be wary of foreign teaching. Select that which is good and cast out everything else. Finally, never bring blame upon Shintoism.

Portions of the nature worship practiced by many of the rural people came from the early animistic religions of the country people. Later, Shintoism absorbed elements of Confucianism, Taoism, and Buddhism. Since the mid-nineteenth century Shintoism has been torn between the old ways and the modern ways. During the Heian period, 794 to 1185, Shinto stressed courtly elegance. When the Kamakura period arrived, 1185 to 1333, the austere approach of the bold and courageous warrior came to predominate. It was the age of the **Samurai** warrior. There have been several occasions when the Shinto followers have tried to root out Buddhism altogether, but they found the faith too firmly entrenched. The Tokugawas tried to maintain a tight control over this very nationalistic faith because they saw it as the central philosophy to absolute control. Much of this approach reappeared in the period from the late 19th century through the Second World War.

By the close of the 17th century there were several Shinto sects which endeavored to merge Shintoism with Neo-Confucianism. Beginning in the 18th century there was a classical revival wherein scholars researched ancient Japanese art, poetry, and literature. These scholars were called "*Kokugaku*" which meant "Japanese Studies." One of these scholars, Kamo Mabauchi, 1697-1769, wanted Shintoists to reject both Buddhist and Confucian applications in an effort to purify the faith. Many poor and oppressed men and women were convinced that they should join the Kokugaku reform movement.

When the Meiji came to power in 1867, they favored the concept of the unity of religion and the state. They also wanted to see the complete modernization of Japan. The following year, 1868, the department of Shinto was established. They issued an edict designed to abolish the common pattern of Buddhist-Shinto coexistence. Buddhist priests who had been connected with Shinto shrines must either return to lay life or be reordained as Shinto priests. The following year, 1869, the department of Shinto was made independent of the cabinet and placed above the Grand Council of State. In 1871, Shintoism was proclaimed the **national religion**. Shinto shrines were decreed the proper place of worship for all subjects, and everyone was ordered to worship the emperor. All Shinto priests were to be appointed by the government from 1871 on. Emperor worship was stressed more and more throughout Japan. Even though the Meiji dynasty wanted to kill Buddhism by issuing these decrees, Buddhism survived. Many ordinary citizens built small Shinto shrines in one corner of a room. It was considered a very loyal and patriotic thing to do.

THE AINU

The earliest inhabitants in the islands of Japan were, so far as we know, the **Ainu**. Another early inhabitant of the islands was referred to in the literature as the **Emishi**, who may or may not have been related to the Ainu. No one knows when these early people arrived or where they came from, but they do have Caucasian features such as fair skins, more hair than most Oriental people, and some have blue eyes. They lived a subsistence life by hunting and gathering and seem to have made little progress in developing Japan in the early years. Although they once inhabited the four main islands, they were pushed northward by the later invaders from China, Manchuria, and Korea in very much the same manner as the American Indian was constantly pushed westward during the settlement of the United States.

The Ainu religion has always been strongly **animistic** with the conviction that the world is filled with spiritual forces called **kami** which control our every move. The Japanese government began to try to integrate the Ainu into their society as early as the Tokugawa era, 1603-1868. All of those who have wanted to remain separate from the mainstream have been moved to Hokkaido in modern times. About 24,000 continue to claim that they are Ainu, but only about 200 of them have a good grasp of their people's culture. The Japanese government has made some effort since World War II to save some of the Ainu culture, but much has been lost already. The problem is further complicated by the fact that these people never developed a written language. Most Ainu today are content to join the mainstream of Japanese culture and to forget their past.

IN SUMMARY

The Prehistoric period in Japan is the very foundation upon which modern Japan rests today. Even though the majority of the original settlers almost certainly came from China, Korea, and Manchuria, by the close of the Prehistoric period the inhabitants let it be known that "foreigners" were not welcome. As a consequence, the Japanese have been selective about the foreign people and culture which they have allowed into their island nation. Religions such as Buddhism, Taoism, Confucianism, and finally Christianity, when they have come to Japan have been allowed into the country on a selective basis. Writing, art, music, and many other cultural aspects are also imports from continental Asia, but they have come in on Japanese terms. They think of their race as relatively pure. Japanese intermarriage with outsiders is politely condoned in recent years, but not totally accepted.

Shinto is no longer the national religion but many Japanese still patronize the Shinto temples and believe in the basic tenents of the faith. Others are not ready to opt for another one of the religious faiths in Japan with the consequence that since World War II there are many Japanese who do not claim any religious faith. History is still very important to the Japanese people. Virtually all Japanese are very protective of their homeland. They do not want to be corrupted by outside influences which may come if more people arrive and take up permanent residence as businessmen. This is one reason why Japan is reluctant to allow western countries to

Prehistoric Japan

operate freely within their borders, even though they are pleased to open businesses in other countries. Japan has probably made more radical changes in its lifestyle and culture since 1945 than it had in all the years before 1945.

It is possible that all the inhabitants of Japan, including the Ainu, have arrived as immigrants. For hundreds of years the daily routine was based upon subsistence agriculture--just one step ahead of starvation. Education and learning were strictly secondary considerations. Consequently, Japan lacks an early written history of their own. They supported a relatively small population on the sparse soil which nature had endowed them. The aristocrats spent a considerable amount of time in warfare while the peasant farmers worked long hours to support themselves and the way of life enjoyed by the aristocrats. Each nobleman hoped to some day control all of the Yamato Plain in southern Honshu. Japan did move from the Hunting and Gathering stage to fixed agriculture, but at a much later date than in India, China, or Korea.

BOOKS FOR FURTHER READING

Carmody, Denise L., & Carmody, John T., *Ways to the Center: An Introduction to World Religions* (1993).

Collcutt, M., Jansen, M., & Kumakura, I., *Cultural Atlas of Japan* (1991).

Earhart, H. Byron, *Japanese Religion: Unity and Diversity* (1982).

Fenton, John Y., *et. al., Religions of Asia* (1988).

Hall, John W., *Japan from Prehistory to Modern Times* (1970).

Meyer, Milton W., *Japan: A Concise History* (1993).

Reischauer, Edwin O., *Japan: The Story of a Nation* (1981).

Reischauer, E.O., Fairbank, J.K., & Craig, A.M., *East Asia: Tradition & Transformation* (1989).

Ross, F.H., & Hills, T., *The Great Religions by Which Men Live* (1956).

Sansom, George B., *A History of Japan*, 3 Volumes (1963).

Smith, Huston, *The Religions of Man* (1986).

Figure 33

Chapter 36
THE EARLY HISTORY OF JAPAN TO A.D. 710

YAMATO JAPAN, c.400-c.700

It should be obvious at this point that Japan was slower in the overall chronology of world history in developing their civilization than was the case in some of the other major nations such as India, China, and Korea. Japan had begun to develop an early agricultural economy in the late Neolithic period, but to move from a **culture** to a **civilization** it was first necessary to develop cities and to have a written language. It should also be noted that Japan's early culture developed in varying places throughout the island archipelago and at different times, some of them overlapping.

A relatively small nobility, composed of the heads of the clans, controlled the land worked by peasants and slaves. Warfare often dominated society in those early years as they fought the native **Ainu** people for their land, then the nobility from the various clans battled one another for the control of the conquered territory. Warfare was a way of life in Japan from their earliest history, quite a contrast to the Chinese, whose civilization was based upon scholar-bureaucrats who rose to power through the Confucian educational process. The two-class system of society in Japan, and the cost of warfare, was all supported by the peasant farmers, who struggled to keep society a step ahead of starvation.

The first area of consideration in seizing precious land from one another was the most attractive farmland--the plains areas. This seemed to be the **Kansai Plain**, the area of modern Osaka-Kyoto-Nara. The **Kanto Plain** in the vicinity of presentday Tokyo was still largely under the control of the Ainu--it was Japan's frontier area. Every nobleman envisioned himself a great power who hoped to someday control not only the Kansai Plain, but all of the island of Honshu.

The first period of historical Japan did not begin until about the 5th century A.D. The early records discuss an area known as "Yamato," therefore, the entire early history of this part of Honshu can be referred to as the **Yamato Period**. The Yamato Plain (Kansai Plain) was agriculturally productive and capable of supporting the large armies of the noblemen. It was the Yamato area where the early ruler Himiko reigned, and the same area where Jimmu Tenno became the first emperor of Japan. Even though the emperor was always granted divine status, the real power in the Yamato period rested with the armed noblemen, the *uji*.

Both the *uji* nobility and the emperor were supported by their incomes from the large-scale rice lands which had been irrigated from a very early time. Since rice was not a native plant in Japan, it is believed that some Korean immigrant brought the seed to Japan about 1,000 B.C. It quickly caught on in Japan as a high yielding grain crop which would support more people than other grain crops. Within a few years, even the taxes were assessed in so many measures of rice. It required reasonably level land because of flooding and a supply of water. These were the essentials of life as well as the economy.

If an *uji* nobleman wanted to expand his economic base, he would simply try to conquer more rice land. By A.D. 500 it was recorded that the nobility had built huge log warehouses to store the surplus rice they had received in taxes. The *uji* also received tribute from fishermen, potters, weavers, and other artisans. Building or supporting a Shinto shrine during this early period was such a commendable act that several were constructed by the *uji* or the emperor. Some of the Shinto shrines became quite elaborate with such heavy financial support. Everyone wanted to have the Shinto gods on their side.

The shrines were entered through a sacred gateway built with two uprights and two crosspieces called a **torii**. A stream of running water or a lake should be available at the shrine for purification. There were many lanterns, the symbol of light favored by the sun goddess. Emperors and noblemen contributed sacred objects (*kami*) to the temple treasury, such as mirrors or swords. It was believed that these objects harbored good spirits. Every temple was favorably situated and beautifully landscaped. The ruling class made Shintoism an integral part of the religious life of Japan before the beginning of the Nara period.

THE SOGA CLAN, c.534 TO c.710

The **Soga Clan**, one of several living on the Yamato Plain, became very wealthy traders and aristocrats. By the close of the 5th century the Soga had emerged as the leading clan in Japan. They seem to have committed themselves to Buddhism and a more intense participation in the affairs of southern Korea. They were interested in learning, especially as it pertained to Buddhism.

Even before the 7th century, the Japanese had been busy at copying the Chinese culture. They were curious to know how the Chinese government and institutions functioned, even to the last detail. They then tried to place these principles in operation in Japan, sometimes with only minor modification. The principles which they borrowed from China were considered so monumental that they have often been referred to as the **Asuka Enlightenment**. Japanese missions to China continued to gather ideas about education, writing, government operations, technology, and Buddhism from the 7th into the 9th century. Such a heavy Chinese influence was soon experienced throughout Japan. This marked a sharp divide with Japan's isolated past.

While the various Japanese missions were in China, they often recruited Chinese artisans and Buddhist priests who would be willing to travel to Japan and to work there. These Chinese in Japan became leaders in teaching the Japanese the various arts and crafts, a fact which helps to explain, at least in part, why the styles are often very similar. Many Korean artisans were also recruited during this same period.

Forty-six Buddhist temples were founded during this period, including the famous **Horyuji Temple** at Nara. The Chinese priests and scholars who went to Japan also taught the Japanese their style of writing. Some of this had already begun prior to the Soga period, but it was now moving at an accelerated rate. Just as they had copied China's principles of government and craftsmanship, the Japanese also copied China's system of classical writing.

There was considerable opposition to the foreign ideas coming into Japan but the head of the Soga clan battled the opposition, killed an emperor who would not go along, and installed his neice as the ruler of Japan. Empress **Suiko**, the first woman to be invested as a ruler in Japan, ordered the court nobles to support Buddhism. Her nephew and regent, **Prince Shotoku**, 574 to 622, became the principal sponsor of Japanese Buddhism. As regent for his aunt, the Empress, he managed to destroy the leading opponents to the new faith at the court, then plunged into an extensive **Sinification** and temple building project throughout his area of control on Honshu

Island. The prefixes "sini-" and "sino-" are used to indicate things which relate to the Chinese. Although some Sinification had already taken place, because the Japanese recognized that China had a much higher level of living and culture than Japan, the pace was accelerated considerably under Prince Shotoku.

In 603 Shotoku introduced the system known as the "**twelve ranks**," a system which was in current use by Chinese court officials. This was a departure from Japanese tradition to appoint the highest governmental offices on merit. It was an old system in China and was used for the next several hundred years in Japan. The following year, 604, Shotoku adopted the Chinese calendar. This is interesting because the Chinese calendar was used to fix the date of **660 B.C.** when Jimmu Tenno came to rule over the Yamato. In 607 he sent a six hundred member commission to the Sui court to gather still more information about China. Missions of this kind continued for the next two hundred years.

The same year the Chinese calendar was adopted, Shotoku issued his "**Seventeen Article Constitution**," sometimes referred to as the "**Seventeen Injunctions.**" This document was a pronouncement of Confucian and Buddhist ethics rather than a true constitution in the western tradition. The Seventeen Articles called for a strongly centralized government with a supreme ruler to administer a bureaucracy based on merit. While Shotoku was deeply involved with reshaping the government of Japan, he gave equal attention to Buddhism.

In 593 the prince ordered **Shitennoji Temple** to be built in nearby Osaka. He then ordered the **Horyuji Temple** built in 607 near his palace in Nara, and it remains the premier temple of Japan to the present time. This is a large temple site with 45 buildings, 17 of which are classified as "major national treasures." Among the temple buildings he set up a residence and a study known as the "Hall of Dreams." Some of the buildings at Horyuji Temple now date from the early 15th century. It has been said that Horyuji Temple is the most beautiful in Japan, and they are the oldest surviving wooden buildings in the world. In those days the road from the Imperial Court passed the site of the temple. Monks carried the Buddhist religion from Horyuji Temple to all parts of Japan. It is interesting that of the 1,385 Buddhist clerics at Horyuji Temple in 614, over half were Korean.

As a consequence of his deep interest in Buddhism Shotoku is credited with being the first Japanese with the Buddhist perception of the world as illusion. Shotoku became so learned and devout in Buddhism that many Japanese still consider him a saint with superhuman powers. But not everyone in Japan was pleased with Shotoku and his Chinese and Buddhist reforms. By the year 643 there occurred enough feeling against all of the Chinese influence at the court, along with the importation of Buddhism, that a serious revolt occurred and Shotoku's son and his family were killed.

An unsettled period followed when various approaches were tried in an effort to reduce the power of the clans. Some suggestions came from the Japanese students who had been sent to China and had now returned. Other suggestions came from Chinese scholars and artisans who were then working inside Japan, and still other suggestions came from several Koreans who were living in exile in Japan after China had taken a large percentage of the Korean peninsula. The Soga clan continued to remain very powerful and involved in palace politics after the revolt.

Clan control was finally accomplished by creating a new structure of ranks and honors. The old *uji* system hindered effective control from the central administration. Just before Prince

333

Shotoku took control, an incident occurred where a leading *uji* in Kyushu refused to support an imperial campaign into Korea in 562. The consequence was that Japan lost its control over their outpost there called **Mimana** (Kaya). Many agreed that the government could not function properly when just one *uji* could block the action of all the others.

THE TAIKA REFORMS, 645

When the government regained its strength following the death of Shotoku in 622, the winning clan to emerge were the Nakatomi *uji*, a Shinto-oriented group that had earlier opposed Buddhism but by this time, 645, had agreed to accept the new Chinese faith. The Nakatomi are much better known in history as the **Fujiwara clan**, a powerful family that would provide a long line of nobility who would dominate court politics for several years.

Buddhist temples were assigned to a new government appointed bureaucracy. Raising sufficient revenue to support the government led to census surveys and registers. Rice fields were allocated uniformly and they were to be redivided regularly according to needs and population changes. Both land and people were to be controlled from the center. Taxes were collected both "in kind" and by labor for those who had no money or other wealth. Many local governmment officers were appointed by a central administration. The sovereign in this system came to be called the **Tenno**, and he ruled with the blessings and the assistance of the Japanese gods. In the end, not all of Prince Shotoku's suggested reforms were retained because they were judged too Chinese, but the Japanese chose to borrow and adapt them on a **selective** basis.

The reforms of the *Taika* ("great change") were not designed as a liberal effort to seize the land as in modern revolutions, but rather it was an effort to command and dominate those stubborn *uji* who used their land revenue to fight against the central government. By redistributing the land it was placed in the hands of relatively small holders who could not easily afford to make war against the state. With the power now centralized under the Fujiwara clan the others could not afford to start a war. In the end, it was an even greater reform than Prince Shotoku had ever envisioned.

The land redistribution was recorded in a thorough census which was kept up to date during the following years. The result was that taxes were levied more equitably throughout the country. All the provinces were brought into this giant system in such a way that everyone paid a fair share and the government had more money than ever before. A code of laws was adopted which further centralized the government's power. This required one of the most drastic changes because it overruled the old hereditary privilege of powerful clans. The central legal system was the most difficult to inaugurate. It experienced three failures over a half a century to complete the process. Resistance in the provinces continued for many years.

The capital was moved from Nara to Osaka (Naniwa) to symbolize the new centralization of power. The port city had the advantage of both land and water access. The Fujiwara often were able to sense that one of the *uji* in an outlying province was unhappy. In many cases he would be brought into the central government, given a position, and hopefully won over. Titles often changed but the centralization of power continued. As the process neared completion it was adopted as the **Taiho Code,** in **701**, and that was then revised as the **Yoro Code** in 718. The new governing structure which was created by the legal codes was patterned after that of China's T'ang dynasty, 618-907, but modified to suit the Japanese situation.

Chapter 37

THE NARA AND THE HEIAN PERIOD IN JAPANESE HISTORY
710-794 and 794-1185

This period in Japanese history is divided according to which city houses the imperial court--Nara or Heian (Kyoto). The **Nara Period** is one of the greatest ages in the development of the Japanese civilization. The city served as Japan's **first** permanent capital from 710 to 784, and it has continued to be the nation's chief center of Buddhism. Chinese ideas were obvious throughout the city. The streets were laid out with very broad avenues in a checkerboard-grid pattern which radiated out from the imperial palace situated in the north central part of the city. It was planned to be similar to the Chinese city of Ch'ang-an except that it was to be only half the size and it was not walled, a major departure from most Chinese cities. However, the city was surrounded by a moat instead of a wall. Even though the original Japanese plan for the city was never completed, it was Japan's most beautiful city at that time. In the early history of the capital city it was called **Heijo** rather than Nara. It seemed that anything which was patterned after the Chinese was good.

Nara and its surroundings soon became the home for Japan's noble and aristocratic elite. It was the center for a rapidly expanding Buddhist religion which served alongside the native Shinto shrines. The capital city also became a cultural and intellectual center. It is usually considered that the Nara period marks the beginning of written records in Japan. Undoubtedly there had been a great amount of writing before the Nara period, especially Buddhist materials, but unfortunately there are very few examples of any writing from the earlier periods. Best estimates are that writing with Chinese characters began in Japan about A.D. 400. For a little less than a century, the city developed as a political, religious, social, and a cultural center.

It was during the Nara Period that the great Buddhist temple of **Todaiji** (Great Eastern Temple), one of the world's largest wooden buildings, was begun in 745 and dedicated in 752. Inside this temple is the famous 53-foot statue of **Vairocana Buddha** (Daibutsu). Todaiji Temple is so large that it cannot be properly photographed from the ground. Its exterior dimensions measure 284 feet by 166 feet by 160 feet high. Since it has endured major rebuilding after both fires and earthquakes, it is presently only two-thirds its original size. Even now, any photograph fails to do justice to the beauty of the entire temple complex. It is truly the Japanese Taj Mahal except that it is much older than the Indian monument.

The Chinese bureaucratic system seemed to permeate all aspects of Japan in this era. The Buddhist temples were under government control and were also supported by the imperial court. Imperial control was extended very intimately over all aspects of the land and the people. A Chinese-type penal and administrative law called *ritsuryo* was almost a direct copy of the Chinese code during the Sui and early Tang dynasties except that in Japan it was called the **Yoro Penal and Administrative Code**. This code was completed during the reign of **Tenchi Tenno**, 661 to 671. The two and a half centuries spanning the Nara period, as well as immediately before and after, have often been described as a time of intense **Sinification** in Japanese history.

In their effort to imitate the Chinese system, the Japanese began minting coins, roads were constructed, and post stations were built. An edict by Emperor **Gemmei** in 713 ordered all provinces to submit information on their geography, traditions, and produce. These reports from five of the provinces are still preserved in Japanese archives. The *Konjiki*, or "Record of Ancient Matters," completed in 712, and the *Nihon shoki*, or "Chronicles of Japan," completed in 720, are the earliest written sources of Japanese history. Among other things, this mythological record traces the emperors, or *tennos*, from the creation of the sun goddess **Amaterasu**. Many Japanese continue to comprehend history as a continuous connection of the emperors and the gods ruling over a very nationalistic nation with great achievements from the time of **Jimmu Tenno** to the end of World War II.

Although the clans had been brought under some semblance of control preceeding the Nara period, it was inevitable that there would be one clan or family which would rise to the top. In the late 7th or early 8th century that clan was the **Fujiwara**. The leader of this clan, or *uji*, was **Fujiwara Fuhito**, 659 to 720.   The clan had been providing imperial concubines for several years and important Fujiwara men were frequent visitors at the court. As they became more familiar with the imperial family they began intermarrying with a number of high-ranking members of the emperor's family. Then, at the time **Mommu Tenno** was emperor, and Fuhito was the head of the Fujiwara clan, Fuhito, managed to marry his son to the emperor's daughter. Not only did he accomplish that feat, he managed to get the son of this marriage named the crown prince.

The **Fujiwara Fuhito** years saw many ambitious projects undertaken by the monarchy. Government projects in Nara included many new buildings for the palace and the Buddhist temples. This meant a need for more money, and more money called for higher taxes. By 711 there were many workers who deserted the government projects because they were required to work so hard and their pay was so little. Many farmers also left their land and became vagabonds rather than raise crops and then surrender a high percentage to the tax collector. Population continued to increase, rice production fell during this time, and there was not enough land suitable for rice farming to give each registered household a plot of the prescribed size and productivity.

After the death of Fujiwara Fuhito in 720, the Fujiwara clan continued its scheming to marry into the imperial family. On one occasion in 729, even the crown prince, Nagaya, was murdered, presumably because he would not cooperate with the Fujiwara clan. Although nearly everyone suspected the Fujiwara, no one was ever brought to justice. In the end, a Fujiwara woman was designated the empress or *kogo*. Her four sons were given prominent positions within the Council of State, where they assisted their mother in ruling Japan. There was no question which clan was now in control. This period has often been referred to as the period of the "four Fujiwara brothers." Then in 737, all four of the brothers died in a smallpox epidemic. From 737 to 764 there was much rivalry among the powerful Japanese *uji*, each trying to gain control. Many ordinary people suffered as these powerful men bid for the control of Japan.

During these same years the Tang dynasty ruled in China. They seemed to do well and Buddhism in China was very strong. Therefore, the Japanese reasoned that in such a time of troubles they could solve all their problems with a heavy dose of Buddhism. As was mentioned earlier, Prince Shotoku, 574 to 622, had already established the Buddhist religion in Japan. During the years following Prince Shotoku, there had been many more Buddhist buildings erected and more Buddhist statues made, more Buddhist sutras came to Japan, and Buddhist rites were ordered throughout Japan.

Nara & Heian Japan, 710-1185

It was during a serious smallpox epidemic in 739 that emperor **Shomu Tenno**, 701-756, ordered each province to pray to Buddha to end the smallpox plague. In 740 he ordered that each province should build a seven-story Buddhist pagoda. Each pagoda should have **ten** copies of the *Lotus Sutra*. A year later, 741, Shomu Tenno ordered every province to maintain two temples-- one for monks and another for nuns. All were ordered to pray for good health, good harvests, and a prosperous nation. Japan became even more Buddhist than China.

The largest single project of Shomu Tenno was to proclaim in 743 that the entire country's resources would be used to erect a monumental statue of **Vairocana Buddha** at **Todaiji Temple**. This project was nine years in the making under the supervision of a Korean sculptor named Kuninaka no Kimimaro. When completed the Buddha statue was 53 feet tall. The huge bronze base, which is 68 feet in circumference, represents Buddha seated upon a lotus blossom with 56 petals. Since the statue was made by using the "lost wax" method of casting, it required seven hundred tons of wax to form the mold. The statue contained 437 tons of bronze, which included 8.5 tons of tin and lead, and one ton of mercury. Five hundred pounds of gold were required to guild the statue.

The statue was so large that it could not be poured in one piece, so they cast it in sections which were each 10 feet by 12.5 feet, then they were fastened together. The head was cast in one piece. The raised right hand of Buddha symbolizes the "promise of peace." The statue looks very crowded inside the down-sized temple following the last fire in the 16th century.

It was an extremely costly project, but it did seem that Buddha was wellpleased because in the middle of the period when they were casting the huge statue, gold was discovered in northern Japan. Since they had already planned to cover the entire statue with gold leaf, it was now possible to use the government's own gold rather than having to import gold from a foreign source. Although the building has been destroyed by fire, it has been rebuilt twice. Buddhist monks came from as far away as India for the dedication of the great temple. It has been estimated that as many as 10,000 people attended the magnificent dedication ceremony.

Emperor Shomu Tenno also gave the temple tax-free lands to assist in its maintenance. When he died in 756, his daughter **Koken** arranged an elaborate Buddhist service for him and had his treasured belongings collected and presented at the Temple. His widow gave the monastery a log cabin warehouse to store many of the personal belongings of the imperial family. Since many of Shomu Tenno's possessions still exist at Todaiji, it gives us a good insight into the Nara period of Japan. In addition to the usual documents of state and personal letters, there were precious works of art, various implements, medicines of the period, and fine imported articles from as far away as Persia.

Since that time, there have been other items added to the warehouse from as far away as Rome. These include rare screens and paintings, as well as such diverse items as furniture, armor, swords, musical instruments, books, coins, jewelry, and a magnificent collection of theatrical masks. The heavy log structure tends to maintain a constant temperature and humidity, which helps to preserve the more delicate items. All of these items display evidence of the rich culture and talent which developed around the Nara court.

Although the influence of Buddhism waned slightly as the Nara period began to decline about 770, it continued to remain a powerful force throughout Japan's history. The Todaiji has continued to hold its place as the national temple of Japan. American bombers spared the cities of Nara and Kyoto during World War II because of the many valuable art treasures and the buildings. The great temple with its huge statue of Buddha, along with the emperor's collection, made Todaiji the center of a statewide system of Buddhism which has continued to the present day.

The physical representation of Buddhism, however, was simply a manifestation of the blossoming of Japanese religious ideas. In the 9th century, at Heian (Kyoto), Buddhism became even more widespread and popular. It was at this time that it began to spread beyond the upper classes and the imperial court, reaching out to very ordinary people. New Buddhist concepts took root in Japan as traveling monks brought back a deeper understanding of their religion by studying in China. One of these missions in 804 had two monks who went to different parts of China where each received a different type of training in Chinese Buddhism. When they returned to Japan, they each founded a new sect. The new sects they founded are known as the **Tendai** and the **Shingon**. Although both sects made important contributions to Heian Japan, they offered rival concepts to the interpretation of the Buddhist faith in Japan.

BUDDHISM IN JAPAN

Buddhism (**Bukkyo**) was the first major institution borrowed from China. The route Buddhism followed from its origin in India saw the faith first move north from India into Central Asia, then it followed the trade routes to China. The Chinese introduced Buddhism to northern Korea and from there it moved south through the peninsula until it arrived in Japan. The form of Buddhism adopted in China, Korea, and Japan followed the **Mahayhana** tradition, also known as the **Greater Vehicle**. This form placed a great emphasis upon the concept of **salvation by faith**, not only faith in Buddha, but in several other enlightened, or exalted, Buddhas. Among these were **Amida**, the Buddha of the Western World of Paradise; **Dainichi**, the Universal Buddha; and **Yakushi**, the Buddha of Medicine and Healing.

Another important aspect of Japanese Buddhism was the reverence for compassionate **bodhisattvas**. These were enlightened beings of wisdom who had already achieved **nirvana**, but out of compassion for mankind, had postponed their own salvation in order to show others the way. Japanese Buddhism also placed a very strong emphasis on the concept of an afterlife in a western paradise where believers would be rewarded and unbelievers would be eternally punished and tormented.

The Buddhists of Japan adopted the concept of the **Tripitaka**, which means the Three Baskets. These are first, right **conduct**, which included the rules for monks and nuns. Secondly, an emphasis upon the discourses or **sutras**--the sayings of Buddha. And, third, **supplementary doctrines**, which included works of Buddhist psychology and metaphysics. The interpretations of the **Tripitaka** did vary from one part of Japan to another and from one monastery to another. It also varied somewhat from the **Tripitaka** as it was interpreted in Korea and China. It is important to remember that Japan adopted this foreign religion on their own terms and shaped it to the needs of their own people.

Buddhism had originated in far away India about a thousand years before it really began to be practiced in Japan. The foreign faith had been first interpreted to suit the Chinese style, then the Koreans reshaped the Chinese version to their satisfaction. Finally, it arrived in Japan, where it was again styled to suit the social and religious climate there. Buddhism did serve to fill a religious vacuum in the lives of the Japanese because it was filled with moral teachings, whereas Shintoism had no moral code as far as ahimsa and reincarnation was concerned. Reverence for ancestors had already become a part of the Japanese thinking, later to be buttressed by Confucian principles, which had also arrived from China via Korea. Since natural resources in Japan had always been limited, the Japanese readily accepted the "natural" attributes of Taoism.

This gave the Japanese people a four-segment faith. Their native Shintoism stressed the ancient gods and goddesses of the state with the emperor as the divine incarnation on earth. Confucianism amplified their connection with the past by reverence for their ancestors. Buddhism provided both a moral code and a path for living to achieve enlightenment and paradise. Buddhism also had its connection with the past and hope for the future through reincarnation. The Taoism unquestionably influenced the Japanese love of nature, their landscaping, and their painting. The four-faiths-in-one made sense to the Japanese mind and some varying level of accommodation was adopted by each individual in Japan. When Christianity arrived, there were many who accepted the faith in Jesus Christ as another enlightened savior in the same manner they had embraced Mahayana Buddhism. There was no major conflict on that point.

The first recorded introduction of Buddhism came in the form of a religious image and some sutras presented to the Yamato leadership by a mission from Paekche when it solicited aid in its quarrels with Silla. Dates regarding the introduction of Buddhism to Japan vary with 538, 552, and 587 all given.

The new faith was not immediately embraced by all the Japanese and the issue touched off a serious court debate. Two powerful *uji*, one representing the devout Shintoists, the other a powerful group of warriors, opposed Japan's acceptance of Buddhism. The Soga, a rival *uji*, and a supporter of Paekche, accepted Buddhism, but worshipped alone. Efforts to promote the new religion were hindered when on two different occasions epidemics such as smallpox were blamed on the new Buddhist religion.

The court adopted Buddhism, however, when a new emperor, who had been influenced by his Buddhist uncle, converted before he died in 587. His death led the anti-Buddhists into a succession war, but the Soga group and its allies won the struggle. The victory was twofold: the Soga now dominated the Yamato court, and Buddhism was to become the vehicle for a general dispersion of Chinese culture in Japan.

SOCIETY AND CULTURE AT NARA AND HEIAN

The capital remained at Nara until **784** when a new location for it was ordered by **Emperor Kammu** (r.781-806), possibly to get away from the large monasteries that had become excessively involved in the operation of the government by this time. The construction of the new site at **Nagaoka**, to the north of Nara, was abruptly and more mysteriously shifted again in 794 to a location a few miles away at **Heian**, the presentday **Kyoto**. One speculation suggests that some personal misfortune experienced by the imperial family may have prompted the move. This new capital city, prophetically called Heian, which means **"peace and tranquility,"** was a little larger but designed very similar to Nara. This became the imperial home of the Japanese emperor until **1868**.

Nara & Heian Japan, 710-1185

Although the move from Nara to Heian is sometimes used as a demarcation between two historic periods, the historical process does not work quite so abruptly. Political, social, economic, and cultural changes develop only through the passage of time. In the case of early Japan, it can be observed that the centralization which had occurred at the beginning of the Nara period was followed by decentralization towards the closing years. This was accompanied by the loss of imperial power to a rival family, the Fujiwara, a process which began between 850 and 900. It is the initial and transitional periods of Japan's political and economic life which should be considered.

THE GOVERNMENT and ECONOMY

An effective centralized government logically required a strong emperor, a well-organized structure, and close liaison with other parts of Japan. In developing their new system, the Japanese followed the Chinese pattern, but made modifications appropriate to their experience. The emperor, for example, was to be a strong political leader in the Chinese tradition, but in Japan he had a religious role as well, and was frequently preoccupied with Shinto ceremonial affairs. Unlike the Chinese emperor, who attained his position by receipt of the "Mandate of Heaven," the emperor of Japan was considered to have had divine origins from the earliest times. Despite the continuity of Japan's emperor from antiquity, his power was generally checked by the domination of influential court-related families and the practice of early abdications in favor of a future heir. As in China, feminine rule was an accepted practice from early times, but at Nara after 770 there was a dramatic shift to male dominance in the emperor's position.

A Buddhist monk, **Dokyo**, had personally aspired to the throne and succeeded in influencing the empress to grant him the title of **Ho-o**, a title reserved for priestly emperors. This so irritated the court nobles that when she died in 770, they exiled the monk and were determined to avoid female leadership that might again give in to masculine charms and threaten the purity of the imperial line. With remarkable persistence, only two empresses acceded to the throne over the following nine centuries.

The structure of government established at Nara resembled the Chinese central bureaucracy but was altered significantly to accommodate the Japanese requirements for a divine religious leadership. Beneath the emperor, the government was divided into two equal parts: (1) the **Grand Council of State**, to handle political and administrative affairs, and (2) the **Office of Dieties**, to deal with religious matters such as performing Shinto rituals and tending to shrines. Each of the three officeholders was considered to be on an equal level, pointing up the importance given to the religious responsibilities of government.

As the political arm of government, the Grand Council of State included the various administrative agencies. In charge of these were the Grand Minister of State with his Minister of the Left (the chief administrator in practice) and Minister of the Right, an arrangement not greatly unlike the government under the earlier Yamato. The functional agencies of government were the same six departments found in the T'ang political system, that is, public works, ceremonial, civil, military, judicial, and financial affairs. The Japanese added two other departments, one for Central Administration and another for the Imperial Household. Ministeries that dealt with court matters were regarded as the most important and prestigeous. It is easy to see from the administrative structure alone that religion, ceremony, and imperial affairs were given greater attention in Japan than in China.

Another very significant difference between the Japanese and Chinese governments was that Japan failed to adopt a bureaucratic system based upon merit and determined by examination. Although a weak effort was made to adopt such a system, it was limited to the aristocracy and never developed into a universal practice as it was in China. This meant that hereditary authority always took precedence over any type of civil service.

The tie of the central administration with the provinces was significant in assuring the emperor's rule throughout Japan, but the full development of local government was accomplished more slowly. Japan was divided into provinces, smaller than those in China, and subdivided into districts and villages. On the lowest level, farmers were organized into five-family units which had the responsibility of checking on each family's behavior and fulfillment of their tax obligations, another practice common in China. In some areas distant from Nara, political control had yet to be consolidated. By the early 9th century, shortly after the capital was established at Kyoto, Japan reportedly had 66 provinces and 600 districts. These were tied together by a system of roads like the **Tokaido** (eastern sea road) along the Inland Sea, which continued to be a vital artery into modern times. Trade and culture moved along the road as well as government administrators.

The lack of any significant foreign threat or internal civil disturbance after 764 eliminated the necessity for peasant armies, which were drafted to serve as in China. Although they were organized, they were used primarily for various labor requirements of the state. A small corps of capital guards, largely for ceremony and police duties, was the extent of Japan's military establishment during the Heian period. The frontier in Japan, however, did expand toward northern Honshu. This was due to a growing independence and expansion of private holdings in the provinces.

THE SHOEN

In additon to government control, the financial health of the provinces was of interest to the capital. To accomplish the dual objective of political and economic dominance in the provinces, the system of appointing trusted officials and taxing the land was a matter of regular policy. In practice, however, the system was often altered by favoritism. Aristocrats with government positions were given tax-free lands either because of their status or as special rewards. Buddhist temples and Shinto shrines were also eligible for tax-free lands. This privilege granted to both aristocrats and religious institutions deprived the government of the income that the tax system normally anticipated. At the beginning of the Nara period, the drift toward increasing tax-free lands had become a recognizable problem for the new government. Some of the injustices were corrected in the Taika Reforms, but the system had a tendency to drift back to favoritism.

Despite this trend, the need to develop wilderness land became paramount as Japan's population and the government's responsibilities grew. To encourage development early in the 8th century, the Nara government gave tax exemptions to wealthy landowners who would cultivate new lands. At first, there were restrictions on the length of time such lands could be retained in private hands. Before the end of the century, however, limitations had been dropped and new lands had in fact become permanent acquisitions.

In additon to developing reclaimed land, another manner of increasing the size of an estate was to allow small landowners--who wanted to either avoid tax payments or seek protection from government incrimination--to commend their land to an aristocratic family or religious institution. Between the evasive methods of reclamation and commendation, the large tax-free estates known as **shoen**, or **sho**, grew increasingly larger. A variety of devious methods were also employed by the court aristocracy to avoid taxes and to illegally acquire public lands. Consequently, the expansion of the **shoen** system continued over several centuries. By the 13th century there were an estimated 5,000 **shoen** in Japan, owned by only a few hundred major proprietors, each with widely scattered holdings.

The ability of the **shoen** to survive and expand was due largely to the protection of aristocratic court families and other special interests. There were several layers of personnel that were involved in the workings of a **shoen**. At the top was a **patron**, either a court noble who could facilitate appointments to the provinces and gain special favors, or a prestigeous member of a monastery. Beneath either of these was the **proprietor**, who was important for his influence at the court. He was always an absentee landlord. Further down the line were the **managers**, or administrators of the estates. They served on the scene to collect the taxes and see that the roads were maintained. Next, there were the **peasants**, who still held "nominal" ownership to the land they had surrendered, but they still worked the land and lived there. Last were the dependent workers.

All those who were at the highest levels in the **shoen** arrangement held **shiki**, or rights, to a portion of the estate's income. Other people who benefitted from the **shoen** were appointed officials, either on the provincial or local level, whose corrupt practices included manipulating financial accounts and bribery.

These developments over several centuries resulted in the eventual collapse of the public ownership of the land. By the late 9th, and early 10th centuries, it was very evident that Japan had returned to the private ownership of large landholdings reminiscent of the *uji* practice in the Yamato era. The number of independent farmers who paid taxes on their agricultural land had now come nearly to an end. Obviously, this had a material effect upon the imperial court's ability to support and govern the country. In an effort to restore control, the court tightened its central administration by establishing new agencies and increasing the power of the ruler and his advisers. The executive function of government was now centered in the newly created body known as the **Bureau of Archivists**. The court also added agencies to carry out law enforcement, provincial administration, and tax collection.

IMPACT OF BUDDHISM

While these political and economic changes were taking place during the Nara and the early Heian periods, the country underwent a spiritual and ethical growth in the spread of Buddhism. By the 8th or 9th centuries, Buddha would never have recognized the plan he had given to his original followers. Perhaps more importantly, Buddhism began to be an important political force. While it did not replace Shintoism at the imperial court, it assumed a much more dominant role in the administration of affairs at the imperial court and in the everyday life of the people of Japan.

There were various aspects of Buddhism that had a special appeal and an affect upon Japanese life. One attraction was the image of Buddha as a source of healing, which stemmed from a chapter in the "**Golden Light**" sutra that tied together religion and medicine. This sutra, with its Mahayana doctrines, significantly influenced the expansion of Buddhism by Emperor Temmu in 672. All the trappings of Buddhism, such as the art and ceremonies, also held a strong appeal to the Japanese people at the court. As Buddhism developed at Nara, temples and monasteries were constructed in the Chinese architectural style. Religious practices such as the confession of sins became commonplace at the court. When Buddhism later expanded, the travels of monks led to the building of bridges and roads and the mapping of Japan's terrain. Hence, in both religious and secular matters, Buddhism made an important contribution.

By the time Buddhism reached Japan, it had already been refined by a thousand years of evolutionary growth. In its effort to transmit the Buddhism of T'ang China, the Buddhist schools at Nara established a philosophical teaching which was categorized as the "**Six Sects.**" The concepts these teachings illustrate reflected the Buddhist belief in change, as contrasted to the Han Confucian model of maintaining the established order. These concepts included complex doctrines concerning enlightenment, cosmology, and metaphysics. Originating in India and developing in China, these Buddhist ideas were quite sophisticated for the Japanese, whose religious experiences had been limited to the simplistic practice of Shinto.

Because of its complex teachings, Buddhism remained an elite doctrine with a limited following among the court nobility and aristocracy for over a century and a half after its arrival in Japan. At Nara during the eighth century, however, Buddhism became a state cult and was spread throughout Japan by imperial encouragement. In the reign of **Emperor Shomu** (r.724-749) monasteries and nunneries were ordered to be built in each province. The effort by the imperial court to give emphasis to Buddhism was also demonstrated in their huge expenditure to build **Todaiji Temple.**

TENDAI BUDDHISM

Saicho, 767 to 822, was the first of the two Japanese monks who had been studying in China who returned in 805. Later he was to be known as **Dengyo Daishi**, a great teacher. He established the **Tendai Sect**, or T'ien-t'ai in Chinese, in the Enryakuji Temple at **Mt. Hiei**. In time this sect grew to become a large and influential center of Buddhist learning. His primary concept of a basic unity in the world emphasized the belief that everyone had the potential of achieving Buddhahood. More easily understood ideas of moral development were stressed rather than the complexities of metaphysics. In the Chinese tradition, truth as set forth in different Buddhist doctrines was compartmentalized into various categories, each acceptable in their own right. The main text for Tendai was the **Lotus Sutra** which symbolizes the lotus flower, laying on the water's surface, as exemplifying beauty and truth having risen above evil. The discipline for monks studying these concepts at Mt. Hiei was long and arduous, but the fresh ideas apparently aided recruitment.

A growing affiliation with the court and consequent honor and attention given to the Tendai sect at Heian also helped Saicho. Furthering the closeness no doubt was Saicho's own writings that revealed his admiration for the court and his willingness to play a subordinate role in court-religious relations. This attitude contrasted markedly with the somewhat haughty monks at Nara, who soon became embittered at the imperial favoritism granted to Saicho's monastery and Tendai Buddhism. For Emperor Kammu and his successors, Mt. Hiei became a spiritual "protector" of the capital.

SHINGON BUDDHISM

In the following year, 806, **Kukai**, 744 to 835, known after his death as **Kobo Daishi**, which also means "great teacher," returned from his study in China. It was ten years after his return that he established the **Shingon**, or **True Word**, sect at **Mt. Koya**. In some ways, Kukai was the more colorful figure. He was a talented youth who his parents hoped would have a successful government career. The court's move from Nara changed his direction, and he took an interest in Buddhism, which he believed was superior to all other philosophies. In China, Kukai went to Ch'ang-an where he studied with the Buddhist leader, Hui-kuo, 746-805, who treated him as a favorite.

The form of Buddhism that Kukai brought back from China--Shingon--means "True Word sect." In this form of Buddhism there is a great emphasis on secretiveness, formulas, ceremonies, and magic. It is much more private as opposed to the openness in other forms of Buddhism. In Shingon, the transmission of wisdom was made privately and orally by the master shortly before he died to his best student. Kukai was attracted to this private (esoteric) form in the belief that to understand Buddha's true inner experience it could only be revealed through secret formulas to other outstanding disciples who already knew the way. The average follower of Shingon Buddhism found it highly aesthetic and intellectually stimulating--it synthesized all concepts regarding the principles of the universe as experienced in the Taoist teachings about *yin and yang*.

Both Tendai and Shingon Buddhism had already become important in the religious life of the Japanese while the founders were still living. These two schools also began to influence other Buddhist philosophical schools as well. The relations between the two monks were cordial at first, and Saicho became quite impressed with the esoteric teachings of his friend Kukai. A break occurred when Saicho sent one of his disciples to study with Kukai, after which Kukai would not allow the student to return to Mt. Hiei.

Following the death of Kukai, another of the disciples of Saicho by the name of **Ennin**, 794-864, founded a form of Tendai esotericism. Ennin had spent nine years in China studying with Tendai masters and had made many penetrating observations of China in his diary. Within a few years, both the Tendai and the Shingon became very esoteric (private) in their teachings. Then the two sects began to compete with one another. In the end, Tendai won because Shingon had no truly great leaders to take up the message after Kukai died. Sometimes the clashes between the rival schools led to violent encounters, especially during the reign of Emperor Shirakawa (r.1072-1086). This struggle between the two sects led to the expression of "the warrior monks."

Nara & Heian Japan, 710-1185

FUJIWARA DOMINANCE AT THE IMPERIAL COURT

During the time that the private estates--**shoen**--altered Japan's economy, and the development of Japanese **Buddhism** laid the foundation for a new spiritual world, court politics began to change the imperial structure during the late Heian period. During the 9th century, one branch of the rich and prestigeous **Fujiwara** house again attained a dominant influence over the imperial family. Through the marriage of Fujiwara women to key members of the court, they were able to monopolize high government positions and ultimately place related sons on the throne.

Success in dominating the court came in 858 when Yoshifusa, 804-872, then the Fujiwara leader, was made regent for his young grandson. This unprecedented act of allowing an individual outside the imperial family to serve as regent was viewed as the first step toward complete dominance. Yoshifusa was also regent for successive adult emperors, and by 884, Fujiwara regents were given the additional title of **kampaku**, a term which suggested increased authority. A couple of efforts were made to place one of their own as emperor, but these did not prove successful. This was especially true during the years when Michinaga (966-1027) held power.

THE INSEI GOVERNMENT

By the eleventh century the court emperors made new efforts to reassert their control. This weakened, but did not eliminate, the power of the Fujiwara. Most notable was the system devised after the abdication of Emperor Shirakawa in 1086 to maintain his own headquarters from which he continued to exert political power. The retired emperor's office, known as **insei**, meaning "cloistered government," was well-staffed with loyal aristocrats. They functioned as a competing agency with the Fujiwara regents to dominate the actual emperor for a century after Shirakawa's death in 1129.

And, for still another century, the system continued, but less vigorously and with periods of interruption. After 1185 the feudal government replaced the imperial court as the viable political power. Consequently, by the end of the eleventh century Japan experienced **three levels** of imperial government, one backing up the other. There was the emperor who was followed by the regent who stood behind him, and the **insei** emperor who stood behind him. It also became an accepted practice at this time for the emperor to retire long before he was approaching death.

LATE HEIAN BUDDHISM

The touch of magic and ritual that developed through esoteric (secret) Buddhism actually became an attraction that helped popularize these foreign sects throughout Japan. The opposite philosophy was expressed in the simplicity of the **Pure Land** sect. They said that the prospect of easy salvation was assured through the simplicity of worship whereby one only needed to express their faith in the **Amida Buddha** by the mere chanting of his name. The broadened support gained by Buddhism began to overtake the importance of both Confucianism and Shintoism, both of which were not to emerge significantly from their secondary roles until much later. Moreover,

Buddhism has held firm in the Japanese thinking and practice into modern times. It is interesting that the faith has lost ground in both India and China.

With the spread of Buddhism came a growth in power and influence that was to actually rival the aristocratic houses. Monasteries grew larger and more numerous. They steadily increased their land holdings and accumulated considerable wealth. The monasteries grew so large that they established special administrative bureaucracies to manage their estates. Several monasteries had to hire workers to cultivate their lands. Such great wealth had to be protected, and gradually monasteries began to support their own armies. Rivalries and land disputes often caused embittered conflicts, sometimes spilling over into the imperial capital itself. These developments were to set the stage for further division and political weakness in Japan leading to a feudal society by 1185.

THE DEVELOPMENT OF JAPANESE ART, LITERATURE, and MUSIC

THE ART and ARCHITECTURAL SCENE

Despite Japan's turmoil during the evolution of its early tradition, cultural gains made great strides. The artistic achievements from the 6th through the 12th century stand as monuments of a remarkable blend of Chinese form accompanied by Japanese talents. In the beginning, Japanese fascination with Buddhist iconography and temples paralleled their interest in religious concepts. Consequently, the early years--those between the introduction of Buddhism in 552 and the Taika reforms in 645--had witnessed the adoption of Chinese art in a very precise form, so much so that some structures in Japan remain the best examples of Chinese design today.

Prince Shotoku's role in Japan in the spread and popularization of Buddhism was similar to that of the Indian leader, Ashoka, as a patron of the same faith. **Horyuji Temple**, one of Japan's most beautiful monasteries, attests to his interest in this new religion brought from China. The temple was built not far from Nara in **607**, but fire later in the same century destroyed most of the buildings. Those standing today are believed to be the early replacements and are considered the **oldest timber structures in the world**. This is a remarkable fact since most of Japan's old temples have been wholly or partially destroyed by the elements on one or more occasions since their construction.

The character of **Horyuji Temple** reflects the architecture of the T'ang period in China-- wooden structures which blend gracefully and discretely into their natural setting. The structures are topped by tile roofs which rest on pillars with forked brackets to hold the crossbeams. Variations of this style became commonplace in Buddhist temple architecture from the seventh century onward. Horyuji is a magnificent example of the architecture of the seventh century in Japan.

The main portion of the monastery is the square, surrounded by a colonnade whose main feature is the gate, which is protected by fearsome guardian gods. The painting was influenced by a linear, abstract style from India and Inner Asia. A five-story pagoda is no longer functional but is symbolic of the unity of heaven and earth. The Horyuji is the principal temple of the Shotoku sect. There are a total of forty-five buildings in the complex, seventeen of which are classified as **national treasures**. Likewise, the architectural feats of Horyuji temple were matched by the adaptation of Chinese-style sculpturing that went into the monastery's statuary. It has become one of the "Seven Great Temples of Nara," and one of the reasons why Nara became the great center of Buddhism in Japan.

The spread of Buddhism in Nara was accompanied by a burst of artistic creation. Art historians divide the period into two parts: **Hakuho**, 645 to 710, and **Tempyo**, 710 to 794. The latter period was especially important because it was in 737 when the provinces were ordered to erect an image of Buddha. This was followed by instructions in 740 to build a seven-story pagoda in the provincial capital and a neighboring monastery. Under such encouragement from the emperor, all forms of art were stimulated, but sculpturing was the most prominent.

In the late Heian period--894 to 1185--native Japanese influences became much more apparent. The ending of official embassies to China after 898 greatly decreased the flow of mainland influence. This then allowed Japanese ideas to blossom. Temples were no longer placed on remote mountainsides in accord with the esoteric need for privacy and secrecy, but were constructed in or near the capital. They were also more elaborate and decorative than those built earlier.

An exceptional example of the late Heian architecture, still standing from this period, is the **Byodoin Temple,** which was built in **1052** at Uji, near Heian. It is symmetrically designed and represents a mythical phoenix, a good luck symbol, with its wings outstretched after having descended to the ground. Sculpturing continued to lack the grandeur of earlier periods and was done almost entirely in wood with artists often working in groups.

Painting in late the Heian period was the most creative. A predominantly Japanese style known as **Yamato-E**, which means "Yamato pictures," replaced the earlier Chinese techniques. In more simple forms and flowing lines, Japanese artists depicted popular stories and scenes from novels, using the *e-makimono* or long scroll. This style flourished in about the eleventh and twelfth centuries. One of the finest examples remaining is the scroll illustrating the *Tale of Genji*, which was painted by an artist of the Fujiwara family.

One of the most intriguing illustrations is that painted by a Buddhist priest, Toba Sojo, in the twelfth century. Excellently drawn in black-line painting, animal caricatures depict members of the clergy--a stately looking frog represents Buddha, while hares and other animals dressed in priestly robes chant the sutras. The satire is an apparent effort by a talented and reformist-minded priest to poke fun at what he viewed to be a foolish and corrupt clergy. In all these efforts, Japanese subjects and techniques prevail.

JAPANESE LITERATURE

The earliest written records of Japan were in the pictographic script adopted from China. To the Japanese it was difficult to learn and cumbersome to use because it did not easily express some of the Japanese thoughts. Furthermore, the Chinese script contained some meanings which were unfamiliar in Japan. As a first step to simplify Chinese, a system of diacritical marks were created to indicate the order in which the characters were to be read to form a Japanese sentence. In time, selected characters were used to form a phonetic Japanese script known as *kana*. Users of either form--characters or *kana*--eventually combined the two, and a **third** form of writing emerged. It is this mixed construction of characters and *kana* which is used today.

347

Nara & Heian Japan, 710-1185

The simplification of Japan's writing system did stimulate literary production. Novels, poems, and diaries became a written method to record the behavior and thought at Nara and Heian. The writers, however, were members of the court, and the daily life shown in their prose and poetry is not that of the peasant, warrior, cleric, or craftsman, but rather the luxurious life of an elite group who did not live in the "real" world. The accounts reflect the charm and grace of this privileged leisure class and tell of the loves and intrigues that preoccupied those who were members and attendants at the court. Although it only shows one side of life in Japan, the peasants, warriors, and others, were illiterate and unable to tell their story.

Talented court members, it should be noted, actually began their writing of poetry before the development of *kana*. Poems were written on a variety of topics which used Chinese characters for the Japanese phonetic sound given to them. Even though Chinese influence abounded at Nara, there was little evidence of Confucian ideas of a classically educated civil service having overwhelmed the members of the court. Japanese concerns were paramount. Many of the poems revealed a strong feeling for the natural world, possibly a Taoist influence. Some dealt with the hazards of daily living, while others were celestial phenomenon like the moon and the stars. There is a general spirit of simplicity and sincerity about the poems, and not one deals with war, even though it was an accepted way of settling disputes and acquiring new territory.

Compassion and devotion are felt in the numerous love poems. For example, there is the story of Sakura-ko, the "Cherry-flower-maiden," who wanted to end the embittered rivalry between two men who fought over her and chose to do so by taking her own life. In expression of their grief, they prepared a poem about how they would each grieve every spring for their fallen "Cherry Blossom." Over 4,500 of these poems were compiled in the mid-eighth century in what is known as the *Mayoshu*, "Myriad Leaves." At the beginning of the tenth century, another anthology of 1,100 poems was compiled, entitled *Kokinshu*, "Collection of Ancient and Modern Poetry," which served as a model for numerous anthologies over the next several centuries. The poetry in the *Kokinshu* was written in the Japanese *kana* by the court nobles. The exceptional beauty and skill of their writing shows that the upper classes did receive an excellent education.

Early Japanese prose contained tales of both legendary and realistic episodes recounted in poetry. It was from these poems that the Japanese novel developed. The work of a court lady, **Murasaki Shikibu's**, 978? to 1015?, masterful *The Tale of Genji* is known as one of the world's great novels. The story is a sensitive tale about the loves of a young prince viewed by a consort of low rank. Most revealing is the frivolity of court life at Heian, since it seemed so very isolated from the world about it. Life at the imperial court was also recorded by Lady Murasaki's account in her diary. A very talented individual, she was also known in her lifetime as a court painter and a musician.

Other court ladies have also contributed to our knowledge of court splendor through their personal accounts. One that shares with us brief impressions, which express a great wit and candor, is **Sei Shonagon's** *Pillow Book*, 1002. Both the prose and the diary accounts form a record of a talented literary style at the imperial court as well as a picturesque account of a system that yielded its strength and dynamism to decadent pleasures and excesses. The excellent quality of writing of these court ladies provides good evidence that Japanese women were educated far beyond the level of women in the other Asian countries.

Nara & Heian Japan, 710-1185
JAPANESE MUSIC

Another important artistic expression was in the area of music. Ancient Chinese and Japanese records confirm this accomplishment as early as the third and the fifth centuries in Japan, and its later development parallels that in other fields. The court music at Nara, for example, seems to have originated in India, China, or Korea. It was mainly instrumental in nature and was played by foreign musicians. During the Heian period, however, these influences began to yield to native contributions and a growing musical talent among the Japanese. In addition to secular ceremonies, religious music had already developed in both Shintoism and Buddhism. Sometimes religious music was interchangeable between the two faiths, since music created for Shinto chants was applied to Buddhist hymns. Folk festivals for both religions were filled with music and accompanied by entertaining dances, and they usually involved songs accompanied by flute and percussion instruments.

The earliest court music, *gagaku*, "refined music," is known to have been played at important ceremonies in the eighth century. It was constantly used at the court in Heian and was very formal and reserved. *Gagaku* music has been played throughout the centuries and still remains an historic tie with Japan's ancient past. When this music is used to accompany dances, it is known as *bugaku*. The Japanese also enjoy making beautiful costumes for their festivals. The precision movements of the dancers, combined with the *gagaku* music, are both observed very closely by the audience. Any misrepresentation is carefully noted by the critics. In music, as in art and literature, Japanese tastes gradually overtook the originally dominant Chinese influences. If an imported cultural attribute is to survive in Japan, it must ultimately conform to the Japanese way of thinking.

A SUMMARY OF JAPANESE HISTORY FROM 710 TO 1185
THE NARA & THE HEIAN PERIOD

At first this period saw great advances in art, literature, and religion. Towards the close of the Heian period, the Japanese masters began to branch out and to create their own styles and fashions in all fields. Their successes in doing so soon rivaled--some would say exceeded--what was occurring simultaneously in China. Culturally, it was one of Japan's greatest periods.

The great successes in Japan were soon reduced to some extent by rivalry between Buddhism and Shinto, the traditional religion of Japan. In some cases the patriotic Japanese were reduced to presenting Shinto deities as manifestations of Buddha. Furthermore, there were rivalries between the various sects of Buddhists, especially the Tendai and the Shingon. Religion came more and more to have a separate role from the political world, whereas in the early years the worship of the divine emperor and the state were one. Naturally, the state suffered as this relationship changed.

With the conquest of northern Honshu Island in the 9th century, the native Ainu were pushed on north to Hokkaido. The emperors began to devote more time to leisure and various scholarly pursuits and less time to governing their possessions. The courtly functions required so much of each emperor's time that it created an opening for a noble family known as the Fujiwara to hold an ever increasing number of important court posts. Over a long period of intermarriage with the most important members of the court, the Fujiwara eased themselves into a power position which they continued to hold for several centuries.

Nara & Heian Japan, 710-1185

During the years the Fujiwara family dominated the court, there was a tendency to concentrate on luxury, especially at Heian (Kyoto). At the same time, the power of the **samurai** or "warrior class" was on the rise. They began to build up their own armed forces and they were prepared to defend their autonomy anytime the occasion arose. Leading Samurai families moved into the court where they also began to intermarry and to hold very important political posts in the same manner as the Fujiwara had over the past few generations.

As the period at Heian began to draw to a close, it became increasingly apparent that Japanese society had slowly undergone some fundamental changes since the Taika Reforms of 645 and the Taiho and Yoro codes of 701 and 718. Although these legal principles were never formally repealed, the evolution of court politics and administration at the imperial level, and the role played by the Fujiwara family, which was being rivaled by the leading samurai families, brought about a governmental structure which was far different in the 12th century from that planned in the 8th century. The weakening of the imperial power and the establishment of the *insei* reduced the authoritarian appearance of the government at a time when they needed to assert more power over the families who were feuding to achieving the inside control over government operations.

The Japanese had placed a great emphasis upon the small, independent, landholding class of farmers--that was what the reforms of the late 7th and early 8th centuries had been about. The *shoen* system of tax manipulation not only placed the control of the agricultural land in the hands of a few powerful men, it also deprived the government of revenue at a time when they needed money for modernizing their operations.

Even though the political and the economic systems were both in need of major readjustments, other aspects of Japanese life continued to make progress. More lands were cultivated in the frontier settlements, especially in northern Honshu, and Japan's artistic growth spread far beyond the capital at Heian. As contact with China began to decrease after the 9th century, Japanese culture began to make major modifications to the Chinese and Korean cultures which they had so freely adopted in the preceding centuries. This created an entirely new culture which suited the Japanese way of thinking. Cultural trends emphasized aesthetic qualities, which, along with the emergence of Buddhism in a Japanese mold, was to be very significant in future years.

As the end of the Heian period approached, the imperial family seemed incapable of asserting leadership. Other families began to want the same position at the imperial court which the Fujiwara family had enjoyed for so many years. Even the Fujiwaras were more interested in the niceities at the court than they were in attending to the government. At the same time there were increasingly powerful families who were gaining military power. It was only a question of time. The Fujiwara family was first overthrown in favor of the **Taira** clan who ruled briefly before being ousted by the **Minamoto** family, also known as the **Genji**. The Heian (Kyoto) era came to a close.

Chapter 38

FEUDAL JAPAN, 1185-1600

THE KAMAKURA PERIOD
1185 to 1333

The roots of the Feudal Period reach far back into Japanese history. The entire period was plagued by almost constant civil war as one warlord after another tried to establish control over an area, then to expand that area at the expense of his neighbor. The island nation had always been governed by a few powerful men. The family which came to dominate Japanese politics just before the Feudal Period, the Fujiwara, came to ignore practical politics in favor of sophisticated court manners. They failed to see government as a serious business, but rather as a struggle to maintain good relations with the divine emperor--everything else would simply follow naturally. The imperial court became a little world of its own with little attachment to, or interest in, the outside world. Those at the court were wealthy and comfortable--for the moment.

There was news of increasing disorder, rising military factions, feuding Buddhist sects, a weak economy accompanied by increasing poverty--all of these should have been signals that there could be an impending revolt. The Fujiwara ignored all signs. After all, they had weathered political storms before. On previous occasions there had always been a member of the clan with sufficient brilliance to pull it all back together.

By the 10th century the Fujiwara family had so entrenched themselves within the imperial court, its administrative branch, and the military, that there were very few opportunities for the young men of the emperor's own family. Consequently, the imperial family created some new clans as a favor to certain ambitious young members who could forsee no future simply staying around the palace. The **Minamoto** and the **Taira** were two of these new clans.

Although many of these new clan members held government administrative posts, others joined the military. It is the military group of leaders who generally receive the attention of historians. The **Seiwa Genji branch** of the Minamoto clan became the most powerful by building up an army of faithful retainers. However, the emperor chose the Taira clan as his own supporters, referring to the men assigned to the palace as the "teeth and claws" of the emperor. The powerful Seiwa Genji could not bear to see the Taira clan on the inside where there were many favors to be granted. The two fought a short war and the Taira clan won the initial struggle.

That was not the end of the power contest. The Seiwa branch of the Minamoto remained quiet for a few years but began building their strength. In 1180 the Taira provoked the Minamoto to fight again--they probably wanted to destroy the power base of the Minamoto forever. This struggle, known as the Gempei War, 1180-1185, turned out unexpectedly for the Taira-- **Minamoto Yoritomo**, 1147 to 1199, emerged the victor. A leader accustomed to taking risks, he had a dedicated group of followers who admired his style. Yoritomo concluded that if any of the Taira clan leaders survived, they would continue to trouble the Minamoto; therefore, the members of the Taira leadership were brutally eliminated. In **1185**, Minamoto Yoritomo decided to set up his own government at **Kamakura**--about 10 miles south of Tokyo--rather than at Heian (Kyoto). The emperor continued to reside at Kyoto, but without support.

Feudal Japan, the Kamakura Period

Yoritomo ruled Japan from Kamakura with his own **samurai** warrior class, which was supported by a feudal system very similar to the European Medieval arrangement. In 1192 Minamoto Yoritomo took the title of **shogun**--*sei-i tai shogun*, which means "generalissimo for the suppression of the eastern barbarians." He is generally thought of as establishing the first *bakufu* separate from the emperor. This is referred to as the **Kamakura Period** of Japanese history--1185-1333.

Concluding that discretion was the better part of valor, the emperor granted Yoritomo the right to hold government in Kamakura, to collect taxes, and to maintain order. He was further granted the power to make grants of land to his followers, the *shugo*, who were armed leaders very similar to the great barons of Europe at this same time. Yoritomo also granted parcels to another class known as *jito*, who served as tax collectors. The *shugo* and the *jito* served as judges in minor cases, and were granted the power to enforce law and order. This meant they were authorized to raise and support an army.

The emperor was allowed to maintain his own residence and to have his own court and officials in Kyoto, but the real power and the final military decisions really came from Kamakura. Still, Yoritomo did not consider himself a military dictator and the governmental powers of the emperor were moved over to the shoguns on a gradual basis over the next several years. When Minamoto Yoritomo's family died out in 1219, the **Hojo** family of the Minamoto clan assumed power.

The Hojo are interesting because they were related to Yoritomo through his wife, **Hojo Masako**. The family had been a branch of the Taira clan, but later established their own name of Hojo, which was named after their land grant. Hojo Masako fell in love with Minamoto Yoritomo while he was in jail. She pleaded with her father, the jailer, to marry the young rebel. He consented and from that time forward the Hojo were allied to the Minamoto. It was said that Masako was a great assistant to Yoritomo.

Probably the most important of the Hojo rulers was **Hojo Tokimune**. He was only seventeen when he became shogun in 1268. That was the same year Kublai Khan, the Mongol ruler of China, sent a message to Japan to surrender and become a tributary state of China. All of Tokimune's advisors thought they should accept, since Japan was not prepared. He disagreed. He sent a strongly worded message to China that Japan had no intention of surrendering. Six years later, 1274, the Mongols arrived with an army of 25,000 men which quickly captured the outer islands. Just as they were ready to invade the mainland, a typhoon came up and destroyed or damaged their ships. At that point they returned to the mainland.

Seven years later, 1281, Kublai Khan invaded Japan a second time. This time he brought a much larger fleet and 140,000 troops of mixed Mongols, Chinese, and Koreans. Many of the Chinese and the Koreans had been drafted into the campaign against their will. During the seven year interval between invasions, Tokimune ordered that walls should be built on Japan's western coast. Even so, the Mongols did manage to land. The battle raged for two months at which time a second typhoon came across Japan. The Mongol fleet was destroyed by the storm and Japan was saved a second time by a *kamikaze*, a "divine wind." The Japanese took no prisoners. There were probably as many as 100,000 Mongols killed. Japan had defeated the dreaded Mongols!

The costly preparations which had dragged out over several years, plus the damages of the war placed the Minamoto clan's finances on a shaky footing. They continued to maintain a sizeable force along Japan's western coast for several years in fear the Mongols would return. In 1333 the Kamakura period was ended by an army sponsored by the emperor **Go-Daigo**, 1318 to 1339. The emperor saw the weakness of the shoguns at Kamakura and decided to recoup his imperial powers. It was only a three-year period until Go-Daigo was driven out by **Ashikaga Takauji**, a former military supporter in 1338.

Figure 34

Figure 35

354

Chapter 39
THE ASHIKAGA SHOGUNATE,1358-1573
(The Muromachi Period)

Ashikaga Takauji, 1305 to 1358, did not think that he and his forces had been properly rewarded for reinstating the emperor Go-Daigo in what is known as the **Kemmu Restoration**. Among other points of dissatifaction, Ashikaga Takauji wanted to be named shogun. The emperor, Go-Daigo, believed in direct imperial rule without any *bakufu* to interfere. Ashikaga and his followers expressed their dissatisfaction by turning against the emperor militarily. The emperor had made one serious error when he decided to establish direct imperial rule--he had no strong military power to back him in a period when military power was everything. He had several of the great nobles for support, but most of them had too little power individually and they were each selfishly wanting to control the imperial court since the Fujiwara family was now out of power. Ashikaga forced Go-Daigo into exile and named his own man to become emperor.

The next period of 240 years is often referred to as the **Muromachi Period** because the Ashikaga shoguns moved the capital from Kamakura back to a district of Kyoto called Muromachi. Instead of tending to ignore the emperors and let them govern from the imperial court as the Kamakura shoguns had, Ashikaga preferred to be in Kyoto where he could watch over the emperors.

The governmental structure Ashikaga established at Muromachi was different than it had been in Kamakura since the government in the provinces was now administered on a much more delegated basis. Each of the provinces was administered by a *shugo* governor, whose governing powers were very similar to one of the great earls, dukes, or barons of Medieval Europe. The *shugo* maintained his own military, but was a sworn vassal of the shogun. Many of the *shugo* were members of the shogun's close family, but that did not mean they were any more trustworthy than an outsider. Many of the *shugo* commonly brought in lower class men to serve as warriors to supplement their **samurai** leaders. The *jito* tax collectors and local administrators were retained, but they often raised money for the *shugo* to build his army instead of sending it to the shogun in Muromachi. The *shugo* met occasionally to advise the shogun or to select a new one in case of a vacancy.

On the surface it appeared to be a strong government, but the shoguns never achieved complete control from Muromachi. It was an unstable warrior-based government from the beginning. The exercise of power varied considerably from one shogun to another. Ashikaga Yoshimitsu, 1358-1408, was one of the stronger shoguns. He felt powerful enough to call himself the "King of Japan," and he used some of the imperial court titles for his own vassals. Power at the top seemed to decline after the death of Yoshimitsu.

Although each *shugo* was guilty of building his own power base, there were generally three geographic areas which formed their *shugo* groups. There was the northern group in the Tokyo area. They had the advantage of the Kanto Plain for an agricultural base and they had been kept militarily alert for many years fighting the Ainu. The second group centered on Muromachi in the Kyoto area. Money did flow into that area for the shogun and that was where the emperor most often resided. The third group was in the far southern islands, especially Kyushu, and up along the west coast. They were isolated enough that they did pretty much as they pleased and ignored the government regardless of which city they occupied. In a way, the three groups were fairly evenly balanced.

Such a situation might have continued for several years, but in 1467 they needed to name another shogun. Since the preceding one had been a weak ruler, the local *shugo* had built their military forces to a greater size than ever before as a matter of self defense--they could not depend on assistance from the shogun. When they all met, they began to strongly disagree among themselves about their new leader. The result was outright warfare known as the **Onin War**, 1467-1477.

One of the leaders during this ten-year civil war decided in his anger to burn Kyoto. Both monks and nobility were forced to flee the city. Every one of the *shugo* needed money badly. They had their pirate ships which raided along their own coast as well as the coasts of China and Korea. All three countries--Japan, China, and Korea--were weakened by piracy. Since none of them could agree on a strong leader, they tended to name a succession of weak men to be shogun. Many small and independent armies were formed by even peasants, guildsmen, and religious houses.

This period is often referred to as the *sengoku jidai*, the "**age of warring provinces**." Many of the powerful *shugo* lost their control to the small independent armies which were formed for "protection," sometimes within their own province. Before this period ended there were thousands of people killed by either military action or by starvation, since agricultural production was greatly disturbed in some areas. By the end of the Feudal Period, there were around 250 different domains where there had formerly been 50 or 60. The shoguns had practically no control over the situation. Many powerful *daimyo*, theoretically the vassals of the shogun but military warriors with their own armies, rose to lead these groups. The ones which exercised the greatest power were the ones who had the most effective armies.

ODA NOBUNAGA, 1534-1582

One of these powerful *daimyo* was **Oda Nobunaga**. He was a restless and ruthless warlord who gained the advantage over his adversaries by arming his followers with muskets to make up for his smaller army. He began his climb to power by overthrowing several rival *daimyo* on Honshu Island. Nobunaga's style endeared him to the people who served with him as much as anything. His father had been a very minor military man and Nobunga did not inherit any great amount of land, position, or power. His dream was to unite Japan as one country and to end the long period of useless warfare.

Some of his most difficult battles were against the armies of the various religious communities. The Buddhist army at Mount Hiei were so persistent they required several years to overcome. In 1571 he managed to destroy the monastery of the Tendai sect of Buddhism. The Ikko sect was fanatically religious. When they allied with several *daimyo*, it meant that Nobunaga had to defeat them all, a task which required ten years. The fortress-monastery of Hongan-ji at Osaka did not surrender until 1580.

There were also armies of independent warlords, leagues of peasants, townspeople and guild members, and armies which claimed to be representing the old regime. In 1568 Nobunaga marched into Kyoto and took over the city. He had hoped to work with the shogun to establish some order, but in 1573 he defeated the last Ashikaga shogun and forced him into exile. That action brought **an end to the Muromachi *bakufu*.** Interestingly, Oda Nobunaga did not assume the title of shogun because he had not been properly appointed by the ***shugo*.** Nobunaga was simply the most powerful warlord in the central Honshu area.

The defeat of the shogun had two important effects. Several of the important warlords and ***shugos*** decided to ally with Nobunaga, since he was obviously the most powerful of the warlords. The other side of the issue caused several of the other military leaders to settle their differences and form alliances against him. He was obviously a powerful warlord who had come from a very modest background. What right did such a commoner have to all that power and territory?

The secret of Oda Nobunaga's success rested upon several things. He managed to attract and recruit some really brilliant military leaders who remained loyal to him. Whereas many of the other warlords simply swept through the countryside, Nobunaga made alliances with factories and mines to supply his army with new and better equipment. One of the first important cities to ally with Nobunaga was Nagoya. Situated in the fertile Owari Plain, Nagoya was important to him as a source of equipment and rice--many of the farmers were pleased to supply his army with food. Peace was maintained in the area surrounding Nagoya and people were busy working without fear of immediate conquest. There was an air of stability which the people enjoyed and were willing to support him. This established a model for his future conquests.

Once an area was brought under military control, Nobunaga would order that the castles and other fortifications should be destroyed and even the peasants were disarmed. Trade began to increase in his area of control. All his subordinates were fully accountable to him. Those who ruled outside his immediate area of control were rotated to prevent them from establishing their own power base. Those who broke his rules were subject to severe penalties, including death. It was the most stable rule since the "warring states" period had begun. Trusted samurai were given grants of land. Coming largely from upper class families, the samurai were an important stabilizing influence upon a conquered area.

One interesting aspect of Nobunaga's rule was that when the Christian missionaries began to arrive in Japan, he welcomed them. He even assisted the Jesuits in building a seminary in the Kyoto area. Nobunaga was fascinated by western culture and products, but he also planned to use the Christians as a counter to the Buddhists, who had grown powerful both politically and militarily.

Under such a military dictatorship it was inevitable that there would be opponents and ambitious leaders who believed they could defeat Nobunaga. He died in the Kyoto temple while under attack by one of his own deputies in 1582. Seriously wounded, Oda Nobunaga committed suicide. By that time he had brought between one-third and one-half of all of Japan under his control.

TOYOTOMI HIDEYOSHI, 1536-1598

Toyotomi Hideyoshi was another commoner who rose to the top level of control in Japan during the late 16th century. The son of a farmer, he began his military training at the lowest ranks at the age of fifteen and worked his way up. At age twenty-two he joined the service of

Feudal Japan--the Ashikaga Period, 1358-1600

Oda Nobunaga. As a capable and loyal soldier, he rose quickly to become a general who was considered trustworthy enough to conquer Japan's west coast. Hideyoshi was a master military strategist. This was accompanied by what might be termed a theatrical military style. Nobunaga so appreciated Hideyoshi's abilities and his loyalty that he often rewarded him with lands and castles. When Nobunaga died, Hideyoshi appealed to the members of their alliance to join with him in a joint effort to unify Japan--to fulfill the dream of Oda Nobunaga.

Many did join Hideyoshi in this venture. The others he gave time to consider their decision. Everyone was so weary of the "warring states" period, a hundred years of fighting and suffering, that many agreed to ally with Hideyoshi. Going to battle became one of his last resorts. It was easier to make concessions than it was to engage in continuous fighting.

Hideyoshi established a Japanese version of a federal state wherein he allowed a tremendous amount of governing power to each *daimyo*--a much less centralized model than in the Nobunaga period. At the time of Hideyoshi's death there were about 200 *daimyo* under his alliance. Each one was allowed to maintain a military force, but for the defense of Japan, not for conquering a neighboring piece of real estate. Beyond the powers of governance, Hideyoshi maintained control over the large cities, the seaports, all natural resources, and all foreign relations. He established a uniform system of weights and measures as well as coinage. He eliminated piracy, a favorite method of financing the warlord armies. In 1588 he ordered that all farmers and townsmen should be disarmed. He ordered a very detailed census of people and resources in order that taxes could be levied fairly.

Hideyoshi could also be a very personable man. He invited the emperor to his castle as a social event. Many of his vassals, especially the generals, the important administrators, and some of the more famous samurai, were also invited to join him in the tea ceremony. Drinking tea and participating in the tea ceremony became very popular during this period. Hideyoshi built new castles and repaired old ones. He rebuilt some of the Buddhist monasteries which had recently been destroyed in the wars. The city of Kyoto was completely rebuilt with wider streets and everything was brought up to modern standards for his own time. There was peace and visible progress on every hand. Most Japanese were very pleased with the government of their country.

In Hideyoshi's later years, there were historians who actually questioned his sanity. Once he had completed the unification and pacification of Japan, he became concerned about the large numbers of samurai who had nothing more to do since the wars were over. He therefore decided to conquer China! His ultimate goal in this massive undertaking is not entirely clear, perhaps just because it was there. He decided to approach China by way of Korea. In 1592 he attacked the Koreans because they would not grant him permission to cross their country.

The Korean campaign went extremely well at the outset, but it soon became bogged down. Probably one of the chief handicaps was that the farther Japan went north into Korea, the longer their supply lines became. Furthermore, the Chinese decided to come to the defense of the Koreans rather than wait until the Japanese had crossed into their territory. Most importantly, the Koreans had developed their armored "turtle boats," which proved almost unsinkable. With heavy rams on each end of each boat they would move in close for the kill. The Japanese could not come up with an effective counter to these vessels, which meant that their troop and supply ships could not operate around the Korean shoreline. Hideyoshi tried twice to take Korea--1592 and 1597. He failed on both occasions. Not only did he plan to conquer both Korea and China, but he said he also wanted to conquer India, and the Philippines. Perhaps it was an early vision of Japan's "Greater Order for East Asia."

Other seemingly insane actions in his later years included the execution of his favorite tea master, Sen no Rikyu, 1522 to 1592. Tea apparently first arrived in Japan about 815. It was the late 12th century before it began to be popular. Sen no Rikyu had traveled to China where the ceremony known as *Chajing*, "the classic of tea," had originated much earlier. Although he could perform a "high" tea ceremony for guests at a performing art program, Rikyu preferred a much simpler tea ceremony *cha no ya* "hot water for tea." In this ceremony with peasant characteristics, the guests went into a tiny mud-walled tea house smaller than two mats. The doorway was so small and low that the guests had to crawl inside. He used rough domestic ceramics, bamboo flower vases, and wooden water containers which he said separated one from the things of this world. It was all closely associated with Zen Buddhism.

Rikyu had served as tea master to Oda Nobunaga, then as tea master to Toyotomi Hideyoshi. Hideyoshi liked this form of tea ceremony so much that he invited his favorite friends and guests. In 1587 he staged a tea party to which he invited all classes of society. For some unknown reason, he then forced Rikyu to perform *harikari*. There are those who believe it was because Rikyu placed his own statue at the entrance to a tea ceremony, while others believe it was because Rikyu refused to allow the old general to see the tea master's daughter. In any event, the popularity of tea did not perish with Sen no Rikyu. Zen Buddhists proclaimed the many health benefits of tea drinking. Hundreds of people built the tiny tea houses in their gardens. Tea contests also became popular where the guests were asked to guess the tea and to tell where it came from. This became a popular form of gambling with very high stakes.

Hideyoshi also placed his favorite nephew, who had been in charge of the Korean invasion, in the same situation as the tea master. He was apparently so distraught by the unsuccessful nature of the Korean campaign in 1598 that the old military leader died at age 62. He had no children by his formal wife, but he had a son who was six years of age by a concubine. He asked his leading general, **Tokugawa Ieyasu**, to care for him and prepare him to rule Japan. By 1600, Ieyasu had consolidated the rule for himself. The Japanese Feudal Period is generally thought to have ended about 1600 with the beginning of the Tokugawa regime.

THE ROLE OF THE SAMURAI

The samurai might very well be thought of as Japan's **warrior caste**. In this way it was similar to India's Kshatriya caste, especially during Japan's feudal period. Its code of **Bushido** has many similarities to the western world's code of **chivalry**. The samurai did not make up a separate religion but rather it was one part of the national **Shinto religion**. The late Feudal Period marks the beginning of an intensely nationalistic period which was based upon militarism. It began around the late Heian period and continued until the Japanese defeat in 1945.

The wars advocated and fought by the samurai from the 11th century on were fought in the name of national unity and for territorial expansion. During the Feudal Period, many samurai came to feel that Korea was like "a dagger pointed at the heart of Japan." Furthermore, they had long considered the Koreans to be inferior people, even though a great amount of Korean culture had formed the foundation of Japanese culture. Entrance to the samurai was relatively easy up to the beginning of the Tokugawa takeover, about 1600. As peace settled in following 1600,

Feudal Japan--the Ashikaga Period, 1358-1600

entrance to the samurai became more difficult. The Meiji realized that too many samurai could become a threat to them, and even though several samurai had supported the Meiji Restoration, they were encouraged to pursue business and intellectual pursuits rather than to become lifelong warriors. But the glory of the samurai does live on as a part of Japan's heroic past in much the same way that the age of the frontier and the cowboy live on in American tradition.

To further understand the significance of the samurai's role in Japan's history and culture, it is well to look at the procedure for making a **Samurai Sword**, a *Nippon-to*. A very elaborate ceremony--**a rite of purification**--was held at the very beginning to cleanse the shop where the sword was to be made. The smiths wore special ceremonial dress and the smithy was completely encircled with paper symbols of cleanliness. Women were not allowed anywhere near the forge from start to finish of the project.

Once the site was purified, the smiths began by heating two lumps of iron. These were hammered into a steel base plate to which more iron was added as necessary. The entire piece was wrapped in tissue paper, then covered with a mixture of clay, powdered charcoal, and water. This process was designed to add carbon to the metal. The embryo sword was beaten with heavy hammers until it was a thin sheet of steel of fairly uniform texture. The tempering was such a sensitive process that the craftsmen believed that it should be attempted only at dawn when the day was fresh and the air was sweet and still.

In the next stage of the manufacturing process the entire blade was first covered with a pack of wet clay. After it had been allowed to set in this manner for some time, usually overnight, they removed the clay along the cutting edge, leaving a coating of clay on the back portion of the steel blade. The forge was then darkened to enable the smith to judge the temperature of the blade by the color of the heated steel. The clay and steel were heated to approximately 800 degrees, then plunged into a trough of water. The cutting edge of the blade cooled quickly, making the edge very hard and brittle. The back of the blade, which had been thickly coated with clay, cooled much more slowly, thus retaining the same degree of flexibility it possessed before tempering.

The tempering was followed by a series of twelve stages of polishing the sword. They varied from the use of coarse stones to thin slices of limestone. In the final stages, the blade was polished with cotton dipped in a mixture of hot oil and powdered cinnabar. Finally, it was burnished with a steel pencil to give it a deep lustre. The craftsman engraved the blade, made the hilt and the scabbard, and then it was ready to be tested. Each sword was an individual work of art and craftsmanship. These old samurai swords are now worth thousands of dollars. Many of those which were manufactured during World War II were mass produced and have a much lower value.

The final step in the sword-making process was to test the blade. The smith-craftsman would do the testing himself in a near-religious rite. The blade was swung at a bundle made of bamboo wrapped in straw and sprinkled with water. This was believed to be the nearest substitute for human flesh and bones, while the water was supposed to represent the blood. Such a dummy, eight to ten inches in diameter, would be sliced in 28 different strokes to make certain that the sword functioned properly. Since the blade was long and heavy, the hilt was designed for two-handed operation. The swish of the knife and the cleavage of the dummy was positively frightening because one realized that the blade could slice a body in two just as neatly as it had sliced the bundle of wet straw and bamboo.

Feudal Japan--the Ashikaga Period, 1358-1600

The armor of the feudal Japanese warrior was also very different from the European style of armor. By late feudal times in Europe, the suits of armor were complete metal suits. In Japan they were thin strips of lacquered metal, or sometimes heavy leather, which were fastened together in various ways, often with either links,leather, or a specially made lacing. The inside was often padded to absorb some of the blow from a heavy sword. There was elaborate shoulder protection and helmets with horrible masks for faces, some of them with visors. Many of these suits of armor looked positively frightening--and that was what they were supposed to do. They had both a breastplate and armor on the back. The legs were also very well protected with shin guards. The suits enhanced the actual size of the warrior to make him look large and ferocious. His weapons were a bow with a quiver full of arrows, his sacred samurai sword, and a dagger. He was not completely equipped without his horse.

The classic samurai battle was a series of duels set up between individuals rather than massed armies rushing toward one another as was often the case in western Europe. A warrior was always expected to be freshly washed and groomed before any encounter. He always expected to win. The conduct of the fight came to be more and more closely regulated by the code of bushido, except all rules seemed to be abandoned during the "warring states" period.

True **bushido**, the "Way of the Warrior," was not totally accepted until the Tokugawa period at which time all the shoguns were samurai. It was an elaborate code of etiquette designed to regulate the behavior between samurai as well as a samurai's behavior toward those who were non-samurai. Various aspects of the code had been in the process of development for centuries with portions taken from Shintoism, Confucianism, and Buddhism. Confucianism required the samurai warrior to show absolute loyalty. Like western chivalry, the samurai was expected to show benevolence to the weak and the helpless--he should see that justice was carried out in all cases. All insults were to be avenged. The samurai always spoke the truth. He should show endless endurance and remain under total self-control at all times. His honor was his life. Any hint of disgrace and shame were to be totally avoided.

Buddhism taught that life is impermanent. This made it possible to face death with serenity. Shame and disgrace could therefore be rectified by *seppuku*, better known as *harikari*-- the taking of one's own life by ritual suicide. Such a grisly ritual required the samurai to disembowel himself before an aide who then drew his sword and lopped off the warrior's head. This was often resorted to when there was no way out of a situation because surrender, or pleading for mercy, were the worst of all possible forms of disgrace. Likewise, a man who was bested in battle could expect no mercy in case he should be down and helpless. It was expected that his adversary would finish him off rather than take him prisoner.

It should be noted that the samurai were not constantly engaged in battle. Outside the battle dress, the samurai normally dressed simply. He could be recognized by his triangular *eboshi*, a hat made from rigid black cloth. Although all were expected to follow the code of bushido to the letter, there were many who played politics during their "off hours." During these times they were sometimes known to "stretch the truth" as they laid plots to obtain high political positions. Beginning in the Tokugawa era they were encouraged to take administrative positions, concentrate on obtaining a good education, becoming proficient in literature and poetry, or, on some occasions, to engage in business.

Feudal Japan--the Ashikaga Period, 1358-1600

THE WEST ARRIVES IN JAPAN

In 1543, the very period when Oda Nobunaga, Toyotomi Hideyoshi, and Tokugawa Ieyasu were contesting for the absolute control of Japan, a terrible storm drove a Portuguese vessel bound for China northward to the small island of Tanegashima off the southern tip of Kyushu. The shipwrecked visitors were well received, almost like men from another planet. The firearms which they were carrying were soon dubbed **Tanegeshima teppo**, or "iron rods." The Japanese were quick to recognize their value and soon began manufacturing copies in Japan.

Other Portuguese followed who were primarily interested in trade. Six years after the original contact, **Francis Xavier** arrived accompanied by two fellow Jesuit missionaries, two servants, and three Japanese who had been won to the faith in some of the South Asian stations. Saint Francis Xavier, 1506 to 1552, has been called the "**Apostle of the Indies**." He had come from an upper class family with both land and money in Navarre, Spain, but the fighting between France and Spain ruined the family fortune and left his father with practically nothing. It is said his father died of sorrow over his losses. There was little for young Francis to do but to join the church.

While young Xavier was studying at the University of Paris, he met **Ignatius Loyola**, the founder of the **Jesuits**. He became one of Loyola's first converts, passed the Spiritual Exercises, and went to Rome where he worked as a priest and teacher. In 1540 King John III of Portugal sent Xavier and one other Jesuit to minister to the Portuguese empire in the East. He arrived in Goa in 1542. There were already Dominicans, Augustinians, and Franciscan missionaries in Goa. Francis Xavier thought of himself as the collaborator of this mission field and carried a letter from the Pope which certified his authority as the head of the Goa mission.

In September 1545 he went to Malacca where he worked until 1549, at which time he went to Japan. His hopes were high that this country would prove to be the nucleus for a Far Eastern Christian church. When he landed at Kagoshima, Japan, there is no record of any missionary having been there before him. He was received kindly and was assisted by Japanese converts from the Moluccas who acted as his interpreters. Between August of 1549 and November of 1551, Xavier preached to many and baptised about 2,000, mostly from the lower classes as well as a few from the military class.

On his way from the Moluccas to Japan, the ship which carried his small group made a stop at Hong Kong. Xavier was impressed by the Chinese who he met there while at the same time recognizing that the Japanese who were with him almost grudgingly esteemed the Chinese culture. China was closed to foreigners at that time, but Xavier believed that he must try to bring Christianity to them as well. In the meantime, back in Portugal, Loyola had divided the eastern missionary field, splitting the Far East away from India. When the letter caught up with Xavier, he was informed that he had been named the first Provincial of the Jesuits in the Far East.

When the Portuguese Commandant in charge of civil and economic affairs in the Hong Kong area learned of Xavier's goal of a mission to China, he stated that he was opposed to the entire idea--China was to be **his** plum, not the Jesuits. When he forbade Xavier to leave the Malacca area to go to China, Francis went anyway. He landed on an island near **Canton, China**, now Guangzhou, in 1552 and for the next three months he tried to obtain permission to work on

Feudal Japan--the Ashikaga Period, 1358-1600

the mainland. He then fell seriously ill. Virtually everyone abandoned him, and he died on December 3, 1552.

Francis Xavier's style of working in the mission field was to first study the language, the local religions and the customs of the native people where he was planning to work. This method has been copied by missionaries of all faiths as well as many governments and businesses. He was canonized in 1622. It would be left for others to open the mission field in China.

For the next fifty years after Francis Xavier, the work of the Christian missionaries and their teachings in Japan went well. The Jesuits were all well educated and had preliminary training to prepare them on the background of Japanese culture. Just as in China, the Jesuits pitched their appeal to the samurai and the daimyo class because they were the respected leaders of the community, but the bulk of their converts were from the lower classes--the farmers and the fishermen. Winning the people in the top leadership roles was never accomplished in China. Most of the Christian converts in both China and Japan were simple, ordinary people.

Aside from a few missionaries working in Japan, the country was closed to outsiders. There were strict bounds of social classes--not quite caste but approaching caste levels--and even less interest in the outside world than in China within the same time frame. The Jesuits had more appeal than ordinary traders might have had because the Japanese viewed them as being militarily organized, masters of their fate, courteous, and courageous. As the Jesuits won the respect of the Japanese, the western merchants more or less crept in under the cover of the respect the Japanese held for the missionaries. Western merchants often had to grudgingly call upon missionaries to act as interpreters or to settle a dispute which often got out of hand.

At the outset, it was only the Portuguese who tapped this trade. When Japanese relations broke down with the Chinese Ming, the Portuguese shippers were the only source of Chinese goods such as silks. Once a year the "great ships" of the Portuguese came from Macao to change missionaries, bring in news, pick up information on the mission field, and bring the latest products from Portugal and the West. The Japanese in turn wanted to buy these goods from the missionaries so in the end, the Jesuits established themselves at **Nagasaki**, on Kyushu Island, and entered into trade on a permanent basis. The daimyo at Nagasaki was impressed by the western missionaries and ordered his retainers to become Christians. He burned Buddhist temples and strongly favored the Jesuits as an element which would weaken the militarily powerful Buddhists during the Feudal Period. Nagasaki became the **only** port through which foreign ships might enter until the 19th century.

Oda Nobunaga, the Japanese leader who began unifying Japan rather than have the country divided into small warring principalities, was, in a Japanese sense, an Asian king Alfred or Otto von Bismarck. Fortunately for the West, he favored the Jesuits. This was especially significant since Nobunaga did not consider other Japanese as being quite equal.

His successor, Toyotomi Hideyoshi, had been born of humble parents and moved up as a general under Nobunaga. As he completed unification, he looked overseas for new lands to conquer. However, his plan for conquering most of East Asia never came close following his inability to succeed in conquering Korea.

Hideyoshi had a very different attitude toward the Christians in Japan than did his predecessor, Nobunaga. He was anxious for the trade, but a few years after he took control, there were several Spanish Franciscan missionaries who arrived from Manila. Within a very short period of time they began quarreling with the Portuguese Jesuits over which level of the Japanese society should be Christianized. At this time the Jesuits were convinced that they would do better by concentrating on the upper class Japanese while the Franciscans thought they should Christianize the lower and working class people. As Hideyoshi learned more about the missionaries, he came to lose most of his original respect for them because they preached a gospel of equality and love in as many things as possible, yet they engaged in these impossible debates about the smallest points of theology and the best method of preaching in Japan. He also failed to understand their allegiance to a foreign leader, the pope, while they were living in Japan.

By 1587, Hideyoshi drafted a list of charges against the Christians and ordered all missionaries to leave Japan. He claimed the missionaries were forcing the Japanese people to become Christians. He said that they taught their disciples to wreck temples, they ate useful animals, and they took Japanese people as slaves to the Indies. He claimed he was also very upset about the growing number of Christian converts who owed their allegiance to a foreign pope at a time when he was establishing a highly nationalistic state in Japan. As Hideyoshi completed the unification of Japan and the Buddhists had been suppressed as a political and a military force, he could no longer see a need to cultivate them in the same manner as had his predecesor, Nobunaga.

None of the Catholic Orders wanted to leave Japan, and for a brief time it seemed to be little more than an order without enforcement. The Jesuits sent some of their Japanese missionaries to China and tried to maintain a very low profile. The Franciscans and Dominicans insisted on taking their message to the people by preaching openly on the streets.

In 1596 a Spanish galleon was wrecked off the coast of Japan. The pilot feared that his cargo would be looted and in an effort to gain Hideyoshi's protection he said that the Spanish king would seize Japan, just as he had other Christian countries, unless they left his cargo alone until he had time to salvage it. Although the pilot was making an empty threat, that was too much! The persecution of the Japanese Christians began almost immediately. Hideyoshi looked upon them as foreigners trying to secure a foothold in his country as well as leading his own people to join in the conspiracy. At this time it became difficult for any Japanese native to be a Christian; it became impossible to be a foreign missionary. The preferred religion was supposed to be Shintoism.

SUMMARIZING JAPAN TO 1600

It is interesting to compare Japan with the other countries of Asia and with Europe in the same time frame. Surrounded by sea, Japan was the most isolated of any of the Asian countries. Their prehistoric period has many comparisons to the prehistoric period in Korea and northern China, the area of presentday Manchuria. This has led many authorities to assume that many of the people who moved into the island archipelago originally came from these areas. No one positively knows the origin of the very earliest inhabitants, the Ainu people.

While India, China, and Korea developed urban communities and writing at a very early time in their history, Japan lagged far behind the other three. Ultimately, they borrowed the Chinese system of writing and although they have modified that system, Japan has never developed their own writing system. Writing became important in India to record their religious

Feudal Japan--the Ashikaga Period, 1358-1600

epics. The Chinese system of writing began recording their history at a very early age. Neither religion nor history seemed to be a major consideration in Japan in their earlier history.

Japan's only purely native religion is Shintoism. It is so closely linked to their nationalistic traditions that it has never attracted widespread attention outside their own borders. Their major religious faith became Buddhism by the 7th or 8th century, an imported religion which had originated in northern India, came through Central Asia to China, from China to Korea, then finally Buddhism arrived in Japan. Two other religious imports from China via Korea were Confucianism and Taoism. All four faiths--Shintoism, Buddhism, Confucianism, and Taoism--had been integrated into the Japanese religious system by the mid-sixteenth century at which time Christianity arrived. All five religions seem to interchange characteristics with each other in the Japanese way of thinking. It is a unique religious understanding.

Japan's early system of governance was intimately tied to Shintoism. From a time before recorded history, the emperor (Mikado) of Japan was not only the political head of Japan, but he was the spiritual head as well--he was a god. The amount of political power exercised by these men (and a few women) has varied considerably through the ages. Generally speaking, the emperors were powerful leaders up to the 11th and 12th centuries. After that time they seem to have allowed power to slowly slip away from them, first by becoming too closely allied to one of the leading clans, then by concentrating on courtly manners when they should have been attending to the affairs of state and building a strong military base. While the emperors failed to build the national economy, they lost the good will of their subjects. At the same time they allowed the leaders of the great clans to each build huge armies. It was inevitable that these armies would clash with one another for the control of Japan. The feudal period in Japan began about 1185 and did not end until 1600. The emperors did not regain their power until the Meiji Restoration in 1868.

Japan's Feudal Period was shorter than Europe's Feudal Age, but it seemed to have less regard for the individual. Europe sank into its feudal period because of a weakening of Rome's government, a circumstance similar to the weakening government in Japan, but Europe was overrun by barbaric invaders from the East and the North. Japan had no successful outside invaders during their feudal age. The death and destruction in Japan was more of a gigantic civil war with several major armies in the field at the same time. The suffering of the Japanese people and the helplessness of the imperial government to effect a remedy was **not** imposed upon them by any outside force--it was brought upon them totally by their own people.

While Europe's period of the early Medieval Ages--often called the Dark Ages--was an unhappy period for most people, it did improve with the passing of time. The barbarians became more humane as the Christian church performed a civilizing effect which tended to lift Europe out of the worst aspects of barbarity. In Japan, the Buddhists were the most powerful single religion in 1185. Instead of easing the barbarism of their feudal period, the Buddhists armed themselves "for protection," and became one of the lethal participants in the wars which raged through their small country.

While Europe's governments seemed to become better organized in time, Japan's reasonably well organized government of the 8th and 9th centuries seemed to sink lower and to become weaker with each passing year. About all the emperor had left by 1600 was his "divinity;" there was no political power. The office of emperor often became a pawn of the great

Feudal Japan--the Ashikaga Period, 1358-1600

warlords as they seated and unseated emperors as the power shifted. Some of the emperors lived near the poverty level. They seemed as helpless as the peasants and the townspeople.

It is impossible to say how much lower Japan might have fallen after a century of serious conflict known as the "warring states" period had it not been for three great leaders, all military men, who had a vision of a great and unified Japan at peace. These men were **Oda Nobunaga, Toyotomi Hideyoshi,** and **Tokugawa Ieyasu**. Instead of trying to seize control by military victory and assassination, as was so common in the Feudal Period, they developed a form of Japanese federalism. Power was shared among the great daimyo who realized after so many years of warfare that no one man could have it all. Japan's Feudal Period was two or three hundred years shorter than in Europe, but it was a very unsettled and dangerous period as men fought to the death to achieve total individual control.

Perhaps one of the most amazing things about Japan's Feudal Period was that art, music, literature, drama, and sculpture all moved forward during this terribly troubled period. Old castles and monasteries were reduced to rubble as the war progressed, but often they were rebuilt better than before. Historians would be interested in the very old documents which often perished in flames--only a few survived. The buildings would be a unique feature to observe today but sometimes warfare does lead to a brighter new age at the end. Those who remember the past do not want to repeat it again and again. Even business and agriculture expanded during these troubled times, especially as Oda Nobunaga began to demonstrate that peace was better than war. With the arrival of the first Europeans at the close of this period, Japan was poised to launch out on a bright new age. Instead, the Tokugawa shoguns slammed the door to outside influences from 1600 until the door was forced open in 1854. Like Korea, Japan became a "Hermit Nation."

BOOKS FOR FURTHER READING

Anderson, G. L., editor, *Masterpieces of the Orient* (1961).

Akira Iriye, *The Pacific: An Inner History of American-East Asian Relations* (1967).

Beardsley, Richard K., Hall, John W., & Ward, Robert E., *Village Japan* (1959).

Bottomley, I., & Hopson, A. P., *Arms and Armor of the Samurai* (1988).

Bowring, Richard, & Kornicki, Peter, editors, *The Cambridge Encyclopedia of Japan* (1993).

Boxer, Charles R., *The Christian Century in Japan, 1549-1650* (1974).

Cleary, Thomas, *The Japanese Art of War: Understanding the Culture of Strategy* (1992).

Clyde, Paul H., & Beers, Burton F., *The Far East* (1975).

Collcutt, Martin; Jansen, Marius; & Kumakura, Isao, *Cultural Atlas of Japan* (1991).

Cotterell, Arthur, *East Asia: From Chinese Predominance to the Rise of the Pacific Rim* (1993).

Feudal Japan--the Ashikaga Period, 1358-1600

Dower, John W., *Origins of the Modern Japanese State: Selected Writings of E. H. Norman* (1975).

Earhart, H. Byron, *Japanese Religion: Unity and Diversity* (1982).

Fairbank, John K., Reischauer, Edwin O., & Craig, *East Asia: Tradition and Transformation* (1989).

Fenton, John Y. *et. al., Religions of Asia* (1988).

Groot, Gerard J., *The Prehistory of Japan* (1972).

Hall, John Whitney, *Japanese History: New Dimensions of Approach and Understanding* (1966).

Hall, John Whitney, *Japan from Prehistory to Modern Times* (1970).

Kitagawa, Joseph M., *Religion in Japanese History* (1966).

Kitagawa, Joseph M., editor, *The Religious Traditions of Asia* (1989).

Lane, Richard, *Images from the Floating World: The Japanese Print* (1978).

Mackenzie, Donald A., *China and Japan: Myths and Legends* (1992).

Mason, R. H. P., & Caiger, J. G., *A History of Japan* (1992).

Mass, Jeffrey P., *Warrior Government in Early Medieval Japan* (1974).

Meyer, Millton W., *Japan: A Concise History* (1993).

Mikiso Hane, *Japan: A Historical Survey* (1972).

Morris, Ivan, translator, *The Pillow Book of Sei Shonagon* (1967).

Morris, Ivan, *The World of the Shining Prince: Court Life in Ancient Japan* (1979).

Morton, W. Scott, *Japan: Its History and Culture* (1994).

Myers, Bernard S., & Copplestone, Trewin, *The History of Asian Art* (1987).

Philippi, Donald L, translator, *Konjiki* (1969).

Plummer, Katherine, *The Shogun's Reluctant Ambassadors: Sea Drifters* (1984).

Reischauer, Edwin O., *Japan: The Story of a Nation* (1981).

Reischauer, Edwin O., *The Japanese* (1981).

Ross, Nancy W., *Buddhism: A Way of Life and Thought* (1980).

Feudal Japan--the Ashikaga Period, 1358-1600

Ryusaku Tsunoda, de Bary, Wm. Theodore, & Keene, Donald, editors, *Sources of Japanese Tradition* (1958).

Sansom, George B., *A History of Japan*, 3 Volumes (1963).

Sansom, G. B., *Japan, A Short Cultural History* (1962).

Schirokauer, Conrad, *A Brief History of Chinese and Japanese Civilizations* (1989).

Seidensticker, Edward G., translator, *The Tale of Genji* (1976).

Stanley-Baker, Joan, *Japanese Art* (1984).

Trewartha, Glenn T., *Japan: A Geography* (1965).

Varley, H. Paul, *Japanese Culture* (1984).

Yutaka Mino, *The Great Eastern Temple: Treasures of Japanese Buddhist Art from Todai-ji* (1986).

Figure 36

SOUTHEAST ASIA TO 1600

Chapter 40
THE GEOGRAPHIC CHARACTERISTICS OF SOUTHEAST ASIA

When we consider the area known as Southeast Asia today, we generally understand this to include Thailand, Kampuchea (Cambodia), Laos, Vietnam, Malaysia, and Singapore. These separate countries are divided partly by their geographic situation but more often by their many ethnic and linguistic groupings. In addition, Southeast Asia includes the islands, both large and small, such as Java, Sumatra, Borneo, the Philippines, and many more. The study of Southeast Asia becomes one of the most complex of all of Asia because of this vast and varied geography. Even though some of these are relatively small countries, there are often several ethnic and language groups within any one country.

Mainland Southeast Asia is a large projection of land jutting out apart from the major Asian land mass, but not including the Indonesian archipelago, the Philippines, or Australia and New Zealand. The Indian Ocean is to the west and the Pacific Ocean is to the east. The combined area of the peninsula includes 625,000 square miles, and it is about 660 miles from east to west and about 1,500 miles from north to south. In addition, the island nation of Indonesia alone covers 741,000 square miles with thousands of islands, many of them too small to be inhabited.

Southeast Asia's climate is tropical since it lies mostly between the Tropic of Cancer and the Equator. Most of the area has moderate to rough terrain, except for the river valleys, yet the highest ridges seldom reach more than 5,000 to 6,000 feet. This is still enough elevation to cause a noticeable variation in temperature due to altitude. The islands of Southeast Asia have been formed largely by volcanic action; a few are still active. Most of the tillable land is in the extensive river valleys of the peninsula or the weathered volcanic soil in the islands. Two of Asia's largest rivers--the Mekong and the Irrawaddy--are located in Southeast Asia. The densest areas of population in Southeast Asia are found in these and the other river valleys.

The population of Southeast Asia is not nearly as dense as most other Asian countries such as their immediate neighbor to the north, China. Although some infiltration from China has definitely taken place, this is not as great as might be expected due to the rugged terrain across the north of the peninsula. Because of the rugged terrain, Southeast Asia has most often been infiltrated via the coastal areas and the river valleys. Even many Chinese have arrived by water rather than by land. It should be noted that most of the rivers run from north to south in Southeast Asia. This has been important in their history and culture because there is little east-west communication within the peninsula since each of the river valleys has a ridge of mountains which tends to separate the people into several river valley cultures.

Water is quite important to the style of agriculture in this area. The Red, the Mekong, and the Chao Phraya rivers are what are often call drowned rivers. That is, they are flat rivers with vast deltas and swamps. Rainfall varies, but is over 60 inches throughout most of the area; however, there are some parts of Southeast Asia which have twice this amount. This is considerably more than the American Midwest, with an average annual rainfall of 45 to 50 inches per year. The consequence of the flat rivers and swamps, along with a normally heavy rainfall, causes a great amount of humidity throughout the area. Clouds often form quickly and dump

The Geography of Southeast Asia

torrential rain upon an already wet area. Crops which grow well in a hot, wet, and humid climate do well throughout Southeast Asia.

Much of the uncultivated upland area of Southeast Asia is a permanent rain forest with palms on the higher ground and mangrove swamps in the lower areas. Tigers, rinoceros, elephants, water buffalo, and a profusion and diversity of birds and insects also inhabit the monsoon rain forests. It is estimated that the human population of this area has grown ten-fold within the last 170 years. This has had a tremendous impact upon the wildlife of the area, since many people view the wildlife in very much the way the frontier farmers in America saw wildlife: that is, as destroyers of their crops and a potential danger to their children.

Aside from a few large cities such as Singapore and Bangkok, most of the people in Southeast Asia are either directly or indirectly involved in agriculture or timber for their living. The principal crops include rice, sugarcane, coffee, tea, fruits, nuts, spices, peanuts, soybeans, and cotton. Since the discovery of America in 1492, maize (corn), cassava, and tobacco have become important crops as well. Modern agricultural techniques, combined with intensive labor practices, has not only given the area a sufficient amount of food, but has made several agricultural products available for export. Most of the work is labor intensive with little in the way of farm tractors or other agricultural machinery.

The water buffalo, a native of Southeast Asia, provides much of the power for tilling the paddies, pulling the heavy loads, providing milk, and a multitude of other dairy products. Other cattle, sheep, goats, pigs, and chickens have been raised in Southeast Asia for thousands of years. The fisheries contribute between 3 and 4 percent of the gross national product in countries such as Malaysia, Cambodia (Kampuchea), and Thailand. A great amount of the manufacturing tends to involve either the food or lumber products.

The lumber industry has grown immensely in the 20th century, so much so that many Southeast Asians are becoming concerned about the rapid depletion of slow-growing varieties as well as the long-range effect upon the ecological system of the area. Rubber production reached its peak in the pre-World War II era, but it is still a very important agricultural export.

Water transportation in Southeast Asia can be verified long before recorded history. From simple dugout canoes to modern ocean liners, the area has used the abundant water resources, along with several good seaports, for the majority of their transportation needs. Water transportation is the least expensive form of transport, but it is also the slowest form. Most of the river systems do rise during the monsoon season, but flooding is never as severe as in nearby Bangladesh.

Except for water transportation, the highways and the railroads are very poor. Singapore and Malaysia now have some excellent highways, but their secondary roads are largely two-lane blacktops. Many of the hard surfaced roads have been built since World War II. Outside the range of the big cities, some roads are little more than trails. Most of the highways parallel the rivers and the mountain ranges, which means that the majority of them run in a north-south direction. There are no major east-west highways throughout the peninsula. Many of the rivers, such as the Irrawaddy, are lacking bridges. Southeast Asia is terribly in need of a better infrastructure to improve their business and manufacturing sector.

Chapter 41
PREHISTORIC SOUTHEAST ASIA

THE FIRST DISCOVERY--JAVA MAN

The first major archaeological find of a very old human being was **Java Man** in 1891. A young Dutch doctor named **Eugene Dubois** was inspired by reading the work of Charles Darwin and others. Dubois became thoroughly convinced that mankind, and the remainder of the animal world, had evolved from earlier types. Dubois further believed that mankind's earliest ancestors would be found on the island of Sumatra in the Dutch East Indies. He further speculated that mankind had migrated from the neighboring island of Borneo, the home of both the gibbon and the orangutan. Dubois thought the gibbon was one of the oldest primates and the orangutan was one of the most intelligent. Such an environment was the ideal location, he believed, for the transition to take place from lower animals to the human animal. Many were referring to such a transition person--half man and half ape--as the "**missing link**." Since the areas where Dubois planned to explore were under Dutch control at that time, his task would be easier.

Dubois had trouble getting any financial backing for his expedition so he financed his own travels. While he was saving enough money for the expedition, he read widely and talked with several scholars in the field of anthropology and biology. When he set out, he still had very limited resources.

Everything he found on Sumatra was of very recent origin--there was nothing which would even come close to being a missing link. By 1890 he was suffering ill health due to malaria and decided to transfer his search to Java where there were more medical facilities. This proved to be a much richer source of fossils. Dubois then learned that the local Javanese people had been selling fossil bones to the Chinese for many years. The Chinese purchased the bones to pulverize into powder and then sell them for medical cures.

Dubois complained to the Dutch government about this. Even though he offered to pay for the bones neither the Javanese nor the Chinese would sell him any of the bones. About this time the Dutch governmental officials began to take an interest. First, they prohibited the sale of fossil bones to the Chinese merchants. Then the Dutch government provided Dubois with a crew of workers and two Dutch military officers to supervise them.

In August 1891, his workers selected a site in north central Java near **Trinil** and began digging down through the strata along the **Solo River**. It was difficult to remove the upper crust, but once they had passed that point, the fossils began to be found. The first find was a single apelike tooth. A few weeks later a human skull was discovered. Dubois reported that "both specimens came from a great manlike ape." Shortly after this the rainy season arrived and the digging was suspended.

About a year after his first discovery, a second turned up. About fifty feet from the place where the man's skull was found they uncovered the left femur of a primate that had walked erect. Although a little heavier than modern man's bones, it was otherwise identical. Teeth and other bits of human remains began to round out an image of a man with a skull which was partly ape and partly man, with legs already fully adapted for walking. Such an early man had been described by a German scientist, Ernst Haeckel, who had given the name to such a person as

Prehistoric Southeast Asia

Pithecanthropus.   This was taken from the Greek words *__pithecos__* (ape) and *anthropus* (man). Dubois then added the word *erectus* (upright) to indicate that he had found the erect ape man. He fully believed he had found the "missing link."

Since the time of Dubois, there have been four important fossil locations discovered in Java. The first of these was excavated in the 1930s and the latest excavations began in the 1960s and continues to the present. Overall these have yielded a number of very old and interesting fossil crania and parts of lower jaws. There still seems to be difficulty in establishing accurate dates for all the Javanese finds. The dates range, for instance, from 2 million years down to as little as 500,000--obviously quite a wide variation. In any event, they are very old. At the present time the only human remains which might surpass the remains of Java Man are those which have been found in central Africa by Louis, Mary, and Richard Leakey.

It is also interesting that no **pre-*Homo erectus*** bones such as those of ***Homo habilis*** have yet been found in Java as they have in Africa. Does this mean that these people moved into Java from elsewhere? And, if this is true, where did they come from? It should also be pointed out that other ***Homo erectus*** bones have been found in Europe and Asia as well as elsewhere in Africa since the Dubois discovery in 1891. Did the people of Europe and Asia all arrive as migrants from another area? These are mysteries which must still be solved.

Controversy began almost immediately over the Dubois find. Were the bones genuine? Did they all belong to one person? Were they really as old as Dubois had reported? The biggest question was, were these the bones from the "missing link" between the apes and mankind in the sequence of evolution?

Dubois was twenty-nine years of age when he found the bones. He spent the remainder of his life carrying the bones around and doing additional research. A sensitive man, Dubois was quite disturbed by the criticism which he received from both theologians and fellow scientists. He withdrew from the argument about the significance of the bones for nearly thirty years, but the controversy raged on. When Dubois eventually came out of seclusion, he continued to say that his Java Man was indeed the "missing link."

It has now been a little over a century since this remarkable and controversial discovery, and it can still cause great controversy among both scientists and theologians. The bones were found at a depth of approximately 50 feet and within a distance of about 50 feet of one another. They were found on a curve of the Solo River in Sangiran near Trinil, Java, Indonesia. This area in 1891 was referred to in the West as the Dutch East Indies. The most significant part of the find consists of a tooth, the cranial cap, and a thigh or femur bone. Measurements of the bones indicated that the man was about 5 feet, 8 inches tall. The bones of his head were much thicker and heavier than modern man. The top of the head also had a heavy sagittal ridge across the top for the attachment of powerful jaw muscles and a heavy browridge as well. The thick skull meant that he had a cranial capacity of about 900 cubic centimeters compared to modern man who has about 1200 cubic centimeters. The shape of the femur indicated that the person did walk fully erect.

The teeth are somewhat larger than modern man's and have traces of an enamel collar called ***cingulum*** around some of the crowns. The canine teeth which were found at this dig tend to overlap slightly. They were set in a heavy jawbone which had a receding chin. If the fragmentary evidence is placed on Lyell's geologic column, and when the other archaeological finds at this site are considered, they definitely belong to the **Paleolithic Age**. Very few things at the Solo River have been dated later than 700,000 years ago. Java Man is therefore currently regarded as one of the oldest human finds. Further digs at this site in 1932, 1936, and 1939 all confirm this general time period. Undoubtedly there is much more to be discovered about our early ancestors in Java.

This find does not measure nearly as old in time as the Leakey discoveries in Central Africa or some of the bones found in South Africa. Java Man is most notable for the early date at which it was found by Dubois, 1891, and the controversy which it stirred because it was a close follow-up to the writings of Darwin and others concerning human evolution.

It should also be kept in mind that Eugene Dubois was more than just an interested citizen who went to Indonesia on a wild hunch that he could find the "missing link." He had received an excellent education and was teaching anatomy at the Royal Normal School in Amsterdam before his departure for Southeast Asia. He had read widely from the best authorities in the field during the late 19th century. It is unfortunate that Eugene Dubois died a bitter man. Had he had the good fortune to live until our present age, he would have better understood that everyone who has discovered some new archaeological find has been subjected to the same kind of close scrutiny. Dubois would be pleased to know that mankind are now believed to have first moved into the Southeast Asian peninsula about one million years ago.

LIFE IN THE STONE AGE PERIOD

The lifestyle of *Homo erectus* in the Paleolithic Age was certainly not easy. The term "Paleolithic" refers to the old tool age, better known as the Old Stone Age. A large share of this type of specimens have been found in the warmer climates such as Africa and Java. Those who moved north, such as Peking Man, must have either learned to shelter themselves from the elements and to live with the four seasons, or else they suffered a lot. We do know that they used simple tools made from stone. It is safe to assume that they also had tools of wood and bone which have not survived to the present time.

All studies of tooth wear indicates that Paleolithic Man ate roots, bulbs, tubers, and other vegetables and fruits. These kinds of food can be easily dug with a stick and they can be carried long distances through barren areas to provide both food and some water without spoiling. It is not inconceivable that they learned to save nut crops, a ready source of fat, protein and minerals for colder weather, or between crops of natural fruits and grains, which were gathered when they were in season. Perhaps they were able to trap fish or small game animals. We have no evidence of the bones of small mammals or of birds because the frail bones would have long since decomposed.

It is safe to assume that they dried some fruits or other crops to tide them through dormant seasons. None of the Java sites from this period indicate the manufacture of pottery. Without jars for storage there would have been a problem keeping dried fruits or vegetables clean, dry enough so they would not mold, and safe from insects, rats, and other rodents. There is no evidence that they did any cultivating or that they had domesticated any animals. In conclusion, they were strictly hunters and gatherers.

Prehistoric Southeast Asia

When Dubois and his team continued digging in the second year, they unearthed a number of specimens of fossil pig, primitive elephant bones, rhinoceros, deer, tiger, hyaena and many other species. This certainly indicates that *Homo erectus* might have been a heavy meat eater. No one is completely certain how they obtained the meat, since the ability to throw things such as spears is not believed to have been developed in the human brain at this early time. Since wildlife was abundant, there are those who believe that they ate the young, the old, and the sick and crippled animals which would have been easier to catch. Some speculate that they drove away the lions or other animals which had originally killed the larger beast and seized it for themselves.

Still another theory centers on the idea that a sizeable number of the community would hunt cooperatively in order to drive the animals into swamps where the heavy animals would get mired down and thus become easy prey. Perhaps they were caught at the water's edge as they came down to drink. In any event, nearly all the sites of *Homo erectus* have sizeable numbers of bones from both large and small wild animals. At some sites the skeletal remains were even arranged carefully in rows, which would indicate some possible religious significance.

Another interesting discovery about the sites of *Homo erectus*, regardless of which part of the world they are located, is that they used a "basic tool kit." This was first noted at a dig being conducted at St. Acheul in France and it has since been referred to as the "**Acheulean Tool Kit**." Such a kit included a simple but versatile range of chopping, cutting, piercing, scraping and pounding tools. There was a handaxe for chopping and pounding, and a long-edged cleaver for butchering included in every kit. The cleavers do vary somewhat in style or shape, but basically they are pretty much alike. The same can be said for the other small tools found on each site. Spearpoints, axes, awls, scrapers, and later the arrow-points also have an amazing similarity wherever they are found around the world.

Does this mean that they all developed the same tools coincidentally, or does it mean that they all came originally from the same location on the earth and then branched out to places as far separated as South Africa, Europe, Java and China? The *Homo erectus* people used this same kit well into **Mesolithic--Middle Stone Age--times**. In northern Europe it was still used as late as 100,000 years ago. No really marked refinement of these tools occurred over several hundred thousand years regardless of location. Some would say that since there was so little degree of design change over time and distance, it would imply that *Homo erectus* had few skills and little imagination compared with the later *Homo sapiens*. It should also be remembered that advancements were introduced much more slowly than in modern times. Prehistoric peoples discovered ways of coping and surviving and they were basically very conservative. They did not want to change too rapidly because when they knew what worked for survival, any change might lead to a disastrous end. Their very survival depended upon repeating the seasons and tools of the past.

All of the early stone tools were either picked up in riverbeds during the dry season and used in their natural state, or if they were worked on a stone anvil, it was by pounding off chips with another rock, that is by "percussion." During the Mesolithic Age they began to "flake" the tools to their desired shape from flint and chert type rocks. It is difficult for us to imagine the primitive stage in which our early ancestors lived some 700,000 or more years ago.

So far as we know the remains of people of this early Paleolithic Age were just "common folks." There is a long chronological gap in archaeological finds between these people and the beginning of people's bones of a much later age. Southeast Asia today is an anthropologist's paradise. In its mountains and jungles live the remnants of a great variety of peoples representing early stages of its ethnological history. There are still pigmy Negritos living as primitive nomads, peoples akin to the Australian aborigines, and others that would appear to be Indonesians in earlier stages of development. These people are often referred to simply as the **"hill tribes**." There has obviously been a great deal of intermixture between the earlier inhabitants and the people who arrived later.

Some of the bones discovered in later years in Java show that they are related to both Java Man and to Peking Man (*Sinanthropus*), as well as some of the earliest cultures from northwest India and Burma. This has led some authorities to speculate that one branch of *Homo sapiens* ("thinking man") may even have originated in the area of Southeast Asia. The archaeological finds in Southeast Asia do not confirm this theory. It is more likely that the earliest people were migrants who moved into the peninsula rather than natives who developed a culture uniquely different. At least the tools which were used by these people are almost identical to tools from the same time from around the world. The digs in Southeast Asia also indicate that there were people with different physical and cultural characteristics who inhabited the Southeast Asian peninsula at various times.

Figure 37

Figure 38

376

Chapter 42
THE NATURE OF CIVILIZATION IN SOUTHEAST ASIA TO c.1600

THE CULTURAL DIVERSITY OF SOUTHEAST ASIA

The original inhabitants of mainland Southeast Asia were probably an Australoid people who intermarried with the earliest migrants coming from the Indian subcontinent. When the two races joined, it formed a new group of people called Melanesoid. Later, around the third to the second centuries B.C., groups of people began migrating south out of southern and southwestern China. Of all the peoples who moved south, the Tai and the Vietnamese were the most Sinicized. The Tibeto-Burmans brought an entirely different culture to the Southeast Asian peninsula. Nearly all of those who migrated south out of the China and Tibetan areas followed the river valleys through the mountain passes into the Southeast Asian peninsula.

About the same time the European traders began to arrive, sometime after 1500, the Chinese traders from the north began accelerating their trading interests in the peninsula. The Chinese were followed very shortly by another wave of Indian and some Arabic traders. Like the Chinese, the Arabic traders were eager to become the middlemen merchants. Most of the Chinese merchants bought for the the Chinese market, whereas the Arabic traders planned to wholesale the goods produced by the local Melanesians to the European merchants. A trade which was profitable for both the merchants and the people of Southeast Asia grew from this foreign trade. A few of these traders intermarried with the people of Southeast Asia, primarily the Indians and the Chinese. The combination of dozens of ethnic groups who came from southern China, Tibet, and India, along with the merchants, has produced a very mixed ethnic people, especially in the large port cities. The rural villages have remained much more ethnically conservative.

Indian traders and missionaries brought Hinduism and Buddhism in the wake of trade. Both of these religions slowly penetrated the area over a period of several centuries. The Arabic traders brought the Islamic faith, which soon overwhelmed the two older faiths in Indonesia and Malaysia, spreading as far as the Island of Mindinao in the Philippines. Christianity was introduced by the Europeans just after 1500, but never made more than a limited impact on the peninsula. Christianity won more converts in the Philippines.

SOUTHEAST ASIA IN PREHISTORIC TIMES

It has often been a great temptation of western historians to look at Southeast Asia as the "Balkans of Asia," and to write about the Chinese influence, the Indian influence, the Arabic influence, and the European influence. It should be clearly understood at the outset that the people of Southeast Asia did have--and continue to have--their own distinctive culture and past history. The art and architecture which blossomed so wondrously in Angkor, Pagan, central Java, and the old kingdom of Champa are strangely different from that of Hindu and Buddhist art and architecture in India or China, even though they did borrow heavily from those areas, especially philosophical ideas. Each area of Southeast Asia developed its own culture and no two of them are alike. Each of the areas of Southeast Asia has been selective concerning what they would keep and what they rejected about each of the outside philosophies.

Southeast Asia--the Ancient Period

The archaeological evidence of early man in the area is quite rich but as yet much of it still awaits the funds to do the archaeology. All of the discoveries in Southeast Asia have been shown to be closely related to the same type as **Peking Man**, a couple of thousand miles to the north. No one knows at this time exactly what course the development of early mankind followed in the two areas--China and Southeast Asia. It is also interesting that their artifacts have a remarkable resemblance to those of the early cultures of northwest India and similar human remains found in Burma. Some of the Paleolithic finds in Vietnam are believed to be as old as 500,000 years ago. There is reasonably good evidence that agriculture began as early as 7000 B.C. The problem with archaeology in all of Southeast Asia is that there was no system of writing in place until rather late, and all interpretation must be done on the basis of archaeology or their stone carvings. Not all of these early cultures carved on stone.

Best archaeological and anthropological evidence indicates that the people of Southeast Asia from the earliest Paleolithic to possibly as late as the early Neolithic ages very likely practiced some form of ritual cannibalism. There was a division of labor with the men serving as hunters, fishermen, and food collectors, while the women tended to the family affairs and a little later, cultivated the soil with a primitive mattock. The men plowed the fields and built the houses. They made the tools, and weapons, and in many of the cultures, they wove the cloth. They traveled throughout the region, including many of the islands, with heavy canoes made from hollowed out tree trunks. Small tools and utensils were made of bone and pottery. Their stone tools are unique in that they were only worked on one edge. Slate was used for knives, scrapers, and sickles for harvesting grain. The characteristics of the people of this region were, therefore, not very different from any other prehistoric people from any other part of the world.

The origins of agriculture in Southeast Asia are as yet unknown. Best speculation is that some form of cultivation began as early as 6,000 to 7,000 B.C. within most of the peninsula, and the islands followed with some farming by about 3,000 B.C. Many of the people in Southeast Asia lived in the mountainous areas. The soil was not very rich and every two or three years they would have worn out the productivity of the soil and be forced to move on. Slash-and-burn cultivation was very common in the mountains. Once the area had been burned over, they would punch holes in the soil with a sharpened stick, then drop a few seeds in the hole. The crop which was most often planted in this form of farming was millet. There is evidence of tools made of stone which served an agricultural purpose as early as 6,000 B.C. Some of the shell tools found in their middens also point to this date.

There were also whorls, usually made of clay, for spinning which date from about the same time. No one knows at this time whether cotton was grown agriculturally or whether it was gathered wild. Pottery also came into general usage around the same time. Mankind was beginning to move from a forager to a settled, self-sufficient farmer. Many of these sites are from northern Vietnam with some indication that the knowledge of rice and other agricultural crops was shared by the people living along the coast of southeastern China. The culture which developed in northeast Thailand also dates to about this same time.

It is impossible at this time to pinpoint the origin of the Neolithic peoples described above. Anthropologists have used both the tool-weapon approach as well as tracing origins by linguistics. The best guess on the location of the earliest cultures in Southeast Asia seems to center in either Cambodia or Vietnam. A few authorities would move this farther north because of the number of innovations which seem to have originated in southern and western China, then moved south along the river valleys into Southeast Asia.

Southeast Asia--the Ancient Period

THE DONG-SON CULTURE

By around 500 B.C. these people were beginning to work in bronze and iron. This was several years later than most other areas of either Asia or Europe. This early Southeast Asian culture has been given the name **Dong-Son** from a village in Tongking (Vietnam). Another term, the "Malay culture" should be thought of as pertaining to a large portion of the Southeast Asian peninsula, not just presentday Malaysia.

The Dong-Son culture shared many characteristics with the people from the province of Yunnan in southwestern China. Anthropologists also believe that these early people of Dong-Son may have had a communal society during their formative period. Within a relatively short time they had established a very hierarchial society. The upper and the ruling classes were buried in graves rich in artifacts which they planned to carry into the next world.

Since Dong-Son was a Bronze Age culture, they manufactured all kinds of bronze products from plowshares to fishhooks. One of their specialties seems to have been large, beautifully decorated bronze kettle drums. With finer quality bronze tools, their wood carving and boat building improved substantially. With better boats their hardy seafarers acquired some knowledge of geography, astronomy, and navigation, all of which led them to travel great distances as both merchants and explorers. Some of their trade names for weights and measures are still used in both India and China. Some of the families accompanied these seafarers to colonize other uninhabited islands scattered around the South Pacific.

There is no indication that they learned to work with bronze from the Chinese. Most authorities believe they either discovered the technique themselves or they borrowed it from northeastern Thailand. In any event, the raw copper and tin came from Thailand. Dong-Son became quite wealthy because they were on a reasonably level route from the Tibetan highlands to the South China Sea. It was still a thriving area when it was conquered by the Han Chinese in A.D. 43. This seems to have effectively ended the Dong-Son culture in northern Vietnam.

The peoples of Southeast Asia have had a long and settled culture. Although the influx of traders from the West, from India, China, and from Japan have altered them to some degree, their basic culture has remained unchanged over thousands of years. Major changes are quite evident in the large coastal cities, but the modernization becomes less evident in the rural areas.

THE REGIONAL AND ETHNIC GROUPS IN SOUTHEAST ASIA

The people of Southeast Asia fall broadly into three groups according to the general areas they inhabit. There are those who inhabit the **coastal areas** from Bangladesh on the west to the area of southeastern China, including the river deltas. Secondly, there were those people who inhabit the **island areas**. The extent of this area can be stretched all the way to the Hawaiian Islands but pertains primarily to Indonesia, Sumatra, Java, Borneo, the Moluccas, etc. The third group inhabits the **upper river valleys** and the **mountainous areas.** Those who live along the coastal areas, especially the large port cities, seem to be the most advanced. Those who live in the mountainous areas seem to be the least advanced. Many of the port cities were considered large by the earliest European traders of the 16th and 17th centuries. The people who live in the mountains and the hidden valleys, often referred to as the "**hill tribes**," have changed little in the last thousand years.

Each of these three areas developed its own unique characteristics. Some concentrated upon wood carving, some set up huge megalithic stones with burial jars around them, some gave a remarkably high status to women, while others were at one stage or another of the evolution of tools, housing, navigation, agricultural cultivation, and the domestication of livestock.

On the mainland there were the **Chams** in **Annam**, what is today central and northern Vietnam. Annam's most important city was **Hue**. The people known as the **Khmers** lived in the Mekong delta and the middle Mekong region, the area of presentday Cambodia (Kampuchea). The Khmers have lived in the same area for thousands of years. They speak a language which is a mixture of many of the small minority groups who inhabit the Cambodian area. It is closely related to the language of the Mons.

Another important ethnic group of Southeast Asia are the **Mons** (Talaing). The Mons were once a large group of people who lived in what is now Burma (Myanmar) and Thailand (Siam). Around the first century A.D. this was a large and prosperous group who spread into other areas of Southeast Asia, especially the Malay peninsula. The Mons have long wanted their own national state and have fought wars with neighboring ethnic groups to accomplish their goal. They once had their own independent country at the mouth of the Irrawaddy River in Burma. All of their wars in more recent history can be considered unsuccessful. Many have been killed in those wars and the remainder of the Mons have merged with the local people of the area and their identity as a separate ethnic group seems to be disappearing.

Among the very earliest known inhabitants of presentday Burma were an ethnic group known as the **Pyus**. The Pyus were living in Burma possibly as long as a thousand years **before** the arrival of the **Tibeto-Burmans** and the **Mons** in that area. It is believed that the Pyus laid the foundations of the great civilization which developed at **Pagan** and the less cultured Tibeto-Burmans simply adopted a large share of the Pyus culture as their own. There has been so little archaeological work done to date in this area that conclusive answers are impossible. It is known that the Pyus buried their dead in large urns. They were also a progressive group of people who were directly involved in the India-China trade with the West, well before the first century B.C.

Another important ethnic group of Southeast Asia is the **Malay** (Melayu) people, primarily inhabiting the area of Malaysia. Originally, the term Malay referred to someone who was a descendant of a select few from Sumatra. The original Malay people were apparently from both sides of the **Straits of Malacca** (Melaca). The people of Melaka differentiated themselves from others by their behavior, dress, language, and manners until the arrival of Islam in the 14th century. At that time Islam became yet another distinguishing factor. Anyone who was not a Muslim was not a true Malay. Although some of these distinguishing factors have faded in recent times, they were very important up to the arrival of the Europeans.

THE INDIAN INFLUENCE

It is very difficult to assess the impact of the Indians upon Southeast Asia. Exact dates when the Indian traders began visiting Southeast Asia seem to be sketchy and varied, each expert selecting his own period. Some authors trace this back as far as the Dravidian era of South India.

Southeast Asia--the Ancient Period

This theory cannot discern whether the people of Southeast Asia had the greater influence upon India or whether the Indians of South India fled to Southeast Asia at the time of the Aryan invasions. All do agree that the seafarers and merchant-traders were quite significant in this exchange of culture.

The main influence came at about the time of the dawn of the Christian era, that is roughly 200 B.C. to A.D. 200. The Indian settlers did have an impact at that time, particularly along the coastal areas. Most of them were merchants, or in some way associated with trade. It has been speculated that they might have come to trade, were caught there by the monsoon season, and decided to stay. The monsoons are known to have governed the way people lived then a great deal more than today. As the Indian traders moved in, they did exert an "influence" rather than to appear as a horde of invaders or conquerors. They "settled in" and became almost like the locals except that they introduced their two major religions, Hinduism and Buddhism.

Some writers prefer the term "**Hinduization**" when writing about this era of Southeast Asian history. That would not be entirely correct because **Buddhism** also left an indelible impact. **Theravada Buddhism** ultimately became the dominant faith of Burma and Arkan, the Thai states and Cambodia. The Theravada school of Buddhism believe that Buddha showed us the way as the great teacher. It is now up to each individual to seek and follow Buddha's path to Enlightenment. Enlightenment **is** the goal of thousands of Buddhist monks throughout most of Southeast Asia. The term "**Indianization**" is therefore a better term to apply to the cultural transfer from the subcontinent.

Vietnam, heavily influenced by China for about a thousand years, more closely follows the **Mahayana Buddhist** teaching, whereby the practice of the faith is on a broader basis than the often narrow teachings of Theravada Buddhism. It should be added immediately, however, that in Southeast Asia one finds Hinduism intermixed with Buddhism to such an extent that the mixture itself has become almost a new religion. Local animistic traditions are also often mixed with the other major faiths. In the western world we see the two faiths as distinctly separate, but in Southeast Asia they have experienced no major conflict in mixing them together.

To carry this even further, several of the areas of Southeast Asia which have huge Buddhist temples, at the same time had Brahmin priests playing an important part in the court ceremonies. This seems to have been a local adaptation, or invention of convenience, in countries such as Myanmar (Burma), Siam (Thailand), and Kampuchea (Cambodia). The Buddhist countries which employed Brahmin court advisors liked the idea of the ruler as Vishnu or Shiva incarnate. As a living god it made them more powerful to their people. The Hinduism which swept across Java has left its impact on the next island to the east, **Bali**. Here, Hindu temples abound even today. Buddhism also swept across Java and left its most lasting monument at the huge temple of **Borobudur**.

A large share of our early knowledge of this area comes from the Hindu writings. Even the earliest Sanskrit inscriptions in Southeast Asia only date back to the 4th century. There do not seem to be valid chronicles of early times composed by the Southeast Asians themselves. Chinese writings do touch upon the area, but they also are very sketchy and sometimes biased. The earliest Roman contacts with the area were in the first century A.D. This trade was largely confined to India and areas to the west. There is very little mention by the Roman chroniclers of lands to the east of India. The Romans seemed to know about a place they called **Chryse** (gold land), now identified as Myanmar (Burma), but there is no proof that any of them had gone there.

Southeast Asia--the Ancient Period

By A.D. 165, the Roman imbalance of payments was beginning to slow down their trade with the eastern world. When the barbarians began to invade the Roman empire, they broke off their trade with the East altogether in order to have resources to defend Rome itself. Contact was not re-established until the 16th and the 17th centuries.

The discussion of the Indian influence in Southeast Asia has so far been concerned with the sea routes. Whether the Indians came from the South, the Madras area, or from the Bengali area in the northeast of India, the fact remains that the Southeast Asians were also extremely competent as navigators traveling westward towards India. With the smaller, less-seaworthy vessels of those early times, travel tended to follow wind direction as dictated by the monsoon. In the spring and early summer months the trade followed the southwesterly winds from India to Southeast Asia. When the winds reversed in the wintertime, the trade flowed from the northeast towards India.

Not to be overlooked, however, was a northerly land route from India to China through Assam, Upper Myanmar and connecting with Yunnan Province in southwestern China. Historical evidence shows this route to have been in use as early as 128 B.C. This benefited South China as well as the Southeast Asian area, and in A.D. 69, the Chinese established a special district to control the access to the upper Mekong River valley. The headquarters of this district was only 60 miles from the present Myanmar frontier on the north. This same overland route was used by many Buddhist pilgrims from China as they journeyed to the India-Nepal-Ceylon area to study Buddhism. This land route was either closed or its usefulness was uncertain following about 342.

Figure 39

Chapter 43
THE SOUTHEAST ASIAN NATIONS TO c.1600

Since each of the several nations of Southeast Asia have had such very different political histories, it is appropriate to study each of them individually. The nation with the oldest record of development, so far as we now are aware, was Vietnam. One of the most powerful of the nations of Southeast Asia in the early years was Cambodia. The Thai were probably the most fiercely independent. The Burmese were different than the remainder of the Southeast Asian nations in that they were settled by a different ethnic group and they were very expansionist. The island nations were interested primarily in trade. Vietnam was most influenced by Chinese culture, partly because they were a part of China for about 1000 years. The remainder of Southeast Asia has been influenced more by India.

VIETNAM

All of the very old remains which have been discovered so far have been found in limestone caves in the cliffs of northern Vietnam. The stone tools in this area have been made from a rock called basalt rather than from flint or slate as in most other parts of the world. Although there are Paleolithic discoveries, the majority of the artifacts belong to the Mesolithic or the Neolithic cultures of this area. The legends covering this period of at least 2000 years before recorded history are probably as interesting as the actual artifacts.

Tradition tells how their early leaders were descendants of **Lac Long Quan**, a dragon lord who had risen from the sea. It was Lac Long Quan who taught the people how to grow rice and that it was proper to wear clothes. Once he had driven the evil spirits from the land the people were allowed to safely occupy Vietnam and to till the soil. They seem to have been doing very well until one day a Chinese lord tried to conquer Vietnam and to rule it for himself. Lac Long Quan returned to earth, captured the Chinese ruler's wife, and she gave birth to the sons which were to rule over Vietnam as the **Lac lords**.

In order to escape crossing the ridge of mountains across the north of Vietnam, the Chinese have always been inclined to move down the coastal area. As a consequence, Chinese influence has been heavy, especially in the northern area at least as far south as Hue. Since the Chinese kept records, sometimes biased in favor of China, they claim that the early Chinese who moved into Vietnam were the ones who taught the Vietnamese how to change from a hunting and gathering stage to the production of rice under settled agriculture. The Chinese records claim that the Vietnamese were still farming by the slash-and-burn technique. All sources would agree that the Chinese influence was significant, but the Vietnamese had probably already moved to a state of fixed agriculture before the Chinese arrived.

Chinese interference in Vietnamese affairs increased during the Han dynasty, 206 B.C. to A.D. 9, and by 111 B.C., the Chinese simply took over Vietnam and ruled it as one of their provinces. They were often totally overbearing in their effort to Sinicise their culture, and in A.D. 40 the Vietnamese, who have always been very independently minded, staged a revolt against their Chinese rulers. This revolt was led by two sisters--Trung Trac and Trung Nhi--who were daughters of one of the Lac lords. Apparently their revolution was quite successful. However, China was not willing to give up their most southern province so easily. They invaded with an army of 20,000 men and actually strengthened their hold over the area. One tradition says that the Chinese general beheaded the two ladies, while another claims they jumped into a river and committed suicide rather than to fall into the hands of the Chinese. Lac Long Quan, the sea dragon, did not reappear to rescue the sisters.

The Chinese government encouraged settlers to move down into Vietnam. Many of them developed land, settled down and soon began intermarrying with the Vietnamese. The Chinese did introduce the metal plow, they brought in more domesticated animals, and the irrigation dikes were greatly improved. It was at this time that the people of Vietnam began growing wet rice extensively. As the Chinese conquered land to the south of the Red River, moving along the Vietnamese coast, they encountered another Vietnamese ethnic group south of Hue who controlled an area they called **Champa**. This independent little country followed the area between the mountains and the sea down into the Mekong River delta. Champa was a wealthy country with a rich rice-growing area. They had been influenced for many years by the Indian traders, who had an active business going with Champa. Both Hinduism and Buddhism were popular, along with some Sanskrit.

It was in Champa that the Indian influence and the Chinese influence met. They were two very different approaches. The Chinese came to conquer and control the area while the Indians were interested primarily in the trade goods. The Indian influence was largely a voluntary acceptance on the part of the Vietnamese--the Chinese influence was often forced upon the people by the men who came to govern Vietnam. India had also heavily influenced Cambodia, Pagan (Burma), and Srivijaya (Sumatra) in the same manner--through trade. Throughout these several centuries the Chinese had always thought of themselves as the center of the universe and they were doing the "barbarians" in Vietnam a great favor by bringing their civilization to them.

Chinese influence in Vietnam increased during the period of troubles between the end of Han dynasty about 220 and the beginning of the T'ang in 618. During this disturbing period of China's history the dynasties came and went. China was often divided into three or more parts during this 400-year period due partially to internal dissention and partially to outside invaders, largely from the north. Throughout these troubled years China never gave up their claims to Vietnam. Furthermore, thousands of Chinese moved south to take up residence in the more peaceful environment of Vietnam. Vietnam staged a revolt to achieve their independence in 541, but China sent an army down and defeated the independence movement within three years. The area of Laos had sent an army to help Vietnam, but it was not enough. It is said that the Chinese offered to pay for the Vietnamese leader's head with gold. In 547 he was assassinated bringing to an end Vietnam's hopes of an independent status for many years.

It was the T'ang Chinese, 618 to 906, who began calling Vietnam **Annam**, "the pacified south." But it was not totally peaceful. In 855 the Tai combined with Vietnam to expel a growing Chinese influence throughout Southeast Asia. This proved to be a long struggle, but in 939 the Vietnamese declared their independence. This led to another effort by China to hold on before Vietnam was totally lost. Order was not restored again until 968 by **Dinh Bo Linh**, one of Vietnam's heroes. During his years there were many Buddhist monasteries built, a reward for Buddhist support during the long struggle for independence. Vietnam promised to cooperate with China in exchange for the Chinese promise that they would recognize the Vietnamese independence. They also had to promise to pay tribute to China, but it was not that heavy a tax. At last they had won their independence after 1000 years of Chinese occupation and domination.

Southeast Asia to 1600--Vietnam

Vietnam's first emperor was **Le Long Dinh**, 1010 to 1029. It was Le who built the capital city at presentday **Hanoi**, a city surrounded with huge earthen walls. He adopted a Chinese style of government, since the Vietnamese had not known any other system for hundreds of years. Confucianism was not popular at first in Vietnam, but by this time the orderly system of government did have its appeal, especially to the educated class in Vietnam. Le Long Dinh built Vietnam's first university where Confucianism was not to be the central educational theme, but as in government, they were so intimately tied to China's culture that the elimination of Confucianism proved impossible. The university graduates did win the government positions and Vietnam began to build their own system of government and an educated class. Le also promoted agriculture, and established flood control projects along the Red River.

The Chinese tried often to come back, and the rising power of Cambodia, sensing the weakened state of Vietnam, decided to attack them from the other side under their warrior king, Suryavarman II. Not content with one try, Suryavarman II tried again, also unsuccessfully. He then decided to campaign in Champa, followed by an attack on the old city of Angkor. These diversionary expeditions on the part of the Cambodians gave Vietnam some relief. At the same time, the Khymers and the Chams both made efforts to steal a piece of Vietnamese territory. All of these outside attacks were repelled by one of Vietnam's most successful generals, **Ly Thuong Kiet**, 1019 to 1105. Ly was a eunuch general whose fame was established when he captured the Cham king in 1069. He carried his victory on into the Cham territory and incorporated the rich rice growing Mekong River delta to Vietnam's borders. This conquest also added the Cham-Indian culture to the Vietnamese culture. From 1075-1077 Ly led a preemptive strike against the Sung Chinese which resulted in the capture of Nanning. It was during this campaign that he wrote a poem stating Vietnam's right to be independent.

The Tran dynasty, 1225-1400 succeeded the Le Long Dinh period. They had scarcely begun to restore order and recover from their wars for independence, when the Mongols staged three invasions of their country--1257, 1258, and 1287. At the same time they invaded Champa and Cambodia in 1283, and Pagan in Burma fell in 1287. When the Mongols seized Yunnan province in southwest China, they forced many of the Tai people to flee into presentday Thailand. All of Southeast Asia was thrown into a state of confusion by these tough warriors form the northern steppes.

Three times they invaded Vietnam and there was no other country able to assist them--even India was suffering. Kublai Khan demanded the right to cross Vietnam to attack Champa. This demand was refused and the Mongols arrived with an army estimated at 500,000 and crossed Vietnam anyway. The Vietnamese cut their supply lines and forced the Mongols to withdraw. This was only temporary and they returned again. The situation looked hopeless but the Vietnamese, under general **Tran Hung Dao**, set bamboo stakes with steel points in the bottom of the Bach Dang River at low tide. When the tide was running high, the Vietnamese army began retreating up the river. They prolonged the battle while the tide began going out. They had not gone far when their boats became impaled on the bamboo stakes. Their entire force was lost--about 300,000 men. The Vietnamese knew there was no way their army could win a head-on battle with the Mongol forces. They resorted more and more to guerrilla tactics which were much more effective. At least they made the price of staying in Vietnam more costly than any rewards possible from a country of rice paddies. Besides, the Mongol tactics of fighting from horseback did not work well in the rice paddies.

Southeast Asia to 1600--Vietnam

General Tran Hung Dao made it so uncomfortable for the Mongols that they were able to consider a peace arrangement regarding Vietnam. The Tran monarch sent a mission to the court of Kublai Khan where an arrangement was made which recognized Vietnam's independence as a tributary state of China. Vietnam also agreed to make a payment to the Chinese every three years. It was not a perfect solution but it "saved face" for both countries and it ended the war between them. A period of great literary achievement occurred at this time. The government commissioned a thirty-volume official history of **Dai-Viet**, the name they now gave their country. There were several other histories written of Vietnam's struggles as a nation along with several biographies of their kings and heroes. Interestingly they were all written in Chinese. Vietnam was beginning to discover its own rich past as a nation.

The economy did not flourish following the wars because the costs had been too great. Other countries were still suffering under the Mongols and the Vietnamese had little market for their goods. The government suddenly seemed weak and helpless. A regent named Ho Qui Ly thought the return of the Chinese would be good for his country. They were only too happy to return in 1407. The result was a crushing level of taxation accompanied by forced Chinese culture and other indignities. Many of the poor ended up in slave labor. The Chinese even took the Vietnamese archives, along with several scholars, back to China. This was one of Vietnam's darkest periods.

One of the rich landlords who was known for his generosity decided to raise an army to push the Chinese out forever. The Lam Son Uprising began in 1418 with several Vietnamese defeats. **Le Loi** managed to avoid capture and kept up a series of guerrilla attacks until the Chinese were obviously losing. In 1428 he declared himself emperor as Ly Thai To, the first of the **Le dynasty**, 1428-1524.

The Le dynasty was known for its policy of land redistribution and agrarian reforms. Le's armies began to add territory at the expense of the weakened Chams. Laos was forced to recognize Vietnam as their overlord. Writing in the Vietnamese language was encouraged. Women were given an almost legal status under the law. But Vietnam was still divided between the northern part and the southern part. The **Trinh Lords** ruled over the northern part with the power of Dutch guns, while the **Nguyen Lords** in the south purchased their arms from the Portuguese who had the better weapons. The Nguyen Lords extended their control into the Cambodian area to broaden their power base. The Trinh Lords controlled Hanoi and the wealthy Red River area. Both sides were fairly evenly divided with the consequence that the civil war continued for years. It was 1673 before the two factions could resolve their differences and bring peace to Vietnam. Both the Trinh and the Nguyen were strong supporters of Buddhism.

According to the Chinese records, the first Europeans had arrived in the delta area of the Red River in A.D. 166. This initial contact was not followed up until the arrival of the Portuguese in Da Nang in 1516. Dominican missionaries arrived in 1527. About this same time a trade began to grow at the port of Hoi An near Da Nang. In 1580 some Franciscan missionaries arrived from the Philippines. When the Jesuits were forced to leave Japan under Hideyoshi's expulsion order, several of them came to Vietnam. Trade began to grow with the western world during the 17th century.

CAMBODIA

Cambodia (Kampuchea) also has a dragon story about their very early history. One day a Brahmin, **Kaundinya**, appeared in a boat off the shore of Cambodia. One version says that the local dragon-princess rowed out to greet him. The Brahmin fired an arrow into her boat. The arrow caused her to be unable to resist him and she agreed to marry him. Her father, a great dragon lord, gave them a rich dowry. The Brahmin used his power to dry off the land so it could be farmed. The early coastal kingdom which developed in Cambodia was called **Funan**.

The other version has the Brahmin firing the arrow onto the land and with about the same consequences. The dragon forces were all lined up at the shore and the arrow hit one of them. The dragon-princess surrendered to the Brahmin immediately and they were married, thus beginning the first Khmer dynasty. The Cambodian court did have Brahmins as advisors for many years. They liked the Hindu concept that as rulers, the Brahmins claimed they were a living god, a reincarnated Shiva, a Vishnu, or Harihara. As gods they therefore could exercise absolute power over their subjects. Their capital at Angkor was designed to be a suitable sanctuary of the ruler-god. Since both stories have a Brahmin involved, it shows the close tie between India and Cambodia from the very earliest times. Hinduism was readily accepted throughout Funan but they did **not** adopt the caste system. Furthermore, women had many more rights than in India.

Between the prehistoric legends of the founding of Cambodia and the 5th and 6th centuries A.D., records are virtually nonexistent. The first reasonably reliable accounts do not begin until the early 9th century when a powerful ruler named **Jayavarman II** established the kingdom of Angkor. There are some Chinese accounts of the missing years, but these were constructed from the stories of Buddhist monks who had come to Cambodia in search of religious understanding, not as historians. China also sent some ambassadors to Funan. They referred to the people of Funan using an Indian script and having libraries and archives, but no record of these archives seems to exist.

The ethnic group living in the lower Mekong Valley and the delta area were referred to as the Funanese. The Chams lived just north of them, and the Khmers lived north of the Chams in the upper Mekong River valley. Many migratory peoples seem to have passed through the lower Mekong Valley with a general tendency of the northern groups to push south. A Mon-Khmer language seems to dominate linguistically, but there are evidences of many other influences, including the Indian-Sanskrit influence.

Funan was the first state to develop in the area. Apparently it was a merger which took place over a period of time with first the Chams, then the Khmers. The Khmer seem to have been a more dominating ethnic group. Funan's rise in importance was due to its port city of **Oc Eo** which was well situated to engage in the trade which passed from India to China. As the economy flourished, Oc Eo encouraged the expansion of the state of Funan to the north and to the south and west into the isthmus area of presentday Burma and Thailand. Their interest in the isthmus centered around a control of the east-west traffic, which seldom went south through the Straits of Malacca, but landed on the west side of the isthmus, transported the goods overland to the other side, then loaded it in other ships to complete the journey to India or China.

Southeast Asia--Cambodia

As the volume of trade at Oc Eo grew, the archaeological indications are that their contacts reached all the way to the Mediterranean world. Oc Eo expanded until it was a large walled city, one of the most prosperous in all of Southeast Asia. The trade brought in gold, silver, and jewels. The kings lived in luxury with harems, fine palaces, and they rode on the backs of elephants. The Chinese accounts marveled at the richness of their pageants. Many people owned slaves. Cock fighting was one of their spare time entertainments. Although the rulers professed Hinduism, it survived peacefully alongside Buddhism.

A new state to the north of Funan known as **Chenla** gradually began to overtake Funan between 539 and 802. The Chenla kingdom did not seem to cultivate the trade aspect as much as the Funanese and over time many ships going from India to China, or vice versa, bypassed the area by going around the southwestern shore of Sumatra and then heading north through the Strait of Sunda. A lot of the trade revenue which bypassed Chenla then created another new empire in the islands of Indonesia which was known as Srivijaya. By the 7th and 8th centuries the Chenla were under the control of the Khmers. The old economic glow was fading, but there was a burst of creative art which did utilize some Indian influences, but it was strictly Khmer at heart.

Cambodia's **Imperial Age**, from 802 to 1440, is also called the **Khmer Empire**. By 802 the northern and southern parts of Chenla seemed to be permanently separated. The ruler who pulled them together was **Jayavarman II**, 802 to 850. He utilized the old Funan as a nucleus-- what some called "Water Chenla"--the Mekong delta area. There was a connection between Jayavarman II and Java which is still not very clear, probably through intermarriage of the royal courts. Jayavarman II was a Mahayana Buddhist, but apparently his son was converted to the Theravada school of thought. He introduced this into Cambodia and it eventually replaced the Mahayana Buddhism. When the fortunes of the Khmer Empire began to sag again in 877, **Indravarman I** usurped the throne and began adding territory and building temples. Irrigation projects included a huge reservoir. He built a large pyramidal temple of stone called the **Bakong** with walls and moats. It was a "temple mountain" which housed a lingam, the phallic symbol of Shiva.

Indravarman I's son, **Yasovarman I**, 889 to 910, laid out an all new capital north of Lake Tonle Sap. It was to serve as Cambodia's capital until 1432. The new capital was called **Angkor Wat**, "the city that has become a Buddhist temple." Yasovarman I had temples built to Shiva, Vishnu, and Buddha, plus over a hundred temples in the provinces outside Angkor. Each successive ruler felt bound to add to the huge temple complex.

Even though Jayavarman II and his successors were influenced by both Javanese ideas and Hinduism, they became independent rulers uncontrolled by either Java or India. The king became a sacred personality who people were expected to worship. The Bakong became for these people the very center of their universe. This meant that the rulers were universal rulers in the world and hence they were not subservient to any other state. This philosophy knit the Khmer and the several other ethnic peoples of the area into one very powerful state known as the **Kingdom of Angkor**. Angkor's boundaries were approximately the same as presentday Kampuchea.

THE KINGDOM OF ANGKOR

The kingdom of Angkor's power eventually extended out to control large portions of Laos, Thailand, Burma, and the Malay Peninsula in addition to Cambodia.

Angkor was established in a fertile area north of the "Great Lake" known as **Tonle Sap**. This large lake acts as a reservoir when the Mekong River begins to flood. Instead of the water spreading out over the land as in most other river valleys, it backs up into Tonle Sap. This natural wonder caused the people to conceive other man-made reservoirs such as Indrataka (Indra's lake), the Eastern Baray, and the Western Baray. Canals then linked each of these bodies of water with a complex of other canals and reservoirs which ranged from small irrigation ditches to huge moats which connected the rural areas with the major cities and shrines.

Such a well-developed system of water management made the Angkor-Khmer people wealthy from the production of wet-rice and their fisheries. Some of their rice was "floating rice," a quick-growing rice from Champa that was able to grow in three meters of water. This variety of rice gave them at least two crops per year, which, along with fishing from the lakes and reservoirs, provided for rapid population growth and their imperial expansion.

Angkor's cultural life was strongly influenced by India. Even though their Hindu priests were called Brahmins and their warriors were called Kshatriyas, these positions were not hereditary and firm lines of social class were not drawn as in India. There was an inherited class for the upper nobility, there was a slave class--everyone else simply ranged in between but without firm dividing lines. The Indo-Aryan writing known as Sanskrit was used in the imperial courts and on the temple carvings. Most of the Angkor empire's temples were located in the area southeast of modern Siem Reap, the site of Angkor's successive capitals.

The best-known of these religious monuments is called **Angkor Wat**. The word **Angkor** designates either the capital city or the kingdom which was ruled from that city. A *wat* is normally a Buddhist temple or monastery, but most of the religious buildings at Angkor Wat are **Hindu** temples which were built to honor Vishnu. Many of the buildings were built by king **Suryavarman II**, who reigned from c.1113 to 1150. The king first made an agreement with China, then attacked Dai Viet (Vietnam) through Laos. In 1144 he defeated Champa in southern Vietnam and annexed it to the Khmer Empire. Suryavarman II sent 700 of his junks to harass the Vietnamese at the Gulf of Tonkin. It was a busy reign with its temple building and foreign campaigns. After his death the Chams pulled together and expelled the Khmers, then came to Cambodia and attacked Angkor.

Angkor Wat is the largest of several of this type of temple-mountains--possibly the largest temple in the world. All of these temples were created by a succession of Khmer rulers to demonstrate **Mount Meru**, where it was believed all the Hindu gods lived. Its five towers represent the five peaks of Meru. The outer walls symbolize the walls at the edge of the world, and the 540 foot wide moat outside the walls represents the oceans beyond.

The plan of the Angkor Wat complex is a huge rectangle which is oriented to the cardinal points. The overall dimensions of the temple are about 4,650 feet by 5,400 feet. The main approach to the temple-tomb was from the west, over a causeway, and through two terraced courtyards. The entire temple was built to represent an elaborate cosmographic and astronomical symbol. The walls of the outer gallery were decorated with bas-reliefs more than six feet high, a total of over 4,800 running feet of reliefs. The scenes depict kings, soldiers on the march, and mythological scenes from Hindu epics and texts. Angkor Wat was dedicated to Vishnu, but the patron saint of most of the temples in the Angkor area was Shiva.

Within the inner sanctuary of Angkor Wat was a gold statue of Vishnu mounted on the fabled winged Garuda. The image of the face of Vishnu was a representation of king Suryavarman. For all the temples dedicated to Hindu gods, it should be emphasized that the Khmer state was **not exclusively** a Hindu state. Buddhism was also practiced by many of the common people. The ruling class preferred Hinduism because it made them gods here on earth, some of them incarnations of Shiva, some of Vishnu.

THE BEGINNING OF DECLINE

Suryavarman was undoubtedly thought of as a great ruler by his own people. Looking back from the advantage of nearly a thousand years it is possible to see the beginning of the end of the Khmer Empire. The king had an almost constant warfare going against his neighbors. These campaigns were expensive and failed to achieve his goal of subjecting Vietnam, or the other kingdoms, to his total control. The great temple at Angkor Wat must have cost an enormous amount of money. Even though the Angkor Empire was the wealthiest one of Southeast Asia, the heavy taxes and the almost constant warfare drained the resources of his empire. A year before Suryavarman's death, c.1150, the Chams decided to invade the Khmer frontiers. Other minority groups began wanting their freedom. His successors began having both peasant and slave revolts. The people rose up and killed one of their kings. By 1177 the Chams thought they were strong enough to attack the capital at Angkor. The untimely death of the ruler and the fall of Angkor brought total chaos to the Khmer state. It appeared the Khmers were doomed.

It was at this moment in their history that Jayavarman VII, c.1181 to 1218, brought about a great change. He worked very hard to reestablish the Khmer state to its full status as it had been in previous years. Several successful campaigns were launched against the Chams along with a magnificent period of temple construction. Again, the enormous cost of the wars and the building of the temples and other public buildings hastened their eventual decline and fall.

It was during the reign of Jayavarman VII that the **Angkor Thom** temple complex was built. Second only to Angkor Wat, it cost the country a huge amount of money. Jayavarman is often characterized as the most active builder of all the Angkorian monarchs at a time when the empire was definitely not in a good financial condition.

Jayavarman VII centered his new city on the Bayon Buddhist shrine dedicated to the Buddhist bodhisattva Avalokiteshvara. The king built a wall over twenty feet high to encircle the city. Just outside the wall was a moat about 300 feet wide. There were five different gateways entering the city on causeways. The gateways, as well as the towers of Bayon, were ringed by four massive sculpted faces. Although it was centered on the older Buddhist shrine, the whole city embodied a Hindu myth of creation.

These two great temples--Angkor Wat and Angkor Thom--were just two examples of several in what was once the Khmer Empire's capital city. All were staffed by either priests or eminent teachers, usually from the wealthy families who had endowed the complexes. We have found no contemporary description of how the ceremonies were performed or the actual use of the temples on a daily basis. Some of the carving on the bas-reliefs include Sanskrit verse which gives the family history of the donor. It has always been assumed that they were built for religious purposes.

Jayavarman's victory over the Cham capital gave the Khmers an opportunity to sack the city and to take a great amount of wealth. Champa then remained under Khmer control from 1203 until 1220. By the end of his reign, Jayavarman controlled the area from Vientiane in Laos on the north, a large percentage of southern Thailand, and a large portion of the Malay peninsula on the south.

Even before the death of Jayavarman VII in 1218, yet another foreign threat was looming. The Tais had been filtering into the Chao Phraya valley since before the beginning of the 12th century. The Khmer people considered the Tai as ill-disciplined and strangely dressed men of little civilization.

No significant building took place at Angkor after the death of Jayavarman. Within two years, 1220, they had lost control over Champa. In 1238 a Tai chieftain mounted a successful coup d' etat against the Khmer governor and founded his own state. The Malay area simply drifted away. But, for the greater part of the 13th century Angkor remained a glittering and wealthy city. The king still came forth in great pomp and ceremony. The 13th century saw a shift away from the Khmer style of Hinduism toward the Theravada school of Buddhism, at least among the ruling class. No one can be sure about the religion of the general populace.

Since Theravada Buddhism came into the Khmer Empire, it was less socially demanding than either the Mahayana Buddhists or the Hindus. Each person was expected to work out his or her own plan of salvation. Among other things, Sanskrit disappeared and the Theravada Buddhists placed no priority on temple building. **Pali** became the sacred language.

Angkor fell to Tai attacks in 1369 and again in 1389. On both occasions the capital was occupied by the Tai forces. A third attack came in 1444 and after that time the Khmers abandoned their city. As the attacks became more frequent it was increasingly difficult to maintain the intricate hydraulic system upon which Angkor's economy had depended. Furthermore, thousands of prisoners of war were shipped out by the Tais. Many of these prisoners were the men who had formerly maintained the dikes and canals. Often they were the peasants who had worked the land and fed their own families as well as producing a surplus for the state. Squabbles among the members of the royal family about how to best combat their problems further weakened the Khmers.

The Khmers moved their capital south to modern **Phnom Penh** in 1444. This did not mean that Angkor and its temples suddenly disappeared. Since they had been based primarily upon Hindu traditions--while it was Buddhism which was now becoming the majority faith--the temples which the Buddhists did not occupy simply fell into disuse and eventual decay. The Vietnamese moved west against the shrinking Khmer state while the Tais moved east. The Khmers were squeezed in between the two in a small and weakened state. Only once, 1566-1576, did the Khmers have the military strength to reoccupy their capital city of Angkor. Finally, the greatly weakened Khmers were captured by the Tais in 1594.

Southeast Asia--Cambodia

One of the last desperate moves of the Khmer government was to seek assistance from the Portuguese and the Spanish who were now getting established in Southeast Asia. For a brief period the Spanish soldiers became arbiters of power within the Khmer state. A Spanish expedition arrived in Kampuchea in 1596 with the intention of giving aid to King Satha. Before they arrived, Satha had been deposed and a usurper, Chung Prei, occupied the throne. After a series of disagreements, and the sacking of the Chinese quarter of Phnom Penh by the Spanish forces, they attacked the king in his palace. Both the usurper king and his son were killed. About a year after this incident the Spanish found one of Satha's sons living in Laos. They took him back to Kampuchea and installed him as king in 1597.

Before the Spanish were able to stabilize the political situation the totally confused Khmers massacred the Spanish garrison. The Spanish left the area in disgust and Kampuchea was free of European domination until the French arrived in the mid-19th century.

IN SUMMARY

The beginning of the decline of the Khmers dates back to the 13th and the 14th centuries. There are no details preserved of the final collapse at Angkor, but the following are various theories, some of which are no longer considered very reliable.

Some authorities believe that the change from their modified Hinduism and Mahayana Buddhism to the Theravada caused a weakening of the drive and purpose which had long been exemplified by the earlier rulers. There were no major campaigns mounted to conquer vast new territories. In fact, they seemed powerless to defend what they already claimed.

Other researchers say they were overcome by malaria. This resulted when the elaborate system of reservoirs and irrigation canals broke down and was no longer maintained in the later years. The stagnant water allowed the mosquitoes to breed, the carriers of malaria. This theory is questionable today. Most authorities agree that the collapse of their complex irrigation system did lead to the breakdown of their economy. The previous years of expansion had been based upon the profits from the land which supported the armies and the massive temple building projects. Their population also declined due to less available food. This meant they had less men for their fighting forces. At the same time that they were losing their agricultural base, there was an increase in coastal trade, which shifted the center of population away from the interior city of Angkor to the coastal trading cities.

There is little doubt that the repeated attacks by the Tais and the Vietnamese sapped both their military and economic strength as well as taking the men for military service who normally maintained their elaborate reservoir and canal system. No one was safe to work on these for fear of attack. The Khmer government seemed helpless to provide the protection necessary for such work.

All authorities agree that overspending on elaborate temples and shrines would have destroyed the economy of any nation in the world at that time. Angkor Wat alone required hundreds of workers for thirty years to complete. Even though a high percentage of the work was done by slaves, they still needed to be fed and housed. There was also the additional cost of quarrying the stone and transporting it to the site. But in addition to the enormous temple buillding program, there was an almost constant war of aggression which also cost the economy dearly.

Finally, their inability to agree on a regular succession to the throne in the later years provided the lethal blow. They seemed to accept palace revolts and coup d'etats as the order of the day. The ordinary people had no say in the management of their government at all. There was no civil service worthy of the name as in China, Japan, or Vietnam. In this regard, it is amazing the Khmers lasted as long as they did. The answer to this is probably because they provided a neutral buffer between the Tais and the Vietnamese. It was not that they were declared neutrals, but rather that both of their neighbors knew in the last years that they were too helpless to initiate any major campaigns. Both Tai and Vietnamese policies were directed toward keeping the Khmers an inactive power. The Spanish might have been of some assistance to lend stability in order to tap the trade of the area. Even they seem to have concluded that the confusion outweighed the profits to be made.

Figure 40

THE KINGDOM OF NANCHAO

Nanchao was a Tai kingdom that arose in the 8th century in the Yunnan province of southwestern China. It tended to center around Lake Tali between the upper reaches of the Mekong, the Yangtze, and the Red rivers. The new province was formed with the encouragement of the Chinese government to act as a buffer between themselves and the aggressive Tibetans. Six Tai kingdoms joined together to form the Kingdom of Nanchao in 729. The term Nanchao means "Southern Princedom" in the Chinese language.

The first king of Nanchao was **Pi-lo-ko**, the king of one of the six small kingdoms. He encouraged the other five to join with him in the fertile valley around Lake Tali. Once the kingdom was established, China then tried to conquer it twice--751 and 754. Both attempts failed as the fiercely independent Tai fought for their freedom. The little kingdom was a reasonably rich valley area surrounded by mountains, thus making it difficult to attack.

Another source of wealth for the Nanchao came from their dominance of the overland trade routes from China to India on the west and Vietnam and the Tonking area to the southeast. As Nanchao's wealth and military power strengthened, they became more aggressive. They attacked Burma in 832 and Tongking in 862. They maintained a high level of culture throughout their brief history. Many of their people became skilled weavers of cotton and silk gauze. They mined both salt and gold. Nanchao was doing fine as a landlocked country until the military forces of Kublai Khan arrived in 1253.

Many of the Tai of Nanchao had been moving south through the mountain passes for many years. Their destinations included northern Vietnam, Laos, northern Thailand, and northern Burma. When Kublai Khan and his Mongol army captured Nanchao in 1253, thousands more Tai people moved south. It could be argued that if more of them had stayed in Nanchao they could have defeated the Mongols, especially since one of their armies destroyed a T'ang army of 50,000 men. At least some understanding of the place of Nanchao is necessary to comprehend the pressures placed upon northern Vietnam, Laos, Thailand, and Burma in these difficult times. The people from southern China, such as the Tai, placed a tremendous pressure upon the Khmers in Cambodia, the Malaysians, and even caused some migrating people to move off the Southeast peninsula onto the island kingdom of what is now Indonesia. The Mongols ultimately attacked as far from their base as Burma, Java, and Japan. Such a movement of people has had a profound effect upon all of Southeast Asia.

Of those who moved south out of Nanchao after Kublai Khan's capture of the area, the ones in northern Burma were called **Shans**, those in Laos were called **Lao**, those in Vietnam were called either **Thai Dam** (Black), or **Thai Deng** (Red). Those who moved into the valley of the Chao Phraya were known as **Siamese**. The largest single number of Tai moved into the Chao Phraya Valley to form what ultimately became Thailand. The Khmers of Cambodia were growing weaker which made it easier to move into the area.

THAILAND: AN INTRODUCTION

The area commonly known as Thailand today was once a part of Cambodia, Burma, and Laos. Thailand came into being after the Mongol domination of Southeast Asia began to diminish. As the struggle for Angkor in Cambodia continued, several of the Tai chiefs in the Chao Phraya River valley concluded that the time was right for them to push for separate statehood. Burma to the west had also been substantially weakened by Mongol aggression. Many of the Tai people who had formerly lived in the valleys of southern China and in Laos had pushed south with the advance of the Mongols. Once the Mongol power diminshed, while the other powers were weak and struggling toward recovery, there was no one predominant power in Southeast Asia. Thailand was formed during that power vacuum.

Sometime during the 13th century, the local Tai, and other chiefs who had survived as vassals of the Angkor rulers, began to establish independent principalities. One of the earliest of these, which dates back to the 1240s, has been identified as **Sukothai**. Another which was established in 1296 was the kingdom of **Chiang Mai**. Both were founded in the northern part of what is today Thailand. Once they had made the break with Angkor, several other principalities in the south began to follow the same pattern. These early efforts at state building, like several before the 13th century, were fragile and based largely around personalities who were able to provide the people with good leadership. Most of these were confined to only one mountain valley in the earliest stages--more of a city-state which was ruled over by a king. Such was the case with Sukhothai.

THE KINGDOM OF SUKOTHAI

The kingdom of **Sukothai** is generally accepted as the first Siamese kingdom in what is today Thailand. During its first century it was under the loose administration and influence of the Cambodian empire of Angkor. Its local chiefs had been given Khmer titles and regalia. The Sukhothai towns had both Hindu and Buddhist monuments. Many of the local Tai chiefs and their people had been moving from northern Laos into northern Thailand for over a century.

The kingdom of Siam began in the 1240s when two of these chiefs joined together to evict the Angkorian governor and to establish their own regime at the city of Sukothai. One of the chiefs, **Sri Indraditua**, became king and ruled over the region between the Ping and the Nan rivers for the next thirty years. The third king in the early dynasty, **Ramkhamhaeng**, who ruled from about 1279 to 1298, greatly expanded the kingdom by using a combination of diplomacy and warfare. In this fashion, Ramkhamhaeng gained vassals as far away as Luang Prabang in Laos.

At the same time that Ramkhamhaeng was trying to expand his kingdom, he collided with another newly forming Thai kingdom of **Lan Na (Chiang Mai)** and **Phayao** to the north. There were also the remnants of the old Angkorian power which was centered at the city of **Lopburi** in southern Thailand.

Some Tai historians give Ramkhamhaeng credit for his genial, patriarchial style in winning chieftains to his support, while others claim he was a military genius who pulled Thailand together by force. Still others say his successes can be attributed to the slowness of his powerful rivals to respond to his advances. In any event, by the end of the 13th century there was a Tai state where none had existed a century before.

Ramkhamhaeng's successors were not nearly so successful. The other emerging kingdoms began to challenge the growth of the state of Sukothai. Their greatest challenge came from the kingdom of **Ayudhya** in the south in the years following its founding by **U Thong** in 1351. King **Borommaracha I**, the ruler of Ayudhya from 1370 to 1388, made it his policy to eliminate his Thai rivals.

Other little kingdoms, such as **Lan Sang**, sprang up in **Laos** in 1353. From this time forward they pressured Sukothai, and by 1378 Sukothai was a vassal of Ayudhya. The last true king of Sukothai was **Mahathammarcha III**, 1398 to 1419. **Mahathammarcha IV** ruled over the area of Sukothai from 1419 to 1438, but he was only a puppet of the kingdom of Lan Sang in Laos. Upon his death the kingdom of Sukothai was incorporated as a province of Ayudhya.

THE KINGDOM OF AYUDHYA
1351-1767

The kingdom of **Ayudhya**, also known as Ayutthaya, is the classical kingdom of **Old Siam**. The kingdom's dates are generally accepted as 1351 to 1767. It centered on a vast level plain with ample water from the **Chao Phraya River** system. There is a legend in Laos that a great leader named Khun Borom, the divine originator of agriculture, handicrafts, manners, learning, and ritual, ruled over Dien Bien Phu for twenty-five years. At the end of that time, the legend says he sent his seven sons to rule over seven different Tai kingdoms which were scattered from North Vietnam diagonally across Southeast Asia. Since none of them were powerful enough to protect their people individually, U Thong founded Ayudhya as a central rallying point for all Tai people.

By the 14th century the power over this region which had been exercised by the Cambodian kingdom of Angkor and the neighboring kingdom of Lopburi had weakened to the point where the Tai, who were moving in from the northeast, joined with the local Mon minority to become an independent kingdom. Tai history shows that **Prince Ramathibodi I**, better known as **U Thong**, became the guiding light who led his people in joining with the people of the Ayudhya area to form the new kingdom on March 4, 1351. Their newly constructed capital city was located on an island in the Chao Phraya River. This was a wise location because it was easier to defend as an island, and the river was navigable from that point to the sea for sea-going vessels in the 14th century. They produced a surplus of agricultural goods, were militarily well organized, and became an acceptable independent kingdom to most of their neighbors from the very beginning.

During the kingdom's first century they aspired to become the power successors to the old Angkor kingdom and sent military expeditions to attack Angkor. Their chief rival in this quest for regional supremacy was the kingdom of Sukothai. As a consequence of their desire to dominate the area, they endeavored to win the support of other small kingdoms of the Indochinese peninsula who might be opposed to the Khmers of Cambodia and to Sukothai.

Ayudhya succeeded in overcoming Sukothai in 1438. By this time they had grown from a small local kingdom to a regional power in Southeast Asia. This left two large challengers to their dominance of the area--the kingdom of **Lan Na** to the north and **Burma** to the west. In the mid-sixteenth century the monarchs of Lan Sang (Laos), Lan Na, and Burma all joined against King **Chakkraphat** of Ayudhya (r.1548-1569), in a major war which lasted for about a decade. At the end, the Burmese sacked the capital city of Ayudhya in August 1569. The Tai were made subjects of Burma from 1569 to 1593.

It was another thirty years before Ayudhya fully recovered under King **Naresuan the Great** who ruled from 1590 to 1605. In 1593, he believed he had recovered sufficiently to renew the war for Tai independence. The crucial battle was called Nong Sarai. King Naresuan rode into the battle on a white elephant. This was very important because the last incarnation of Buddha before his birth as the Buddha was believed to have been as a white elephant. The Tai king reached out with his long-handled sword and killed the Burmese commander. At that point the Burmese troops fled from the battlefield. They were chased far into Burma, an action which tended to reunify the discouraged Tai.

The Tai operated with a very centralized government. The king appointed governors to all of the areas under his control. There was only one Tai army since the king did not allow each province to maintain one of its own. The government established social ranks and they defined each individual's social rank within the system. Slavery was allowed. Ayudhya became the most organized government in all of Southeast Asia.

By this time the kingdom began to attract European shipping and trade, and during the reign of King **Narai**, 1656 to 1688, the French made an abortive attempt to seize the kingdom as a colony. In the end, the French were evicted. Many European traders then viewed Ayadhya as an unfriendly area and the Dutch, the English, and other European traders avoided them for several years.

Figure 41

THE EARLY HISTORY OF BURMA

Many ethnic and nationality groups have come and gone in the country known as Myanmar (Burma) today. Very little archaeological work has been done to establish the earliest beginnings of civilization in the area. Some of the earliest discoveries go back to about 13,000 years ago to a Neolithic culture. Apparently there were many little city-states which developed in the area and became small ethnic kingdoms by about 200 B.C.

THE PYU KINGDOM

One of the early powers in what is today Myanmar (Burma) was the little kingdom founded by a group of people called the **Pyus**. They moved into the upper valley of the Irrawaddy River in the period about 200 B.C., an advance group of people from the Tibeto-Burman area. They established their capital city at **Srikshetra**, the "City of Splendor," supposedly founded in 638, but it was probably there much earlier. China considered the Pyu people their southern anchor for the overland trade route which linked China and India during the 3rd and 4th century. The trade goods which moved into northern Burma from China, was transported across the mountains to the coast of the Bay of Bengal. Ships then carried it across the Bay of Bengal to the Calcutta area, where the merchandise could begin its journey on the Grand Trunk Highway across northern India. This route not only accommodated the people of southwestern China, but it could also bypass a large portion of Central Asia, an area which was often difficult to negotiate because of political disturbances. Buddhism first entered the area of northern Burma by way of the Pyu traders.

THE MON KINGDOM OF HANTHAWADDY

A second early ethnic group to inhabit the area of presentday Burma were the **Mons**, also known as the Talaing. They have left an impact upon nearly all the languages of Southeast Asia to one extent or another. They first appeared in the area of the Chao Phraya Valley and west into Burma about A.D. 500. Having lived for several years in the Khmer state of Cambodia, they carried that culture westward into the Chao Phraya Valley and on into Burma. They adopted the Therevada Buddhist tradition from Ceylon (Sri Lanka) and from southern India. They established their capital city at **Pegu** in 825. The Mons were scarcely able to get their kingdom organized when the Burmans began attacking the Mon settlements in the delta region of the Irrawaddy, including Pegu.

THE SHAN

Another minority group in the Southeast Asian family of people is the **Shan** or Chan. There are pockets of Shan people scattered all over presentday Burma, parts of Thailand, and southwestern China. Although they see themselves as a very distinctive ethnic group, there are several different groups of Shan, probably one of the reasons why they have never been able to get organized into a single power bloc for political action. Closely associated with the Tai language group, they are separate from the Tai and live largely in Burma rather than in Thailand.

There are a sufficient number of Shan to have caused problems for the other ethnic groups in Burma.

THE TIBETO-BURMESE

The Tibeto-Burmese began leaving the area of southern Tibet sometime about 500 B.C. They slowly made their way through the mountains across northern Burma, following the best routes they could locate, because they concluded they would rather endure the hardships of the journey than to stay in the area of conflict between Tibet and China. The Pyu, the Mon, and the Shan were already in the area of the Irrawaddy River valley. Several of the Tai along the Chao Phraya River valley had also spilled over into modern Burma. And, there were dozens of other small ethnic groups in the northern parts of Laos, Thailand, and Burma who seemed to have moved around the area looking for new opportunities to found a nation. Many of them moved into the area of Burma. Even today, there are over one hundred different languages spoken in Burma. The Tibeto-Burmese had to struggle for supremacy with those who already occupied the valley of the Irrawaddy as well as those who tried to enter later.

In a sense, the Tibeto-Burmans passed through the Pyu territory, absorbing many of the Pyu on their way south to the fertile valley of the Irrawaddy. Many of the Pyus moved farther north in the valley and established a new capital. The Mons, firmly established in the delta region, held firm. The Tibeto-Burmans seemed confined between the Pyus on the north and the Mons to the south. Then, the Tai-Shans mounted an offensive throughout the Southeast Asian peninsula from Vietnam on the east to Burma in the west. The Mons suffered from this Tai-Shan offensive, but held on in the delta region. The Pyus were nearly destroyed. The Tibeto-Burmese seem to have survived this aggressive move by the Tai-Shans to emerge as the strongest power in the Irrawaddy River valley.

In 849, the Tibeto-Burmans built the city of **Pagan** and encircled it with a huge wall. The **Kingdom of Pagan** survived from 849 to 1287. The Mons were powerful enough at this time to have destroyed the fledgling city of Pagan, but they were less aggressive people. The Irrawaddy Valley became more arid as one progressed to the north, and many believe they simply preferred the rich delta lands, along with the trading options, open in the lower river valley. Their capital at Pegu was doing well.

By 1044, the religious situation in Burma was becoming very confused. The Indian influence through trade was quite important. The Tibeto-Burmese had been influenced by the Mahayana Buddhism, which had traveled from Nanchao in southwestern China along the trade routes. The religious situation in India first changed from Theravada Buddhism toward the Mahayana school, then toward Tantrism, and finally Hinduism overcame all the Buddhist schools of thought. Situated between the Chinese influence on the northeast and the Indian influence on the southwest, many of the Tibeto-Burmans became confused and returned to animistic worship. The Mons began accepting more and more Hinduism in their culture. One of the Buddhist priests from the Mon area was so displeased that he fled to Pagan where he converted the king to the Theravada teaching. Burma would follow the individual route to Buddhist salvation with its many temples and thousands of monks seeking enlightenment.

The ruler who made the decision to accept Theravada Buddhism was **Anawrahta**, who ruled from 1044 to 1077. He was one of the most able administrators and military leaders in all of Burma's history. He began a gradual encroachment upon the Mon territories to the south to obtain seaports to open his landlocked state of Pagan to the sea. The Tai-Shan were placed on the defensive as he sent armies into Thailand to diminish their rising power. He even challenged the powerful Chola Empire of southern India when they began encroaching in the Southeast Asian area. Pagan subsidized an army in Sri Lanka, which promised to assist in controlling the Cholas.

The more advanced culture of both the Pyus and the Mons was absorbed by his largely peasant farmer Tibeto-Burman people. The kingdom of Pagan prospered and population increased. This meant that more land was placed under cultivation, and King Anawrahta ordered that adequate irrigation works should be provided to increase agricultural productivity. He also provided for the succession to the throne in order that Pagan would not be left leaderless following his passing from the scene.

It was the Mongols who finally finished off the Pagan kingdom in 1287. They demanded that Pagan recognize them as their overlord and pay tribute. The Pagan Burmans adamantly refused--they killed the Mongol envoy. That was certainly not a very intelligent move, considering the power and resources of the Mongols at that time. The Mongols invaded the valley kingdom and very shortly their stout little army succumbed to the invading horde. The Mongol occupation was not easy. The Burmese constantly sniped at them, tribute was difficult to collect, and eventually the Mongols quietly withdrew from Burma--the cost was greater than the reward. The neighboring Thailand managed to survive by recognizing the Mongols and agreeing to make themselves subjects of the Great Khan. This gave the Tai-Shan an opportunity to move into the Irrawaddy Valley at the close of the Mongol period and to have their period of domination over Burma before the Burmese in Pagan could recover from the Mongols.

Burmese territories were already established reasonably close to their presentday borders before the Mongols arrived. So also was their economic system from the irrigated rice fields of central Burma to their ports in the delta region. The beautiful temples of Pagan were all constructed before the arrival of the Mongols. The temple known as **Ananda** was built during the reign of Anawrahta and his son, **Kyanzittha**, 1084 to 1112. The round temple is set on a square base with the upper portion shaped like a bee hive with a stupa at the very top. There are minatures of this shape on each of the four corners of the base. This style set the tone for dozens of other Buddhist temples throughout Burma. Altogether there are 1,424 Buddha statues inside and outside the Ananda temple. The royal palace once stood nearby and there are many other important buildings still standing such as the monastery and an important library of Buddhist sources, which was begun by King Anawrahta. It was Buddhism which united all the ethnic residents of Burma more than kings, armies, or geography.

Although one of the minority groups within Burma's borders has sometimes carved off a piece of territory for a few years, the chief power struggle has most often been between Mons, Tai-Shan, and the Tibeto-Burmans for the control of the Irrawaddy Valley. The Burmese have most often been in political and military control, and when they are not, their cultural heritage has carried on even in defeat.

After the departure of the Mongols, the Shans began to have more influence at the court, but times were difficult and life was uncertain as every ethnic group within their borders seemed to want to form the new Burma. The power which unified Burma again centered in upper Burma at the city of **Ava**, not far from Mandalay. Beginning in 1368, the kings at Ava claimed to be half-Burmese and half-Shan. Their capital was too far upstream to take advantage of the growing interest in the rapidly developing India-China trade, which was followed in the 16th century by the European traders. The kings of Ava fully recognized this problem and fought a long succession of unsuccessful wars with a reconstituted Mon state in the delta region. Aside from their long period of wars, Ava encouraged education and scholarship. The 250 years following the establishment of Ava witnessed some of Burma's finest literary accomplishments.

The troubled ethnic situation flared again in 1540 when a group of animistic Shan refugees from Nanchao decided the time was right to attack Ava. They showed no respect for anyone, especially Buddhists, and thousands of monks were slain without resistance in the temples and monasteries. The refugees who managed to escape from Ava went south to **Toungoo**, a city on the Sittang River northeast of Pegu. Toungoo had been founded in 1510 by King Minkyinyo, who ruled from 1486 to 1531. When the people from Ava came to the city in 1540, it was decided to move the capital to the old capital of Lower Burma at Pegu, a distance of about 125 miles. It was still generally called the Toungoo dynasty as the kings sallied forth to bring Shans, Mons, and other ethnic groups, all under their control. This became easier for the Toungoo kings because they invested in the latest Portuguese firearms while most of the ethnic armies fought with the old weapons.

The greatest of the Toungoo kings was **Bayinnaung**, who ruled from 1551 to 1581. He picked up the momentum where his brother-in-law had left off on unifying Burma. It was Bayinnaung who finalized control over the entire Irrawaddy Valley in a series of campaigns from 1554 to 1558. The nearby king of Siam (Thailand) feared the rising power of the Toungoo kings and mounted a campaign to bring Burma under his control. The Tai campaign extended from 1563 to 1569, and at the end of the long war the Tai of Siam came under the complete control of Burma. Many regarded King Bayinnaung as the strongest ruler of Asia outside of China. Unfortunately, after the death of the king, each of the ethnic groups considered going independent. The only thing which held Bayinnaung's loose confederation together after his death was the rising power of Portugal in Southeast Asia. Some still drifted away. The most important group which was lost to Burma was Siam.

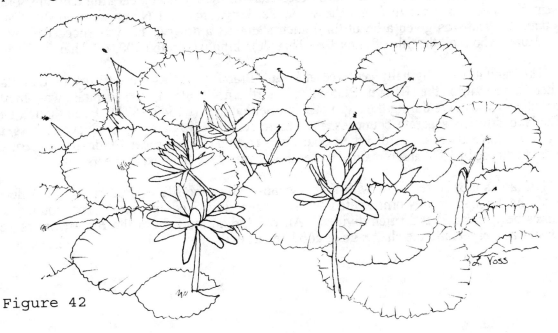

Figure 42

THE PLACE OF LAOS IN EASTERN CIVILIZATION

Laos is a small landlocked nation on the northern edge of the Southeast Asian mainland. Hemmed in by mountains and by powerful and ambitious neighbors, it has been difficult to even survive through the centuries. The immediate neighbors are Vietnam, China, Burma (Myanmar), Thailand (Siam), and Cambodia (Kampuchea). Most of its inhabitants today are farmers in a mountainous country as they have been since the beginning of habitation in the area. They have also suffered from the same problems over thousands of years--malaria, poor sanitation, and impure water--combined with poor dietary habits.

The Mekong River forms a large percentage of its borders with Burma and Thailand. The Mekong River has been a very important river in the life of Laos. The Lao people are one branch of the people who migrated out of China beginning as early as the Han dynasty in China (202 B.C.-A.D. 221) and increasing in the 8th century. The Mongols caused further population adjustments during their control of China from 1279 to 1368. Most of the migrants consider themselves directly or indirectly related to the Tai. The Theravada school of Buddhism predominates in Laos.

Laos was originally a part of the old Khmer Empire, but they have seen major invasions from Siam (Thailand) and from Vietnam. India and the West has had about as great an influence upon Laos as has China or Vietnam because of the mountain ridges on the north and the east. The first united kingdom of the little principalities was created by **Fa Ngum**, who reigned from 1353 to 1373. Fa Ngum seems to have had a fondness for beautiful women and when he seduced one of his father's concubines, he was exiled to Cambodia.

The Khmer ruler encouraged him to reclaim his throne, which he did in 1353, by deposing his father and naming his newly organized kingdom Lan Xang (Lan Sang), "the land of a million elephants." It was said that Fa Ngum was a descendant of the mythological king Khoum Borum, who sent his seven sons out to found the seven Tai kingdoms. Fa Ngum married the Khmer king's daughter and was given a beautiful golden statue as a dowry. He was succeeded by his son, Un Huan, who took the title of Sam Saen Thai, "the king who ruled 300,000 Thai."

The capital was originally centered at Luang Prabang, but as the territory of Lan Xang expanded across into the Khorat Plateau of northern Thailand, the capital was moved permanently to Vientiane during the reign of King Setthathirat (r.1547-1571). Even though Laos and Thailand are two separate countries, the ethnic relationships are close. Nevertheless, the rulers of Laos have always regarded their country as having its own separate identity. Vientiane fell to the Burmese in 1570 and remained under their control for the next 30 years.

Lao art is mostly religious with many scenes telling the life of Buddha in great detail. Some of the Laotian richly ornamented art has been destroyed in wars. The country has sometimes been invaded and often divided. An old Indian story from the *Ramayana* is very popular in Laos, especially the challenge of good versus evil.

MALAYSIA: A COUNTRY AT THE CROSSROADS OF ASIA

There has not yet been a great amount of archaeology in the Malay peninsula but what has been done has been mostly Neolithic sites which date to around 1500 to 2500 B.C. The Paleolithic sites do go back to 35,000 years ago, but there is too little to draw any strong conclusions. Sometime about 2500 B.C., a group of people began migrating down the peninsula from China. They were already in an advanced Neolithic stage by the time they entered the peninsula. They were followed shortly thereafter by a Bronze Age people, who, like the early Bronze Age culture in North Vietnam, made beautiful bronze drums and bells. Small Malayan kingdoms began to appear in the second and third centuries of the Christian era, many of them already influenced by the culture of India at that time. This combination of ethnic Chinese and an Indianized culture were mostly rice farmers who lived in bamboo houses, which were built on stilts. Women filled a very prominent role from the earliest times in Malaysia.

The early Malays buried their dead in enclosed caskets or in jars. The royalty were buried in huge megalithic tombs made by setting two flat stones upright and placing a third stone across, then covering it all in a hill of dirt. There is good evidence of ancestor worship and phallic worship, while animism seemed to be the base religion for many years. As Indian influence came in, they were influenced first by Hinduism, then by Buddhism, and finally by Islam. They borrowed a great amount of their art from India in the early years.

Indian merchants probably came to Malaysia to purchase tin, a metal which the peninsula still exports. The Khmer kingdom of Funan was the first to dominate in the area because of their interest in the East-West trade between China and India. The route across the isthmus was the first area of importance as a trade route, followed later by the passage through the Straits of Malacca (Melaka). The inhabitants of Malaysia were also great seafarers and many of them engaged in the East-West trade. This brought the Malays the best of the cultures which passed through their ports. Since Malaysia also has gold mines, it was possible for them to purchase some of the goods which passed through their area.

Another rich source of revenue came from the fees paid to ship the goods across the isthmus, or from the tolls charged on ships passing through the straits. There were several times when the pirates operating out of the Srivijayan ports made it unprofitable to attempt the straits passage. During those times the traffic sometimes passed through the Sunda straits and avoided Malaysia altogether.

Geographically, the Malaysian area was caught between the Khmer kingdom in Cambodia, a Tai desire to control the peninsula and the straits, and the Sumatran kingdom of Srivijaya. This was complicated by the Srivijayan struggle with the rising power of kingdoms on the nearby island of Java. Under such unsettled conditions, piracy thrived throughout the area. The Chinese often simply decided to stop the trade altogether. When that occurred there were Chinese merchants who still came to the area to risk one more cargo. Since the Malaysian's economy depended so much upon the trade in their area, any interruption of the traffic created a tremendous hardship.

The history of the founding of the two cities on the Straits of Malacca--Singapore and Melaka--are so entwined in myths and legends of the local people that without any written accounts before the 15th century there is nothing authentic. Accepting the best parts of the

Southeast Asia--Malaysia

legends, it seems that the aggressive little kingdoms of Java began harassing the Srivijayan capital at Palembang so much that one of the members of the court, or of the royal family, took a group of followers across the Straits of Malacca and founded the city of **Temasek**, later called Singapura (Singapore), the "lion city." The local prince at **Melaka**, a ruler attached to Ayudhya (Thailand) was killed in this change of government, and the area came under new control. Melaka on the mainland was always the most important in those years, and Singapore did not become important until the British took the island over following 1819.

The change of ownership at Melaka seems to have occurred about 1400 or 1403. The prince's name was apparently Paramesvara. After this date, tolls through the straits seem to have been fair and Melaka policed the pirates who operated in the area. This action made trade at the straits a much more acceptable route than previously. Furthermore, ships were being built much more durably to withstand long sea voyages so that some ships now made the entire voyage from China to India and back again. Ships prior to 1400 were seldom interested in making a complete passage from one end of the market range to the other. It was a new type of trade which Melaka, and later Singapore, both exploited. The European traders with the East also became excited about the area around the Straits of Malacca, especially the Portuguese.

Once trade through the straits area became commonplace, the tolls went up. Those who failed to stop and pay the proper amount were caught and executed. Apparently one of these executions angered the Chola king, Rajendra I, who raided both the straits area and Srivijaya. It was not easy being at the crossroads of trade and commerce from three worlds--India, China, and Europe.

Islam had already arrived before the changes took place in 1400. Muslim traders from India were the first to introduce the new religion to the ports on the northwest coast of Sumatra. Within a relatively short time it spread throughout Sumatra and across the straits to Malaysia. The period often called Malacca's Golden Age covers the time from 1400 to 1511. They prepared their first history during the 15th century. Although it is the best available, there are many myths and legends because there were so few written records and no major stone records to work from as in many other countries.

When the trade began to increase through the straits area, everyone wanted a share of the revenue. One of the first to press their demands was the kingdom of Ayudhya. When Muzaffar Shah refused to pay a portion of the revenue to Ayudhya, the Siamese kingdom sent two expeditions to force payment--1445 and again in 1456. The Siamese succeeded in acquiring some land along the straits area but they did not get the tolls. The next sultan, Mahmud Shah was more aggressive. He declared Malacca was his empire and incorporated all of the Malay peninsula and eastern Sumatra. Mahmud's revenue increased greatly from tolls, fees, and from the money spent by the ships which purchased provisions and entertainment. It was such a temptation that the Portuguese moved in and took the area as a colony in 1511.

The Muslim sultans began to have a recurring problem. When one of their sultans began to age, they customarily named one of their sons as the crown prince. Everyone in the kingdom understood who the successor was supposed to be, and rarely did anyone ever challenge his choice. When the old sultan died, the decision was actually made at the funeral or on the following day. By the time of Mahmud Shah, the other Muslim leaders established the custom that they would select the person who they thought would be the **best** leader. By 1511, that meant they selected the weakest person they could respectfully name because he would be

404

beholden to them throughout his lifetime. As a consequence the other Muslim leaders could extract bribes and favors in an endless fashion. With all the revenue available at Malacca, there was a lot of intrigue behind the back of the royalty. This obviously resulted in weak sultans which tempted **Alfonso de Albuquerque**, the Portuguese, to successfully take Malacca in 1511.

The sultans were particularly upset that a European Christian was in control of the Straits of Malacca. Several efforts were made to recapture Malacca following 1511, but they all failed. Many of the Muslims decided to spend their time carrying the Islamic faith to the various islands throughout the region instead of engaging in military adventures against the superior Portuguese. Many of them believed that they would accomplish more by religious crusading before the Christian missionaries converted all of Asia. They managed to convert Borneo, many of the people on the little islands, and they extended their faith as far as Mindanao, the southern island of the Philippines.

A high percentage of the trade which moved through the Straits of Malacca was luxury goods. The Chinese bought ivory, rhinocerous horn, camphor, and various hardwoods. The Chinese market was also interested in goods produced in Malaysia such as hornbill, ivory, various tree resins, and edible birds' nests from Borneo. China sold wine, rice, silk, and porcelain. The Arabs and the Indians came to buy tin. The Arabs sold glassware, cloth, and tapestries. The Indians sold cotton textiles. Both the Arabs and the Indians bought spices, some for local consumption, but the majority of the spices they purchased was for resale to the Mediterranean world. As early as the 11th century, the Europeans were convinced they had to have spices to live. The West (Europe) had few goods the Chinese wanted. As a consequence, it was a one-sided trade for the West--they wanted the spice and they paid the price.

Figure 43

SRIVIJAYA AND THE ISLAND POWERS

The old **Srivijaya** of the late 7th to the early 13th century is now the modern state of Indonesia. The country today is a long archipelago composed of nearly 14,000 islands, 6,000 of which are uninhabited. In the period following the 7th century, Srivijaya made its money from the East-West trade which passed through the Straits of Malacca between India and China. They also controlled the Sunda Straits on the eastern end of Sumatra, where ships passed through between Java and Sumatra. Besides the price of tolls, Srivijaya took in revenue from re-supplying ships before they set out for the long journey to China or to India. At that time, few ships made the entire distance--usually they operated only in the Indian Ocean area or only in the South China Sea.

In addition to the lucrative trade passing through their straits and their ports, the Sumatran area was the world's largest producer of pepper, a product which was in demand from Britain on the west to China on the east. The nearby island of Java produced tea and other spices, as well as acting as a merchant-wholesaler for all kinds of spices from the Moluccas, the Celebes, Borneo, and other islands in that general area. All of these spices were in great demand throughout the South Asian area, as well as the Arab world, and had been over a long period of time. After the 11th century it seemed they could not produce enough spice to satisfy the European market.

Srivijaya actually preceded the rise of the trading cities on the mainland such as Melaka and Singapore. As trade prospered between India and China, so also did the state of Srivijaya prosper. Political disturbances in either country greatly disrupted their prosperity. At the outset, the trade operated largely through the port at Palembang in northeastern Sumatra. As business and profits increased, Srivijaya came to control all of Sumatra, all of the area in the Straits of Malacca and the Sunda Straits, and most of nearby Java.

Chola was also a powerful trading nation in South India. Probably founded around A.D. 200, they were expansionist from the beginning. They came to control a strip along the Coromandel coast of the Indian subcontinent around Trichinopoly (Tiruchchirappalli) in the southeast. This was a good position from which to launch trading expeditions to Sri Lanka and across the Indian Ocean. They were a prosperous, staunchly Hindu country with a well-organized government which irrigated the land and began adding territory. They acquired northern Ceylon (Sri Lanka) in 996. By 1014 they acquired the Laccadive and the Maldive Islands. They took **all** of Ceylon, overran the Deccan and reached the Ganges River by 1023. This was a proud achievement as the victorious army carried water from the holy Ganges back to Trichinopoly.

Some of the Indians thought they were charged too much for tolls and too high a markup on the goods which they purchased in Srivijaya. They began acquiring territory along the Malay peninsula to circumvent these high prices. This did not seem to be satisfactory and in 1025 they decided to challenge the power of Srivijaya by capturing their capital city of Palembang. It was a more successful campaign than they imagined as they took the city, captured the king, and hauled his treasure back to Chola. This one campaign broke up the fragile relationships which the rulers in Palembang had spliced together over the years. It showed that even though they were good businessmen, they had no military power capable of protecting themselves, their friends, or their allies. By the 12th century, mighty Srivijaya was reduced to a small kingdom trying to balance its budget. At the end they were replaced by a rising kingdom on Java called Majapahit.

406

Southeast Asia--Indonesia

JAVA MAKES A MOVE FOR POWER

Several little kingdoms came and went in the years both before and after Srivijaya. One of the major problems in reconstructing the history of the island kingdoms is the lack of any writing or permanent records. Both Sumatra and Java were heavily Indianized. Stone statues and temples dedicated to either Hinduism or Buddhism have been found in abundance. This would lead to the presumption that the monks did read and write. Some of the stone inscriptions indicate that scholars came from great distances to study in Central Java. There are a few rulers listed--some dynasties kept better records than others--but it would be impossible to reconstruct a full and complete history of Java.

The **Sailendra** was just one of the family-kingdom-dynasties from Central Java which came to power about the mid-eighth century. Their leaders took the title of *maharaja* from their knowledge of Indian rulers. Such an imposing title was designed to overawe their subjects. This was not unusual in Java and Sumatra, where the kings ruled in a more absolute manner than was ever imagined in the western monarchies. To further mystify their positions, they often married into other royal families from distant kingdoms rather than to marry local women. The Sailendra rulers preferred to bring their brides from the powerful kingdom of Srivijaya. By the late 9th century, the Sailendra family had so intermarried with the Srivijaya house that when they lost their throne in Central Java, they were the next closest heirs in Srivijaya, and they ruled there for several years.

THE BUDDHIST TEMPLE OF BOROBUDUR

The rulers also liked to connect themselves, whenever possible, with the spiritual world. As a consequence, the kings of the Sailendra dynasty built many temples on the Kedu Plain in central Java. The most notable of all their temples was the massive Buddhist temple of **Borobudur**. Built between the years 778 and 824 on the Kedu Plain in central Java, this temple was constructed to fit on top of a natural mound of earth. It was designed to be a gigantic *mandala*, an earthly model of the universe. The square base was designed to represent the earth, which they believed was flat and square. On top of the earth was the round temple which was designed to represent the heavens. On the very top of the round part was a sacred stupa.

The temple is amply supplied with some 2000 raised relief panels illustrating the nine previous lives of the Buddha as based on several different versions of Mahayana Buddhist texts. The panels are supplemented by 400 statues of the Buddha from different stages of his life, and showing him in many different poses. At the very lowest level there are some of the monarchs in stone, probably to remind the Buddhist pilgrim of the power of the ones who built this 150-foot high temple of stone.

Borobudur was designed to be a gigantic textbook covering all the important teachings of Buddha. If one follows the pilgrim path, one circles the entire monument nine times in the same direction the sun circles the earth. Each panel of Buddha's life and teaching should be studied carefully. As the pilgrim passes through one of these sections it is like a narrow corridor, constructed in such a manner that the pilgrim must focus on Buddhism--they cannot see the world outside. If the entire journey is completed to the top, the pilgrim would have walked several miles and studied the raised relief panels. At the top they should achieve enlightenment or Buddahood.

OTHER LITTLE KINGDOMS OF JAVA

The last Indianized state in the area was **Majapahit** which was based in eastern Java from the 13th to the 16th centuries. The last king of Majapahit was **Kertanagara**, who ruled from 1268 to 1292. Toward the end of Kertanagara's reign, Kublai Khan sent an envoy to his court who demanded that the Javanese kingdom recognize Kublai Khan as their overlord and pay tribute. The king ordered that the envoy should have his face and ears permanently disfigured and scarred, then sent him back to China. This bold and unnecessary action brought a Mongol fleet of 1000 ships to Java in an effort to capture the island.

The Mongols were not successful in this campaign because the Javanese resorted to such intense guerrilla warfare. In the end, the Mongols finally loaded as much loot on their ships as possible and abandoned the venture. Other kings were angry at the king of Majapahit for causing all the trouble. Besides, they were in a contest among themselves for the rich trade through the Sunda Straits, area since the kingdom of Srivijaya was obviously in decline. The year after the Mongol episode, the king of **Kadiri**, Jayakatwang, rebelled and killed Kertanagara.

Hinduism and Buddhism had coexisted in Java for many years. **Kadiri** had risen as a Hindu state about the 11th century. They then began expanding their empire to include parts of Borneo and all of nearby Bali. They had tried to control Srivijaya, but had failed. Later they reorganized and formed the kingdom of **Singosari**, 1222 to 1292.

And, there were many other little kingdoms which came and went, sometimes lasting through only the lifetime of a single ruler. By the time the Europeans arrived in the 17th century, the center of power had passed from Sumatra to Java. Both islands were Muslim. The European traders--the Portuguese, the Dutch, the French, and the English--all wanted Java which they believed was the source of the rich spices. Actually, most of the spices came from the Moluccas--they were brought to Java as a central market place. Chinese and Indian merchants also began frequenting the island of Java for their spices, thus reducing the importance of the Straits of Malacca to some extent.

THE STORY OF SPICES

The Europeans had known about the spices of the East as early as the time of Alexander the Great, possibly even earlier. The spices were relatively light in weight, they were easy to transport because they were not subject to spoilage, and they brought a nice market price outside their immediate area of production. Many of the spices from the Moluccas, the Celebes, and various parts of Borneo were not even raised in India. Some of the more popular spices were cultivated in Ceylon. The Arabs discovered what spices could do to enhance the flavor of lamb at least a thousand years before the beginning of the Christian era.

The Romans became interested in spices early in the Christian era and developed a good trade with the Arabs, which continued for a couple of hundred years. By around 300, the Romans began to run low on cash to purchase these "luxury" goods. The Romans had little to sell which was of interest to the Arab traders, there were no gold mines in western Europe, and what little gold remained was needed to either purchase military equipment or to pay heavy bribes to the barbarians to prevent them from sacking a city. Rome had an unfavorable balance of payments and terminated the trade.

The most intense interest in the eastern spice trade built up during and following the Crusades, after 1095. By the the 12th century, more Europeans became acquainted with the highly spiced food of the eastern world and they liked it. Europe was beginning to enter a transition period from the High Middle Ages to the early Renaissance--they were looking for new and exciting experiences. Since there was no refrigeration in those times, smoking and salting were the only means available for preserving meat. Europe had experimented with several herbs to flavor the meat but the spices seemed to add a whole new dimension to their food, especially slightly tainted meat. A brisk trade began to develop, particularly as the Italian merchant ships hauled crusaders to the Holy Land they could carry spices on the return trip. Besides, the profits were great.

The Arabs acted as the middlemen in this trade, buying the spices from the East and selling them to the western traders. The demand rose so quickly that it was difficult to keep up with the supply. When the sharp Arab traders discovered they could get almost any price for a shipment of spices--the prices went up even more. Several European merchants who dealt in this trade began asking questions about the places from which the spices had originated. In an effort to protect their monopoly situation as middlemen, the Arabs told all kinds of stories about the hardships they had to endure in order to obtain the spices. There were hazardous sea voyages through dragon-infested waters, spice gardens inhabited with poisonous snakes, as well as strange winged creatures like huge bats or small dinosaurs which often would snatch a caravan driver right off his camel. When the Arab trader had finished his fantastic tale, it made the spices seem like a bargain, and no thinking European would want to endure such hardships.

But as the prices continued to climb, several Europeans realized the spices came from somewhere in the Far East. The Muslim Arabs controlled the access routes across the Middle East, totally closing all the spice trade when a militant group of "Turks" captured Constantinople (Istanbul) in 1453. Even though the Europeans desired the spices very much, there was no groundswell of enthusiasm to mount a military campaign to cross the Middle East. The Europeans had tried military force in eight or nine Crusades to seize the Holy Land--every one of them had ended in failure sooner or later. The only way was to find a way around the huge continent of Africa, if that were possible.

It is interesting that the Italian merchants, who had profited so handsomely from the spice trade, decided to wait until the Arab Muslims decided to reopen the trade routes. The Portuguese decided to find a way around Africa. The Spanish gambled on sending Christopher Columbus across the Atlantic Ocean on the boldest venture of all--to reach the East by sailing out toward the west. The Portuguese were the first to succeed in their venture by rounding the end of the African continent in 1488, and Vasco da Gama reached India in 1498. By the early 16th century the spices were beginning to enter the European trade again, this time bypassing the Arab world by the long voyage around Africa.

Columbus was less successful. After four voyages he never did arrive in China, Japan, or the Indies--the Americas blocked his route. The English sent out John Cabot to find a way around America by a northern route. It was Ferdinand Magellan, sailing under a Spanish flag,

Southeast Asia--Indonesia

who followed the route of Columbus to America, then found a way around the south end of America. It was one of Magellan's ships that became the first to circumnavigate the globe. The cargo of spices--largely cloves--which Magellan's ship carried, more than offset the cost of the entire expedition. By 1522 the Spanish knew the world really was round. Magellan and his sailors had discovered the Spice Islands--the East Indies. An Englishman, Francis Drake, repeated the circumnavigation in 1577. The Dutch were already sufficiently interested in the spice trade that their government chartered the Dutch East India Company to exploit that trade in 1602. The European race to the realms of Asia was on.

Figure 44

THE PHILIPPINES TO c.1600

THE GEOGRAPHY

The **Philippine Islands** are situated about 500 miles off the coast of the Southeast Asian mainland. The islands are a part of the long archipelago of largely volcanic islands which begin far to the north off the coast of Alaska and stretch down the coast of the East Asian mainland to include the islands of Indonesia. There are over 7000 islands in the group known as "the Philippines." Some of the islands in the Philippine group either have active volcanoes, or they have been active in this century. The islands are generally mountainous with most of the population living in the fertile plains areas of Luzon and Panay.

The climate of the Philippines is tropical. The islands are situated in the typical two-season monsoon pattern. The wet season begins in May and continues until late November or early December. The cooler and drier season extends through the winter months. Typhoons are very common in the Philippines during the wet season, sometimes as many as thirty in a single season.

THE EARLY HISTORY

Practically nothing is known of the prehistoric period in the Philippines. Best judgment by racial characteristics indicates that the early people were immigrants who arrived in successive waves by island-hopping in their small outrigger boats, while a few may have come directly from the mainland. Each immigrant group seems to have settled to itself in an area with sufficient hunting and fishing which was supplemented by gathering roots and fruits from the lush forests. Most of the immigrants seem to have had a small knowledge of a shifting agriculture, but "farming" was not a major consideration. The only evidence of settled agriculture are the very old rice terraces in the mountains of northern Luzon, dating to about A.D. 1000. This would indicate some contact with another area where rice was grown rather than a local development.

There are other evidences of contact with more developed civilizations. Some of the settlements were using a Sanskrit-based writing system when the first Europeans arrived. Best guesses are that this knowledge of writing came from the Indianized kingdoms of Srivijaya or Mahapahit in what is currently Indonesia. Chinese traders also recorded that they had stopped in the Philippines about the year 1000. Since there was no manufacturing in the Philippines at that time, and no money economy, the traders evidently did not see a need to follow up on their initial contact.

The people were governed largely through dozens of kinship groups, similar to a small tribe, which were called *barangays*. Each of these was under a chief who was known as the *datu*. These were small groups of people of often 100 or less. The people seem to have also had a social class system with the *datu* and the royal family at the top and the slaves at the bottom. Most of the slaves were either prisoners captured in their numerous petty wars, or they were slaves because they could not pay their debts.

Their religion was polytheistic animism. They envisioned hundreds of evil spirits which constantly needed to be appeased. There was little uniformity of evil spirits from one area of the

Philippines to another. They are unique in that they are the only area which was not touched by either Hinduism or Buddhism in all of Asia. The Philippine Islands are also unique since no one ever united all the islands until the Europeans arrived. Islam arrived in Mindanao and the Sulu Islands in the 15th century; Christianity arrived in the 16th century.

The actual "history" of the Philippines began with the arrival of the Europeans. The first to arrive was Ferdinand Magellan in 1521. In his desire to capture the islands for the king of Spain, Magellan engaged in a skirmish with the natives of Cebu and was killed. When his ship and crew returned to Spain with a cargo of spices, it whetted the Spanish desire to tap the spice market of the Moluccas, and in 1565 they founded their first permanent colony at Cebu. Manila was founded six years later because of its very attractive harbor. Most of our knowledge of the early Philippines comes from Spanish records of observations and stories which they recorded. Christian missions were founded from the very beginning and the spread of Islam was checked before it overcame the entire island group. It is one of the few places where Christian missions were successful throughout Asia. The Philippines are also important since they introduced several American food products such as corn (maize), tomatoes, potatoes, tobacco, and several other crops unknown in Asia.

A SUMMARY OF SOUTHEAST ASIA

Southeast Asia is one of the most interesting areas of all of Asia. The earliest record of mankind in the entire world, except for the still disputed finds in Africa, continues to be Java Man from the island of Java. Mainland Southeast Asia has been heavily influenced by China. In the case of northern Vietnam the influence has been quite heavy. It is much less so for the other areas of the large peninsula. However, many of the other peoples of Southeast Asia, such as the Tai and the Tibeto-Burmans, came from the area of southwestern China and southeastern Tibet to escape from oppressive conditions placed upon their freedom and independence in their land of origin. They apparently carried very little Chinese culture with them.

The general movement of population in Southeast Asia has been from the north toward the south, following the river valleys south between the ranges of mountains--most of the rivers and the mountains are arranged in a north to south direction. Many of the people who migrated into Southeast Asia followed the Malay Peninsula down to the Straits of Malacca, crossed over to Sumatra or to Java, then continued island-hopping in their small outrigger boats until they had reached the Philippines. Some journeyed on as far as Hawaii and Easter Island. One theory believes some of these early seafarers came as far as America.

By the 5th or 6th centuries, Southeast Asia had become the geographic crossroads of Asia. The Straits of Malacca, which had been a place to cross on the way to Sumatra, now became a place where the trade and commerce of eastern Asia met the trade and commerce of the western markets. Sometimes those markets were as far away as the Mediterranean world. By the 15th century it became an even more strategic location with the European interest in the spice trade.

Two old religions--Hinduism and Buddhism--have had a profound effect upon the people of Southeast Asia. These two faiths traveled primarily with the merchants and traders who introduced their faiths on a casual basis and they caught on. Culture and literacy moved with the religions. Two newer religions--Christianity and Islam--arrived with the missionaries, who often tried to force their faith upon the people. The Muslims were more successful than the Christians

Southeast Asia--the Philippines

in their mission work. The Muslims were less forceful in Southeast Asia than in India, the Middle East, or in North Africa. The only really successful Christian mission area in all of Asia before 1600 was in the Philippines.

Agriculture is the predominant occupation throughout Southeast Asia. Rice is the staple food, supplemented with vegetables and a wide variety of fruit. Meat consumption depends largely upon religious persuasion. Some areas of Southeast Asia have been so careful about taking life to further the individual's personal needs that they will not even wear silk because the worm must be killed in order to unwind the cocoon. The timber industry and the fish markets are centuries old occupations. Manufacturing has not been a high priority beyond the basic needs in metals, pottery, and woodworking.

The women of Southeast Asia have enjoyed a higher status than anywhere else in the world. Generally, the women are considered equal in every way except that the division of labor has left them primarily in charge of domestic affairs. The unequal aspects of women under Hinduism and Islam have been tossed aside, even in areas where those religions predominate in Southeast Asia. Women have not only been able to inherit property, but in several areas, the family tree is traced through the mothers rather than the fathers.

Maintaining historical records, or even genealogical records, has seldom held a very high priority in Southeast Asia. Writing almost always accompanied religion once the people moved from animism to one of the major faiths such as Hinduism or Buddhism. While the Chinese--and many others--kept at least some records, the Southeast Asians either failed to maintain such records or many of them have been lost. Areas such as the Philippines seem to have had no interest in record keeping at any time before the 16th century. The wet climate--accompanied by many buildings which were constructed of perishable materials such as mats, bamboo poles, and thatch--has made even archaeological records difficult. There are many beautiful stone monuments, but they are primarily religious in nature--they have very few records of rulers or other information which could assist the modern historian in reconstructing their past.

Figure 45

BOOKS FOR FURTHER READING

Agoncillo, Teodoro A., *A Short History of the Philippines* (1975).

Andaya, Barbara Watson, & Andaya, Leonard Y., *A History of Malaysia* (1982).

Cady, John F., *Thailand, Burma, Laos, & Cambodia* (1966).

Cressey, George B., *Asia's Lands and Peoples* (1963).

Eliot, Joshua, *et. al.*, editors, *Thailand, Indochina, & Burma Handbook* (1992).

Fairbank, John K., Reischauer, Edwin O., & Craig, Albert M., *East Asia: Tradition & Transformation* (1989).

Forman, Bedrich, *Borobudur, The Buddhist Legend in Stone* (1980).

Lattimore, Owen & Eleanor, *Silks, Spices and Empire* (1968).

Legge, J. D., *Indonesia* (1964).

Marzuki, Yazir, & Heraty, Toeti, *Borobudur* (1985).

Reid, Anthony, editor, *Southeast Asia in the Early Modern Era: Trade, Power, and Belief* (1993).

Robinson, Harry, *Monsoon Asia: A Geographical Survey* (1967).

Tarling, Nicholas, editor, *The Cambridge History of Southeast Asia*, Volume I (1992).

Tarling, Nicholas, *A Concise History of Southeast Asia* (1966).

Chapter 44
A BRIEF SUMMARY OF EASTERN CIVILIZATIONS TO 1600

There is a great geographic distance between Great Britain and Spain in western Europe and Japan and China in the Far East, yet they both are a part of Eurasia, the largest single land mass in the world. There are many ways in which the *cultural* differences are almost as great as the geographic differences. In our modern age, there are many maps and geography books which clearly portray the geographic differences. In the period before 1600, neither the East nor the West understood the simplest geographic features of the other. The only connections had been through trade, and even that had been handled largely by Arabs, who served as the middlemen between East and West. The only notable exception was the military campaigns of Alexander the Great to the East, and the Mongol campaigns to the West.

Geography has played a major role in the history of eastern civilizations. This has been true on every one of the continents, but nowhere has this been of greater significance than in Asia. The Alps of Europe are still rugged mountains to cross, but that barrier was beginning to break down as early as the time of Julius Caesar--even before the beginning of the Roman Empire--when Caesar crossed the mountains and conquered Gaul (France). The Himalaya Mountains continue to be a major barrier in Asia. There are many airports which practically close in the mountainous areas of Asia in the wintertime, while it is a most unusual day when flights in and out of Switzerland are not running on schedule. Neither are there any super highways through the Himalayas.

Another geographic barrier in Asia, which is unknown in western Europe, is the desert area. Some parts of northern China, Mongolia, and Central Asia, all have vast desert areas. In addition, there are thousands of square miles of grassy steppes and timbered areas across the far northern stretches of Asia, while Europe has only a small area of this type of landform in northern Scandinavia.

While the Rhine and the Danube rivers of Europe have tied that area together on an east-west basis, many of Asia's rivers flow north into the Arctic Ocean. The Volga and the Ural rivers flow south, but they both end in the Caspian Sea, which has no outlet to the major oceans. It is interesting that one of the main rivers of the Indian subcontinent, the Indus River, flows south and was the birthplace of India's first civilization. The Ganges River does tie northern India into one unit. Likewise the Yangtze and the Huang Ho both flow easterly over a large area, and have been instrumental in tying China together as one united area. There are are no rivers which tie several nations of Asia together as in the case of the European Danube River.

Mountains, deserts, and rivers have more often separated the peoples of Asia than they have ever brought them together. Geography has also caused many more small, isolated ethnic and nationality groups to form, often within the borders of a single country such as China. Nowhere is this more evident than in Southeast Asia.

Even though China has its minority groups who live in the little mountainous regions, most of the Chinese feel they are one nationality group. To be "Chinese" is more important than being Mandarin, or to be from any one province--it is much more than having been born within the borders of the old Han Empire. For centuries, the Chinese believed they were at the center of the universe--everyone else was a "barbarian." There have been some secession movements by

A Summary of Asia to 1600

nationality groups, but this has never been a major problem. Peoples such as the Manchurians and the Mongolians have often migrated to China to become a part of "being Chinese."

It is interesting that India never developed any such feeling of nationality in their geographic area, the subcontinent, before 1600. Whenever unity was accomplished in India, it was often done by force of arms. The only time they were unified in these early years was because of the Muslims--the Mughals. Japan's unification came late, following a period of great violence and turmoil, but Japan has not been seriously divided since 1600. The nations of Southeast Asia have never been united under a single government and there are no immediate signs they will be soon.

The terrain, the nature of the river valley, the elevation, the latitude, and the amount of rainfall, have all determined **where** the people live, and **how many** the land will support in that area. The type of food which can be grown has also been important in Asia for centuries. Naturally, the best land has most often been at the heart of much of Asia's warfare. Rice has been the grain of choice in Asia for the last 4,000 years or more, and rice is limited by water supply and latitude. Overpopulation in proportion to the area's ability to produce food has long ago determined that meat products are a supplementary part of the diet rather than the main dish. Good grazing land has often been placed under cultivation.

Both Europe and Asia have had their leaders who were not content to rule over only their land of national inheritance--they wanted more. There can be little doubt that the western conqueror, Alexander the Great, would have conquered even more of Asia had he lived longer. The greatest territorial expansion of all of history was that of the Mongols. From China in the eastern world, to a sizeable area of Russia and Eastern Europe in the western world, from the wide steppes of the north to the Indian Ocean--the Mongols controlled it all. But Kublai Khan tried twice to conquer Japan, he tried to take Java, and he made heavy inroads into Southeast Asia. How much more could one man want? How much more could he rule effectively?

Everyday life in Asia for thousands of years has been guided by religion. Buddhism, Confucianism, and Taoism have been powerful forces to pull very disparate peoples together under one umbrella. Just as Christian nations have fought one another to the death in western Europe, so also have Muslims often ruined the lives of thousands of people in their lust for power. Before the Muslims, the Indian rajahs fought one another for the control of a particular area of India. The ordinary citizen of any one of the Asian nations has preferred to work out their own religious philosophy regardless of the wars or suffering which may rage about him or her.

Literature and philosophy, history and art, education and architecture--all are heavily imbued with religion in Asia. Europe experienced a similar period during the medieval period, but beginning with the Renaissance they came to believe that mankind could change their lives if they only set their minds to do so, a movement referred to as Humanism. This was followed by the age of science and discovery, which soon led to many technological inventions. All of that groundwork was laid prior to 1600 in Europe. Many Asians are still engaged in the "Long Search" for religious fulfillment. Beyond survival, religion is the single most important thing in one's life. Although many different inventions were discovered in Asia long before the Europeans even thought about them, manufacturing those inventions for profit was not a primary goal--religion was the goal.

A Summary of Asia to 1600

The Christianity which developed in western Europe was thoroughly researched by hundreds of great scholar-theologians. It was then presented to the ordinary layman as the single path to eternal bliss in the next world. The Asian religious approach is different. Hinduism is composed of thousands of pages of theology which must be thought through, then meditated about, in order to achieve moksha. Buddha gave his followers a path to achieve enlilghtenment. In both of those major faiths, the person who fails to achieve their oneness or enlightenment will be reborn to try again. It is a lifelong quest for each individual. There are no arrangements for a last minute, deathbed confession of faith. Most do not believe that simple faith alone will achieve their religious goal.

For this reason, more people spend more time in religious pursuits in Asia than in the western world. Christians would hope that everyone would make the same lifelong quest, but more often they are so involved in everyday affairs that they depend upon a deathbed confession. There is even a Zen way of conducting business. Any journey through Asia, however short, will certainly impress the western traveler of the obvious sincerity of this depth of faith and conviction.

Finally, there are inevitably many generalizations necessary in a survey course which covers 35,000 years or more. Even under the best circumstances, sources covering the period before 1600 are very sketchy. Although a large amount of archaeology has been done, there are undoubtedly many entire cities buried beneath the loess and the mud of China, or simply swept out to sea in the floods of Bangladesh. The wooden temples of all of Asia have had their problems with fires, especially in Japan. The practice of cremation has left no grave-goods. In many cases the ashes are swept into the river to return to nature. Furthermore, paper and bamboo products do not keep well over the centuries, especially in alkaline soils. Asian archaeology is still in its infancy.

The Chinese have kept written records longer than any other civilization. They do contribute the names of many rulers through several dynasties, but only a few have any details recorded about them. Often there is only one account where one does exist. This means there are no cross-references to check. Many of the everyday stories deal with court life, such as *The Tale of Genji* by Lady Murasaki. No one seems to have written a story about the man who forged the samurai sword, or the potter who designed and fired the Ming piece of pottery. Village life has been pieced together largely through archaeology. The obsession of the Indian writer with great epic tales has told us very little about the houses and daily life of an early Aryan family. Myths and legends abound in the early history of every Asian nation.

This lack of more precise records presents a real challenge for even a survey history. Still, the quest is worthwhile. Like a giant mystery unfolding, Asian history is rich in resources which everyone in the western world should read alongside their knowledge of the West. It has been a long journey to 1600, and hopefully an enjoyable one. The story is only beginning. Be sure to read the history of this area from 1600 to the present. Only then will East and West begin to understand one another as people rather than as total strangers.

A Summary of Asia to 1600

BOOKS FOR FURTHER READING

The following list of books is submitted as a basic reference shelf for those who would like to pursue the study of Asia in more depth. Ask your librarian for help. In the end, you must travel through Asia to really understand the people, their culture, and their history.

Basham, A. L., *The Wonder That Was India* (1984).

Bechert, Heinz, & Gombrich, Richard, editors, *The World of Buddhism* (1984).

Berger, Carl, *The Korean Knot: A Military-Political History* (1964).

The Bible (any good translation).

Blunden, Caroline, & Elvin, Mark, *Cultural Atlas of China* (1983).

Bowring, Richard, & Kornicki, Peter, editors, *The Cambridge Encyclopedia of Japan* (1993).

The Cambridge History of India, 5 Volumes (1922-1937).

Collcutt, M. Jansen, & Kamakura,I., *Cultural Atlas of Japan* (1991).

Cotterell, Arthur, *China, A Cultural History* (1988).

Cotterell, Arthur, & Morgan, David, *China's Civilization* (1975).

Creel, H. G., *The Birth of China* (1937).

Cressey, George B., *Asia's Lands and Peoples* (1963).

Eckert, Carter J. *et. al.*, *Korea Old and New: A History* (1990).

Embree, Ainslie T., editor, *Encyclopedia of Asian History*, Four Volumes (1988).

The New Encyclopedia Britannica, 29 Volumes (1987 or newer).

Fairbank, John K., *China: A New History* (1992).

Fairbank, John K., Reischauer, Edwin O., & Craig, Albert M., *East Asia: Tradition and Transformation* (1989).
[Note: Any book by any of these three authors is excellent.]

Fenton, Hein, *et. al., Religions of Asia* (1988).

Gernet, Jacques, *Ancient China from the Beginnings to the Empire* (1968).

Gernet, Jacques, *A History of Chinese Civilization* (1987).

A Summary of Asia to 1600

Hall, John W., *Japan from Prehistory to Modern Times* (1970).

Henthorn, William E., *A History of Korea* (1971).

Hopkirk, Peter, *The Great Game: The Struggle for Empire in Central Asia* (1992).

Kitagawa, Joseph, M., editor, *The Religious Traditions of Asia* (1989).

The Koran (any good translation).

Loewe, Michael, *The Pride That Was China* (1990).

Mason, R. H. P, & Caiger, J. G., *A History of Japan* (1992).

Myer, Milton W., *Japan: A Concise History* (1993).

Myers, Bernard S., & Copplestone, Trewin, *The History of Asian Art* (1987).

Rawlinson, H. G., *India: A Short Cultural History* (1952).

Rawson, R. R., *The Monsoon Lands of Asia* (1963).

Robinson, Harry, *Monsoon Asia: A Geographical Survey* (1967).

Sansom, George B., *A History of Japan*, 3 Volumes (1963).

Shirokauer, Conrad, *A Brief History of Chinese and Japanese Civilizations* (1989).

Sivin, Nathan, *The Contemporary Atlas of China* (1988).

Smith, Huston, *The Religions of Man* (1986).

Smith, Vincent A., *The Oxford History of India*, edited by Sir Mortimer Wheeler & A.L. Basham (1967).

Tarling, Nicholas, *The Cambridge History of Southeast Asia*, Two Volumes (1992).

Thapar, Romila, *A History of India* (1966).

Thomas, P., *Hindu Religion, Customs and Manners* (1975).

Trewartha, Glenn T., *Japan: A Geography* (1965).

Waldron, Arthur, *The Great Wall of China from History to Myth* (1990).

Webster's New Geographical Dictionary (1988).

Zwalf, W., editor, *Buddhism: Art and Faith* (1985).

INDEX to VOLUME I

Index

Index

Index